GloBE Rules Made Easy

GloBE Rules Made Easy

Kuldeep Sharma

Wolters Kluwer

Published by:
Kluwer Law International B.V.
PO Box 316
2400 AH Alphen aan den Rijn
The Netherlands
E-mail: lrs-sales@wolterskluwer.com
Website: www.wolterskluwer.com/en/solutions/kluwerlawinternational

Sold and distributed by:
Wolters Kluwer Legal & Regulatory U.S.
7201 McKinney Circle
Frederick, MD 21704
United States of America
E-mail: customer.service@wolterskluwer.com

ISBN 978-94-035-1156-6

e-Book: ISBN 978-94-035-1166-5
web-PDF: ISBN 978-94-035-1176-4

About the Author

Kuldeep Sharma, an erstwhile officer of the Indian Revenue Service, has worked for over thirty years in the Income Tax Department, New Delhi, wherein he has had the opportunity to work at multiple levels in Direct Taxes, i.e., in field dispensations as well as tax policy department under the aegis of Central Board of Direct Taxes (CBDT) and has garnered wide experience in taxation of corporates and non-corporates (including individuals).

The last ten years of his service were completely dedicated to the field of International Taxation and Transfer Pricing (IT&TP), wherein he has accredited himself in a variety of roles involving Transfer Pricing audits and processing of Advance Pricing Agreements (APAs). For four years, he has worked in the Foreign Tax and Tax Research Division of CBDT, wherein, apart from handling policy issues related to non-residents, Country-by-Country Reporting, Tax Treaty Negotiations and complex APA, Mutual Agreement Procedure (MAP) cases, he has been actively engaged in matters involving Base Erosion and Profit Shifting (BEPS) and the Multilateral Convention to Implement Tax Treaty Related Measures to Prevent Base Erosion and Profit Shifting (MLI).

He has travelled extensively internationally and attended important events on tax, which includes representing the country during plenary meetings at OECD, Paris. Also, he has attended a number of seminars, workshops and meetings on IT&TP.

Presently, he is actively engaged in writing books on IT&TP, wherein he has shared his deep insights and experience in the niche areas of taxation. His maiden book titled *MLI Made Easy* (ISBN 978-94-035-3260-8) was published by Wolters Kluwer in April 2021, and his second book titled *Evolution of APA Regime* (ISBN 978-94-035-3551-7) was published by Wolters Kluwer in July 2021. Both publications have been widely appreciated.

About the Author

Kuldeep Sharma holds a BSc (Physics) Hons. as well as an MBA (Finance). His years of practical experience in Direct Taxes have enabled him to successfully achieve the status of ADIT Graduate accredited by the Chartered Institute of Taxation, UK and Fellow Member issued by The Tax Institute, Australia.

In addition, he is an Insolvency Professional under the Insolvency and Bankruptcy Code, 2016 and has been registered since September 2021 with the Insolvency and Bankruptcy Board of India.

For any clarification, he may be contacted at cooldip.sharma@gmail.com

Table of Contents

List of Boxes

List of Illustrations

List of Figures

List of Tables

List of Abbreviations

ADS	Automated Digital Services
AE	Associated Enterprise
AEOI	Automatic Exchange of Information
ALP	Arm's Length Principle
AoA	Authorised OECD Approach
APA	Advance Pricing Agreement
BAPA	Bilateral Advance Pricing Agreement
BBBA	Build Back Better Act
BEAT	Base Erosion Anti-Abuse Tax
BEPS	Base Erosion and Profit Shifting
CbCR	Country-by-Country Reporting
CE	Constituent Entity
CFC	Controlled Foreign Corporation
CFS	Consolidated Financial Statements
CIT	Corporate Income Tax
CRS	Common Reporting Standard
DMT	Domestic Minimum Top-Up Tax
ETR	Effective Tax Rate
EU	European Union
FAQ	Frequently Asked Questions
FAR	Functions Performed, Assets Utilised and Risks Assumed
FX	Foreign Currency Exchange
FXGL	Foreign Currency Exchange Gain or Loss
G20	Group of Twenty
GDP	Gross Domestic Product
GILTI	Global Intangible Low-Taxed Income

GloBE	Global Anti-Base Erosion
IAS	International Accounting Standards
ICT	Information and Communications Technology
IF	Inclusive Framework
IFRS	International Financial Reporting Standards
IIR	Income Inclusion Rule
IMF	International Monetary Fund
JV	Joint Venture
LTCE	Low-Taxed Constituent Entity
MLI	Multilateral Convention to Implement Tax Treaty related measures to prevent Base Erosion and Profit Shifting
MNE	Multinational Enterprise
OCI	Other Comprehensive Income
OECD	Organisation for Economic Co-operation and Development
OECD MTC	OECD Model Tax Convention
PE	Permanent Establishment
POPE	Partially Owned Parent Entity
QDMTT	Qualified Domestic Minimum Top-Up Tax
SMEs	Small and Medium Enterprises
SOR	Switch-Over Rule
STTR	Subject to Tax Rule
TCJA	Tax Cuts and Jobs Act
TP	Transfer Pricing
UAPA	Unilateral Advance Pricing Agreement
UN MTC	United Nations Model Tax Convention
UPE	Ultimate Parent Entity
UTPR	Undertaxed Profits Rule

Preface

The primary purpose of the OECD/G20 project on digitalisation addresses how taxing rights on income generated from cross-border activities in the digital age should be allocated among countries. It involves development of a solution to various mechanisms (and proposals) so as to bridge the requirements of capital/technology exporting countries vis-à-vis capital/technology importing countries and, in the process, *inter alia*, shore up tax revenues of market jurisdictions to account for the contribution made by users in the market jurisdictions and compensate such jurisdictions for the revenue generated by them for the MNEs. This is being achieved through the Two-Pillar Solution, wherein Pillar One intends to ensure a fairer distribution of profits and taxing rights among countries with respect to the largest and most profitable MNEs. It will reallocate some taxing rights over MNEs from their home countries to the markets where they have business activities and earn profits, regardless of whether firms have a physical presence there. The secondary purpose of the OECD/G20 project is to address the remaining BEPS issues related to low-tax jurisdictions. This is being addressed by Pillar Two, which *inter alia* deals with:

- global minimum tax rate of 15 % in all countries with an intent to curb shifting of profits from higher tax jurisdiction to lower tax jurisdiction or tax havens;
- to discourage 'race to the bottom', i.e., competition among countries to charge lower corporate taxes to attract foreign investment; and
- to place a floor on tax competition between jurisdictions, ensuring the sustainability of corporate income tax (CIT) as a major source of government revenues while leaving appropriate flexibility for countries to use CIT as a policy lever for supporting business investment and innovation.

The book clearly brings out the evolution of GloBE Rules in a harmonious manner, highlighting each step of development and culminating with the release of Commentary and Examples to the rules. While drafting the book, a conscious effort has been made to incorporate all technical, policy and implementation aspects of GloBE Rules in a manner which will be found useful by a wide array of stakeholders, i.e., Tax

Officers, Tax Professionals, Tax Advisors, Taxpayers, Academicians and others (such as Law students) in any part of the academic world.

As far as the structure of the book is concerned, it is divided into seven chapters. *Chapter 1* is introductory and provides an overview of the Two-Pillar Solution, revenue implications of the proposals and information on jurisdictions which have agreed and not agreed to these proposals. *Chapter 2* provides a background discussion of the Pillar Two Solution and a recap of the advancement and changes made in salient Pillar Two Proposals since the release of Report on Pillar Two Blueprint and subsequent agreements made by IF members, as reflected in OECD's statements dated 1 July 2021 and 8 October 2021 respectively, culminating with the release of GloBE Model Rules on 20 December 2021. *Chapter 3* provides an overview of operating provisions of GloBE Rules, involving various steps in determining the top-up tax liability for an MNE in order to apply the GloBE Rules, *inter alia*, explained through flow-charts, as released by the OECD and accompanied by discussions that the GloBE Rules are to be implemented as part of a common approach.

Chapter 4 covers comprehensive discussions in respect of each article of GloBE Rules, its Commentary and Examples released by the OECD. These provisions, being complex, have been explained in the book in the following differentiating manner:

- each article contained in Chapters 1 to 9 of the GloBE Rules has been summarised in a box as a prelude, providing the readers with a quick summary of the ensuing discussions;
- at appropriate places, the provisions have been explained through flow-charts, tables or diagrams for a better and faster understanding of the readers;
- the technical provisions contained in each article of GloBE Rules are discussed para-wise, and each paragraph invariably carries a brief italicised header/narration;
- the Examples and Definitions (as contained in Chapter 10 of GloBE Rules) released by the OECD have been inserted at relevant places where the corresponding articles of GloBE Rules are discussed. Further, the Examples have been encapsulated in flow-charts for a better and faster understanding of the readers. At the same time, for the ease of readers, an index of definitions (which is specific to the book) has also been incorporated in Chapter 4.

Chapter 5 covers elaborate technical discussions amidst specific policy considerations, accompanied by an analysis of all the 141 IF member countries on certain parameters with suitable recommendations, whereas *Chapter 6* discusses the GloBE implementation process of certain jurisdictions, namely, Canada, European Union, Jersey, New Zealand, Singapore, South Africa, Switzerland, United Arab Emirates, the United Kingdom and the United States of America. *Chapter 7* is the concluding chapter and, in line with the title of the book, provides a comprehensive FAQ-cum-quick summary of the salient issues of all articles contained in Chapters 1 to 9 of GloBE Rules as a ready reckoner for reference and understanding of readers. Accordingly, a checklist titled 'GloBE Rules at a Glance' has been devised, encapsulating the features, application and nuances of GloBE Rules.

The various publications and releases by the OECD up to 31 May 2022 in the form of Press Releases, GloBE Rules, Commentary on GloBE Rules, Fact sheets, FAQs and Examples on GloBE Rules have been considered and duly explained in this book.

The dates (period) of statistical data discussed in this book are duly mentioned at appropriate and relevant places and are not later than 31 May 2022.

Acknowledgements

In continuation to my earlier two publications by Wolters Kluwer, namely, *MLI Made Easy* (ISBN 978-94-035-3260-8, published in April 2021) and *Evolution of APA Regime* (ISBN 978-94-035-3551-7, published in July 2021), my third book titled *GloBE Rules Made Easy*, providing an overview of Pillar Two Proposals and detailing the finer nuances of GloBE Rules, in particular, was a logical forward-looking action on my part.

GloBE Rules have caused much consternation in the world of taxation as they are an innovative, self-contained, but complex set of provisions. Merely following the developments in Pillar Two through OECD's statements, various publications by OECD and analysis thereof by tax experts from time to time may not suffice to fully comprehend the nuances contained in these rules. Hence, for the benefit of all stakeholders, this self-contained book provides deep insight and a liberal dose of elaborate discussions on legal aspects of GloBE Rules in the form of text, illustrations, diagrams, flowcharts, tables, boxes and my observations at appropriate places.

My profound gratitude to my family, which has been my constant pillar of support and has gladly permitted me to devote time meant for them to my academic pursuits. In addition, I would like to acknowledge that my elder daughter Ms Raunicka Sharma, a BBA LLB student (final year) from Symbiosis Law School, Noida, India, provided insights into the contours of the book, data collection and research, including its final proof reading, whereas, my younger daughter, Ms Paavnieka Sharma (student of Class XII) designed the tables, diagrams and flowcharts of the book.

My association with Wolters Kluwer began with my maiden literary venture titled *MLI Made Easy*, and it continued with *Evolution of APA Regime*. I would like to express my sincere gratitude to the entire Wolters Kluwer team for agreeing to continue with our association through my third venture, titled *GloBE Rules Made Easy*. These publications may not have been possible without the confidence and faith Wolters Kluwer has in me.

Executive Summary

1. The primary purpose of the OECD/G20 project on digitalisation addresses how taxing rights on income generated from cross-border activities in the digital age should be allocated among countries. Accordingly, in order to progress towards a consensus-based solution, the IF agreed on a Policy Note in January 2019 that grouped the targeted proposals into two pillars:

- one of nexus and profit allocation, and
- another on ensuring a minimum level of taxation (the GloBE).[1]

2. Recommendations of the Two-Pillar Solution, as approved by the IF member countries, are summarised below:

1. Refer 'Transfer Pricing Developments Around the World 2020, Edited by Michael Lang, Raffaele Petruzzi, published by Wolters Kluwer, Chapter 6: Recent developments on the tax challenges arising from the digitalization of the Economy: New Profit Allocation Rules, by Giammarco Cottani, pg. 153' accessed on 31 May 2022.

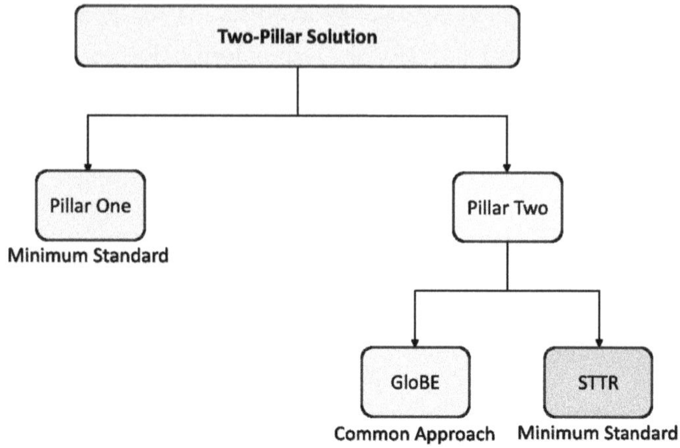

3. A brief overview of objectives of Pillar One and Pillar Two is provided in Chapter 1. Pillar Two (refer paragraph 5) *inter alia* deals with:

- global minimum tax rate of 15% in all countries with an intent to curb shifting of profits from higher tax jurisdiction to lower tax jurisdiction or tax havens;
- to discourage 'race to the bottom', i.e., competition among countries to charge lower corporate taxes to attract foreign investment; and
- to place a floor on tax competition between jurisdictions, ensuring the sustainability of corporate income tax (CIT) as a major source of government revenues while leaving appropriate flexibility for countries to use CIT as a policy lever for supporting business investment and innovation.

4. Tax revenue implications involving the Two-Pillar Solution are discussed in Chapter 1. As per OECD's FAQs on Global Anti-Base Erosion Model (GloBE) Rules (Pillar Two), with a minimum effective tax rate (ETR) of 15%, the GloBE Rules are expected to generate around USD 150 billion in additional global tax revenues per year (refer paragraph 11).

5. The OECD, vide its statement dated 8 October 2021, reported that 136 jurisdictions (out of the 140 members of the OECD/G20 Inclusive Framework (IF) on Base Erosion and Profit Shifting (BEPS)) joined the Statement on the Two-Pillar Solution to 'Address the Tax Challenges Arising from the Digitalisation of the Economy', ensuring that the firms pay a fair share of tax wherever they operate and generate profits. It was also reported that four countries, namely Kenya, Nigeria, Pakistan and Sri Lanka, have not yet joined the agreement. Subsequently, OECD reported that 137 member jurisdictions of IF have agreed to it as of 4 November 2021 (refer paragraph 13).

6. The Pillar Two Proposals have been discussed in Chapter 2. The Pillar Two blueprint is the mother document containing innovative and complex rules as approved by the IF members, subject to certain pending agreements. In addition, discussions in Chapter 2 have been made in respect of OECD's statement dated 1 July

2021 in respect of Pillar Two (refer paragraph 31), OECD's statement dated 8 October 2021 in respect of Pillar Two (refer paragraph 32), OECD's Pillar Two Model Rules dated 20 December 2021 and its Commentary (refer paragraphs 33, 34). A quick recap of the advancement and changes made in salient Pillar Two Proposals since release of Report on Pillar Two Blueprint and subsequent agreements made by IF members, as reflected in OECD's statements dated 1 July 2021 and 8 October 2021, respectively, culminating with the release of GloBE Model Rules on 20 December 2021 has also been done in Chapter 2 (refer paragraph 35).

7. Discussions on Operating Provisions of GloBE Rules have been made in Chapter 3. The various steps in determining the top-up tax liability for an MNE in order to apply the GloBE Rules are also discussed in Chapter 3, *inter alia*, explained through flow-charts, as released by the OECD (refer paragraphs 38, 39). It is important to note that the GloBE Rules are to be implemented as part of a common approach (refer paragraphs 40-42).

8. After comprehensive discussions among IF members and taking the views of various stakeholders through public consultations, the GloBE Model Rules were released on 20 December 2021, which consist of ten chapters and 49 articles in total. Thereafter, the Commentary and Illustrative Examples on Pillar Two Model Rules were released by the OECD on 14 March 2022. The Commentary and Illustrative Examples provide tax administrations and taxpayers with guidance on the interpretation and application of these rules. Comprehensive discussions have been made in Chapter 4 in respect of each article of GloBE Rules, its Commentary and Examples released by the OECD. These provisions, being complex, have been explained in the book in the following differentiating manner:

- each article contained in Chapters 1 to 9 of the GloBE Rules has been summarised in a box as a prelude, providing the readers with a quick summary of the ensuing discussions;
- at appropriate places, the provisions have been explained through flow-charts, tables or diagrams for a better and faster understanding of the readers;
- the technical provisions contained in each article of GloBE Rules are discussed para-wise, and each paragraph invariably carries a brief italicised header/narration;
- The Examples and Definitions (as contained in Chapter 10 of GloBE Rules) released by the OECD have been inserted at relevant places where the corresponding articles of GloBE Rules are discussed. Further, the Examples have been encapsulated in flow-charts for a better and faster understanding of the readers. At the same time, for the ease of readers, an index of definitions (which is specific to the book) has also been incorporated in Chapter 4.

9. Accordingly, Chapter 4 of the book contains technical discussions on various articles of GloBE Rules, as summarised below:

S.N	*Article*	*Title of Article*	*Paragraphs*
1	1.1.	Scope of GloBE Rules	47-59
2	1.2.	MNE Group and Group	60-66
3	1.3.	Constituent Entity	67-74
4	1.4.	Ultimate Parent Entity	75-79
5	1.5.	Excluded Entity	80-106
6	2.1.	Application of the IIR	109-141
7	2.2.	Allocation of Top-Up Tax under the IIR	142-159
8	2.3.	IIR Offset Mechanism	160-169
9	2.4.	Application of the UTPR	170-192
10	2.5.	UTPR Top-up Tax Amount	193-213
11	2.6.	Allocation of Top-Up Tax for the UTPR	214-235
12	3.1.	Financial Accounts	237-254
13	3.2.	Adjustments to determine GloBE Income or Loss	255-379
14	3.3.	International Shipping Income exclusion	380-401
15	3.4.	Allocation of Income or Loss between a Main Entity and a Permanent Establishment	402-422
16	3.5.	Allocation of Income or Loss from a Flow-through Entity	423-438
17	4.1.	Adjusted Covered Taxes	440-458
18	4.2.	Definition of Covered Taxes	459-467
19	4.3.	Allocation of Covered Taxes from one Constituent Entity to another Constituent Entity	468-495
20	4.4.	Mechanism to address temporary differences	496-530
21	4.5.	The GloBE Loss Election	531-546
22	4.6.	Post-filing Adjustments and Tax Rate Changes	547-562
23	5.1.	Determination of Effective Tax Rate	564-577
24	5.2.	Top-up Tax	578-592
25	5.3.	Substance-based Income Exclusion	593-624
26	5.4.	Additional Current Top-up Tax	625-637
27	5.5.	*De minimis* exclusion	638-654
28	5.6.	Minority-Owned Constituent Entities	655-670
29	6.1.	Application of Consolidated Revenue Threshold to Group Mergers and Demergers	677-685
30	6.2.	Constituent Entities joining and leaving an MNE Group	686-696
31	6.3.	Transfer of Assets and Liabilities	697-710
32	6.4.	Joint Ventures	711-722
33	6.5.	Multi-Parented MNE Groups	723-732
34	7.1.	Ultimate Parent Entity that is a Flow-through Entity	734-752

S.N	*Article*	*Title of Article*	*Paragraphs*
35	7.2.	Ultimate Parent Entity subject to Deductible Dividend Regime	753-768
36	7.3.	Eligible Distribution Tax Systems	769-795
37	7.4.	Effective Tax Rate Computation for Investment Entities	796-813
38	7.5.	Investment Entity Tax Transparency Election	814-826
39	7.6.	Taxable Distribution Method Election	827-843
40	8.1.	Filing obligation	845-869
41	8.2.	Safe Harbours	870-878
42	8.3.	Administrative Guidance	879-884
43	9.1.	Tax Attributes Upon Transition	886-897
44	9.2.	Transitional relief for the Substance-based Income Exclusion	898-903
45	9.3.	Exclusion from the UTPR of MNE Groups in the initial phase of their international activity	904-918
46	9.4.	Transitional relief for filing obligations	919-921
47	10.1.	Defined Terms	922-923
48	10.2.	Definitions of Flow-through Entity, Tax Transparent Entity, Reverse Hybrid Entity, and Hybrid Entity	
49	10.3.	Location of an Entity and a Permanent Establishment	

10. GloBE Rules are endowed with innovative and complex provisions which require elaborate discussions amidst specific policy considerations, as conducted in Chapter 5 on the following lines:

(a) Interaction between GloBE Rules and existing BEPS measures has been discussed in paragraphs 924-926.

(b) Interaction and Relation of IIR with UTPR has been discussed in paragraphs 927-931.

(c) Interaction and Relation of IIR with CFC Rule has been discussed in paragraphs 932-939.

(d) Interaction and Relation of GloBE Rules with Global Intangible Low-Taxed Income (GILTI) and BEAT has been discussed in paragraphs 940-943.

(e) Interaction of GloBE Rules with tax-sparing provisions has been discussed in paragraphs 944-955.

(f) GloBE Rules contain enough measures to ease compliance burden, as discussed in paragraphs 956-957.

(g) GloBE Rules contain anti-abuse provisions and measures so that in the course of their implementation, MNEs do not exploit them to their advantage, as discussed in paragraph 958.

(h) Although the taxpayers are required to maintain adequate and robust documentation to demonstrate that GloBE Rules have been sufficiently complied with, it has been outlined in the Commentary to GloBE Rules that there is a need for supporting documentation to facilitate adequate examination and satisfaction of tax authorities, as discussed in paragraph 959.

(i) Analysis of all the 141 IF Member Countries has been done in Chapter 5 (refer paragraph 960) in respect of the following parameters:
   - Applicability of CIT regime
   - Whether the CIT rate is equal to or more than 15%
   - Availability of TP provisions
   - Commitment to Automatic Exchange of Information (AEOI).

Based on the above analysis, further discussions have been made in Chapter 5, along the following lines:

(i) Introduction of CIT regime in jurisdictions which do not have it as yet and appropriate CIT rate (refer paragraphs 961-964).

(ii) GloBE Model Rules released on 20 December 2021 have added a new concept of Qualified Domestic Top-up Tax (QDMTT), a concept that previously was not included in the OECD Report on Pillar Two Blueprint. In order to preserve tax sovereignty and their tax base, IF member countries may consider incorporating the QDMTT as it allows the jurisdiction in which a low-taxed entity is resident to levy the top-up tax before application of the IIR at the level of the parent company (refer paragraphs 965-966).

(iii) While computing GloBE income, the *inter se* transactions between CEs within or across jurisdictions are required to be aligned with the Arm's Length Principle (ALP) (refer paragraphs 967-968).

(iv) To bring in transparency is a prime objective of all anti-BEPS measures. Implementation of CRS for AEOI is a positive demonstration by a country that it is committed to being a transparent, compliant and reputable jurisdiction (refer paragraphs 969-970).

(v) Pillar Two compliances will be over and above the tax returns and filings that are already being executed by taxpayers. The GloBE has been designed as a global set of rules that will be targeted at large MNE groups and will overlay the domestic regime of a jurisdiction. Accordingly, the design of IIR and UTPR as Top-up Taxes does not restrict a jurisdiction from legislating the rules under a CIT system in its domestic law, for which jurisdictions may take further necessary steps in their respective domestic law (refer paragraphs 971-972).

11. OECD's October statement has set out an aim for jurisdictions to legislate GloBE Rules into their respective domestic laws in 2022 so that these rules take effect from 2023. It may also be noted that IF members have agreed that the earliest the UTPR will come into effect is in 2024, as mentioned in paragraph 25 of the Commentary on

Chapter 9 (Transition Rules). Accordingly, many jurisdictions have got activated to kick-start the implementation process, which reflects the way various tax administrations have perceived GloBE Rules and their respective mechanism of implementation. Since the approach to understanding and implementation of GloBE Rules among all jurisdictions has to be common and consistent, the elaborate discussion, as carried out in Chapter 6 of the book, on certain jurisdictions' implementation processes demonstrates just that. Also, readers will get acquainted with the implementation process at global level, which, coupled with the theoretical discussion on GloBE Rules carried out in Chapter 4 of the book and Technical and Policy discussions in Chapter 5 of the book, is expected to further enhance and deepen their understanding of these rules. The GloBE implementation process of the following jurisdictions has been discussed in Chapter 6:

(a) Implementation by Canada (refer paragraphs 974-978),
(b) Implementation by the European Union (refer paragraphs 979-981),
(c) Implementation by Jersey (refer paragraph 982),
(d) Implementation by New Zealand (refer paragraph 983),
(e) Implementation by Singapore (refer paragraphs 984-985),
(f) Implementation by South Africa (refer paragraph 986),
(g) Implementation by Switzerland (refer paragraph 987),
(h) Implementation by the United Arab Emirates (refer paragraphs 988-993),
(i) Implementation by the United Kingdom (refer paragraphs 994-1004), and
(j) Implementation by the United States of America (refer paragraph 1005).

12. In line with the title of the book, for the benefit of readers, the concluding Chapter 7 of the book contains a comprehensive FAQ-cum-quick summary of the salient issues of all articles contained in Chapters 1 to 9 of GloBE Rules as a ready reckoner for reference and understanding. Accordingly, a checklist titled 'GloBE Rules at a Glance' has been devised *inter alia* encapsulating the features, application and nuances of GloBE Rules (refer paragraph 1008).

13. As part of the GloBE Implementation Framework, discussed in Chapter 7 of the book, the OECD is expected to render Administrative Guidance (under Article 8.3), which will be released and made publicly available, to facilitate transparent, consistent, coordinated, uniform and efficacious implementation of the GloBE Rules by tax administrations and MNE Groups respectively (refer paragraphs 1009-1010).

14. Jurisdictions are expected to protect their turf; accordingly, most countries which decide to implement the GloBE Rules may opt to introduce domestic minimum tax (DMT) in their domestic legislation. A DMT would ensure that any additional tax on local economic activities and profits that results from the Pillar Two minimum tax framework is to the benefit of the local exchequer. Also, a DMT could significantly reduce compliance burdens on local groups by preventing them from being subject to the UTPR in multiple countries in respect of their local domestic operations.

15. The Two-Pillar solution is expected to have an impact on MNE investment, innovation and economic activity at global level. By raising additional tax revenues, the proposals would increase (after-tax) investment costs for the MNEs affected. This would likely have a negative effect on investment and activity, but the magnitude of this effect is estimated to be relatively small, i.e., less than 0.1% of gross domestic product (GDP) in the medium to long term.

CHAPTER 1
Introduction

One of the salient purposes of the OECD/G20 project is to address remaining BEPS issues related to low-tax jurisdictions. This is being addressed by Pillar Two, which inter alia *deals with:*

- *global minimum tax rate of 15% in all countries with an intent to curb shifting of profits from higher tax jurisdiction to lower tax jurisdiction or tax havens;*
- *to discourage 'race to the bottom', i.e., competition among countries to charge lower corporate taxes to attract foreign investment; and*
- *to place a floor on tax competition between jurisdictions, ensuring the sustainability of CIT as a major source of government revenues while leaving appropriate flexibility for countries to use CIT as a policy lever for supporting business investment and innovation.*

As per OECD's FAQs on GloBE Rules (Pillar Two), with a minimum ETR of 15%, the GloBE rules are expected to generate around USD 150 billion in additional global tax revenues per year.

OECD has reported that 137 member jurisdictions of IF, out of a total of 141, have agreed to the Two-Pillar Solution as of 4 November 2021. Kenya, Nigeria, Pakistan and Sri Lanka have not yet joined the agreement.

1.1 BACKGROUND

1. The transformative processes brought in by information and communication technology (ICT) have resulted in proliferation of the digital economy, which has made technologies cheaper, more powerful, and widely standardised, improving business processes and bolstering innovation across all sectors of the economy. Digitalisation and globalisation have had a profound impact on economies and the lives of people around the world, and this impact has only accelerated in the 21st century. These changes have brought with them challenges to the rules for taxing international business income, which have prevailed for more than a hundred years and resulted in Multinational Enterprises (MNEs) not paying their fair share of tax despite the huge profits many of these businesses have garnered as the world has become increasingly interconnected. The importance of ICT and the resultant digital economy was abundantly evident and has gained immense acceleration during the COVID-19 period. Because the digital economy is increasingly becoming the economy itself, it would be difficult, if not impossible, to ring-fence the digital economy from the rest of the economy for tax purposes.[2]

2. Shoring up pertinent policy measures against tax base erosion, in particular in developing countries, and ensuring a fair allocation of tax revenues would be vital for financing sustainable development and effectively pursuing the Sustainable Development Goals.[3] Some MNEs have rampantly indulged in tax planning devices which made use of gaps in the interaction of different tax systems and tax treaties to artificially reduce taxable income or shift profits to low-tax jurisdictions in which little or no economic activity was performed. MNEs, aided by digital means, became capable of generating profits from market jurisdictions without physical presence and were able to escape the tax net as treaty rules predominantly relied on physical presence and nexus approach for levy of tax. It is important to establish tax regimes aimed at foreign suppliers without a physical presence in the countries of consumption as:

- it is an action to develop the principle of tax equality, which allows maintaining equity in the economies of the countries since it balances the conditions in which suppliers abroad compete with national suppliers; and
- it strengthens the fiscal sovereignty of the countries in which foreign suppliers generate value through their activities.[4]

3. In order to establish a tax on cross-border digital operations, the best international practices recommend adapting the tax legislation of market jurisdictions in a manner that they adopt the 'destination principle', which allows the taxation of transactions carried out on goods, services, and intangibles supplied from abroad that are consumed in that market jurisdiction.[5]

1.2 OBJECTIVE OF PILLAR ONE (IN BRIEF)

4. The primary purpose of the OECD/G20 project on digitalisation addresses how taxing rights on income generated from cross-border activities in the digital age should

2. Refer 'Action 1: BEPS 2015 Final Report, OECD/G20 Base Erosion and Profit Shifting Project' http://www.oecd.org/tax/beps-2015-final-reports.htm.
3. Refer 'Sustainable Development Goals' https://www.un.org/sustainabledevelopment/sustainable-development-goals/ accessed on 5 April 2022.
4. Refer 'Handbook developed by CIAT/NORAD titled Digital Economy Compliance' https://www.ciat.org/Biblioteca/DocumentosTecnicos/Ingles/2021-DEC-Handbook-ing.pdf accessed on 7 April 2022.
5. *Id.* Although the discussions in the Handbook are in context of VAT, the concept of taxation based on destination principle (may be read as appropriate to the 'source rule' of taxation applicable to market jurisdictions) can be broadly applied on corporate income tax also.

be allocated among countries.[6] It involves development of a solution to various mechanisms (and proposals) so as to bridge the requirements of capital/technology exporting countries vis-à-vis capital/technology importing countries and, in the process, *inter alia*, shore up tax revenues of market jurisdictions to account for the contribution made by users in the market jurisdictions and compensate such jurisdictions for the revenue generated by them for the MNEs. This is being achieved through the Two-Pillar Solution, wherein, *inter alia*, Pillar One intends to ensure a fairer distribution of profits and taxing rights among countries with respect to the largest and most profitable MNEs. It will reallocate some taxing rights over MNEs from their home countries to the markets where they have business activities and earn profits, regardless of whether firms have a physical presence there. The rules provide that MNEs with global sales above EUR 20 billion and profitability above 10% will be covered, with 25% of profit above the 10% threshold to be reallocated to market jurisdictions.[7]

1.3 OBJECTIVE OF PILLAR TWO (IN BRIEF)

5. The secondary purpose of the OECD/G20 project is to address remaining BEPS issues related to low-tax jurisdictions.[8] This is being addressed by Pillar Two, which *inter alia* deals with:

- global minimum tax rate of 15% in all countries with an intent to curb shifting of profits from higher tax jurisdiction to lower tax jurisdiction or tax havens;
- to discourage 'race to the bottom', i.e., competition among countries to charge lower corporate taxes to attract foreign investment; and
- to place a floor on tax competition between jurisdictions, ensuring the sustainability of CIT as a major source of government revenues while leaving appropriate flexibility for countries to use CIT as a policy lever for supporting business investment and innovation.

6. Countries that choose to introduce the GloBE rules have agreed to do so in a consistent and coordinated way. The interlocking nature of the GloBE Rules means that their adoption by a critical mass of jurisdictions will be sufficient to ensure that MNEs are required to pay the minimum level of tax on their profits arising in each jurisdiction where they operate. The GloBE Rules incorporate an agreed rule order together with backstop or secondary rules that apply if a country where an MNE is based does not apply the primary rule. For instance, if the country where the MNE is headquartered

6. Refer 'BEPS Project Public Consultation Document on Addressing the Tax Challenges of the Digitalisation of the Economy' https://www.oecd.org/tax/beps/public-consultation-document-addressing-the-tax-challenges-of-the-digitalisation-of-the-economy.pdf accessed on 7 April 2022.
7. Refer 'OECD's Press Release dated 8 October 2021 titled International community strikes a ground-breaking tax deal for the digital age' https://www.oecd.org/tax/international-community-strikes-a-ground-breaking-tax-deal-for-the-digital-age.htm accessed on 7 April 2022.
8. Refer 'South Centre Tax Cooperation Policy Brief 22, 12 January 2022 by Kuldeep Sharma titled Global Minimum Corporate Tax: Interaction of Income Inclusion Rule with Controlled Foreign Corporation and Tax-sparing Provisions' https://www.southcentre.int/tax-cooperation-policy-brief-22-12-january-2022/ accessed on 7 April 2022.

does not subject the ultimate parent entity (UPE) of the MNE group to the primary income inclusion rule (IIR), another parent entity in the group, further down in the ownership chain, must apply the IIR under the agreed rule order. If even this does not result in the income of the MNE Group being subject to tax at the 15% minimum tax rate, the further backstop of the UTPR kicks in, which ensures the payment of the minimum tax through a denial of deduction or similar mechanism in all the countries where the MNE has a presence. The interlocking nature of these rules therefore ensures that top-up tax will be collected in jurisdictions that have introduced the GloBE rules, even where the MNE operates in or through other jurisdictions that have not implemented the rules. While countries are not required to adopt the GloBE rules, jurisdictions that adopt the GloBE rules will apply an ETR test using a common tax base and a common definition of covered taxes to determine whether an MNE is subject to an ETR below the agreed minimum rate of 15% in any jurisdiction where it operates. Thus, the objective of Pillar Two is to help in creating a level playing field for all developed and developing countries and put a floor under tax competition.[9]

7. All countries are sovereign and can set the tax policy of their choice, but harmful tax competition and aggressive tax planning need to end. Tax havens[10] have thrived over the years by offering secrecy (like bank secrecy) and shell companies (where the company doesn't need to have any employees or activity in the jurisdiction) and no or low tax on profits booked there. The work of the G20 and the OECD-hosted Global Forum on Transparency and Exchange of Information for Tax Purposes has ended bank secrecy (including leading to the automatic exchange of bank information), and the OECD BEPS Project requires companies to have a minimum level of substance to put an end to shell companies along with important transparency rules so that tax administrations can apply their tax rules effectively. Pillar Two will now ensure that those companies pay a minimum ETR of 15% on their profits booked there (subject to carve-outs for real, substantial activities). The cumulative impact of these initiatives means that tax havens may no longer exist. Those jurisdictions that offer international financial services may continue to find a market for their services, but on the basis that they add real economic value for their customers and support commercial transactions that are not tax-driven.[11]

9. Refer 'FAQ No. 1 on OECD's Model GloBE Rules dated 20 December 2021' https://www.oecd.org/tax/beps/pillar-two-model-GloBE-rules-faqs.pdf accessed on 7 April 2022.
10. Action 5: BEPS 2015 Final Report, OECD/G20 Base Erosion and Profit Shifting Project states the four key factors to define a 'tax haven' are: (i) no or nominal tax on the relevant income; (ii) lack of effective exchange of information; (iii) lack of transparency; (iv) no substantial activities. No or nominal tax is not sufficient in itself to classify a jurisdiction as a tax haven.
11. Refer 'FAQ No. 7 on OECD's statement dated 8 October 2021' https://www.oecd.org/tax/beps/faqs-statement-on-a-two-pillar-solution-to-address-the-tax-challenges-arising-from-the-digitalisation-of-the-economy-october-2021.pdf accessed on 5 April 2022.

1.4 RECOMMENDATIONS[12] OF UNITED NATIONS ON TAX CHALLENGES ARISING OUT OF DIGITALISATION

8. Since existing permanent establishment (PE) provisions in United Nations Model Tax Convention (UN MTC) do not cover in their ambit any income arising in market jurisdictions from automated digital services (ADS), the UN Committee of Experts on International Co-operation in Tax Matters (UN Tax Committee) took this subject as a matter of priority to be dealt with and decided to focus on a tax treaty provision under the UN MTC that would enable jurisdictions to apply their domestic legislation levying taxes on income derived from digital business models. The work of the UN Tax Committee on taxation of digitalised economies is duly reflected in the provisions of Article 12B in the UN MTC. Article 12B is deemed to automatically apply once the ADS (having minimal human intervention and administered through electronic network, internet) has been provided and has no thresholds in terms of its application. This ability to derive income from a country with little or no physical presence there is considered by the UN Tax Committee to justify source taxation of income from ADS. However, unlike OECD's wider recommendations comprising Pillar One (to reallocate taxing rights over MNEs from their home countries to the markets where they have business activities and earn profits, regardless of whether firms have a physical presence there) and Pillar Two (to address remaining BEPS issues related to low-tax jurisdictions), the recommendations of UN Tax Committee reflected in the provisions of Article 12B in the UN MTC are restricted to ADS only. Further, OECD's recommendations propose modifications in domestic laws and tax treaties of jurisdictions opting for the Two-Pillar Solution, whereas, on the other hand, the UN's recommendations are restricted to tax treaties alone.

1.5 TAX REVENUE IMPLICATIONS INVOLVING THE TWO-PILLAR SOLUTION

9. The Organisation for Economic Co-operation and Development (OECD), in its report titled 'Tax Challenges Arising from Digitalisation – Economic Impact Assessment',[13] projected the global tax revenue effects from the Two-Pillar Solution as given in Table 1.1.

12. Refer 'South Centre Tax Cooperation Policy Brief 14, June 2021 by Kuldeep Sharma titled The Tax Sovereignty Principle and Its Peaceful Coexistence with Article 12B of the UN Model Tax Convention' https://www.southcentre.int/wp-content/uploads/2021/06/Tax-PB-14.pdf accessed on 5 April 2022.
13. Refer 'OECD's report titled Tax Challenges Arising from Digitalisation – Economic Impact Assessment (Table 1.1.)' https://www.oecd-ilibrary.org/docserver/0e3cc2d4-en.pdf?expires=1645597172&id=id&accname=guest&checksum=BCDA456EF4506AF36EFDBF9351B85E5E accessed on 7 April 2022.

Table 1.1 Estimated Global Tax Revenue Gains from the Two-Pillar Solution

Estimated Global Fax Revenue Gains		*In % of Global CIT Revenues*	*In USD Billion*
Pillar One		0.2-0.5	5-12
Pillar Two	Direct revenue gains	0.9-1.7	23-42
	Additional gains from reduced profit shifting	0.8-1.1	19-28
	Total Pillar Two	1.7-2.8	42-70
Total Pillar One and Pillar Two		**1.9-3.2**	**47-81**
US GILTI regime		0.4-0.8	9-21
Total, including GILTI		**2.3-4.0**	**56-102**

Source: OECD's report titled 'Tax Challenges Arising from Digitalisation – Economic Impact Assessment' (Table 1.1).

10. Subsequently, it was reported[14] by the OECD that under Pillar One, taxing rights on more than USD 125 billion of profits are expected to be reallocated to market jurisdictions each year. Developing country revenue gains are expected to be greater than those in more advanced economies as a proportion of existing revenues.

11. As per OECD's FAQs on GloBE Rules (Pillar Two),[15] with a minimum ETR of 15%, the GloBE rules are expected to generate around USD 150 billion in additional global tax revenues per year. It is important to remember that 15% is the ETR to be paid by multinationals, which is not the statutory rate set out in a country's tax laws. Many countries have reasonable corporate tax rates in their laws, but most multinationals currently pay a lot less as a result of deductions, exemptions, loopholes, or tax avoidance strategies. As a result, even though 15% may sound low to some, it is quite significant as it is the rate of tax actually paid. The minimum tax puts a floor on tax competition and is expected to generate around USD 150 billion in additional global tax revenues.[16]

12. However, on a country-specific basis, the additional revenue generation arising from GloBE Rules shall depend on many factors, *inter alia* mentioned below:

- adherence by the IF member countries to the timeline prescribed for implementation of GloBE Rules;

14. Refer 'OECD's Press Release dated 8 October 2021 titled International community strikes a ground-breaking tax deal for the digital age' https://www.oecd.org/tax/international-community-strikes-a-ground-breaking-tax-deal-for-the-digital-age.htm accessed on 7 April 2022.
15. Refer 'OECD's FAQs on Global Anti-Base Erosion Model Rules (Pillar Two)' https://www.oecd.org/tax/beps/pillar-two-model-GloBE-rules-faqs.pdf.
16. Refer 'How global corporate tax deal was struck, OECD official Grace Perez-Navarro recounts' https://cfo.economictimes.indiatimes.com/news/how-global-corporate-tax-deal-was-struck-oecd-official-grace-perez-navarro-recounts/87010778 accessed on 7 April 2022.

- number of in-scope MNEs in a particular country;
- adoption and position taken by a critical mass of IF member countries;
- the effects of different policy choices made by other IF members given the common approach nature of GloBE Rules;
- the unfolding pattern of domestic minimum top-up tax (DMT) adoption and implementation by other jurisdictions;
- longer-term behavioural changes by both MNEs and jurisdictions in response to the GloBE framework.

1.6 COUNTRIES IN AGREEMENT OR OPPOSED TO THE TWO-PILLAR SOLUTION

13. The OECD, vide its statement dated 8 October 2021,[17] reported that 136 jurisdictions (out of the 140 members of the OECD/G20 Inclusive Framework (IF) on BEPS) joined the Statement on the Two-Pillar Solution to 'Address the Tax Challenges Arising from the Digitalisation of the Economy', ensuring that the firms pay a fair share of tax wherever they operate and generate profits. It was also reported that four countries, namely Kenya, Nigeria, Pakistan and Sri Lanka, have not yet joined the agreement. Subsequently, OECD reported that 137 member jurisdictions of IF have agreed to it as of 4 November 2021.[18] Additionally, as of 31 May 2022, it has been reported that Poland[19] has raised concerns that the minimum tax could enter into force without the new rules preventing big multinationals from booking profits in the most favourable countries. Poland is of the view that the October 2021 global agreement on a Two-Pillar Solution was premised on simultaneous implementation of the two pillars, and the Pillar Two rules, therefore, should not be adopted on a stand-alone basis. The Implementation of GloBE Rules by various Jurisdictions is further discussed in detail in Chapter 6 of the book.

17. Refer 'OECD's Press Release dated 8 October 2021 titled International community strikes a ground-breaking tax deal for the digital age' https://www.oecd.org/tax/international-community-strikes-a-ground-breaking-tax-deal-for-the-digital-age.htm accessed on 7 April 2022.
18. Refer 'OECD's Statement on a Two-Pillar Solution to Address the Tax Challenges Arising from the Digitalisation of the Economy – 8 October 2021' https://www.oecd.org/tax/beps/statement-on-a-two-pillar-solution-to-address-the-tax-challenges-arising-from-the-digitalisation-of-the-economy-october-2021.htm accessed on 7 April 2022.
19. Refer 'Poland blocks EU compromise on global minimum corporate tax deal' https://www.reuters.com/world/europe/poland-blocks-eu-compromise-global-minimum-corporate-tax-deal-2022-04-05/ accessed on 7 April 2022 (Poland has subsequently agreed, while Hungary has objected to implementation of a global minimum tax in the EU).

CHAPTER 2
Pillar Two Proposals

The Pillar Two blueprint is the mother document containing innovative and complex rules as approved by the IF members, subject to certain pending agreements. Subsequent additional developments to Pillar Two rules as a result of agreement of IF members are reflected in 1 July 2021 and 8 October 2021 statements released by the OECD, which got culminated with the release of GloBE rules on 20 December 2021. The GloBE rules are further explained by the Commentary and Illustrative Examples released by the OECD on 14 March 2022.

2.1 EVOLUTION OF PILLAR TWO PROPOSALS

14. Eliminating opportunities for cross-border tax avoidance, evasion and the effective/efficient prevention of double taxation are critical to building an international tax system that supports economic growth and a resilient global economy. Globalisation has exacerbated the impact of gaps and frictions among different countries' tax systems. As a result, some features of the current bilateral tax treaty system facilitated BEPS, which needed to be addressed. BEPS[20] refers to tax planning strategies used by MNEs that exploit gaps and mismatches in tax rules to avoid paying tax. Work on BEPS *inter alia,* including taxation of digital economies, gained momentum with the release of the report by the OECD titled 'Addressing Base Erosion and Profit Shifting' in February 2013, following which OECD and G20 countries adopted a 15-point Action Plan to address BEPS in September 2013. BEPS practices cost countries USD 100-240 billion in lost revenue annually. Working together within OECD/G20 Inclusive Framework (IF)[21] on BEPS, 141 countries and jurisdictions are collaborating on the implementation of 15 measures to tackle tax avoidance, improve the coherence of international tax rules and ensure a more transparent tax environment. The Action Plan identified 15 actions along three key pillars:

20. Refer 'OECD – What is BEPS?' http://www.oecd.org/tax/beps/about/ accessed on 8 April 2022.
21. Refer 'Members of the OECD/G20 Inclusive Framework on BEPS' https://www.oecd.org/tax/beps/inclusive-framework-on-beps-composition.pdf accessed on 8 April 2022.

(1) introducing coherence in the domestic rules that affect cross-border activities;
(2) reinforcing substance requirements in the existing international standards;
(3) improving transparency as well as certainty.

15. In subsequence to adoption of the 15-point Action Plan to address BEPS in September 2013, after two years of work, measures in response to 15 actions were delivered to G20 Leaders in November 2015, comprising BEPS 2015 Final Reports. The 15 Actions[22] equip governments with domestic and international rules and instruments to address tax avoidance, ensuring that profits are taxed where economic activities generating the profits are performed. Implementation of these 15 BEPS Action Reports is now underway, out of which BEPS Action Reports 2, 6, 7 and 14 are being implemented through the BEPS Action 15 Report titled the 'Multilateral Convention to Implement Tax Treaty related measures to prevent Base Erosion & Profit Shifting (MLI)',[23] with an objective to modify existing bilateral tax treaties solely in order to swiftly implement the tax treaty measures developed in the course of the OECD/G20 BEPS Project.

16. The BEPS Action 1 Final Report[24] titled 'Addressing the Tax Challenges of the Digital Economy' provides that the digital economy is the result of a transformative process brought by ICT, which has made technologies cheaper, more powerful, and widely standardised, improving business processes and bolstering innovation across all sectors of the economy. Some of the key features of the digital economy and its business models exacerbate BEPS risks. To address broader tax challenges raised by the digital economy, the following options were analysed:

(i) a new nexus in the form of a significant economic presence;
(ii) a withholding tax on certain types of digital transactions; and
(iii) an equalisation levy.

Countries were given the option to introduce any of the above three options in their domestic laws as additional safeguards against BEPS, provided they respect existing treaty obligations or in their bilateral tax treaties.

17. At the request of the G20, the IF continued to work on the issue of tax challenges arising from the digitalisation of the economies, delivering an interim report in March 2018.[25] In January 2019,[26] members of the IF agreed to examine proposals in two pillars, which could form the basis for a consensus solution to the tax challenges arising

---

22. Refer 'OECD – BEPS Actions' http://www.oecd.org/tax/beps/beps-actions/ accessed on 8 April 2022.
23. Refer 'MLI Made Easy' by Kuldeep Sharma (paragraphs 9, 10), published by Wolters Kluwer https://law-store.wolterskluwer.com/s/product/mli-made-easy/01t4R00000Oibvu accessed on 8 April 2022.
24. Refer 'Action 1: BEPS 2015 Final Report, OECD/G20 Base Erosion and Profit Shifting Project' http://www.oecd.org/tax/beps-2015-final-reports.htm.
25. Refer 'OECD's Tax Challenges Arising from Digitalisation – Interim Report 2018' https://www.oecd.org/ctp/tax-challenges-arising-from-digitalisation-interim-report-9789264293083-en.htm accessed on 8 April 2022.

from digitalisation. Pillar One is focused on nexus and profit allocation, whereas Pillar Two is focused on a global minimum tax intended to address remaining BEPS issues. A programme of work to be conducted on Pillar One and Pillar Two was adopted in May 2019[27] and later endorsed by the G20 in June 2019.[28] As part of the May 2019 programme of work, the OECD Secretariat was also mandated to carry out an economic analysis and impact assessment of the Pillar One and Pillar Two proposals. On 30 January 2020,[29] a statement was released by the OECD/G20 IF on BEPS intimating that the IF has agreed upon an outline of the architecture of a Unified Approach on Pillar One as the basis for negotiations and welcomed the progress made on Pillar Two. In respect of Pillar Two, it was *inter alia* further reported in the said statement that significant work on key issues is advancing at a fast pace with good technical progress on many aspects of the GloBE proposal, but significant work still remains. In July 2020, the G20 mandated the IF to produce reports on the Blueprints of Pillar One and Pillar Two to be presented before the G20 Finance Ministers meeting in October 2020. This report (blueprint) was approved by the IF on 8-9 October 2020 and published on 14 October 2020[30] by the OECD Secretariat.

18. The Pillar Two blueprint[31] is the mother document containing innovative and complex rules as approved by the IF members, subject to certain pending agreements. Subsequent additional developments to Pillar Two rules as a result of agreement of IF members are reflected in 1 July 2021[32] and 8 October 2021[33] statements released by the

26. Refer 'OECD's Policy Note: Addressing the Tax Challenges of the Digitalisation of the Economy as approved by the IF on BEPS on 23 January 2019' https://www.oecd.org/tax/beps/policy-note-beps-inclusive-framework-addressing-tax-challenges-digitalisation.pdf accessed on 8 April 2022.
27. Refer 'OECD's Programme of Work to Develop a Consensus Solution to the Tax Challenges arising from the Digitalisation of the Economy' https://www.oecd.org/tax/beps/programme-of-work-to-develop-a-consensus-solution-to-the-tax-challenges-arising-from-the-digitalisation-of-the-economy.pdf accessed on 8 April 2022.
28. Refer 'OECD Secretary-General Tax Report to G20 Leaders in Osaka, Japan in June 2019 (pg. 9, 13)' https://www.oecd.org/tax/oecd-secretary-general-tax-report-g20-leaders-june-2019.pdf accessed on 8 April 2022.
29. Refer 'Statement by the OECD/G20 IF on BEPS on the Two-Pillar Approach to Address the Tax Challenges Arising from the Digitalisation of the Economy, as approved on 29-30 January 2020' https://www.oecd.org/tax/beps/statement-by-the-oecd-g20-inclusive-framework-on-beps-january-2020.pdf accessed on 8 April 2022.
30. Refer 'Report on Pillar Two Blueprint by IF on BEPS' https://www.oecd.org/tax/beps/tax-challenges-arising-from-digitalisation-report-on-pillar-two-blueprint-abb4c3d1-en.htm accessed on 8 April 2022.
31. *Id.*
32. Refer 'OECD's Statement on a Two-Pillar Solution to Address the Tax Challenges Arising From the Digitalisation of the Economy dated 1 July 2021' https://www.oecd.org/tax/beps/statement-on-a-two-pillar-solution-to-address-the-tax-challenges-arising-from-the-digitalisation-of-the-economy-july-2021.pdf accessed on 8 April 2022.
33. Refer 'OECD's Statement on a Two-Pillar Solution to Address the Tax Challenges Arising from the Digitalisation of the Economy dated 8 October 2021' https://www.oecd.org/tax/beps/statement-on-a-two-pillar-solution-to-address-the-tax-challenges-arising-from-the-digitalisation-of-the-economy-october-2021.pdf accessed on 8 April 2022.

OECD, which got culminated with the release of GloBE rules on 20 December 2021.[34] The GloBE rules are further explained by the Commentary[35] and Illustrative Examples[36] released by the OECD on 14 March 2022.

2.2 BLUEPRINT ON PILLAR TWO

19. The blueprint on Pillar Two states[37] that Pillar Two would address remaining BEPS challenges and sets out rules that would provide jurisdictions with a right to 'tax back' where other jurisdictions have not exercised their primary taxing rights or the payment is otherwise subject to low levels of effective taxation. These rules would ensure that all large, internationally operating businesses pay at least a minimum level of tax. Jurisdictions are free to determine their own tax systems, including whether they have a CIT and the level of their tax rates, but also consider the right of other jurisdictions to apply an internationally agreed Pillar Two regime where income is taxed below an agreed minimum rate. The so-called tax back is achieved via a number of interlocking rules[38] that seek to (i) ensure minimum taxation while avoiding double taxation or taxation where there is no economic profit, (ii) cope with different tax system designs by jurisdictions as well as different operating models by businesses, (iii) ensure transparency and a level playing field, and (iv) minimise administrative and compliance costs.

20. *Interlocking rules under Pillar Two* – Ensuring minimum taxation under Pillar Two is achieved through IIR, together with the Undertaxed Profits Rule (UTPR)[39] acting as a backstop. The IIR and UTPR are complemented by Switch-Over Rule (SOR) and Subject to Tax Rule (STTR). These rules are briefly described hereunder:

- IIR – The operation of the IIR is, in some respects, based on traditional controlled foreign company (CFC) rule principles and triggers an inclusion at the level of the shareholder where the income of a controlled foreign entity is

34. Refer 'OECD's Global Anti-Base Erosion Model Rules (Pillar Two)' https://www.oecd.org/tax/beps/tax-challenges-arising-from-the-digitalisation-of-the-economy-global-anti-base-erosion-model-rules-pillar-two.pdf accessed on 8 April 2022.
35. Refer 'OECD's Commentary to the Global Anti-Base Erosion Model Rules (Pillar Two)' https://www.oecd.org/tax/beps/tax-challenges-arising-from-the-digitalisation-of-the-economy-global-anti-base-erosion-model-rules-pillar-two-commentary.pdf accessed on 8 April 2022.
36. Refer 'OECD's Global Anti-Base Erosion Model Rules (Pillar Two) Examples' https://www.oecd.org/tax/beps/tax-challenges-arising-from-the-digitalisation-of-the-economy-global-anti-base-erosion-model-rules-pillar-two-examples.pdf accessed on 8 April 2022.
37. Refer 'Cover Statement by the OECD/G20 IF on BEPS on the Reports on the Blueprints of Pillar One and Pillar Two' as contained on pages 10-12 of the Report on Pillar Two Blueprint.
38. Refer Executive Summary (paragraph 8) of the Report on Pillar Two Blueprint.
39. Earlier referred to as Undertaxed Payments Rule. Now referred to as Undertaxed Profits Rule as in 'The HMRC's OECD Pillar 2 Consultation on implementation (paragraphs 1.16 and 7.1)' https://assets.publishing.service.gov.uk/government/uploads/system/uploads/attachment_data/file/1045663/11Jan_2022_Pillar_2_Consultation_.pdf accessed on 12 April 2022 and in 'International Tax Measures announced in Budget 2022 by Canada, Pillar Two – Global Minimum Tax' https://budget.gc.ca/2022/report-rapport/tm-mf-en.html#a4_1_2 accessed on 15 May 2022.

taxed below the effective minimum tax rate.[40] The primacy of the IIR and use of the top-down approach[41] is largely driven by:
- simplicity and lower compliance costs;
- the ease of obtaining the necessary income and tax information required to make an ETR determination;
- the fact that the IIR will generally require only one adjustment to be made by a single taxpayer and the availability of mechanisms to avoid the risk of double taxation; and
- the general decision to use a top-down rather than a bottom-up approach for the use of the IIR in connection with multi-tier MNE Groups is driven in significant part by compliance and simplicity considerations. The top-down approach will limit the number of jurisdictions applying the IIR, thereby reducing the need for coordination and, by extension, complexity, administrative burden, and the risk of double taxation under the rules.

- UTPR – It is a secondary rule and only applies where a Constituent Entity (CE) is not already subject to an IIR. The UTPR is nevertheless a key part of the rule set as it serves as backstop to the IIR, ensures a level playing field and addresses inversion risks that might otherwise arise.[42]
- SOR – IIR is complemented by a SOR that removes treaty obstacles from its application to certain branch structures and applies where an income tax treaty otherwise obligates a contracting state to use the exemption method.[43]
- STTR – It complements the above rules. It acknowledges that denying treaty benefits for certain deductible intragroup payments made to jurisdictions (i.e., jurisdiction of the payee) where those payments are subject to no or low rates of nominal taxation may help source countries (i.e., jurisdiction of the payer) to protect their tax base, notably for countries with lower administrative capacities.[44] STTR allows the source jurisdiction to impose additional taxation on certain covered payments up to the agreed minimum rate.[45] It is based on a nominal tax rate test, thereby avoiding the conceptual and administrative challenges of using an ETR test.[46]

21. *Scope*[47] *of Pillar Two:* The above-stated rules apply to MNE Groups and their CEs within the consolidated group as determined under applicable financial accounting standards. They only apply to businesses that meet or exceed a EUR 750 million annual gross revenue threshold. This threshold has certain benefits, as mentioned below:

- creates synergies with the current BEPS Action 13 Country-by-Country Reporting (CbCR) rules, thereby reducing compliance costs;

40. Refer Executive Summary (paragraph 9) of the Report on Pillar Two Blueprint.
41. *Id.* (pg. 18).
42. *Id.* (paragraph 10).
43. *Id.* (paragraph 9).
44. *Id.* (paragraph 11).
45. *Id.* (paragraph 20).
46. *Id.* (pg. 18).
47. *Id.* (paragraph 12).

- avoids adverse impacts on Small and Medium Enterprises (SMEs) while preserving the impact of the rules with in-scope MNE Groups still earning over 90% of global corporate revenues.

22. *Exclusions*[48] *from Pillar Two:* The Pillar Two rules exclude the following from its scope:

- certain parent entities, including investment and pension funds;
- governmental entities such as sovereign wealth funds and international and non-profit bodies, which typically benefit from an exclusion or exemption from tax under applicable domestic tax law.

23. *Entities subject to special rules:*[49] Special rules under Pillar Two may apply to Associates, joint ventures and so-called orphan entities that are not part of the consolidated group.

24. *Tax base:*[50] Both the IIR and the UTPR use a common tax base. The determination of the base starts with the financial accounts prepared under the accounting standard used by the parent of the MNE Group to prepare its consolidated financial statements (CFS). This must be International Financial Reporting Standards (IFRS) or another acceptable accounting standard. The use of financial accounts as a common basis ensures certain benefits as mentioned below:

- a level playing field for both jurisdictions and MNEs;
- enhances transparency; and
- leverages off existing systems, thereby minimising compliance cost.

Certain adjustments are then made to the financial accounts to eliminate specific items of income from the tax base, such as intragroup dividends and to incorporate certain expenses, such as tax-deductible stock-based compensation. This is necessary where the outcomes of the financial accounting rules would otherwise distort the tax policy objectives of Pillar Two.

25. *Covered Taxes:*[51] The IIR and the UTPR use a common definition of taxes, referred to as 'covered taxes', which is derived from the definition of taxes used for statistical purposes by many international organisations, including the OECD, European Union (EU), International Monetary Fund (IMF), World Bank and the United Nations (UN). The definition is deliberately kept broad for the purposes mentioned below:

- to avoid legalistic distinctions; and
- accommodate different tax systems provided they substantively impose taxes on an entity's income or profits.

---

48. *Id.* (paragraph 13).
49. *Id.* (paragraph 13).
50. *Id.* (paragraph 14).
51. *Id.* (paragraph 15).

26. *ETR:*[52] The ETR is determined by applying the tax base and covered taxes on a jurisdictional basis. This requires an assignment of the income and taxes among the jurisdictions in which the MNE operates and to which it pays taxes. The GloBE tax computation calculation also includes two important additional adjustments; a mechanism to mitigate the impact of volatility in the ETR from one period to the next and a formulaic substance carve-out. Any top-up tax imposed under the STTR will be taken into account in determining the ETR for purposes of the IIR and the UTPR.[53]

27. *Mechanism of operation of Pillar Two:*[54] If an MNE's jurisdictional ETR is below the agreed minimum rate, the MNE will be liable for an incremental amount of tax that is sufficient to bring the total amount of tax on the excess profits up to the minimum rate. The ETR calculation therefore operates both as a trigger for the imposition of the tax liability and as a measure of the amount of top-up tax imposed under the rules. This design ensures a level playing field as all MNEs pay a minimum level of tax in each jurisdiction in which they operate, while the top-up mechanism coupled with the common base makes sure that they face the same level of top-up tax irrespective of where they are based. The amount of top-up tax is collected either by application of the IIR or, where no IIR applies, by the application of the UTPR.

28. *Implementation of Pillar Two:*[55] While the IIR and the UTPR do not require changes to bilateral treaties and can be implemented by way of changes to domestic law, both the STTR and the SOR can only be implemented through changes to existing bilateral tax treaties. The latter could be implemented through bilateral negotiations and amendments to individual treaties or as part of a multilateral convention.

29. *GILTI coexistence:* GILTI is the income earned by foreign affiliates of US companies from intangible assets such as patents, trademarks, and copyrights. The Tax Cuts and Jobs Act 2017 (TCJA) imposes a new minimum tax on GILTI. GILTI is intended to approximate the income from intangible assets (such as patents, trademarks, and copyrights) held abroad so as to discourage US firms from shifting these assets offshore.[56] Given the pre-existing nature of the GILTI regime and its legislative intent, there are reasons for treating GILTI as a qualified IIR for purposes of the GloBE rules, provided that the coexistence achieves reasonably equivalent effects.[57] Further consideration is required as to how the interactions between the GILTI and the GloBE rules would be coordinated.

30. The application of GloBE rules to wholly owned CEs of an MNE group is depicted below through a flow diagram in Figure 2.1.

---

52. *Id.* (paragraph 16).
53. *Id.* (paragraph 20).
54. *Id.* (paragraph 19).
55. *Id.* (paragraph 21).
56. Refer 'Tax Policy Center's Note titled What is global intangible low-taxed income and how is it taxed under the TCJA?' https://www.taxpolicycenter.org/briefing-book/what-global-intangible-low-taxed-income-and-how-it-taxed-under-tcja accessed on 9 April 2022.
57. Refer Executive Summary (paragraph 27) of the Report on Pillar Two Blueprint.

Figure 2.1 Flow Diagram on Application of GloBE Rules

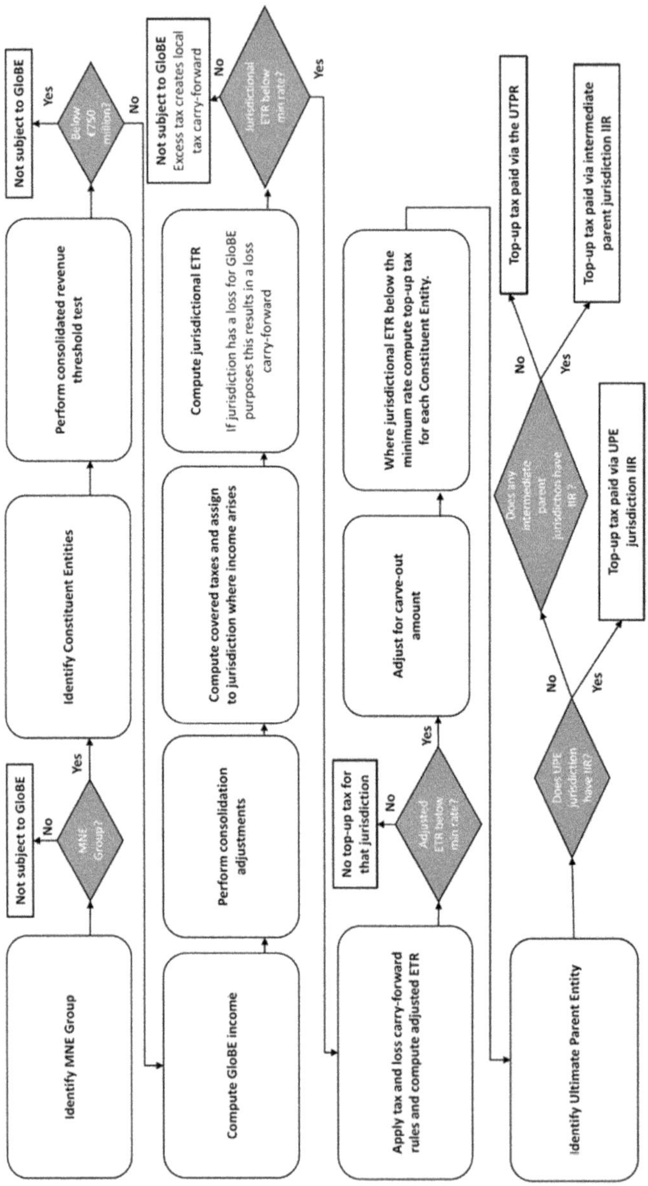

Source: Executive Summary of the Report on Pillar Two Blueprint (pg. 21).

2.3 OECD'S STATEMENT DATED 1 JULY 2021 IN RESPECT OF PILLAR TWO

31. The OECD's statement dated 1 July 2021[58] was an update on the IF discussions on the Two-Pillar Solution. The statement primarily continued with Pillar Two Proposals reported in the blueprint (as mentioned *supra*) and provided an overview of certain additional agreements between the IF members, as mentioned below:

- *Rule Status*: In the Pillar Two blueprint, no agreement was reached between the IF members over the status of IIR and UTPR as a common approach, including an acceptance of the right of all members of the IF to implement them as part of an agreed Pillar Two regime. However, the OECD's statement dated 1 July 2021 reported that the GloBE Rules will have the status of a common approach, which means that IF members:
  - are not required to adopt the GloBE rules, but if they choose to do so, they will implement and administer the rules in a way that is consistent with the outcomes provided for under Pillar Two, including in light of model rules and guidance agreed to by the IF;
  - accept the application of the GloBE rules applied by other IF members, including agreement as to rule order and the application of any agreed safe harbours.
- *Scope*: Countries are free to apply the IIR to MNEs headquartered in their country even if they do not meet the threshold of EUR 750 million.
- *Rule Design*: The IIR allocates top-up tax based on a top-down approach subject to a split-ownership rule for shareholdings below 80%.[59] The UTPR allocates top-up tax from low-tax constituent entities, including those located in the UPE jurisdiction, under a methodology to be agreed upon.
- *ETR calculation:* In respect of existing distribution tax systems, there will be no top-up tax liability if earnings are distributed within three to four years[60] and taxed at or above the minimum level.
- *Minimum rate*: The minimum tax rate used for purposes of the IIR and UTPR will be at least 15%.
- *Carve-outs*: The GloBE rules will provide for a formulaic substance carve-out that will exclude an amount of income that is at least 5% (in the transition period of five years, at least 7.5%) of the carrying value of tangible assets and payroll.
- *De minimis exclusion*: The GloBE rules will provide for a *de minimis* exclusion.

58. Refer 'OECD's Statement on a Two-Pillar Solution to Address the Tax Challenges Arising From the Digitalisation of the Economy dated 1 July 2021' https://www.oecd.org/tax/beps/statement-on-a-two-pillar-solution-to-address-the-tax-challenges-arising-from-the-digitalisation-of-the-economy-july-2021.pdf.
59. In the Pillar Two blueprint, the percentage was not agreed upon.
60. In the Pillar Two blueprint (paragraph 228), the discussion was to increase ETR to the extent an equal amount of distribution tax is not paid within a reasonable period of time, e.g., two to four years.

- *Exclusion for international shipping income*: The GloBE rules provide for an exclusion for international shipping income using the definition of such income under the OECD Model Tax Convention (MTC).
- *Safe harbour*: To ensure that the administration of the GloBE rules is as targeted as possible, to promote simplification and to avoid compliance and administrative costs that are disproportionate to the policy objectives, the implementation framework will include safe harbours and/or other mechanisms.
- *STTR*: IF members that apply nominal CIT rates below the STTR minimum rate to interest, royalties and a defined set of other payments would implement the STTR into their bilateral treaties with developing IF members when requested to do so. The taxing right will be limited to the difference between the minimum rate and the tax rate on the payment. The minimum rate for the STTR will be from 7.5% to 9%.
- *Implementation:* Pillar Two should be brought into law in 2022 to be effective in 2023. The implementation plan will include:
  - GloBE Model rules with proper mechanisms to facilitate over time the coordination of the GloBE rules that have been implemented by IF members, including the possible development of a multilateral instrument for that purpose.
  - An STTR model provision together with a multilateral instrument to facilitate its adoption.
  - Transitional rules, including the possibility of a deferred implementation of the UTPR.
- *GILTI coexistence*: Consideration will be given to the conditions under which the US GILTI regime will coexist with the GloBE rules to ensure a level playing field.

2.4 OECD'S STATEMENT DATED 8 OCTOBER 2021 IN RESPECT OF PILLAR TWO

32. The OECD's statement dated 8 October 2021[61] was an update on the IF discussions on the Two-Pillar Solution. The statement primarily continued with Pillar Two Proposals reported in the blueprint and statement dated 1 July 2021 (as mentioned *supra*) and provided an overview of certain additional agreements between the IF members, as mentioned below:

- *IF members in agreement*: The landmark deal, agreed by 136 countries and jurisdictions representing more than 90% of global GDP, is supported by all

61. Refer 'OECD's Statement on a Two-Pillar Solution to Address the Tax Challenges Arising from the Digitalisation of the Economy dated 8 October 2021' https://www.oecd.org/tax/beps/statement-on-a-two-pillar-solution-to-address-the-tax-challenges-arising-from-the-digitalisation-of-the-economy-october-2021.pdf

OECD and G20 countries. Four countries, namely Kenya, Nigeria, Pakistan and Sri Lanka, have not yet joined the agreement.

- *Rule Design*: The UTPR allocates top-up tax from low-tax constituent entities, including those located in the UPE jurisdiction. The GloBE rules will provide for an exclusion from the UTPR for MNEs in the initial phase of their international activity, defined as those MNEs that have a maximum of EUR 50 million tangible assets abroad and that operate in no more than five other jurisdictions. This exclusion is limited to a period of five years after the MNE comes into the scope of the GloBE rules for the first time. For MNEs that are in scope of the GloBE rules, when they come into effect, the period of five years will start at the time the UTPR rules come into effect.[62]
- *ETR calculation*: In respect of existing distribution tax systems, there will be no top-up tax liability if earnings are distributed within four years[63] and taxed at or above the minimum level.
- *Minimum rate*: The minimum tax rate used for purposes of the IIR and UTPR will be 15%.[64]
- *Carve-outs*: The GloBE rules will provide for a formulaic substance carve-out that will exclude an amount of income that is 5% of the carrying value of tangible assets and payroll. In a transition period of ten years, the amount of income excluded will be 8% of the carrying value of tangible assets and 10% of payroll, declining annually by 0.2 percentage points for the first five years and by 0.4 percentage points for tangible assets and by 0.8 percentage points for payroll for the last five years.[65]
- *De minimis exclusion*: The GloBE rules will provide for a *de minimis* exclusion for those jurisdictions where the MNE has revenues of less than EUR 10 million and profits of less than EUR 1 million.[66]
- *STTR*: The minimum rate for the STTR will be 9%.[67]
- *Implementation:* The UTPR shall come into effect in 2024.[68]

2.5 OECD'S PILLAR TWO MODEL RULES DATED 20 DECEMBER 2021

33. OECD's statement dated 8 October 2021 was followed by release of Pillar Two Model Rules on 20 December 2021,[69] which define the scope and set out the

62. In OECD's statement dated 1 July 2021, the methodology was not agreed upon.
63. In OECD's statement dated 1 July 2021, the period mentioned was three to four years.
64. In OECD's statement dated 1 July 2021, the minimum tax rate mentioned was at least 15%.
65. In OECD's statement dated 1 July 2021, the percentage and period of carve-outs was different.
66. In OECD's statement dated 1 July 2021, the quantum was not specified.
67. In OECD's statement dated 1 July 2021, the minimum rate was undecided and was mentioned in the range of 7.5% to 9%.
68. In OECD's statement dated 1 July 2021, the period of entering into effect of UTPR was not agreed among the IF members.
69. Refer 'OECD's Global Anti-Base Erosion Model Rules (Pillar Two)' https://www.oecd.org/tax/beps/tax-challenges-arising-from-the-digitalisation-of-the-economy-global-anti-base-erosion-model-rules-pillar-two.pdf.

mechanism for GloBE rules under Pillar Two. Taxpayers that either have no foreign presence or that have less than EUR 750 million in consolidated revenues are not in scope of the Model Rules.[70] The Model Rules have *inter alia* introduced certain new features, which are briefly discussed below:

- the Pillar Two Model Rules contemplate the possibility that jurisdictions may introduce their own DMT based on the GloBE mechanics, which is then fully creditable against any liability under GloBE, thereby preserving a jurisdiction's primary right of taxation over its own income;
- the UTPR rule works by requiring an adjustment (such as a denial of a deduction or making an equivalent adjustment) that increases the tax at the level of the subsidiary. The adjustment is an amount sufficient to result in the group entities paying their share of the top-up tax remaining after the IIR. The share of the top-up tax is calculated based on a formula in proportion to the relative share of assets and employees. This not only helps to ensure the rule is administrable but also attaches the adjustment to entities that are most likely to have the capacity to pay the required amount of top-up tax. Increase in payment of tax at the level of the subsidiary based on relative share of assets and employees also ensures sharing of top-up tax with jurisdictions having substantial activity so as to compensate such jurisdictions for the intensity in Functions Performed, Assets Utilised and Risks Assumed (FAR) arising out of enhanced deployment of assets and employees. It would be pertinent to state here paragraph 81 of the Commentary of Chapter 2, as below:

> The UTPR Percentage is determined on the basis of factors that reflect the relative substance of the MNE Group in each UTPR Jurisdiction. Relying on substance factors provides for a simple and transparent allocation key which facilitates the coordination among tax administrations. It is also expected that the jurisdictions where the MNE Group has more substance on a relative basis will be those where there is more tax capacity (such as deductible expenditure) to absorb adjustments under the UTPR. This approach, together with the exclusion mechanism in Article 2.6.3, is intended to reduce the risk of allocating Top-up Tax to a jurisdiction that does not have enough capacity to impose the UTPR adjustment.

2.6 COMMENTARY ON PILLAR TWO MODEL RULES

34. The Commentary[71] and Illustrative Examples[72] on Pillar Two Model Rules were released by the OECD on 14 March 2022. The Commentary provides tax

70. Refer 'OECD's The Pillar Two Rules in a Nutshell (Overview)' https://www.oecd.org/tax/beps/pillar-two-model-rules-in-a-nutshell.pdf.
71. Refer 'OECD's Commentary to the Global Anti-Base Erosion Model Rules (Pillar Two)' https://www.oecd.org/tax/beps/tax-challenges-arising-from-the-digitalisation-of-the-economy-global-anti-base-erosion-model-rules-pillar-two-commentary.pdf
72. Refer 'OECD's Global Anti-Base Erosion Model Rules (Pillar Two) Examples' https://www.oecd.org/tax/beps/tax-challenges-arising-from-the-digitalisation-of-the-economy-global-anti-base-erosion-model-rules-pillar-two-examples.pdf

administrations and taxpayers with guidance on the interpretation and application of these rules. The Commentary is intended to promote a consistent and common interpretation of the GloBE Rules that will facilitate coordinated outcomes for both tax administrations and MNE Groups. The Commentary explains the intended outcomes under the rules and clarifies the meaning of certain terms. It also includes examples which illustrate the application of the rules to certain fact patterns.

2.7 RECAP OF ADVANCEMENT MADE IN SALIENT PILLAR TWO PROPOSALS

35. The core concepts of Pillar Two Proposals, as agreed by the IF members, are incorporated in the Report on Pillar Two Blueprint, which addresses all the key technical aspects of the design of GloBE Rules. Continued discussions, including public consultations, paved the way for the blueprint to undergo modifications in a few areas from time to time. A quick recap of the advancements and changes made in salient Pillar Two Proposals commencing from the release of Report on Pillar Two Blueprint and subsequent agreements made by IF members, as reflected in OECD's statements dated 1 July 2021 and 8 October 2021, respectively, culminating with the release of GloBE Model Rules on 20 December 2021, is captured in Table 2.1.

Table 2.1 Advancements and Changes Made in Salient Pillar Two Proposals Commencing from Blueprint Report Till the Release of GloBE Model Rules

S.N	*Particulars of Proposal under Pillar Two*	*Blueprint*	*OECD Statement Dated 1 July 2021*	*OECD Statement Dated 8 October 2021*	*GloBE Model Rules*
1	GloBE Rules will have the status of a common approach.	No such agreement between IF members as yet.	Agreement is reached between IF members that GloBE Rules will have the status of a common approach.	Agreement is continued with.	Agreement is continued with.
2	Threshold test of EUR 750 million – period thereof.	MNE Groups having total consolidated group revenue below EUR 750 million or equivalent in the immediately preceding fiscal year of the Group, are to be excluded from the application of the GloBE rules.	No mention of period.	No mention of period.	There is a four-year test period determining whether the threshold is met. Generally, if revenue of EUR 750 million is exceeded in two of the previous four fiscal years, the threshold is met.
3	Countries are free to apply the IIR to MNEs headquartered in their country even if they do not meet the threshold of EUR 750 million.	Not decided as yet.	This provision is introduced.	This provision is continued with.	This provision is continued with.

S.N	*Particulars of Proposal under Pillar Two*	*Blueprint*	*OECD Statement Dated 1 July 2021*	*OECD Statement Dated 8 October 2021*	*GloBE Model Rules*
4	Exclusion of international shipping income.	Not decided as yet.	To be excluded.	To be excluded.	To be excluded.
5	Methodology to allocate the UTPR top-up tax.	The top-up tax is allocated to a UTPR Taxpayer in two steps as follows: (a) First, if the UTPR Taxpayer makes any deductible payments to the low-tax Constituent Entity during the relevant period, the top-up tax of such CE is allocated to the UTPR Taxpayer in proportion to the total of deductible payments made to that entity by all UTPR Taxpayers;	No mention of agreed methodology.	No mention of agreed methodology.	Allocation based on relative number of employees and the value of tangible assets in the jurisdiction in proportion to the number of employees and the value of tangible assets in all the UTPR jurisdictions.

S.N	*Particulars of Proposal under Pillar Two*	*Blueprint*	*OECD Statement Dated 1 July 2021*	*OECD Statement Dated 8 October 2021*	*GloBE Model Rules*
		(b) Second, if the UTPR Taxpayer has net intragroup expenditure, in proportion to the total amount of net intragroup expenditure incurred by all UTPR Taxpayers. The top-up tax allocated to a UTPR Taxpayer under each step is limited to an amount equal to the domestic covered tax rate multiplied by the gross amount of deductible intragroup payments taken into consideration in calculating its portion of top-up tax.			
6	Rule Design for period of exclusion under the UTPR.	Methodology to be agreed.	Methodology to be agreed.	Exclusion limited to a period of five years after the MNE comes into the scope of the GloBE rules for the first time.	Exclusion limited to a period of five years after the MNE comes into the scope of the GloBE rules for the first time.

S.N	*Particulars of Proposal under Pillar Two*	*Blueprint*	*OECD Statement Dated 1 July 2021*	*OECD Statement Dated 8 October 2021*	*GloBE Model Rules*
7	ETR calculation in respect of existing distribution tax systems.	No top-up tax liability if earnings are distributed within 2-4 years and taxed at or above the minimum level.	No top-up tax liability if earnings are distributed within 3-4 years and taxed at or above the minimum level.	No top-up tax liability if earnings are distributed within four years and taxed at or above the minimum level.	No top-up tax liability if earnings are distributed within four years and taxed at or above the minimum level.
8	Minimum tax rate for purposes of IIR and UTPR.	Not decided as yet.	At least 15%.	15%.	15%.
9	Carve-outs.	Not decided as yet.	Formulaic substance carve-out that will exclude an amount of income that is at least 5% (in the transition period of five years, at least 7.5%) of the carrying value of tangible assets and payroll.	Formulaic substance carve-out that will exclude an amount of income that is 5% of the carrying value of tangible assets and payroll. In a transition period of ten years, the amount of income excluded will be 8% of the carrying value of tangible assets and 10% of payroll, declining annually by 0.2 percentage points for the	Formulaic substance carve-out that will exclude an amount of income that is 5% of the carrying value of tangible assets and payroll. In a transition period of ten years, the amount of income excluded will be 8% of the carrying value of tangible assets and 10% of payroll, declining annually by 0.2 percentage points for the

S.N	*Particulars of Proposal under Pillar Two*	*Blueprint*	*OECD Statement Dated 1 July 2021*	*OECD Statement Dated 8 October 2021*	*GloBE Model Rules*
				first five years, and by 0.4 percentage points for tangible assets and by 0.8 percentage points for payroll for the last five years.	first five years, and by 0.4 percentage points for tangible assets and by 0.8 percentage points for payroll for the last five years.
10	Adjustments for timing differences in calculating jurisdictional ETR.	Local tax carry-forwards will be taken into account to determine the jurisdictional ETR.	No comment on this issue.	No comment on this issue.	Deferred tax accounting approach to determine the jurisdictional ETR.
11	Whether Real Estate Investment Vehicle that is a UPE is considered as an Excluded Entity.	No	No	No	Yes
12	Mechanism to bring JVs into the scope of GloBE Rules.	A simplified IIR may apply to the income attributable to interests in JVs.	No comment on this issue.	No comment on this issue.	Top-up Tax of the JV Group shall be computed in accordance with Chapters 3 to 7 and Article 8.2 as if the members of the JV Group were CEs of a separate MNE Group and as if the JV was the UPE of that Group. The JV or its JV Subsidiaries

S.N	*Particulars of Proposal under Pillar Two*	*Blueprint*	*OECD Statement Dated 1 July 2021*	*OECD Statement Dated 8 October 2021*	*GloBE Model Rules*
					to not apply the IIR or the UTPR directly. Rather, the MNE Group to determine Top-up Tax in respect of a JV (or its JV Subsidiaries) located in a Low-Taxed Jurisdiction and allocate any resulting Top-up Tax to a CE within the MNE Group under the IIR or the UTPR.
13	*De minimis* exclusion.	Amounts not agreed upon as yet.	Amounts not agreed upon as yet.	Revenues of less than EUR 10 million and profits of less than EUR 1 million.	Revenues of less than EUR 10 million and profits of less than EUR 1 million.
14	Minimum rate for the STTR.	No agreement on rate.	7.5% to 9%.	9%.	STTR is not part of GloBE Rules.
15	Provision of domestic minimum top-up tax in a low-tax jurisdiction.	No	No	No	Introduced.

CHAPTER 3

Overview of Operating Provisions of GloBE Rules

GloBE Rules were released on 20 December 2021 and consist of ten chapters and 49 articles in total. These rules apply a system of top-up taxes that brings the total amount of taxes paid on an MNE's excess profit in a jurisdiction up to the minimum rate of 15%. The tax imposed under the GloBE Rules is a top-up tax calculated and applied at a jurisdictional level. The GloBE Rules are to be implemented as part of a common approach.

3.1 INTRODUCTION TO GLOBE RULES

36. GloBE Rules[73] were released on 20 December 2021 and consist of ten chapters and 49 articles in total. These rules provide for a coordinated system of taxation intended to ensure large MNE groups pay a minimum level of tax on the income arising in each of the jurisdictions where they operate. It does so by imposing a top-up tax on profits arising in a jurisdiction whenever the ETR, determined on a jurisdictional basis, is below the minimum rate of 15%. A bird's eye view of various chapters and articles of GloBE Rules is provided in Table 3.1.

73. Refer 'OECD's Global Anti-Base Erosion Model Rules (Pillar Two)' https://www.oecd.org/tax/beps/tax-challenges-arising-from-the-digitalisation-of-the-economy-global-anti-base-erosion-model-rules-pillar-two.pdf.

Table 3.1 List of Chapters and Articles of GloBE Rules

S.N	*Chapter*	*Title of Chapter*	*S.N*	*Article*	*Title of Article*
1	1	Scope	1	1.1.	Scope of GloBE Rules
			2	1.2.	MNE Group and Group
			3	1.3.	Constituent Entity
			4	1.4.	Ultimate Parent Entity
			5	1.5.	Excluded Entity
2	2	Charging Provisions	6	2.1.	Application of the IIR
			7	2.2.	Allocation of Top-Up Tax under the IIR
			8	2.3.	IIR Offset Mechanism
			9	2.4.	Application of the UTPR
			10	2.5.	UTPR Top-up Tax Amount
			11	2.6.	Allocation of Top-Up Tax for the UTPR
3	3	Computation of GloBE Income or Loss	12	3.1.	Financial Accounts
			13	3.2.	Adjustments to determine GloBE Income or Loss
			14	3.3.	International Shipping Income exclusion
			15	3.4.	Allocation of Income or Loss between a Main Entity and a Permanent Establishment
			16	3.5.	Allocation of Income or Loss from a Flow-through Entity
4	4	Computation of Adjusted Covered Taxes	17	4.1.	Adjusted Covered Taxes
			18	4.2.	Definition of Covered Taxes
			19	4.3.	Allocation of Covered Taxes from one Constituent Entity to another Constituent Entity
			20	4.4.	Mechanism to address temporary differences

S.N	*Chapter*	*Title of Chapter*	*S.N*	*Article*	*Title of Article*
			21	4.5.	The GloBE Loss Election
			22	4.6.	Post-filing Adjustments and Tax Rate Changes
5	5	Computation of Effective Tax Rate and Top-up Tax	23	5.1.	Determination of Effective Tax Rate
			24	5.2.	Top-up Tax
			25	5.3.	Substance-based Income Exclusion
			26	5.4.	Additional Current Top-up Tax
			27	5.5.	*De minimis* exclusion
			28	5.6.	Minority-Owned Constituent Entities
6	6	Corporate Restructurings and Holding Structures	29	6.1.	Application of Consolidated Revenue Threshold to Group Mergers and Demergers
			30	6.2.	Constituent Entities joining and leaving an MNE Group
			31	6.3.	Transfer of Assets and Liabilities
			32	6.4.	Joint Ventures
			33	6.5.	Multi-Parented MNE Groups
7	7	Tax neutrality and distribution regimes	34	7.1.	Ultimate Parent Entity that is a Flow-through Entity
			35	7.2.	Ultimate Parent Entity subject to Deductible Dividend Regime
			36	7.3.	Eligible Distribution Tax Systems
			37	7.4.	Effective Tax Rate Computation for Investment Entities
			38	7.5.	Investment Entity Tax Transparency Election
			39	7.6.	Taxable Distribution Method Election

S.N	*Chapter*	*Title of Chapter*	*S.N*	*Article*	*Title of Article*
8	8	Administration	40	8.1.	Filing obligation
			41	8.2.	Safe Harbours
			42	8.3.	Administrative Guidance
9	9	Transition rules	43	9.1.	Tax Attributes Upon Transition
			44	9.2.	Transitional relief for the Substance-based Income Exclusion
			45	9.3.	Exclusion from the UTPR of MNE Groups in the initial phase of their international activity
			46	9.4.	Transitional relief for filing obligations
10	10	Definitions	47	10.1.	Defined Terms
			48	10.2.	Definitions of Flow-through Entity, Tax Transparent Entity, Reverse Hybrid Entity, and Hybrid Entity
			49	10.3.	Location of an Entity and a Permanent Establishment

3.2 OVERVIEW OF OPERATION OF GLOBE RULES IN EACH CHAPTER

37. Prior to article-wise discussion of GloBE Rules in detail and in order to obtain an initial insight into the operative provisions[74] of rules contained in each chapter, refer to Figure 3.1.

74. Refer 'OECD's Global Anti-Base Erosion Model Rules (Pillar Two)' https://www.oecd.org/tax/beps/tax-challenges-arising-from-the-digitalisation-of-the-economy-global-anti-base-erosion-model-rules-pillar-two.pdf.

Figure 3.1 Operative Provisions[75] Contained in Each Chapter of GloBE Rules

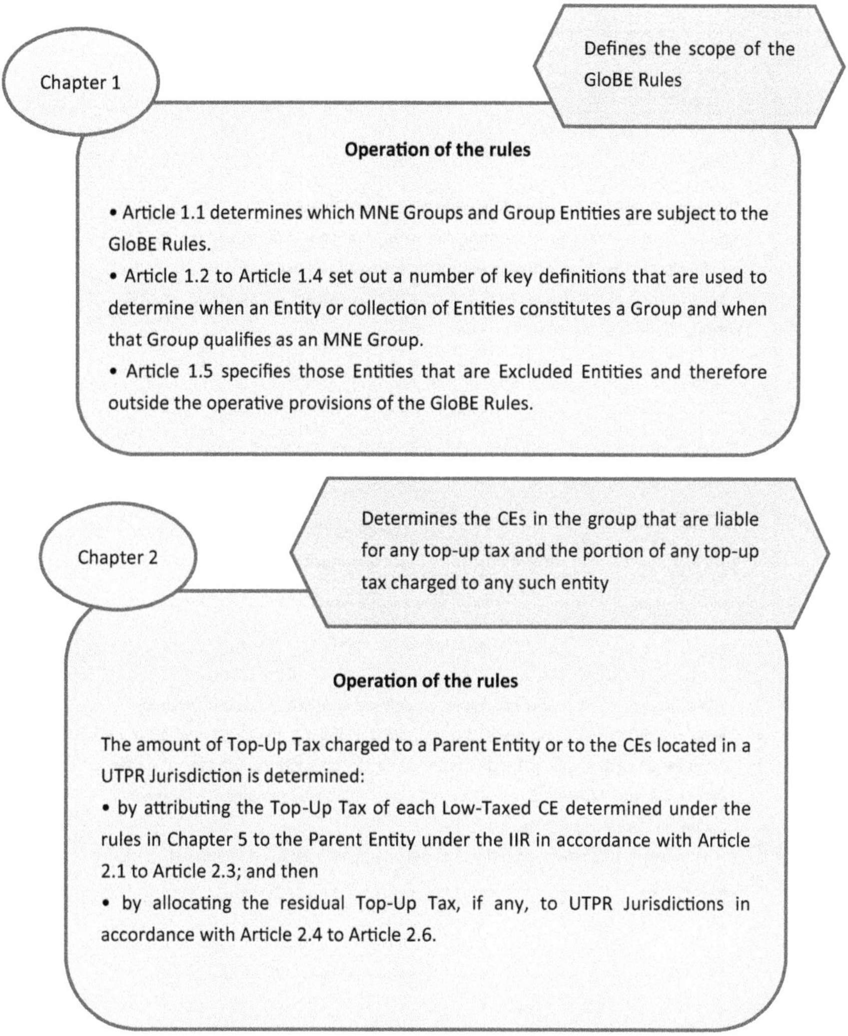

75. Refer 'OECD's Global Anti-Base Erosion Model Rules (Pillar Two)' https://www.oecd.org/tax/beps/tax-challenges-arising-from-the-digitalisation-of-the-economy-global-anti-base-erosion-model-rules-pillar-two.pdf.

Chapter 3

Determines the income (or loss) for the period for each CE in the MNE Group

Operation of the rules

The amount of GloBE Income or Loss of a CE is determined:

- by taking the Financial Accounting Net Income or Loss determined for the CE for the Fiscal Year in accordance with Article 3.1; and then
- by adjusting this amount under Article 3.2 to Article 3.5 to arrive at that Entity's GloBE Income or Loss.

Chapter 4

Identifies the taxes attributable to income for the period for each CE in the MNE Group

Operation of the rules

The amount of a CE's Covered Taxes, as defined in Article 4.2 is determined

- by taking the current taxes determined for the CE for the Fiscal Year in accordance with Article 4.1, adjusted to reflect certain timing differences under Article 4.4 and Article 4.5; by allocating Covered Taxes from one CE to another in certain cases under Article 4.3; and
- by taking into account the effect of certain post-filing tax adjustments under Article 4.6.

Chapter 5

Aggregates the income and taxes of all CEs located in the same jurisdiction to determine the ETR for that jurisdiction. Also includes an elective substance-based income exclusion that may reduce the amount of profits subject to any top-up tax.

Operation of the rules

The Top-up Tax of each Low-Taxed CE is determined:

- by aggregating each CE's GloBE Income or Loss, determined under Chapter 3, and Adjusted Covered Taxes, determined under Chapter 4, with those of other CEs located in the same jurisdiction to determine an ETR for the jurisdiction;
- by identifying which jurisdiction is a Low-Tax Jurisdiction (i.e. has an ETR that is below the Minimum Rate);
- by computing a jurisdictional Top-Up Tax Percentage for each Low-Tax Jurisdiction;
- by applying the Substance-based Income Exclusion to the Net GloBE Income in the Low-Tax Jurisdiction to determine the Excess Profits in that jurisdiction;
- by multiplying the Top-up Tax percentage by such Excess Profit and reducing the result by the amount of any Qualified Domestic Minimum Top-up Tax to determine the Top-Up Tax for each Low-Tax Jurisdiction; and
- by allocating such Top-up Taxes to the Constituent Entities in the Low-Tax Jurisdiction in proportion to their GloBE Income.

The resulting Top-up Tax of each Low Tax CE is then charged to a Parent Entity or to CEs located in a UTPR Jurisdiction under Chapter 2. This chapter also includes a de minimis exclusion for the CEs located in the same jurisdiction when their aggregated revenue and income does not exceed certain thresholds. Special rules are provided in Article 5.6 for calculating the ETR in respect of Minority-Owned CEs.

Chapter 6

Contains rules relating to acquisitions, disposals and joint ventures

Operation of the rules

Contains rules relating to acquisitions, disposals and Joint Ventures.

- Article 6.1 supplements Article 1.1 by providing further rules for applying the consolidated revenue threshold in the case of merger and demerger transactions that took place in the prior four year period.
- Article 6.2 provides special rules for the application of the GloBE Rules that apply when a CE enters or leaves an MNE Group during the Fiscal Year.
- Article 6.3 provides special rules for the treatment of transfers of assets and liabilities including as part of a reorganisation.
- Article 6.4 brings certain Joint Ventures within the scope of the GloBE Rules.
- Article 6.5 provides special rules for Multi-Parented MNE Groups.

Chapter 7

Deals with the application of the GloBE Rules to certain tax neutrality and other distribution regimes

Operation of the rules

Deals with the application of the GloBE Rules to certain tax neutrality and other distribution regimes.

• Article 7.1 and Article 7.2 provide special rules in relation to UPEs that are subject to a tax neutrality regime (such as a tax transparency regime or a Deductible Dividend Regime).

• Article 7.3 provides special rules in relation to certain tax regimes that subject an Entity to tax on its earnings when those earnings are distributed or deemed distributed.

• Article 7.4 to Article 7.6 provide special rules in relation to controlled Investment Entities that seek to preserve the tax neutrality of these Entities without giving rise to any leakage under the GloBE Rules.

Chapter 8

Covers administrative aspects of the GloBE Rules including information filing requirements as well as the application of any safe-harbours

Operation of the rules

Addresses certain administrative aspects of the GloBE Rules.

• Article 8.1 sets out an MNE Groups obligation to file a standardised information return in each jurisdiction that has introduced the GloBE Rules in order to provide information on the tax calculations made by the MNE under the GloBE Rules.

• Article 8.2 allows for the development of certain safe harbours.

• Article 8.3 facilitates co-ordination between tax administrations in the application of the GloBE Rules through the development of Agreed Administrative Guidance.

Chapter 9

Sets out certain transitional rules

Operation of the rules

Sets out certain Transitional Rules.

- Article 9.1 provides the transition rules that apply where an MNE Group enters within the scope of the GloBE Rules.
- Article 9.2 modifies the percentages to be applied in the calculation of the Substance-based Income Exclusion under Article 5.3 during a transitional period.
- Article 9.3 provides an exclusion from the UTPR for MNE Groups that are in the initial phase of their international activity.
- Article 9.4 provides transitional relief for filing obligations.

Chapter 10

Sets out defined terms used in the GloBE Rules

Operation of the rules

Sets out defined terms used in the GloBE Rules.

- Article 10.1 sets out general definitions that are used in the GloBE Rules.
- Article 10.2 sets out certain definitions in respect of Flow-through Entities.
- Article 10.3 sets out definitional rules for determining the location of an Entity for the purposes of applying the GloBE Rules.

3.3 STEPS[76] IN DETERMINING TOP-UP TAX LIABILITY FOR AN MNE

38. The GloBE rules apply a system of top-up taxes that brings the total amount of taxes paid on an MNE's excess profit in a jurisdiction up to the minimum rate of 15%. The tax imposed under the GloBE Rules is a top-up tax calculated and applied at a jurisdictional level. The GloBE rules use a standardised base and definition of covered taxes to identify those jurisdictions where an MNE is subject to an ETR below 15%. It then imposes a coordinated tax charge that brings the MNE's ETR on that income up to the minimum rate (after taking into account a substance-based carve-out). The design of the GloBE Rules as a top-up tax facilitates the coordinated application of the GloBE Rules.

39. The various steps[77] in determining top-up tax liability for an MNE in order to apply the GloBE Rules are as below:

- In Step 1, an MNE Group determines whether it is within the scope of the GloBE Rules and identifies the CEs within the Group and their location.
- Step 2 and Step 3 determine the ETR of each CE.
- In the event an MNE is subject to an ETR below 15% in any jurisdiction, Step 4 sets out the mechanism for calculating the top-up tax in respect of that low-tax jurisdiction.
- This top-up tax is then imposed on a group entity under an IIR or UTPR under Step 5.

Each of the above-mentioned steps is described in further detail through flow-charts[78] in Figure 3.2.

76. Refer 'OECD's Pillar Two Model Rules Fact Sheets titled Overview of the Key Operating Provisions of the GloBE Rules' https://www.oecd.org/tax/beps/pillar-two-GloBE-rules-fact-sheets.pdf accessed on 11 April 2022.
77. *Id.*
78. *Id.*

Figure 3.2 Steps in Determining Top-Up Tax Liability for an MNE in Order to Apply the GloBE Rules

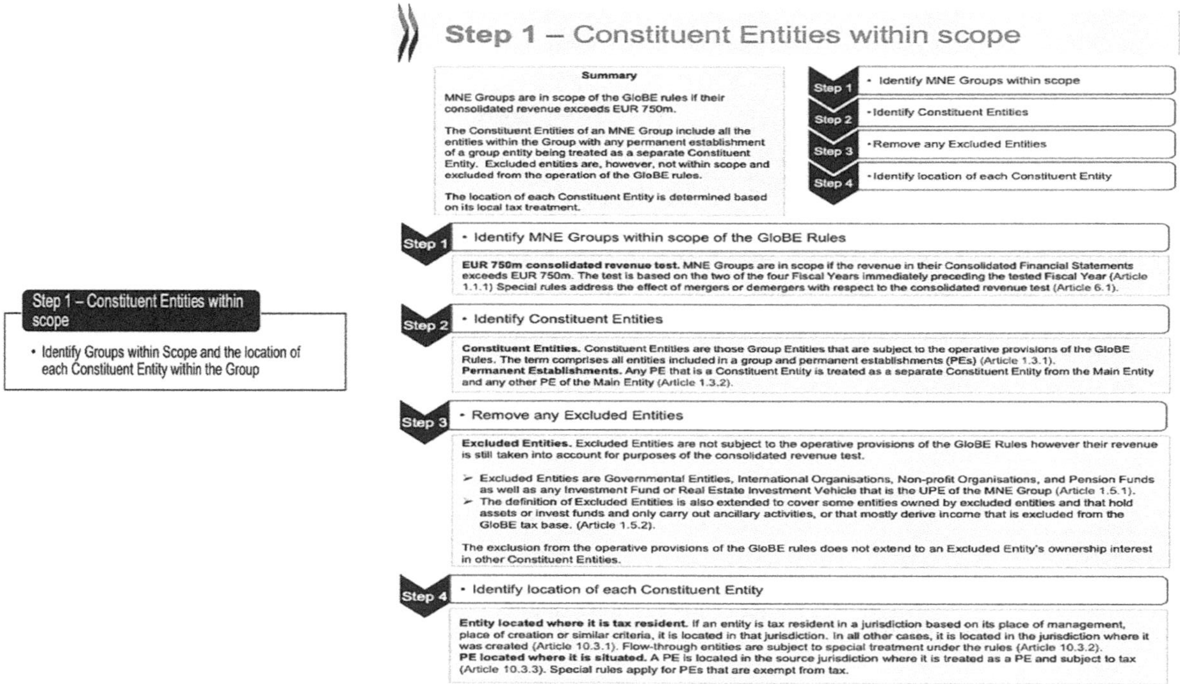

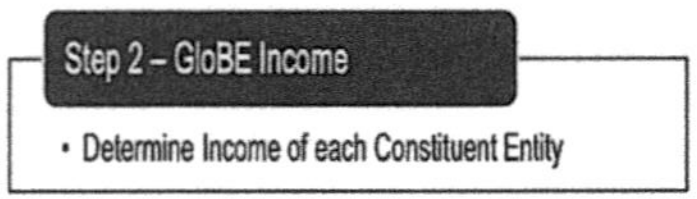
Step 2 – GloBE Income
• Determine Income of each Constituent Entity

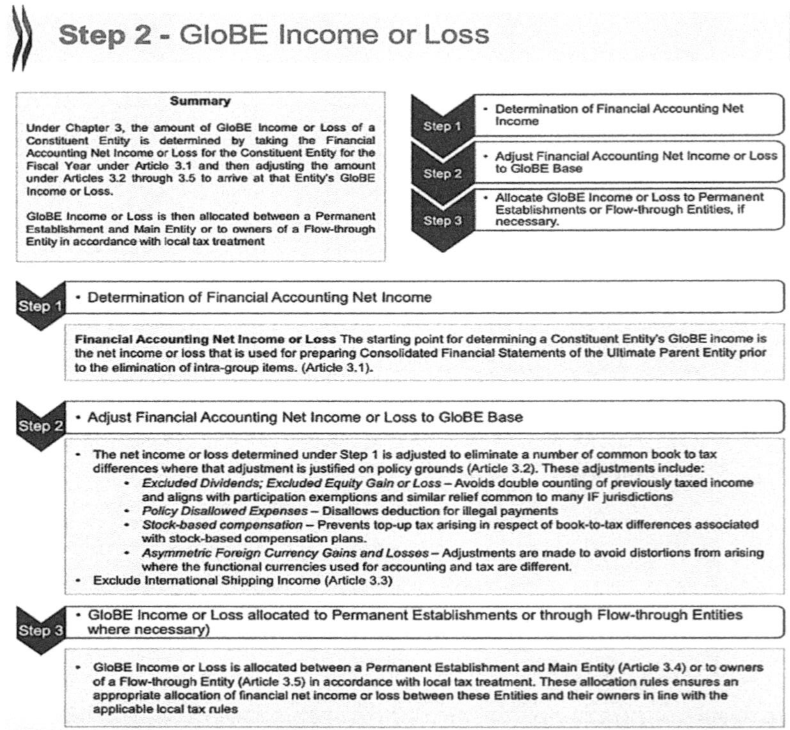
Step 2 - GloBE Income or Loss
Summary
Under Chapter 3, the amount of GloBE Income or Loss of a Constituent Entity is determined by taking the Financial Accounting Net Income or Loss for the Constituent Entity for the Fiscal Year under Article 3.1 and then adjusting the amount under Articles 3.2 through 3.5 to arrive at that Entity's GloBE Income or Loss.
GloBE Income or Loss is then allocated between a Permanent Establishment and Main Entity or to owners of a Flow-through Entity in accordance with local tax treatment
Step 1
• Determination of Financial Accounting Net Income
Step 2
• Adjust Financial Accounting Net Income or Loss to GloBE Base
Step 3
• Allocate GloBE Income or Loss to Permanent Establishments or Flow-through Entities, if necessary.
Step 1
• Determination of Financial Accounting Net Income
Financial Accounting Net Income or Loss The starting point for determining a Constituent Entity's GloBE income is the net income or loss that is used for preparing Consolidated Financial Statements of the Ultimate Parent Entity prior to the elimination of intra-group items. (Article 3.1).
Step 2
• Adjust Financial Accounting Net Income or Loss to GloBE Base
• The net income or loss determined under Step 1 is adjusted to eliminate a number of common book to tax differences where that adjustment is justified on policy grounds (Article 3.2). These adjustments include:
• Excluded Dividends; Excluded Equity Gain or Loss – Avoids double counting of previously taxed income and aligns with participation exemptions and similar relief common to many IF jurisdictions
• Policy Disallowed Expenses – Disallows deduction for illegal payments
• Stock-based compensation – Prevents top-up tax arising in respect of book-to-tax differences associated with stock-based compensation plans.
• Asymmetric Foreign Currency Gains and Losses – Adjustments are made to avoid distortions from arising where the functional currencies used for accounting and tax are different.
• Exclude International Shipping Income (Article 3.3)
Step 3
• GloBE Income or Loss allocated to Permanent Establishments or through Flow-through Entities where necessary)
• GloBE Income or Loss is allocated between a Permanent Establishment and Main Entity (Article 3.4) or to owners of a Flow-through Entity (Article 3.5) in accordance with local tax treatment. These allocation rules ensures an appropriate allocation of financial net income or loss between these Entities and their owners in line with the applicable local tax rules

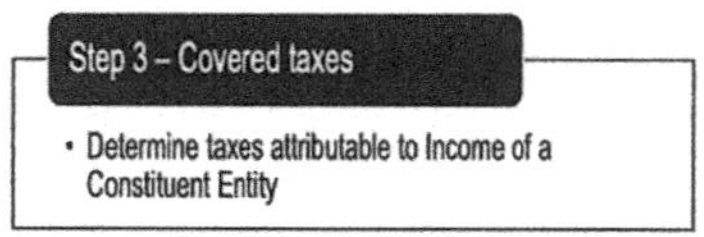
Step 3 – Covered taxes
• Determine taxes attributable to Income of a Constituent Entity

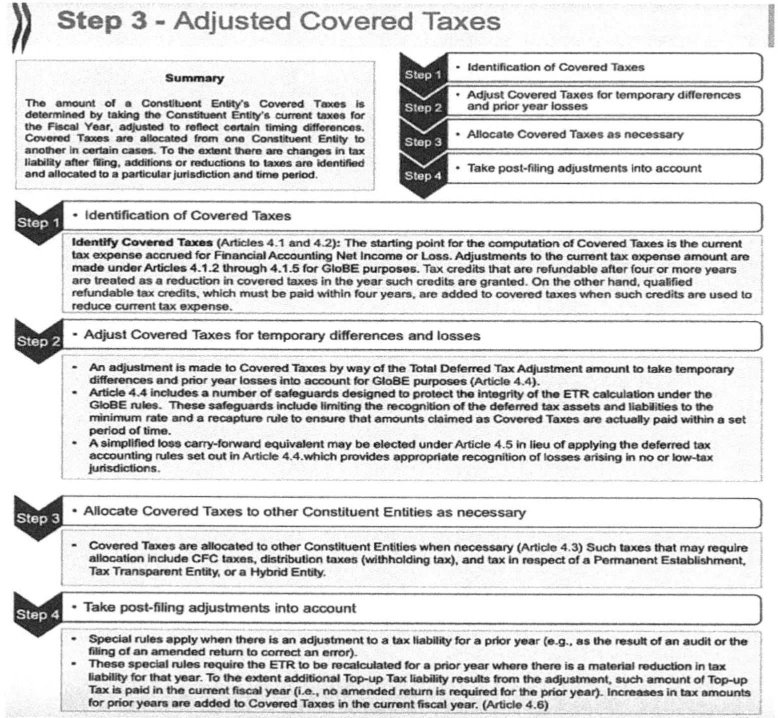
Step 3 - Adjusted Covered Taxes
Summary
The amount of a Constituent Entity's Covered Taxes is determined by taking the Constituent Entity's current taxes for the Fiscal Year, adjusted to reflect certain timing differences. Covered Taxes are allocated from one Constituent Entity to another in certain cases. To the extent there are changes in tax liability after filing, additions or reductions to taxes are identified and allocated to a particular jurisdiction and time period.
Step 1
• Identification of Covered Taxes
Step 2
• Adjust Covered Taxes for temporary differences and prior year losses
Step 3
• Allocate Covered Taxes as necessary
Step 4
• Take post-filing adjustments into account
Step 1
• Identification of Covered Taxes
Identify Covered Taxes (Articles 4.1 and 4.2): The starting point for the computation of Covered Taxes is the current tax expense accrued for Financial Accounting Net Income or Loss. Adjustments to the current tax expense amount are made under Articles 4.1.2 through 4.1.5 for GloBE purposes. Tax credits that are refundable after four or more years are treated as a reduction in covered taxes in the year such credits are granted. On the other hand, qualified refundable tax credits, which must be paid within four years, are added to covered taxes when such credits are used to reduce current tax expense.
Step 2
• Adjust Covered Taxes for temporary differences and losses
• An adjustment is made to Covered Taxes by way of the Total Deferred Tax Adjustment amount to take temporary differences and prior year losses into account for GloBE purposes (Article 4.4).
• Article 4.4 includes a number of safeguards designed to protect the integrity of the ETR calculation under the GloBE rules. These safeguards include limiting the recognition of the deferred tax assets and liabilities to the minimum rate and a recapture rule to ensure that amounts claimed as Covered Taxes are actually paid within a set period of time.
• A simplified loss carry-forward equivalent may be elected under Article 4.5 in lieu of applying the deferred tax accounting rules set out in Article 4.4.which provides appropriate recognition of losses arising in no or low-tax jurisdictions.
Step 3
• Allocate Covered Taxes to other Constituent Entities as necessary
• Covered Taxes are allocated to other Constituent Entities when necessary (Article 4.3) Such taxes that may require allocation include CFC taxes, distribution taxes (withholding tax), and tax in respect of a Permanent Establishment, Tax Transparent Entity, or a Hybrid Entity.
Step 4
• Take post-filing adjustments into account
• Special rules apply when there is an adjustment to a tax liability for a prior year (e.g., as the result of an audit or the filing of an amended return to correct an error).
• These special rules require the ETR to be recalculated for a prior year where there is a material reduction in tax liability for that year. To the extent additional Top-up Tax liability results from the adjustment, such amount of Top-up Tax is paid in the current fiscal year (i.e., no amended return is required for the prior year). Increases in tax amounts for prior years are added to Covered Taxes in the current fiscal year. (Article 4.6)

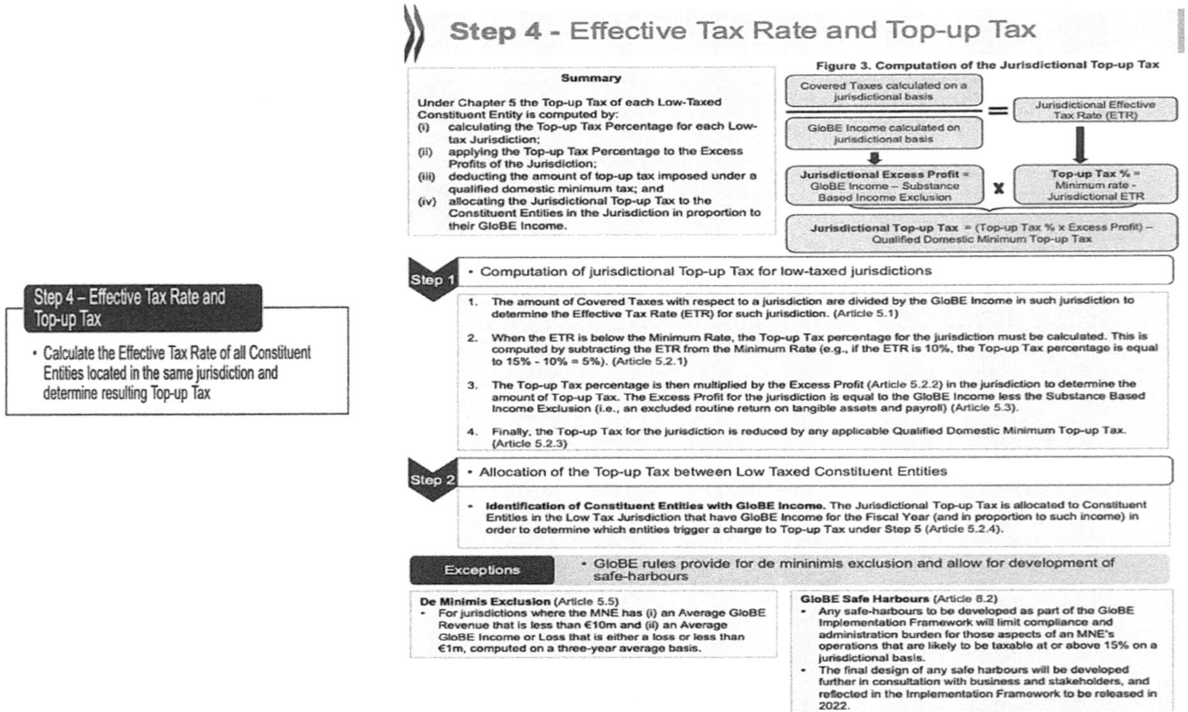
Step 4 – Effective Tax Rate and Top-up Tax
• Calculate the Effective Tax Rate of all Constituent Entities located in the same jurisdiction and determine resulting Top-up Tax
Step 4 - Effective Tax Rate and Top-up Tax
Summary
Under Chapter 5 the Top-up Tax of each Low-Taxed Constituent Entity is computed by:
(i) calculating the Top-up Tax Percentage for each Low-tax Jurisdiction;
(ii) applying the Top-up Tax Percentage to the Excess Profits of the Jurisdiction;
(iii) deducting the amount of top-up tax imposed under a qualified domestic minimum tax; and
(iv) allocating the Jurisdictional Top-up Tax to the Constituent Entities in the Jurisdiction in proportion to their GloBE Income.
Figure 3. Computation of the Jurisdictional Top-up Tax
Covered Taxes calculated on a jurisdictional basis
GloBE Income calculated on jurisdictional basis
=
Jurisdictional Effective Tax Rate (ETR)
Jurisdictional Excess Profit = GloBE Income – Substance Based Income Exclusion
x
Top-up Tax % = Minimum rate - Jurisdictional ETR
Jurisdictional Top-up Tax = (Top-up Tax % x Excess Profit) – Qualified Domestic Minimum Top-up Tax
Step 1
• Computation of jurisdictional Top-up Tax for low-taxed jurisdictions
1. The amount of Covered Taxes with respect to a jurisdiction are divided by the GloBE Income in such jurisdiction to determine the Effective Tax Rate (ETR) for such jurisdiction. (Article 5.1)
2. When the ETR is below the Minimum Rate, the Top-up Tax percentage for the jurisdiction must be calculated. This is computed by subtracting the ETR from the Minimum Rate (e.g., if the ETR is 10%, the Top-up Tax percentage is equal to 15% - 10% = 5%). (Article 5.2.1)
3. The Top-up Tax percentage is then multiplied by the Excess Profit (Article 5.2.2) in the jurisdiction to determine the amount of Top-up Tax. The Excess Profit for the jurisdiction is equal to the GloBE Income less the Substance Based Income Exclusion (i.e., an excluded routine return on tangible assets and payroll) (Article 5.3).
4. Finally, the Top-up Tax for the jurisdiction is reduced by any applicable Qualified Domestic Minimum Top-up Tax. (Article 5.2.3)
Step 2
• Allocation of the Top-up Tax between Low Taxed Constituent Entities
- Identification of Constituent Entities with GloBE Income. The Jurisdictional Top-up Tax is allocated to Constituent Entities in the Low Tax Jurisdiction that have GloBE Income for the Fiscal Year (and in proportion to such income) in order to determine which entities trigger a charge to Top-up Tax under Step 5 (Article 5.2.4).
Exceptions
• GloBE rules provide for de mininimis exclusion and allow for development of safe-harbours
De Minimis Exclusion (Article 5.5)
- For jurisdictions where the MNE has (i) an Average GloBE Revenue that is less than €10m and (ii) an Average GloBE Income or Loss that is either a loss or less than €1m, computed on a three-year average basis.
GloBE Safe Harbours (Article 8.2)
- Any safe-harbours to be developed as part of the GloBE Implementation Framework will limit compliance and administration burden for those aspects of an MNE's operations that are likely to be taxable at or above 15% on a jurisdictional basis.
- The final design of any safe harbours will be developed further in consultation with business and stakeholders, and reflected in the Implementation Framework to be released in 2022.

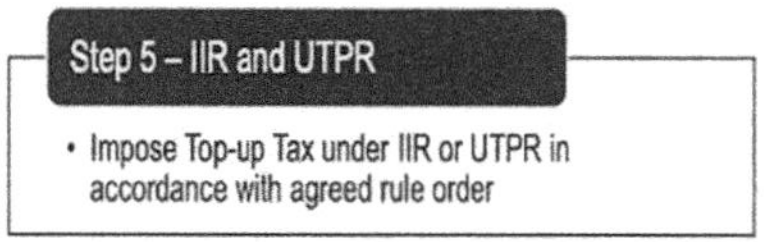
Step 5 – IIR and UTPR
• Impose Top-up Tax under IIR or UTPR in accordance with agreed rule order

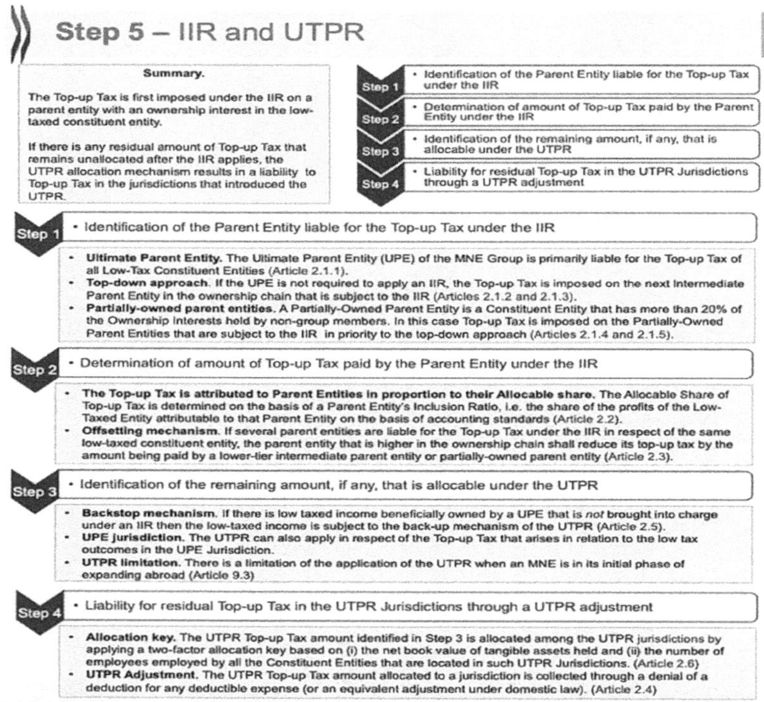
Step 5 – IIR and UTPR
Summary.
The Top-up Tax is first imposed under the IIR on a parent entity with an ownership interest in the low-taxed constituent entity.
If there is any residual amount of Top-up Tax that remains unallocated after the IIR applies, the UTPR allocation mechanism results in a liability to Top-up Tax in the jurisdictions that introduced the UTPR.
Step 1
• Identification of the Parent Entity liable for the Top-up Tax under the IIR
Step 2
• Determination of amount of Top-up Tax paid by the Parent Entity under the IIR
Step 3
• Identification of the remaining amount, if any, that is allocable under the UTPR
Step 4
• Liability for residual Top-up Tax in the UTPR Jurisdictions through a UTPR adjustment
Step 1
• Identification of the Parent Entity liable for the Top-up Tax under the IIR
• Ultimate Parent Entity. The Ultimate Parent Entity (UPE) of the MNE Group is primarily liable for the Top-up Tax of all Low-Tax Constituent Entities (Article 2.1.1).
• Top-down approach. If the UPE is not required to apply an IIR, the Top-up Tax is imposed on the next Intermediate Parent Entity in the ownership chain that is subject to the IIR (Articles 2.1.2 and 2.1.3).
• Partially-owned parent entities. A Partially-Owned Parent Entity is a Constituent Entity that has more than 20% of the Ownership Interests held by non-group members. In this case Top-up Tax is imposed on the Partially-Owned Parent Entities that are subject to the IIR in priority to the top-down approach (Articles 2.1.4 and 2.1.5).
Step 2
• Determination of amount of Top-up Tax paid by the Parent Entity under the IIR
• The Top-up Tax is attributed to Parent Entities in proportion to their Allocable share. The Allocable Share of Top-up Tax is determined on the basis of a Parent Entity's Inclusion Ratio, i.e. the share of the profits of the Low-Taxed Entity attributable to that Parent Entity on the basis of accounting standards (Article 2.2).
• Offsetting mechanism. If several parent entities are liable for the Top-up Tax under the IIR in respect of the same low-taxed constituent entity, the parent entity that is higher in the ownership chain shall reduce its top-up tax by the amount being paid by a lower-tier intermediate parent entity or partially-owned parent entity (Article 2.3).
Step 3
• Identification of the remaining amount, if any, that is allocable under the UTPR
• Backstop mechanism. If there is low taxed income beneficially owned by a UPE that is not brought into charge under an IIR then the low-taxed income is subject to the back-up mechanism of the UTPR (Article 2.5).
• UPE jurisdiction. The UTPR can also apply in respect of the Top-up Tax that arises in relation to the low tax outcomes in the UPE Jurisdiction.
• UTPR limitation. There is a limitation of the application of the UTPR when an MNE is in its initial phase of expanding abroad (Article 9.3)
Step 4
• Liability for residual Top-up Tax in the UTPR Jurisdictions through a UTPR adjustment
• Allocation key. The UTPR Top-up Tax amount identified in Step 3 is allocated among the UTPR jurisdictions by applying a two-factor allocation key based on (i) the net book value of tangible assets held and (ii) the number of employees employed by all the Constituent Entities that are located in such UTPR Jurisdictions. (Article 2.6)
• UTPR Adjustment. The UTPR Top-up Tax amount allocated to a jurisdiction is collected through a denial of a deduction for any deductible expense (or an equivalent adjustment under domestic law). (Article 2.4)

3.4 GLOBE RULES TO BE IMPLEMENTED AS A COMMON APPROACH

40. The GloBE Rules are to be implemented as part of a common approach. A jurisdiction that joins the common approach is not required to adopt the GloBE Rules, but if it chooses to do so, it agrees to implement and administer them in a way that is consistent with the outcomes provided under the GloBE Rules and its Commentary. Consistency in the implementation and administration of the GloBE Rules is intended to result in a transparent and comprehensive system of taxation that provides predictable outcomes for MNEs and avoids the risk of double or over-taxation. Accordingly, jurisdictions which adopt GloBE Rules cannot make significant changes to the policy design agreed upon in the OECD.

41. In practice, multinational groups with subsidiaries in countries that operate at a rate below the agreed minimum rate will ultimately also have to face the consequences of Pillar Two. This is because the rules test the ETR per jurisdiction and apply a top-up tax to companies in the low-tax jurisdictions. As a result of either the IIR or the UTPR, a State will collect the top-up tax due at the level of the entire group if some jurisdictions where entities are based impose tax below the minimum level and do not impose any domestic top-up tax. In other words, owing to the common approach, failing to apply the Pillar Two rules will not protect jurisdictions from effectively being subject to tax, at least at the agreed minimum rate.[79]

42. The GloBE Model Rules are the product of extensive international negotiation and have been agreed to by IF members. A country's failure to adhere in its domestic implementing legislation to the common approach set out in the Model Rules runs the risk of the implementing country's IIR not being a 'qualified' IIR under the Model Rules, leaving MNEs based in that country open to the application of other countries' UTPRs.[80]

---

79. Refer 'European Commission's Questions and Answers on Minimum corporate taxation' https://ec.europa.eu/commission/presscorner/detail/en/qanda_21_6967 accessed on 1 May 2022.
80. Refer 'International Tax Measures announced in Budget 2022 by Canada, Pillar Two – Global Minimum Tax' https://budget.gc.ca/2022/report-rapport/tm-mf-en.html#a4_1_2 accessed on 15 May 2022.

Chapter 4
Detailed Discussions on GloBE Rules[81]

The GloBE Model Rules were released on 20 December 2021, which consist of ten chapters and 49 articles in total. Thereafter, the Commentary and Illustrative Examples on Pillar Two Model Rules were released by the OECD on 14 March 2022. The Commentary and Illustrative Examples provide tax administrations and taxpayers with guidance on the interpretation and application of these rules. These provisions, being complex, have been explained in the following differentiating manner:

- *each Article contained in Chapters 1 to 9 of the GloBE Rules has been summarised in a box as a prelude, providing the readers with a quick summary of the ensuing discussions;*
- *at appropriate places, the provisions have been explained through flow-charts, tables or diagrams for a better and faster understanding of the readers;*
- *the technical provisions contained in each article of GloBE Rules are discussed para-wise, and each paragraph invariably carries a brief italicised header/narration;*
- *the Examples and Definitions (as contained in Chapter 10 of GloBE Rules) released by the OECD have been inserted at relevant places where the corresponding articles of GloBE Rules are discussed. Further, the Examples have been encapsulated in flow-charts for a better and faster understanding of the readers. At the same time, for the ease of readers, an index of definitions (which is specific to the book) has also been incorporated.*

43. It has been discussed in the foregoing text that OECD/G20's initiative to address remaining BEPS issues related to low-tax jurisdictions led to the formulation of a very innovative and complex set of rules in the form of Pillar Two Proposals. After comprehensive discussions among IF members and taking the views of various stakeholders through public consultations, the GloBE Model Rules[82] were released on

81. Based on OECD's GloBE Model Rules, its Commentary and Illustrative Examples.
82. Refer 'OECD's Global Anti-Base Erosion Model Rules (Pillar Two)' https://www.oecd.org/tax/beps/tax-challenges-arising-from-the-digitalisation-of-the-economy-global-anti-base-erosion-model-rules-pillar-two.pdf.

20 December 2021, which consist of ten chapters and 49 articles in total. Thereafter, the Commentary[83] and Illustrative Examples[84] on Pillar Two Model Rules were released by the OECD on 14 March 2022. The Commentary and Illustrative Examples provide tax administrations and taxpayers with guidance on the interpretation and application of these rules.

44. The GloBE Rules have been developed as part of the solution for addressing the tax challenges of the digital economy. They are designed to ensure large MNEs pay a minimum level of tax on the income arising in each jurisdiction where they operate. The GloBE Rules are drafted in the form of model rules in order to provide jurisdictions with a template for domestic implementation. Comprehensive discussions on the GloBE Model Rules are conducted hereunder.[85]

4.1 CHAPTER 1 OF GLOBE RULES (SCOPE OF GLOBE RULES)[86]

45. Chapter 1 defines the scope of GloBE Model Rules and sets out the rules for determining whether a taxpayer is within its scope. The GloBE Rules will apply to the Constituent Entities of an MNE Group that meets the consolidated revenue threshold as set out in Article 1.1. Also, Article 1.1 is modified by Article 6.1, which sets out further rules clarifying the application of the consolidated revenue threshold in the case of mergers and demergers. Chapter 1 also includes a number of key definitions that are used to determine when an entity or collection of entities constitutes a Group and when that Group qualifies as an MNE Group.

46. The term Entity is defined in Article 10.1. as below:

> Entity means:
>
> (a) any legal person (other than a natural person); or
> (b) an arrangement that prepares separate financial accounts, such as a partnership or trust.

A broad definition of entity ensures that the term captures separate legal persons as well as arrangements such as partnerships and trusts. Entities form a Group when they are under common control such that their income is (or would be) included in the same CFS. The term CE is then used to identify the Group Entities that are subject to the GloBE Rules. In this context, an entity with one or more PEs is divided into separate CEs. The chapter also sets out those entities (Excluded Entities) that are excluded from the rules.

83. Refer 'OECD's Commentary to the Global Anti-Base Erosion Model Rules (Pillar Two)' https://www.oecd.org/tax/beps/tax-challenges-arising-from-the-digitalisation-of-the-economy-global-anti-base-erosion-model-rules-pillar-two-commentary.pdf
84. Refer 'OECD's Global Anti-Base Erosion Model Rules (Pillar Two) Examples' https://www.oecd.org/tax/beps/tax-challenges-arising-from-the-digitalisation-of-the-economy-global-anti-base-erosion-model-rules-pillar-two-examples.pdf.
85. Based on OECD's GloBE Model Rules, its Commentary and Illustrative Examples.
86. *Id.*

4.1.1 Article 1.1. (Scope of GloBE Rules)

47. Article 1.1 limits the application of the GloBE Rules to MNE Groups whose annual consolidated revenues in at least two of the four preceding Fiscal Years[87] equal or exceed EUR 750 million. These scope rules ensure that smaller Groups and purely domestic Groups remain unaffected by the GloBE Rules. The article also clarifies that Entities that are Excluded Entities are not subject to the GloBE Rules.

48. The term GloBE Rules mentioned above is defined in Article 10.1 as below:

> GloBE Rules means this set of rules as developed by the OECD/G20 Inclusive Framework on Base Erosion and Profit Shifting.

49. Prominent features of Article 1.1 are provided in Box 4.1.

Box 4.1 Prominent Features of Article 1.1

- Limits the application of the GloBE Rules to MNE Groups whose annual consolidated revenues in at least two of the four preceding Fiscal Years equal or exceed EUR 750 million.
- Consolidated revenue for the current year (i.e., the tested Fiscal Year) is not factored into the four-year calculation.
- The revenue threshold takes into account the consolidated revenue as reported in the CFS of the Group.
- The revenues taken into account in the determination of the MNE Group's total revenue under the consolidated revenue threshold should be the one reflected in the CFS and should not be reduced by the amount attributable to minority interest holders.
- The threshold applies based on the consolidated revenue of the MNE Group, not the aggregate of the revenues of each Group Entity, i.e., revenues from transactions with other Group Entities that are eliminated in the consolidation process are excluded from the revenue threshold test.
- The definition of Fiscal Year aligns with the test used in CbCR and ensures consistency in the application of the threshold for GloBE and CbCR purposes.
- The scope rules ensure that smaller Groups and purely domestic Groups remain unaffected by the GloBE Rules.
- Addresses cases where a Fiscal Year of an MNE Group is a period other than twelve months.
- Clarifies that entities that are Excluded Entities are not subject to the GloBE Rules (except for purposes of calculating the revenue threshold).

87. For this purpose, the Fiscal Year refers to the period covered by the CFS.

4.1.1.1 Article 1.1.1.

50. The GloBE Rules apply to CEs that are members of an MNE Group that has annual revenue of EUR 750 million or more in the CFS of the UPE in at least two of the four Fiscal Years immediately preceding the tested Fiscal Year. It may be noted that consolidated revenue for the current year (i.e., the tested Fiscal Year) is not factored into the four-year calculation. Excluding the current year's results from the revenue threshold test ensures that an MNE Group knows, at the beginning of the tested Fiscal Year, whether it will be subject to the GloBE Rules in that year. The rules set out in this article build on the definitions and methodology currently used by IF members under BEPS Action 13 for Country-by-Country Reporting (CbCR) purposes. The GloBE rules generally apply to the MNE Groups and their CEs that are subject to CbCR obligations described in the BEPS Action 13 Report.

51. *Benefits of using the CbCR monetary threshold*: Using the same monetary threshold as that used for CbCR purposes limits the incremental compliance costs associated with the introduction of the GloBE Rules and will make it easier for tax administrations to monitor compliance with the rules based on existing information collection and exchange systems.

52. *Reasons for using a two-out-of-four years test*: Where the MNE Group has EUR 750 million or more of reported revenue in at least two Fiscal Years in the four-year period immediately preceding the tested Fiscal Year, the CEs that make up the MNE Group will be within the scope of the GloBE Rules. The consolidated revenue threshold applies to the revenue that is reported in the CFS of the MNE Group. The threshold uses a two-out-of-four-years test in order to reduce volatility in the application of the rules.

53. *CFS unavailable for the four Fiscal Years immediately preceding the tested Fiscal Year*: It may happen in some cases that the CFS may not be available in respect of the four Fiscal Years immediately preceding the tested Fiscal Year. This could happen in the following situations:

- The entities that make up the Group may have been recently created, so that there are no financial statements for entities in any prior year. In such cases where the entities forming the Group were recently created such that there are no financial statements for the Group in prior years, then the third year is the first year in which the GloBE Rules can apply since, at that point, there will be two prior years to test. If the revenue threshold is met for the two prior years, the Group will be within the scope of the GloBE Rules in year three, notwithstanding that the Group does not have four prior years of CFS.
- Prior to the tested Fiscal Year, the entities forming the Group were stand-alone entities that were not required to consolidate. Article 6.1.1(b) deals with such a situation. In the case of two single entities that come together to form a Group, the revenue of each entity (as reflected in the financial statements of each of the entities for the prior Fiscal Years) is aggregated for the purposes of applying the consolidated revenue threshold. In the case of an entity that joins

a Group, the revenue included in that entity's financial statements for a given year must be added to the consolidated revenue of the Group for the same year. This deeming rule is applied to each of the four Fiscal Years prior to the tested Fiscal Year in order to determine whether the newly formed Group falls within the scope of the GloBE Rules. This means that if the combined revenue in two out of the four Fiscal Years prior to the tested Fiscal Year equals or exceeds EUR 750 million, then the consolidated revenue threshold in Article 1.1 is met, and the MNE Group is subject to the GloBE Rules in the tested Fiscal Year. This rule shall be redundant where the acquiring MNE Group already meets the revenue threshold under Article 1.1 in the Fiscal Year in which the merger takes place.

Illustration # 1: Let us consider a situation that in Year 1, A Co and B Co are incorporated and form the AB Group. CFS are prepared for the AB Group. In Years 1 and 2, the AB Group has consolidated revenue of EUR 750 million. In this case, the AB Group is not within the scope of the GloBE Rules in Years 1 and 2 because Article 1.1.1 requires the AB Group to have consolidated revenues of EUR 750 million or more in at least two of the four Fiscal Years preceding the tested Fiscal Year. In Year 3, the consolidated revenue threshold has been met because the consolidated revenue of the AB Group equals EUR 750 million in two Fiscal Years preceding the tested Fiscal Year, which is Year 3.

54. Illustration # 2: The concept of Scope of GloBE Rules is further explained through a flow-chart given below:

In Scope

Consolidated revenue (EUR million) in CFS of UPE (A Co)
(CEs of the MNE Group comprise A Co in Jurisdiction A and A Sub in Jurisdiction B)

Year 1	Year 2	Year 3	Year 4	Tested Fiscal Year
500	800	750	900	500

Reason : Annual revenue of EUR 750 million or more in the CFS of the UPE in three of the four Fiscal Years immediately preceding the tested Fiscal Year.

Consolidated revenue (EUR million) in CFS of UPE (A Co)
(CEs of the MNE Group comprise A Co in Jurisdiction A and A Sub in Jurisdiction B)

Year 1	Year 2	Year 3	Year 4	Tested Fiscal Year
500	400	750	900	500

Reason : Annual revenue of EUR 750 million or more in the CFS of the UPE in at least two of the four Fiscal Years immediately preceding the tested Fiscal Year.

Consolidated revenue (EUR million) in CFS of UPE (A Co)
(CEs of the MNE Group comprise A Co in Jurisdiction A and A Sub in Jurisdiction B)

Year 1	Year 2	Year 3	Year 4	Tested Fiscal Year
CFS not available	CFS not available	750	900	500

Reason : In this example, the third year, i.e., Tested Fiscal Year is the first year in which the GloBE Rules can apply, since, at that point, there will be two prior years to test. Since the revenue threshold is met for the two prior years, the Group will be within the scope of the GloBE Rules in year three, which is the Tested Fiscal Year, notwithstanding that the Group does not have four prior years of CFS.

Not in Scope

Consolidated revenue (EUR million) in CFS of UPE (A Co)
(CEs of the MNE Group comprise A Co in Jurisdiction A and A Sub in Jurisdiction B)

Year 1	Year 2	Year 3	Year 4	Tested Fiscal Year
500	400	740	900	500

Reason : Annual revenue of EUR 750 million or more in the CFS of the UPE in only one of the four Fiscal Years immediately preceding the tested Fiscal Year.

Consolidated revenue (EUR million) in CFS of UPE (A Co)
(CEs of the MNE Group comprise A Co in Jurisdiction A and A Sub in Jurisdiction B)

Year 1	Year 2	Year 3	Year 4	Tested Fiscal Year
500	400	740	900	800

Reason : Annual revenue of EUR 750 million or more in the CFS of the UPE in only one of the four Fiscal Years immediately preceding the tested Fiscal Year. Consolidated revenue for the current year (i.e., the tested Fiscal Year) is not factored into the four-year calculation

Consolidated revenue (EUR million) in CFS of UPE (A Co)
(CEs of the MNE Group comprise A Co in Jurisdiction A and A Sub in Jurisdiction B)

Year 1	Year 2	Year 3	Year 4	Tested Fiscal Year
CFS not available	CFS not available	CFS not available	900	800

Reason : There are no two prior years to test. Consolidated revenue for the current year (i.e., the tested Fiscal Year) is not factored into the four-year calculation

55. *Computation of Revenue Threshold*: The revenue threshold takes into account the consolidated revenue as reported in the CFS of the Group. The definition of CFS is provided in Article 10.1 as below:

(a) the financial statements prepared by an Entity in accordance with an Acceptable Financial Accounting Standard, in which the assets, liabilities, income, expenses and cash flows of that Entity and the Entities in which it has a Controlling Interest are presented as those of a single economic unit;
(b) where an Entity meets the definition of a Group under Article 1.2.3, the financial statements of the Entity that are prepared in accordance with an Acceptable Financial Accounting Standard;
(c) where the UPE has financial statements described in paragraph (a) or (b) that are not prepared in accordance with an Acceptable Financial Accounting Standard, the financial statements are those that have been prepared subject to adjustments to prevent any Material Competitive Distortions; and
(d) where the UPE does not prepare financial statements described in the paragraphs above, the CFS of the UPE are those that would have been prepared if such entity were required to prepare such statements in accordance with an Authorised Financial Accounting Standard that is either an Acceptable Financial Accounting Standard or another financial accounting standard that is adjusted to prevent any Material Competitive Distortions.

The above definition *inter alia* includes a deeming provision to address those situations where the MNE Group is only a single Entity with foreign branch operations or does not otherwise prepare CFS under such a standard. In ascertaining the revenue threshold, the following pertinent issues may also be noted:

- Where the income of an entity is consolidated with that of an MNE Group, then the threshold in Article 1.1.1 is applied to the total amount of the entity's revenue that is reflected in the CFS of the Group, even if a portion of the interests in that Group Entity is owned (directly or indirectly) by minority interest holders. In accounting terms, this means that the revenues taken into account in the determination of the MNE Group's total revenue under the consolidated revenue threshold should be the one reflected in the CFS and should not be reduced by the amount attributable to minority interest holders.
- The threshold applies based on the consolidated revenue of the MNE Group, not the aggregate of the revenues of each Group Entity, i.e., revenues from transactions with other Group Entities that are eliminated in the consolidation process are excluded from the revenue threshold test.
- An Excluded Entity (is not a CE and is, therefore, not subject to the GloBE Rules) will qualify as a Group Entity for purposes of determining the revenue threshold to the extent its income is consolidated with the rest of the Group. In this case, the revenue of that Excluded Entity must be taken into account in applying the consolidated revenue threshold. This ensures consistency with the threshold for reporting under CbCR and avoids requiring additional rules to address the treatment of revenues attributable to transactions between the Excluded Entity and the rest of the Group (including anti-avoidance rules to protect against fragmentation).

- In cases where the revenue threshold is set in a currency other than the Euro and such amount changes on a yearly basis, the applicable revenue threshold for the Fiscal Year is the last revenue threshold in effect as of the beginning of the Fiscal Year.

56. The term Group Entity mentioned above is defined in Article 10.1 as below:

> Group Entity, in respect of any Entity or Group, means an Entity that is a member of the same Group.

4.1.1.2 Article 1.1.2.

57. If one or more of the Fiscal Years of the MNE Group taken into account for purposes of Article 1.1.1 is of a period other than twelve months, for each of those Fiscal Years, the EUR 750 million threshold is adjusted proportionally to correspond with the length of the relevant Fiscal Year. Accordingly, Article 1.1.2 addresses cases where a Fiscal Year of an MNE Group is a period other than twelve months. The definition of Fiscal Year aligns with the test used in CbCR and ensures consistency in the application of the threshold for GloBE and CbCR purposes. The term Fiscal Year is defined in Article 10.1 as below:

> Fiscal Year means an accounting period with respect to which the UPE of the MNE Group prepares its CFS. In the case of CFS as defined in paragraph (d) of its definition, Fiscal Year means the calendar year.

58. Illustration # 3: If the Fiscal Year of the MNE Group is comprised of nine months and the consolidated revenue for the period is EUR 562.5 million, then the tax authority shall require the revenue to be grossed up by the ratio of the number of months in the year to twelve. Under these facts, the MNE Group's consolidated revenue for the year for purposes of applying the threshold would be EUR 750 million (= EUR 562.5 million x 12/9).

4.1.1.3 Article 1.1.3.

59. Article 1.1.3 states that entities that meet the definition of Excluded Entities are excluded from the GloBE Rules. These entities are excluded from the definition of CEs, thereby taking them outside the scope of the GloBE Rules (except for purposes of calculating the revenue threshold). The various types of Excluded Entities are explained further in Article 1.5 *infra*. The term Entity mentioned above is defined in Article 10.1. as below:

> Entity means:
>
> (a) any legal person (other than a natural person); or
> (b) an arrangement that prepares separate financial accounts, such as a partnership or trust.

4.1.2 Article 1.2. (MNE Group and Group)

60. Article 1.2. defines the terms 'MNE Group' and 'Group' for the purposes of the GloBE Rules. These terms, which are used to determine the scope of the GloBE Rules under Article 1.1, perform two key functions. First, they restrict the GloBE Rules to those Groups or Entities with foreign subsidiaries or branches. Second, they define the degree of common ownership and control required for two or more entities to be members of the same Group.

61. Prominent features of Article 1.2 are provided in Box 4.2.

Box 4.2 Prominent Features of Article 1.2

- Defines the terms 'MNE Group' and 'Group' for the purposes of GloBE Rules.
- A Group will be an MNE Group if it has one or more entities or PEs located in a jurisdiction other than the UPE jurisdiction.
- Group is defined based on an accounting consolidation test.
- An entity and its foreign PE meet the definition of Group and MNE Group.
- Stateless PE excluded in determination of a Group.

4.1.2.1 Article 1.2.1.

62. An MNE Group means any Group that includes at least one entity or Permanent Establishment (PE) that is not located in the jurisdiction of the UPE. There are two elements to this definition:

(1) Whether two or more entities form a Group is based on an accounting consolidation test. This consolidation test is determined based on the CFS prepared by the UPE. Subparagraph (d) of the definition of CFS in Article 10.1 includes a deeming provision for those UPEs that do not prepare CFS.
(2) A Group will be an MNE Group if it has one or more entities or PEs located in a jurisdiction other than the UPE jurisdiction.

63. Article 1.2.1 requires a UPE of the Group to have, directly or indirectly, at least one foreign subsidiary or PE before the Group will be considered an MNE Group. A single subsidiary or PE (even one that does not earn income) located in a jurisdiction other than the one where the UPE is located is sufficient to bring a Group within the definition of an MNE Group. Definition of PE is provided in Article 10.1 as below:

> Permanent Establishment means:
>
> (a) a place of business (including a deemed place of business) situated in a jurisdiction and treated as a permanent establishment in accordance with an applicable Tax Treaty in force provided that such jurisdiction taxes the income

attributable to it in accordance with a provision similar to Article 7 of the OECD MTC on Income and on Capital;

(b) if there is no applicable Tax Treaty in force, a place of business (including a deemed place of business) in respect of which a jurisdiction taxes under its domestic law the income attributable to such place of business on a net basis similar to the manner in which it taxes its own tax residents;

(c) if a jurisdiction has no CIT system, a place of business (including a deemed place of business) situated in that jurisdiction that would be treated as a permanent establishment in accordance with the OECD MTC on Income and on Capital provided that such jurisdiction would have had the right to tax the income attributable to it in accordance with Article 7 of that model; or

(d) a place of business (or a deemed place of business) that is not already described in paragraphs (a) to (c) through which operations are conducted outside the jurisdiction where the Entity is located provided that such jurisdiction exempts the income attributable to such operations.

4.1.2.2 Article 1.2.2.

64. Article 1.2.2 defines a Group based on an accounting consolidation test. This definition is used for purposes of defining a CE in Article 1.3. A Group means a collection of entities that are related through ownership or control such that the assets, liabilities, income, expenses and cash flows of those entities:

(a) are included in the CFS of the UPE. This means that the assets, liabilities, income, expenses, and cash flows (i.e., the financial results) of the entity (including the ones of its PEs) are consolidated on a line-by-line basis in the CFS that the UPE prepares for the MNE Group. If no consolidated accounts exist, a collection of entities would still be considered a Group if these entities would have been so consolidated if an entity were required to prepare such accounts with respect to the entities it controls because the definition of the term CFS in Article 10.1 also includes a 'deemed consolidation test' in paragraph (d) which considers these entities consolidating together and therefore, forming part of the same Group. Whether an entity is part of a Group depends on whether it meets the definition of an 'Entity' under Article 10.1 and the requirements set out in the said paragraph (a); or

(b) are excluded from the CFS of the UPE solely on size or materiality grounds or on the grounds that the entity is held for sale. This type of entity is also treated as part of the Group as long as it remains sufficiently within the control of the UPE to fall within the general consolidation requirements of the relevant Acceptable Financial Accounting Standard.

4.1.2.3 Article 1.2.3.

65. In order to ensure MNE Groups that meet the consolidated revenue threshold and engage in cross-border operations through PEs rather than subsidiaries are also subject to the GloBE Rules, Article 1.2.3 provides a supplementary definition of Group. A Group also means an entity that is located in one jurisdiction and has one or more PEs located in other jurisdictions, provided that the entity is not a part of another Group described in Article 1.2.2. Thus, in combination with Article 1.2.1, an entity and its foreign PE will meet the definition of Group and MNE Group.

66. *Stateless PE excluded*: Article 1.2.3 will not apply where the entity only has a stateless PE in accordance with paragraph (d) of the definition of PE in Article 10.1 and Article 10.3.3(d) because such a PE is not recognised under the laws of any other jurisdiction. This narrow situation only occurs where a stand-alone entity has a PE as defined by paragraph (d) of the definition of PE in Article 10.1.

4.1.3 Article 1.3. (Constituent Entity)

67. The term Constituent Entity (CE) defines those Group Entities that are subject to the GloBE Rules. For example, a Group Entity must be a CE before it can be treated as a Low-Taxed Constituent Entity (LTCE) and subject to charge under the IIR or UTPR.

68. The term LTCE mentioned above is defined in Article 10.1 as below:

> Low-Taxed Constituent Entity means a Constituent Entity of the MNE Group that is located in a Low-Tax Jurisdiction or a Stateless Constituent Entity that, in respect of a Fiscal Year, has GloBE Income and is subject to an Effective Tax Rate (as determined under Chapter 5) in that Fiscal Year is lower than the Minimum Rate.

69. Prominent features of Article 1.3 are provided in Box 4.3.

Box 4.3 Prominent Features of Article 1.3

- Defines the term CE.
- Provides that a PE that is a CE shall be treated as separate from the Main Entity and any other PE of that Main Entity.
- Provides for independence of foreign PE.
- Provides that a CE does not include an entity that is an Excluded Entity.

4.1.3.1 Article 1.3.1.

70. A CE is:

(a) any entity that is included in a Group. Each of the entities of the Group, as determined in Article 1.2.2, will be a CE unless it is an Excluded Entity under Article 1.5; and
(b) any PE of a Main Entity that is within paragraph (a). A PE, as defined in Article 10.1, of a Main Entity that is itself a CE is treated as a separate CE. This paragraph applies to any of the four types of PEs described in the definition of PE in Article 10.1.

4.1.3.2 Article 1.3.2.

71. A PE that is a CE under Article 1.3.1(b) above shall be treated as separate from the Main Entity and any other PE of that Main Entity. This means a company with two PEs would be treated as three separate CEs for the purposes of the GloBE rules.[88]

72. *Requirement for independence of foreign PE:* The need to distinguish the separate business operations undertaken in the foreign PE is essential for the jurisdictional blending calculations under Chapter 5. It ensures that the income earned through PEs in another jurisdiction and the tax imposed on that income is not blended with the tax and income of the Main Entity or another PE in a different jurisdiction. Accordingly, it ensures parity in the treatment of foreign subsidiaries and PEs of the MNE Group.

4.1.3.3 Article 1.3.3.

73. Article 1.3.3 provides that a CE does not include an entity that is an Excluded Entity, which is therefore outside the GloBE Rules.

74. The concept of a CE is further explained through a flow-chart in Figure 4.1.

88. Refer 'The HMRC's OECD Pillar 2 Consultation on implementation' https://assets.publishing.service.gov.uk/government/uploads/system/uploads/attachment_data/file/1045663/11Jan_2022_Pillar_2_Consultation_.pdf accessed on 12 April 2022.

Figure 4.1 Determination of a Business Unit as a CE

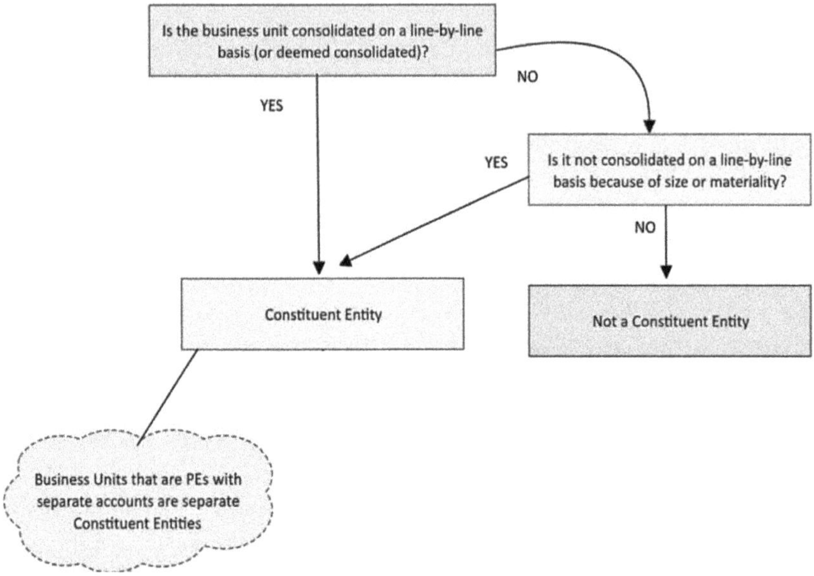

Source: Annexure of the Report on Pillar Two Blueprint (pg. 182).

4.1.4 Article 1.4. (UPE)

75. The definition of UPE is set out in Article 1.4. The UPE definition is used as part of the definition of a Group and is the starting point for identifying all the entities that comprise the MNE Group. The identification of the UPE is also relevant in other parts of the GloBE Rules. For example, the GloBE Rules give priority in the application of the IIR to the jurisdiction in which the UPE is located (the UPE Jurisdiction), and it will generally be the financial accounting standard of the UPE that is used as the basis for calculating the GloBE Income or Loss of CEs under Chapter 3.

76. Prominent features of Article 1.4 are provided in Box 4.4.

Box 4.4 Prominent Features of Article 1.4

- Defines the term UPE.
- To be a UPE of the Group, the entity must comply with two requirements, i.e., the UPE is an entity that directly or indirectly owns a Controlling Interest in another entity and disqualifies an entity from being the UPE of a Group if the Controlling Interests in that entity are held by another entity.
- In cases where the Group is a single entity with one or more foreign PEs, then the Main Entity is the UPE.

4.1.4.1 Article 1.4.1.

77. UPE means either:

(a) an Entity that:
   (i) owns directly or indirectly a Controlling Interest in any other entity; and
   (ii) is not owned, with a Controlling Interest, directly or indirectly by another entity; or
(b) the Main Entity of a Group that is within Article 1.2.3.

78. Paragraph (a) above is the most common scenario. It describes the UPE of a Group as defined in Article 1.2.2, i.e., the UPE of a Group comprised of at least two entities. To be a UPE of the Group, the entity must comply with two requirements. The first condition is set out in subparagraph (i), which states that the UPE is an entity that directly or indirectly owns a Controlling Interest in another entity. The definition of Controlling Interest uses a consolidation test (including a deemed consolidation test) to determine whether an entity owns a Controlling Interest in another entity. Definition of Controlling Interest is provided in Article 10.1 as below:

> Controlling Interest means an Ownership Interest in an entity such that the interest holder:
>
> (a) is required to consolidate the assets, liabilities, income, expenses and cash flows of the entity on a line-by-line basis in accordance with an Acceptable Financial Accounting Standard; or
> (b) would have been required to consolidate the assets, liabilities, income, expenses and cash flows of the entity on a line-by-line basis if the interest holder had prepared CFS.
>
> A Main Entity is deemed to have the Controlling Interests of its PEs.

Therefore, the requirement in subparagraph (i) is met if an entity is required to consolidate the assets, liabilities, income, expenses and cash flows of another entity on a line-by-line basis in accordance with an Acceptable Financial Accounting Standard or if it would have been so required if the first-mentioned entity had prepared CFS in accordance with an Authorised Financial Accounting Standard that is either an Acceptable Financial Accounting Standard or another financial accounting standard that is adjusted to prevent any Material Competitive Distortions. The second requirement is set in subparagraph (ii), which states that the Controlling Interests of the entity should not be owned directly or indirectly by another entity that is described in subparagraph (i). Therefore, it disqualifies an entity from being the UPE of a Group if the Controlling Interests in that entity are held by another entity. Stated differently, an entity is not considered the UPE of a Group if there is another entity higher in the ownership chain that is required, or that would have been required, to consolidate the first-mentioned entity on a line-by-line basis.

79. Paragraph (b) above describes the UPE of a Group as defined in Article 1.2.3 (i.e., a Group that is made up of a Main Entity and one or more PEs). In this case, the Main Entity is treated as the UPE of the Group. This paragraph provides that in those cases where the Group is a single entity with one or more foreign PEs, then the Main Entity is the UPE. This extended definition of UPE is necessary to ensure that a domestic entity that engages in cross-border operations through PEs is subject to the GloBE Rules. Main Entity is defined in Article 10.1 as below:

> Main Entity, in respect of a PE, is the entity that includes the Financial Accounting Net Income or Loss of the PE in its financial statements.

4.1.5 Article 1.5. (Excluded Entity)

80. Article 1.5 specifies those entities that are Excluded Entities and therefore not subject to the GloBE Rules.

81. Prominent features of Article 1.5 are provided in Box 4.5.

Box 4.5 Prominent Features of Article 1.5

- Specifies those entities that are Excluded Entities and therefore not subject to the GloBE Rules.
- IIR and UTPR do not apply to Excluded Entities.
- GloBE attributes of Excluded Entities are removed from the various computations under the GloBE Rules, except for the application of the revenue threshold.
- Excluded Entities do not have any administrative obligations under the GloBE Rules.
- Investment Fund that is a UPE and Real Estate Investment Vehicle that is a UPE are treated as Excluded Entities in order to protect their status as tax neutral investment vehicles.

- Article 1.5.2 recognises that Excluded Entities may be required, for regulatory or commercial reasons, to hold assets or carry out specific functions through separate controlled entities.
- Reason for Article 1.5.2 not to apply if entity is held by Pension Service Entity is that allowing a Pension Services Entity to establish a further separate controlled entity that qualified for Excluded Entity status would dilute the intended effect of the rules in Article 1.5.2, which are intended to be limited to those controlled entities that carry out functions for the Excluded Entity (such as the Governmental Entity, International or Non-profit Organisations or Pension Fund itself).
- Article 1.5.2(a) addresses the situation where an Excluded Entity under Article 1.5.1 sets up an entity to hold its assets or invest its funds, or to carry out activities that are ancillary to the Excluded Entity's activities.
- In order to qualify as an Excluded Entity under Article 1.5.2(a), the entity must meet two tests: an ownership test and an activities test.
- Article 1.5.2(a) also applies if the Excluded Entity under Article 1.5.1 owns at least 95% of the value of the entity through a chain of Excluded Entities.
- Excluded Entity under Article 1.5.2(b) includes one which owns at least 85% of the value of another entity whose Financial Accounting Net Income or Loss primarily composes Excluded Dividends or Excluded Equity Gains or Losses that are excluded from GloBE Income.
- The type of holding vehicles under Article 1.5.2(b) is not expected to be subject to a top-up tax under the GloBE Rules because all of their income is excluded from the GloBE Income. The practical effect of this provision is that it prevents these entities from applying the charging provisions in Chapter 2.
- Article 1.5.3 provides for an option for a Filing Constituent Entity to not treat an entity as an Excluded Entity.
- The reason for providing an option to an MNE Group to not elect an entity as an Excluded Entity is to allow that entity to apply the IIR to its subsidiaries instead of subjecting all of its CEs to the UTPR.

82. *Consequences (practical effects) for an Excluded Entity under the GloBE Rules*: Qualification as an Excluded Entity has three practical effects under the GloBE Rules:

(a) First, the IIR and UTPR do not apply to Excluded Entities. For example, only CEs are required to apply the IIR in accordance with Article 2.1. Therefore, an Excluded Entity that is the UPE of the MNE Group is not required to apply the IIR, and the rule must be applied by the next Entity in the ownership chain (that is not itself an Excluded Entity).

(b) Second, the GloBE attributes of Excluded Entities (including their profits, losses, taxes accrued, tangible assets, and payroll expenses) are removed from the various computations under the GloBE Rules, except for the application of the revenue threshold as described above.

(c) Third, Excluded Entities do not have any administrative obligations under the GloBE Rules, such as the filing of a GloBE Information Return, and information related to their income, taxes, assets, etc., is not reported in the GloBE Information Return (other than the information relating to Excluded Entities required under Article 8.1.4(b) (which refers to information on the overall corporate structure of the MNE Group including the Controlling Interests in the CEs held by other CEs) and any other information as agreed in the GloBE Implementation Framework).

83. The term GloBE Information Return mentioned *supra* is defined in Article 10.1 as below:

> GloBE Information Return means that standardized return to be developed in accordance with the GloBE Implementation Framework that contains the information described in Article 8.1.4.

84. The term GloBE Implementation Framework mentioned *supra* is defined in Article 10.1 as below:

> GloBE Implementation Framework means the procedures to be developed by the Inclusive Framework on BEPS in order to develop administrative rules, guidance, and procedures that will facilitate the coordinated implementation of the GloBE Rules.

4.1.5.1 Article 1.5.1.

85. Generally, Excluded Entities would not be consolidated on a line-by-line basis with a Group of operating entities and, therefore, would not have been considered as CEs of such Group under the tests set out in Article 1.3. However, for completeness, consistency and to improve certainty of outcomes, Article 1.5.1 explicitly provides a list of Excluded Entities, as shown in a flow-chart in Figure 4.2.

Figure 4.2 Excluded Entities

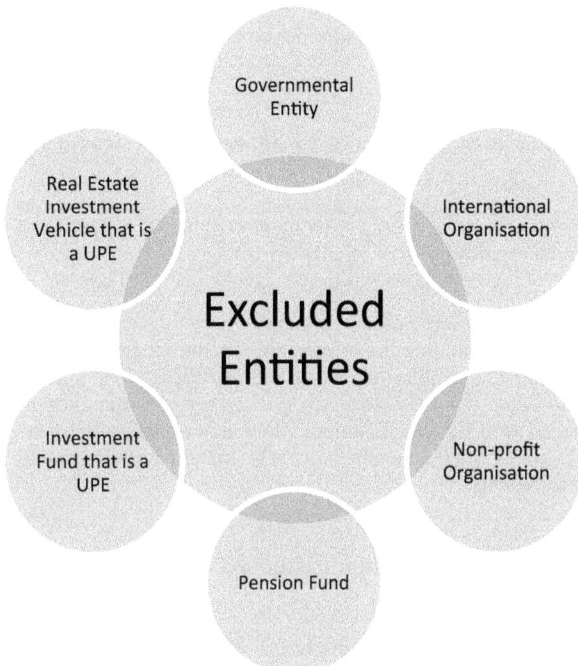

86. *Reason for treating Investment Fund that is a UPE and Real Estate Investment Vehicle that is a UPE as Excluded Entities*: These entities are excluded from the GloBE Rules in order to protect their status as tax neutral investment vehicles. If an Investment Fund or Real Estate Investment Vehicle is not the UPE of the MNE Group, it can still be treated as a CE of the MNE Group, provided it otherwise meets the consolidation requirements of Article 1.2 and Article 1.3. However, such Investment Funds and Real Estate Investment Vehicles are considered Investment Entities and are subject to special rules for calculation of ETR in Articles 7.4 through 7.6.

87. The term Governmental Entity mentioned above is defined in Article 10.1 as below:

> Governmental Entity means an Entity that meets all of the following criteria set out in paragraphs (a) to (d) below:
>
> (a) it is part of or wholly-owned by a government (including any political subdivision or local authority thereof);
> (b) it has the principal purpose of:
> (i) fulfilling a government function; or
> (ii) managing or investing that government's or jurisdiction's assets through the making and holding of investments, asset management, and related investment activities for the government's or jurisdiction's assets;
> and does not carry on a trade or business;

(c) it is accountable to the government on its overall performance, and provides annual information reporting to the government; and
(d) its assets vest in such government upon dissolution and to the extent it distributes net earnings, such net earnings are distributed solely to such government with no portion of its net earnings inuring to the benefit of any private person.

88. The term International Organisation mentioned above is defined in Article 10.1 as below:

> International Organisation means any intergovernmental organisation (including a supranational organisation) or wholly-owned agency or instrumentality thereof that meets all of the criteria set out in paragraphs (a) to (c) below:
>
> (a) it is comprised primarily of governments;
> (b) it has in effect a headquarters or substantially similar agreement (for example, arrangements that entitle the organisation's offices or establishments in the jurisdiction (e.g., a subdivision, or a local, or regional office) to privileges and immunities) with the jurisdiction in which it is established; and
> (c) law or its governing documents prevent its income from inuring to the benefit of private persons.

89. The term Non-profit Organisation mentioned above is defined in Article 10.1 as below:

> Non-profit Organisation means an entity that meets all of the following criteria:
>
> (a) it is established and operated in its jurisdiction of residence:
> (i) exclusively for religious, charitable, scientific, artistic, cultural, athletic, educational, or other similar purposes; or
> (ii) as a professional organisation, business league, chamber of commerce, labour organisation, agricultural or horticultural organisation, civic league or an organisation operated exclusively for the promotion of social welfare;
> (b) substantially all of the income from the activities mentioned in paragraph (a) is exempt from income tax in its jurisdiction of residence;
> (c) it has no shareholders or members who have a proprietary or beneficial interest in its income or assets;
> (d) the income or assets of the entity may not be distributed to, or applied for the benefit of, a private person or non-charitable entity other than:
> (i) pursuant to the conduct of the entity's charitable activities;
> (ii) as payment of reasonable compensation for services rendered or for the use of property or capital; or
> (iii) as payment representing the fair market value of property which the entity has purchased, and
> (e) upon termination, liquidation or dissolution of the entity, all of its assets must be distributed or revert to a Non-profit Organisation or to the government (including any Governmental Entity) of the entity's jurisdiction of residence or any political subdivision thereof;
>
> but does not include any entity carrying on a trade or business that is not directly related to the purposes for which it was established.

90. The term Pension Fund mentioned above is defined in Article 10.1 as below:

> Pension Fund means:
>
> (a) an entity that is established and operated in a jurisdiction exclusively or almost exclusively to administer or provide retirement benefits and ancillary or incidental benefits to individuals:
>   i. regulated as such by that jurisdiction or one of its political subdivisions or local authorities; or
>   ii. those benefits are secured or otherwise protected by national regulations and funded by a pool of assets held through a fiduciary arrangement or trustor to secure the fulfilment of the corresponding pension obligations against a case of insolvency of the MNE Group; and
>
> (b) a Pension Services Entity.

91. The term Investment Fund mentioned above is defined in Article 10.1 as below:

> Investment Fund means an entity that meets all of the criteria set out in paragraphs (a) to (g) below:
>
> (a) it is designed to pool assets (which may be financial and non-financial) from a number of investors (some of which are not connected);
> (b) it invests in accordance with a defined investment policy;
> (c) it allows investors to reduce transaction, research, and analytical costs, or to spread risk collectively;
> (d) it is primarily designed to generate investment income or gains, or protection against a particular or general event or outcome;
> (e) investors have a right to return from the assets of the fund or income earned on those assets, based on the contributions made by those investors;
> (f) the entity or its management is subject to a regulatory regime in the jurisdiction in which it is established or managed (including appropriate anti-money laundering and investor protection regulation); and
> (g) it is managed by investment fund management professionals on behalf of the investors.

92. The term Real Estate Investment Vehicle mentioned above is defined in Article 10.1 as below:

> Real Estate Investment Vehicle means an entity the taxation of which achieves a single level of taxation either in its hands or the hands of its interest holders (with at most one year of deferral), provided that that person holds predominantly immovable property and is itself widely held.

4.1.5.2 Article 1.5.2.

93. Article 1.5.2 is an extension of the definition of an Excluded Entity in Article 1.5.1 that covers entities owned by an Excluded Entity and states as below:

> An Excluded Entity is also an Entity:

(a) where at least 95% of the value of the Entity is owned (directly or through a chain of Excluded Entities) by one or more Excluded Entities referred to in Article 1.5.1 (other than a Pension Services Entity) and where that Entity:
  i. operates exclusively or almost exclusively to hold assets or invest funds for the benefit of the Excluded Entity or Entities; or
  ii. only carries out activities that are ancillary to those carried out by the Excluded Entity or Entities; or

(b) where at least 85% of the value of the Entity is owned (directly or through a chain of Excluded Entities), by one or more Excluded Entities referred to in Article 1.5.1 (other than a Pension Services Entity) provided that substantially all of the Entity's income is Excluded Dividends or Excluded Equity Gain or Loss that is excluded from the computation of GloBE Income or Loss in accordance with Articles 3.2.1(b) or (c).

94. *Reason for Excluded Entities provided under the Article:* Article 1.5.2 recognises that Excluded Entities may be required, for regulatory or commercial reasons, to hold assets or carry out specific functions through separate controlled entities. For example, commercial or regulatory requirements may prevent an Investment Fund referred to in Article 1.5.1(e) from investing directly in an asset and may require the investment to be made through a separate vehicle to limit the Investment Fund's liability. The rule in Article 1.5.2 addresses these types of situations and may permit such a holding vehicle to qualify as an Excluded Entity.

95. *Reason for Article 1.5.2 not to apply if entity held by Pension Service Entity*: Pension Services Entities are special purpose vehicles that may perform similar functions to the Entities described in Article 1.5.2. Allowing a Pension Services Entity to establish a further separate controlled entity that qualified for Excluded Entity status would dilute the intended effect of the rules in Article 1.5.2, which are intended to be limited to those controlled entities that carry out functions for the Excluded Entity (such as the Governmental Entity, International or Non-profit Organisations or Pension Fund itself). Pension Services Entity is defined in Article 10.1 as below:

> Pension Services Entity means an entity that is established and operated exclusively or almost exclusively:
>
> (a) to invest funds for the benefit of entities referred to in paragraph (a) of the definition of Pension Fund; or
>
> (b) to carry out activities that are ancillary to those regulated activities carried out by the entities referred to in paragraph (a) of the definition of Pension Fund provided that they are members of the same Group.

96. Article 1.5.2(a) addresses the situation where an Excluded Entity under Article 1.5.1 sets up an entity to hold its assets or invest its funds, or to carry out activities that are ancillary to the Excluded Entity's activities. In order to qualify as an Excluded Entity under Article 1.5.2(a), the entity must meet two tests: an ownership test and an activities test.

97. Article 1.5.2(a) also applies if the Excluded Entity under Article 1.5.1 owns at least 95% of the value of the entity through a chain of Excluded Entities. This aspect is explained through an illustration given below:

> **Illustration # 4:** Let's assume A Co is an Excluded Entity under Article 1.5.1. A Co wholly owns B Co (another Excluded Entity), which in turn owns 95% of the value of C Co. In this case, C Co meets the ownership test under paragraph (a) because 95% of its value is indirectly owned by A Co. In contrast, if A Co owned 95% of Ownership Interests of B Co, then the ownership test is not met with respect to C Co because the value owned by A Co has been diluted to 90% (95% x 95%).

98. *Reason for 95% threshold in Article 1.5.2(a):* The 95% threshold allows for situations in which there is a small minority interest holder, such as where a fund manager holds a small percentage of an Investment Fund or where domestic law requires at least two shareholders to incorporate a corporation or where an Excluded Entity invests through a partnership and is required to have another entity acting as the general partner for domestic law purposes.

99. *Activities test under Article 1.5.2(a)(i):* Subparagraph (i) of Article 1.5.2(a) requires that the entity operates 'exclusively or almost exclusively to hold assets or invest funds'. The words 'exclusively or almost exclusively' denote a facts and circumstances test that requires all or almost all of the entity's activities to be related to holding assets or investing funds. This language further means that in order to be an Excluded Entity under paragraph (a), the entity must not actively carry out activities other than holding assets or investing funds. For example, subparagraph (i) could apply to a sovereign wealth fund owned by a government (in case it does not already meet the definition of a Governmental Entity under Article 10.1) that is holding assets and investing funds for the benefit of the government, but it would not extend to an airline company owned by the government, because an airline's activities go beyond holding assets and investing funds. Subparagraph (i) also requires that the assets are held or funds invested 'for the benefit of the Excluded Entity'. This condition has to be read in conjunction with the other conditions of this article. For example, this condition is still met even if the fund manager benefits from the investments made by such entity in proportion to its ownership percentage.

100. *Activities test under Article 1.5.2(a)(ii):* The activities test is met under subparagraph (ii) of Article 1.5.2(a) if the entity only carries out activities that are ancillary to the activities carried out by an Excluded Entity. This 'alternative activities' test was included because, in some situations, the activities that would otherwise be performed by the Excluded Entity referred to in Article 1.5.1 are outsourced to a separate legal entity that is wholly owned by the Excluded Entity (including those that are 95% owned). For example, if an Excluded Entity sets up an information technology service company that provides services exclusively to the Excluded Entity, then such company would meet the requirement under subparagraph (ii).

101. *Reason for incorporating paragraph (b) of Article 1.5.2:* Paragraph (b) covers the case where an Excluded Entity referred to in Article 1.5.1 (other than a Pension Services

Entity) owns at least 85% of the value of another entity whose Financial Accounting Net Income or Loss would otherwise be excluded from the GloBE Income or Loss because it is primarily composed of Excluded Dividends or Excluded Equity Gains or Losses that are excluded from GloBE Income in accordance with Article 3.2.1(b) or (c). These types of holding vehicles would not be expected to be subject to a top-up tax under the GloBE Rules because all of their income is excluded from the GloBE Income. The practical effect of this provision is that it prevents these entities from applying the charging provisions in Chapter 2.

102. *Reason for keeping a lower threshold of 85% in Article 1.5.2(b):* The ownership percentage in paragraph (b) is lower than in paragraph (a) in order to provide greater flexibility, in particular, in the context of vehicles held by Investments Funds where third parties may hold a greater stake or where the interests in the holding vehicle are issued to management or other employees of the operating company.

103. *Reason for incorporating the phrase 'substantially all of the Entity's income' in Article 1.5.2(b):* This phrase was included to avoid a situation where the entity fails to qualify under paragraph (b) solely because it receives a small amount of income other than dividend and other equity returns on controlled companies. For example, the interest received from a bank on money that passes through the entity's bank account should not prevent the entity from qualifying as an Excluded Entity under paragraph (b), provided that such interest income represents an insignificant amount of its overall income.

4.1.5.3 Article 1.5.3.

104. A Filing Constituent Entity may elect not to treat an entity as an Excluded Entity under Article 1.5.2. An election under this article is a Five-Year Election. Filing Constituent Entity is defined in Article 10.1 as below:

> Filing Constituent Entity is an entity filing the GloBE Information Return in accordance with Article 8.1.

105. The term Five-Year Election mentioned above is defined in Article 10.1 as below:

> Five-Year Election means an election made by a Filing Constituent Entity with respect to a Fiscal Year (the election year) that cannot be revoked with respect to the election year or the four succeeding Fiscal Years. If a Five-Year Election is revoked with respect to a Fiscal Year (the revocation year), a new election cannot be made with respect to the four Fiscal Years succeeding the revocation year.

106. *Reason for providing an option to not elect an entity as an Excluded Entity:* When the election is made, the GloBE Rules will apply to the Entity described in Article 1.5.2 in the same manner as they apply to any other CE of the MNE Group. For example, a Filing Constituent Entity may elect to treat an entity as a CE rather than an Excluded Entity under Article 1.5.2 in order to apply the IIR and not the UTPR with respect to the top-up tax of the LTCE. Take, for example, an MNE Group with a UPE that is an

Investment Fund which is an Excluded Entity, but which consolidates on a line-by-line basis with its subsidiaries under the Acceptable Financial Accounting Standard used to prepare its CFS. Such MNE Group may make this election such that the entity can apply the IIR to its subsidiaries instead of subjecting all of its CEs to the UTPR.

4.2 CHAPTER 2 OF GLOBE RULES (CHARGING PROVISIONS)[89]

107. *Overview*: Chapter 2 pertains to charging provisions in the form of two interlocking rules, IIR and UTPR. The GloBE Rules apply a system of top-up taxes, i.e., an IIR and a UTPR, which are designed to bring the total amount of taxes paid on an MNE's excess profit in a jurisdiction up to the minimum rate of 15% (as defined in Article 10.1). This top-up tax (means the top-up tax computed for the jurisdiction or CE pursuant to Article 5.2, as defined in Article 10.1) does not operate as a typical direct tax on income of an entity. Rather it applies to the excess profits calculated on a jurisdictional basis and only applies to the extent those profits are subject to tax in a given year below the minimum rate of 15%. Rather than a typical direct tax on income, the tax imposed under the GloBE Rules is closer in design to an international alternative minimum tax that uses standardised base and tax calculation mechanics to identify pools of low-taxed income within an MNE Group and imposes a coordinated tax charge that brings the Group's ETR on that income in each jurisdiction up to the minimum rate of 15%. The design of the GloBE Rules as a top-up tax facilitates the coordinated application of the GloBE Rules by ensuring that the aggregate amount of incremental tax payable under the rules in each jurisdiction does not cause the ETR to exceed the minimum rate. The design of the IIR and UTPR as top-up taxes, however, does not restrict a jurisdiction from legislating those rules under a CIT system in its domestic law.

108. *SOR*: Taken together, the IIR and UTPR provide a systematic solution to ensure all in-scope MNE Groups pay a minimum level of tax on their profits in excess of a routine return in the jurisdictions in which they operate. However, concerns about the intended application of these rules can arise where a Parent Entity jurisdiction, which would otherwise apply the IIR in accordance with the provisions of Article 2, has entered into bilateral tax treaties in which it has adopted the exemption method (instead of a credit method) to eliminate double taxation of income arising in the other jurisdiction. In this case, a SOR in a Tax Treaty could facilitate the application of the IIR by the jurisdiction of residence of the Parent Entity to tax the income of the PE in those cases where the IIR applies as a matter of domestic law. The SOR could safeguard the application of the IIR by the residence state with respect to a PE. The rule would, by virtue of its domestic law trigger, only apply when and to the extent that a resident of a Contracting State was required to apply the IIR with respect to a PE in the other Contracting State.

89. Based on OECD's GloBE Model Rules, its Commentary and Illustrative Examples.

4.2.1 Article 2.1. (Application of the IIR)

109. Article 2.1 identifies the entities in the MNE Group that are required to apply the IIR rule.

110. Prominent features of Article 2.1 are provided in Box 4.6.

Box 4.6 Prominent Features of Article 2.1

- Identifies the entities in the MNE Group that are required to apply the IIR rule.
- Provides the main rule for application of the IIR.
- Amount of ownership Interests held by the UPE in the LTCE is not directly relevant to apply IIR, as a prerequisite for applying IIR is that the LTCE should be a CE (or treated as such in the case of JVs) and should be a member of the MNE Group.
- Holding period is not relevant as IIR applies if the UPE holds Ownership Interests of the LTCE at any time during the Fiscal Year.
- Provides rules for application of the IIR by an Intermediate Parent Entity.
- PEs are not treated as Parent Entities under the GloBE Rules. In this context, Ownership Interests in an LTCE that are held through a PE are treated instead as held by the Main Entity.
- Intermediate Parent Entity's Allocable Share of the top-up tax is not limited by the UPE's allocable share.
- Amount of ownership Interests held by the Intermediate Parent Entity in the LTCE is not relevant for applying Article 2.1.2.
- Embodies the 'top-down approach', which generally gives priority to applying the IIR to the Parent Entities at the top of the ownership chain.
- Prevents the application of the IIR at the level of an Intermediate Parent Entity when the Controlling Interests of such entity are held directly or indirectly by another Intermediate Parent Entity which is required to apply a Qualified IIR.
- Provides that a Partially-Owned Parent Entity (POPE) located in a jurisdiction which has implemented GloBE rules and that owns (directly or indirectly) an Ownership Interest in an LTCE at any time during the Fiscal Year shall pay tax of an amount equal to its Allocable Share of the top-up tax of that LTCE for the Fiscal Year.
- Prevents the application of the IIR at the level of a POPE when the Controlling Interests of such entity are held directly or indirectly by another POPE, which is required to apply a Qualified IIR.
- Provides for the application of IIR by the Parent Entity to LTCEs that are located outside the implementing jurisdiction of the Parent Entity.

- IIR can be applied domestically in order to avoid discriminating between domestic and foreign CEs that are members of the same MNE Group and by a Parent Entity to itself.

111. The IIR is applied by a Parent Entity, which is defined in Article 10.1 as below:

> Parent entity means a UPE that is not an Excluded Entity, or an Intermediate Parent Entity, or a Partially-Owned Parent Entity (POPE).

112. The term Intermediate Parent Entity mentioned above is defined in Article 10.1 as below:

> Intermediate Parent Entity means a CE (other than a UPE, POPE, PE, or Investment Entity) that owns (directly or indirectly) an Ownership Interest in another CE in the same MNE Group.

113. The term Partially-Owned Parent Entity mentioned above is defined in Article 10.1 as below:

> Partially-Owned Parent Entity means a CE (other than a UPE, PE, or Investment Entity) that:
>
> (a) owns (directly or indirectly) an Ownership Interest in another CE of the same MNE Group; and
> (b) has more than 20% of the Ownership Interests in its profits held directly or indirectly by persons that are not CEs of the MNE Group.

114. The term Ownership Interest mentioned above is defined in Article 10.1 as below:

> Ownership Interest means any equity interest that carries rights to the profits, capital or reserves of an Entity, including the profits, capital or reserves of a Main Entity's Permanent Establishment(s).

4.2.1.1 Article 2.1.1.

115. Article 2.1.1 provides the main rule for application of the IIR. It applies when a CE, that is, the UPE of an MNE Group, located in a jurisdiction that has implemented IIR and that owns (directly or indirectly) an Ownership Interest in an LTCE at any time during the Fiscal Year shall pay tax of an amount equal to its Allocable Share of the top-up tax of that LTCE for the Fiscal Year.

116. *Amount of ownership Interests held by the UPE in the LTCE not relevant for application of the Article*: The amount of the Ownership Interests held by the UPE in the LTCE is not directly relevant in the determination of whether this article applies because a prerequisite of this rule is that the LTCE is a CE (or treated as such in the case of JVs) and a member of the MNE Group.

117. The term Joint Venture (JV) mentioned above is defined in Article 10.1 as below:

> Joint Venture (JV) means an Entity whose financial results are reported under the equity method in the Consolidated Financial Statements of the UPE, provided that the UPE holds directly or indirectly at least 50% of its Ownership Interests. A Joint Venture does not include:
>
> (a) a UPE of an MNE Group that is subject to the GloBE Rules;
> (b) an Excluded Entity as defined by Article 1.5.1;
> (c) an Entity whose Ownership Interest held by the MNE Group are held directly through an Excluded Entity referred in Article 1.5.1 and the Entity:
> (i) operates exclusively or almost exclusively to hold assets or invest funds for the benefit of its investors;
> (ii) carries out activities that are ancillary to those carried out by the Excluded Entity; or
> (iii) substantially all of its income is excluded from the computation of GloBE Income or Loss in accordance with Articles 3.2.1(b) and (c).
> (d) an Entity that is held by an MNE Group composed exclusively of Excluded Entities; or
> (e) a JV Subsidiary.

118. *The Article contains the main charging provision of the IIR*: Article 2.1.1 requires the UPE to pay a tax of an amount equal to its Allocable Share of the top-up tax of that LTCE for the Fiscal Year. The determination of a Parent Entity's Allocable Share is carried out in accordance with Article 2.2.

119. *Relevance of Holding period for the purposes of applying the Article*: The IIR applies if the UPE holds Ownership Interests of the LTCE 'at any time during the Fiscal Year'. This means that the UPE is required to apply the IIR with respect to a CE that was disposed of or acquired during the Fiscal Year. The holding period of the interests during the Fiscal Year is not relevant for purposes of applying Article 2.1.1 because this is already reflected in the computation of the top-up tax under Chapter 5. The calculation of the top-up tax takes into account the amount of income reported in the CFS, which takes into account the holding period in which the UPE owns an LTCE for the Fiscal Year. The special rules under Article 6.2.1 provide greater detail on how the GloBE Rules operate under these circumstances, including how the IIR and top-down approach apply.

4.2.1.2 Article 2.1.2.

120. Article 2.1.2 provides the rules for application of the IIR by an Intermediate Parent Entity. It provides that an Intermediate Parent Entity of an MNE Group located in a jurisdiction that has implemented IIR and that owns (directly or indirectly) an Ownership Interest in an LTCE at any time during a Fiscal Year shall pay tax of an amount equal to its Allocable Share of the top-up tax of that LTCE for the Fiscal Year.

121. *PEs not treated as Parent Entities under the GloBE Rules:* In order to avoid difficult factual determinations and disputes as to whether the Ownership Interests in LTCEs are held by the PE or the Main Entity, PEs are not treated as Parent Entities under the GloBE Rules. In this context, Ownership Interests in an LTCE that are held through a PE are treated instead as held by the Main Entity.

122. *Allocable Share of the top-up tax*: The Intermediate Parent Entity's Allocable Share of the top-up tax is not limited by the UPE's allocable share. For example, a UPE (that is located in a jurisdiction without a Qualified IIR) owns 90% of the Ownership Interests of an Intermediate Parent Entity that, in turn, owns 100% of the Ownership Interests of an LTCE. The Allocable Share of these two Parent Entities in the LTCE is based on the Ownership Interests that they directly or indirectly hold in the LTCE. Therefore, the Intermediate Parent Entity's Allocable Share of the LTCE's Top-up Tax is 100%, while the UPE's Allocable Share of the same LTCE would be 90%.

123. *Amount of ownership Interests not relevant for applying Article 2.1.2*: The amount of Ownership Interests held by the Intermediate Parent Entity in the LTCE is not relevant for applying Article 2.1.2. Accordingly, the Intermediate Parent Entity is not required to have a Controlling Interest in the LTCE to apply the IIR as long as the LTCE is a member of the same MNE Group. For example, an Intermediate Parent Entity may hold a 10% Ownership Interest in an LTCE and still be required to apply the IIR in accordance with Article 2.1.2. The amount of Top-up Tax that the Intermediate Parent Entity is required to pay, however, is limited to the Intermediate Parent Entity's Allocable Share in respect of its Ownership Interest (i.e., equity interest) as set out in Article 2.2.1.

4.2.1.3 Article 2.1.3.

124. Article 2.1.3 states as below:

> Article 2.1.2 shall not apply if:
>
> (a) the UPE of the MNE Group is required to apply a Qualified IIR for that Fiscal Year; or
> (b) another Intermediate Parent Entity that owns (directly or indirectly) a Controlling Interest in the Intermediate Parent Entity is required to apply a Qualified IIR for that Fiscal Year.

125. *Top-down approach defined:* The 'top-down approach' is embodied in Article 2.1.3, which generally gives priority to applying the IIR to the Parent Entities at the top of the ownership chain. The mechanics of this provision limit the application of Article 2.1.2 to prevent instances of double taxation that would be caused by multiple Parent Entities applying the IIR with respect to the same Ownership Interest in the LTCE.

126. *Role of Article 2.1.3(a):* Article 2.1.3 (a) deactivates Article 2.1.2 and prevents the application of the IIR at the Intermediate Parent Entity level when the UPE is required to apply a Qualified IIR for the Fiscal Year. The phrase 'required to apply a Qualified IIR' ensures that the exclusion in Article 2.1.3(a) operates only where the domestic tax legislation of the UPE jurisdiction requires the UPE to apply a Qualified IIR. Article

2.1.3(a) would not apply, for example, where the UPE jurisdiction has introduced a Qualified IIR, but it is still not in force, or the UPE is an Excluded Entity that is outside the scope of such rules.

127. The term Qualified IIR mentioned above is defined in Article 10.1 as below:

> Qualified IIR means a set of rules equivalent to Article 2.1 to Article 2.3 of the GloBE Rules (including any provisions of the GloBE Rules associated with those articles) that are included in the domestic law of a jurisdiction and that are implemented and administered in a way that is consistent with the outcomes provided for under the GloBE Rules and the Commentary provided that such jurisdiction does not provide any benefits that are related to such rules.

128. The term Commentary mentioned above is defined in Article 10.1 as below:

> Commentary means the Commentary to the GloBE Rules as developed by the OECD/G20 Inclusive Framework on Base Erosion and Profit Shifting.

129. *Role of Article 2.1.3(b):* Article 2.1.3(b) regulates the 'top-down approach' where two or more Intermediate Parent Entities are required to apply the IIR to the same LTCE. It prevents the application of the IIR at the level of an Intermediate Parent Entity when the Controlling Interests of such entity are held directly or indirectly by another Intermediate Parent Entity which is required to apply a Qualified IIR. However, Article 2.1.3(b) shall not apply, and the IIR shall not get deactivated if one Intermediate Parent Entity does not have a Controlling Interest in the other Intermediate Parent Entity. Accordingly, the IIR can be applied by more than one Intermediate Parent Entity in the same MNE Group.

130. Illustration # 5: The illustration, through a flow-chart, explains the application of the top-down approach under Article 2.1.3 in a situation where the UPE is not required to apply a Qualified IIR.

Application of Top-down approach under Article 2.1.3

Facts

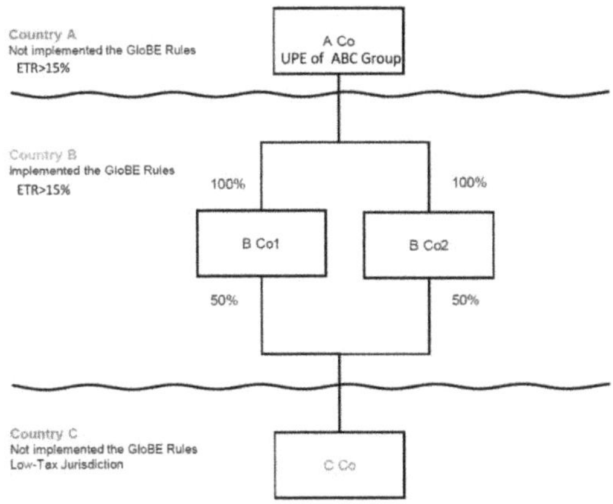

Impression – Country C is a Low-Tax Jurisdiction and C Co is a LTCE for the purposes of the GloBE Rules and any top-up tax determined for C Co under Chapter 5 will therefore be subject to charge under an applicable IIR.

Solution – A Co is the UPE and would have the priority to apply the IIR under Articles 2.1.1 and 2.1.3, if Country A had introduced a Qualified IIR. In this case, however, only Country B has introduced a Qualified IIR and thus, the Intermediate Parent Entities (B Co 1 and B Co 2) are required to apply the IIR in accordance with Article 2.1.2 because the conditions in Article 2.1.3(a) are not met. B Co 1 and B Co 2 must apply the IIR in accordance with Article 2.1.2 based on their Allocable Share of the Top-up Tax (50% each) of C Co. B Co 1 and B Co 2 pay the Top-tax under the IIR equal to the full amount of C Co's Top-up Tax.

131. Illustration # 6: This example illustrates the application of the top-down approach under Article 2.1.3 and Offset Mechanism under Article 2.3 in a situation where an Intermediate Parent Entity required to apply a Qualified IIR owns an Ownership Interest in another Intermediate Parent Entity that is also required to apply a Qualified IIR with respect to the same LTCE.

Application of Top-down approach under Article 2.1.3 and Offset Mechanism under Article 2.3

Facts

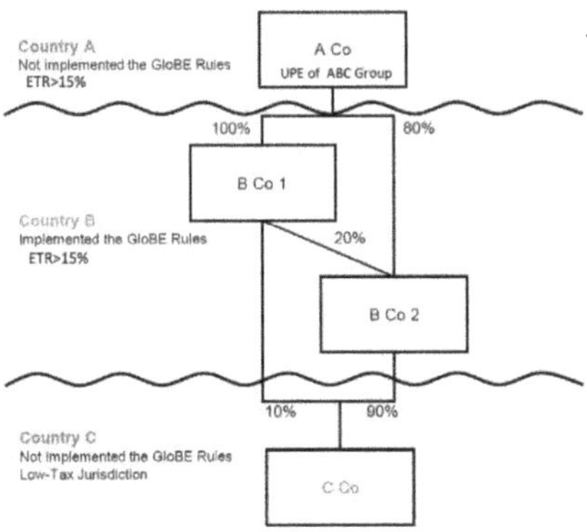

Impression – One of the Intermediate Parent Entities (B Co 1) that is required to apply the IIR holds some of the Ownership Interests of another Intermediate Parent Entity (B Co 2). Article 2.1.3(b) does not prevent the lower-tier entity (B Co 2) from applying the IIR because B Co 1 does not own a Controlling Interest in B Co 2.

Solution – Both B Co 1 and B Co 2 are required to apply the IIR under Article 2.1.2 based on their Allocable Share of the top-up tax in accordance with Article 2.2. In this case, since B Co 2's Allocable Share of C Co's Top-up Tax is 90% (based on its direct shareholding in C Co) and that B Co 1's Allocable Share of the top-up tax is 28% (10% due to its direct ownership and 18% due to its indirect ownership). However, in order to avoid double taxation, Article 2.3 requires B Co 1 to reduce the top-up tax attributable to its indirect ownership in C Co by the amount that will be brought into charge by B Co 2.

4.2.1.4 Article 2.1.4.

132. Article 2.1.4 provides the rules for the application of the IIR by a POPE. Notwithstanding Articles 2.1.1 to 2.1.3, a POPE located in a jurisdiction which has implemented GloBE rules and that owns (directly or indirectly) an Ownership Interest in an LTCE at any time during the Fiscal Year shall pay tax of an amount equal to its Allocable Share of the top-up tax of that LTCE for the Fiscal Year.

133. *Reason for incorporating 'notwithstanding' clause in the Article*: The reference in Article 2.1.4 'notwithstanding Articles 2.1.1 to 2.1.3' means that the rules apply regardless of whether the UPE or an Intermediate Parent Entity is also required to apply a Qualified IIR.

4.2.1.5 Article 2.1.5.

134. In accordance with the top-down approach, Article 2.1.5 provides a priority rule for scenarios in which two or more POPEs are situated in the same ownership chain and are required to apply the IIR with respect to the same LTCE. Therefore, Article 2.1.4 shall not apply if the POPE is wholly owned (directly or indirectly) by another POPE that is required to apply a Qualified IIR for that Fiscal Year.

135. *Difference between Article 2.1.5 and Article 2.1.3(b)*: Article 2.1.5 applies only where the POPE is wholly owned by another POPE. This differs from the language of paragraph (b) of Article 2.1.3 (the priority rule for Intermediate Parent Entities), which requires a direct or indirect Controlling Interest by a higher tier Intermediate Parent Entity to deactivate the rule. This nuance is deliberate and addresses structures with minority interests at each level in a partially owned subgroup. Utilising a control test in this context would apply the IIR at higher levels in the partially owned chain and leave the top-up tax attributable to lower-tier minority interests outside the scope of the rule. Accordingly, to prevent distortions and ensure that the appropriate amount of top-up tax is taken into account, a POPE must apply the IIR unless it is wholly owned (directly or indirectly) by another POPE that is required to apply a Qualified IIR for the Fiscal Year.

136. Illustration # 7: The illustration, through a flow-chart, explains the application of the split-ownership rules and the top-down approach in a situation where the UPE and POPE are required to apply a Qualified IIR under Article 2.1.5 with respect to the same LTCE.

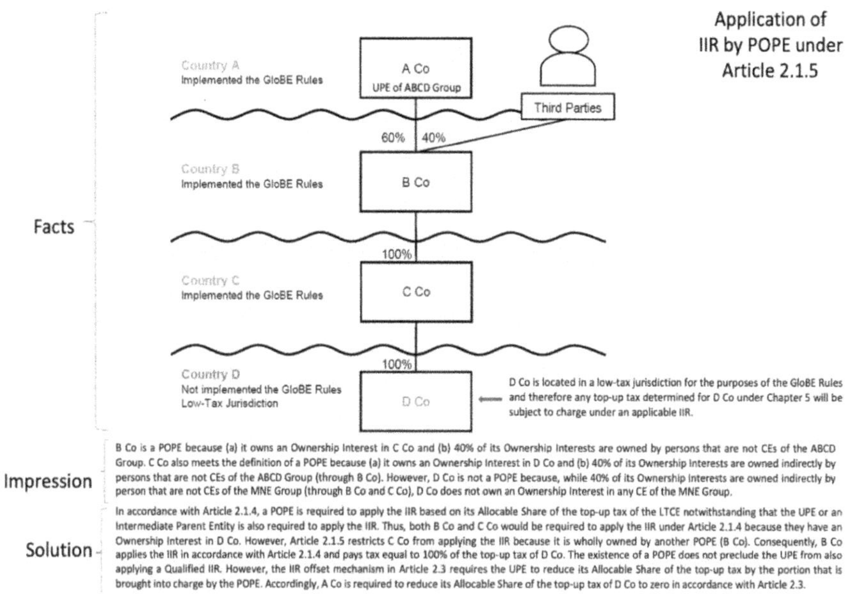

137. Illustration # 8: The illustration, through a flow-chart, explains the application of the split-ownership rules and the top-down approach under Articles 2.1.4 and 2.1.5 in a situation where two POPEs are required to apply a Qualified IIR with respect to the same LTCE.

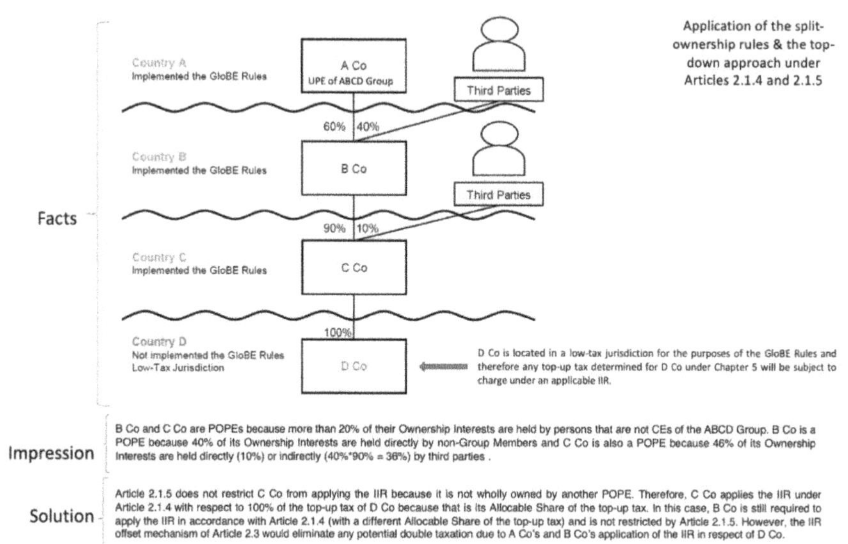

4.2.1.6 Article 2.1.6.

138. Article 2.1.6 requires the application of the IIR by the Parent Entity to LTCEs that are located outside the implementing jurisdiction of the Parent Entity. It states that a Parent Entity located in a jurisdiction that has implemented GloBE Rules shall apply the provisions of Articles 2.1.1 to 2.1.5 with respect to an LTCE that is not located in that jurisdiction.

139. *IIR can be applied domestically and by a Parent Entity to itself*: It is possible to extend the application of the IIR domestically in order to avoid discriminating between domestic and foreign CEs that are members of the same MNE Group. In these cases, an implementing jurisdiction may introduce further rules that require a Parent Entity to bring into account its share of top-up tax attributable to its Ownership Interest in domestic LTCEs together with any top-up tax allocated to that Parent Entity itself. Under this approach, a Parent Entity located in a Low-tax Jurisdiction would apply an IIR to its allocable share of top-up tax of any domestic LTCEs and also apply the IIR in respect of any top-up tax that would otherwise be allocated to the Parent Entity under Article 5.2.4. An IIR that is applied to a Parent Entity's Ownership Interest in its domestic LTCEs shall be treated as a Qualified IIR, provided it meets the other requirements set out in the GloBE Rules and the Commentary. The application of such a domestic IIR will remain subject to the operation of the agreed rule order in Chapter 2, including the top-down approach and the split-ownership rules, and any top-up tax collected under a domestic IIR should be recognised as an IIR tax by other jurisdictions in accordance with the ordinary rules in Chapter 2. Similarly, where a jurisdiction also requires the Parent Entity to apply a domestic IIR to itself, any top-up tax payable as a result of the application of that rule is treated as having been brought into charge under an IIR, notwithstanding that the tax imposed relates to the top-up tax allocated to the Parent Entity itself. Such IIR will be treated as a Qualified IIR under the GloBE Rules, provided the circumstances in which such tax is imposed and the amount of tax brought into charge is the same as the tax that would have been imposed had the Parent Entity held 100% of the Ownership Interests in itself. The application of a domestic IIR in this situation should be distinguished from a DMT that could be applied to all the CEs located in the same jurisdiction and regardless of whether that CE was a Parent Entity required to apply an IIR.

140. The term Low-tax Jurisdiction mentioned above is defined in Article 10.1 as below:

> Low-Tax Jurisdiction, in respect of an MNE Group in any Fiscal Year, means a jurisdiction where the MNE Group has Net GloBE Income and is subject to an Effective Tax Rate (as determined under Chapter 5) in that period that is lower than the Minimum Rate.

141. Illustration # 9: The illustration, through a flow-chart, explains the provisions of Article 2.1.6.

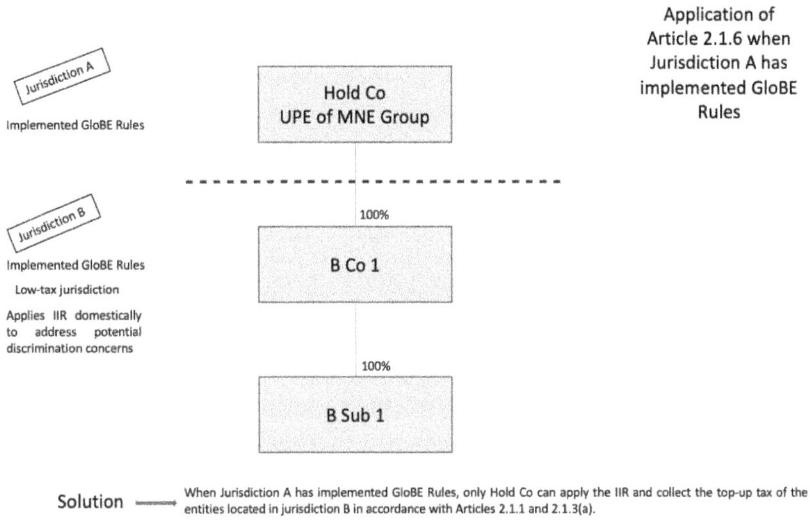

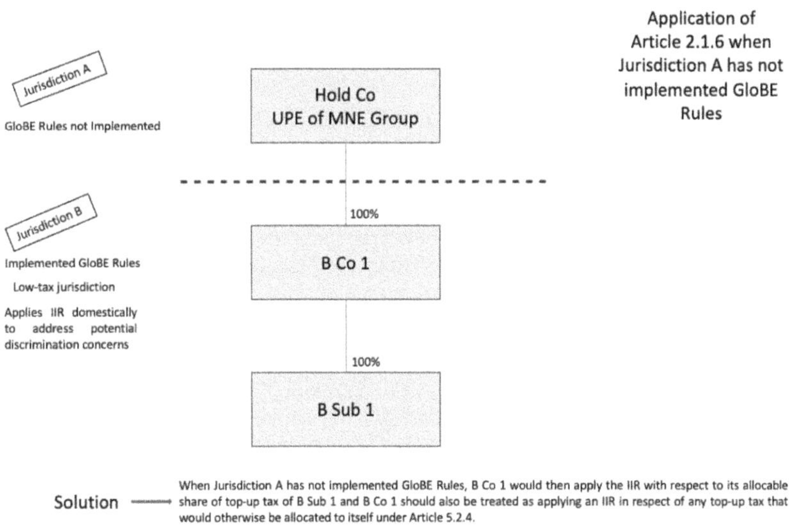

4.2.2 Article 2.2. (Allocation of Top-Up Tax under the IIR)

142. Article 2.2 provides a formula for attributing the top-up tax to the relevant Parent Entity based on its interest in the LTCE's income. Entities subject to the IIR pay tax in an amount equal to their 'Allocable Share' of top-up tax. Article 2.2 contains the rules for the attribution of top-up tax under this rule.

143. Prominent features of Article 2.2 are provided in Box 4.7.

Box 4.7 Prominent Features of Article 2.2

- Provides the formula for the allocation of top-up tax.
- Provides that a Parent Entity's Allocable Share of the top-up tax of an LTCE is an amount equal to the top-up tax of the LTCE as calculated under Chapter 5 multiplied by the Parent Entity's Inclusion Ratio for the LTCE for the Fiscal Year.
- Provides that a Parent Entity's Inclusion Ratio for an LTCE for a Fiscal Year is the ratio of (a) the GloBE Income of the LTCE for the Fiscal Year, reduced by the amount of such income attributable to Ownership Interests held by other owners, to (b) the GloBE Income of the LTCE for the Fiscal Year.
- Provides the methodology of computation of amount of GloBE Income of an LTCE allocable to Ownership Interests held by other owners.
- Provides that the CE's income is determined on a separate entity basis and transactions between Group Entities are generally respected.
- Clarifies that in the case of a Flow-through Entity, any amount that is allocated to a person that is not a Group Entity is excluded for purposes of determining a Parent Entity's Inclusion Ratio.

4.2.2.1 Article 2.2.1.

144. Article 2.2.1 provides the formula for the allocation of top-up tax. A Parent Entity's Allocable Share of the top-up tax of an LTCE is an amount equal to the top-up tax of the LTCE as calculated under Chapter 5 multiplied by the Parent Entity's Inclusion Ratio for the LTCE for the Fiscal Year. This article allocates to the Parent Entity applying the IIR (as determined by Article 2.1) its Allocable Share of top-up tax liability. The Allocable Share is the amount of top-up tax owed in respect of an LTCE, determined by reference to the Parent Entity's Ownership Interest in the income of the LTCE. This is achieved by multiplying the top-up tax of the LTCE by the Parent Entity's Inclusion Ratio (defined in Article 2.2.2).

4.2.2.2 Article 2.2.2.

145. A Parent Entity's Inclusion Ratio for an LTCE for a Fiscal Year is the ratio of (a) the GloBE Income of the LTCE for the Fiscal Year, reduced by the amount of such income attributable to Ownership Interests held by other owners, to (b) the GloBE Income of the LTCE for the Fiscal Year. The above may be depicted as below:

$$\text{Parent Entity's Inclusion Ratio} = \frac{\text{GloBE Income of the LTCE for the Fiscal Year} - \text{The amount of such income attributable to Ownership Interests held by other owners}}{\text{GloBE Income of the LTCE for the Fiscal Year}}$$

146. Article 2.2.2 defines the Parent Entity's Inclusion Ratio for the purposes of applying the IIR. The Inclusion Ratio is, in essence, the ratio of the Parent Entity's share of an LTCE's GloBE Income to its total GloBE Income for the Fiscal Year. Where a subsidiary is wholly owned, the Inclusion Ratio will always be 1, and no additional computations are required. However, Article 2.2.2 achieves that result by subtracting the amount of GloBE Income allocable to Ownership Interests held by other owners from the total GloBE Income and dividing the difference by the total GloBE Income of the Entity. The determination of the amount of GloBE Income allocable to Ownership Interests held by other owners is determined under Article 2.2.3.

4.2.2.3 Article 2.2.3.

147. The amount of GloBE Income of an LTCE allocable to Ownership Interests held by other owners as set out in Article 2.2.2(a), is determined under Article 2.2.3, which is the amount that would have been treated as attributable to such owners under the principles of the Acceptable Financial Accounting Standard used in the CFS of the UPE if the LTCE's net income were equal to its GloBE Income and:

(a) the Parent Entity had prepared CFS in accordance with that accounting standard (the hypothetical CFS);
(b) the Parent Entity owned a Controlling Interest in the LTCE such that all of the income and expenses of the LTCE were consolidated on a line-by-line basis with those of the Parent Entity in the hypothetical CFS;
(c) all of the LTCE's GloBE Income were attributable to transactions with persons that are not Group Entities; and
(d) all Ownership Interests not directly or indirectly held by the Parent Entity were held by persons other than Group Entities.

148. The starting point to determine 'the amount of GloBE Income of an LTCE allocable to Ownership Interests held by other owners' is the GloBE Income or Loss computation for a CE in Chapter 3, which starts with the entity's Financial Accounting Net Income or Loss and makes adjustments from there. The CE's income is determined on a separate entity basis, and transactions between Group Entities are generally respected; the GloBE Income computation generally does not take into account elimination adjustments that would be made in the financial statement consolidation process. Article 3.2.8 allows the MNE Group to apply its consolidated accounting elimination adjustments, but only in respect of transactions between Group Entities in the same jurisdiction. Thus, in most cases, it is unlikely that an LTCE's GloBE Income will exactly equal the accounting income that is ultimately reflected in the CFS. In some cases, the Financial Accounting Net Income or Loss of an LTCE may be zero after consolidation adjustments. However, it is the GloBE Income, not the Financial Accounting Net Income, that must be allocated to the Parent Entity applying the IIR.

149. *Consolidated profit and loss statement of the UPE takes into account its subsidiaries' portion of income or loss belonging to minority owners (partially owned by third parties)*: CFS generally reflect all of the assets, liabilities, income, expenses and cash flows of controlled subsidiaries. However, the owners of the UPE do not have an interest in 100% of those items if the subsidiary is partially owned by third parties. Thus, the UPE must evaluate the extent to which the assets, liabilities, income, expenses and cash flows of its subsidiaries belong to minority interest holders in order to properly report the portion that belongs to its owners in the CFS. The consolidated profit and loss statement will include a reduction to the total income for the portion that belongs to minority owners in arriving at the UPE's consolidated net income. Similarly, the consolidated balance sheet includes a line item reflecting the cumulative equity of the minority owners in the total assets of the consolidated group. Without these adjustments, the CFS would overstate the portion of the income of the consolidated group that belongs to or inures to the benefit of the owners of the UPE.

150. *Need for hypothetical allocation in the Article*: The GloBE Rules leverage the principles that the UPE applies, or would need to apply, in its CFS to determine the share of income of the Financial Accounting Net Income or Loss that belongs to other owners of an LTCE that it does not wholly own. When the IIR is applied by an Intermediate Parent Entity or a POPE, the rules further require that Parent Entity apply the same principles that the UPE applies to minority owners to their separate ownership interests in LTCEs. To this end, Article 2.2.3 requires a hypothetical allocation (in accordance with those principles) of an amount of financial accounting income that is equal to the LTCE's GloBE Income based on the assumptions in paragraphs (a) to (d).

151. The first assumption contained in paragraph (a) is explained in Figure 4.3.

Figure 4.3 First Assumption Contained in Article 2.2.3(a)

What is first assumption?	•The first assumption is that the Parent Entity performing this hypothetical allocation, prepared CFS (the hypothetical CFS) using the same accounting standard used in the UPE's CFS.
Where is it necessary to apply?	•This assumption is necessary where the Parent Entity is not the UPE. Although the UPE actually prepared CFS, the statements prepared by Parent Entity are the hypothetical CFS for purposes of Article 2.2.3.
Purpose of first assumption?	•The assumption sets a uniform accounting standard to properly allocate the LTCE's GloBE Income, and in turn top-up tax, among Parent Entities applying the IIR. •Because all Parent Entities will be applying the same accounting standard to determine their Inclusion Ratio, there will be no leakage (or duplication) of top-up tax liability. •there will be a proper coordination under Article 2.3 between the application of the IIR by a Parent Entity and a POPE in respect of the same LTCE.

152. The second assumption contained in paragraph (b) is explained in Figure 4.4.

Figure 4.4 Second Assumption Contained in Article 2.2.3(b)

What is second assumption?	•The second assumption is that the Parent Entity owned a Controlling Interest in the LTCE such that the income and expenses of the LTCE were consolidated on a line-by-line basis with those of the Parent Entity in the hypothetical CFS (i.e. the amount of each item of income and expense of the LTCE accrued under the accounting standard for the Fiscal Year is included in the consolidated amount of each item of income and expense reflected in the hypothetical CFS).
Where and when is it necessary to apply?	•The LTCE is a CE because the UPE owns a Controlling Interest in it. However, the UPE's Controlling Interest may not be held through the Parent Entity required to apply the IIR. That Parent Entity may only hold a minority interest in the LTCE, in which case the Parent Entity would not be required to consolidate its accounts on a line-by-line basis with the LTCE. The Parent Entity might otherwise, for example, include only the net profit or loss of the LTCE under the equity method in the CFS if it only took into account its Ownership Interests for this purpose.
Purpose of second assumption?	•The assumption is intended to clarify that the LTCE is treated as if it were controlled by the Parent Entity preparing these hypothetical CFS even if it does not own a Controlling Interest in the LTCE. This brings all of the LTCE's income and expenses into the Parent Entity's hypothetical CFS on a line-by-line basis so that it would be necessary to determine the share of its income allocable to other owners under the relevant accounting standard. •This assumption is limited to the consolidation of the income and expense of the LTCE. This limitation is intended to avoid any confusion that might arise as a result of the assumption that its income were equal to GloBE Income.

153. The third assumption contained in paragraph (c) is explained in Figure 4.5.

Figure 4.5 Third Assumption Contained in Article 2.2.3(c)

What is third assumption?	•The third assumption is that all of the LTCE's GloBE Income is attributable to transactions with persons that are not Group Entities.
Why is it necessary to apply?	•Because, the normal process of preparing CFS eliminates income and expenses attributable to transactions between group members.
Purpose of third assumption?	•This assumption is intended to clarify that the amount that should be allocated in the hypothetical allocation is the total GloBE Income of the LTCE, irrespective of whether some or all of that income was earned through transactions with Group Entities and would have been eliminated in preparing actual CFS. The entire amount of GloBE Income needs to be allocated in the hypothetical allocation, even if some or all of it is in fact derived from transactions with other Group Entities.

154. The fourth assumption contained in paragraph (d) is explained in Figure 4.6.

Figure 4.6 Fourth Assumption Contained in Article 2.2.3(d)

What is fourth assumption?	•The fourth and final assumption is that all other owners (including other CEs) are treated as not holding any Controlling Interests in the LTCE.
How is it applied?	•This assumption treats other CEs of the MNE Group that own an interest in the LTCE in the same manner as persons that are not Group Entities. Thus the income attributable to other CEs is treated as income attributable to a non-Group Entity.
Purpose of fourth assumption?	•This ensures that only the income attributable to direct and indirect Ownership Interests owned by the Parent Entity is included in the Parent Entity's Inclusion Ratio.

155. Illustration # 10: This example illustrates, through a flow-chart, the computation of the Inclusion Ratio and a Parent Entity's Allocable Share of the Top-up Tax Amount as per Article 2.2.3.

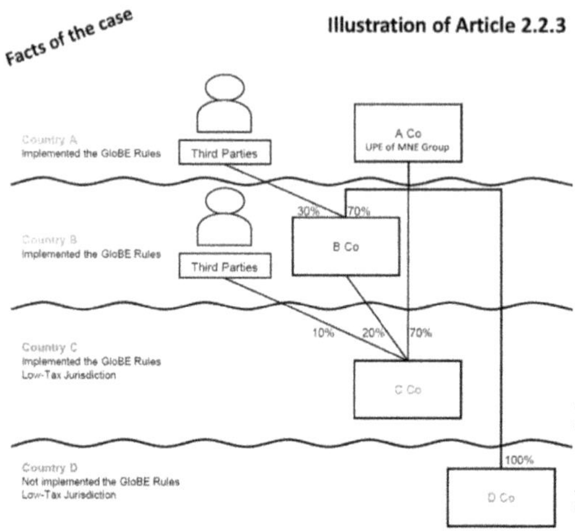

Assumptions made

Entity	C Co	D Co
Financial Accounting Net Income reflected in CFS of A Co	18,000	0
GloBE Income	20,000	35,000
Difference	2,000	35,000
Reasons for difference between entity's GloBE income & its income reflected in the CFS	Attributable to expenses of 2,000 that are not taken into account in computing GloBE income or loss.	Attributable to the fact that all of its transactions were conducted with Group Entities located outside of Country D.

Top-up tax computed for Country C and allocated to C Co for the Fiscal Year is 1,000

Top-up tax computed for Country D and allocated to D Co for the Fiscal Year is 500

Solution

Computation of B Co's Allocable Share of the top-up tax of C Co	Computation of A Co's Allocable Share of the top-up tax of C Co	Computation of A Co's Allocable Share of the top-up tax of D Co
If B Co actually prepared CFS pursuant to UPE's financial accounting standard, it would not consolidate the income and expenses of C Co because B Co only owns a 20% Ownership Interest in C Co. However, pursuant to Article 2.2.3(a), B Co assumes that it owns a Controlling Interest in C Co such that it would be required to consolidate its income, expense, assets, liabilities and cash flows with C Co for purposes of the hypothetical CFS.	The first step is computing the amount of GloBE Income attributable to the Ownership Interests held by "other owners" in accordance with Article 2.2.3. In this case, 3,200 of the GloBE Income is attributed to Ownership Interests held by other owners (2,000 in relation to the 10% Ownership Interests owned directly by non-Group Entities and 1,200 in relation to the 6% Ownership Interests indirectly owned by other non-Group Entities through B Co). This amount is different from the amount attributed to persons that are non-Group Entities as reflected in the CFS because Article 2.2 uses the GloBE Income and not the Financial Accounting Net Income.	The first step is computing the amount of GloBE Income attributable to Ownership Interests held by "other owners" in accordance with Article 2.2.3. In this case, that amount is zero because D Co is wholly-owned by A Co.
The first step in determining B Co's Inclusion Ratio is computing the amount of GloBE Income attributable to Ownership Interests held by "other owners" in accordance with Article 2.2.3, which includes the Ownership Interests held by A Co. Under paragraph (d), Ownership Interests held by A Co are treated as Ownership Interests held by non-Group Entities for purposes of applying the UPE's financial accounting standard for allocating income to non-Group Entities that do not have a Controlling Interest in the LTCE. In this case, 16,000 of the GloBE Income is attributed to Ownership Interests held by other owners (2,000 in relation to the 10% owned by a person that is not a Group Entity and 14,000 in relation to the 70% owned by A Co).	The second step is to compute A Co's "Inclusion Ratio" for C Co in accordance with Article 2.2.2. A Co's Inclusion Ratio is 84% (= [20,000 GloBE Income – 3,200 other owners' interest] /20,000 GloBE Income).	The second step is to compute A Co's Inclusion Ratio with respect to D Co. A Co's Inclusion Ratio is 100% (= [35,000 GloBE Income – 0 other owners' interest] / 35,000 GloBE Income). The fact that D Co's income was eliminated in the actual consolidation process does not change the outcome of the hypothetical allocation because Article 2.2.3(c) requires an allocation on the basis of the GloBE Income and not the CE's income reflected in the CFS of A Co.
The second step is to compute B Co's "Inclusion Ratio" for C Co in accordance with Article 2.2.2. B Co's Inclusion Ratio is 20% (= [20,000 GloBE Income – 16,000 other owners' interest] / 20,000 GloBE Income). The final step is calculating B Co's Allocable Share of the top-up tax of C Co in accordance with Article 2.2.1. B Co's Allocable Share of the top-up tax is 200 (= 1,000 top-up tax x 20% Inclusion Ratio).	The final step is to calculate A Co's Allocable Share of the top-up tax of C Co in accordance with Article 2.2 and Article 2.3. A Co first computes a tentative Allocable Share of the top-up tax under Article 2.2.1 of 840 (= 1,000 top-up tax x 84% Inclusion Ratio). Then, A Co reduces its Allocable Share by an amount equal to the portion that is brought to charge under the IIR applicable to B Co, or 14% (= B Co 20% x 70%). Thus, A Co's Allocable Share of the top-up tax for purposes of applying Chapter 2 is 700 (= 840 tentative Allocable Share – 140 offset).	The final step is to calculate A Co's Allocable Share of the Top-up Tax of D Co in accordance with Article 2.2.1. A Co's Allocable Share of the Top-up Tax is 500 (= 500 Top-up Tax x 100 % Inclusion Ratio).

Summary of each Parent Entity's Allocable Share of the top-up tax of each LTCE and the Article 2.3 Offset Mechanism

	A Co	B Co	Non-Group	Total
Allocable Share of C Co Top-up Tax	840	200	100	1,140
Article 2.3 Offset	-140	-	-	-140
Allocable Share of D Co Top-up Tax	500	-	-	500
Total Top-up Tax allocated	1,200	200	100	1,500

It may be noted in this illustration that even though B Co's Allocable Share of C Co top-up tax is 200, the Offset provided to A Co under Article 2.3 is 140 (which is computed in the ratio of indirect ownership interest of A Co of 14% in C Co through B Co).

4.2.2.4 Article 2.2.4.

156. In the case of a Flow-through Entity, GloBE Income under this article shall not include any income allocated, pursuant to Article 3.5.3, to an owner that is not a Group Entity. This article clarifies that in the case of a Flow-through Entity, the total GloBE income for purposes of the Inclusion Ratio is the total GloBE Income that is attributable to Ownership Interests held by CEs of the MNE Group. Thus, any amount that is allocated to a person that is not a Group Entity pursuant to Article 3.5.3 is excluded for purposes of determining a Parent Entity's Inclusion Ratio.

157. In this context, Article 3.5.3 states that prior to the application of Article 3.5.1, the Financial Accounting Net Income or Loss of a Flow-through Entity shall be reduced by the amount allocable to its owners that are not Group Entities and that hold their Ownership Interest in the Flow-through Entity directly or through a Tax Transparent Structure.

158. Definitions of the terms Flow-through Entity, Tax Transparent Entity, Reverse Hybrid Entity, and Hybrid Entity in the above context are provided in Article 10.2 as below:

> 10.2.1. An Entity is a Flow-through Entity to the extent it is fiscally transparent with respect to its income, expenditure, profit or loss in the jurisdiction where it was created unless it is tax resident and subject to a Covered Tax on its income or profit in another jurisdiction.
>
> (a) A Flow-Through Entity is a **Tax Transparent Entity** with respect to its income, expenditure, profit or loss to the extent that it is fiscally transparent in the jurisdiction in which its owner is located.
> (b) A Flow-Through Entity is a **Reverse Hybrid Entity** with respect to its income, expenditure, profit or loss to the extent that it is not fiscally transparent in the jurisdiction in which the owner is located.
>
> 10.2.2. An Entity is treated as fiscally transparent under the laws of a jurisdiction if that jurisdiction treats the income, expenditure, profit or loss of that Entity as if it were derived or incurred by the direct owner of that Entity in proportion to its interest in that Entity.
>
> 10.2.3. An Ownership Interest in an Entity or a Permanent Establishment that is a Constituent Entity shall be treated as held through a **Tax Transparent Structure** if that Ownership Interest is held indirectly through a chain of Tax Transparent Entities.
>
> 10.2.4. A Constituent Entity that is not a tax resident and not subject to a Covered Tax or a Qualified Domestic Minimum Top-up Tax (QDMTT) based on its place of

management, place of creation, or similar criteria shall be treated as a Flow-Through Entity and a Tax Transparent Entity in respect of its income, expenditure, profit or loss to the extent that:

(a) its owners are located in a jurisdiction that treats the Entity as fiscally transparent;
(b) it does not have a place of business in the jurisdiction where it was created; and
(c) the income, expenditure, profit or loss is not attributable to a Permanent Establishment.

10.2.5 An Entity that is treated as a separate taxable person for income tax purposes in the jurisdiction where it is located is a **Hybrid Entity** with respect to its income, expenditure, profit or loss to the extent that it is fiscally transparent in the jurisdiction in which its owner is located.

159. Illustration # 11: This example illustrates, through a flow-chart, application of Article 2.2.4 and the determination of the Inclusion Ratio and the Allocable Share of the top-up tax in a situation where some of the LTCE's income is allocated to non-Group Entities under Article 3.5.3.

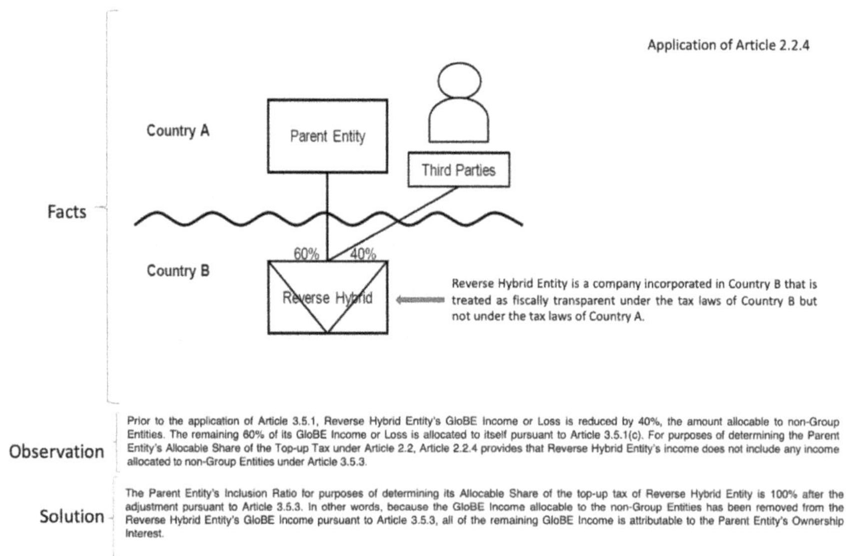

4.2.3 Article 2.3. (IIR Offset Mechanism)

160. Article 2.3 provides a mechanism for offsetting the top-up tax allocated to a Parent Entity by the amount of top-up tax allocated to another Parent Entity that is also required to apply the IIR to the same LTCE in order to avoid double taxation. These rules are intended to coordinate the application of the IIR in certain tiered or split-ownership structures to ensure that any portion of the profits of the MNE Group is subject to the IIR in only one jurisdiction.

161. Prominent features of Article 2.3 are provided in Box 4.8.

Box 4.8 Prominent Features of Article 2.3

- Provides IIR Offset Mechanism to prevent double taxation.
- Reduces the Top-up Tax that has been allocated to a Parent Entity where two Parent Entities in the same ownership chain are required to apply an IIR to the same top-up tax amount, and the potential for overlapping application of the IIR is not solved by the ordering rules.
- Provides that the reduction in tax will be an amount equal to the portion of the Parent Entity's Allocable Share of the top-up tax that is brought into charge by the Intermediate Parent Entity or the POPE under a Qualified IIR.
- Provides that the reduction in tax is made at the moment of allocating the amount of top-up tax among Parent Entities and not after the full amount or a portion of the top-up tax is effectively paid.

4.2.3.1 Article 2.3.1.

162. A Parent Entity that owns an Ownership Interest in an LTCE indirectly through an Intermediate Parent Entity or a POPE that is not eligible for an exclusion from the IIR under Article 2.1.3 or 2.1.5 shall reduce its allocable share of a top-up tax of the LTCE in accordance with Article 2.3.2.

163. *The Article prevents double taxation*: Article 2.3.1 reduces the Top-up Tax that has been allocated to a Parent Entity where two Parent Entities in the same ownership chain are required to apply an IIR to the same top-up tax amount, and the potential for overlapping application of the IIR is not solved by the ordering rules in Articles 2.1.3 or 2.1.5. This can occur, for example, where an upper-tier Intermediate Parent Entity has a non-Controlling Interest in a lower-tier Intermediate Parent Entity, which, in turn, holds all the Ownership Interests in an LTCE. In this case, both Parent Entities will be required to apply the IIR under Article 2.1.2 in respect of the LTCE. A similar situation can arise under Articles 2.1.4 and 2.1.5, where a POPE does not hold all of the Ownership Interests of a lower-tier POPE. In this case, both POPEs in the same ownership chain are required to apply the IIR. Article 2.3.1 prevents double taxation in these situations.

4.2.3.2 Article 2.3.2.

164. The reduction in Article 2.3.1 will be an amount equal to the portion of the Parent Entity's Allocable Share of the top-up tax that is brought into charge by the Intermediate Parent Entity or the POPE under a Qualified IIR.

165. *Purpose of the Article and its operation*: Article 2.3.2 determines the amount of the top-up tax reduction required pursuant to Article 2.3.1. Article 2.3.2 reduces the top-up tax that would otherwise be payable under the IIR by the upper-tier Parent Entity by the amount that is brought into charge under a Qualified IIR applied by the lower-tier Parent Entity. The reduction of top-up tax is limited to 'the portion' of the top-up tax that has been allocated to the upper-tier Parent Entity and that 'is brought into charge' by the lower-tier Intermediate Parent Entity or POPE. In other words, the reduction is limited to the amount of the upper-tier Parent Entity's Allocable share of the LTCE's top-up tax that is attributable to Ownership Interests held indirectly through the lower-tier Intermediate Parent Entity or POPE that is also obligated to apply the IIR.

166. *Stage of IIR Offset*: Article 2.3 reduces a Parent Entity's allocable share of a top-up tax by the amount allocated to a POPE or Intermediate Parent Entity located at a lower level of the ownership chain. This reduction is made at the moment of allocating the amount of top-up tax among Parent Entities and not after the full amount or a portion of the top-up tax is effectively paid.

167. Illustration # 12: This example illustrates, through a flow-chart, the application of the IIR offset mechanism in Article 2.3.2 in a situation where a UPE and a POPE apply a Qualified IIR with respect to the same LTCE.

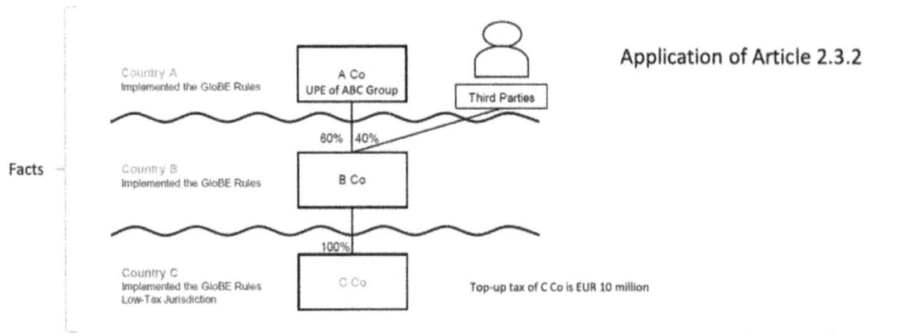

Observation

- B Co is a POPE because it has Ownership Interests in another CE of the ABC Group and 40% of its Ownership Interests are held by third parties (i.e. non-group Entities). B Co is therefore required to apply the IIR in accordance with Article 2.1.4 because it is a POPE that owns an Ownership Interest in a LTCE.
- A Co is also required to apply the IIR in accordance with Article 2.1.1 because it is the UPE.
- To prevent double taxation, Article 2.3.1 reduces the top-up tax that has been allocated to A Co because it owns an Ownership Interest in an LTCE (C Co) through a POPE (B Co). The reduction of top-up tax is limited to "the portion" of the top-up tax that has been allocated to the upper-tier Parent Entity (A Co) and that "is brought into charge" by the lower-tier Intermediate Parent Entity or POPE (B Co) in accordance with Article 2.3.2.

Solution

B Co is required to apply the IIR and its Allocable Share of the top-up tax is EUR 10 million. A Co is also required to apply the IIR but its Allocable Share of the top-up tax (EUR 6 million) is reduced to zero by the top-up tax brought into charge by B Co, as explained in the table below:

Entity	Direct Ownership Interest in C Co	Indirect Ownership Interest in C Co	Inclusion Ratio	Allocable Share of top-up tax	IIR offset	Final top-up tax liability
B Co	100%	-	1	EUR 10 million	-	EUR 10 million
A Co	-	60% (60%*100%)	0.6	EUR 6 million	EUR 6 million	0

168. Illustration # 13: This example illustrates, through a flow-chart, the application of the IIR offset mechanism in Article 2.3.2 in a situation where a UPE has a direct Ownership Interest in an LTCE and an indirect Ownership Interest in the LTCE that is owned through a POPE and both the UPE and the POPE apply a Qualified IIR with respect to the LTCE.

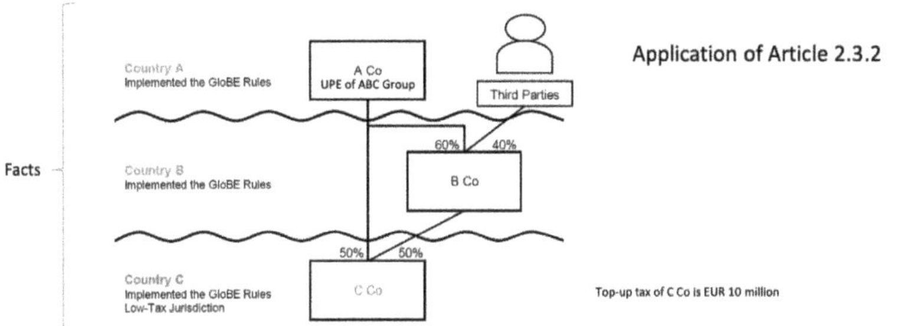

Observation

- B Co is a POPE because it has 50% Ownership Interests in another CE of the ABC Group and 40% of its Ownership Interests are held by third parties (i.e. non-group Entities). B Co is therefore required to apply the IIR in accordance with Article 2.1.4 because it is a POPE that owns an Ownership Interest in a LTCE.
- A Co is also required to apply the IIR in accordance with Article 2.1.1 because it is the UPE that owns, directly and indirectly, 80% of an LTCE (C Co).
- To prevent double taxation, Article 2.3.1 reduces the top-up tax that has been allocated to A Co because it owns a 30% Indirect Ownership Interest in an LTCE (C Co) through a POPE (B Co). The reduction of top-up tax is limited to "the portion" of the top-up tax that has been allocated to the upper-tier Parent Entity (A Co) and that "is brought into charge" by the lower-tier Intermediate Parent Entity or POPE (B Co) in accordance with Article 2.3.2.

Solution

B Co is required to apply the IIR and its Allocable Share of the top-up tax is EUR 5 million. A Co is also required to apply the IIR but its Allocable Share of the top-up tax (EUR 8 million) is reduced by EUR 3 million to EUR 5 million by the top-up tax brought into charge by B Co, as explained in the table below:

Entity	Direct Ownership Interest in C Co	Indirect Ownership Interest in C Co	Inclusion Ratio	Allocable Share of top-up tax	IIR offset	Final top-up tax liability
B Co	50%	-	0.5	EUR 5 million	-	EUR 5 million
A Co	50%	30% (60%*50%)	0.8	EUR 8 million	EUR 3 million	EUR 5 million

169. Illustration # 14: This example illustrates, through a flow-chart, the application of the IIR offset mechanism in Article 2.3.2 in a situation where two Intermediate Parent Entities apply a Qualified IIR with respect to the same LTCE.

Application of Article 2.3.2

Facts

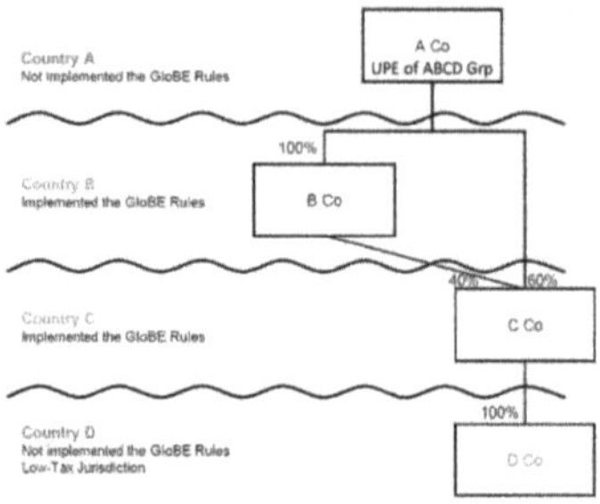

B Co has 40% Ownership Interest in C Co, which is not a Controlling Interest for the purposes of this example.

The top-up tax of D Co is EUR 10 million

Observation

- The UPE (A Co) is not required to apply the IIR as Country A has not implemented the GloBE Rules.
- C Co is an Intermediate Parent Entity and is therefore required to apply the IIR in accordance with Article 2.1.2 because it owns an Ownership Interest in an LTCE (D Co). C Co's obligation to apply the IIR is not switched-off under Article 2.1.3 because the Parent Entity holding its Controlling Interests (A Co) is not required to apply the IIR.
- B Co is also required to apply the IIR because it is an Intermediate Parent Entity that owns 40% of an LTCE (D Co) and its Controlling Interests are not held by a Parent Entity that is required to apply the IIR (A Co is not required to apply the IIR). B Co's Allocable Share of the top-up tax, however, is reduced by the amount that is equal to the portion brought into charge by the lower-tier Parent Entity (C Co) through which its Ownership Interest in D Co is held.

Solution

The outcome is explained in the table below:

Entity	Direct Ownership Interest in D Co	Indirect Ownership Interest in D Co	Inclusion Ratio	Allocable Share of top-up tax	IIR offset	Final top-up tax liability
A Co	-	100% (40% + 60%)	-	-	-	-
B Co	-	40%	0.4	EUR 4 million	EUR 4 million	0
C Co	100%	-	0.1	EUR 10 million	0	EUR 10 million

4.2.4 Article 2.4. (Application of the UTPR)

170. The UTPR provides a mechanism for making an adjustment in respect of the top-up tax that is calculated for an LTCE to the extent that such top-up tax is not brought within the charge of a Qualified IIR. This article sets out the UTPR adjustment mechanism to be applied by a UTPR Jurisdiction.

171. Prominent features of Article 2.4 are provided in Box 4.9.

Box 4.9 Prominent Features of Article 2.4

- Sets out the UTPR adjustment mechanism to be applied by a UTPR Jurisdiction as a backstop mechanism when IIR is not applied.
- Provides that the CEs of an MNE Group located in a jurisdiction that has implemented GloBE Rules shall be denied a deduction (or required to make an equivalent adjustment under domestic law) of an amount resulting in those CEs having an additional cash tax expense equal to the UTPR top-up tax amount for the Fiscal Year allocated to that jurisdiction.
- Provides that the additional cash tax expense is in addition to the amount that would otherwise have been paid under the ordinary domestic rules for calculating a CE's tax liability.
- Provides that the UTPR applies after any provisions of domestic law that affect the deductibility of expenses incurred by CEs.
- Does not prescribe the mechanism by which the adjustment must be made. This is a matter of domestic law implementation that is left to the UTPR jurisdictions.

- Provides that the allocation among the CEs within a UTPR Jurisdiction should be addressed under that UTPR Jurisdiction's domestic law.
- Provides that the payer of additional cash tax expense can be different from the CE that was denied a deduction (or required to make an equivalent adjustment).
- Provides that the UTPR adjustment is imposed as soon as possible and sets out a carry-forward mechanism to address the situation where the UTPR adjustment is subject to some limitations.
- Provides that the earliest taxable period a UTPR adjustment can be made is the CEs' taxable year which commences during that Fiscal Year and that ends on the same day or after the Fiscal Year ends.
- Provides that the UTPR adjustment ensures that the maximum amount is collected from the CEs as early as possible.
- Provides that the UTPR Jurisdiction should impose the adjustment in priority on those CEs that will have an immediate additional cash tax expense in that year.
- Provides that the carry-forward mechanism applies if the UTPR top-up tax amount allocated to a UTPR Jurisdiction exceeds the additional cash tax expense that will be incurred (in the current or a future taxable year) by CEs located in such jurisdiction as a result of the UTPR.
- Provides that the carry-forward mechanism applies only to the extent of securing additional cash tax expense equivalent to the UTPR top-up tax amount allocated to a jurisdiction.
- Provides that the carry-forward mechanism operates indefinitely. A jurisdiction may have a domestic statute of limitation that prevents its tax administration from applying the carry-forward mechanism to its full extent. In such a situation, the top-up tax amount that has not yet been collected is not allocated to another jurisdiction.
- Provides that the carry-forward mechanism operates even if the MNE Group's revenue falls below the threshold of EUR 750 million or the CE that is allocated UTPR top-up tax amount under the UTPR is not part of the MNE Group in future years.
- Provides that a UTPR Jurisdiction may reallocate the UTPR top-up tax amount among the CEs located in that jurisdiction, in subsequent years, in order to ensure that the UTPR top-up tax amount is collected as soon as possible.
- Excludes a controlled Investment Entity from the application of the UTPR.

4.2.4.1 Article 2.4.1.

172. The CEs of an MNE Group located in a jurisdiction that has implemented GloBE Rules shall be denied a deduction (or required to make an equivalent adjustment under domestic law) of an amount resulting in those CEs having an additional cash tax expense equal to the UTPR top-up tax amount for the Fiscal Year allocated to that *jurisdiction*. The timing of the UTPR adjustment is addressed in Article 2.4.2. UTPR operates through two forms:

(1) denial of a deduction; or
(2) equivalent adjustment.

The UTPR does not prescribe the mechanism by which the adjustment must be made. This is a matter of domestic law implementation that is left to the UTPR jurisdictions.

173. *Denial of a deduction*: Denying a taxpayer a deduction generally increases the cash tax expense for that taxpayer by increasing the net income subject to tax in that jurisdiction. The increase in the tax payable as a result of the denial of a deduction is an amount equal to the taxpayer's rate of tax multiplied by the amount of the payment (or other expense) for which the deduction was denied. If the UTPR in a jurisdiction relies on a denial of deduction mechanism, then the amount of deductions that need to be denied under the rule can be determined by dividing the UTPR Top-up Tax Amount allocated to the jurisdiction under Article 2.6 by the taxpayer's applicable rate of tax on such income. For instance, if a Constituent Entity located in a UTPR Jurisdiction is allocated a UTPR top-up tax amount of 100 and the CIT rate is 25%, then denying the deduction for an otherwise deductible payment of 400 (= 100 / 25%) results in an incremental cost equal to the UTPR top-up tax amount allocated under the rule (400 x 25% = 100). Certain issues pertaining to denial of a deduction in the course of implementation of UTPR are as below:

- Denial of a deduction under Article 2.4.1 means the denial of a deduction for local tax purposes in respect of expenditure or similar items that are taken into account in calculating ordinary net income for tax purposes in that jurisdiction.
- The denied deduction need not be attributable to a transaction with another CE.
- The denied deduction includes the denial of an allowance for depreciation or amortisation and extends to a denial of a deduction for a purely notional expense or non-economic loss (such as a deemed interest expense).
- Deemed or notional expenses incurred by a PE or Main Entity in respect of the application of the ALP may also be taken into account for the purposes of the UTPR, provided such amounts are taken into account in calculating ordinary net income for tax purposes in that jurisdiction.
- A denial of a deduction does not include an item to the extent that it is already subject to separate limitation under another rule (such as an interest limitation rule).
- An adjustment that took the form of a denial of a deduction recorded against non-taxable income and that therefore does not result in an additional amount

of cash tax expense payable by the CEs, would not constitute a valid denial of a deduction for the purposes of a UTPR adjustment.

174. *Equivalent adjustment:* Article 2.4.1 further provides that the UTPR may take the form of an adjustment that is equivalent to a denial of a deduction. The adjustment under the UTPR will depend on the existing design of the domestic tax system and should be coordinated with other domestic law provisions and a jurisdiction's international obligations, including those under Tax Treaties. For example, the adjustment under the UTPR could take the form of an additional tax levied directly on a resident taxpayer in an amount equal to the allocated UTPR top-up tax amount. *Alternatively*, a jurisdiction could include an additional amount of deemed income representing a reversal of deductible expenses incurred in the current or prior period, or a jurisdiction could choose to reduce an allowance or deemed deduction to reflect an allocation of top-up tax.

175. *Additional cash tax expense:* Whichever form the UTPR adjustment may take, Article 2.4.1 provides that the adjustment should result in an additional cash tax expense (either in the current year or, under a carry-forward mechanism, in a future year) for the CEs of the MNE Group in the jurisdiction that equals the UTPR top-up tax amount allocated to this jurisdiction for each Fiscal Year. For this purpose, the additional cash tax expense is in addition to the amount that would otherwise have been paid under the ordinary domestic rules for calculating a CE's tax liability. Certain issues pertaining to additional cash tax expense in the course of implementation of UTPR are as below:

- The resulting additional cash tax expense should be determined in respect of the taxable year in which the Fiscal Year ends and should be due in addition to the amount of tax that would otherwise be payable for such taxable year under the normal tax rules in the jurisdiction applicable to the CE.
- The additional cash tax expense increases the amount of tax that the CE or Entities would otherwise have paid under the ordinary domestic rules for calculating their taxable income. This means that the UTPR applies after any provisions of domestic law that affect the deductibility of expenses incurred by CEs.
- The filing requirements associated with the tracking of the payment of the additional cash tax expense over time are addressed in Article 8.1.4(c).
- For purposes of Article 2.4.1, an additional cash tax expense for a taxable year does not cover an amount of tax that will be payable by the CEs in respect of a future period. This means that a reduction of the amount of losses, which could otherwise be carried forward for CIT purposes, will not give rise to an additional cash tax expense for the taxable year within the meaning of this article until a corresponding amount of income has arisen in the subsequent period.
- Article 2.4.1 provides that the CEs of an MNE Group shall be denied a deduction for otherwise deductible expenses (or be subject to an equivalent

adjustment under domestic law) of an amount sufficient to result in the CEs located in the UTPR jurisdiction having an additional cash tax expense equal to the UTPR top-up tax amount allocated to that jurisdiction.

176. *The article does not prescribe how the UTPR top-up tax amount is allocated among the CEs that are located in the UTPR Jurisdiction*: The allocation among the CEs within a UTPR Jurisdiction should be addressed under that UTPR Jurisdiction's domestic law, which would ensure that such allocation mechanism is best coordinated with other existing domestic tax rules. The UTPR Jurisdiction may provide in its domestic law that the UTPR adjustment is imposed on only one CE or several CEs that are located in the jurisdiction. For instance, several CEs may, for domestic tax purposes, belong to the same tax consolidated group such that the most straightforward way of making the adjustment required under the UTPR is at the level of the local tax consolidated group rather than on an entity-by-entity basis. CEs may also be treated differently for this purpose, depending on whether they are wholly owned or almost wholly owned by the MNE Group or whether they are partially owned CEs. Allocating top-up tax to a partially owned CE would result in the minority interest holders of such CE bearing indirectly a portion of the tax cost incurred by the application of the UTPR. A UTPR Jurisdiction may therefore provide that the top-up tax is allocated first to those CEs that are wholly owned or almost wholly owned by the MNE Group in order to minimise the extent to which those minority interest holders share the burden of top-up tax allocated from LTCEs in which they do not have an economic interest.

177. *Payer of additional cash tax expense can be different from the CE that was denied a deduction (or required to make an equivalent adjustment)*: Article 2.4.1 does not require that the additional cash tax expense is paid by the same CEs as those that were denied a deduction (or required to make an equivalent adjustment). For instance, the UTPR jurisdiction may deny a deduction to (or impose an equivalent adjustment) on a Tax Transparent Entity, the effect of which flows through to the owners. In this case, the additional cash tax expense collected by the UTPR Jurisdiction may be levied or borne by the owners of the Tax Transparent Entity itself. As such, this additional cash tax expense may be taken into account for the purposes of assessing whether the adjustment has resulted in an additional cash tax expense that is equal to the UTPR top-up tax amount.

178. Illustration # 15: This example illustrates how to assess whether CEs located in a UTPR Jurisdiction have an additional cash tax expense equal to the UTPR top-up tax amount allocated to that jurisdiction for purposes of applying Article 2.4.1.

(a) The following assumptions are made in the illustration:
- Jurisdiction, where the CE is located, allows losses to be carried forward indefinitely.
- The UTPR top-up tax amount allocated to that jurisdiction is EUR 60 for Year 1.
- The jurisdiction has a CIT rate of 20%.

- There are no other CEs in that jurisdiction.

(b) Particulars of the CE (prior to UTPR adjustment) and consequent tax liability are assumed to be as below:

	Particulars	*Year 1*	*Year 2*
Prior to UTPR Adjustment	Revenue	200	200
	Deductible Expenses	-300	-100
	Profit or loss (before UTPR adjustment)	-100	100
	Loss carry-forward generated or (used) (before UTPR adjustment)	100	-100
	Loss carry-forward balance (before UTPR adjustment)	100	0
	Tax due in the jurisdiction (before UTPR adjustment)	0	0

(c) The jurisdiction denies EUR 300 of deductions (= 60/20%) under its UTPR in order to produce an additional tax expense of EUR 60, equal to the UTPR top-up tax amount. The following table summarises the income tax liability of the CE in the UTPR Jurisdiction after the UTPR adjustment:

	Particulars	*Year 1*	*Year 2*
Post UTPR Adjustment	*Revenue*	200	200
	Deductible Expenses	-300	-100
	UTPR Adjustment (denial of deduction)	300	0
	Profit or loss (after UTPR adjustment)	200	100
	Loss carry-forward generated or (used) (after UTPR adjustment)	0	0
	Loss carry-forward balance (after UTPR adjustment)	0	0
	Tax due in the jurisdiction (after UTPR adjustment)	40	20

(d) The additional cash tax expense is in addition to the amount of additional tax that the CEs would otherwise have paid under the ordinary domestic rules for calculating their taxable income and tax liability. Therefore, the additional cash tax expense is determined by comparing the amount of tax that is due after the UTPR adjustment is made with the amount of tax that would have been paid under the ordinary domestic rules for calculating taxable income. The following table illustrates the computations that are made to assess the additional cash tax expense that the CE had in respect of Year 1 and Year 2:

Computation of the additional cash tax expense	*Year 1*	*Year 2*
Tax due in the jurisdiction (before UTPR adjustment) [i]	0	0
Tax due in the jurisdiction (after UTPR adjustment) [ii]	40	20
Additional cash tax expense [ii] – [i]	40	20

(e) Thus, the application of the UTPR in Year 1 eliminates the loss that can be carried forward to Year 2 and results in an additional cash tax expense over the two-year period that equals the UTPR top-up tax amount. Therefore, no additional UTPR adjustment is needed in Year 2.

4.2.4.2 Article 2.4.2.

179. The adjustment mentioned in Article 2.4.1 shall apply to the extent possible with respect to the taxable year in which the Fiscal Year ends. If this adjustment is insufficient to produce an additional cash tax expense for this taxable year equal to the UTPR top-up tax amount allocated to the GloBE Rules implementing jurisdiction for the Fiscal Year, the difference shall be carried forward to the extent necessary to the succeeding Fiscal Years and be subject to the adjustment mentioned in Article 2.4.1 to the extent possible for each taxable year. Through this article, it is provided that the UTPR adjustment is imposed as soon as possible and sets out a carry-forward mechanism to address the situation where the UTPR adjustment is subject to some limitations.

180. *The earliest taxable period when a UTPR adjustment can be made:* The UTPR top-up tax amount is calculated based on the low-tax profits arising during a given Fiscal Year. The earliest taxable period a UTPR adjustment can be made is the CEs' taxable year which commences during that Fiscal Year and ends on the same day or after the Fiscal Year ends.

181. *When will a taxpayer or tax administration become aware of UTPR top-up tax amount*: It may not be possible for a taxpayer or tax administration to know the UTPR top-up tax amount that has been allocated to a jurisdiction until the GloBE Information Return is actually filed. While the GloBE Information Return is required to be filed no later than fifteen months after the last day of the MNE's Fiscal Year, this date may be after the due date for the tax return of the relevant taxable year. When the UTPR adjustment takes the form of a denial of a deduction, jurisdictions may require the CEs to file an amended tax return with respect to the relevant taxable year in order to affect the relevant deductions for that year. When the adjustment requires the submission of an amended tax return, the CEs located in the UTPR Jurisdiction should not suffer any penalties for late filing or payment that results from any increase in tax payable due solely to the application of the UTPR. If it is not possible to make a full adjustment in that period, then the adjustment should be made in the following period or as soon as reasonably practicable.

182. *Meaning of 'to the extent possible'*: Article 2.4.2 *inter alia* provides that the adjustment provided under Article 2.4.1 shall apply to the extent possible with respect to the taxable year in which the Fiscal Year ends. There may be situations, however, where the UTPR adjustment will be limited in its amount for a given taxable year, for instance, because there is only a limited amount of deductible expenses. Nevertheless, the UTPR adjustment shall ensure that the maximum amount is collected from the CEs as early as possible.

183. *UTPR Jurisdiction should impose the adjustment in priority on those CEs that will have an immediate additional cash tax expense in that year:* There may also be situations where the additional cash tax expense of the CEs in an MNE Group will depend on the facts and circumstances of the particular CEs on which the UTPR adjustment will be imposed. As mentioned previously, denying a deduction to a CE that is in a loss position may not result in an immediate additional cash tax expense for that CE. Therefore, in order to impose the adjustment to the extent possible with respect to a given taxable year, the UTPR Jurisdiction should, to the extent possible, taking into account the limitations under applicable laws, impose the adjustment in priority on those CEs that will have an immediate additional cash tax expense in that year.

184. *Carry forward mechanism for additional cash tax expense*: Article 2.4.2 provides a carry-forward mechanism to address the situation where the UTPR adjustment made with respect to the taxable year in which the Fiscal Year ends did not result in enough additional cash tax expense to equal the UTPR top-up tax amount allocated to the jurisdiction for that Fiscal Year and will not result in enough additional cash tax expense without a further adjustment being made. In other words, the carry-forward mechanism provided under Article 2.4.2 applies if the UTPR top-up tax amount allocated to a UTPR Jurisdiction exceeds the additional cash tax expense that will be incurred (in the current or a future taxable year) by CEs located in such jurisdiction as a result of the UTPR. Article 2.4.2 provides that under such circumstances, it may be necessary for the difference between the UTPR top-up tax amount and the amount of the additional cash tax expense of the CEs that resulted from the application of the UTPR to be carried over to the following Fiscal Year and imposed in the taxable year in which the following Fiscal Year ends, which is expected to be the immediately subsequent taxable year. This difference shall be subject to an adjustment provided in Article 2.4.1 in the next year but remains with the jurisdiction where it was first allocated and is not subject again to the general allocation mechanism in Article 2.6 in a later year.

185. *Carry forward mechanism to apply only to the extent of securing additional cash tax expense equivalent to UTPR top-up tax amount allocated to a jurisdiction:* Article 2.4.2 further provides that the carry-forward mechanism is only applied to the extent it is necessary to impose another adjustment to ensure that the CEs will have an additional cash tax expense that equals the UTPR top-up tax amount allocated to the jurisdiction. There may be situations where it is not necessary to impose another adjustment, for instance, because the first adjustment will result in the CEs having, over time, an additional cash tax expense that equals the UTPR top-up tax amount allocated to the jurisdiction. This may be the case when the adjustment consists of a reduction of the amount of losses, and those losses can be carried forward indefinitely under the laws of the UTPR jurisdiction (refer **Illustration # 15** above). However, if the losses cannot be carried forward indefinitely, the UTPR adjustment may need to be carried forward because the first adjustment will not necessarily result in an additional cash tax expense in the period during which the losses can be carried forward and a further adjustment would be necessary at the end of this period (refer **Illustration # 16** below).

186. *Carry forward mechanism operates indefinitely*: Article 2.4.2 is not limited to the first taxable year that follows the one when the allocated UTPR top-up tax amount could not result in an additional cash tax expense. The design of the carry-forward mechanism in Article 2.4.2 should subject the untaxed portion of the UTPR top-up tax amount to the adjustment provided in Article 2.4.1 in the next year and each following year to the extent necessary to achieve the full adjustment under Article 2.4.1. If the top-up tax that has been pushed back into Article 2.4.1 does not result in an additional cash tax expense in that year, then Article 2.4.2 would apply again in the following year, thereby providing an indefinite carry-forward mechanism for any portion that further remains untaxed in the second and subsequent years. Article 2.4.2 also applies to the carried forward portion of the UTPR adjustment and provides that this adjustment shall apply '*to the extent possible*' to that following taxable year. While Article 2.4.2 provides for an indefinite carry-forward mechanism, domestic law, in certain circumstances, may limit the practical application of the carry-forward after a certain period of time. For example, a jurisdiction may have a domestic statute of limitation that prevents its tax administration from applying the carry-forward mechanism to its full extent. In such a situation, the top-up tax amount that has not yet been collected is not allocated to another jurisdiction.

187. *Carry forward mechanism operates even if the MNE Group's revenue falls below the threshold of EUR 750 million or the CE that is allocated UTPR top-up tax amount under the UTPR is not part of the MNE Group in future years:* Article 2.4.2 is not limited to the Fiscal Years in which the MNE Group is within the scope of the GloBE Rules or the Fiscal Years when the CE that is allocated UTPR top-up tax amount under the UTPR is part of the MNE Group. If the MNE Group's revenues fall below the threshold of Article 1.1, the CEs that were allocated UTPR top-up tax amounts that did not give rise to an additional cash tax expense would still be liable for the UTPR top-up tax amounts they were allocated.

188. *Reallocation of UTPR top-up tax amount among CEs*: Article 2.4.1 does not prescribe how the UTPR top-up tax amount is allocated among the CEs that are located in the UTPR Jurisdiction. Therefore, a UTPR Jurisdiction may reallocate the UTPR top-up tax amount among the CEs located in that jurisdiction, in subsequent years, in order to ensure that the UTPR top-up tax amount is collected as soon as possible. In such a case, the adjustment provided in Article 2.4.1 in that later year does not need to be imposed on the CEs located in that jurisdiction that were initially allocated top-up tax under domestic law. It may be applied against any CEs of the same MNE Group that are located in that jurisdiction, subject to the requirement in Article 2.4.2 that the adjustment shall be made to the extent possible with respect to the taxable year in which that Fiscal Year ends. Similarly, a jurisdiction may adopt a mechanism to reallocate the UTPR top-up tax amount to other constituent entities in the jurisdiction that remain with the MNE Group to address the situation where a CE would be separated from the MNE Group after being allocated top-up tax that did not give rise to an additional cash tax expense. A UTPR jurisdiction may also provide that this CE is still liable for the top-up tax that it was allocated under a jurisdiction's Qualified UTPR, even if it has been separated from the MNE Group. A UTPR jurisdiction may also consider the possibility of imposing a final tax charge under the UTPR in respect of a liquidation or similar transaction that will result in there being no remaining CEs in the UTPR jurisdiction for the MNE Group.

189. The term Qualified UTPR mentioned above is defined in Article 10.1 as below:

> Qualified UTPR means a set of rules equivalent to Article 2.4 to Article 2.6 of the GloBE Rules (including any provisions of the GloBE Rules associated with those articles) that are included in the domestic law of a jurisdiction and that are implemented and administered in a way that is consistent with the outcomes provided for under the GloBE Rules and the Commentary provided that such jurisdiction does not provide any benefits that are related to such rules.

190. Illustration # 16: This example illustrates a situation where the carry-forward mechanism provided under Article 2.4.2 is necessary for the CEs located in a UTPR Jurisdiction to have an additional cash tax expense equal to the UTPR top-up tax amount allocated to that jurisdiction for the purposes of applying Article 2.4.1.

(a) The following assumptions are made in the illustration:
  - Jurisdiction, where the CE is located, does not allow losses to be carried forward.
  - The UTPR top-up tax amount allocated to that jurisdiction is EUR 60 for Year 1.
  - The jurisdiction has a CIT rate of 20%.
  - There are no other CEs in that jurisdiction.

(b) Particulars of the CE (prior to UTPR adjustment) and consequent tax liability:

	Particulars	*Year 1*	*Year 2*
Prior to UTPR Adjustment	Revenue	200	200
	Deductible Expenses	-300	-100
	Profit or loss (before UTPR adjustment)	-100	100
	Loss carry-forward generated or (used) (before UTPR adjustment)	0	0
	Loss carry-forward balance (before UTPR adjustment)	0	0
	Tax due in the jurisdiction (before UTPR adjustment)	0	20

(c) The jurisdiction denies EUR 300 of deductions (= 60/20%) under its UTPR in order to produce an additional tax expense of EUR 60, equal to the UTPR top-up tax amount. The following table summarises the income tax liability of the CE in the UTPR Jurisdiction after the UTPR adjustment in respect of Year 1:

	Particulars	*Year 1*	*Year 2*
Post UTPR Adjustment	Revenue	200	200
	Deductible Expenses	-300	-100
	UTPR Adjustment (denial of deduction)	300	0
	Profit or loss (after UTPR adjustment)	200	100
	Loss carry-forward (after UTPR adjustment) – not available	0	0
	Tax due in the jurisdiction (after UTPR adjustment)	40	20

(d) In this example, the additional cash tax expense incurred by the CE amounts to EUR 40 in respect of Year 1 and EUR 0 in respect of Year 2 unless an additional adjustment is made under Article 2.4.2 (as carried out below). There is no additional cash tax expense in Year 2 that results from the UTPR adjustment made in Year 1. Therefore, to impose an additional cash tax expense under the UTPR in Year 2, so that additional cash tax expense over the two-year period equals the UTPR top-up tax amount, the UTPR Jurisdiction will need to deny another EUR 100 of deductions in Year 2 to increase the profit to EUR 200 (thereby imposing an additional EUR 20 of tax by virtue of the application of the UTPR).

(e) The following table summarises the income tax liability of the CE in the UTPR Jurisdiction after the UTPR adjustment made in respect of Year 1 and the additional adjustment made in respect of Year 2:

<table>
<tr><td rowspan="7">Post UTPR Adjustment</td><th>Particulars</th><th>Year 1</th><th>Year 2</th></tr>
<tr><td>Revenue</td><td>200</td><td>200</td></tr>
<tr><td>Deductible Expenses</td><td>-300</td><td>-100</td></tr>
<tr><td>UTPR Adjustment (denial of deduction)</td><td>300</td><td>100</td></tr>
<tr><td>Profit or loss (after UTPR adjustment)</td><td>200</td><td>200</td></tr>
<tr><td>Loss carry-forward (after UTPR adjustment) – not available</td><td>0</td><td>0</td></tr>
<tr><td>Tax due in the jurisdiction (after UTPR adjustment)</td><td>40</td><td>40</td></tr>
</table>

(f) The following table illustrates the computations that are made to assess the additional cash tax expense that the CE had in respect of Year 1 and Year 2:

Computation of the additional cash tax expense	*Year 1*	*Year 2*
Tax due in the jurisdiction (before UTPR adjustment) [i]	0	20
Tax due in the jurisdiction (after UTPR adjustment) [ii]	40	40
Additional cash tax expense [ii] – [i]	40	20

(g) Thus, with the application of the UTPR in Year 1 and no carry-forward of losses to Year 2, additional UTPR adjustment is needed in Year 2 so that additional cash tax expense over the two-year period equals the UTPR top-up tax amount.

4.2.4.3 Article 2.4.3.

191. Article 2.4.1 shall not apply to a CE that is an Investment Entity. This article excludes a controlled Investment Entity from the application of the UTPR. This exclusion is to avoid interfering with the intended tax neutrality of these entities with respect to owners that are not Group Entities. It may be noted that Investment Entities that are the UPE of the MNE Group are Excluded Entities and are, therefore, already outside the scope of the GloBE Rules.

192. The term Investment Entity mentioned above is defined in Article 10.1 as below:

Investment Entity means:

(a) an Investment Fund or a Real Estate Investment Vehicle;
(b) an Entity that is at least 95% owned directly by an Entity described in paragraph (a) or through a chain of such Entities and that operates exclusively or almost exclusively to hold assets or invest funds for the benefit of such Investment Entities; and
(c) an Entity where at least 85% of the value of the Entity is owned by an Entity referred to in paragraph (a) provided that substantially all of the Entity's income is Excluded Dividends or Excluded Equity Gain or Loss that is excluded from the computation of GloBE Income or Loss in accordance with Articles 3.2.1 (b) or (c).

4.2.5 Article 2.5. (UTPR Top-Up Tax Amount)

193. Article 2.5 calculates the Total Amount of an MNE Group's top-up tax that is allocable under the UTPR. The Total UTPR top-up tax amount is determined by reference to the total amount of top-up tax that is due (as provided in Article 2.5.1) and that is not already subject to a Qualified IIR (as provided in Articles 2.5.2. and 2.5.3). Like the IIR, the UTPR relies on the same computation made in accordance with Chapter 5 for determining the MNE Group's jurisdictional ETR and the amount of top-up tax. This includes the same methodology for determining GloBE Income or Loss, the amount of Covered Taxes on such income and the rules for determining the application of the Substance-based Income Exclusion. Equally, the exclusions to the definition of CE (for example, in respect of Government Entities) apply to the ETR calculation used for determining the top-up tax such that no top-up tax would arise, or be allocable under the UTPR, in respect of these entities.

194. The term Total UTPR top-up tax amount mentioned above is defined in Article 10.1 as below:

Total UTPR Top-up Tax Amount means the total amount of Top-up Tax that is allocable under the UTPR as defined in Article 2.4.1.

195. Prominent features of Article 2.5 are provided in Box 4.10.

Box 4.10 Prominent Features of Article 2.5

- Provides the starting point for the computation of the UTPR top-up tax amount and ensures that the aggregate adjustments made under the UTPR in each jurisdiction do not exceed the total amount of top-up tax computed for all Low-tax Jurisdictions where the MNE Group is operating.
- Calculates the Total Amount of an MNE Group's top-up tax that is allocable under the UTPR.
- Provides that the Total UTPR top-up tax amount is determined by reference to the total amount of top-up tax that is due and that is not already subject to a Qualified IIR.

- Stipulates that the IIR takes priority over the UTPR.
- Provides that there is single computation of the top-up tax under the IIR and the UTPR.
- Provides that the determination of top-up tax is made for each LTCE.
- Provides that under certain conditions, despite the UPE applying a Qualified IIR, there could still be situations and scope for the operation of the UTPR with respect to CEs located in the UPE Jurisdiction and allocated to each UTPR Jurisdiction in accordance with Article 2.6.
- Addresses situations on operation of UTPR where UPE is located in a jurisdiction without a Qualified IIR and owns a larger interest in the LTCE than the Intermediate Parent Entity.

196. *Benefit of single computation of the top-up tax under the IIR and the UTPR:* Common and single computation of the top-up tax under the IIR and the UTPR improves coordination between GloBE Rules in each jurisdiction and reduces implementation and compliance costs while ensuring that the rules do not result in over-taxation or taxation in excess of economic profits. In addition, relying on the same top-up tax computation under both the IIR and the UTPR aligns the expected outcomes under both rules, which allows the UTPR to operate as a meaningful backstop to the IIR. Not having a single computation of the top-up tax under both the IIR and the UTPR would either lead to less effective or harsher outcomes under the UTPR than under the IIR.

4.2.5.1 Article 2.5.1.

197. The total UTPR top-up tax amount for a Fiscal Year shall be equal to the sum of the top-up tax calculated for each LTCE of an MNE Group for that Fiscal Year (determined in accordance with Article 5.2), subject to the adjustments set out in the said Article 2.5 and Article 9.3 (which pertains to the exclusion from the UTPR of MNE Groups in the initial phase of their international activity). This article provides the starting point for the computation of the UTPR top-up tax amount and ensures that the aggregate adjustments made under the UTPR in each jurisdiction do not exceed the total amount of top-up tax computed for all Low-tax Jurisdictions where the MNE Group is operating.

198. In accordance with the methodology described in Article 5.2, the amount of top-up tax that is allocable under the UTPR is determined in respect of each CE located in a jurisdiction where the MNE's jurisdictional ETR is below the Minimum Rate (i.e., an LTCE). The total UTPR top-up tax amount is equal to the sum of the top-up tax calculated for each of these LTCEs, taking into account the relevant provisions of the GloBE Rules that may affect the calculation of the top-up tax, such as:

- Article 5.6 for a Minority-Owned Constituent Entity (means a Constituent Entity where the UPE has a direct or indirect Ownership Interest in that Entity of 30% or less, as defined in Article 10.1); and
- Article 7.4 or Article 7.6 for an Investment Entity.

199. The top-up tax calculated for each of these LTCEs may be subject to adjustments, as provided in Articles 2.5.2, 2.5.3 and Article 9.3. In relation to JVs and JV Subsidiaries, Article 6.4.1(c) increases the total UTPR top-up tax amount taken into account for purposes of Article 2.5.1 in respect of a JV Group top-up tax that has not been brought into charge under a Qualified IIR. The total UTPR top-up tax amount taking into account those adjustments is then allocated among the UTPR Jurisdictions in accordance with the mechanism set out in Article 2.6.

200. The term JV Group mentioned above is defined in Article 10.1 as below:

> JV Group means a Joint Venture and its JV Subsidiaries.

201. The term JV Group top-up tax mentioned above is defined in Article 10.1 as below:

> JV Group Top-up Tax means the UPE's Allocable Share of the Top-up Tax of all members of the JV Group.

4.2.5.2 Article 2.5.2.

202. The top-up tax calculated for an LTCE that is otherwise taken into account under Article 2.5.1 shall be reduced to zero if all of the UPE's Ownership Interests in such LTCE are held directly or indirectly by one or more Parent Entities that are required to apply a Qualified IIR in the jurisdiction where they are located with respect to that LTCE for the Fiscal Year. Thus, the IIR takes priority over the UTPR.

203. *Charging of IIR at the level of UPE and Intermediate Parent Entity levels removes application of UTPR*: The IIR will not be switched off when the higher-tiered Intermediate Parent does not control the lower-tiered Intermediate Parent. In this circumstance, the lower-tiered Intermediate Parent will charge its IIR, and the higher-tiered Intermediate Parent will reduce its share of the top-up tax by the tax charged by the lower-tiered Intermediate Parent. This maximises the amount of top-up tax collected under the IIR, which in turn reduces the residual top-up which is collected through the UTPR.

Illustration # 17: Let's consider top-up tax of 100 has been calculated for Entity A. Parent A holds 20% of Parent B, which holds 100% of Entity A, as depicted in a flow-chart below:

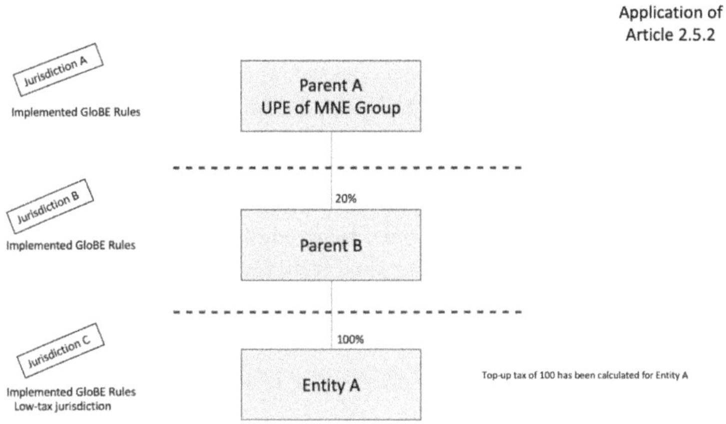

If Parent A applies IIR and collects the top-up tax, then 20 of the top-up tax would be collected, and the remainder would be taxed under the UTPR. However, if Parent B also applies its IIR, in that case, the full 100 of the top-up tax is collected through IIR, so that there is no need to apply the UTPR. Parent A reduces its top-up tax of 20 to nil under the IIR Offset Mechanism provided in Article 2.3 because this has already been charged by Parent B (so that double taxation is prevented).

204. *The Article applies on an entity-by-entity basis*: In the situation where no IIR applies at the UPE level, a lower-level Parent Entity may be required to apply the IIR as provided under Article 2.1. If the UPE's Ownership Interest in an LTCE is held indirectly through a Parent Entity that is required to apply the IIR, then no top-up tax shall be allocated under the UTPR for such LTCE. Whether or not the amount of top-up tax may be reduced to zero in accordance with this rule is determined on an entity-by-entity basis. This means that the determination is made for each LTCE.

205. *UTPR allocation when several Parent Entities are involved*: It is possible that several Parent Entities are required to apply a Qualified IIR in respect of several LTCEs. It is also possible that the Ownership Interests of a given LTCE are held by several Parent Entities that are located in the same jurisdiction and required to apply a Qualified IIR. In such a case, the Ownership Interests held by each Parent Entity are taken into account for the purposes of this test. If all of the UPE's Ownership Interests in an LTCE are held through various Parent Entities that are required to apply a Qualified IIR, no top-up tax shall be allocated under the UTPR in respect of such LTCE.

206. *Situation where UTPR may operate in respect of CEs located in UPE's jurisdiction despite application of Qualified IIR by UPE*: The fact that the UPE is required to apply a Qualified IIR does not mean there is no scope for the operation of the UTPR with respect to CEs located in the UPE Jurisdiction. Where the UPE is required to apply a Qualified IIR for the Fiscal Year, it may only be required under the laws of the UPE Jurisdiction to apply the IIR in respect of PEs and subsidiaries located in other jurisdictions. In this case, no top-up tax will be allocated under the UTPR in respect of foreign LTCEs (i.e., located outside of the UPE Jurisdiction). There could be, however, top-up tax allocable under the UTPR in respect of the domestic LTCEs (i.e., located in the UPE Jurisdiction) if the ETR of the UPE Jurisdiction is below the Minimum Rate. That top-up tax may be reduced to zero by virtue of a QDMTT payable in the UPE Jurisdiction under Article 5.2.3. In the case where the UPE is required to apply a domestic IIR with respect to domestic LTCEs, the top-up tax may also be reduced to zero under Article 2.5.2 (refer Commentary on Article 2.1.6 providing an option to jurisdictions to extend the application of the IIR domestically in order to avoid discriminating between domestic and foreign CEs that are members of the same MNE Group). If the top-up tax arising in the UPE Jurisdiction is not reduced to zero, it will be included in the UTPR top-up tax amount and allocated to each UTPR Jurisdiction in accordance with Article 2.6.

207. The term UPE Jurisdiction mentioned above is defined in Article 10.1 as below:

> UPE Jurisdiction means the jurisdiction where the Ultimate Parent Entity is located.

208. The term UTPR top-up tax amount mentioned above is defined in Article 10.1 as below:

> UTPR Top-up Tax Amount means the amount of Top-up Tax allocated to a UTPR Jurisdiction under the UTPR.

4.2.5.3 Article 2.5.3.

209. Where Article 2.5.2 does not apply, the top-up tax calculated for an LTCE that is otherwise taken into account under Article 2.5.1 shall be reduced by a Parent Entity's Allocable Share of the top-up tax of that LTCE that is brought into charge under a Qualified IIR.

210. *Difference between Article 2.5.2 and Article 2.5.3:* Article 2.5.2 applies when the Parent Entity or Entities that apply the IIR collectively hold all of the UPE's Ownership Interests in the LTCE, whereas, Article 2.5.3 applies in situations where the Parent Entity or Entities that apply the IIR do not hold all of the UPE's Ownership Interests in the LTCE. Unlike the exclusion mechanism adopted under Article 2.5.2, deduction mechanism is the characteristic of Article 2.5.3.

211. *The article inter alia addresses situations where UPE is located in a jurisdiction without a Qualified IIR and owns a larger interest in the LTCE than the Intermediate Parent Entity*: It is expected that, in most cases, either the LTCEs will be wholly owned by another CE that is subject to a Qualified IIR (and the UTPR will not apply) or their shares will be wholly owned by other CEs that are not subject to an IIR (and the UTPR will apply). There may be situations, however, where an Intermediate Parent Entity owns an interest in an LTCE and applies the IIR in respect of its share of the income of such LTCE under Article 2.1.2, but the application of the IIR in the Intermediate Parent Entity's jurisdiction does not result in all the top-up tax attributable to the UPE's

Ownership Interests being brought into charge under a Qualified IIR. This situation could arise, for example, where the UPE (located in a jurisdiction without a Qualified IIR) owns a larger interest in the LTCE than the Intermediate Parent Entity does. In this case, rather than excluding the whole amount of top-up tax from charge under Article 2.5.2, the amount of top-up tax levied under the Qualified IIR in the Intermediate Parent Entity's jurisdiction is deducted from the total top-up tax of the LTCE. This mechanism ensures that the IIR has priority over the UTPR and avoids multiple taxation of the same low-taxed income as a result of the GloBE Rules. The Ownership Interests in the LTCE may also be held by different Parent Entities that, together, own less than the UPE's Ownership Interests in the LTCE. In such cases, the sum of top-up taxes that is allocated to each Parent Entity under IIR is deducted from the total top-up tax amount that is allocated under the UTPR pursuant to Article 2.5.3.

212. *In certain situations, Article 2.5.3 allows for a greater tax expense:* Article 2.5.3 reduces the total UTPR top-up tax amount by the amount of top-up tax subject to the IIR (rather than reducing it to zero), and thus, it leaves within the charge to tax, low-taxed income that is beneficially owned by minority shareholders. Unlike the exclusion mechanism under Article 2.5.2, this deduction mechanism under Article 2.5.3 does not allow the MNE Group to limit the total amount of top-up tax payable to the allocable share of top-up tax that would have been allocated to the UPE if the UPE had been subject to a Qualified IIR with respect of the LTCE. Equally, it does not require a determination of whether a POPE would have been subject to tax under the IIR because of the ownership structure of the MNE Group or the Allocable Share of top-up tax that would have been allocated to that POPE. Instead, Article 2.5.3 deducts the tax due under an IIR from the amount of top-up tax that is computed on the total amount of income of the LTCE, irrespective of the UPE's Allocable Share of the top-up tax due in respect of the LTCE. Applying the UTPR to the total amount of top-up tax of an LTCE (i.e., not limited to the UPE's Ownership Interest in the LTCE) simplifies its application. It allows for a greater tax expense than the top-up tax that would have been collected under the IIR if it had applied at the UPE level because it is not limited to the UPE's Allocable Share of the top-up tax due in respect of LTCE.

213. Illustration # 18: This example illustrates, through a flow-chart, computation of the UTPR top-up tax amount under Article 2.5.3.

Application of Article 2.5.3

Facts

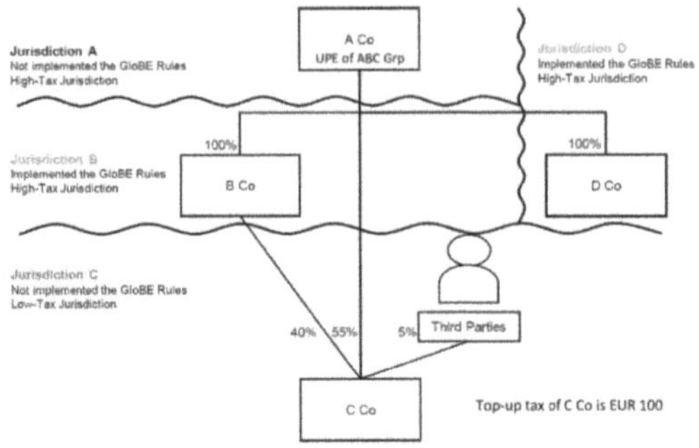

Observation

- A Co is not required to apply a Qualified IIR.
- B Co's allocable share of the Top-up Tax of C Co equals 40%. Therefore, as provided under Article 2.1.2, B Co is required to apply a Qualified IIR with respect to 40% of the Top-up Tax of C Co.
- A Co's Ownership Interest in C Co equals to 95% in total (40% indirectly held via B Co and 55% directly held). Therefore, not all of A Co's Ownership Interest in C Co are held by a Parent Entity that is required to apply a Qualified IIR with respect to C Co (which is B Co in this example) and Article 2.5.3 applies respectively.

Solution

- B Co is liable for a Top-up Tax of EUR 40.
- Article 2.5.3 provides that the Top-up Tax of EUR 100 of C Co is reduced by the amount of B Co's allocable share of C Co's Top-up Tax (EUR 40) to compute the UTPR Top-up Tax Amount that is allocated under the UTPR. In this example, the UTPR Top-up Tax Amount is EUR 60 (= 100 – 40).

4.2.6 Article 2.6. (Allocation of Top-Up Tax for the UTPR)

214. Article 2.6 provides the methodology (formula) for allocating such top-up tax to each UTPR Jurisdiction on the basis of a substance-based allocation key.

215. The term UTPR Jurisdiction mentioned above is defined in Article 10.1 as below:

> UTPR Jurisdiction means a jurisdiction that has a Qualified UTPR in force.

216. Prominent features of Article 2.6 are provided in Box 4.11.

Box 4.11 Prominent features of Article 2.6

- Provides the methodology (formula) for allocating top-up tax to each UTPR Jurisdiction on the basis of a substance-based allocation key.
- UTPR Percentage of a jurisdiction implementing GloBE Rules shall be determined each Fiscal Year for each MNE Group.
- The UTPR Percentage is determined on the basis of factors that reflect the relative substance of the MNE Group in each UTPR Jurisdiction. Jurisdictions, where the MNE Group has more substance on a relative basis, will be those where there is more tax capacity (such as deductible expenditure) to absorb adjustments under the UTPR.
- Provides that the top-up tax is allocated only among UTPR Jurisdictions. Allocating any of the UTPR top-up tax amount to jurisdictions that do not have a UTPR would significantly reduce the effectiveness of the rule because the top-up tax allocated to those jurisdictions would not be collected.

- Provides two types of exclusions in computing a jurisdiction's UTPR percentage (pertaining to number of employees employed and the net book value of tangible assets held by an investment entity and a flow-through entity).
- Provides that a UTPR Jurisdiction shall be excluded from the allocation mechanism when the UTPR top-up tax amount allocated to that jurisdiction in a prior year has not yet resulted in an equivalent additional cash tax expense for the CEs located in that jurisdiction. When that is the case, the UTPR percentage for the jurisdiction is zero. This mechanism:
  - ensures that no more top-up tax is allocated to such a jurisdiction until it has been able to impose the requisite amount of tax.
  - applies on an annual basis for each Fiscal Year when the UTPR applies and that the exclusion mechanism is specific to a particular MNE Group.
  - does not apply for a Fiscal Year if all jurisdictions with a Qualified UTPR in Force for the Fiscal Year have a UTPR Percentage of zero for the MNE Group for that Fiscal Year.

4.2.6.1 Article 2.6.1.

217. Subject to Articles 2.6.2 and 2.6.3, the UTPR top-up tax amount allocated to a jurisdiction implementing GloBE Rules shall be determined by multiplying the Total UTPR top-up tax amount determined in Article 2.5.1 by the jurisdiction's UTPR Percentage. The UTPR Percentage of a jurisdiction implementing GloBE Rules shall be determined each Fiscal Year for each MNE Group as follows:

Determination of UTPR Percentage for the jurisdiction implementing GloBE Rules for each Fiscal Year for each MNE Group

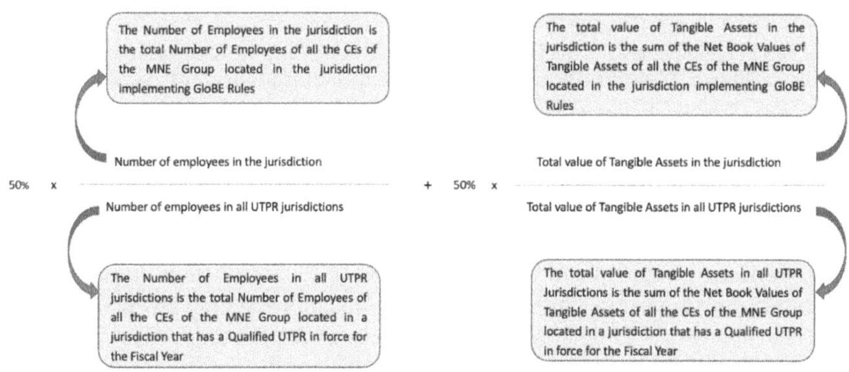

218. The term Number of Employees mentioned above is defined in Article 10.1 as below:

> Number of Employees, for the purposes of the UTPR percentage, means the total number of employees on a full-time equivalent (FTE) basis of all the Constituent Entities resident for tax purposes in the relevant tax jurisdiction. For this purpose, independent contractors participating in the ordinary operating activities of the Constituent Entity are reported as employees. With regard to Permanent Establishments, employees should be allocated to the tax jurisdiction in which the Permanent Establishment is located when the payroll costs of such employees are included in the separate financial accounts of that Permanent Establishment as determined by Article 3.4.1 and adjusted in accordance with 3.4.2. The Number of Employees attributed to the tax jurisdiction of a Permanent Establishment shall not be taken into account for the Number of Employees of the tax jurisdiction of the Main Entity.

219. The term Tangible Assets mentioned above is defined in Article 10.1 as below:

> Tangible Assets, for the purposes of the UTPR percentage and for Article 9.3, means the Tangible Assets of all the Constituent Entities resident for tax purposes in the relevant tax jurisdiction. Tangible Assets do not include cash or cash equivalents, intangibles, or financial assets. With regard to Permanent Establishments, Tangible Assets should be allocated to the tax jurisdiction in which the Permanent Establishment is located provided those Tangible Assets are included in the separate financial accounts of that Permanent Establishment as determined by Article 3.4.1 and adjusted in accordance with Article 3.4.2. The Tangible Assets allocated to the tax jurisdiction of a Permanent Establishment shall not be taken into account for the Tangible Assets of the tax jurisdiction of the Main Entity.

220. The term Net Book Value of Tangible Assets mentioned above is defined in Article 10.1 as below:

> Net Book Value of Tangible Assets means the average of the beginning and end values of Tangible Assets after taking into account accumulated depreciation, depletion, and impairment, as recorded in the financial statements.

221. The term UTPR Percentage mentioned above is defined in Article 10.1 as below:

> UTPR Percentage means the percentage of Total UTPR Top-up Tax Amount that is allocated to a UTPR Jurisdiction in accordance with the formula provided in 2.6.1.

222. *Objective of determination of UTPR percentage:* Article 2.6.1 provides that the UTPR Top-up Tax Amount determined under Article 2.5.1 is allocated among UTPR Jurisdictions by applying their respective UTPR Percentages. Article 2.6.1 then sets out the formula for computing the UTPR Percentage of each UTPR Jurisdiction and is drafted from the perspective of the implementing UTPR Jurisdiction. In other words, the formula determines the amount allocable to the implementing UTPR Jurisdiction. The UTPR Percentage is determined on the basis of factors that reflect the relative substance of the MNE Group in each UTPR Jurisdiction. Relying on substance factors provides for a simple and transparent allocation key which facilitates the coordination among tax administrations. It is also expected that the jurisdictions where the MNE Group has more substance on a relative basis will be those where there is more tax capacity (such as deductible expenditure) to absorb adjustments under the UTPR. This approach, together with the exclusion mechanism in Article 2.6.3, is intended to reduce the risk of allocating Top-up Tax to a jurisdiction that does not have enough capacity to impose the UTPR adjustment.

223. *UTPR percentage is based on quantitative factors comprising number of employees and the net book value of tangible assets of the CEs located in respective jurisdictions:* Article 2.6.1 provides that the UTPR Percentage is determined on the basis of quantitative factors that are aggregated at the jurisdictional level. These factors are based on information required in the MNE Group's CbCR. More specifically, Article 2.6.1 provides that the substance of UTPR jurisdictions is determined on the basis of a ratio based on the Number of Employees and the Net Book Value of Tangible Assets of the CEs that are located in those respective jurisdictions. The Number of Employees and the Net Book Value of Tangible Assets were determined to be the most appropriate for reflecting a consistent measure of substance in jurisdictions. In addition, the factors used under the UTPR provide both MNE Groups and tax administrations with bright-line measures based on existing compliance mechanisms. Using quantitative factors that can be available in CbCR facilitates coordination between UTPR Jurisdictions and minimises the risk of disputes. Other factors (such as payroll) were considered and rejected by the IF.

224. *Reason for adopting a 50% weight for each factor*: The Number of Employees and the Net Book Value of Tangible Assets each account for half of the UTPR percentage of the UTPR Jurisdiction. This is to reflect that substance can be measured both on the basis of the Number of Employees and the Net Book Value of Tangible Assets across jurisdictions, recognising that substance may take various forms, depending on the industry and the business model of the MNE Group. Using a 50% weight for each factor avoids favouring one of the two factors over the other in the formula.

225. *Scope of UTPR percentage:* The UTPR Percentage is only computed for purposes of allocating the UTPR Top-up Tax Amount and for jurisdictions that introduced a Qualified UTPR ('UTPR Jurisdictions'). The UTPR Percentage is determined for all UTPR Jurisdictions where the MNE Group is operating, even if those UTPR Jurisdictions are Low-Tax Jurisdictions under the GloBE Rules for that MNE Group. This means that:

- a Low-Tax Jurisdiction that is also a UTPR Jurisdiction is allocated a portion of the UTPR Top-up Tax Amount if its UTPR Percentage is not zero (it could be zero, for instance, as a result of the provisions in Article 2.6.3).
- the UPE Jurisdiction itself could be a Low-Tax Jurisdiction under the GloBE Rules and be allocated a portion of the UTPR Top-up Tax Amount that arises in respect of the CEs that are located in the UPE Jurisdiction. In addition, the UPE Jurisdiction may apply a Qualified IIR with respect to the CEs of the MNE Group that are not located in the UPE Jurisdiction (in accordance with Article 2.1.6), but this would not be relevant for purposes of determining the UTPR Top-up Tax Amount that arises in respect of the CEs in the UPE Jurisdiction.

226. *Top-up Tax allocated only among UTPR Jurisdictions*: Article 2.6.1 further provides that only the substance factors of CEs of the Group located in a UTPR Jurisdiction (including those of the implementing jurisdiction) are taken into account in the denominator of the fraction. Therefore, the top-up tax is allocated only among UTPR Jurisdictions. The substance factors of CEs that are not located in a UTPR Jurisdiction are not taken into account for purposes of the allocation key because doing so would have the effect of allocating some of the UTPR top-up tax amount to jurisdictions without a Qualified UTPR. Allocating any of the UTPR top-up tax amount to jurisdictions that do not have a UTPR would significantly reduce the effectiveness of the rule because the top-up tax allocated to those jurisdictions would not be collected. The UTPR Percentage is determined on an annual basis for each Fiscal Year. However, it is not expected to be significantly different from one year to the next unless the MNE Group undertakes a significant acquisition, disposal or restructuring of its operations.

227. Illustration # 19: If five jurisdictions implement the UTPR and four of those jurisdictions have 25% of the group's tangible assets and employees, and the fifth has 0%, in that case, the first four jurisdictions would each be allocated 25% of the top-up tax under the UTPR.

4.2.6.2 Article 2.6.2.

228. Article 2.6.2 provides two types of exclusions in computing a jurisdiction's UTPR percentage, as mentioned below:

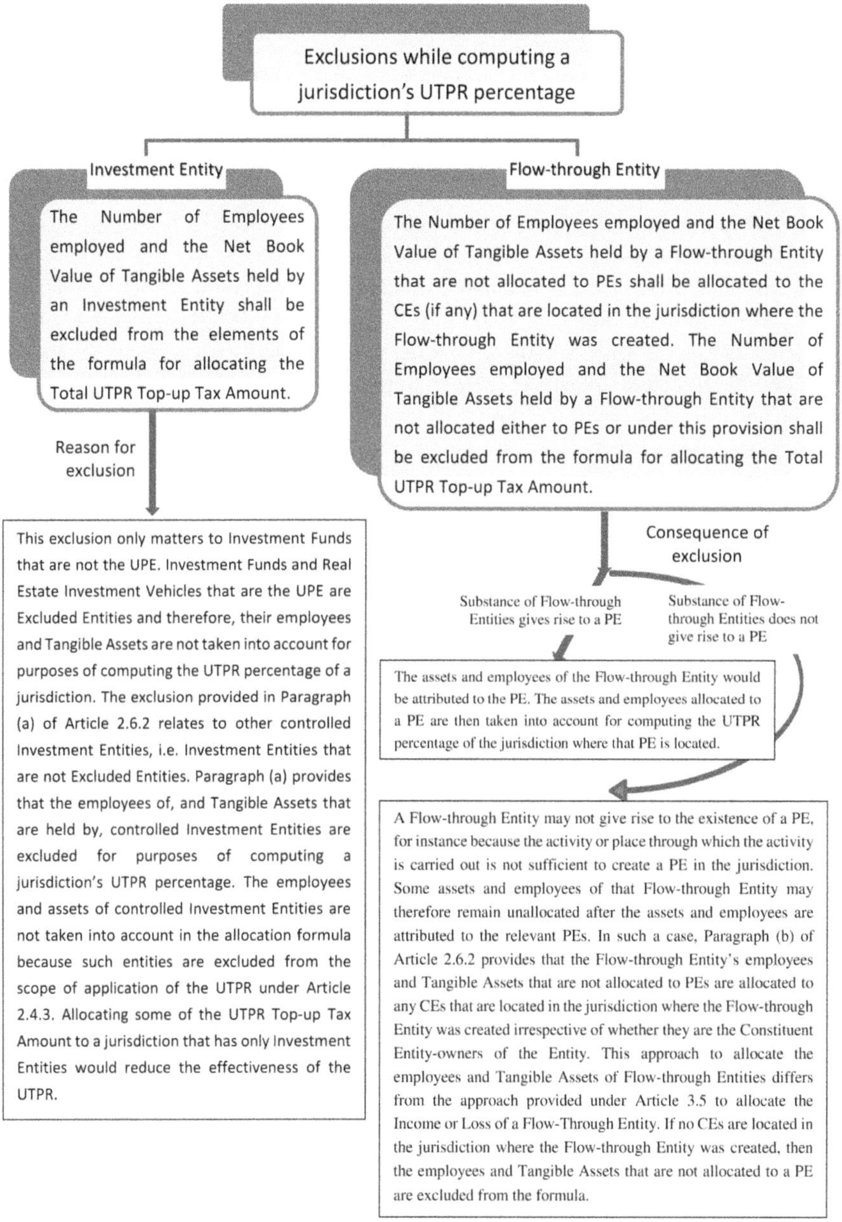

4.2.6.3 Article 2.6.3.

229. Notwithstanding Article 2.6.1, the UTPR percentage of a jurisdiction introducing the GloBE Rules for an MNE Group is deemed to be zero for a Fiscal Year as long as the top-up tax amount allocated to that jurisdiction in a prior Fiscal Year has not resulted in the CEs of this MNE Group located in that jurisdiction having an additional cash tax expense equal, in total, to the UTPR top-up tax amount for that prior Fiscal Year allocated to that jurisdiction. The Number of Employees and the Tangible Assets of the CEs of this MNE Group located in a jurisdiction with a UTPR percentage of zero for a Fiscal Year shall be excluded from the formula provided under Article 2.6.1 for allocating the Total UTPR Top-up Tax Amount for that Fiscal Year.

230. *Purpose of the Article*: Article 2.6.3 provides that a UTPR Jurisdiction shall be excluded from the allocation mechanism provided under Article 2.6.1 when the UTPR top-up tax amount allocated to that jurisdiction in a prior year has not yet resulted in an equivalent additional cash tax expense for the CEs located in that jurisdiction. Article 2.6.3 provides that, when that is the case, the UTPR percentage for the jurisdiction is zero. This mechanism ensures that no more top-up tax is allocated to such a jurisdiction until it has been able to impose the requisite amount of tax. Article 2.6.3 further provides that the Number of Employees and Tangible Assets of the CEs located in such a jurisdiction are excluded from the denominator of the formula for purposes of the allocation key. This ensures that the top-up tax that would have been allocated to the UTPR Jurisdiction with a UTPR percentage of zero is actually allocated to the other UTPR Jurisdictions.

231. *Exclusion mechanism under the Article is specific to a particular MNE Group:* Article 2.6.3 applies on an annual basis for each Fiscal Year when the UTPR applies and further provides that the exclusion mechanism is specific to a particular MNE Group. This is because the capacity to impose an adjustment under the UTPR may depend on the specificities of the CEs of that MNE Group in the UTPR Jurisdiction. For instance, the capacity to impose the adjustment may be limited in the situation where the MNE Group has losses in the UTPR Jurisdiction. For the avoidance of doubt, when the rule applies to an MNE Group, it does not preclude the UTPR Jurisdiction from being allocated UTPR top-up tax amount computed in respect of other MNE Groups with employees and tangible assets in the jurisdiction.

4.2.6.4 Article 2.6.4.

232. Article 2.6.3 does not apply for a Fiscal Year if all jurisdictions with a Qualified UTPR in Force for the Fiscal Year have a UTPR Percentage of zero for the MNE Group for that Fiscal Year.

233. *Purpose of exception provided in the Article:* Article 2.6.4 provides that Article 2.6.3 does not apply in circumstances where the UTPR percentage for all UTPR Jurisdictions in which CEs of an MNE Group are located would be zero for a given Fiscal Year. This exception ensures that in such circumstances, the UTPR top-up tax amount is still allocated to the UTPR Jurisdictions. Since it applies in situations where all UTPR Jurisdictions may have limited capacity to impose an additional top-up tax, this exception acknowledges that the UTPR top-up tax amount allocated in that year may also need to be carried forward as provided in Article 2.4.2 and be collected in a future year.

234. Similar to Article 2.6.3, Article 2.6.4 applies on an annual basis for each Fiscal Year when the UTPR applies and on an MNE Group-by-MNE Group basis.

235. Illustration # 20: This example illustrates, through a flow-chart, the effect of Article 2.6.4 on the UTPR Percentages of the UTPR Jurisdictions.

Illustration of Article 2.6.4

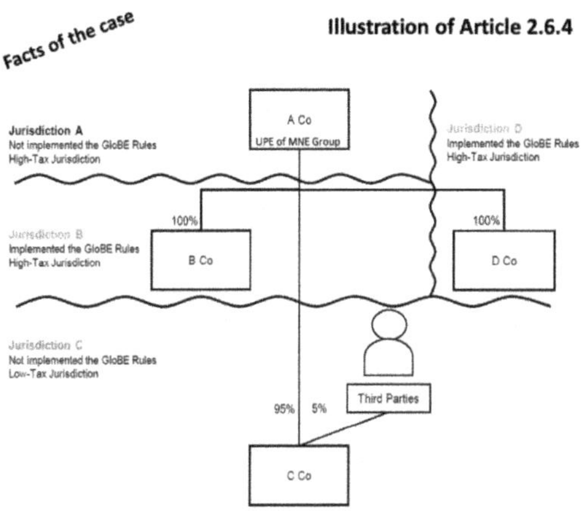

Assumptions made

1	Assume the UTPR Top-up Tax Amount in respect of C Co is EUR 100 for each of Fiscal Years 1 to 4
2	UTPR Percentages of Jurisdictions B and D are 50% each over the same period based on the formula under Article 2.6.1
3	Assume that Jurisdiction B is not able to collect the whole amount of EUR 50 for the taxable year in which Fiscal Year 1 ends
4	Assume that Jurisdiction B is again not able to collect the whole amount of UTPR Top-up Tax of EUR 50 (allocated in respect of Fiscal Year 1) for the taxable year in which Fiscal Year 2 ends. Further, Jurisdiction D is also not able to collect the whole amount of EUR 100 (allocated in respect of Fiscal Year 2) for the taxable year in which Fiscal Year 2 ends.
5	Finally, assume that all remaining UTPR Top-up Tax Amounts are collected in both Jurisdictions B and D for the taxable year in which Fiscal Year 3 ends.

Summary of Solution

1	No CE is required to apply a Qualified IIR with respect to the Top-up Tax of C Co because Jurisdiction A has not implemented the GloBE Rules and B Co and D Co do not have Ownership Interests in C Co. Therefore, the total amount of Top-up Tax is allocated under the UTPR.
2	For Fiscal Year 1, Jurisdiction B and D are each allocated an amount of Top-up Tax of EUR 50.
3	In view of Assumption No. 3, Article 2.6.3 provides that Jurisdiction B's UTPR Percentage is deemed to be zero for Year 2 (and following Years) as long as the UTPR Top-Up Tax Amount of EUR 50 allocated to Jurisdiction B in Year 1 has not resulted in B Co having an equivalent additional cash tax expense. This means that no more UTPR Top-up Tax Amount is allocated to Jurisdiction B until it has been able to impose the relevant Tax. Hence, in Fiscal Year 2, Jurisdiction B has a UTPR percentage of zero. As a consequence, the whole UTPR Top-up Tax calculated for Fiscal Year 2 (EUR 100) is allocated to Jurisdiction D.
4	In view of Assumption No 4 and as provided in Article 2.6.3, both Jurisdictions B and D would have a UTPR percentage of zero for Fiscal Year 3. However, Article 2.6.4 stipulates that Article 2.6.3 would not apply when it would result in all UTPR Jurisdictions' UTPR percentages being reduced to zero. Pursuant to Article 2.4.2, in Fiscal Year 3, the Total UTPR Top-up Tax Amount of EUR 100 is therefore allocated to Jurisdictions B and D in respect of their UTPR Percentage based on the formula under Article 2.6.1 (50%/50%) without the application of Article 2.6.3. An amount of EUR 50 of Top-up Tax is added to the other UTPR Top-up Tax Amounts that are still to be collected by each Jurisdiction.
5	In view of Assumption No. 5, in Fiscal Year 4, the UTPR Top-up Tax Amount of 100 is allocated to Jurisdictions B and D based on their respective UTPR Percentages determined using the formula in Article 2.6.1.

Summary of the amount of UTPR Top-up Tax allocated to each jurisdiction:

Year	UTPR Top-up Tax Amount	Allocation Jurisdiction B	Allocation Jurisdiction D
1	EUR 100	EUR 50 (UTPR Percentage of 50%)	EUR 50 (UTPR Percentage of 50%)
2	EUR 100	EUR 0 (UTPR Percentage of 0%)	EUR 100 (UTPR Percentage of 100%)
3	EUR 100	EUR 50 (UTPR Percentage of 50%)	EUR 50 (UTPR Percentage of 50%)
4	EUR 100	EUR 50 (UTPR Percentage of 50%)	EUR 50 (UTPR Percentage of 50%)

4.3 CHAPTER 3 OF GLOBE RULES (COMPUTATION OF GLOBE INCOME OR LOSS)[90]

236. Chapter 3 of the GloBE Rules sets out the computation of GloBE Income or Loss for each CE, and it operates to convert Financial Accounting Net Income or Loss to the GloBE Income or Loss, which is then utilised in subsequent chapters to determine the ETR and Excess Profits for purposes of determining whether top-up tax is payable with respect to a particular jurisdiction.

4.3.1 Article 3.1. (Financial Accounts)

237. The starting point for computation of GloBE Income or Loss for each CE is the Financial Accounting Net Income or Loss of the CE calculated in accordance with the rules of Article 3.1.

238. Prominent features of Article 3.1 are provided in Box 4.12.

Box 4.12 Prominent Features of Article 3.1

- Provides that the computation of GloBE Income or Loss begins with the Financial Accounting Net Income or Loss of the CE. That amount is adjusted for the items of income, gain, loss and expense that are set out in Articles 3.2 to Article 3.5.
- States that the Financial Accounting Net Income or Loss is the net income or loss determined for a CE (before any consolidation adjustments eliminating intragroup transactions) in preparing CFS of the UPE.
- The net income or loss of the CE has to be determined using the accounting standard that was used to determine the CE's income or loss in preparing the CFS.
- Provides that the items reported under Other Comprehensive Income (OCI) section are excluded from the computation of GloBE Income or Loss.
- Addresses the situation where the CE maintains its entity-level financial accounts using an accounting standard that is different from the standard used in the preparation of the UPE's CFS, and it is not reasonably practicable to accurately calculate its Financial Accounting Net Income or Loss in conformity with the accounting standard used by the UPE in the CFS.

4.3.1.1 Article 3.1.1.

239. The GloBE Income or Loss of each CE is the Financial Accounting Net Income or Loss determined for the CE for the Fiscal Year adjusted for the items described in Article

90. Based on OECD's GloBE Model Rules, its Commentary and Illustrative Examples.

3.2 to Article 3.5. In accordance with the said Article, the computation of GloBE Income or Loss begins with the Financial Accounting Net Income or Loss of the CE. That amount is adjusted for the items of income, gain, loss and expense that are set out in Articles 3.2 to Article 3.5.

4.3.1.2 Article 3.1.2.

240. Financial Accounting Net Income or Loss is the net income or loss determined for a CE (before any consolidation adjustments eliminating intragroup transactions) in preparing CFS of the UPE. It is the net income or loss determined for the CE by taking into account all of the Entity's income and expenses, including from transactions with other members of the Group and the income tax expense.

241. Stated differently, the starting point for calculating GloBE income or loss is the bottom-line net income or loss of the Group Entity before making any consolidation adjustments that would eliminate income or expense attributable to intragroup transactions. The following aspects in computing the Financial Accounting Net Income or Loss of a CE may *inter alia* be taken into account:

- Elimination of income and expenses from intragroup transactions that occur in the accounting consolidation process are not taken into account in the computation of a CE's Financial Accounting Net Income or Loss.
- In addition, adjustments to income or expense attributable to purchase accounting for an acquired business (irrespective of when the business was acquired) that are reflected in the MNE Group's consolidated accounts, rather than a CE's separate accounts, are not taken into account in the computation of a CE's Financial Accounting Net Income or Loss.
- Items of income and expense, other than those attributable to purchase accounting, that are reflected in the consolidated accounts, rather than a CE's separate accounts, may be taken into account in computing the CE's Financial Accounting Net Income or Loss and GloBE Income or Loss only to the extent they can be reliably and consistently traced to the relevant Entity (e.g., stock-based compensation).

242. Depending on the date of business acquisition, certain adjustments are called for while computing a CE's Financial Accounting Net Income of Loss and its Adjusted Covered Taxes, as below:

- *Acquisition is prior to 1 December 2021* – In the case of a business combination for which the acquisition date is prior to 1 December 2021, the CE may use the carrying value[91] reflected in its separate accounts after the application of 'push

91. Carrying value, also known as carrying amount, is the cost of an asset less accumulated depreciation.

down' accounting,[92] if permitted, or the carrying value of assets and liabilities determined as per the financial accounting standard used by the UPE, but only if the MNE Group does not have sufficient records to determine its Financial Accounting Net Income or Loss with reasonable accuracy based on the unadjusted carrying values of the acquired assets and liabilities. In such cases, however, the CE must also take into account any deferred tax assets and liabilities arising in connection with the purchase in the computation of its Financial Accounting Net Income or Loss and its Adjusted Covered Taxes.

- *Acquisition is on or after 1 December 2021* – A CE may not take into account 'push down' adjustments to the carrying value of assets and liabilities attributable to the purchase of a business if the acquisition date is on or after 1 December 2021.

243. *Application of accounting standards*: The net income or loss of the CE has to be determined using the accounting standard that was used to determine the CE's income or loss in preparing the CFS (except as provided in Article 3.1.3, discussed below). In general, CFS are the financial statements prepared by a UPE in accordance with an Acceptable Financial Accounting Standard. If a UPE does not have financial statements prepared in accordance with one of those standards, its CFS are the statements that are, or would be prepared, using an Authorised Financial Accounting Standard, which is required to be adjusted to prevent Material Competitive Distortions, as necessary. It may be noted that only Authorised Financial Accounting Standards that are not Acceptable Financial Accounting Standards may require adjustment for Material Competitive Distortions, whereas the list of international and national accounting standards that are Acceptable Financial Accounting Standards do not require such adjustment.

244. The term Acceptable Financial Accounting Standard mentioned above is defined in Article 10.1 as below:

> Acceptable Financial Accounting Standard means International Financial Reporting Standards (IFRS) and the generally accepted accounting principles of Australia, Brazil, Canada, Member States of the European Union, Member States of the European Economic Area, Hong Kong (China), Japan, Mexico, New Zealand, the People's Republic of China, the Republic of India, the Republic of Korea, Russia, Singapore, Switzerland, the United Kingdom, and the United States of America.

245. The term Authorised Financial Accounting Standard mentioned above is defined in Article 10.1 as below:

> Authorised Financial Accounting Standard, in respect of any Entity, means a set of generally acceptable accounting principles permitted by an Authorised Accounting Body in the jurisdiction where that Entity is located.

92. Push down accounting is a method of accounting for the purchase of another company at the purchase price rather than its historical cost. The target company's assets and liabilities are written up (or down) to reflect the purchase price.

246. The term Authorised Accounting Body mentioned above is defined in Article 10.1 as below:

> Authorised Accounting Body is the body with legal authority in a jurisdiction to prescribe, establish, or accept accounting standards for financial reporting purposes.

247. The term Material Competitive Distortion mentioned above is defined in Article 10.1 as below:

> Material Competitive Distortion in respect of the application of a specific principle or procedure under a set of generally accepted accounting principles means an application that results in an aggregate variation greater than EUR 75 million in a Fiscal Year as compared to the amount that would have been determined by applying the corresponding IFRS principle or procedure. Where the application of a specific principle or procedure results in a Material Competitive Distortion, the accounting treatment of any item or transaction subject to that principle or procedure must be adjusted to conform to the treatment required for the item or transaction under IFRS in accordance with any Agreed Administrative Guidance.

248. Various advantages of using the information to prepare the CFS as the starting point for calculating GloBE Income or Loss are given in Figure 4.7.

Figure 4.7 Advantages of Using the Information in Preparation of CFS as the Starting Point for Calculating GloBE Income or Loss

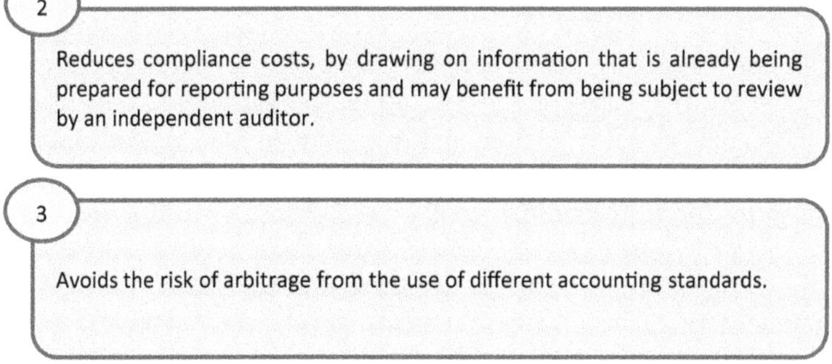

249. *Items reported under OCI section are excluded*: Since the rules for computing GloBE Income or Loss begin with the Financial Accounting Net Income or Loss reflected in the profit and loss statement; hence, income or expense items that are reported under certain financial accounting standards in the OCI section of the CFS (rather than in the profit and loss statement) are generally excluded from the computation of GloBE Income or Loss. The items included in OCI may include gains and losses on certain debt and equity investments, foreign currency exchange gains and losses, and changes in liabilities under pension plans.

250. The term OCI mentioned above is defined in Article 10.1 as below:

> Other Comprehensive Income means items of income and expense that are not recognised in profit or loss as required or permitted by the Authorised Financial Accounting Standard used in the Consolidated Financial Statements. Other Comprehensive Income is usually reported as an adjustment to equity in the statement of financial position (balance sheet).

251. *Materiality threshold*: Since the accounting standards used to prepare the CFS include a materiality threshold, minor or inconsequential deviations from a strict application of the UPE's accounting standard in the computation of a particular CE's Financial Accounting Net Income or Loss for purposes of preparing the CFS do not need to be adjusted when such threshold is not exceeded. On the one hand, the financial accounting auditor's acceptance of a deviation in the CFS without a qualification to the auditor's opinion is good evidence that the difference is immaterial. On the other hand, an auditor's opinion that contains a qualification with respect to the accounting treatment of a specific item or items of income and expense is relevant, but not conclusive, evidence that the deviation is material. In addition, if a UPE uses an accounting standard permitted by the Authorised Accounting Body in the UPE Jurisdiction and the Authorised Accounting Body permits the UPE to apply a different accounting standard to compute the Financial Accounting Net Income or Loss of foreign CEs (for purposes of preparing the CFS), the Financial Accounting Net Income or Loss computed for those foreign CEs using the different accounting standard need not be adjusted to strictly conform to the UPE's accounting standard.

4.3.1.3 Article 3.1.3.

252. If it is not reasonably practicable to determine the Financial Accounting Net Income or Loss for a CE based on the accounting standard used in the preparation of CFS of the UPE, the Financial Accounting Net Income or Loss for the CE for the Fiscal Year may be determined using another Acceptable Financial Accounting Standard or an Authorised Financial Accounting Standard if:

(a) the financial accounts of the CE are maintained based on that accounting standard;
(b) the information contained in the financial accounts is reliable; and
(c) permanent differences in excess of EUR 1 million that arise from the application of a particular principle or standard to items of income or expense or transactions that differs from the financial standard used in the preparation of

the CFS of the UPE are conformed to the treatment required under the accounting standard used in the CFS of the UPE.

253. *Purpose of the Article*: This article is intended to address a situation where the CE maintains its entity-level financial accounts using an accounting standard that is different from the standard used in the preparation of the UPE's CFS, and it is not reasonably practicable to accurately calculate its Financial Accounting Net Income or Loss in conformity with the accounting standard used by the UPE in the CFS. In this event, the Financial Accounting Net Income or Loss may be determined using another Acceptable Financial Accounting Standard or Authorised Financial Accounting Standard (adjusted for Material Competitive Distortions). This rule is not expected to apply in many cases because an MNE Group will typically have mechanisms in place to convert a subsidiary's entity-level accounts to the UPE's accounting standard in connection with the preparation of the CFS. In those circumstances, it is reasonably practicable to accurately calculate the CE's Financial Accounting Net Income or Loss based on the standard used in the preparation of the UPE's CFS. However, the rule could apply, for example, when the MNE Group has undertaken a recent acquisition of a group of entities that have historically used a different accounting standard to that of the acquiring MNE Group, and it is not reasonably practicable for the MNE Group to convert the acquired entities' financial accounting systems from their historical financial accounting standard to the UPE's standard.

254. *Use of an alternative accounting standard is limited by three conditions*: Where it is not reasonably practicable to use the UPE's financial accounting standard to compute the CE's Financial Accounting Net Income or Loss, the use of an alternative accounting standard is limited by three conditions as mentioned below:

- The first condition of Article 3.1.3 is that the financial accounts of the CE are maintained based on an Acceptable Financial Accounting Standard or Authorised Financial Accounting Standard. Financial accounts maintained under an Authorised Financial Accounting Standard must be adjusted for Material Competitive Distortions. A CE may not use an accounting standard under Article 3.1.3 other than the one used in its financial accounts. If the CE does not maintain its financial accounts based on an Acceptable Financial Accounting Standard or Authorised Financial Accounting Standard, it must compute its financial accounting income using the UPE's financial accounting standard, notwithstanding any practical difficulties;
- The second condition under Article 3.1.3 is that the information in the financial accounts maintained according to the other accounting standard is reliable. This means that there must be appropriate mechanisms in place to ensure that the information is recorded accurately. In this regard, the financial accounting internal controls and accounting processes employed by the CE must be tested and deemed acceptable to the financial accounting auditor pursuant to generally accepted auditing standards applicable in the location of the UPE or the CE (in the case of a Flow-through Entity in the jurisdiction of

creation). If the CE does not meet this requirement in a Fiscal Year, it must determine the actual income and expenses for that year and develop and implement mechanisms to ensure that the information in the accounts is reliable.

- The final condition of Article 3.1.3 is that the use of the other accounting standard must not result in permanent differences in excess of EUR 1 million from the financial accounting standard of the UPE. If the permanent differences, in the aggregate, exceed EUR 1 million, the treatment of the relevant items in the CE's financial accounts must be adjusted to conform to the treatment that would apply under the UPE's financial accounting standard. This condition only applies to permanent differences between the accounting standards. For example, if a financial instrument is treated as debt under the UPE's financial accounting standard and equity under the other accounting standard, the UPE's standard will reflect payments received on the instrument in the financial accounting net income and the other standard will not. This will result in a permanent difference in the Financial Accounting Net Income or Loss of the holder of the instrument. Timing differences, including differences in the financial accounting period used under the different accounting standards, are not subject to this condition.

4.3.2 Article 3.2. (Adjustments to Determine GloBE Income or Loss)

255. The Financial Accounting Net Income or Loss of the CE calculated in accordance with the rules of Article 3.1 is then adjusted under Article 3.2 for common differences between financial accounting and taxable income in order to reflect intended policy outcomes (such as the exclusion of dividend income and adding-back of illegal payments). Differences between financial accounting standards and tax accounting rules generally can be categorised as giving rise either to permanent differences[93] that will not reverse in a future period or temporary differences[94] (i.e., timing differences) that will reverse in a future period. The adjustments required in Article 3.2 are generally related to permanent differences between the treatment required under financial accounting rules and local tax rules. Temporary differences are addressed in

93. A permanent difference is a business transaction that is reported differently for financial and tax reporting purposes, and for which the difference will never be eliminated. An example of a permanent difference is a company incurring a fine or penalty. Tax codes seldom allow a deduction in the event of a fine or penalty, but fines and penalties are often deducted from income in book accounting. A permanent difference will cause a difference between the statutory tax rate and the effective tax rate. Also, because the permanent difference will never be eliminated, this tax difference does not generate deferred taxes, as in the case of temporary differences.

94. Temporary differences are differences between pre-tax book income and taxable income that will eventually reverse itself or be eliminated. Temporary differences arise when business income or expenses are recognised in different periods on the financial statements than on the tax returns. These differences might include revenue recognition, expenses incurred but not yet paid or depreciation calculation differences.

Chapter 4. To the extent an adjustment required by Article 3.2 excludes an amount of income from the GloBE Income or Loss computation, any Covered Taxes associated with that income must also be excluded from Adjusted Covered Taxes pursuant to Article 4.1.3(a). While the number of adjustments has been kept at a minimum to minimise complexity, the adjustments set out in Article 3.2 reflect cases that are sufficiently material and widely accepted in IF jurisdictions.

256. Prominent features of Article 3.2 are provided in Box 4.13.

Box 4.13 Prominent Features of Article 3.2

- The Financial Accounting Net Income or Loss of the CE calculated in accordance with the rules of Article 3.1 is then adjusted under Article 3.2 for common differences between financial accounting and taxable income in order to reflect intended policy outcomes (such as the exclusion of dividend income and adding-back of illegal payments).
- To the extent, an adjustment required by Article 3.2 excludes an amount of income from the GloBE Income or Loss computation, any Covered Taxes associated with that income must also be excluded from Adjusted Covered Taxes pursuant to Article 4.1.3(a).
- Article 3.2.1 sets out nine adjustments to the Financial Accounting Net Income or Loss that are required in the computation of each CE's GloBE Income or Loss:
  (a) While income taxes and other covered tax liabilities that accrue during the Fiscal Year can be expected to reduce net income for financial reporting purposes, these tax expenses must be added back to income in order to accurately calculate the tax on total income for the year for GloBE purposes. This is important for the purposes of computation of ETR.
  (b) Dividends and distributions from controlled entities and entities reported under the equity method will generally be excluded from the calculation of the group's consolidated income.
  (c) Excluded Equity Gain or Loss:
    - Fair value method gains or losses on Ownership Interests other than Portfolio Shareholdings are excluded from the GloBE Income or Loss computation.
    - Equity method income or loss is excluded from the computation of GloBE Income or Loss irrespective of whether that income or loss, or a portion thereof, is included in the owner's taxable income computation under the laws of the jurisdiction in which the owner is located.
    - The GloBE Rules eliminate most of the permanent differences by generally excluding gains and losses from dispositions of Ownership Interests from the seller's GloBE Income or Loss computation.

However, gains and losses from the disposition of a Portfolio Shareholding are included in the GloBE Income or Loss.

(d) To eliminate the effect of reporting gains or losses in OCI under the revaluation model on the computation of GloBE Income or Loss, all Included Revaluation Method Gain or Loss for the Fiscal Year to be included in the computation of GloBE Income or Loss.

(e) To the extent gain is excluded under Article 6.3, a negative adjustment is required under Article 3.2.1(e), and to the extent a loss is excluded, a positive adjustment is required while determining GloBE Income or Loss.

(f) No Foreign currency exchange gain or loss (FXGL) adjustments are required when the functional currencies are the same, whereas FXGL adjustments are required when the functional currencies are different.

(g) There is a materiality threshold that prevents the rule from applying in the case of *de minimis* fines and penalties that equal or exceed EUR 50,000. There is no such threshold for bribes and kickbacks, which are always disallowed.

(h) Paragraph (h) requires an adjustment for prior period errors and changes in Accounting Principles.

(i) Pension liabilities are allowed as expenses in the computation of GloBE Income or Loss to the extent of contributions to a Pension Fund during the Fiscal Year.

- Article 3.2.2 provides an election to substitute in the computation of GloBE Income or Loss the amount of stock-based compensation allowed as a deduction in the computation of a CE's taxable income in place of the amount expensed in its financial accounts. The election must be made by the Filing CE. The scope of the election is limited to compensation expenditures in the form of stock, stock options, or stock warrants (or an equivalent), where the amount allowed as an expense is computed differently for local tax purposes than for financial accounting purposes.
- Provides for adherence to ALP:
  - Any transaction between CEs located in different jurisdictions that is not recorded in the same amount in the financial accounts of both CEs or that is not consistent with the ALP must be adjusted so as to be in the same amount and consistent with the ALP. No case for adjustment under Article 3.2.3 when cross-border transactions between Group Entities are at ALP. Adjustments may be made to prevent double taxation or double non-taxation. Adjustments may not be made when such actions give rise to double taxation or double non-taxation.
  - For GloBE purposes, additional adjustments to conform with the ALP in respect of wholly domestic transactions should not generally be required because the effect of these transactions will generally be eliminated under the jurisdictional blending rules of Chapter 5. However, ALP requirement for same-country (domestic) transactions is essential to prevent deliberate manufacturing of losses. Transactions between

Minority-Owned CEs and other CEs, as well as, Investment Entities and other CEs must be recorded in accordance with the ALP. Transactions between CEs in the same jurisdiction must be recorded in the same amount in both CEs.

- Provides that Qualified Refundable Tax Credits shall be treated as income in the computation of GloBE Income or Loss of a CE, whereas, Non-Qualified Refundable Tax Credits shall not be treated as income in the computation of GloBE Income or Loss of a CE.
- Article 3.2.5 provides for an election to use the realisation method for assets and liabilities that are accounted for in the CE's financial accounts using the fair value method or impairment accounting. The election is a Five-Year Election and applies to all CEs located in the jurisdiction to which the election applies. The election applies to all assets and liabilities of such CEs unless the Filing Constituent Entity chooses to limit the election to tangible assets of such CEs or to CEs that are Investment Entities.
- Provides that where there is Aggregate Asset Gain in a jurisdiction in a Fiscal Year, the Filing Constituent Entity may make, under Article 3.2.6, an Annual Election for that jurisdiction to adjust GloBE Income or Loss in a prescribed manner with respect to each previous Fiscal Year in the Look-back Period. The objective is to mitigate the effect of recognising the entire gain in a single year on the MNE Group's jurisdictional ETR computation. The election is an Annual Election made on a jurisdictional basis and applies only with respect to gains and losses attributable to disposition of Local Tangible Assets.
- Provides that the computation of a Low-Tax Entity's GloBE Income or Loss shall exclude, subject to conditions, any expense attributable to an Intra-group Financing Arrangement. Purpose of this rule is to prevent MNE Groups from engaging in transactions that are intended to increase the ETR in a jurisdiction that is below the Minimum Rate.
- Provides that a UPE may elect to apply its consolidated accounting treatment to eliminate income, expense, gains, and losses from transactions between CEs that are located and included in a tax consolidation group in the same jurisdiction for purposes of computing each such CE's Net GloBE Income or Loss. The election under this article is a Five-Year Election. The election applies to transactions between CEs located in the same jurisdiction.
- Provides that an insurance company shall exclude from the computation of GloBE Income or Loss amounts charged to policyholders for Taxes paid by the insurance company in respect of returns to the policyholders. An insurance company shall include in the computation of GloBE Income or Loss any returns to policyholders that are not reflected in Financial Accounting Net Income or Loss to the extent the corresponding increase or decrease in liability to the policyholders is reflected in its Financial Accounting Net Income or Loss.
- Provides that amounts recognised as a decrease to the equity of a CE attributable to distributions paid or payable in respect of Additional Tier One Capital issued by the CE shall be treated as an expense in the computation of

its GloBE Income or Loss. Amounts recognised as an increase to the equity of a CE attributable to distributions received or receivable in respect of Additional Tier One Capital held by the CE shall be included in the computation of its GloBE Income or Loss.

- Article 3.2.11 requires adjustments to a CE's Financial Accounting Net Income or Loss where necessary to reflect the requirements of Chapters 6 and 7.

4.3.2.1 Article 3.2.1

257. A CE's Financial Accounting Net Income or Loss is adjusted for the following nine items to arrive at that entity's GloBE Income or Loss:

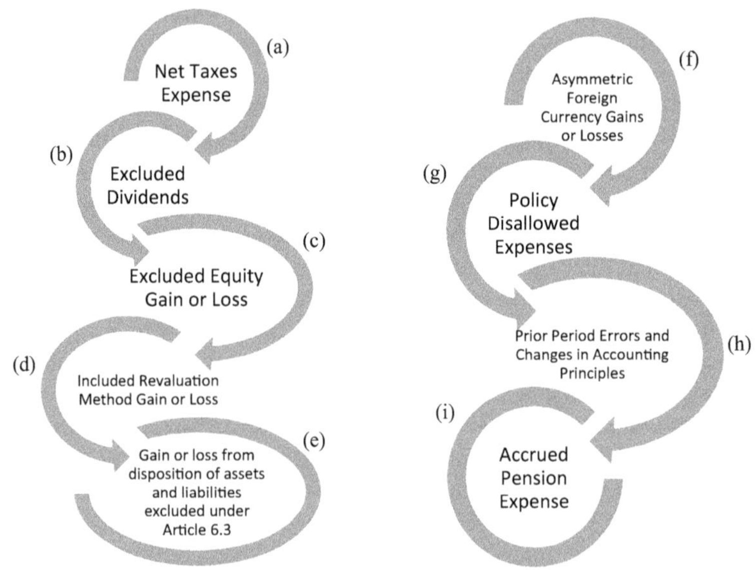

258. Article 3.2.1 sets out the adjustments to the Financial Accounting Net Income or Loss that are required in the computation of each CE's GloBE Income or Loss. These adjustments bring the CE's GloBE Income or Loss more into alignment with the computation of taxable income under a typical CIT (for example, exclusion of equity method income or loss from a non-Controlling Interest in a corporation) and prevent double taxation of the MNE Group's income under the GloBE Rules, (for example, exclusion of dividends received from CEs).

(a) Net Taxes Expense

259. Net Taxes Expense is defined in Article 10.1 as below:

> Net Taxes Expense means the net amount of:
>
> (a) any Covered Taxes accrued as an expense and any current and deferred Covered Taxes included in the income tax expense, including Covered Taxes on income that is excluded from the GloBE Income or Loss computation;
> (b) any deferred tax asset attributable to a loss for the Fiscal Year;
> (c) any Qualified Domestic Minimum Top-up Tax accrued as an expense;
> (d) any taxes arising pursuant to the GloBE rules accrued as an expense; and
> (e) any Disqualified Refundable Imputation Tax accrued as an expense.

260. While income taxes and other covered tax liabilities that accrue during the Fiscal Year can be expected to reduce net income for financial reporting purposes, these tax expenses must be added back to income in order to accurately calculate the tax on total income for the year for GloBE purposes. This is important for the purposes of computation of ETR, as demonstrated by an illustration below.

Illustration # 21: This example illustrates computation of ETR by taking into account the treatment of net taxes expense.

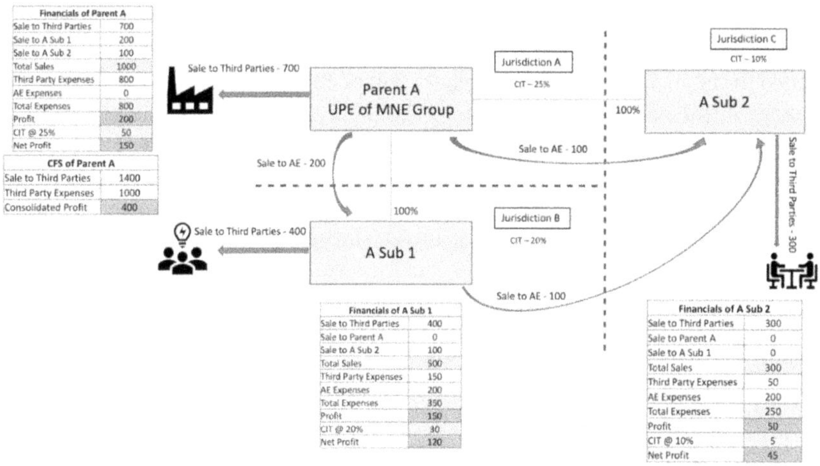

Financials of Parent A	
Sale to Third Parties	700
Sale to A Sub 1	200
Sale to A Sub 2	100
Total Sales	1000
Third Party Expenses	800
AE Expenses	0
Total Expenses	800
Profit	200
CIT @ 25%	50
Net Profit	150

CFS of Parent A	
Sale to Third Parties	1400
Third Party Expenses	1000
Consolidated Profit	400

Financials of A Sub 1	
Sale to Third Parties	400
Sale to Parent A	0
Sale to A Sub 2	100
Total Sales	500
Third Party Expenses	150
AE Expenses	200
Total Expenses	350
Profit	150
CIT @ 20%	30
Net Profit	120

Financials of A Sub 2	
Sale to Third Parties	300
Sale to Parent A	0
Sale to A Sub 1	0
Total Sales	300
Third Party Expenses	50
AE Expenses	200
Total Expenses	250
Profit	50
CIT @ 10%	5
Net Profit	45

In the above dataset:

- The ETR of Parent A (on a stand-alone basis) is 25% (=50/200) for GloBE purposes and not 33.3% (=50/150).
- The ETR of A Sub 1 is 20% (=30/150) for GloBE purposes and not 25% (=30/120).
- The ETR of A Sub 2 is 10% (=5/50) for GloBE purposes and not 11.1% (=5/45).

261. *Covered Taxes under paragraph (a) of definition of Net Taxes Expense*: Any Covered Taxes that were deducted in the computation of Financial Accounting Net Income or Loss, whether as an above-the-line expense or as a below-the-line income tax, must be added back to the determination of GloBE Income or Loss. As a matter of general tax policy, creditable taxes are generally not deductible against taxable income. Allowing a deduction and a credit for the same taxes would effectively provide a double benefit for the same taxes. However, an amount withheld by a CE in respect of Taxes imposed on another person (i.e., the foreign payee) in lieu of a generally applicable CIT is an expense and is not Covered Taxes of the CE. Accordingly, there is no need to make an adjustment in respect of such an amount in the determination of the CE's GloBE Income. This is the case regardless of whether a foreign payee requires a CE, being the payer, to gross up the payment to reimburse the foreign payee for the withholding tax imposed by the jurisdiction of the CE on the foreign payee's income.

262. *Deferred tax asset attributable to a loss under paragraph (b) of definition of Net Taxes Expense*: A deferred tax asset arising in respect of a loss does not represent Tax paid in advance of the recognition of income for tax purposes. Instead, it arises because a portion of the total loss, i.e., the excess of expenses over income, effectively creates an asset that can be used against tax liability on income arising in the future. As such, it reduces the economic effect of the business loss. The deferred tax asset is determined by reference to the pre-tax accounting loss. Accordingly, the amount of the deferred tax asset must be treated as a negative amount in the computation of the Net Taxes Expense adjustment. For example, A Co incurs an economic loss of 100 in Year 1 and records a deferred tax asset of 15 (assuming a 15% corporate tax rate). The net loss recorded for financial accounting purposes will be 85, given that an asset of 15 has been generated in the same year by virtue of the local tax loss carry forward. In order to accurately reflect the loss for GloBE purposes, the 15 is taken into account in the Net Taxes Expense adjustment as a negative amount. However, to the extent a deferred tax asset is taken into account in the adjustment for Covered Taxes pursuant to paragraph (a) of the definition of Net Taxes Expense, it is not taken into account under paragraph (b).

263. *QDMTT accrued as an expense under paragraph (c) of definition of Net Taxes Expense*: The same reasoning against allowing a deduction for Covered Taxes applies in the case of QDMTTs because those taxes also reduce the MNE Group's potential Top-up Tax liability, albeit as a direct reduction to Top-up Tax liability under Article 5.2.3 rather than as part of the ETR computation under Article 5.2.1. These Taxes are positive amounts that increase the Net Taxes Expense adjustment. It may be noted that a domestic minimum tax that is not a QDMTT but that meets the definition of a Covered Tax and that is deducted in the computation of Financial Accounting Net Income or Loss must be added back under paragraph (a).

264. *Taxes arising pursuant to the GloBE rules accrued as an expense under paragraph (d) of definition of Net Taxes Expense*: Top-up Taxes arising under the GloBE Rules that have been accrued in the financial statements must be added back to the Financial Accounting Net Income or Loss. The amount of tax paid under a Tax regime does not reduce the base on which that Tax is levied. The adjustment for Top-up Taxes arising under the GloBE Rules applies irrespective of whether the taxes are due to an accrual of the estimated liability for the current Fiscal Year or an adjustment to the actual liability for a previous Fiscal Year. These Taxes are positive amounts that increase the Net Taxes Expense adjustment. For example, an MNE Group may report its expected Top-up Tax liability for a Fiscal Year in its financial statements. Such amount must be added back to prevent overstating the ETR, as the amount of GloBE Income would otherwise be understated.

265. *Disqualified Refundable Imputation Tax accrued as an expense under paragraph (e) of definition of Net Taxes Expense:* Disqualified Refundable Imputation Tax is defined in Article10.1 as below:

> Disqualified Refundable Imputation Tax means any amount of Tax, other than a Qualified Imputation Tax, accrued or paid by a Constituent Entity that is:
>
> (a) refundable to the beneficial owner of a dividend distributed by such Constituent Entity in respect of that dividend or creditable by the beneficial owner against a tax liability other than a tax liability in respect of such dividend; or
> (b) refundable to the distributing corporation upon distribution of a dividend.

Disqualified Refundable Imputation Taxes are not Covered Taxes. However, they must be added back to the Financial Accounting Net Income or Loss because such Taxes are essentially deposits that the MNE Group can have refunded at the time of its choosing by simply distributing a dividend. As such, they are not properly treated as an expense in the computation of GloBE Income or Loss. When Disqualified Refundable Imputation Taxes are paid or accrued and included as an expense in the Financial Accounting Net Income or Loss, they must be added back. This would be a positive amount that increases the Net Taxes Expense adjustment. If, however, Disqualified Refundable Imputation Taxes are refunded or credited to the MNE group in a Fiscal Year and treated as an income item or a reduction to a tax expense in the Financial Accounting Net Income or Loss, the amount must be removed from income or added back to the tax expense. This would be a negative amount that decreases the Net Taxes Expense adjustment.

(b) Excluded Dividends

266. Excluded Dividends are defined in Article 10.1 as below:

> Excluded Dividends means dividends or other distributions received or accrued in respect of an Ownership Interest, except for:
>
> (a) a Short-term Portfolio Shareholding, and
> (b) an Ownership Interest in an Investment Entity that is subject to an election under Article 7.6.

267. The term Short-term Portfolio Shareholding mentioned above is defined in Article 10.1 as below:

> Short-term Portfolio Shareholding means a Portfolio Shareholding that has been economically held by the Constituent Entity that receives or accrues the dividends or other distributions for less than one year at the date of the distribution.

268. The term Portfolio Shareholding mentioned above is defined in Article 10.1 as below:

> Portfolio Shareholding means Ownership Interests in an Entity that are held by the MNE Group and that carry rights to less than 10% of the profits, capital, reserves, or voting rights of that Entity at the date of the distribution or disposition.

269. Dividends and distributions from controlled entities and entities reported under the equity method will generally be excluded from the calculation of the group's consolidated income. The underlying income or loss of entities that are consolidated on a line-by-line basis and Entities that are accounted for under the equity method is included directly in the Group's income. CFS exclude distributions from these entities to avoid double-counting of the same income. The GloBE Rules, however, generally require the GloBE Income or Loss and Covered Taxes of CEs to be determined starting with the separate Financial Accounting Net Income or Loss of the CE. Accordingly, the starting point for a CE's income for financial accounting purposes would be to include intragroup dividends, including distributions received or accrued in respect of an Ownership Interest held in a Flow-Through Entity, as well as dividends received in respect of Ownership Interests in JVs, associated entities, and other entities, including dividends on Portfolio Shareholdings. Article 3.2.1(b) adjusts a CE's Financial Accounting Net Income or Loss by reducing that Net Income (or increasing the Loss) by the amount of any Excluded Dividends received during the Fiscal Year. In general terms, Excluded Dividends are dividends or other distributions paid on shares or other equity interests where (i) the MNE Group holds 10% or more of the Ownership Interests in the issuer or (ii) the CE has held full economic ownership of the Ownership Interest for a period of twelve months or more. Paragraph (b) of Article 3.2.1 is intended to provide for a broad exemption for dividends that aligns with the operation and scope of participation exemptions in many IF jurisdictions and covers both substantial and long-term shareholdings while, at the same time, ensuring that the exclusion does not provide unintended benefits for dividend income received by a CE as part of its trading activity.

270. *Dividends received or accrued from Short-term Portfolio Shareholding (less than one year) are included in the GloBE Income or Loss of the CE:* The dividend exclusion rule under the GloBE Rules provides an exception for dividends received from an entity:

- in which the MNE Group owns a low percentage of that Entity's Ownership Interests (i.e., a 'Portfolio Shareholding');
- where the CE has economically owned such Ownership Interest for a short period of time (referred to as 'Short-term Portfolio Shareholdings'). This

means that dividends received or accrued from Short-term Portfolio Shareholding are included in the GloBE Income or Loss of the CE.

271. There could be a discrepancy between the extent of the ownership held throughout the holding period and at the date of the distribution, whereby the dividend received at the date of the distribution may not necessarily reflect the extent of the rights that were held during the holding period. Ordinarily, the dividends or other distributions that are accrued at the date of the distribution reflect the economic ownership of the shareholding that is held at that date. Therefore, the economically held test addresses the potential discrepancy that could arise during the period and at the date of the distribution and provide a requirement that those Portfolio Shareholding are economically held for at least one year to be excluded from the GloBE Income or Loss.

272. Whether the CE has economically held the Portfolio Shareholding for one year is tested on the date of the distribution of the dividends. Fluctuations of the Ownership Interest held in an entity should be taken into account for that purpose. In this respect, for simplification purposes, the disposition of an Ownership Interest in a particular class of shares is deemed to be a disposition of the most recently acquired Ownership Interests of the same class that were acquired the last.

273. The CE is considered as having held the relevant Ownership Interest for one year if it has held that Ownership Interest for an uninterrupted period of at least twelve months. The requirement only relates to the Ownership Interest in respect of which a distribution is received or accrued and does not require a further determination of whether the distribution was funded by another distribution to which the same condition would apply. For example, a CE that receives a distribution in respect of an Ownership Interest in a mutual fund must determine its holding period for that interest but need not determine how long the mutual fund held the equity interest that was the source of the distributed profits. This condition applies to each CE holder separately and in respect of the same class of shares such that the dividends received or accrued in respect of the same class of shares that were held for a year or more are exempted, whereas other dividends are not. Unlike the 10% threshold test, the ownership period requirement applies on a Constituent Entity-by-Constituent Entity basis, which means that an intragroup transfer of shares would be considered an interruption of the holding period. The holding period would not be considered as interrupted, however, in the case of a GloBE Reorganisation between CEs.

274. In relation to Short-term Portfolio Shareholdings, the dividend income is not included in the adjustment for Excluded Dividends and thus would be included in the GloBE Income or Loss. Any taxes paid under local law in respect of those dividends would be included in the Adjusted Covered Taxes (the numerator) of the ETR calculation under Article 4.1.1. The treatment of dividends on Short-term Portfolio Shareholdings applies equally to dividends on stock in domestic and foreign corporations.

275. *Ownership Interest in an Investment Entity that is subject to an election under Article 7.6:* Dividends or other distributions received or accrued in respect of an Ownership Interest in an Investment Entity that is subject to an election under the Taxable Distribution Method set out in Article 7.6 are not Excluded Dividends. Accordingly, those dividends or other distributions must be included in the computation of GloBE Income or Loss of the CE-owner pursuant to the election since such dividends are not Excluded Dividends once the election has been made.

276. Illustration # 22: In respect of Excluded Dividend and Short-term Portfolio Shareholding, this example illustrates, through a flow-chart, how to test the period during which a Portfolio Shareholding was held.

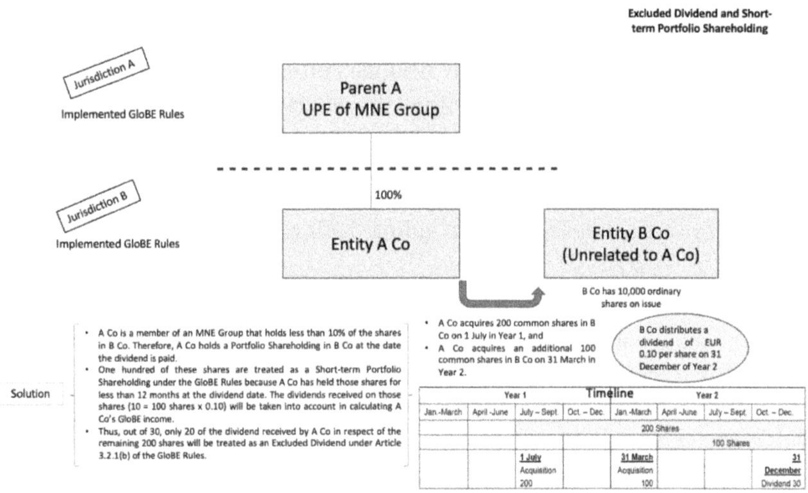

277. Illustration # 23: In respect of Excluded Dividend and Short-term Portfolio Shareholding, this example illustrates, through a flow-chart, the treatment of dividends when a portion of shareholding is sold in Year 2.

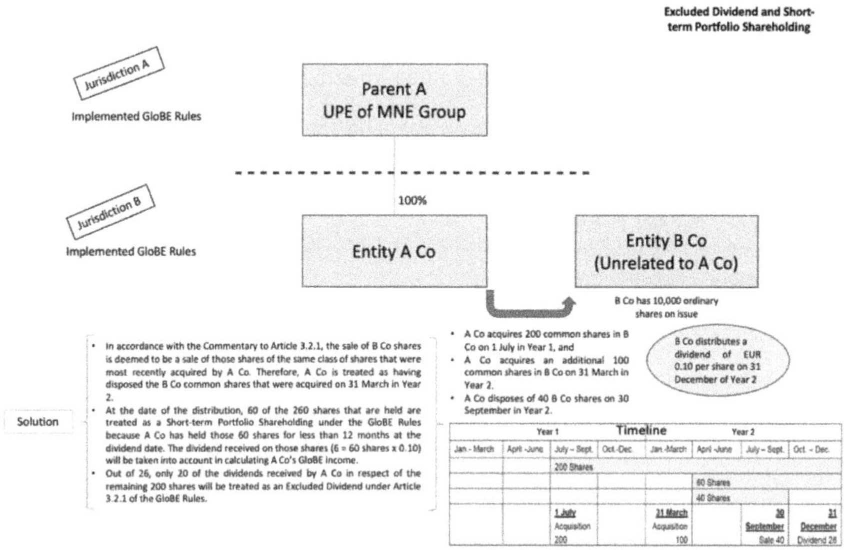

278. Illustration # 24: In respect of Excluded Dividend and Short-term Portfolio Shareholding, this example illustrates, through a flow-chart, the treatment of dividends when a portion of shareholding is sold in Year 1.

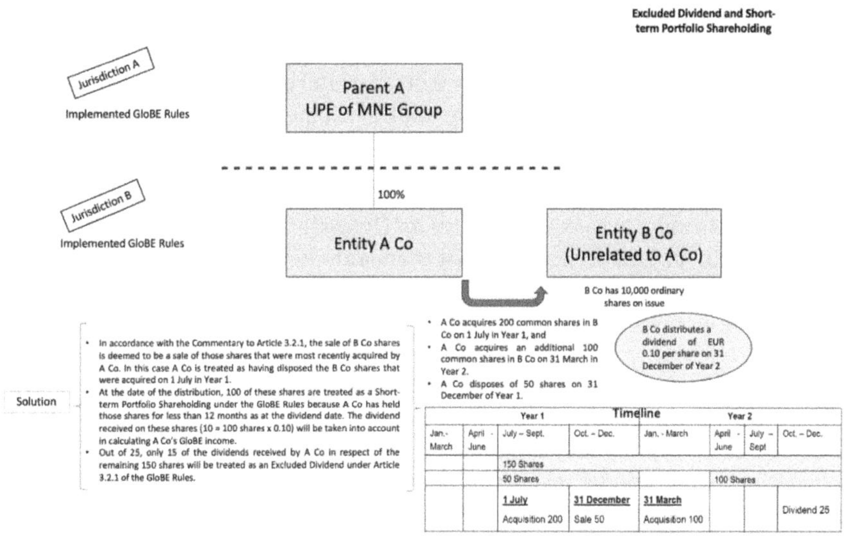

(c) Excluded Equity Gain or Loss

279. Excluded Equity Gain or Loss is defined in Article 10.1 as below:

> Excluded Equity Gain or Loss means the gain, profit or loss included in the Financial Accounting Net Income or Loss of the Constituent Entity arising from:
>
> (a) gains and losses from changes in fair value of an Ownership Interest, except for a Portfolio Shareholding;
> (b) profit or loss in respect of an Ownership Interest included under the equity method of accounting; and
> (c) gains and losses from disposition of an Ownership Interest, except for a disposition of a Portfolio Shareholding.

280. *Changes in fair value:* The first type of Excluded Equity Gain or Loss is attributable to changes in fair value of an Ownership Interest that is accounted for using a fair value accounting method, including mark-to-market. A fair value method revalues the Ownership Interest periodically and changes in its value are reported as gain or loss, either in the profit and loss statement or in the OCI section of the balance sheet. Fair value method gains or losses on Ownership Interests other than Portfolio Shareholdings are excluded from the GloBE Income or Loss computation. Accordingly, excluded fair value gains require a negative adjustment and excluded fair value losses require a positive adjustment to the Financial Accounting Net Income or Loss. The fair value gain or loss for a Fiscal Year, however, must be adjusted to reflect any distributions on that Ownership Interest that were excluded from the computation of GloBE Income or Loss pursuant to Article 3.2.1(b). To the extent such fair value gains and losses are recorded in OCI or equity instead of the profit and loss statement, they may already have been excluded from the GloBE Income or Loss, and no adjustment is necessary under Article 3.2.1(c).

281. *Equity method of accounting:* The second type of Excluded Equity Gain or Loss is attributable to income or loss arising from an Ownership Interest accounted for using the equity method. Financial accounting standards typically require equity method accounting when the MNE Group holds a significant but non-Controlling Interest in an entity, ordinarily between 20% and 50% of the equity interests in an entity. These entities are referred to as joint ventures or associates under financial accounting standards. As explained in the Commentary to Chapter 1, entities that are joint ventures and associates for accounting purposes are not CEs under the definition in Article 1.3 because they are not controlled by the MNE Group. Under the equity method, the owner includes its proportionate share of the Entity's after-tax income or loss in the computation of its Financial Accounting Net Income or Loss. The adjustment required in respect of Ownership Interests accounted for under the equity method may be a positive or negative amount depending upon whether the entity reported net income or net loss. Equity method net income is a negative adjustment to the Financial Accounting Net Income or Loss. An equity method loss is a positive adjustment to the Financial Accounting Net Income or Loss. Equity method income or loss is excluded from the computation of GloBE Income or Loss irrespective of whether that income or loss, or a portion thereof, is included in the owner's taxable income computation under the laws of the jurisdiction in which the owner is located. Thus, if an entity accounted for under the equity method is treated as a Tax Transparent Entity in the owner's tax jurisdiction, the annual income or loss is nevertheless removed from the owner's GloBE Income or Loss computation. In general, entities whose Ownership Interests are accounted for under the equity method are not CEs. However, pursuant to Article 6.4, JVs, as defined in Article 10.1, will be treated as if they were CEs. A JV subject to Article 6.4 is an entity in which the UPE holds directly or indirectly at least 50% of its Ownership Interests. This definition encompasses entities that are considered joint ventures for accounting purposes and some that are considered associates for accounting purposes. The adjustment required by Article 3.2.1(c) also applies to Ownership Interests in JVs as defined in Article 10.1 because they too are accounted for using the equity method.

282. *Gains or losses on disposition*: The third and last type of Excluded Equity Gains or Losses are those gains and losses arising from a disposition of an Ownership Interest in any Entity where the MNE Group holds, in the aggregate, 10% or more of the Ownership Interests at the time of the transfer, i.e., Ownership Interests other than a Portfolio Shareholding. This category includes gains and losses from the sale of Ownership Interests in a CE, JVs as defined in Article 10.1, as well as non-Portfolio Shareholdings in entities that are not CEs or JVs. In many IF jurisdictions, e.g., India, gains arising from the disposition of Ownership Interests are wholly or partially exempt from tax or subject to taxation at reduced rates, and losses arising from the disposition of Ownership Interests may not be tax deductible (or are adjusted with future gains). As with the taxation of dividends, there is significant variance in the way gain or loss from the disposal of an Ownership Interest is taxed under local law. Local tax treatment depends on the nature (and residence) of the issuer of the Ownership Interest and the way the sale transaction is structured. As discussed above, many IF jurisdictions fully or partially exempt from the tax base gains and losses arising from the disposition of Ownership Interests. Gain or loss arising on the disposition of an Ownership Interest, whether measured by reference to the carrying cost of the equity interest or the underlying assets, that is included in the financial accounting income of the seller but excluded from the seller's taxable income, would represent a permanent difference. If the difference is not adjusted for in the GloBE Income or Loss computation, gains on sales of Ownership Interests will result in a lower GloBE ETR for the seller (and potential tax liability under the GloBE Rules). Losses, however, will result in a higher GloBE ETR for the seller (and potentially shield other income from GloBE tax liability). The GloBE Rules eliminate most of these permanent differences by generally excluding gains and losses from dispositions of Ownership Interests from the seller's GloBE Income or Loss computation. However, gains and losses from the disposition of a Portfolio Shareholding are included in the GloBE Income or Loss.

283. *Comparison of Excluded Dividends and Excluded gains or losses from disposition:* The definition of Portfolio Shareholding is used both in the context of Excluded Dividends and in the context of Excluded Equity Gain or Loss. In the context of Excluded Dividends, the potential scope of excluded income is broader than in the context of excluded gains because the ownership period requirement limits the categories of dividends for which an exception to the exclusion is provided. Unlike the rule that applies for purposes of Excluded Dividends, the period during which the Portfolio Shareholding is held is not relevant for determining whether gains and losses arising from the disposition of that shareholding are includible in GloBE Income or Loss. Further comparison between the two is provided in Table 4.1.

Table 4.1 Comparison of Excluded Dividends and Excluded Gains or Losses from Disposition

Period of shareholding	*Portfolio Shareholding (i.e., carrying rights to less than 10% of the profits, capital, reserves or voting rights of the distributing entity)*		*Non-Portfolio Shareholding (i.e., carrying rights to at least 10% of the profits, capital, reserves and voting rights of the distributing entity)*	
	Excluded Dividends	Excluded gain/ loss from disposition	Excluded Dividends	Excluded gain/ loss from disposition
Short-term shareholding (i.e., economically held for less than one year)	Included dividend	Included gain/ loss	Excluded Dividend	Excluded gain/ loss
Non- Short-term shareholding (i.e., economically held for at least one year)	Excluded Dividend	Included gain/ loss	Excluded Dividend	Excluded gain/ loss

(d) Included Revaluation Method Gain or Loss

284. Included Revaluation Method Gain or Loss is defined in Article 10.1 as below:

> Included Revaluation Method Gain or Loss means the net gain or loss, increased or decreased by any associated Covered Taxes, for the Fiscal Year in respect of all property, plant and equipment that arises under an accounting method or practice that:
>
> (a) periodically adjusts the carrying value of such property to its fair value;
> (b) records the changes in value in OCI; and
> (c) does not subsequently report the gains or losses recorded in OCI through profit and loss.

285. *Factors necessitating Included Revaluation Method Gain or Loss accounting to determine GloBE Income*: Under some financial accounting standards, an entity can elect either the cost model or the revaluation model as its accounting policy for property, plant and equipment. Under the revaluation model, an asset is carried at a revalued amount, which is its fair value at the date of the revaluation less any subsequent accumulated depreciation and subsequent accumulated impairment losses. Revaluation increases are generally recognised in OCI rather than profit or loss. Revaluation decreases, however, are generally (but not always) recognised in profit and loss. Absent a corrective measure, the revaluation model would impact the computation of GloBE Income because revaluation gains are generally excluded from Financial Accounting Net Income or Loss, and depreciation expense is determined based on the revalued amount. Therefore, to eliminate the effect of reporting gains or losses in OCI under the revaluation model on the computation of GloBE Income or Loss, paragraph (d) requires all Included Revaluation Method Gain or Loss for the Fiscal Year to be included in the computation of GloBE Income or Loss. Any revaluation losses or subsequent incremental increase in depreciation are allowed in the computation of GloBE Income or Loss to the extent they are attributable to revaluation increases (gains) included in the computation of GloBE Income or Loss pursuant to Article 3.2.1(d).

286. The above definition requires the amount of the gain or loss recorded in OCI to be increased by the amount of any associated Covered Taxes to the extent that gain or loss was recorded net of Covered Taxes. Any Covered Taxes (current or deferred) associated with Included Revaluation Method Gain or Loss are taken into account in the computation of Adjusted Covered Taxes under Article 4.1. The definition includes the amount of associated Covered Taxes to ensure that Covered Taxes are not both deducted (in effect) and taken into account in the ETR computation.

287. An election under Article 3.2.5 may be made with respect to tangible property that includes property subject to the revaluation model. If such an election is made, the gains or losses in the OCI would not be included in the computation of GloBE Income or Loss as they arise but would be deferred until the asset is disposed of. That election also requires the CE to determine its depreciation in respect of the assets subject to the election without regard to increases or decreases in the carrying value of the assets attributable to the revaluation model. The Covered Taxes associated with the gains and losses in OCI would likewise need to be deferred until disposition of the asset.

(e) Adjustment for gain or loss from disposition of assets and liabilities excluded under Article 6.3

288. Gains and losses from the disposition of assets are generally taken into account under the GloBE Rules, even where the buyer is another CE. Financial accounting rules typically include gains and losses from sales of assets. Assets acquired are recorded in the financial accounts at their cost. In the case of sales between members of the Group, however, adjustments to eliminate the intragroup gain or loss and the increase or decrease in the assets' cost are made when the company prepares its consolidated financial accounts so that the intragroup transaction does not affect the Group's income on a consolidated basis. Nevertheless, each CE's separate Financial Accounting Net

Income or Loss should reflect the results of the transaction in the same manner as if it were a transaction with a non-Group member. Article 6.3 generally requires inclusion of gain or loss arising from a transfer of assets (other than Ownership Interests that are not Portfolio Shareholdings) and liabilities in the computation of GloBE Income or Loss. Accordingly, a loss from a transfer of Ownership Interests in another CE is not included under Article 6.3. As noted, this is the normal result of applying the financial accounting rules on a separate entity basis, even for transfers between CEs. However, if the transfer is pursuant to a GloBE Reorganisation, the gain or loss (in respect of the transferred assets and liabilities) is included in the computation of GloBE Income or Loss only to the extent of Non-qualifying Gain or Loss, defined in Article 10.1 generally as the lesser of the taxable or financial accounting gain or loss on the transfer. In most cases, there will not be any Non-qualifying Loss because jurisdictions typically do not allow losses to be taken into account in connection with a tax-free reorganisation. To the extent gain is excluded under Article 6.3, a negative adjustment is required under Article 3.2.1(e), and to the extent a loss is excluded, a positive adjustment is required.

289. The term Non-qualifying Gain or Loss mentioned *supra* is defined in Article 10.1, as below:

> Non-qualifying Gain or Loss means the lesser of the gain or loss of the disposing Constituent Entity arising in connection with a GloBE Reorganisation that is subject to tax in the disposing Constituent Entity's location and the financial accounting gain or loss arising in connection with the GloBE Reorganisation.

(f) Asymmetric Foreign Currency Gains or Losses

290. Asymmetric FXGL are defined in Article 10.1 as below:

> Asymmetric Foreign Currency Gains or Losses means foreign currency gains or losses of an entity whose accounting and tax functional currencies are different and that are:
>
> (a) included in the computation of a Constituent Entity's taxable income or loss and attributable to fluctuations in the exchange rate between its accounting functional currency and its tax functional currency;
> (b) included in the computation of a Constituent Entity's Financial Accounting Net Income or Loss and attributable to fluctuations in the exchange rate between its tax functional currency and its accounting functional currency;
> (c) included in the computation of a Constituent Entity's Financial Accounting Net Income or Loss and attributable to fluctuations in the exchange rate between a third foreign currency and its accounting functional currency; and
> (d) attributable to fluctuations in the exchange rate between a third foreign currency and its tax functional currency, whether or not such foreign currency gain or loss is included in taxable income.
>
> The tax functional currency is the functional currency used to determine the Constituent Entity's taxable income or loss for a Covered Tax in the jurisdiction in which it is located. The accounting functional currency is the functional currency used to determine the Constituent Entity's Financial Accounting Net Income or Loss. A third foreign currency is a currency that is not the Constituent Entity's tax functional currency or accounting functional currency.

291. *No FXGL adjustments when the functional currencies are the same*: The GloBE Rules do not make any adjustments for FXGL when the functional currencies are the same. In those circumstances, any FXGL reflected in the financial accounts are included in the GloBE Income or Loss computation, irrespective of whether the local tax rules impose tax on FXGL. If FXGL is exempt under local tax rules, there will be a permanent difference that does, and should, affect the ETR of the jurisdiction.

292. *FXGL adjustments when the functional currencies are different*: The GloBE Rules do, however, make adjustments to avoid distortions that could arise when the functional currencies used for accounting and tax differ. The definition of Asymmetric Foreign Currency Gain or Loss in Article 10.1 includes four types of FXGL. The FXGL included in the definition are described based on the relationship between the tax functional currency, the accounting functional currency and a third foreign currency.

293. *Application of paragraph (a) of definition of Asymmetric FXGL*: Paragraph (a) of the definition applies to transactions in the accounting functional currency that produce taxable gain or loss because the tax functional currency is different. It brings the tax FXGL into the Financial Accounting Net Income or Loss. Paragraph (a) requires a positive adjustment to Financial Accounting Net Income or Loss in the amount of the tax foreign currency exchange (FX) gain and a negative adjustment to Financial Accounting Net Income or Loss in the amount of the tax FX loss. Paragraph (a) also applies where an asset or liability denominated in the accounting functional currency is retranslated in the tax functional currency so that a tax FXGL arises, despite no FXGL arising for accounting purposes.

294. Illustration # 25: This example illustrates, through a flow-chart, applicability of paragraph (a) of the definition of Asymmetric Foreign Currency Gains or Losses.

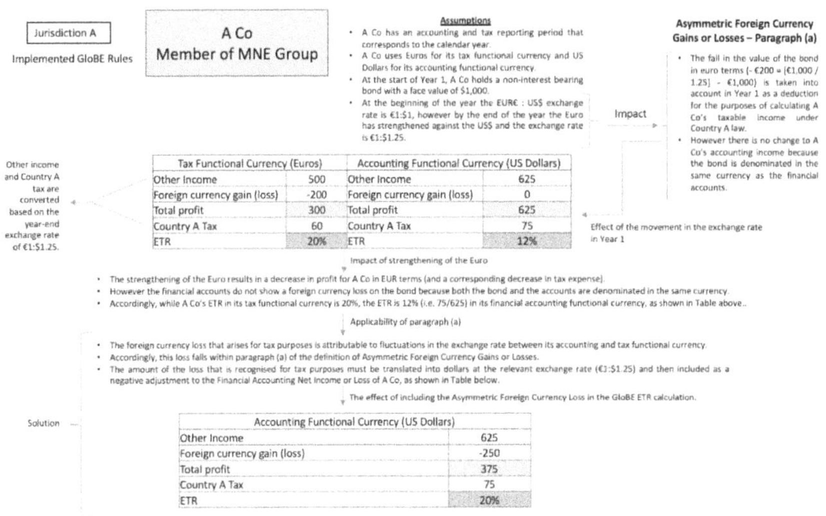

295. *Application of paragraph (b) of definition of Asymmetric FXGL*: Paragraph (b) of the definition applies to transactions in the tax functional currency that produce an accounting gain or loss because the accounting functional currency is different. It removes the accounting FXGL from the Financial Accounting Net Income or Loss. Thus, paragraph (b) requires a negative adjustment to Financial Accounting Net Income or Loss in the amount of the accounting FX gain and a positive adjustment to Financial Accounting Net Income or Loss in the amount of the accounting FX Loss. Paragraph (b) also applies where an asset or liability denominated in the tax functional currency is retranslated in the accounting functional currency so that an accounting FXGL arises, but no FXGL arises for tax purposes.

296. Illustration # 26: This example illustrates, through a flow-chart, applicability of paragraph (b) of the definition of Asymmetric Foreign Currency Gains or Losses.

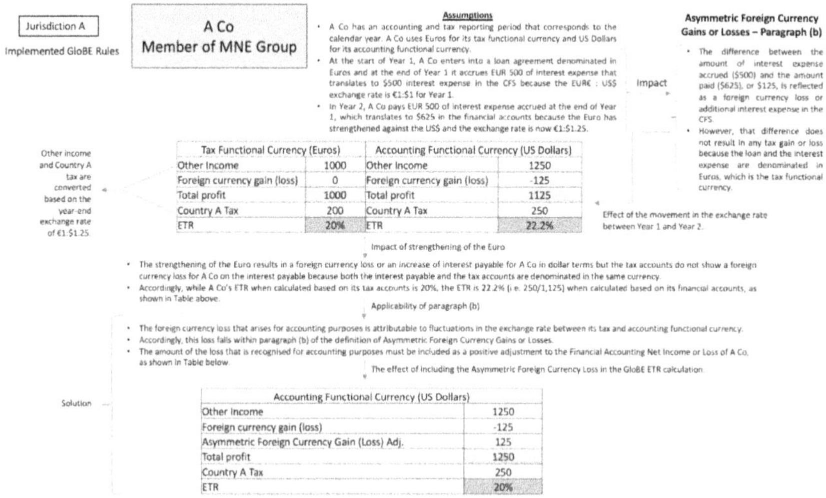

297. *Application of paragraph (c) of definition of Asymmetric FXGL*: Paragraph (c) of the definition is the exclusionary arm of the rule in respect of FXGL arising from transactions in a third foreign currency. These transactions may result in an FXGL vis-à-vis both the accounting and tax functional currencies. However, paragraph (c) only applies to the FXGL in respect of the accounting functional currency. It excludes these gains and losses from the GloBE Income or Loss computation by requiring a negative adjustment to Financial Accounting Net Income or Loss in the amount of the accounting FX gain and a positive adjustment to Financial Accounting Net Income or Loss in the amount of the accounting FX Loss.

298. *Application of paragraph (d) of definition of Asymmetric FXGL*: Paragraph (d) of the definition is the inclusionary arm of the rules for third foreign currency gains. It includes the gain or loss determined with respect to the tax functional currency by requiring a positive adjustment to Financial Accounting Net Income or Loss in the amount of the tax FX gain and a negative adjustment to Financial Accounting Net Income or Loss in the amount of the tax FX loss. This rule applies irrespective of whether the FXGL in the tax functional currency is includible in taxable income or subject to tax in the CE's location. For purposes of paragraph (d), if the FX gain or loss is not subject to tax under local law, the tax FX gain or loss is the amount that would have arisen for tax purposes if the CE had been subject to tax on the gain or loss using the same method for determining FXGL as is used in the financial accounts.

299. Illustration # 27: This example illustrates, through a flow-chart, applicability of paragraphs (c) and (d) of the definition of Asymmetric Foreign Currency Gains or Losses.

Jurisdiction A

Implemented GloBE Rules

A Co
Member of MNE Group

Assumptions

- A Co has an accounting and tax reporting period that corresponds to the calendar year. A Co uses Euros for its tax functional currency and US Dollars for its accounting functional currency.
- In Year 1, the GBP£ : EUR€ exchange rate is £1:€1.1, the GBP£ : US$ exchange rate is £1:$1.8, and the US$: EUR€ exchange rate is $1:€0.61. In Year 1, A Co sells merchandise on account for £100 and accrues a receivable of €110 for local tax purposes and a receivable of $180 in the financial accounts.
- In Year 2, A Co receives £100 in respect of the receivable recorded in Year 1.
- In Year 2, the US$: EUR€ exchange rate remains $1:€0.61.

Impact in Year 2

Asymmetric Foreign Currency Gains or Losses – Paragraph (c) & (d)

- In Year 2, receipt of £100 translates to €121 and $198 because the British Pound Sterling has strengthened:
  - i. against the Euro so that the exchange rate is now £1:€1.21; and
  - ii. against the US Dollar so that the exchange rate is now £1:$1.98.

Other Income and Tax are converted based on the year-end exchange rates of £1:€1.21 and £1:$1.98.

Tax Functional Currency (Euros)		Accounting Functional Currency (US Dollars)	
Other Income	200	Other Income	328
Foreign currency gain (loss)	0	Foreign currency gain (loss)	18
Total profit	200	Total profit	346
Country A Tax	30	Country A Tax	49
ETR	15%	ETR	14%

Effect of the movement in the exchange rate between Year 1 and Year 2.

Impact of strengthening of the British Pound Sterling

- The strengthening of the British Pound Sterling results in a €11 (= 121 – 110) gain for tax purposes because A Co received British Pounds Sterling worth €121 in respect of a receivable that was recorded at €110 in the tax accounts. Furthermore, the strengthening results in a $18 (= 198 - 180) gain for accounting purposes because A Co received British Pounds Sterling worth $198 in respect of a receivable that was recorded at $180 in the financial accounts, as shown in Table above. The gain in euro terms, however, is not taken into account for the purposes of calculating A Co's taxable income under Country A law.

Solution

Applicability of paragraph (c)

- The strengthening of the British Pound Sterling results in an increase of profit for A Co in dollar terms. The foreign currency gain that arises for accounting purposes is attributable to fluctuations in the exchange rate between a third currency (GBP) and the accounting functional currency of A Co. Accordingly, this gain falls within paragraph (c) of the definition of Asymmetric Foreign Currency Gains or Losses. Therefore, the amount of the gain that is recognised for accounting purposes must be included as a negative adjustment to the Financial Accounting Net Income or Loss of A Co, as shown in Table below.

Applicability of paragraph (d)

- The foreign currency gain that is attributable to fluctuations in the exchange rate between a third currency (GBP) and the tax functional currency of A Co falls within paragraph (d) of the definition of Asymmetric Foreign Currency Gains or Losses. Paragraph (d) requires an adjustment to the Financial Accounting Net Income or Loss when there is a gain or loss attributable to such fluctuations irrespective of whether such gain or loss is included in the taxable income of A Co. Accordingly, the amount of the gain in respect of the tax functional currency must be translated into the accounting functional currency and included as a positive adjustment to the Financial Accounting Net Income or Loss of A Co, as shown in Table below.

The effect of including the Asymmetric Foreign Currency Loss in the GloBE ETR calculation.

Accounting Functional Currency (US Dollars)	
Other Income	328
Foreign currency gain (loss)	18
Asymmetric Foreign Currency Gain (Loss) Adj. (para (c))	-18
Asymmetric Foreign Currency Gain (Loss) Adj. (para (d))	18
Total profit	346
Country A Tax	49
ETR	14%

(g) Policy Disallowed Expenses

300. Policy Disallowed Expenses are defined in Article 10.1 as below:

> Policy Disallowed Expenses means:
>
> (a) expenses accrued by the Constituent Entity for illegal payments, including bribes and kickbacks; and
> (b) expenses accrued by the Constituent Entity for fines and penalties that equal or exceed EUR 50,000 (or an equivalent in the functional currency in which the Constituent Entity's Financial Accounting Net Income or Loss was calculated).

301. *Bribes, kickbacks, and other illegal payments*: For purposes of Article 3.2.1(g), a payment is illegal if it is illegal under the laws applicable to the CE that made the payment or the laws applicable to the UPE. Bribes, kickbacks, and other illegal payments are allowed as expenses under financial accounting rules but are not deductible for tax purposes in most IF jurisdictions.

302. *Fines and penalties*: Similar to bribes, fines and penalties imposed by a government are commonly disallowed for tax purposes. However, the policy rationale for denying a deduction for fines and penalties is to limit the economic cost to only the person that committed the act. This rationale would be diluted if the taxpayer were allowed to share the burden of the penalty with all taxpayers (by way of tax deduction for it).

303. *Monetary threshold*: There is a materiality threshold that prevents the rule from applying in the case of *de minimis* fines and because the rule only applies to fines and penalties that equal or exceed EUR 50,000 (or an equivalent amount in the functional currency in which the CE's Financial Accounting Net Income or Loss was calculated). There is no such threshold for bribes and kickbacks, which are always disallowed. The purpose of the threshold is to continue to allow deductions for smaller fines that may not be specifically recorded as separate items in the accounts of the CE. This approach avoids the complexity of tracking small fines and penalties for GloBE purposes while at the same time preventing MNEs from escaping a top-up tax because of a few large, non-deductible fines or penalties. Interest charges for late payment of tax or other liabilities to a governmental unit are not considered fines or penalties for this purpose and do not need to be added back to Financial Accounting Net Income or Loss.

(h) Prior Period Errors and Changes in Accounting Principles

304. Prior Period Errors and Changes in Accounting Principles are defined in Article 10.1 as below:

> Prior Period Errors and Changes in Accounting Principles means all changes in the opening equity at the beginning of the Fiscal Year of a Constituent Entity attributable to:
>
> (a) a correction of an error in the determination of Financial Accounting Net Income in a previous Fiscal Year that affected the income or expenses

includible in the computation of GloBE Income or Loss for such Fiscal Year, except to the extent such error correction resulted in a material decrease to a liability for Covered Taxes subject to Article 4.6; or

(b) a change in accounting principle or policy that affects income or expenses includible in the computation of GloBE Income or Loss.

305. Paragraph (h) requires an adjustment for prior period errors and changes in Accounting Principles. The said paragraph does not apply to an error correction that requires a corresponding decrease in covered taxes in a previous Fiscal Year of EUR 1,000,000 or more. Such error corrections are subject to the rules of Article 4.6.1.

306. As an example, an erroneous exclusion of revenue will generally result in an increase in opening equity and a corresponding increase in income in the computation of the GloBE Income or Loss when the error is corrected. To the extent the equity adjustment is attributable to items of income or expense that were, or would have been, included in the computation of GloBE Income or Loss, it must be treated as an increase or decrease to the Financial Accounting Net Income or Loss of the relevant CE. To the extent that the error is attributable to a Fiscal Year prior to the application of the GloBE Rules to the CE, the adjustment to opening equity does not result in an adjustment under Article 3.2.1(h) because it did not affect the computation of GloBE Income or Loss. Also, if the adjustment is a decrease that requires re-computation of the ETR and top-up tax for a previous Fiscal Year under Article 4.6.1, an adjustment under Article 3.2.1(h) is not required because the adjustment is made in the relevant Fiscal Year pursuant to Article 4.6.1.

307. When an MNE Group changes an accounting principle or policy used in the determination of its Financial Accounting Net Income or Loss, it may be required to re-determine its opening equity as if it had used the new accounting principle or policy in previous Fiscal Years. This may be necessary to prevent the amount from being double-counted or omitted from the MNE Group's income or equity in a subsequent Fiscal Year as a result of the change in principle or policy. In the case of a change in accounting principle or policy, the increase or decrease in equity represents the net income, gain, expense, or loss that under the new accounting principle or policy will be included in the computation of Financial Accounting Net Income or Loss in a future period or that would have been included in that computation in a previous Fiscal Year. The change in accounting principle or policy may require either an increase or decrease in the opening equity. The adjustment under Article 3.2.1(h) should correspond directionally to the adjustment to opening equity. Thus, if a change in accounting principle or policy decreases opening equity, the adjustment under Article 3.2.1(h) would be a negative adjustment that has the same effect as an additional deduction in the computation of GloBE Income or Loss. Conversely, if a change in accounting principle or policy increases opening equity, the adjustment under Article 3.2.1(h) would be a positive adjustment that has the same effect as an additional income in the computation of GloBE Income or Loss.

(i) Accrued Pension Expense

308. The term Accrued Pension Expense is defined in Article 10.1 as below:

> Accrued Pension Expense means the difference between the amount of pension liability expense included in the Financial Accounting Net Income or Loss and the amount contributed to a Pension Fund for the Fiscal Year.

309. Pension liabilities are allowed as expenses in the computation of GloBE Income or Loss to the extent of contributions to a Pension Fund during the Fiscal Year. The adjustment for Accrued Pension Expense required by Article 3.2.1(i) is equal to the difference between:

(a) the amount of pension contributions during the year, and
(b) the amount accrued as an expense in the computation of Financial Accounting Net Income or Loss during the Fiscal Year.

The adjustment to Financial Accounting Net Income or Loss for this difference will be a positive amount if the amount accrued as an expense in the financial accounts exceeds the contributions for the year. It will be a negative amount in Fiscal Years in which the contributions exceed the expense accrued in the financial accounts.

310. Calculating the annual expense for pension liabilities based on contributions to a Pension Fund has two benefits, as mentioned below:

- First, the timing rule for deducting pension liabilities under local tax rules is commonly based on the timing of contributions; consequently, it will better align the timing of the expense from a GloBE Rules perspective with the effect on local tax liability attributable to the contribution.
- Second, it avoids complications and potential competitiveness concerns that would arise under some Acceptable Financial Accounting Standards that reflect some of the effects of pension accounting solely in the OCI.

311. In the company pension schemes of some jurisdictions, the annual accrued pension expense is always equal to the annual contribution amount. In such cases, there would be no adjustment under Article 3.2.1(i).

4.3.2.2 Article 3.2.2.

312. Article 3.2.2 provides an election to substitute in the computation of GloBE Income or Loss the amount of stock-based compensation[95] allowed as a deduction in the computation of a CE's taxable income in place of the amount expensed in its

95. In stock-based compensation, the following terms *inter alia* are crucial:

- Grant date – The date when an entity gives the option to its employee to purchase shares.

financial accounts. In many IF jurisdictions, a corporation is entitled to deduct for tax purposes the value of stock-based compensation that it paid based on the market value of the stock when the option is exercised. For example, a corporation may be able to deduct the present value of the stock option at the time of issuance or over the exercise period and then the difference between the amount originally deducted and the market value when the option is exercised by the holder.

313. Accordingly, at the election of the Filing CE, a CE may substitute the amount allowed as a deduction in the computation of its taxable income in its location for the amount expensed in its financial accounts for a cost or expense of such CE that was paid with stock-based compensation. If the stock-based compensation expense arises in connection with an option that expires without exercise, the CE must include the total amount previously deducted in the computation of its GloBE Income or Loss for the Fiscal Year in which the option expires. The election is a Five-Year Election and must be applied consistently to the stock-based compensation of all CEs located in the same jurisdiction for the year in which the election is made and all subsequent Fiscal Years. If the election is made in a Fiscal Year after some of the stock-based compensation of a transaction has been recorded in the financial accounts, the CE must include in the computation of its GloBE Income or Loss for that Fiscal Year an amount equal to the excess of the cumulative amount allowed as an expense in the computation of its GloBE Income or Loss in previous Fiscal Years over the cumulative amount that would have been allowed as an expense if the election had been in place in those Fiscal Years. If the election is revoked, the CE must include in the computation of its GloBE Income or Loss for the revocation year the amount deducted pursuant to the election that exceeds financial accounting expense accrued in respect of the stock-based compensation that has not been paid.

314. *Financial accounting of stock-based compensation*: For financial accounting purposes, companies generally account for stock-based compensation based on the present value of the stock option at the time of issuance and amortise that amount over the exercise period. The company may adjust its estimate of the amount of the stock-based compensation expense and, thus, the amount taken as an accounting expense based on changes in circumstances during the exercise period. If the market value of the stock increases over the exercise period, the corporation will deduct an amount for tax purposes that is higher than the amount expensed for financial accounting purposes, which is a permanent difference. This disparity between the amount of expense allowed in the computation of financial accounting income and the local tax base would often depress the GloBE ETR, in some cases below the Minimum Rate. The election under Article 3.2.2 brings the GloBE Income or Loss more into line

- Date of vesting – An option is considered to have vested on the date when the employee is allowed to exercise the option to purchase shares, on satisfaction of certain conditions prescribed for exercising the option. The prescribed conditions could be related to performance criteria, completion of certain tenure with the organisation, or attaining specific designation with the organisation.
- Exercise date – The exercise date is when the employee actually uses or exercises his option, i.e., buys the shares.

with the local tax rules in those jurisdictions that allow a deduction based on the value of the stock at the exercise date.

315. *Situation when election is not made*: If the election is not made, the CE simply computes its GloBE Income or Loss, taking into account the amount of stock-based compensation allowed in the computation of its Financial Accounting Net Income or Loss.

316. *Election by the Filing CE only*: The election must be made by the Filing CE. The scope of the election is limited to compensation expenditures in the form of stock, stock options, or stock warrants (or an equivalent), where the amount allowed as an expense is computed differently for local tax purposes than for financial accounting purposes. In principle, the election applies to stock-based compensation for employees and non-employees. However, if the local tax base applies different rules for employees and non-employees, the election will apply differently to stock-based compensation of employees and non-employees in conformity with those local tax rules.

317. *Outcome when an option expires without exercise*: If the election is made in respect of an option that expires without exercise, the CE must treat the amount previously included as an expense in the computation of the GloBE Income or Loss pursuant to the election as additional income under the GloBE Rules. This rule prevents the CE from retaining the benefit of a deduction for an item that will never be paid.

318. *Period of election; election made on jurisdiction basis*: The election is a Five-Year Election and must be applied consistently to the stock-based compensation expense of all CEs located in the same jurisdiction and for the year in respect of which the election is made and all subsequent Fiscal Years, unless and until the election is revoked. The election is essentially made on a jurisdictional basis and thus can be made for some jurisdictions and not for some other jurisdictions. Further, revocation of the election is made on a jurisdictional basis.

319. *Revocation of election*: If an election under Article 3.2.2 is revoked before the end of the exercise period for some or all of the stock-based compensation paid by CEs located in the jurisdiction, those CEs must recapture the excess tax deductions taken in the computation of GloBE Income or Loss up to before the first year to which the revocation applies, but only with respect to stock-based compensation expenses for which an option has not yet been exercised. In other words, revocation of the election only affects stock-based compensation expense for which the final tax deduction has not been determined; it does not affect the amount allowed as a deduction in respect of options that have already been exercised.

320. *Conditions in respect of stock-based compensation expense*: Regardless of whether an election under Article 3.2.2 is made, the entire amount of the stock-based compensation expense is subject to the conditions that:

- The item of expense must be susceptible to being reliably and consistently traced to the CE that received the property, use of property, services, etc., for which the stock-based compensation was provided.

- The election only applies to the CE that incurred the expense and received the property (including use of property) or services for which the stock-based compensation was provided.
- The stock provided does not need to be stock issued by the CE that incurred the relevant expense. However, the expense for stock-based compensation is not allowed to the CE that issued the shares used as compensation unless it received the property, services, etc., for which the compensation was paid. Thus, for example, if a CE provides stock-based compensation to its executives in the form of UPE stock, the CE, not the UPE, deducts the value of the stock.
- Only one CE is allowed to deduct stock-based compensation in excess of the amount allowed in the financial accounts, and only if that CE is allowed a deduction for such stock-based compensation for local tax purposes. Thus, if the accounting expense needs to be moved from the entity whose shares are used as compensation to the entity that incurred the expense, the expense of the entity that issued the shares and the reimbursements from the entity that incurred the expense should be in equal amounts based on the amount of the stock-based compensation expense allowed in the CFS.

4.3.2.3 Article 3.2.3.

321. Any transaction between CEs located in different jurisdictions that is not recorded in the same amount in the financial accounts of both CEs or that is not consistent with the ALP must be adjusted so as to be in the same amount and consistent with the ALP. A loss from a sale or other transfer of an asset between two CEs located in the same jurisdiction that is not recorded consistent with the ALP shall be re-computed based on the ALP if that loss is included in the computation of GloBE Income or Loss. Rules for allocating income or loss between a Main Entity and its PEs are found in Article 3.4. Thus, Article 3.2.3 requires transactions between Group Entities to be priced consistently with the ALP and recorded at the same price for GloBE purposes for all CEs that are parties to the transaction.

322. The term ALP mentioned above is defined in Article 10.1 as below:

> Arm's Length Principle means the principle under which transactions between Constituent Entities must be recorded by reference to the conditions that would have been obtained between independent enterprises in comparable transactions and under comparable circumstances.

(a) Cross-border (international) transactions

323. *No case for adjustment under Article 3.2.3 when cross-border transactions between Group Entities are at ALP*: CEs of an MNE Group typically maintain a transfer pricing policy based on the ALP, and this standard is used to determine the transfer price that is reflected in their financial accounts and in computing the local taxable income. Therefore, it is generally expected that CEs' financial accounts will reflect transactions between Group Entities based on the ALP and at the same price. The MNE Group and the tax administrations examining the tax returns of CEs engaged in the controlled transactions are in the best place to assess compliance with the ALP. Where the MNE Group has used the transfer price reflected in its financial accounts to compute local taxable income and the relevant tax authorities do not require a transfer pricing adjustment, this price should be used in the computation of GloBE Income or Loss. In these circumstances, the MNE Group should not make an adjustment under Article 3.2.3.

324. *Adjustment in cross-border transfer price while computing GloBE Income in pursuance of concurrence between relevant tax authorities:* Where all of the relevant tax authorities agree that a transfer price must be adjusted to the same price in order to reflect the ALP, the counterparties shall adjust their GloBE Income or Loss based on that price for purposes of computing GloBE Income or Loss. For example, such an instance would arise where a Bilateral Advance Pricing Agreement (BAPA) is agreed upon by the competent authorities of all counterparty jurisdictions concerned. The adjustments to the GloBE Income or Loss must be applied consistently for GloBE purposes across all counterparties in line with the ALP agreed under the BAPA. If, in connection with an audit of counterparties' tax returns, the relevant tax authorities agree that a transfer price must be adjusted to the same price, each CE concerned must adjust its GloBE Income or Loss. The adjustment to each counterparty's transfer price is taken into account in the computation of its GloBE Income or Loss pursuant to Article 4.6.1.

325. *Adjustments may be made to prevent double taxation or double non-taxation*: In some cases, the transfer price used in the financial accounts of the counterparties may differ from the transfer price used to compute a counterparty's taxable income but not the transfer price used to compute another counterparty's taxable income in another jurisdiction. These differences may arise where:

(a) a Unilateral Advance Pricing Agreement (UAPA) has been agreed upon;
(b) a CE files a tax return under a self-assessment system that includes (suo moto) book-to-tax adjustments in order to comply with domestic transfer pricing rules; or
(c) a tax authority challenges and adjusts the transfer price used in the local tax return of one of the CEs.

When these differences arise, the transfer price used for taxable income purposes is presumed to be consistent with the ALP. The GloBE Income or Loss should be adjusted accordingly under Article 3.2.3, where necessary, to prevent double taxation or double non-taxation under the GloBE Rules. Specifically, a unilateral transfer pricing adjustment will result in a corresponding adjustment to the GloBE Income or Loss of all counterparties under Article 3.2.3 unless the transfer pricing adjustment increases or decreases the MNE Group's taxable income in a jurisdiction that has a nominal tax rate below the Minimum Rate, or that was a Low-Tax Jurisdiction with respect to the MNE Group in each of the two Fiscal Years preceding the unilateral transfer pricing adjustment (an undertaxed jurisdiction). This rule results in adjustments where necessary to prevent double taxation or double non-taxation. For example, a local transfer pricing adjustment that increases the taxable income in a high-tax jurisdiction results in a corresponding adjustment under Article 3.2.3, where that adjustment is necessary to ensure a corresponding decrease to the GloBE Income of the relevant counterparties in an undertaxed jurisdiction. Without this adjustment, the income included in the high-tax jurisdiction under local law would be subject to double taxation – once in the high-tax jurisdiction and again under the GloBE Rules. Similarly, if an adjustment decreases the taxable income in a high-tax jurisdiction, corresponding adjustments to the GloBE Income or Loss of all counterparties will ensure that the GloBE Income of counterparties in undertaxed jurisdictions is increased by a corresponding amount and exposed to Top-up Tax under the GloBE Rules. Without this adjustment, the income excluded from the high-tax jurisdiction taxable income would benefit from double non-taxation, as it would not be subject to tax in the high-tax jurisdiction or under the GloBE Rules.

326. *Adjustments may not be made when such actions give rise to double taxation or double non-taxation:* Adjustments will not be made under this rule when such adjustments would give rise to double taxation or double non-taxation under the GloBE Rules. For example, a unilateral transfer pricing adjustment that reduces taxable income in a jurisdiction that has a nominal tax rate above the Minimum Rate but that had an ETR below the Minimum Rate in the previous two years should not be reflected in the GloBE Income or Loss because if the counterparties are located in a high-tax jurisdiction, such adjustment will produce double non-taxation under the GloBE Rules (i.e., the adjusted income is not subject to tax in either jurisdiction and is not exposed to Top-up Tax under the GloBE Rules). Finally, a unilateral transfer pricing adjustment that increases taxable income in an undertaxed jurisdiction should not be reflected in the GloBE Income because such adjustment would produce double taxation under the GloBE Rules (i.e., the adjustment would expose the income to top-up tax in the jurisdiction in which the unilateral adjustment is made and the income is already subject to local tax in the other jurisdiction and/or top-up tax if the other jurisdiction is an undertaxed jurisdiction).

327. Illustration # 28: This example illustrates, through a flow-chart, ALP determination for cross-border transactions under Article 3.2.3.

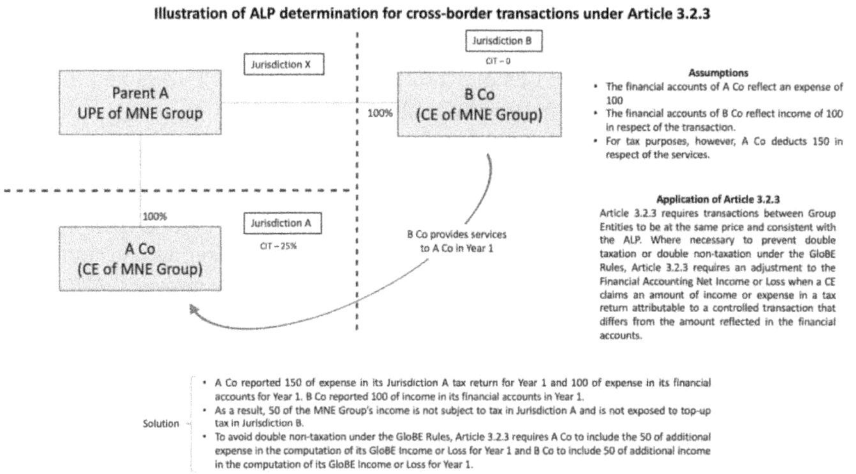

328. Illustration # 29: This example illustrates, through a flow-chart, ALP determination for cross-border transactions under Article 3.2.3 in pursuance of UAPA.

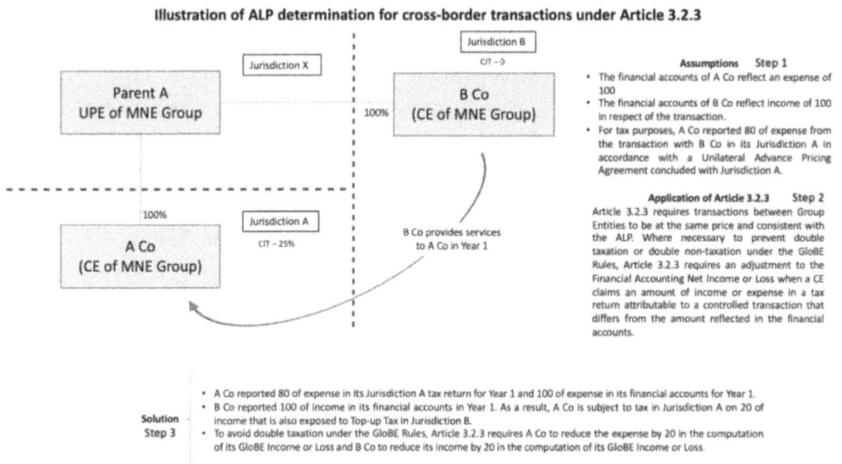

(b) Same-country (domestic) transactions

329. Transactions between CEs located in the same jurisdiction generally are not required to be adjusted, for tax purposes, from the amounts used in preparation of the CFS. This is because the shifting of income from one taxpayer to another within the same jurisdiction will generally not impact the overall amount of income subject to tax in that jurisdiction. These same-country transactions may already be eliminated or otherwise adjusted for local tax purposes pursuant to a consolidation or group tax relief regime. For GloBE purposes, additional adjustments to conform with the ALP in respect of wholly domestic transactions should not generally be required because the effect of these transactions will generally be eliminated under the jurisdictional blending rules of Chapter 5. Furthermore, the CEs may not be applying the ALP to same-jurisdiction transactions in a jurisdiction that does not impose a Covered Tax.

330. *ALP requirement for same-country (domestic) transactions essential to prevent deliberate manufacturing of losses*: At the same time, Article 3.2.3 does require the application of the ALP to transactions between CEs in the same jurisdiction if the sale or other transfer of an asset produces a loss and that loss is taken into account in the computation of GloBE Income or Loss. This rule is intended to prevent MNE Groups from manufacturing losses in a jurisdiction through sales or other transfers between Group members at prices that are not consistent with the ALP. The rule does not apply if the loss is excluded from the CE's GloBE Income or Loss computation. Thus, if the MNE Group has in place an election under Article 3.2.8 to apply consolidated accounting in the jurisdiction in which the loss arises, the loss will be eliminated in consolidation and excluded from the computation of the CE's GloBE Income or Loss.

331. *Transactions between Minority-Owned CEs and other CEs, as well as, Investment Entities and other CEs must also be recorded in accordance with the ALP:* Transactions between Minority-Owned CEs and other CEs must also be recorded in accordance with the ALP. This is necessary because Minority-Owned CEs are not included in the ETR and top-up tax computations for the jurisdiction under Articles 5.1 and 5.2 but instead compute their ETR and top-up tax separately pursuant to Article 5.6. Thus, the income and expense of the parties to the transaction will not be eliminated in the jurisdictional blending computation, and failure to reflect transactions based on the ALP would distort the ETR and top-up tax calculations for the jurisdiction and the Minority-Owned CEs. Similarly, transactions between Investment Entities and other CEs located in the same jurisdiction must also be recorded in accordance with the ALP.

332. *Transactions between CEs in the same jurisdiction must be recorded in the same amount in both CEs*: Although not explicitly stated in Article 3.2.3, transactions between CEs in the same jurisdiction must also be recorded in the same amount in both CEs. This is the expected result of applying a common accounting standard to CEs in the same jurisdiction. The principle applies, however, in all cases to prevent the exclusion of income from, or duplication of expenses in, the GloBE Income or Loss computation.

4.3.2.4 Article 3.2.4.

333. Qualified Refundable Tax Credits shall be treated as income in the computation of GloBE Income or Loss of a CE, whereas, Non-Qualified Refundable Tax Credits shall not be treated as income in the computation of GloBE Income or Loss of a CE.

334. The term Qualified Refundable Tax Credit mentioned above is defined in Article 10.1 as below:

> Qualified Refundable Tax Credit means a refundable tax credit designed in a way such that it must be paid as cash or available as cash equivalents within four years from when a Constituent Entity satisfies the conditions for receiving the credit under the laws of the jurisdiction granting the credit. A tax credit that is refundable in part is a Qualified Refundable Tax Credit to the extent it must be paid as cash or available as cash equivalents within four years from when a Constituent Entity satisfies the conditions for receiving the credit under the laws of the jurisdiction granting the credit. A Qualified Refundable Tax Credit does not include any amount of tax creditable or refundable pursuant to a Qualified Imputation Tax or a Disqualified Refundable Imputation Tax.

335. The term Non-Qualified Refundable Tax Credits mentioned above is defined in Article 10.1 as below:

> Non-Qualified Refundable Tax Credit means a tax credit that is not a Qualified Refundable Tax Credit but that is refundable in whole or in part.

336. The term Qualified Imputation Tax mentioned above is defined in Article 10.1 as below:

> Qualified Imputation Tax means a Covered Tax accrued or paid by a Constituent Entity that is refundable or creditable to the beneficial owner of a dividend distributed by such Constituent Entity (or, in the case of a Covered Tax accrued or paid by a Permanent Establishment, a dividend distributed by the Main Entity) to the extent that the refund is payable, or the credit is provided:
>
> (a) by a jurisdiction other than the jurisdiction which imposed the Covered Taxes under a foreign tax credit regime;
> (b) to a beneficial owner of the dividend that is subject to tax at a nominal rate that equals or exceeds the Minimum Rate on the dividend on a current basis under the domestic law of the jurisdiction which imposed the Covered Taxes on the Constituent Entity;
> (c) to an individual beneficial owner of the dividend who is tax resident in the jurisdiction which imposed the Covered Taxes on the Constituent Entity and who is subject to tax on the dividends as ordinary income; or
> (d) to a Governmental Entity, an International Organisation, a resident Non-profit Organisation, a resident Pension Fund, a resident Investment Entity that is not a Group Entity, or a resident life insurance company to the extent that the dividends are received in connection with a pension fund business and subject to tax in a similar manner as a dividend received by Pension Fund.
>
> For purposes of paragraph (d), a Non-Profit Organisation or Pension Fund is resident in a jurisdiction if it is created and managed in that jurisdiction, and an Investment Entity is resident in a jurisdiction if it is created and regulated in the jurisdiction. A life insurance company is resident in the jurisdiction in which it is located.

337. *Purpose of refundable tax credits*: The refundable tax credits are government incentives delivered via the tax system to engage in certain activities, such as research and development, whereby the government allows the company to offset its taxes for engaging in specified activities or incurring specified expenditures or the government will refund the amount of the unused credit if the company doesn't have any tax liability. In this way, the government effectively pays for the activity or expenditure in a similar manner to a grant. The basic idea is that the incentive or grant is delivered by a tax reduction to the extent possible.

338. The treatment of Qualified Refundable Tax Credit is explained in Figure 4.8.

Figure 4.8 Treatment of Qualified Refundable Tax Credit

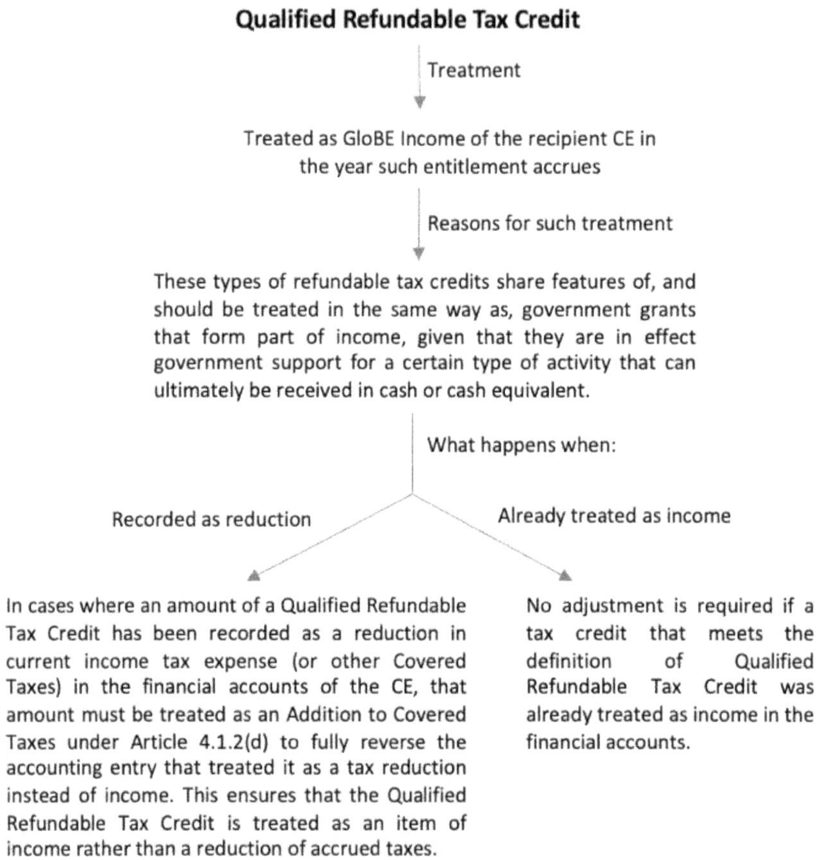

339. Likewise, a Non-Qualified Refundable Tax Credit that was treated as income in the financial accounts must be deducted in full from the measure of net income in the financial statements, and there must be a corresponding reduction of Adjusted Covered Taxes under Article 4.1.3(b).

340. Where the tax credit regime under the laws of a jurisdiction provides for partial refundability, such that only a fixed percentage or portion of the credit is refundable, these rules apply separately and correspondingly to the refundable part and the non-refundable part of the tax credit.

4.3.2.5 Article 3.2.5.

341. Article 3.2.5 provides an election to use the realisation method for assets and liabilities that are accounted for in the CE's financial accounts using the fair value method or impairment accounting. The election generally applies with respect to all assets and liabilities of all CEs in a jurisdiction and may be made with respect to those assets or liabilities after the year in which the asset was acquired. However, the election can be limited to tangible assets of such CEs or to assets and liabilities of such CEs that are Investment Entities. An election under Article 3.2.5 is a Five-Year Election. It cannot be revoked within five Fiscal Years after an Election Year, and another election cannot be made within five Fiscal Years after a revocation year. In the year an election under this article is revoked, the GloBE Income or Loss is adjusted by the difference between the fair value of the asset or liability at the beginning of the year and the carrying value of the asset or liability determined pursuant to the election. This adjustment recaptures the net fair value gain or loss that arose during the pendency of the Article 3.2.5 election.

342. The said article states that with respect to assets and liabilities that are subject to fair value or impairment accounting in the CFS, a Filing Constituent Entity may elect to determine gains and losses using the realisation principle for purposes of computing GloBE Income. The election is a Five-Year Election and applies to all CEs located in the jurisdiction to which the election applies. The election applies to all assets and liabilities of such CEs unless the Filing Constituent Entity chooses to limit the election to tangible assets of such Constituent Entities or to Constituent Entities that are Investment Entities. Under this election:

(a) all gains or losses attributable to fair value or impairment accounting with respect to an asset or liability shall be excluded from the computation of GloBE Income or Loss;
(b) the carrying value of an asset or liability for purposes of determining gain or loss shall be its carrying value at the later of:
  (i) the first day of the election year, or
  (ii) the date the asset was acquired or liability was incurred; and
(c) if the election is revoked, the GloBE Income or Loss of the Constituent Entities is adjusted by the difference at the beginning of the revocation year between the fair value of the asset or liability and the carrying value of the asset or liability determined pursuant to the election.

343. *CE to exclude fair value or impairment gain or loss in respect of assets or liabilities and must include gain or loss determined under the realisation method from the computation of GloBE Income or Loss:* Under the election, gain or loss associated with an asset or liability will arise when the asset is disposed of rather than as its value changes due to changes in market value or impairments. The carrying value of such asset or liability for purposes of determining gain or loss shall be the carrying value of that asset or liability at the later of the time the asset was acquired, or liability was incurred or the beginning of the year for which the election is made. Accordingly, under Article 3.2.5, a CE must exclude fair value or impairment gain or loss in respect of assets or liabilities subject to the election from the computation of GloBE Income or Loss and must include gain or loss determined under the realisation method.

344. *Policy justification for this treatment is to reduce volatility*: The policy justification for this treatment is to reduce volatility by allowing the taxpayer to crystallise the gain for GloBE purposes as of the actual date of disposition rather than from one period to the next, in line with the accounting treatment. For example, if a CE holds convertible debt in a start-up company and the company performs poorly in its first few years, the CE may be required, under the applicable accounting standard, to recognise a fair value loss on the investment. If the start-up is eventually acquired by an unrelated purchaser and the CE disposes of the convertible debt for its original acquisition cost, the 'gain' reported upon sale is not really an economic gain but could be subject to a top-up tax if there are no related Covered Taxes paid in respect of the gain in that year. An election under Article 3.2.5 prevents this result by permitting the CE to determine the gain upon sale based on the original cost of the asset.

4.3.2.6 Article 3.2.6.

345. Where there is Aggregate Asset Gain in a jurisdiction in a Fiscal Year, the Filing Constituent Entity may make, under this article 3.2.6, an Annual Election for that jurisdiction to adjust GloBE Income or Loss with respect to each previous Fiscal Year in the Look-back Period in the manner described in paragraphs (b) and (c) and to spread any remaining Adjusted Asset Gain over the Look-back Period in the manner described in paragraph (d). The ETR and Top-up Tax, if any, for any previous Fiscal Year must be recalculated under Article 5.4.1. When an election is made under this article:

(a) Covered Taxes with respect to any Net Asset Gain or Net Asset Loss in the Election Year shall be excluded from the computation of Adjusted Covered Taxes.
(b) The Aggregate Asset Gain in the Election Year shall be carried back to the earliest Loss Year and set off ratably against any Net Asset Loss of any Constituent Entity located in that jurisdiction.
(c) If, for any Loss Year, the Adjusted Asset Gain exceeds the total amount of Net Asset Loss of all Constituent Entities located in that jurisdiction, the Adjusted Asset Gain shall be carried forward to the following Loss Year (if any) and applied ratably against any Net Asset Loss of any Constituent Entity located in that jurisdiction.
(d) Any Adjusted Asset Gain that remains after the application of paragraphs (b) and (c) shall be allocated evenly to each Fiscal Year in the Look-back Period. The Allocated Asset Gain for the relevant year shall be included in the computation of GloBE Income or Loss for a Constituent Entity located in that jurisdiction in that year in accordance with the following formula:

$$\text{Allocated Asset Gain for relevant year} \times \frac{\text{The specified CE's Net Asset Gain in the Election Year}}{\text{The Net Asset Gain of all specified CE's in the Election Year}}$$

For the purposes of the above formula, a specified Constituent Entity is a Constituent Entity that has Net Asset Gain in the Election Year and was located in the jurisdiction in the relevant year. If there is no specified Constituent Entity for a relevant year, the Adjusted Asset Gain allocated to that year will be allocated equally to each Constituent Entity in the jurisdiction in that year.

346. The term Aggregate Asset Gain mentioned above is defined in Article 10.1 as below:

> Aggregate Asset Gain in respect of an election under Article 3.2.6, means the net gain in the Election Year from the disposition of Local Tangible Assets by all Constituent Entities located in the jurisdiction excluding the gain or loss on a transfer of assets between Group Members.

347. The term Annual Election mentioned above is defined in Article 10.1 as below:

> Annual Election means an election made by a Filing Constituent Entity and that applies only for the Fiscal Year for which the election is made.

348. The term Look-back Period mentioned above is defined in Article 10.1 as below:

> Look-back Period in respect of an election under Article 3.2.6, means the Election Year and the four prior Fiscal Years.

349. The term Adjusted Asset Gain mentioned above is defined in Article 10.1 as below:

> Adjusted Asset Gain in respect of Aggregate Asset Gain that is subject to an election under Article 3.2.6 means an amount equal to the Aggregate Asset Gain in the Election Year, reduced by any amount of such gain that has been applied against the Net Asset Loss in a prior Loss Year under Article 3.2.6 (b) or (c).

350. The term Election Year mentioned above is defined in Article 10.1 as below:

> Election Year in respect of an Annual Election means the year for which the election is made.

351. The term Net Asset Gain mentioned above is defined in Article 10.1 as below:

> Net Asset Gain in respect of an election under Article 3.2.6, means the net gain from the disposition of Local Tangible Assets by a Constituent Entity located in the jurisdiction for which the election was made excluding the gain or loss on a transfer of assets to another Group Member.

352. The term Net Asset Loss mentioned above is defined in Article 10.1 as below:

> Net Asset Loss in respect of a Constituent Entity and a Fiscal Year, means the net loss from the disposition of Local Tangible Assets by that Constituent Entity in that year excluding the gain or loss on a transfer of assets to another Group Member. The amount of Net Asset Loss shall be reduced by the amount of Net Asset Gain or Adjusted Asset Gain which is set off against such loss pursuant to the application of Article 3.2.6(b) or (c) as a result of a previous election made under Article 3.2.6.

353. The term Local Tangible Asset mentioned above is defined in Article 10.1 as below:

> Local Tangible Asset means immovable property located in the same jurisdiction as the Constituent Entity.

354. The term Loss Year mentioned above is defined in Article 10.1 as below:

> Loss Year in respect of jurisdiction for which the Filing Constituent Entity has made an election under Article 3.2.6, means a Fiscal Year in the Look-back Period for which there is a Net Asset Loss for a Constituent Entity located in that jurisdiction and the total amount of Net Asset Loss of all such Constituent Entities exceeds the total amount of their Net Asset Gain.

355. The term Allocated Asset Gain mentioned above is defined in Article 10.1 as below:

> Allocated Asset Gain in respect of an election under Article 3.2.6, means the Adjusted Asset Gain that is allocated to a Fiscal Year in the Look-back Period under Article 3.2.6(d).

356. *Objective is to mitigate the effect of recognising the entire gain in a single year on the MNE Group's jurisdictional ETR computation:* Article 3.2.6 provides an election that permits an MNE Group to spread the effect of gains and losses from the sale of Local Tangible Assets over a period of up to five years to mitigate the effect of recognising the entire gain in a single year on the MNE Group's jurisdictional ETR computation and to match the timing of gains and losses on Local Tangible Assets. The policy justification for this election is that the increase in value of the asset likely accumulated over a period of years and spreading the gain over that period, up to a maximum of five years, and matching it with losses from similar property provides a better measure of whether the MNE Group has been subject to a minimum level of tax in the jurisdiction over that period.

357. *The election is an Annual Election made on a jurisdictional basis*: The election applies only with respect to gains and losses attributable to disposition of Local Tangible Assets. This limitation ensures that relief provided under this section cannot be used to shelter gain on mobile assets. However, the election may be combined with an election under Article 3.2.5 in respect of tangible assets. In that case, fair value gains or losses and impairment adjustments associated with the asset during the pendency of the Article 3.2.5 election will have been excluded from the computation of GloBE Income or Loss, and the carrying value for determining gain or loss will not be adjusted for fair value changes or impairments. The election does not apply to sales between Group Entities because the spread period includes all years in which CEs held the property.

358. The process of Election to spread capital gains over five years is encapsulated in Figure 4.9.

Figure 4.9 Process of Election to Spread Capital Gains over Five Years

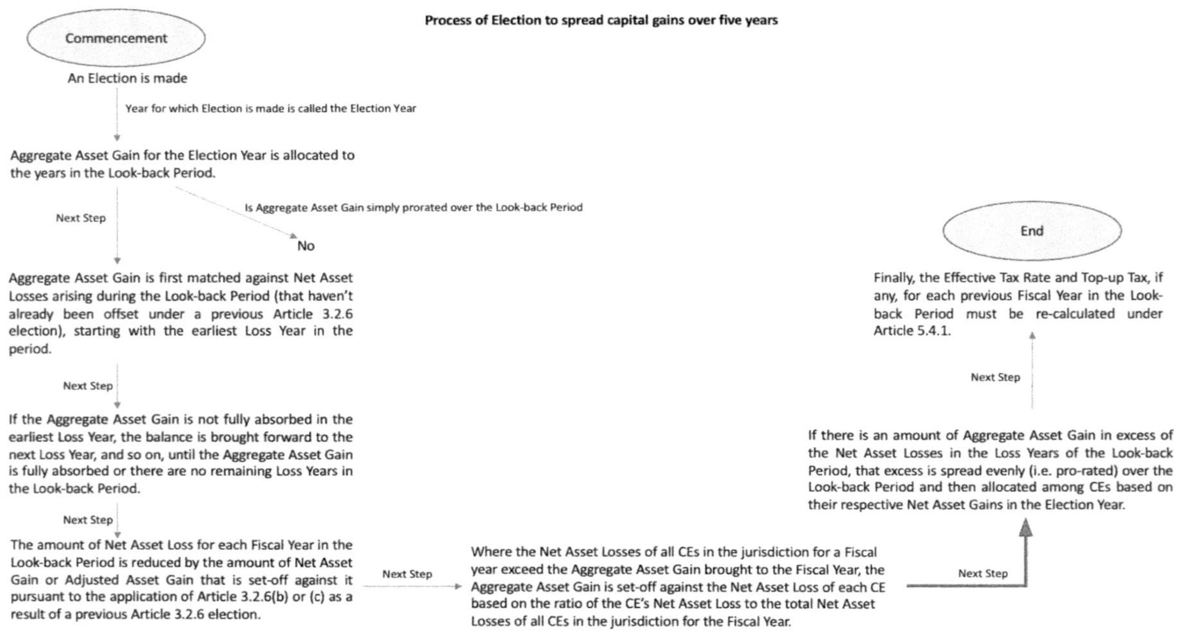

359. *Covered Taxes arising in the Election Year, if any, with respect to Net Asset Gains or Losses are excluded from Adjusted Covered Taxes:* When the election is made, any Covered Taxes (including deferred tax assets) with respect to any Net Asset Gain or Net Asset Loss in the Election Year must be determined based on the facts and circumstances and excluded from the computation of Adjusted Covered Taxes. In many cases, when the election is made, it is being made because there are no Covered Taxes attributable to Net Asset Gains or Net Asset Loss on Local Tangible Assets. To the extent the election is not made and there are Covered Taxes attributable to Net Asset Gains or Net Asset Loss on Local Tangible Assets, such Covered Taxes remain in the ETR computation. Determining the amount of Covered Taxes to apportion to each year would be unduly cumbersome, and the allowance of a carry-back tailored to match losses in prior years is a substantial benefit. Therefore, the Covered Taxes arising in the Election Year, if any, with respect to Net Asset Gains or Losses are excluded from Adjusted Covered Taxes.

360. *Top-up Tax of previous Fiscal Years to be re-computed under certain conditions:* To the extent a GloBE Loss was generated in previous Fiscal Years, such GloBE Loss must be recalculated after the application of this article. To the extent a GloBE Loss is reduced as a result of the operation of this article and such loss had been used in a Fiscal Year, the Top-up Tax for such Fiscal Year must also be re-computed in line with the principles of Articles 4.6 and 5.4.

361. Illustration # 30: This example illustrates, through a flow-chart, the process of Election to Spread Capital Gains Over Five Years.

Illustration of the Process of Election to Spread Capital Gains Over Five Years under Article 3.2.6

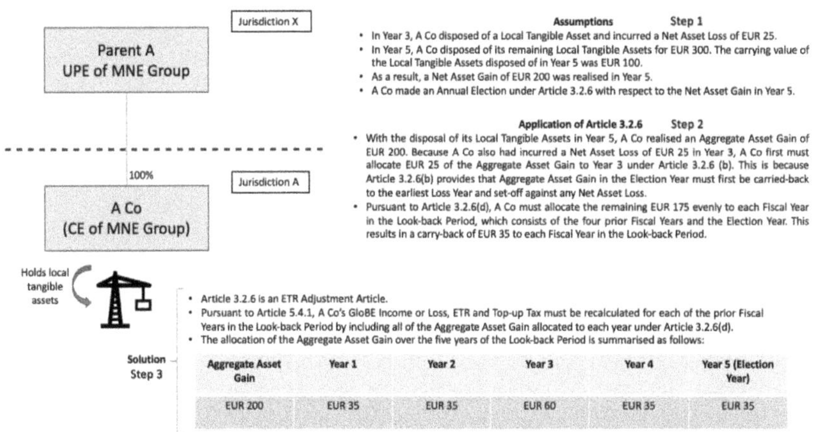

4.3.2.7 Article 3.2.7.

362. The computation of a Low-Tax Entity's GloBE Income or Loss shall exclude any expense attributable to an Intragroup Financing Arrangement that can reasonably be anticipated over the expected duration of the arrangement to:

(a) increase the amount of expenses taken into account in calculating the GloBE Income or Loss of the Low-Tax Entity;
(b) without resulting in a commensurate increase in the taxable income of the High-Tax Counterparty.

363. The term Intragroup Financing Arrangement mentioned above is defined in Article 10.1 as below:

> Intragroup Financing Arrangement means any arrangement entered into between two or more members of the MNE Group whereby a High-Tax Counterparty directly or indirectly provides credit or otherwise makes an investment in a Low-Tax Entity.

364. The term Low-Tax Entity mentioned above is defined in Article 10.1 as below:

> Low-Tax Entity means a Constituent Entity located in a Low-Tax Jurisdiction or a jurisdiction that would be a Low-Tax Jurisdiction if the Effective Tax Rate for the jurisdiction were determined without regard to any income or expense accrued by that Entity in respect of an Intragroup Financing Arrangement.

365. The term High-Tax Counterparty mentioned above is defined in Article 10.1 as below:

> High-Tax Counterparty means a Constituent Entity that is located in a jurisdiction that is not a Low-Tax Jurisdiction or that is located in a jurisdiction that would not be a Low-Tax Jurisdiction if its ETR were determined without regard to any income or expense accrued by that Entity in respect of an Intragroup Financing Arrangement.

366. *Purpose of this rule is to prevent MNE Groups from engaging in transactions that are intended to increase the ETR in a jurisdiction that is below the Minimum Rate:* Article 3.2.7 provides a rule with respect to Intragroup Financing Arrangements that increase the amount of expenses taken into account in computing the GloBE Income or Loss of a Low-Tax Entity and do not result in a corresponding increase to the taxable income of the High-Tax Counterparty to such arrangement. This rule prevents MNE Groups from engaging in transactions that are intended to increase the ETR in a jurisdiction that is below the Minimum Rate by reducing the GloBE Income or Loss in such jurisdiction without increasing the taxable income of the counterparty to the arrangement. A payment should not be treated as increasing the taxable income of a High-Tax Counterparty if it is eligible for an exclusion, exemption, deduction or credit or other tax benefits under local law, and the amount of that benefit is calculated by reference to the amount of payment received. For example, assume that Jurisdiction A has introduced an interest limitation rule that limits a taxpayer's net interest deduction to a percentage of its earnings. The amount of interest expense denied under this interest limitation rule constitutes excess interest capacity that is eligible to be carried forward and set off against interest income in a subsequent year. For example, a High-Tax Counterparty located in Jurisdiction A lends money to a Low-Tax Entity. At the time the loan is entered into, the High-Tax Counterparty has excess interest capacity from previous years that is not expected to be used over the expected term of the loan. In this case, the receipt of interest from the Low-Tax Entity under the loan will not be treated as giving rise to an increase in taxable income to the extent the High-Tax Counterparty can immediately set off such interest income against the carry-forward of excess interest capacity.

367. *Process of determination of an arrangement in place is an objective test:* The term arrangement includes an agreement, plan or understanding (whether enforceable or not) and includes all the steps and transactions that give effect to that arrangement. Whether there is an arrangement in place is an objective test to be inferred from the actual transactions that took place and the information available to those involved in the arrangement. A series of transactions will be treated as part of an Intragroup Financing Arrangement where an objective observer would reasonably conclude that they were part of a plan or arrangement to allow a High-Tax Counterparty to provide credit or make a direct or indirect investment in a Low-Tax Entity. The test is an objective one, based on an assessment of the actual transactions that took place in light of the overall outcomes achieved. A step or transaction can form part of an arrangement even though the details may not be known to all the parties to the arrangement. For example, a member of the MNE Group may act as an intermediary by borrowing money from a High-Tax Counterparty and then on-lending it to a Low-Tax Entity within the same group. In this case, the back-to-back loans could be considered part of an arrangement whereby a High-Tax Counterparty has indirectly provided credit to a Low-Tax Entity. Although the High-Tax Counterparty did not know the ultimate destination of the funds, it would be sufficient that the intermediary borrowed the funds with the specific purpose of on-lending them to the Low-Tax Entity. If the Intermediary operates, however, as a treasury or financing centre for the group that manages the group's working capital requirements, the money borrowed from the High-Tax Counterparty may, on an objective assessment, be considered entirely separate from and independent of the loan made to the Low-Tax Entity such that these loans are not considered part of an Intragroup Financing Arrangement.

368. Illustration # 31: This example illustrates, through a flow-chart, Special Rule for Intragroup Financing Arrangement.

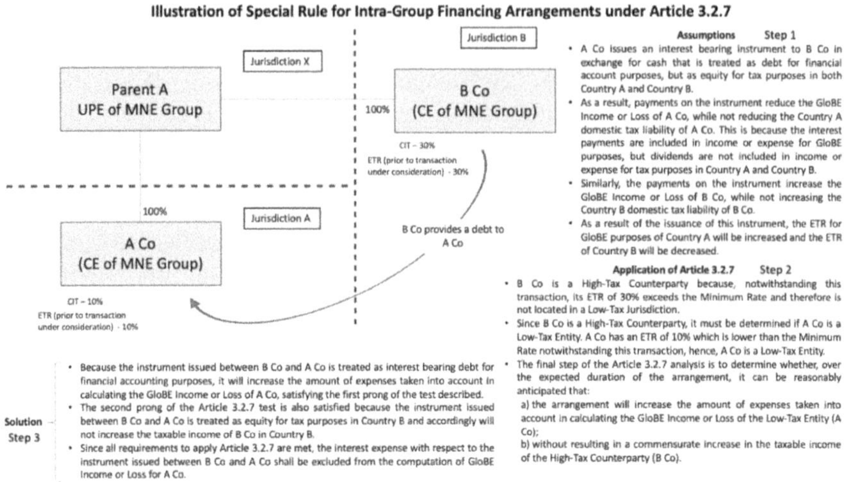

369. Illustration # 32: This example illustrates, through a flow-chart, Special Rule for Intragroup Financing Arrangement and use of tax attributes that would not otherwise be used to increase the ETR of a Low-Tax Entity.

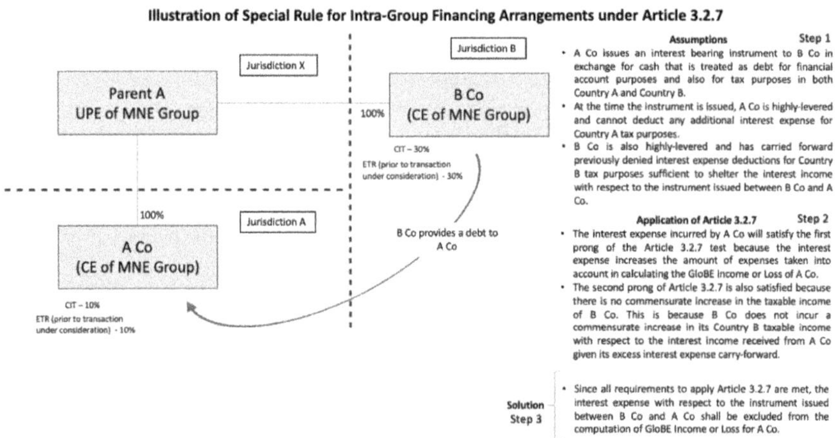

4.3.2.8 Article 3.2.8.

370. A UPE may elect to apply its consolidated accounting treatment to eliminate income, expense, gains, and losses from transactions between CEs that are located and included in a tax consolidation group, in the same jurisdiction for purposes of computing each such CE's Net GloBE Income or Loss. The election under this article is a Five-Year Election. Upon making or revoking such election, appropriate adjustments shall be made for GloBE purposes such that there shall not be duplications or omissions of items of GloBE Income or Loss as a result of having made or revoked the election.

371. *Purpose of election*: If this election is made, income, expenses, gains and losses resulting from transactions between the CEs may be eliminated from the computation of GloBE Income or Loss in the same manner as amounts relating to transactions among members of a consolidated group are eliminated as part of the consolidation adjustments under the Acceptable Financial Accounting Standard used by the UPE in preparing its CFS. This is intended to prevent unintended consequences where income, expense, gains and losses from domestic intragroup transactions are treated as tax-neutral intragroup transactions under local law. The consolidated accounting should neither eliminate the MNE Group's economic income from transactions with third parties nor result in the carrying value of any assets being adjusted to include purchase accounting adjustments held in consolidation. Assets will continue to be held at their original carrying values, and the full economic gain or loss accruing during the MNE Group's ownership of those assets should be brought into account when they are sold outside of the tax consolidated group or outside of that jurisdiction.

372. *The election applies to transactions between CEs located in the same jurisdiction*: The election is limited to transactions between CEs (other than Investment Entities, Minority-Owned CEs, and JVs treated as CEs under Article 6.4) located in the same jurisdiction. Transactions between CEs located in different jurisdictions would continue to be treated in the same manner as transactions with a third party and would not benefit from the netting or income deferral that results from the election. If the manufacturing CE sells its finished product to a resale CE located in another jurisdiction, the manufacturing CE would be required to recognise the MNE Group's profit on that intragroup sale (taking into account the ALP) as if it were a sale to a third-party customer. The MNE Group may prefer an election over the burden of determining arm's length prices for transactions between CEs in the same jurisdiction, particularly in cases where the CEs may not be applying an arm's length standard to same-jurisdiction transactions in a jurisdiction that does not impose a Covered Tax.

4.3.2.9 Article 3.2.9.

373. An insurance company shall exclude from the computation of GloBE Income or Loss amounts charged to policyholders for Taxes paid by the insurance company in respect of returns to the policyholders. An insurance company shall include in the computation of GloBE Income or Loss any returns to policyholders that are not reflected in Financial Accounting Net Income or Loss to the extent the corresponding increase or decrease in liability to the policyholders is reflected in its Financial Accounting Net Income or Loss.

374. The charge of tax (or reduction in policyholder liabilities equivalent to policyholder tax) is excluded from the computation of GloBE Income or Loss under Article 3.2.9, and any taxes arising on the policyholder returns are excluded from the definition of Covered Taxes pursuant to Article 4.2.2(e).

4.3.2.10 Article 3.2.10.

375. Amounts recognised as a decrease to the equity of a CE attributable to distributions paid or payable in respect of Additional Tier One Capital issued by the CE shall be treated as an expense in the computation of its GloBE Income or Loss. Amounts recognised as an increase to the equity of a CE attributable to distributions received or receivable in respect of Additional Tier One Capital held by the CE shall be included in the computation of its GloBE Income or Loss.

376. The term Additional Tier One Capital is defined in Article 10.1 as below:

> Additional Tier One Capital means an instrument issued by a Constituent Entity pursuant to prudential regulatory requirements applicable to the banking sector that is convertible to equity or written down if a pre-specified trigger event occurs and that has other features which are designed to aid loss absorbency in the event of a financial crisis.

377. Additional Tier One Capital is generally treated as equity for financial accounting purposes. However, it is treated as debt for tax purposes in some IF jurisdictions. Thus, for many CEs, payments in respect of Additional Tier One Capital are deductible as interest expense by the issuer and includible as interest income of the holder for tax purposes. This represents a permanent difference between financial accounting and taxable income that is both common and material. Accordingly, Article 3.2.10 provides that increases or decreases to the equity of a CE attributable to distributions in respect of Additional Tier One Capital shall be treated as income or expense in the computation of its GloBE Income or Loss. Equity adjustments attributable to the issuance or redemption of Additional Tier One Capital are not included in the computation of GloBE Income or Loss.

378. Article 3.2.7 does not apply to deny a deduction for distributions treated as an expense pursuant to Article 3.2.10.

4.3.2.11 Article 3.2.11.

379. Article 3.2.11 requires adjustments to a CE's Financial Accounting Net Income or Loss where necessary to reflect the requirements of Chapters 6 and 7. For example, if a CE is required to use the historical carrying value of an asset pursuant to Article 6.2 and it used the fair value of that asset to compute its depreciation expense for the Fiscal Year, it must adjust the depreciation expense to the amount that would have been computed using the historical carrying value of the asset.

4.3.3 Article 3.3. (International Shipping Income Exclusion)

380. Article 3.3 provides a specific exclusion for International Shipping Income and Qualified Ancillary International Shipping Income from the scope of the GloBE Rules.

381. Prominent features of Article 3.3 are provided in Box 14.

Box 4.14 Prominent Features of Article 3.3

- Provides for a specific exclusion for International Shipping Income and Qualified Ancillary International Shipping Income from the scope of the GloBE Rules.
- Provides that where the computation of a CE's International Shipping Income and Qualified Ancillary International Shipping Income results in a loss, the loss shall be excluded from the computation of its GloBE Income or Loss.
- Reasons for keeping shipping industry outside the scope of the GloBE Rules include industry-specific tax rules, as the widespread availability of alternative tax regimes for the shipping industry means that international shipping often operates outside the scope of CIT.
- Provides that the mechanism of operation of Article 3.3 involves adopting a qualified income approach based on the scope of Article 8 of the OECD MTC 2017 and excludes from the scope of the GloBE Rules the profits from transportation of passengers or cargo by ships in international traffic.
- Provides that to an extent, an adjustment required by Article 3.3 excludes an amount of income from the GloBE Income or Loss computation; any Covered Taxes associated with that income must also be excluded from Adjusted Covered Taxes pursuant to Article 4.1.3(a).
- Provides that International Shipping Income excludes the net income obtained from the transportation of passengers or cargo by ships via inland waterways within the same jurisdiction.
- To qualify for the exclusion, the Qualified Ancillary International Shipping Income must be obtained by a CE from the activities listed in Article 3.3.3 that are performed primarily in connection with the transportation of passengers or cargo by ships in international traffic.
- Provides for a limitation on the amount of ancillary income that qualifies for exclusion, which shall not exceed 50% of those CEs' International Shipping Income.
- The Qualified Ancillary Shipping Income for the jurisdiction that exceeds 50% of International Shipping Income does not qualify for the exclusion, i.e., the excess is included in the GloBE Income. The limitation applies on a jurisdictional basis.
- The Qualified Ancillary Shipping Income for the jurisdiction in excess of the limitation must be allocated among CEs in the jurisdiction in proportion to the Qualified Ancillary Shipping Income of each of those CEs.
- Provides that all direct and indirect costs attributed to a CE's International Shipping Income and Qualified Ancillary International Shipping Income shall be excluded from the computation of its GloBE Income or Loss.

- Provides that to the extent direct or indirect costs that are attributable to income from qualified ancillary activities in excess of the 50% limitation under Article 3.3.4, those costs are taken into account in the computation of a CE's GloBE Income or Loss because the related income is included in the computation as well.
- Imposes a substance criterion for International Shipping Income to qualify for the exclusion.

382. *Reasons for keeping shipping industry outside the scope of the GloBE Rules*: The international shipping industry has long been subject to industry-specific tax rules. The capital-intensive nature, the level of profitability and the long economic life cycle of international shipping have led a number of jurisdictions to introduce alternative or supplementary taxation regimes for this industry. The tax regimes applicable to international shipping, such as tonnage taxes, may result in less volatile tax outcomes for shipping and provide a more stable basis for long-term investment. The widespread availability of these alternative tax regimes means that international shipping often operates outside the scope of CIT. Including international shipping within the scope of the GloBE Rules would therefore raise policy questions in light of the policy choices of these jurisdictions.

383. *Mechanism of operation of the Article*: Article 3.3 adopts a qualified income approach based on the scope of Article 8 of the OECD MTC 2017[96] and excludes from the scope of the GloBE Rules the profits from transportation of passengers or cargo by ships in international traffic. Like the adjustments in Article 3.2, the exclusion for International Shipping Income and Qualified Ancillary International Shipping Income is an adjustment to the Financial Accounting Net Income or Loss. The exclusions are computed on a net basis pursuant to Article 3.3.2 to Article 3.3.5. The adjustment will be a negative amount in the situation where the International Shipping Income or Qualified Ancillary International Shipping Income is positive. The adjustment will be a positive amount in the situation where the International Shipping Income or Qualified Ancillary International Shipping Income is negative. To the extent an adjustment required by Article 3.3 excludes an amount of income from the GloBE Income or Loss computation, any Covered Taxes associated with that income must also be excluded from Adjusted Covered Taxes pursuant to Article 4.1.3(a).

4.3.3.1 Article 3.3.1.

384. For an MNE Group that has International Shipping Income, each Constituent Entity's International Shipping Income and Qualified Ancillary International Shipping Income shall be excluded from the computation of its GloBE Income or Loss under Article 3.2 for the jurisdiction in which it is located. Where the computation of a

96. Refer 'OECD's Model Tax Convention 2017' https://www.oecd.org/ctp/treaties/model-tax-convention-on-income-and-on-capital-condensed-version-20745419.htm.

Constituent Entity's International Shipping Income and Qualified Ancillary International Shipping Income results in a loss, the loss shall be excluded from the computation of its GloBE Income or Loss.

4.3.3.2 Article 3.3.2.

385. Article 3.3.2 defines International Shipping Income as the net income obtained by the CE from the activities specified in paragraphs (a) to (f), except to the extent the net income is obtained from the transportation of passengers or cargo by ships via inland waterways within the same jurisdiction, summarised in Figure 4.10.

Figure 4.10 Definition of International Shipping Income

International Shipping Income

Means:

Includes net income obtained by a CE from:

(a) the transportation of passengers or cargo by ships that it operates in international traffic, whether the ship is owned, leased or otherwise at the disposal of the CE. This paragraph excludes the profits or net income obtained by a CE from the transportation of passengers or cargo by ships in international traffic from GloBE computation in line with Article 8(1) of the OECD MTC. For the purposes of the GloBE Rules, the term "international traffic" means any transport by a ship, except when the ship is operated solely between places within a single jurisdiction (regardless of whether such jurisdiction is the same jurisdiction as the one in which the CE is located). This differs slightly from the definition in Article 3 of the OECD MTC, which adds the qualification "and the enterprise that operates the ship or aircraft is not an enterprise of that State". While these words are necessary for the proper operation of Article 8 of the OECD MTC, the transport by a ship, when the ship is operated solely between places in a jurisdiction and the CE that operates the ship is located in that jurisdiction, would also not be considered as international traffic for purposes of the GloBE Rules.

(b) the transportation of passengers or cargo by ships operated in international traffic under slot-chartering arrangements. Consistent with paragraph 6 of the Commentary on Article 8 of the OECD MTC, the exclusion also applies in respect of the transportation of passengers or cargo by ships operated in international traffic under slot-chartering arrangements.

(c) leasing a ship, to be used for the transportation of passengers or cargo in international traffic, on charter fully equipped, crewed and supplied. Consistent with paragraph 5 of the Commentary on Article 8 of the OECD MTC, to benefit from the exclusion, the lessor needs to demonstrate that the ship is expected to be used for the transportation of passengers or cargo in international traffic.

(d) leasing a ship on a bare boat charter basis, for the use of transportation of passengers or cargo in international traffic, to another CE. This income is covered under Paragraph 5 of the Commentary on Article 8 of the OECD MTC only if the leasing (whether or not intragroup) is an ancillary activity of an enterprise engaged in the international operation of ships. The leasing of ships on a bare boat charter basis is considered as international shipping income (instead of ancillary) for purposes of the GloBE Rules as an exception, under the condition that the lessee is also a CE of the same MNE Group and has International Shipping income. Including this item of income ensures that the structure of intragroup transactions involving CEs of the same MNE Group does not affect the characterisation of International Shipping Income.

(e) the participation in a pool, a joint business or an international operating agency for the transportation of passengers or cargo by ships in international traffic. This provision complies with Article 8(2) of the OECD MTC.

(f) the sale of a ship used for the transportation of passengers or cargo in international traffic provided that the ship has been held for use by the CE for a minimum of one year. This provision would normally fall under Article 13 of the OECD MTC. A minimum holding period requirement of 1 year is applied for the purposes of the GloBE Rules to prevent ship trading activities from qualifying for the exclusion. Ships that have been purchased with a view to reselling are usually recorded as inventory in the financial accounts under IAS 2, and gains (or losses) on the sale of such ships when the holding period is not met do not qualify for the exclusion. Legally owned ships used for international shipping operations are recognized as Property, Plant & Equipment assets in the financial accounts under IAS 16 if they are held for use in the production or supply of goods or services, for rental to others, or for administrative purposes, and are expected to be used during more than one period (IFRS Foundation, 2022). Capital gains (or losses) on the sale of such ships recognized as Property, Plant & Equipment assets in the financial accounts would qualify for the exclusion provided that they have been recorded as being held for use in the financial accounts of the CE for 1 year or more.

Excludes net income obtained by a CE from:

Transportation of passengers or cargo by ships via inland waterways within the same jurisdiction, such as rivers, canals and lakes.

4.3.3.3 Article 3.3.3.

386. The ancillary activities identified in this article are limited to those explicitly mentioned in the Commentary on Article 8 of the OECD MTC, 2017. To qualify for the exclusion, the Qualified Ancillary International Shipping Income must be obtained by a CE from the activities listed in Article 3.3.3 that are performed primarily in connection with the transportation of passengers or cargo by ships in international traffic. These activities are summarised in Figure 4.11.

Figure 4.11 Definition of Qualified Ancillary International Shipping Income

Qualified Ancillary International Shipping Income

Means:

Includes net income obtained by a CE from:

(a) leasing a ship on a bare boat charter basis to another shipping enterprise that is not a CE, provided that the charter does not exceed three years. This provision is different from Article 3.3.2(d) where the lessee is a CE. Paragraph 5 of the Commentary on Article 8 of the OECD MTC provides that Article 7, and not Article 8, applies to profits from leasing a ship on a bare boat charter basis except when it is an ancillary activity of an enterprise engaged in the international operation of ships. The Commentary on Article 8 of the OECD MTC does not provide for a time limit for that activity to be considered as ancillary. The three year time-limit condition in Article 3.3.3(a) is intended to limit the eligibility of this exclusion to income from bare-boat chartering-out by a shipping company with short-term over-capacity, and to prevent the exclusion being applied to income from long-term leasing arrangements.

- However, the three-year time limit is not intended to encompass what would be considered an ancillary bare boat charter as referred to in paragraph 5 of the Commentary on Article 8 of the OECD MTC.
- The three year time-limit condition would not be met when the contractual arrangement provides that the bare boat is available to the lessee for a time period that exceeds three years. For that purpose, other bare boat charters of the same ship, concluded with respect to prior or subsequent periods, would need to be taken into account. If a contractual arrangement is agreed for a shorter period than three years, the facts and circumstances would be analysed to determine whether the total period of the charter has exceeded three years. For instance, the renewal of a two-year bare boat charter for another period of two years would be considered as exceeding three years. Therefore, income earned after the date of the renewal would not qualify for the exclusion. Whether the income earned before the date of the renewal would qualify for the exclusion would depend on the facts and circumstances.

(b) sale of tickets issued by other shipping enterprises for the domestic leg of an international voyage (as mentioned in paragraph 8 of the Commentary on Article 8 of the OECD MTC). For this purpose, a shipping enterprise is an enterprise that operates ships.

(c) leasing and short-term storage of containers or detention charges for the late return of containers. For example where the enterprise charges a customer for keeping a loaded container in a warehouse pending delivery, or from detention charges for the late return of containers (as mentioned in paragraph 9 of the Commentary on Article 8 of the OECD MTC). For instance, a period of 5 days or less could be presumed to be short-term for this purpose. Facts and circumstances would, however, need to be taken into account to determine whether the storage was short-term.

(d) provision of services to other shipping enterprises by engineers, maintenance staff, cargo handlers, catering staff, and customer services personnel (as mentioned in paragraph 10 of the Commentary on Article 8 of the OECD MTC).

(e) investment income where the investment that generates the income is made as an integral part of the carrying on the business of operating the ships in international traffic (as mentioned in paragraph 14 of the Commentary on Article 8 of the OECD MTC). This would apply to interest income generated, for example, from cash deposits or other short-term working capital necessary for the carrying on of that business. This would also apply to interest income on bonds posted as security where this is required by law in order to carry on the business; in such cases, the investment is needed to allow the operation of the ships at that location. Paragraph (e) does not apply, however, to interest income derived in the course of the handling of cash-flow or other treasury activities for other CEs regardless of whether such CEs are located within or outside that jurisdiction (centralisation of treasury and investment activities). Nor would it apply to interest income generated by the short-term investment of the profits generated by a shipping operation where the funds invested are not required for that operation.

Excludes net income obtained by a CE from:

Inland transportation, which is not covered as a qualified ancillary activity for the purposes of the international shipping income exclusion.
Excluding income from inland transportation from the scope of Qualified Ancillary International Shipping Income mitigates the risk of competitive distortions, which could otherwise arise from including such transportation as a qualified ancillary activity under the GloBE Rules, between shipping companies that have vertically integrated such services as part of their international shipping operation and independent freight forwarding and land-based logistics service providers.

4.3.3.4 Article 3.3.4.

387. Article 3.3.4 provides a limitation on the amount of ancillary income that qualifies for the exclusion. The aggregated Qualified Ancillary International Shipping Income of all Constituent Entities located in a jurisdiction shall not exceed 50% of those Constituent Entities' International Shipping Income.

388. *Rationale for limitation*: The rationale for the limitation is that ancillary activities should only qualify for the exclusion where they are providing necessary support to the primary activity of the international shipping operation.

389. *Consequences of breach in limitation of 50%*: The Qualified Ancillary Shipping Income for the jurisdiction that exceeds 50% of International Shipping Income does not qualify for the exclusion, i.e., the excess is included in the GloBE Income. The limitation applies on a jurisdictional basis.

390. *Computation of Qualified Ancillary Shipping Income and its allocation, if the limitation is breached*: The Qualified Ancillary Shipping Income for the jurisdiction is the lesser of the total net income from qualified ancillary activities of all CEs located in the jurisdiction or half of the total International Shipping Income of such CEs. Applying the limitation thus requires that the net income of a CE from its international shipping activities under Article 3.3.2 be computed separately from its net income from qualified ancillary activities under Article 3.3.3. The Qualified Ancillary Shipping Income for the jurisdiction in excess of the limitation must be allocated among CEs in the jurisdiction in proportion to the Qualified Ancillary Shipping Income of each of those CEs.

391. Illustration # 33: This example illustrates, through a flow-chart, exclusion of International Shipping Income and Qualified Ancillary International Shipping Income from GloBE Income or Loss.

Illustration of exclusion of International Shipping Income and Qualified Ancillary International Shipping Income from GloBE Income or Loss under Article 3.3

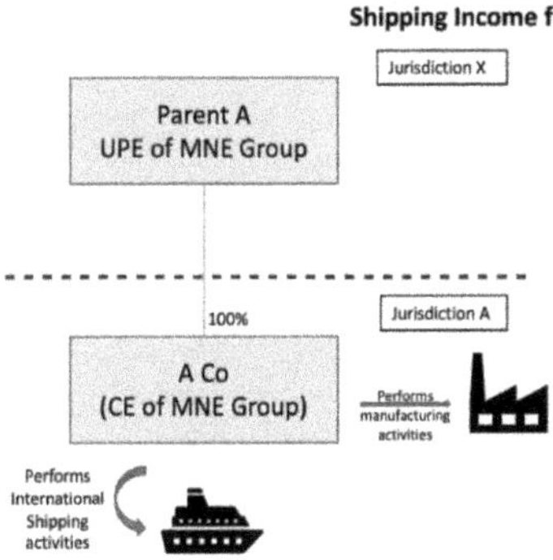

Assumptions Step 1

- Assume a CE has Financial Accounting Net Income of EUR 200.
- This CE has an income of EUR 60 that was derived from performing manufacturing activity that is not covered by Article 3.3.
- In addition, this CE has International Shipping Income of EUR 100 and Qualified Ancillary International Shipping Income of EUR 40.

Application of Article 3.3 Step 2

- No adjustments other than the exclusion of International Shipping Income and Qualified Ancillary International Shipping Income are required to compute the GloBE Income of the Constituent Entity.
- The resulting GloBE Income of the Constituent Entity is EUR 60 (= 200 – (100 + 40)).

Solution Step 3

- The adjustment required under Article 3.3.1 is illustrated in the table below:

Computation of the GloBE Income of the CE	Net Income	
[A] Financial Accounting Net Income or Loss	200	
[B] Income (other than shipping)		60
[C] International Shipping Income		100
[D] Qualified Ancillary International Shipping Income		40
[E] Adjustment under Article 3.3.1 = [C+D]	140	
GloBE Income = [A] – [E]	60	

392. Illustration # 34: This example illustrates, through a flow-chart, exclusion of International Shipping Income and Qualified Ancillary International Shipping Income when Qualified Ancillary International Shipping Income exceeds the limitation provided under Article 3.3.4.

Illustration of exclusion of International Shipping Income and Qualified Ancillary International Shipping Income when Qualified Ancillary International Shipping Income exceeds the limitation provided under Article 3.3.4

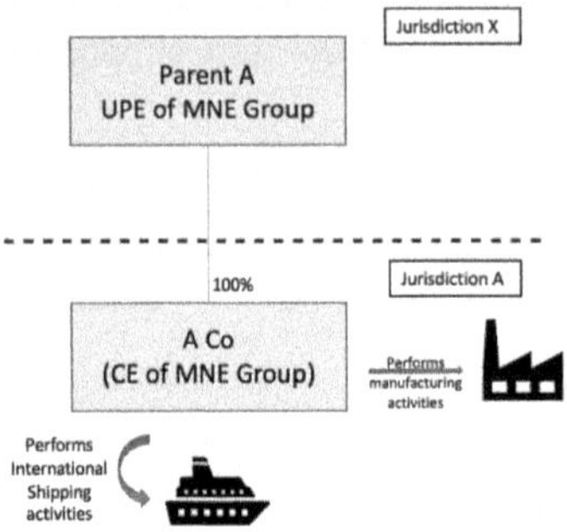

Assumptions Step 1

- Assume a CE has Financial Accounting Net Income of EUR 200.
- This CE has an income of EUR 40 that was derived from performing manufacturing activity that is not covered by Article 3.3.
- In addition, this CE has International Shipping Income of EUR 100 and Qualified Ancillary International Shipping Income of EUR 60.

Application of Article 3.3.4 Step 2

- Article 3.3.4 provides that the aggregated Qualified Ancillary International Shipping Income of all CEs located in a jurisdiction shall not exceed 50% of those CEs' International Shipping Income.
- Therefore, the total amount of Qualified Ancillary International Shipping Income is limited to EUR 50 in this example.
- The resulting GloBE Income of the Constituent Entity is EUR 50 (= 200 – (100 + 50)).

Solution Step 3

- The adjustment required under Article 3.3.1 is illustrated in the table below:

Computation of the GloBE Income of the CE	Net Income	
[A] Financial Accounting Net Income or Loss	200	
[B] Income (other than shipping)		40
[C] International Shipping Income		100
[D] Qualified Ancillary International Shipping Income		60
[E] Negative adjustment under Article 3.3.4 that limits [D] to 50% of [C]		-10
[F] Adjustment under Article 3.3.1 = [C+D+E]	150	
GloBE Income = [A] – [F]	50	

393. Illustration # 35: This example illustrates, through a flow-chart, exclusion of International Shipping Loss and Qualified Ancillary International Shipping Loss.

Illustration of exclusion of International Shipping Loss and Qualified Ancillary International Shipping Loss under Article 3.3

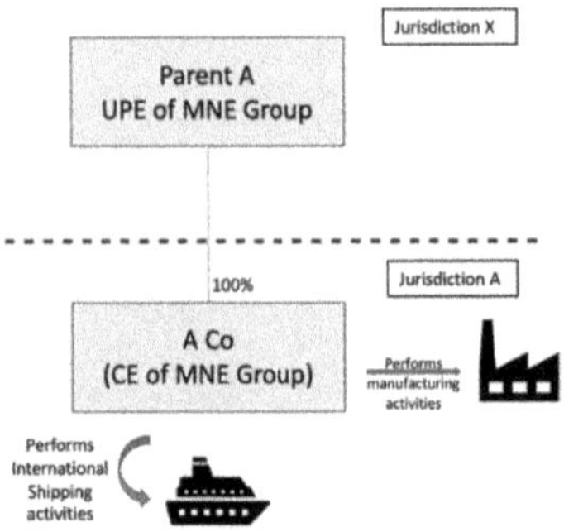

Assumptions Step 1

- Assume a CE has Financial Accounting Net Income of EUR 200.
- This CE has an income of EUR 360 that was derived from performing manufacturing activity that is not covered by Article 3.3.
- In addition, this CE has International Shipping Loss of EUR 100 and Qualified Ancillary International Shipping Loss of EUR 60.

Application of Article 3.3 Step 2

- Although the Financial Accounting Net Income of the CE is EUR 200, the GloBE Income of the CE is EUR 360 (= 200 - (-100 - 60) = 200 + 160).

Solution Step 3

- The adjustment required under Article 3.3.1 is illustrated in the table below:

Computation of the GloBE Income of the CE	Net Income	
[A] Financial Accounting Net Income or Loss	200	
[B] Income (other than shipping)		360
[C] International Shipping Income		-100
[D] Qualified Ancillary International Shipping Income		-60
[E] Adjustment under Article 3.3.1 = [C+D]	-160	
GloBE Income = [A] – [E]	360	

4.3.3.5 Article 3.3.5.

394. The costs incurred by a Constituent Entity that are directly attributable to its international shipping activities listed in Article 3.3.2 and the costs directly attributable to its qualified ancillary activities listed in Article 3.3.3 shall be deducted from the Constituent Entity's revenues from such activities to compute its International Shipping Income and Qualified Ancillary International Shipping Income. Other costs incurred by a Constituent Entity that are indirectly attributable to a Constituent Entity's international shipping activities and qualified ancillary activities shall be allocated on the basis of the Constituent Entity's revenues from such activities in proportion to its total revenues. All direct and indirect costs attributed to a Constituent Entity's International Shipping Income and Qualified Ancillary International Shipping Income shall be excluded from the computation of its GloBE Income or Loss.

395. *Direct Costs*: As an illustration, the directly attributable costs from the operation of an international shipping business (to be ascertained and allocated based on facts and circumstances) are as under:

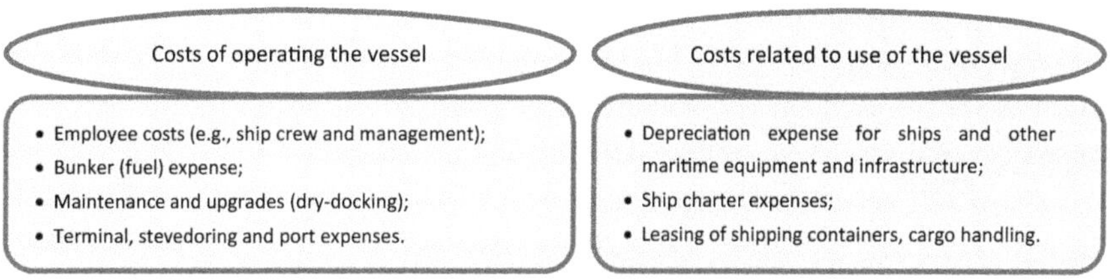

396. *Indirect Costs:* Indirect costs (i.e., all costs that are not direct costs) should be allocated between a CE's international shipping income and other income on a formulaic basis in proportion to its revenues from international shipping over its total revenues.

397. Illustration # 36: This example illustrates, through a flow-chart, allocation of Indirect Costs between a CE's International Shipping Income and Other Income under Article 3.3.5.

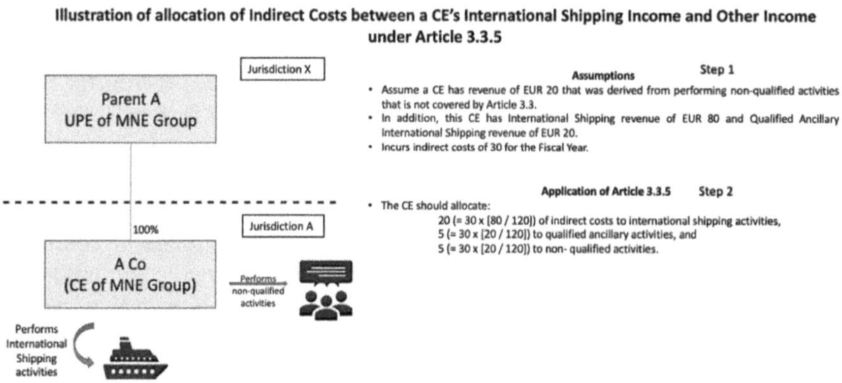

398. To the extent that direct or indirect costs are attributable to income from qualified ancillary activities in excess of the 50% limitation under Article 3.3.4, those costs are taken into account in the computation of a CE's GloBE Income or Loss because the related income is included in the computation as well.

399. Illustration # 37: This example illustrates, through a flow-chart, computation of CE's GloBE Income or Loss when qualified ancillary shipping income is in excess of the 50% limitation under Article 3.3.4.

Illustration of computation of CE's GloBE Income or Loss when qualified ancillary income is in excess of the 50% limitation under Article 3.3.4

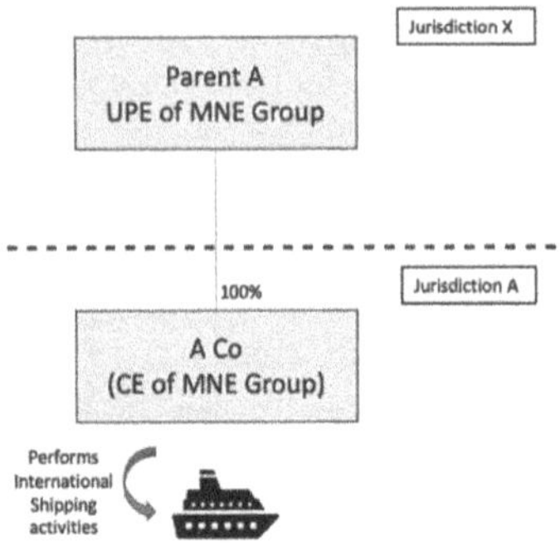

Assumptions **Step 1**

- Assume a CE engaged in international shipping has 200 of revenue from international shipping activities and 130 of direct and indirect costs related thereto, and thus 70 of International Shipping Income.
- The CE also has 100 of revenue from qualified ancillary activities and 60 of direct and indirect costs related thereto and thus 40 of Qualified Ancillary International Shipping Income.

Application of Article 3.3.4 **Step 2**

- The net income from Qualified Ancillary International Shipping Income exceeds 50% of the International Shipping Income by 5 (= 40 - [70 x 50%]) and therefore is not excluded from the computation of GloBE Income or Loss.

Solution **Step 3**

- The CE reduces its Financial Accounting Net Income or Loss of 110 (= 300 revenues – 190 expenses) by (i) the International Shipping Income of 70 and (ii) the allowable Qualified Ancillary International Shipping Income of 35, for the purposes of computing its GloBE Income, as illustrated in the table below:

International Shipping Revenue	[A]	200
International Shipping Direct & Indirect Costs	[B]	-130
International Shipping Income [A] - [B]	[C]	70
Qualified Ancillary International Shipping Revenue	[D]	100
Qualified Ancillary International Shipping Direct & Indirect Costs	[E]	-60
Qualified Ancillary International Shipping Income [D] - [E]	[F]	40
Negative adjustment under Article 3.3.4 that limits [F] to 50% of [C]	[G]	5
Allowable Qualified Ancillary International Shipping Income [F] - [G]	[H]	35
Financial Accounting Revenue [A] + [D]	[I]	300
Financial Accounting Direct & Indirect Costs [B] + [E]	[J]	-190
Financial Accounting Net Income [I] - [J]	[K]	110
GloBE Income [K] - ([C] + [H])	[L]	5

4.3.3.6 Article 3.3.6.

400. In order for a Constituent Entity's International Shipping Income and Qualified Ancillary International Shipping Income to qualify for the exclusion from its GloBE Income or Loss under this article, the Constituent Entity must demonstrate that the strategic or commercial management of all ships concerned is effectively carried on from within the jurisdiction where the Constituent Entity is located.

401. *Substance criterion to qualify for the exclusion*: Article 3.3.6 imposes a substance criterion in order to qualify for the exclusion. Article 3.3.6 is aimed at ensuring that the strategic or commercial management of all ships deployed in earning International Shipping Income is effectively carried on from within the jurisdiction where the CE is located. This condition is consistent with the manner in which many shipping tax regimes are designed in order to establish an economic link between the shipping company and the jurisdiction of the shipping tax regime. The strategic or commercial management of the ships concerned is limited to those deployed in earning International Shipping Income and must be effectively carried out in the jurisdiction where the CE is located in order to qualify for the exclusion. Carrying on strategic or commercial management from within the jurisdiction where the CE is located is effectively determined on the basis of the relevant facts and circumstances and taking into account all relevant factors depending on the item of income. The relevant factors take into account not only the strategic or commercial management activities of the ships concerned that are conducted inside the jurisdiction but also the strategic or commercial management activities of the ships concerned that are conducted outside the jurisdiction. The strategic and commercial management functions are elaborated in Figure 4.12.

Figure 4.12 Strategic and Commercial Management Functions to Establish Substance Criterion for International Shipping to Qualify for Exclusion

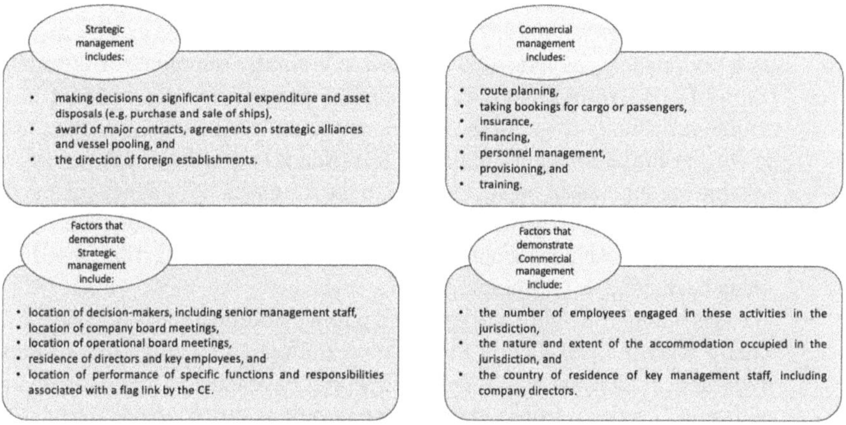

4.3.4 Article 3.4. (Allocation of Income or Loss Between a Main Entity and a PE)

402. Article 3.4 sets out rules for allocating income between a Main Entity and a PE. The definition of a PE stated in Article 10.1 is provided in Figure 4.13.

Figure 4.13 Definition of a PE

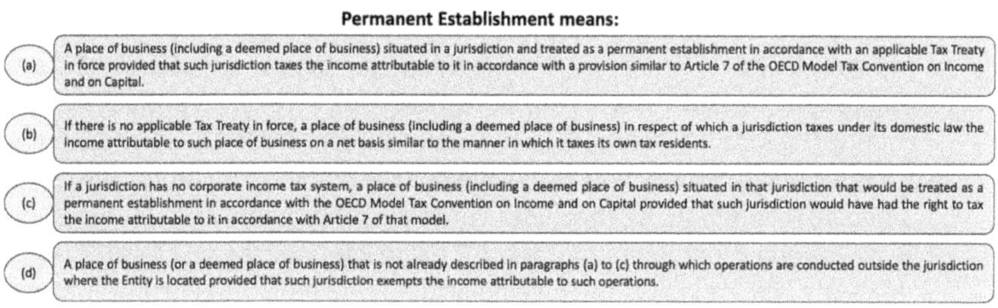

403. The definition of a PE stated above applies for the purposes of GloBE Rules only and refers to cases where:

(a) a PE exists in accordance with a Tax Treaty. The phrase 'deemed place of business' was included for situations in which the non-resident does not have a place of business, but its activities in the source jurisdiction are deemed to be a PE under the terms of the Treaty, for example, a dependent agent PE. Determinations by domestic courts and competent authorities are taken into account while holding existence of a PE for purposes of the Tax Treaty;

(b) a PE exists in accordance with domestic law in cases where there is no Tax Treaty in force between the residence and source jurisdictions. Paragraph (b) requires that the source jurisdiction taxes the income attributable to a 'domestic PE' on a net basis similar to the manner in which it taxes its own tax residents. It does not require that the 'domestic PE' is taxed exactly the same as a tax resident, as long as it is taxed in a similar manner. For instance, a 'domestic PE' would be taxed in a similar manner as a tax resident in the source jurisdiction regardless that the deductibility of its expenses is subject to further limitations not applicable to resident taxpayers. Furthermore, the taxable income has to be attributable to the 'domestic PE', which means that activities have to be carried out through it in the source jurisdiction. Finally, this condition excludes from paragraph (b) any source taxation based on a gross basis (e.g., a withholding tax);

(c) in cases where it would have existed if a jurisdiction without a CIT had a Tax Treaty with the jurisdiction of the Main Entity. This Paragraph requires a hypothetical analysis of whether a PE would have existed in the jurisdiction with no CIT system (referred in this paragraph as the 'source country'). The analysis proceeds as if the residence and source country had a treaty that replicates the last version of the OECD MTC. This means that it takes into account the version of the OECD MTC of the year in which this analysis is made;

(d) paragraph (d) includes cases that are not covered in (a) to (c) above and creates a PE for purposes of the GloBE Rules in situations where the jurisdiction in which a CE is located exempts the income attributable to the operations conducted outside such jurisdiction. By excluding PEs already described in paragraphs (a) to (c), the definition avoids any overlap between PEs falling under this paragraph and the other types of PE listed in the paragraph above. Drawing a clear dividing line between 'stateless PEs' under paragraph (d) and those under paragraphs (a) – (c) is important for determining the location of the PE in accordance with Article 10.2. For example, A Co is located in jurisdiction A and conducts activities in jurisdiction B through a person that habitually concludes contracts in the name of A Co. Jurisdiction B has adopted the definition of a PE of Article 5 of the OECD MTC into its domestic law and taxes the income attributable to it. Jurisdiction A exempts the income earned by A Co through a PE. Jurisdictions A and B do not have a Tax Treaty. In this case, paragraph (b) is triggered because jurisdiction B taxes the income attributable to a PE in accordance with its domestic law. Paragraph (d) is also triggered because jurisdiction A exempts the income attributable to the operations carried out through the PE. In this case, a PE exists in jurisdiction B for purposes of the GloBE Rules. If, however, jurisdiction B does not treat an agent that habitually concludes contracts in the name of its principal as giving rise to a PE under local law, then paragraph (d) would apply, but the PE would be 'stateless' for the purposes of the GloBE Rules, meaning that the income of the PE would be subject to the GloBE Rules on a stand-alone basis without the ability to blend its income with other CEs located in jurisdiction B.

404. Prominent features of Article 3.4 are provided in Box 4.15.

Box 4.15 Prominent Features of Article 3.4

- Article 3.4 ensures that the right amount of Financial Accounting Net Income or Loss is allocated between the PE and Main Entity. In making this allocation, the accounting treatment is followed as far as possible. This is subject, however, to the income and expense allocation rules under a Tax Treaty or domestic tax law.
- A PE is a tax rather than an accounting concept. This means that financial accounting information may not always be separately maintained in respect of the PE.
- Provides that the Financial Accounting Net Income or Loss of a CE that is a PE in accordance with paragraphs (a), (b) and (c) of its definition in Article 10.1 is the net income or loss reflected in the separate financial accounts of the PE.
- Where a PE maintains separate financial accounts, CEs that are PEs and subsidiaries are treated in the same way for the purposes of computing the ETR.
- Provides that if the PE does not have separate financial accounts, then the Financial Accounting Net Income or Loss is the amount that would have been reflected in its separate financial accounts if prepared on a stand-alone basis and in accordance with the accounting standard used in the preparation of the CFS of the UPE.
- Provides for adjustments in the amount and items of income and expenses that can be attributed to the PE for the purposes of determining its Financial Accounting Net Income or Loss under Article 3.4.1.
- Provides that where a PE exists in accordance with paragraph (c) of its definition in Article 10.1, then the income or expenses for determining the Financial Accounting Net Income or Loss of the PE would be the amounts and items that would have been attributed in accordance with Article 7 of the OECD MTC, 2017.
- Article 3.4.3 provides for attribution of income to a PE that arises under paragraph (d) of the PE definition in Article 10.1 when the Main Entity jurisdiction exempts such income from tax, which is attributable to activities occurring outside the jurisdiction.

- The Financial Accounting Net Income or Loss of a PE is not taken into account in determining the GloBE Income or Loss of the Main Entity, except as provided in Article 3.4.5.
- Article 3.4.5 provides a rule relating to the allocation of losses of a PE to the Main Entity under certain conditions.

405. *Concept of a PE:* A PE is a tax rather than an accounting concept. This means that financial accounting information may not always be separately maintained in respect of the PE. In many cases, however, separate accounts may be maintained either for management purposes or to comply with local tax rules. Given that the GloBE Rules primarily rely on accounting information rather than management accounts or local tax information, Article 3.4 ensures that the right amount of Financial Accounting Net Income or Loss is allocated between the PE and Main Entity. In making this allocation, the accounting treatment is followed as far as possible. This is subject, however, to the income and expense allocation rules under a Tax Treaty or domestic tax law.

4.3.4.1 Article 3.4.1.

406. The Financial Accounting Net Income or Loss of a Constituent Entity that is a Permanent Establishment in accordance with paragraphs (a), (b) and (c) of the definition in Article 10.1 is the net income or loss reflected in the separate financial accounts of the Permanent Establishment. If the Permanent Establishment does not have separate financial accounts, then the Financial Accounting Net Income or Loss is the amount that would have been reflected in its separate financial accounts if prepared on a stand-alone basis and in accordance with the accounting standard used in the preparation of the Consolidated Financial Accounts of the UPE.

407. *Situation where the PE has separate financial accounts*: In these situations, the first sentence of Article 3.4.1 provides that Financial Accounting Net Income or Loss of the PE is the net income or loss reflected in its financial accounts. This ensures that CEs that are PEs and subsidiaries are treated in the same way for the purposes of computing the ETR. However, following the principle in the GloBE Rules, such accounts have to be prepared in accordance with an Acceptable Financial Accounting Standard or an Authorised Financial Accounting Standard, subject to adjustments to prevent any Material Competitive Distortions.

408. *Situation where the PE does not have separate financial accounts:* In that scenario, the second sentence of Article 3.4.1 provides that the Financial Accounting Net Income or Loss is the amount that would have been reflected in its separate financial accounts if they existed. Therefore, accounts or reports will need to be prepared in such a scenario to compute the amount that would have been reflected in the financial accounts. Article 3.4.1 requires this determination to be based on the accounting standard used in the preparation of the CFS of the UPE.

4.3.4.2 Article 3.4.2.

409. The Financial Accounting Net Income or Loss of a Permanent Establishment referred to in Article 3.4.1 shall be adjusted, if necessary:

(a) in the case of a Permanent Establishment as defined by paragraphs (a) and (b) of the definition in Article 10.1, to reflect only the amounts and items of income and expense that are attributable to the Permanent Establishment in accordance with the applicable Tax Treaty or domestic law of the jurisdiction where it is located regardless of the amount of income subject to tax and the amount of deductible expenses in that jurisdiction;

(b) in the case of a Permanent Establishment as defined by paragraph (c) of the definition in Article 10.1, to reflect only the amounts and items of income and expense that would have been attributed to it in accordance with Article 7 of the OECD MTC.

410. *Purpose of the Article*: Article 3.4.2 adjusts the amount and items of income and expenses that can be attributed to the PE for the purposes of determining its Financial Accounting Net Income or Loss under Article 3.4.1. Given that a PE is a tax concept, there are no specific accounting rules for determining which items and amounts of income and expenses are taken into account by the Main Entity or the PE for purposes of determining the Financial Accounting Net Income or Loss.

411. *Intent of incorporating 'regardless of the amount of income subject to tax and the amount of deductible expenses in that jurisdiction' in Article 3.4.2(a):* Article 3.4.2(a) provides that the amount and items of income and expenses are those being attributed to the PE in accordance with the Tax Treaty or domestic law of the source jurisdiction. The phrase 'regardless of the amount of income subject to tax and the amount of deductible expenses in that jurisdiction' is intended to distinguish between the tax rules for attributing income to the PE and the tax rules, including timing rules, for computing its taxable income.

412. Illustration # 38: This example illustrates, through a flow-chart, determination of income of a PE as per Financial Accounting under Article 3.4.2(a).

Illustration of determination of income of a PE as per Financial Accounting under Article 3.4.2(a)

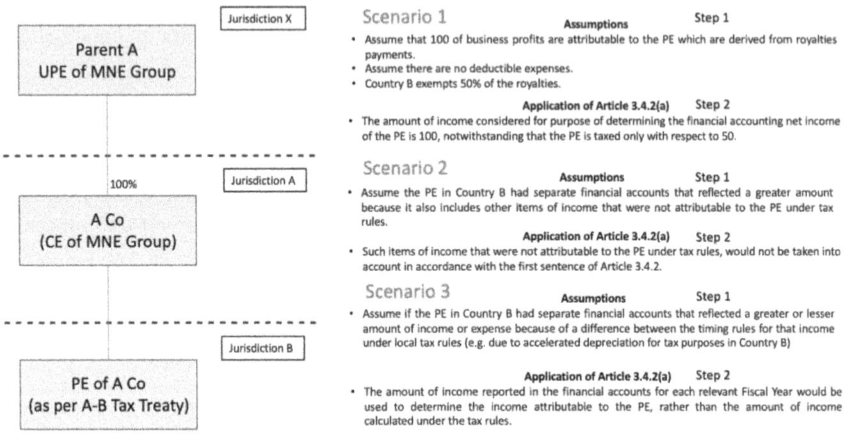

413. *Purpose of the Article*: Article 3.4.2(b) provides that where a PE exists in accordance with paragraph (c) of the definition in Article 10.1, then the income or expenses for determining the Financial Accounting Net Income or Loss would be the amounts and items that would have been attributed in accordance with Article 7 of the OECD MTC, 2017. This sentence accounts for the scenario in paragraph (c) of the definition of PE, which is based on activities in a jurisdiction that would hypothetically create a PE under Article 5 of the OECD MTC, 2017.

4.3.4.3 Article 3.4.3.

414. In case of a Constituent Entity that is a Permanent Establishment in accordance with paragraph (d) of the definition in Article 10.1, its income used for computing Financial Accounting Net Income or Loss is the income being exempted in the jurisdiction where the Main Entity is located and attributable to the operations conducted outside that jurisdiction. The expenses used for computing Financial Accounting Net Income or Loss are those that are not deducted for taxable purposes in the jurisdiction where the Main Entity is located and that are attributable to such operations.

415. *Purpose of the Article*: Article 3.4.3 describes the attribution of income to a PE that arises under paragraph (d) of the PE definition in Article 10.1. Article 3.4.3 attributes to the PE the income that the Main Entity jurisdiction exempts from tax and that is attributable to activities occurring outside the jurisdiction. Similarly, Article 3.4.3 allocates to the PE any expenses that are not taken into account in the jurisdiction of the Main Entity because they are attributable to activities occurring outside the jurisdiction.

4.3.4.4 *Article 3.4.4.*

416. The Financial Accounting Net Income or Loss of a Permanent Establishment is not taken into account in determining the GloBE Income or Loss of the Main Entity, except as provided in Article 3.4.5.

417. *Purpose of the Article is to prevent double-counting or omission:* Article 3.4.4 provides that the Financial Accounting Net Income or Loss of a PE as adjusted by Articles 3.4.2 and 3.4.3 should not be taken into account in determining the GloBE Income or Loss of the Main Entity. Thus, if the Financial Accounting Net Income or Loss of a PE is reflected in the financial accounts of a Main Entity, it must be subtracted from the Financial Accounting Net Income or Loss of the Main Entity. This article is intended to prevent double-counting or omission of Financial Accounting Net Income or Loss in the computation of the GloBE Income or Loss of the Main Entity and the PE.

4.3.4.5 *Article 3.4.5.*

418. A GloBE Loss of a Permanent Establishment shall be treated as an expense of the Main Entity (and not of the Permanent Establishment) for purposes of computing its GloBE Income or Loss to the extent that the loss of the Permanent Establishment is treated as an expense in the computation of the domestic taxable income of such Main Entity and is not set off against an item of income that is subject to tax under the laws of both the jurisdiction of the Main Entity and the jurisdiction of the Permanent Establishment. GloBE Income subsequently arising in the Permanent Establishment shall be treated as GloBE Income of the Main Entity (and not the Permanent Establishment) up to the amount of the GloBE Loss that previously was treated as an expense for purposes of computing the GloBE Income or Loss of the Main Entity.

419. *The Article safeguards domestic tax treatment of absorption of PE losses of certain jurisdictions*: Article 3.4.5 provides a rule relating to the allocation of losses of a PE. Some jurisdictions include the income or loss of a PE in the computation of the domestic taxable income of its Main Entity (e.g., jurisdictions with a worldwide tax system with a foreign tax credit system). However, GloBE Rules calculate the ETR of the Main Entity without taking into account the GloBE Income or Loss of the PE. Absent a special rule, the ETR of the Main Entity may be understated in a Fiscal Year when a PE loss is taken into account for domestic tax purposes but not for GloBE Income or Loss purposes. Under Article 3.4.5, this domestic treatment can be preserved with the necessary corresponding adjustments.

420. A GloBE Loss of a PE shall be treated as an expense of the Main Entity for purposes of computing its GloBE Income or Loss, to the extent that the loss of the PE is treated as an expense in the computation of the domestic taxable income or loss of such Main Entity. This provision applies irrespective of whether the tax base of the Main Entity takes into account the net loss of the PE or each of its items of income and expense. Thus, if the Main Entity takes into account only 80% of a PE loss in computing its domestic taxable income, then the same percentage of the PE's GloBE Loss is treated as an expense in the computation of the Main Entity's GloBE Income or Loss, and the remaining 20% is treated as a loss in computing the PE's GloBE Income or Loss. However, if a PE loss produces a time-limited loss carry-forward for the Main Entity, it is treated as an expense in the computation of the Main Entity's domestic taxable loss, irrespective of whether such carry-forward expires before it is used in full.

421. *Meaning of last part of first sentence of Article 3.4.5 (...is not set off against an item of income that is subject to tax under the laws of both the jurisdiction of the Main Entity and the jurisdiction of the Permanent Establishment):* The last part of the first sentence requires a PE loss not to be set off against an item of income that is subject to tax under the laws of both the jurisdiction of the Main Entity and the jurisdiction of the Permanent Establishment. The limitation on the loss reattribution to the Main Entity is explained by **Illustration # 39**.

Illustration of application of Article 3.4.5

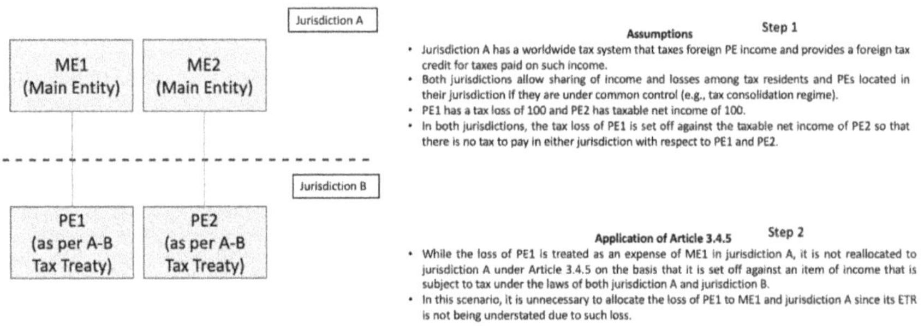

422. *Purpose of second sentence of Article 3.4.5*: The second sentence of Article 3.4.5 requires a corresponding adjustment which treats GloBE income subsequently earned by the PE as GloBE Income of the Main Entity (and not of the PE) up to the amount of the GloBE Loss that previously was treated as an expense for purposes of computing the GloBE Income or Loss of the Main Entity. This rule applies to the full extent of the amount of loss treated as an expense in the computation of the Main Entity's domestic taxable income or loss. Thus, even if the loss became part of a loss carry-forward in the Main Entity's jurisdiction that expired before it was used in full, the PE's income to the extent of that loss is treated as GloBE Income of the Main Entity. This rule avoids difficult tracing issues and complex rules that would be needed to administer a tracing rule.

4.3.5 Article 3.5. (Allocation of Income or Loss from a Flow-Through Entity)

423. Article 3.5 stipulates rules for allocating income derived through a Flow-through Entity to other CEs. The definition of a Flow-through Entity and connected terms defined in Article 10.2 are provided in Figure 4.14.

Figure 4.14 Definition of Flow-Through Entity and Connected Terms Defined in Article 10.2

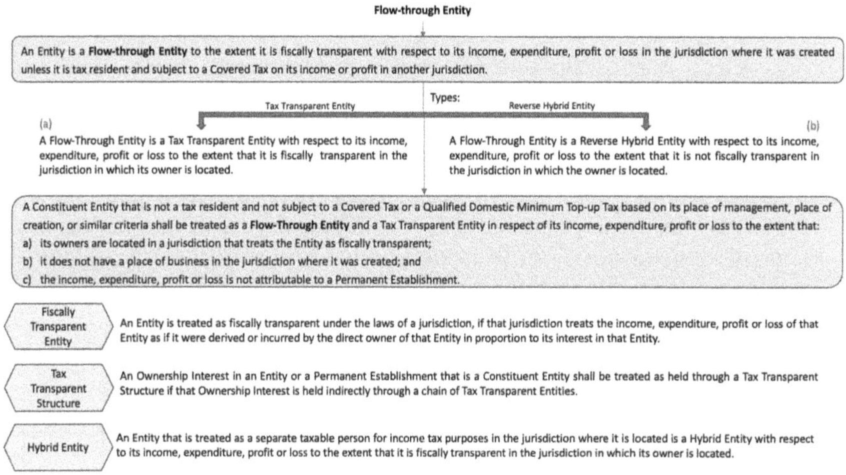

424. The above-stated terms are *inter alia* further explained in the OECD's Commentary on Article 10.2, as below:

(a) *Flow-through Entity*: The last part of the sentence of Article 10.2.1 establishes an exception to its definition. It states that an entity is not a Flow-through Entity if it is a tax resident and subject to a Covered Tax on its income or profit in another jurisdiction. For example, assume an entity incorporated in Country A has its place of effective management in Country B. The entity has elected to be treated as fiscally transparent in Country A (the jurisdiction where it was created). The tax residency test in Country B is a place of effective management, and therefore, Country B taxes the entity as a tax resident. In this case, the entity would not be a Flow-through Entity under the GloBE Rules because it is a tax resident of Country B. Flow-through Entities can further be divided into two categories. The difference between these terms depends on how the direct owners (i.e., holders of their Ownership Interest) are treating them under their domestic tax law:

(1) Tax Transparent Entities: A Flow-through Entity is a Tax Transparent Entity if the domestic tax law of the owners also treats it as fiscally transparent and requires the owner to recognise the income, expenditure, profit or loss of the Flow-through Entity as if it was income earned or expenditure borne by the owners.

(2) Reverse Hybrid Entities: A Flow-through Entity is a Reverse Hybrid Entity if the domestic tax law of the owners is not treating it as fiscally transparent and, therefore, it does not recognise the income, expenditure,

profit or loss when earned or incurred by the entity, but until the entity distributes profits or make an equivalent payment to its owners.

In addition, Article 10.2.4 is a deeming provision that treats a CE as a Flow-through Entity and Tax Transparent Entity if such entity has no tax residency and is not subject to a Covered Tax or a Qualified Domestic Minimum Tax, and its owners treat it as fiscally transparent. The most common case covered by this provision is where a CE with no tax residency is created in a jurisdiction with no CIT, and its owners treat that entity as fiscally transparent. This scenario is not covered by Article 10.2.1 because these entities are not fiscally transparent in the jurisdiction where they are created because they are not subject to a CIT legislation that treats their income, expenditure, profit or loss as derived or incurred by its owners. Article 10.2.4 is only triggered if several conditions are met:

(1) First, the CE shall not have a tax residence and not subject to a Covered Tax or a QDMTT based on its place of management, creation or similar criteria.
(2) Second, the jurisdiction of its owners shall treat the entity as fiscally transparent.
(3) Third, the entity shall not have a place of business in the jurisdiction where it is created.
(4) Lastly, its income, expenditure, profit or loss shall not be attributable to a PE.

(b) *Fiscally Transparent Entity*: Under Article 10.2.2, an Entity is treated as fiscally transparent in the jurisdiction in which it is created if that jurisdiction does not impose a Covered Tax on the Entity and treats the owners of the Entity as earning their respective shares of the Entity's income directly for purposes of that Covered Tax. This rule does not require the jurisdiction to treat the owners as incurring their respective shares of the Entity's net losses. Accordingly, an Entity may also be considered fiscally transparent where the laws of the jurisdiction where it is established allow for the pass-through of income but require net losses to be carried forward by the Entity itself and taken into account in the computation of the Entity's income in a subsequent period. An example of this kind of Entity can be a trust which allocates income of a specific category or class to certain beneficiaries, but it is allowed to carry forward any net loss from one taxable year to the next one in order to be offset against future income in that year. An Entity should not be treated as fiscally transparent under the laws of a jurisdiction solely because it is treated for tax purposes in that jurisdiction as forming part of another Constituent Entity because it is a member of a tax consolidated group.

(c) *Tax Transparent Structure*: Under Article 10.2.3, it is defined as a chain of Tax Transparent Entities through which an owner has an Ownership Interest in an entity or a PE. This term is used to describe the situation in which a non-member of the MNE Group has an Ownership Interest in a Flow-through Entity through a Tax Transparent Structure.

(d) *Hybrid Entity*: Article 10.2.5 defines a Hybrid Entity as an entity that is treated as a separate taxable person for income tax purposes in the jurisdiction where it is located (i.e., a tax resident) but treated as fiscally transparent in the jurisdiction where its owners are located. Similar to other definitions in Article 10.2, the phrase 'with respect to its income, expenditure, profit or loss to the extent that it is fiscally transparent in the jurisdiction in which its owner is located' allows that an entity can be considered a Hybrid Entity only with respect to the owners that treat it as fiscally transparent.

425. Prominent features of Article 3.5 are provided in Box 4.16.

Box 4.16 Prominent Features of Article 3.5

- Stipulates rules for allocating income derived through a Flow-through Entity to other CEs.
- Objective is to ensure the right allocation of Financial Accounting Net Income or Loss between Flow-through Entities and their owners in accordance with the applicable tax rules.
- Income of a Flow-through Entity is first allocated to a PE under Article 3.5.1(a) read with Article 3.4.
- Residual income of a Flow-through Entity post allocation to a PE is allocated to direct owners under Article 3.5.1(b) in accordance with their Ownership Interests in the profits of that entity to reflect the tax treatment in both the entity's and owner's jurisdictions.
- Provides that if the Constituent Entity-owners are also Tax Transparent Entities, then paragraph (b) of Article 3.5.1 applies again and allocates the residual Financial Accounting Net Income or Loss to the next Constituent Entity-owner up the ownership chain (unless the Ownership Interest holder is the UPE, in which case Article 3.5.1(c) applies).
- Provides that if all the CEs are Tax Transparent Entities (i.e., a Tax Transparent Structure), all of the MNE Group's income or loss is ultimately allocated to the UPE under Article 3.5.1 (b) and (c).
- Provides that where the Tax Transparent Entity is the UPE of the MNE Group, the Financial Accounting Net Income or Loss is allocated to the entity instead of the owners because the owners are not CEs of the MNE Group required to apply the GloBE Rules. Article 7.1 provides additional rules that apply when a Flow-through Entity is the UPE of an MNE Group.
- Provides that in the case of a Reverse Hybrid Entity, the Financial Accounting Net Income or Loss remains attributable to the entity, and it is not allocated to its owners because, according to the owner's tax legislation, the entity is not fiscally transparent, and its income or loss is not directly taxed in the hands of its owners.
- Provides that Article 3.5.1 applies separately with respect to each of the Ownership Interests in the Flow-through Entity in accordance with the

applicable tax rules. It recognises that the same Flow-through Entity can be treated as a Tax Transparent Entity by some of its owners and a Reverse Hybrid Entity by its other owners.

- Ensures that the jurisdictional ETR of the CEs is properly computed so that any taxes paid by non-Group members are not taken into account.
- Article 3.5.3 does not apply to a UPE that is a Flow-through Entity or any Flow-through Entity owned by such a UPE (directly or through a Tax Transparent Structure).
- The Financial Accounting Net Income or Loss of a Flow-through Entity is reduced by the amount that is allocated to other CEs (Constituent Entity-owners or PEs). This is necessary to avoid double-counting that income or loss under the GloBE Rules.

426. *Objective of the Article*: Article 3.5 determines how the GloBE Income or Loss of a Flow-through Entity is allocated between different CEs. These rules are necessary because, in many cases, these entities would have their separate financial accounts showing their Financial Accounting Net Income or Loss regardless of the fact that they have no taxable net income or loss because it has been allocated to their owners under the tax rules. Given that the GloBE Rules rely on accounting information, Article 3.5 ensures the right allocation of Financial Accounting Net Income or Loss between these entities and their owners in accordance with the applicable tax rules.

427. The general mechanics of Article 3.5 is *explained* in Figure 4.15.

Figure 4.15 General Mechanics of Article 3.5

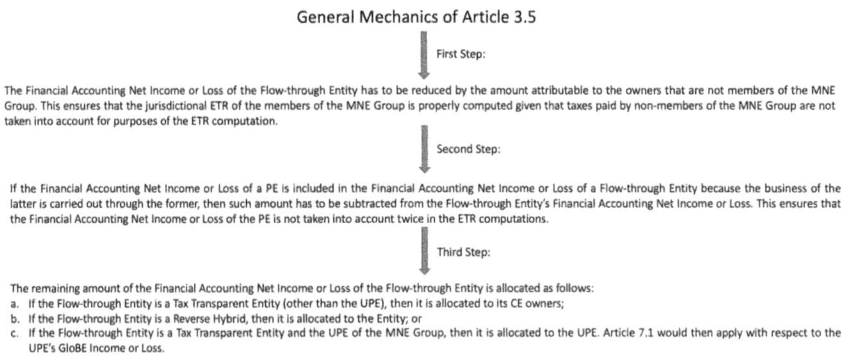

4.3.5.1 Article 3.5.1.

428. The Financial Accounting Net Income or Loss of a Constituent Entity that is a Flow-through Entity is allocated as follows:

(a) in the case of a Permanent Establishment through which the business of the Entity is wholly or partly carried out, the Financial Accounting Net Income or Loss of the Entity is allocated to that Permanent Establishment in accordance with Article 3.4;
(b) in the case of a Tax Transparent Entity that is not the UPE, any Financial Accounting Net Income or Loss remaining after application of paragraph (a) is allocated to its Constituent Entity-owners in accordance with their Ownership Interests; and
(c) in the case of a Tax Transparent Entity that is the UPE or a Reverse Hybrid Entity, any Financial Accounting Net Income or Loss remaining after application of paragraph (a) is allocated to it.

429. *Income of a Flow-through Entity is first allocated to a PE under Article 3.5.1(a):* Paragraph (a) provides that if the business of the Flow-through Entity is partially or totally carried out through a PE, the Financial Accounting Net Income or Loss of the Flow-through Entity is attributed to that PE in accordance with Article 3.4. This rule ensures that the Financial Accounting Net Income or Loss of the PE is removed from the Financial Accounting Net Income or Loss of the Flow-through Entity where it is included.

430. Illustration # 40: This example illustrates, through a flow-chart, allocation of income of a Flow-through Entity to a PE (PE situated in the jurisdiction where the Flow-through Entity was created) under Article 3.5.1(a).

Illustration of allocation of income of a Flow-through Entity to a PE (PE situated in the jurisdiction where the Flow-through Entity was created) under Article 3.5.1(a)

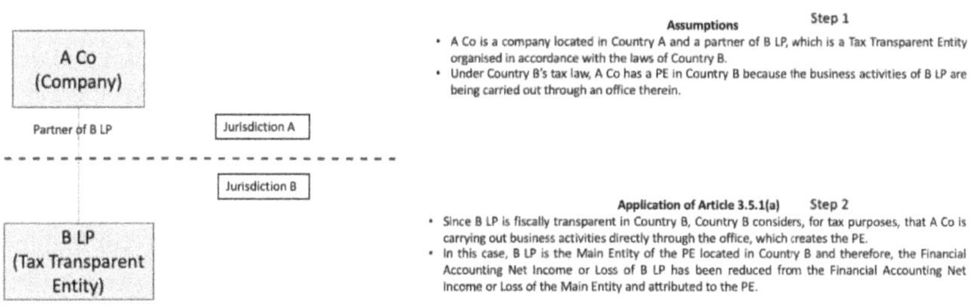

431. Illustration # 41: This example illustrates, through a flow-chart, allocation of income of a Flow-through Entity to a PE (PE situated in third jurisdiction) under Article 3.5.1(a).

Illustration of allocation of income of a Flow-through Entity to a PE (PE situated in third jurisdiction) under Article 3.5.1(a)

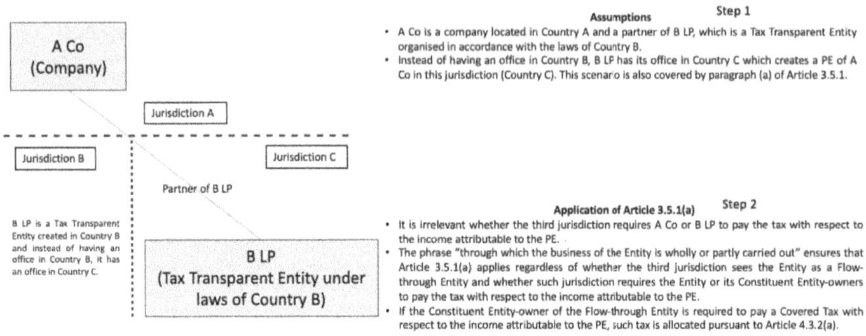

432. *Residual income of a Flow-through Entity post allocation to a PE is allocated to direct owners under Article 3.5.1(b):* Article 3.5.1(b) applies only after the application of the rule in Article 3.5.1(a). This means that the allocation of Financial Accounting Net Income or Loss to the Constituent Entity-owner has to be reduced by any amount already attributed to a PE in accordance with Article 3.5.1(a). This prevents allocation of the same amount of income or loss to the PE and to the Constituent Entity-owner of the Tax Transparent Entity. This also means that no Financial Accounting Net Income or Loss would be allocated to a stateless Tax Transparent Entity. In this case, income or loss of a Tax Transparent Entity that is not the UPE of the MNE Group is allocated to the Constituent Entity-owners in accordance with their Ownership Interests in the profits of that entity to reflect the tax treatment in both the entity's and owner's jurisdictions. If the Constituent Entity-owners are also Tax Transparent Entities, then paragraph (b) of Article 3.5.1 applies again and allocates the residual Financial Accounting Net Income or Loss to the next Constituent Entity-owner up the ownership chain (unless the Ownership Interest holder is the UPE, in which case Article 3.5.1(c) applies). Thus, if all the CEs are Tax Transparent Entities (i.e., a Tax Transparent Structure), all of the MNE Group's income or loss is ultimately allocated to the UPE under Article 3.5.1 (b) and (c). The phrase 'in accordance with their Ownership Interests' is intended to ensure that the amount of Financial Accounting Net Income or Loss remaining after allocation to a PE is allocated among the Constituent Entity-owners in accordance with their interest in such income, as illustrated in **Illustration # 42**:

Illustration of allocation of residual income of a Flow-through Entity to direct owners under Article 3.5.1(b)

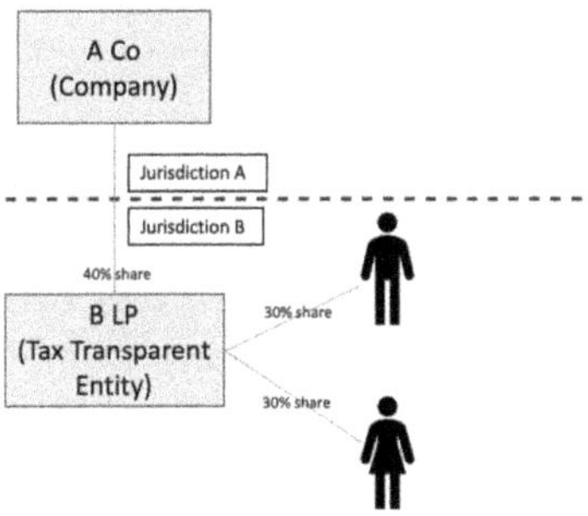

Assumptions Step 1

- The Ownership Interests of a Tax Transparent Entity in Country B are held as follows:
  - 40% by a non-resident Constituent Entity-owner A Co, and
  - the remaining 60% of the Ownership Interests are divided equally by two resident Constituent Entity-owners.
- The Tax Transparent Entity has an office in Country B where it is located.

Application of Article 3.5.1(b) Step 2

- Under the applicable tax provisions in Country B, such fixed place of business creates a PE in that jurisdiction for the non-resident owner, A Co and 40% of the Tax Transparent Entity's income is allocated to a PE of A Co in Country B under Article 3.5.1(a) .
- The remaining 60% of income is allocated to the Constituent Entity-owners in accordance with Article 3.5.1(b) (30% each).

The term Ownership Interests is defined in Article 10.1 as any equity interests that carry rights to the profits, capital or reserves of the entity. In the context of Flow-through Entities, it shall take into account the rights on income or profits attached to the equity interests, including any agreements or contracts that derive from such interests, because Article 3.5.1 is a profit and loss allocation rule. In some situations, however, there could be a mismatch between the amount of profits allocated to the Constituent Entity-owner under the fiscal transparency rules of its jurisdiction and the amount of profits to which the Constituent Entity-owner is entitled in accordance with the rights attached to the equity interests. Article 3.5.1(b) applies to the extent that the entity is treated as a Flow-through Entity and a Tax Transparent Entity in accordance with Article 10.2.1. Therefore, Article 3.5.1(b) follows the treatment under tax law which aligns the allocation of income, expenses, profits or losses under GloBE Rules with the outcome provided by the domestic tax laws of the Constituent Entity-owner and the Flow-through Entity, as illustrated in **Illustration # 43**:

Illustration of allocation of residual income of a Flow-through Entity to direct owners under Article 3.5.1(b) when there is a mismatch between the amount of profits allocated under the fiscal transparency rules of a jurisdiction and the amount of profits entitled as per rights attached to the equity interests

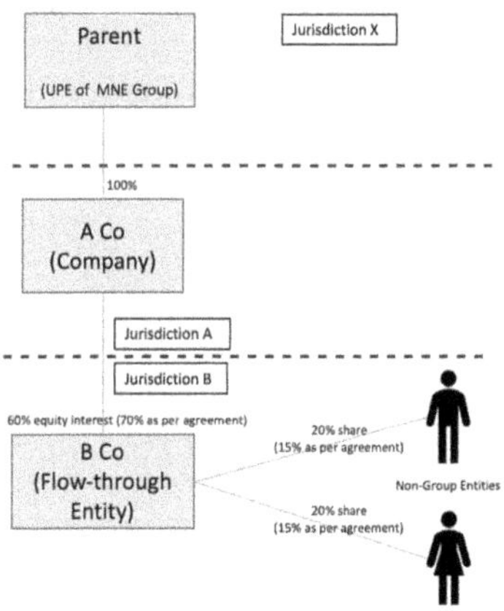

Assumptions Step 1

- A Co is an Entity located in jurisdiction A that holds 60% of the equity interests of B Co, a Flow-through Entity created under the domestic law of jurisdiction B.
- A Co and B Co are CEs of the same MNE Group, while the holders of the remaining 40% of the equity interests are not part of the Group.
- A Co has an agreement with the other equity interest holders that provides A Co with an additional right attached to its equity interest entitling A Co to 70% of B Co's profits (instead of 60%) for a five-year period starting after B Co's incorporation.
- Jurisdiction A treats B Co as fiscally transparent but does not recognise the effect of the agreement between A Co and the rest of the equity interest holders and therefore does not treat the agreement as giving A Co any additional 10% entitlement to the profits of B Co. This means that under jurisdiction A's domestic tax law, only 60% of B Co's profits are considered as being derived by A Co during the five-year period referred to above.

Application of Article 3.5.1(b) Step 2

- Under the GloBE Rules, A Co holds 70% of the Ownership Interests of B Co during the five-year period of the agreement.
- Under Article 3.5.3, 30% of the Financial Net Income of B Co is reduced because it is the amount allocated to owners that are not Group Entities based on their Ownership Interests.
- The remaining 70% of the Financial Net Income is allocated to A Co under Article 3.5.1(b) because jurisdiction A considers that B Co is entirely fiscally transparent such that all of the profits of B Co are being derived by its owners (including A Co).
- The fact that jurisdiction A does not treat the agreement between A Co and the other equity interest holders as giving A Co an additional entitlement to 10% of the profits of B Co is not relevant to the income allocation under Article 3.5.1(b) as long as jurisdiction A treats B Co as entirely fiscally transparent (i.e. a Tax Transparent Entity).

433. *Allocation to UPEs and Reverse Hybrids under Article 3.5.1(c):* Article 3.5.1(c) allocates the Financial Accounting Net Income or Loss of two types of Entities:

(i) a Tax Transparent Entity that is the UPE of the MNE Group, and
(ii) a Reverse Hybrid Entity.

In both cases, the residual Financial Accounting Net Income or Loss is allocated to the Entity itself and not to its Ownership Interest holders. For purposes of applying Article 3.5.1(c), a Tax Transparent Entity shall be treated as the UPE of the MNE Group if that Entity would be the UPE of the MNE Group but for the fact that its Controlling Interests are held by an Excluded Entity. Where the Tax Transparent Entity is the UPE of the MNE Group, the Financial Accounting Net Income or Loss is allocated to the Entity instead of the owners because the owners are not Constituent Entities of the MNE Group required to apply the GloBE Rules. Article 7.1 provides additional rules that apply when a Flow-through Entity is the UPE of n MNE Group. In the case of a Reverse Hybrid Entity, the Financial Accounting Net Income or Loss remains attributable to the Entity, and it is not allocated to its owners because, according to the owner's tax legislation, the Entity is not fiscally transparent, and its income or loss is not directly taxed in the hands of its owners. As in Article 3.5.1(b), the allocation of Financial Accounting Net Income or Losses to the UPE Tax Transparent Entity or Reverse Hybrid Entity has to be reduced by any amount already attributed to a PE in accordance with Article 3.5.1(a) to prevent double-counting.

4.3.5.2 Article 3.5.2.

434. Article 3.5.2 states that Article 3.5.1 applies separately with respect to each of the Ownership Interests in the Flow-through Entity in accordance with the applicable tax rules. It recognises that the same Flow-through Entity can be treated as a Tax Transparent Entity by some of its owners and a Reverse Hybrid Entity by its other owners. In such cases, the rules in Article 3.5.1 are applied separately from the perspective of each Constituent Entity-owner. In other words, Article 3.5.1 applies the Tax Transparent Entity treatment with respect to Constituent Entity-owners that treat the entity as tax transparent and applies the Reverse Hybrid Entity treatment with respect to the other Constituent Entity-owners.

4.3.5.3 Article 3.5.3.

435. Prior to the application of Article 3.5.1, the Financial Accounting Net Income or Loss of a Flow-through Entity shall be reduced by the amount allocable to its owners that are not Group Entities and that hold their Ownership Interest in the Flow-through Entity directly or through a Tax Transparent Structure. This ensures that the jurisdictional ETR of the CEs is properly computed because it does not take into account any taxes paid by non-Group members. If the CFS of the MNE Group include a Covered Tax that is associated with the Financial Accounting Net Income that has been reduced by Article 3.5.3, then the amount of such Covered Tax has to be reduced in the same proportion in accordance with Article 4.1.3(a). The application of Article 3.5.3 is explained through **Illustration # 44**:

Illustration of application of Article 3.5.3

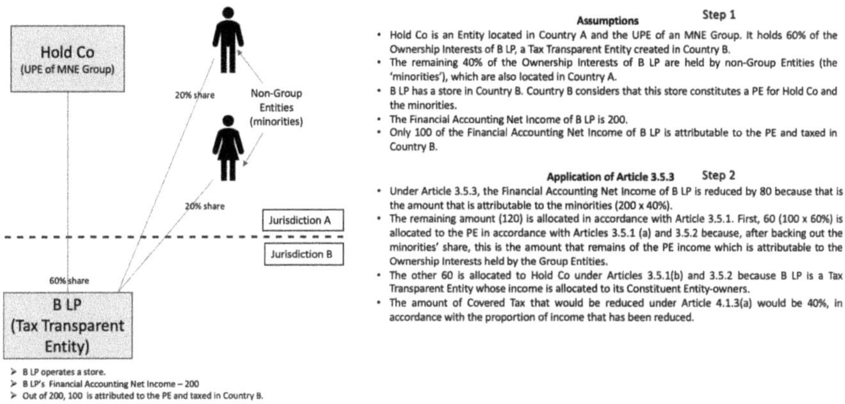

436. This provision also applies where the Ownership Interests of the Flow-through Entity are held by non-Group members through a Tax Transparent Structure (i.e., a chain of Tax Transparent Entities).

4.3.5.4 Article 3.5.4.

437. Article 3.5.3 does not apply to:

(a) a UPE that is a Flow-through Entity; or
(b) any Flow-through Entity owned by such a UPE (directly or through a Tax Transparent Structure).

The above cases are not contemplated in Article 3.5.3 because all of the owners of the Flow-through Entity are non-Group owners, which is covered by Article 7.1.

4.3.5.5 Article 3.5.5.

438. The Financial Accounting Net Income or Loss of a Flow-through Entity is reduced by the amount that is allocated to other CEs (Constituent Entity-owners or PEs). This is necessary to avoid double-counting under the GloBE Rules.

4.4 CHAPTER 4 OF GLOBE RULES (COMPUTATION OF ADJUSTED COVERED TAXES)[97]

439. This chapter contains the rules that determine the amount of taxes that are to be associated with that GloBE Income or Loss for purposes of calculating the ETR, which in turn feeds into the Top-up Tax calculation. The operative term in Chapter 4 is Adjusted Covered Taxes, and only amounts that meet this definition are included in the numerator of the ETR calculation. In order to arrive at the Adjusted Covered Taxes:

- start with Covered Taxes, which:
  - are broadly defined to include Taxes imposed on a CE's income or profits as well as Taxes that are functionally equivalent to such income taxes and Taxes on retained earnings and corporate equity,
  - do not include Taxes such as indirect taxes, payroll and property taxes, which are not based on a measure of income or Top-up Taxes imposed under the GloBE rules themselves.
- then make a number of adjustments, including:
  - a mechanism to take into account Taxes of a CE that are not recorded in the tax line of the profit and loss statement,
  - excluding Taxes that are not related to GloBE Income or Loss,
  - allocating certain cross-border Taxes to the proper CE, such as taxes imposed under a Controlled Foreign Corporation (CFC) regime or upon a Tax Transparent Entity,
  - addressing temporary differences, which is based on the mechanisms of deferred tax accounting (also allowing MNEs to use an optional simplified rule that can be applied in lieu of the deferred tax accounting approach),
  - post-filing changes to a CE's liability for Covered Tax.

4.4.1 Article 4.1. (Adjusted Covered Taxes)

440. Provides the overall mechanism on determination of Adjusted Covered Taxes to be taken into account in the ETR calculation for GloBE Purposes.

441. Prominent features of Article 4.1 are provided in Box 4.17.

Box 4.17 Prominent Features of Article 4.1

- Provides definition of Adjusted Covered Taxes, which starts with covered taxes.
- Provides for certain additions to the Covered Taxes for GloBE purposes in order to ensure that all Covered Taxes are properly captured and attributed to the CE since the range of items identified as income taxes in the financial

97. Based on OECD's GloBE Model Rules, its Commentary and Illustrative Examples.

statements may be narrower than the items that fall within the definition of Covered Taxes for the purposes of the GloBE Rules.

- Requires subtraction of several types of Covered Taxes to ensure that the ETR calculation for the relevant CE reflects only taxes that arise in respect of GloBE Income or Loss and that are expected to be paid within three years.
- Provision requiring reduction to Covered Taxes of any amount of current tax expense that is not expected to be paid within three years of the last day of the Fiscal Year prevents an abuse in situations where a CE could assert that it does not intend to pay the tax in a year where the CE is well over the Minimum Rate, and then subsequently pays the tax liability in a year in which it is below the Minimum Rate, using the rule to escape what would otherwise be Top-up Tax liability. Paragraph (e) of Article 4.1.3 applies with respect to amounts of current tax expense; accordingly, post-filing adjustments, such as additional tax liability resulting from a subsequent audit, will not fall within the scope of this paragraph since such amounts are not included in current tax expense.
- No amount of Covered Taxes may be taken into account more than once.
- An Additional Current Top-up Tax charge will only arise in a Fiscal Year where the local tax loss is greater than the loss that has been recorded for GloBE purposes, and the additional tax loss results from a deduction for a non-economic loss or similar permanent difference between the local tax base and GloBE Income or Loss.
- Article 4.1.5 ensures that the permanent difference giving rise to the inflated tax loss does not result in an overstated ETR for a jurisdiction when the deferred tax attribute is later used.

4.4.1.1 Article 4.1.1.

442. The Adjusted Covered Taxes of a Constituent Entity for the Fiscal Year shall be equal to the current tax expense accrued in its Financial Accounting Net Income or Loss with respect to Covered Taxes for the Fiscal Year adjusted by:

(a) the net amount of its Additions to Covered Taxes for the Fiscal Year (as determined under Article 4.1.2) and Reductions to Covered Taxes for the Fiscal Year (as determined under Article 4.1.3);

(b) the Total Deferred Tax Adjustment Amount (as determined under Article 4.4); and

(c) any increase or decrease in Covered Taxes recorded in equity or OCI relating to amounts included in the computation of GloBE Income or Loss that will be subject to tax under local tax rules.

443. The mechanics of computation of Adjusted Covered Taxes of a CE for the Fiscal Year is explained in Figure 4.16.

Figure 4.16 Mechanics of Computation of Adjusted Covered Taxes under Article 4.1.1

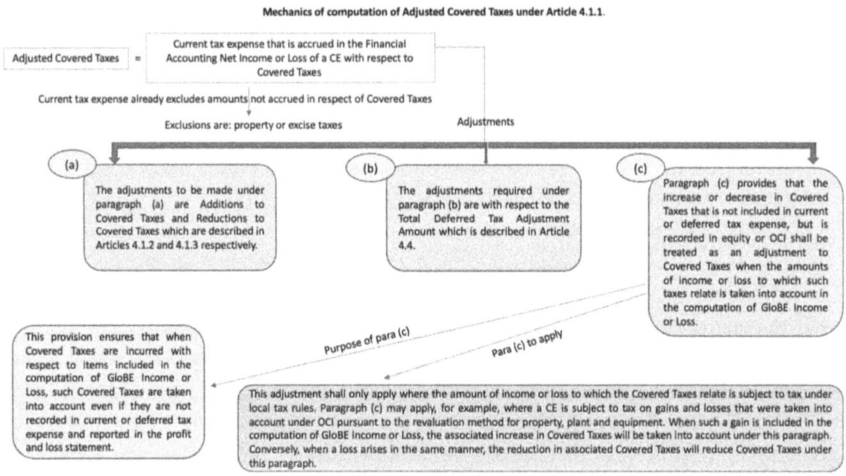

4.4.1.2 Article 4.1.2.

444. The Additions to Covered Taxes of a Constituent Entity for the Fiscal Year is the sum of:

(a) any amount of Covered Taxes accrued as an expense in the profit before taxation in the financial accounts;
(b) any amount of GloBE Loss Deferred Tax Asset used under Article 4.5.3;
(c) any amount of Covered Taxes that is paid in the Fiscal Year and that relates to an uncertain tax position where that amount has been treated for a previous Fiscal Year as a Reduction to Covered Taxes under Article 4.1.3(d); and
(d) any amount of credit or refund in respect of a Qualified Refundable Tax Credit that is recorded as a reduction to the current tax expense.

445. *Objective of the Article:* The said Article requires certain additions to the Covered Taxes to be taken into account for GloBE purposes in order to ensure that all Covered Taxes are properly captured and attributed to the CE. An adjustment may be required under Article 4.1.2 because the range of items identified as income taxes in the financial statements may be narrower than the items that fall within the definition of Covered Taxes for the purposes of the GloBE Rules. There are four types of adjustments required under paragraphs (a) to (d). These are explained in Figure 4.17.

Figure 4.17 Additions to Covered Taxes under Article 4.1.2

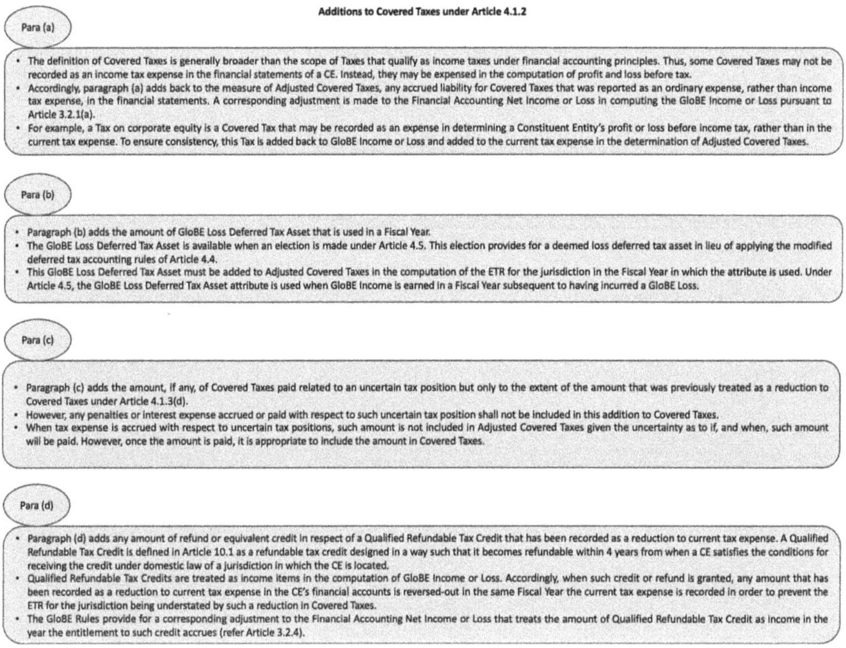

4.4.1.3 Article 4.1.3.

446. The Reductions to Covered Taxes of a Constituent Entity for the Fiscal Year are the sum of:

(a) the amount of current tax expense with respect to income excluded from the computation of GloBE Income or Loss under Chapter 3;
(b) any amount of credit or refund in respect of a Non-Qualified Refundable Tax Credit that is not recorded as a reduction to the current tax expense;
(c) any amount of Covered Taxes refunded or credited, except for any Qualified Refundable Tax Credit, to a Constituent Entity that was not treated as an adjustment to current tax expense in the financial accounts;
(d) the amount of current tax expense which relates to an uncertain tax position; and
(e) any amount of current tax expense that is not expected to be paid within three years of the last day of the Fiscal Year.

447. *Objective of the Article*: The said Article requires subtraction of several types of Covered Taxes to ensure that the ETR calculation for the relevant CE reflects only taxes that arise in respect of GloBE Income or Loss and that are expected to be paid within three years. There are five types of adjustments required under paragraphs (a) to (e). These are explained in Figure 4.18.

Figure 4.18 Reductions to Covered Taxes under Article 4.1.3

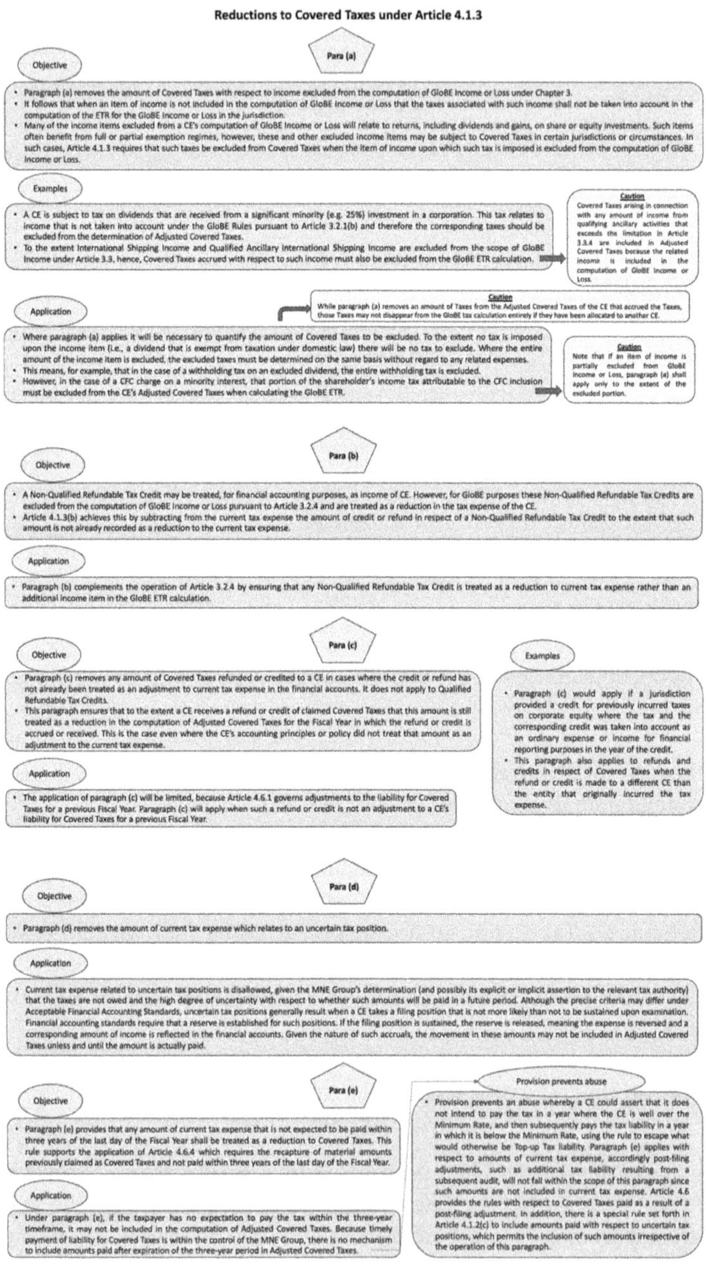

448. The application of Article 4.1.3 is explained through **Illustration # 45**:

Illustration of application of Article 4.1.3

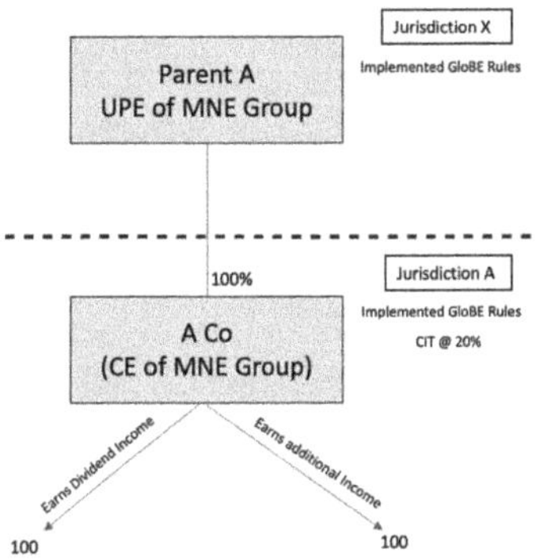

Assumptions **Step 1**

- A Co is member of an MNE Group that is subject to the GloBE Rules and it is located in Country A, which imposes a 20% corporate income tax.
- In a Fiscal Year, A Co receives a dividend of 100 that is excluded from the computation of GloBE Income or Loss under Article 3.2.1(b). The dividend, however, is included in the computation of the taxable income in Country A.
- In the same Fiscal year, A Co earns an additional 100 of Country A taxable income that is also GloBE Income. Accordingly, for Country A tax purposes, A Co records taxable income of 200 (Dividend of 100 + Operating Income of 100) and Country A tax of 40 (20% x 200).

Year 1

A Co Domestic Taxable Income:		A Co GloBE Income:	
Dividend	100	Dividend	0
Operating Income	100	Operating Income	100
Total Taxable Income in Country A	200	Total GloBE Income of A Co	100
Tax in Country A @ 20%	40		

Application of Article 4.1.3(a) **Step 2**

- Article 4.1.3(a) requires that the amount of current tax expense with respect to income excluded from the computation of GloBE Income or Loss must reduce Covered Taxes for a Constituent Entity. Accordingly, the Country A tax relating to the dividend that has been excluded for GloBE purposes must be removed from the Adjusted Covered Taxes of A Co for GloBE purposes.

Solution **Step 3**

- To determine the amount of Article 4.1.3(a) reduction attributable to the excluded income, the amount of excluded income shall be divided by the taxable income for the jurisdiction and then multiplied by the current tax expense.
- In this case, there is excluded income of 100 (the dividend received) and taxable income of 200 (Dividend of 100 + Operating Income of 100). Dividing 100 by 200 results in a 50% reduction of A Co's taxable income in Country A. This percentage is then multiplied by the 40 of A Co's Country A tax, to remove 20 of tax from the Covered Tax computation for A Co.
- As a result, for the Fiscal Year, A Co has GloBE Income of 100 (since the dividend is excluded) and an ETR of 20% (20 Covered Tax / GloBE Income of 100).

4.4.1.4 Article 4.1.4.

449. No amount of Covered Taxes may be taken into account more than once. The adjustments made in Articles 4.1.1 to 4.1.3 may overlap such that a single levy could be described in two adjustment categories. However, Article 4.1.4 clarifies that Covered Taxes can only be included in the Adjusted Covered Taxes of a single CE, and they can be included only once. If a levy is described in two adjustment categories, the amount of Covered Taxes accrued in respect of such levy for the Fiscal Year is therefore not counted twice in the determination of Adjusted Covered Taxes.

4.4.1.5 Article 4.1.5.

450. In a Fiscal Year in which there is no Net GloBE Income for a jurisdiction, if the Adjusted Covered Taxes for a jurisdiction are less than zero and less than the Expected Adjusted Covered Taxes Amount, the Constituent Entities in that jurisdiction shall be treated as having Additional Current Top-up Tax for the jurisdiction under Article 5.4 arising in the current Fiscal Year equal to the difference between these amounts. The Expected Adjusted Covered Taxes Amount is equal to the GloBE Income or Loss for a jurisdiction multiplied by the Minimum Rate.

451. The term Additional Current Top-up Tax mentioned above is defined in Article 10.1 as below:

> Additional Current Top-up Tax is the amount of tax determined in Article 5.4 and any amount treated as Additional Current Top-up Tax determined under Article 5.4, such as the amount determined under Article 4.1.5 or Article 7.3.

452. *When is the Article applicable*: Article 4.1.5 provides a special rule that applies in limited circumstances when there is no Net GloBE Income in a jurisdiction for the Fiscal Year, and the CE has a deferred tax asset that has arisen due to a permanent difference (e.g., a loss attributable to an amount that is not deductible for GloBE purposes) in the same Fiscal Year. This fact pattern may occur when the local tax rules in the CE's jurisdiction grant a deduction from income that is in excess of the amount that would be allowed for financial accounting purposes and where that difference between GloBE and local tax rules will not reverse over time. Examples of items that could give rise to these types of excess losses include notional interest deductions or a deduction that is in excess of economic cost (i.e., a super deduction). Permanent differences that result in such excess losses may also arise where a jurisdiction exempts an item of income or gain that is included in GloBE Income or Loss in a Fiscal Year where the CE still has an overall economic loss for the year. Accordingly, the local tax loss is greater than the amount of loss recognised for GloBE purposes, triggering the application of Article 4.1.5. The generation of a GloBE Loss Deferred Tax Asset under Article 4.5 is not expected to result in Top-up Tax under Article 4.1.5 because, when elected, Article 4.5 applies in lieu of Article 4.4.

453. *What the Article does*: In situations mentioned above, simply allowing a CE to use its local tax loss as the starting point for determining its Total Deferred Tax Adjustment Amount under Article 4.4 would undermine the integrity of the GloBE Rules by effectively allowing the CE to substitute the (more generous) local tax rules for those agreed under the GloBE. One option would have been to require the CE to make an adjustment to the amount of deferred tax asset in these cases to align it with GloBE outcomes. However, this would have required developing an alternative deferred tax accounting methodology for addressing these specific cases as well as mechanisms for tracking and tracing such differences over time, thereby undermining the compliance and administration benefits of relying on deferred tax accounting to address timing differences. Instead, the approach taken under Article 4.1.5 is to tax the excess benefit resulting from the permanent difference in the year it is created at the Minimum Rate but to allow the CE to follow the local tax rules and apply the excess deferred tax asset arising for local tax purposes to shelter income in a future year without giving rise to adverse outcomes under the GloBE Rules.

454. *Computation of Additional Current Top-up Tax under the Article*: An Additional Current Top-up Tax charge will only arise in a Fiscal Year where the local tax loss is greater than the loss that has been recorded for GloBE purposes, and the additional tax loss results from a deduction for a non-economic loss or similar permanent difference between the local tax base and GloBE Income or Loss. For example, if there is a Net GloBE Loss of (100) for a jurisdiction, the maximum amount of deferred tax asset generated in such year for GloBE purposes should be 15 (i.e., the GloBE Loss multiplied by the Minimum Rate). This amount is described in Article 4.1.5 as the 'Expected Adjusted Covered Taxes Amount'. Where the loss allowed for local tax purposes is in excess of the Net GloBE Loss (for example, a local tax loss of 150), and this difference is the result of permanent differences between the local and GloBE tax base, the Total Deferred Tax Adjustment Amount under Article 4.4 will be greater than the Expected

Adjusted Covered Taxes Amount. In this case, Additional Current Top-up Tax of 7.5 (50*15%) would be applicable under Article 4.1.5, which will have the effect of taxing this difference at the minimum rate. Article 5.4.3 provides rules related to the allocation of the Top-up Tax arising under Article 4.1.5 among CEs located in the jurisdiction.

455. *Essence of the Article*: An Additional Current Top-up Tax charge will only arise in a Fiscal Year where the local tax loss is greater than the loss that has been recorded for GloBE purposes, and the additional tax loss results from a deduction for a non-economic loss or similar permanent difference between the local tax base and GloBE Income or Loss, triggering the application of Article 4.1.5, which ensures that the permanent difference giving rise to the inflated tax loss does not result in an overstated ETR for a jurisdiction when the deferred tax attribute is later used.

456. The application of Article 4.1.5 is explained through **Illustration # 46**:

Illustration of Application of Article 4.1.5 and imposition of top-up tax in loss year

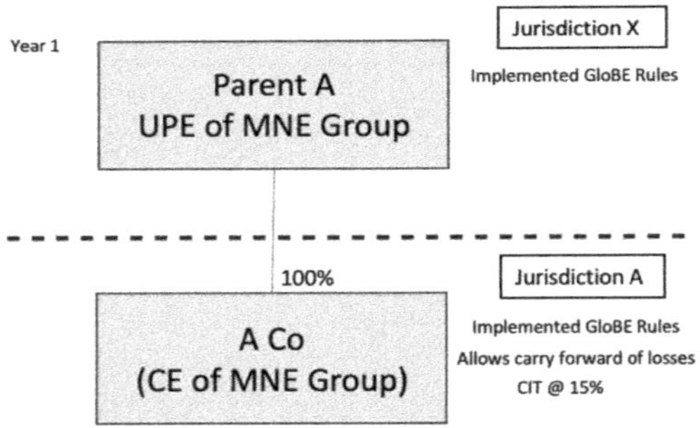

Step 1

Assumptions

- A Co is a CE of an MNE Group that is subject to the GloBE Rules. A Co is the only CE located in Country A. The only tax imposed on A Co under Country A law is CIT which is imposed at the rate of 15%. Country A provides for the carry-forward of tax losses.
- In Year 1, A Co has income of 120 and expenditure of (220) under the GloBE Rules resulting in a total GloBE Loss for the period of (100). However, under the tax laws of Country A, A Co is only treated as having taxable income of 100. This is due to the fact that 20 of A Co's income results from a capital gain that is excluded from tax under Country A law.

Year 1

A Co Domestic Taxable Income:

Income	100
Expenditure	(220)
Total Profit (Loss)	(120)
Tax (Tax benefit) in Country A @ 15%	(18)

A Co GloBE Income:

Income	100
Capital gain excluded under local law	20
Expenditure	(220)
Total Profit (Loss)	(100)
Expected Adjusted Covered Taxes Amount	(15)

Step 2

Application of Article 4.1.5

- The local tax loss of A Co is greater than the loss that has been recorded for GloBE purposes. The additional tax loss of 20 under Country A law results from the fact that Country A law does not include the 20 of capital gain (i.e. the additional loss is a permanent difference in respect of a non-economic loss). A Co's tax loss gives rise to a deferred tax asset for financial accounting purposes equal to the tax loss multiplied by the corporate tax rate (120 x 15% = 18). The generation of this deferred tax asset is incorporated into A Co's Total Deferred Tax Adjustment Amount under Article 4.4.1 and treated as a reduction to A Co's Adjusted Covered Taxes under Article 4.1.1. When the loss carry-forward is used in a subsequent year in Country A, the deferred tax asset is treated as an addition to A Co's Adjusted Covered Taxes under the mechanics of the same provisions.
- In this case A Co has a GloBE Loss and it is the only CE located in Country A. This means there is no Net GloBE Income in Country A. A Co's Expected Adjusted Covered Taxes Amount for the year is A Co's GloBE Loss of (100) multiplied by the Minimum Rate of 15% [(100) x 15% = (15)].

Step 3

Solution

- A Co's Adjusted Covered Taxes (18) are less than A Co's Expected Adjusted Covered Taxes Amount (15). A Co therefore has additional Top-up Tax of 3 in Year 1 under Article 4.1.5.
- Imposing an immediate tax charge on A Co in Year 1 means that the additional tax asset generated for local tax purposes can be recognised in the Adjusted Covered Taxes Amount while preserving the adherence between the deferred tax expense of A Co under the financial accounting rules and the GloBE Rules (i.e., the 18 deferred tax asset determined for financial accounting purposes is also used for GloBE purposes).
- Article 4.1.5 thereby ensures that the permanent difference giving rise to the inflated tax loss does not result in an overstated ETR for Country A when the deferred tax attribute is later used.

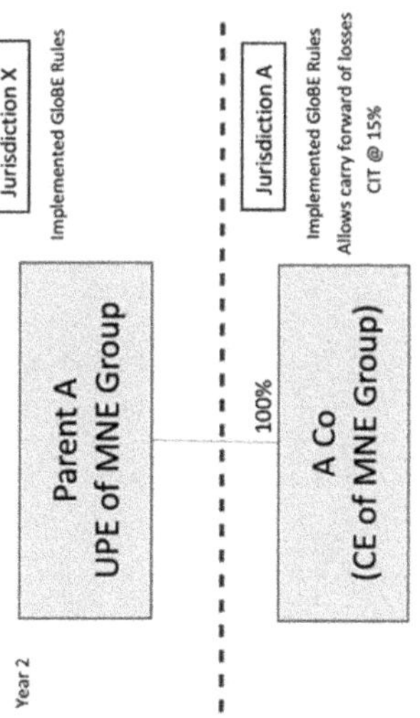

Assumptions **Step 1**

- Assume, in Year 2, A Co has 220 of income and (100) of expenditure resulting in 120 of profit that is included in both GloBE Income and taxable income.

Application of Article 4.1.5 **Step 2**

- As A Co uses 120 loss carry-forward under local tax rules from Year 1, A Co has 120 of GloBE Income, zero taxable income and zero current tax expense in Year 2.
- The full deferred tax asset of 18, is included in the Adjusted Covered Taxes in Year 2 under Article 4.4 and no Top-up Tax is expected to arise.
- The table below illustrates the tax position of A Co for local tax and GloBE purposes in Year 2:

Year 2

A Co Domestic Taxable Income:

Income	220
Expenditure	(100)
Profit (Loss)	120
Loss brought forward	(120)
Total Profit (Loss)	0

A Co GloBE Income:

Income	220
Expenditure	(100)
Total Profit (Loss)	120
Adjusted Covered Taxes	18
GloBE ETR	15%

457. The application of Article 4.1.5, when two CEs exist in a Jurisdiction, is explained through **Illustration # 47**:

Illustration of Application of Article 4.1.5 and imposition of top-up tax in loss year when two CEs exist in a Jurisdiction

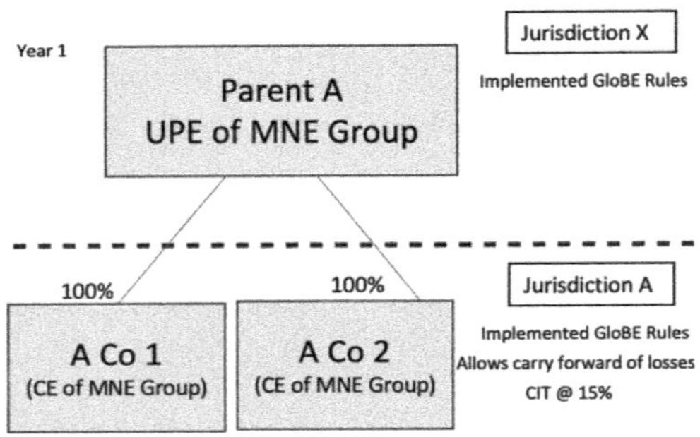

Particulars	A Co 1	A Co 2	Jurisdictional (Country A)
GloBE Income or (Loss)	(100)	50	(50)
Deferred Tax Asset	(18)	-	
Covered Taxes	-	7.5	
Expected Adjusted Covered Taxes Amount			(7.5)
Adjusted Covered Taxes Amount	(18)	7.5	(10.5)
Additional Current Top-up Tax			3

Assumptions Step 1

- In Year 1, A Co 1 has GloBE Loss (100); deferred tax asset of 18, as given below:

Year 1

A Co Domestic Taxable Income:	
Income	100
Expenditure	(220)
Total Profit (Loss)	(120)
Tax (Tax benefit) in Country A @ 15%	(18)

A Co GloBE Income:	
Income	100
Capital gain excluded under local law	20
Expenditure	(220)
Total Profit (Loss)	(100)
Expected Adjusted Covered Taxes Amount	(15)

- In Year 1, A Co 2 has a total GloBE Income of 50.

Application of Article 4.1.5 Step 2

- Under this scenario, if the Adjusted Covered Taxes in Country A are less than zero and less than the Expected Adjusted Covered Taxes Amount, A Co 1 and A Co 2 are treated as having Additional Current Top-up Tax arising in Year 1 and equal to the difference between these two amounts under Article 4.1.5.
- A Co 1 and A Co 2's Expected Adjusted Covered Taxes Amount for Year 1 is equal to the GloBE Income or Loss for the jurisdiction multiplied by the Minimum Rate. For this reason, A Co 1's deferred tax asset of (18) has to be added to A Co 2's Covered Taxes of 7.5 (15% * 50), which results in Adjusted Covered Taxes for Country A of (10.5). A Co 1 and A Co 2's Expected Adjusted Covered Taxes Amount for Year 1, is A Co 1 and A Co 2's GloBE Loss of (50) multiplied by the Minimum Rate of 15% [(50) x 15% = (7.5)].
- As the Adjusted Covered Taxes (10.5) are less than zero and less than the Expected Adjusted Covered Taxes Amount (7.5), an Additional Current Top-up Tax of 3 arises under Article 4.1.5. The Additional Current Top-up Tax of 3 is then allocated to A Co 1 under Article 5.4.3 as A Co 1 recorded an Adjusted Covered Taxes amount that is less than zero and less than the GloBE Income or Loss multiplied by the Minimum Rate.
- A table illustrating the numerical results of this example is given here.

458. Article 4.1.5, when two CEs exist in a Jurisdiction and Adjusted Covered Taxes Amount is more than Expected Adjusted Covered Taxes Amount, is explained through **Illustration # 48**:

Illustration of Article 4.1.5 in loss year when two CEs exist in a Jurisdiction

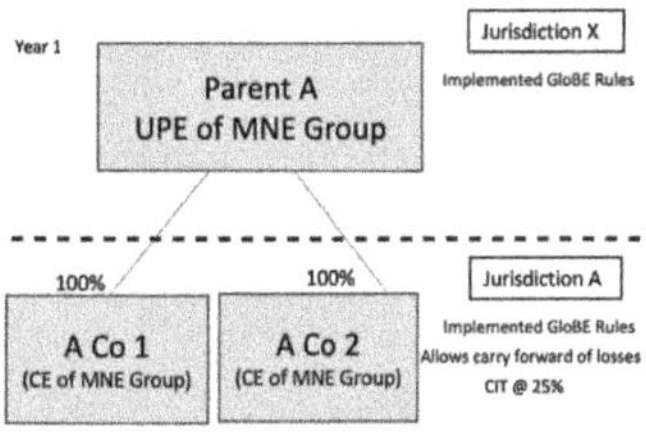

Particulars	A Co 1	A Co 2	Jurisdictional (Country A)
GloBE Income or (Loss)	(100)	50	(50)
Deferred Tax Asset	(18)	-	
Covered Taxes	-	12.5	
Expected Adjusted Covered Taxes Amount			(7.5)
Adjusted Covered Taxes Amount	(18)	12.5	(5.5)
Additional Current Top-up Tax			0

Assumptions **Step 1**

- In Year 1, A Co 1 has GloBE Loss (100); deferred tax asset of 18, as given below:

Year 1

A Co Domestic Taxable Income:	
Income	100
Expenditure	(220)
Total Profit (Loss)	(120)
Tax (Tax benefit) in Country A @ 15%	(18)

A Co GloBE Income:	
Income	100
Capital gain excluded under local law	20
Expenditure	(220)
Total Profit (Loss)	(100)
Expected Adjusted Covered Taxes Amount	(15)

- In Year 1, A Co 2 has a total GloBE Income of 50.

Application of Article 4.1.5 **Step 2**

- In this scenario, A Co 2 has Adjusted Covered Taxes of 12.5 (50 * 25%).
- The Expected Adjusted Covered Taxes Amount of Country A in Year 1 remains (7.5) because the GloBE Loss is always multiplied by the Minimum Rate (15% * (50)).
- As the deferred tax asset of A Co 1 was recast at the Minimum Rate in accordance with Article 4.4.1, it remains (18) and is added to the Adjusted Covered Taxes of A Co 2 of 12.5, which results in Adjusted Covered Taxes for Country A of (5.5).
- Because the Adjusted Covered Taxes amount for Country A of (5.5) is not less than the Expected Adjusted Covered Taxes Amount of (7.5), no adjustment is required in this case under Article 4.1.5.
- The taxes accrued by A Co 2 in Year 1 are sufficient to shelter the permanent difference in A Co 1 from Top-up Tax.
- A table illustrating the numerical results of this example is given here.

4.4.2 Article 4.2. (Definition of Covered Taxes)

459. Article 4.2 provides the definition of Covered Taxes that are taken into account in the determination of Adjusted Covered Taxes under Article 4.1. The definition of Covered Taxes is developed solely for the purposes of the GloBE Rules and has no direct interaction with Article 2 (Taxes Covered) of the OECD MTC 2017, which defines the taxes within the scope of the Convention. Taxes that do not qualify for the definition of Covered Taxes under the GloBE Rules, such as excise taxes and payroll taxes, will be treated as deductible in the computation of the GloBE Income or Loss (i.e., as reductions to the denominator in the ETR calculation under Article 5.1) The fact that a Tax may be deducted from the tax base for another Covered Tax does not, however, mean that the Tax is not eligible to be considered as a Covered Tax. The concept of Covered Taxes is explained in Figure 4.19.

Figure 4.19 Concept of Covered Taxes

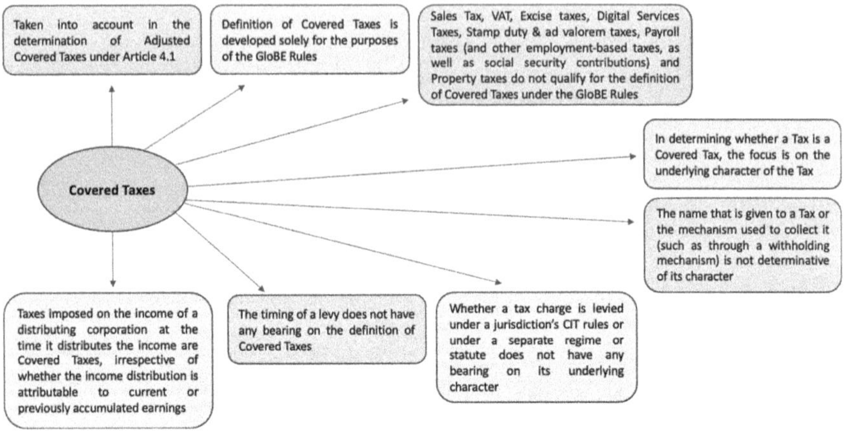

460. Prominent features of Article 4.2 are provided in Box 4.18.

Box 4.18 Prominent Features of Article 4.2

- Provides the definition of Covered Taxes that are taken into account in the determination of Adjusted Covered Taxes under Article 4.1.
- The definition of Covered Taxes is developed solely for the purposes of the GloBE Rules and has no direct interaction with Article 2 (Taxes Covered) of the OECD MTC 2017.
- Provides that Covered Taxes means:
  - any Taxes recorded in the financial accounts of a CE with respect to its income or profits;
  - any Taxes on distributed profits imposed under an Eligible Distribution Tax System;
  - any Taxes imposed in lieu of a generally applicable CIT;
  - any Taxes levied by reference to retained earnings and corporate equity, including a Tax on multiple components based on income and equity.
- Sales Tax, VAT, Excise taxes, Digital Services Taxes, Stamp duty and ad valorem taxes, Payroll taxes (and other employment-based taxes, as well as social security contributions), and Property taxes do not qualify for the definition of Covered Taxes under the GloBE Rules.
- Although Covered Taxes are defined broadly, certain Taxes are specifically excluded from the definition. These excluded Taxes generally fall into two categories: Top-up Taxes and refundable taxes.
- Provides that an ordinary domestic minimum tax that is not a QDMTT is a Covered Tax if it otherwise meets the definition of a Covered Tax.

4.4.2.1 Article 4.2.1.

461. Covered Taxes means:

(a) taxes recorded in the financial accounts of a Constituent Entity with respect to its income or profits or its share of the income or profits of a Constituent Entity in which it owns an Ownership Interest;
(b) taxes on distributed profits, deemed profit distributions, and non-business expenses imposed under an Eligible Distribution Tax System;
(c) taxes imposed in lieu of a generally applicable CIT; and
(d) taxes levied by reference to retained earnings and corporate equity, including a Tax on multiple components based on income and equity.

462. The term Tax mentioned *supra* is defined in Article 10.1 as below:

> Tax means a compulsory unrequited payment to General Government.

Fees and payments for privileges, services, property, or other benefits provided by the government do not qualify as Taxes. Similarly, Taxes neither include fines and penalties nor include interest or similar charges with respect to payments of tax liabilities after the applicable due date.

463. The term Eligible Distribution Tax System mentioned *supra* is defined in Article 10.1, as below:

> Eligible Distribution Tax System means a corporate income tax system that
>
> (a) imposes an income tax on the corporation with the tax generally payable only when the corporation distributes profits to shareholders, is deemed to distribute profits to shareholders, or incurs certain non-business expenses;
> (b) imposes tax at a rate equal to or in excess of the Minimum Rate; and
> (c) was in force on or before 1 July 2021.

464. The definition of Covered Taxes, stated *supra*, includes four types of Taxes described in paragraphs (a) to (d), as explained in Figure 4.20.

Figure 4.20   Definition of Covered Taxes

Para (a)

- Paragraph (a) provides that any Taxes recorded in the financial accounts of a CE with respect to its income or profits are Covered Taxes. Income taxes are generally levied on a flow of money or money's worth that accrues to a taxpayer during a period of time. Income taxes take into account related expenses of producing the flow of money to measure the taxpayer's net increase in wealth for the period. A definition of Covered Taxes that applies to income calculated on a net (rather than gross) basis is in line with the definition of income tax used for financial accounting purposes and therefore it is expected that a Tax recognised as an income tax for financial accounting purposes should generally qualify as a Covered Tax under the GloBE Rules.

<u>Caution</u>
Certain income taxes are specifically excluded from the definition of Covered Taxes under Article 4.2.2.

- The definition encompasses not only Taxes imposed on income at the time such income is derived but also to Taxes that are imposed on a subsequent distribution of profits. Moreover, the definition includes Taxes on the income of the CE as well as its share of income of another CE in which it owns an Ownership Interest. Thus, Taxes imposed on the CE's share of undistributed profits from a Tax Transparent Entity such as a partnership, Taxes imposed under a CFC Tax Regime, as well as Taxes imposed on distributions from another CE are treated as Covered Taxes under paragraph (a).

<u>Caution</u>
A Tax imposed on gross income or revenue without any deductions (i.e. a tax on turnover) would not be considered an income tax. The design and substantive character of such turnover taxes generally have more similarities to consumption or sales taxes. The definition of Covered Taxes therefore does not include a Tax on a gross amount unless such a Tax is in lieu of an income tax.

- Taxes or surcharges imposed on the net income from specific activities, such as banking, or the exploration and production of oil and gas, irrespective of whether or not they apply in addition to a generally applicable income tax, would also fall within the general definition of a Covered Tax. The definition would include a separate levy that is imposed on the net income or profits from natural resource extraction activity (or a part of a multi-component levy that is imposed on net income or profits).

<u>Caution</u>
Natural resource levies closely linked to extractions, for example, those that are imposed on a fixed basis or on the quantity, volume or value of the resources extracted rather than on net income or profits, would not be treated as Covered Taxes except where these levies satisfy the "in lieu of" test described in connection with paragraph (c) of Article 4.2.1.

- Tax on net income of a CE under Pillar One would be treated as a Covered Tax under the GloBE Rules as a tax with respect to income or profits. Since Pillar One applies before the GloBE Rules, any income tax with respect to Pillar One adjustments will be taken into account by the CE that takes into account the income associated with such Tax for purposes of calculating its GloBE Income or Loss.

Para (b)

- Paragraph (b) provides that any Taxes on distributed profits imposed under an Eligible Distribution Tax System are Covered Taxes.

Para (c)

- Paragraph (c) provides that Taxes imposed **in lieu of** a generally applicable CIT are Covered Taxes. A generally applicable CIT could be one that applies to all resident corporations or one that typically applies to those resident corporations that are members of a large multinational group. A generally applicable CIT would also include an income tax imposed on a corporation but which also applies to other taxable persons such as individuals.

Meaning of 'in lieu of' explained

The "in lieu of" test includes Taxes that are not described in the generally applicable income tax definition but which operate as substitutes for such taxes.

This test, which is used in some jurisdictions in the context of their foreign tax credit rules, would generally include withholding taxes on interest, rents and royalties, and other taxes on other categories of gross payments such as insurance premiums, provided such taxes are imposed in substitution for a generally applicable income tax.

Taxes imposed in lieu of a generally applicable CIT would also include taxes arising from the Subject to Tax Rule.

The "in lieu of" concept also covers Taxes that are imposed on an alternative basis (i.e. other than net income), such as Taxes based on the number of units produced or commercial surface area, and which are used as substitutes for a generally applicable income tax under the laws of the jurisdiction. Where, for example, a jurisdiction imposes a simplified methodology for calculating the income on a particular category of business or investment and this Tax is imposed in substitution for a generally applicable income tax, then that Tax falls within the definition of a Covered Tax.

A Tax imposed on an alternative basis levied at state or local government level, which is creditable against a generally applicable income tax levied at the national government level, would also qualify as a Covered Tax under the "in lieu of" test to the extent that it is credited against income tax in the same jurisdiction. Such local taxes can be considered as being in substitution (partially or fully) for a generally applicable income tax and an administratively efficient way of transferring resources from national to local government within the same jurisdiction.

Fails "in lieu of" test → A Tax that is imposed on an alternative basis that applies in addition to, and not as a substitute for, a generally applicable income tax under the laws of the jurisdiction would not fall under the "in lieu of" test for Covered Taxes.

Para (d)

- Paragraph (d) provides that Taxes levied by reference to retained earnings and corporate equity, including a Tax on multiple components based on income and equity, are Covered Taxes. Some jurisdictions impose Taxes on the net equity of a corporation in addition to CIT. The equity or capital of a corporation is composed of its retained earnings (i.e. the undistributed portion of the after-tax income in the Profit and Loss statement) and the contributions made by shareholders. Taxes on corporate equity may be inherently interlinked with the design of the CIT systems.
- For example, it may be possible under the laws of a jurisdiction to credit CIT against a corporate equity tax so that a company is allowed to reduce the corporate equity tax up to the amount of CIT that it pays in that jurisdiction. Taxes on corporate equity may also act as a supplement to CIT as part of a jurisdiction's overall approach to the taxation of a corporation's activities in that jurisdiction.
- For example, some Taxes on corporate equity may incorporate a minimum tax element to their design. Such Taxes on corporate equity are therefore an integral part of the overall system of corporate taxation in those jurisdictions.

- Some jurisdictions impose Taxes that have multiple components to the base. Where all the components of the tax base fall within the definition of income or profit covered by the GloBE Rules, then the tax, as a whole, is included within the definition of Covered Taxes.
- Other taxes may be levied in respect of a corporation's activities in a jurisdiction, and are administratively and conceptually part of the system of corporate taxation in these jurisdictions but may include both an income and a non-income element. Where such taxes are predominately a tax on an entity's income and it would be administratively burdensome to split the Tax into separate income and non-income components then such Taxes should be treated, in full, as Covered Taxes under the GloBE Rules.
- An example of a Covered Tax with multiple components is the corporate Zakat levied by the Kingdom of Saudi Arabia. The Zakat operates as a tax on income or equity or both and is therefore properly considered a Covered Tax for the purposes of the GloBE Rules.

4.4.2.2 Article 4.2.2.

465. Covered Taxes does not include any amount of:

(a) Top-up Tax accrued by a Parent Entity under a Qualified IIR;
(b) Top-up Tax accrued by a Constituent Entity under a QDMTT;
(c) Taxes attributable to an adjustment made by a Constituent Entity as a result of the application of a Qualified UTPR;
(d) A Disqualified Refundable Imputation Tax;
(e) Taxes paid by an insurance company in respect of returns to policyholders.

466. The term QDMTT mentioned *supra* is defined in Article 10.1, as below:

> Qualified Domestic Minimum Top-up Tax means a minimum tax that is included in the domestic law of a jurisdiction and that:
>
> (a) determines the Excess Profits of the Constituent Entities located in the jurisdiction (domestic Excess Profits) in a manner that is equivalent to the GloBE Rules;
> (b) operates to increase domestic tax liability with respect to domestic Excess Profits to the Minimum Rate for the jurisdiction and Constituent Entities for a Fiscal Year; and
> (c) is implemented and administered in a way that is consistent with the outcomes provided for under the GloBE Rules and the Commentary, provided that such jurisdiction does not provide any benefits that are related to such rules.
>
> A Qualified Domestic Minimum Top-up Tax may compute domestic Excess Profits based on an Acceptable Financial Accounting Standard permitted by the Authorised Accounting Body or an Authorised Financial Accounting Standard adjusted to prevent any Material Competitive Distortions, rather than the financial accounting standard used in the Consolidated Financial Statements.

467. Although Covered Taxes are defined broadly, certain Taxes are specifically excluded from the definition. These excluded Taxes generally fall into two categories: Top-up Taxes and refundable taxes, as explained in Figure 4.21.

Figure 4.21 Exclusions from Covered Taxes

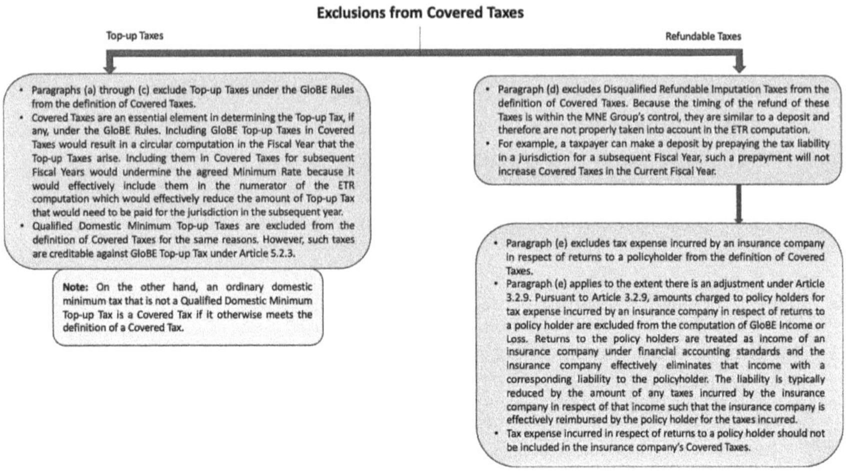

4.4.3 Article 4.3. (Allocation of Covered Taxes from One CE to Another CE)

468. Article 4.3 provides for allocation of Covered Taxes from one CE to another CE. The Tax allocation provisions in Chapter 4 follow the same pattern as the Income allocation provisions.

469. Prominent features of Article 4.3 are provided in Box 4.19.

Box 4.19 Prominent Features of Article 4.3

- Provides for allocation of Covered Taxes from one CE to another CE. The Tax allocation provisions in Chapter 4 follow the same pattern as the Income allocation provisions.
- Provides for allocation of Covered Taxes in respect of PEs, Tax Transparent Entities and Hybrid Entities, as well as the allocation of CFC taxes and taxes on distributions from one CE to another.
- The allocation of Covered Taxes under Article 4.3.1 is not limited to the current Taxes paid or accrued; it applies also to Deferred Taxes under Article 4.4.
- In order to preserve the intended rule order, domestic tax regimes should not provide a foreign tax credit for any tax imposed under a Qualified UTPR or IIR which is implemented in a foreign jurisdiction; otherwise, the application of that domestic tax regime would create circularity issues since those Taxes have already been determined prior to applying the Qualified UTPR or IIR.
- Paragraph (a) of Article 4.3.2 allocates Covered Taxes from a CE to a PE.

- Paragraph (b) of Article 4.3.2 provides that Tax borne by a Tax Transparent Entity that is attributable to a PE is first allocated to the PE, whereas, Tax borne by a Tax Transparent Entity that is not attributable to a PE is then allocated to Constituent Entity-owners.
- Paragraph (c) of Article 4.3.2 allocates taxes imposed pursuant to a CFC Tax Regime.
- Paragraph (d) of Article 4.3.2 allocates Taxes of Constituent Entity-owners arising in connection with the income of Hybrid Entities.
- Paragraph (e) of Article 4.3.2 allocates taxes arising in connection with dividends and other distributions between CEs.
- Article 4.3.3 imposes a limitation on the 'push-down' of Taxes from a Constituent Entity-owner that are attributable to Passive Income of the subsidiary CE.
- Without the rule of Article 4.3.3, an MNE Group could shift mobile income from high-tax jurisdictions to Low-Tax Jurisdictions to reduce overall tax liability (including Top-up Tax liability) in the MNE Group.
- Article 4.3.4 ensures that in cases where the GloBE Income of a PE is treated as GloBE Income of the Main Entity pursuant to Article 3.4.5, any Adjusted Covered Taxes associated with such income are treated as Adjusted Covered Taxes of the Main Entity, in an amount not exceeding such income multiplied by the highest corporate tax rate on ordinary income in the jurisdiction.

4.4.3.1 Article 4.3.1.

470. Covered Taxes are generally allocated to the CE, including a Stateless CE, that includes the corresponding income in the computation of its GloBE Income or Loss and then are taken into account in the ETR computation for the jurisdiction in which the entity is located. Accordingly, Article 4.3.2 applies to the allocation of Covered Taxes in respect of Permanent Establishments, Tax Transparent Entities and Hybrid Entities, as well as the allocation of CFC taxes and taxes on distributions from one Constituent Entity to another.

471. *Application of the Article*: In many cases, Covered Taxes will be paid by the CE with respect to its own income and to a tax authority in the jurisdiction in which it is located, and no allocation of tax is required. However, in some more complicated cases, Covered Taxes may be imposed on the CE in respect of income included in another CE's GloBE Income or Loss computation or by a jurisdiction other than the one in which the CE is located. This is the case with respect to CFC taxes and withholding taxes, for example. In those cases, it is necessary to allocate the Covered Taxes to the relevant CE that earned the income, subject to the limitations of Article 4.3.3. Similarly, rules are needed to properly allocate Covered Taxes of Main Entities in the case of PEs and Constituent Entity-owners in the case of Tax Transparent Entities. Finally, rules are needed to properly allocate Covered Taxes on distributions. Article 4.3.1 provides for the allocation of these Covered Taxes. The allocation of Covered Taxes under Article 4.3.1 is not limited to the current Taxes paid or accrued; it applies also to deferred Taxes under Article 4.4.

4.4.3.2 Article 4.3.2.

472. Covered Taxes are allocated from one Constituent Entity to another Constituent Entity as follows:

(a) the amount of any Covered Taxes included in the financial accounts of a Constituent Entity with respect to GloBE Income or Loss of a Permanent Establishment is allocated to the Permanent Establishment;
(b) the amount of any Covered Taxes included in the financial accounts of a Tax Transparent Entity with respect to GloBE Income or Loss allocated to a Constituent Entity-owner pursuant to Article 3.5.1(b) is allocated to that Constituent Entity-owner;
(c) in the case of a Constituent Entity whose Constituent Entity-owners are subject to a Controlled Foreign Company Tax Regime, the amount of any Covered Taxes included in the financial accounts of its direct or indirect Constituent Entity-owners under a Controlled Foreign Company Tax Regime on their share of the Controlled Foreign Company's income are allocated to the Constituent Entity;
(d) in the case of a Constituent Entity that is a Hybrid Entity, the amount of any Covered Taxes included in the financial accounts of a Constituent Entity-owner on income of the Hybrid Entity is allocated to the Hybrid Entity; and
(e) the amount of any Covered Taxes accrued in the financial accounts of a Constituent Entity's direct Constituent Entity-owners on distributions from the Constituent Entity during the Fiscal Year is allocated to the distributing Constituent Entity.

473. The term Controlled Foreign Company Tax Regime mentioned above is defined in Article 10.1 as below:

> Controlled Foreign Company Tax Regime means a set of tax rules (other than an IIR) under which a direct or indirect shareholder of a foreign entity (the controlled foreign company or CFC) is subject to current taxation on its share of part or all of the income earned by the CFC, irrespective of whether that income is distributed currently to the shareholder.

474. *Purpose of the Article:* Article 4.3.2 provides special allocation rules for certain cross-border taxes. These allocation rules are necessary to align the Covered Taxes with the GloBE Income to which the taxes relate, subject to certain limitations. It is intended that the GloBE Rules apply after the application of the STTR and domestic tax regimes, including regimes for the taxation of PEs or CFCs. Therefore, to preserve the intended rule order, domestic tax regimes should not provide a foreign tax credit for any tax imposed under a Qualified UTPR or IIR which is implemented in a foreign jurisdiction; otherwise, the application of that domestic tax regime would create circularity issues since those Taxes have already been determined prior to applying the Qualified UTPR or IIR.

Allocation of tax to a PE under Paragraph (a) of Article 4.3.2

475. *Purpose of paragraph (a)*: Paragraph (a) allocates Covered Taxes from a CE to a PE. The rule applies to Covered Taxes incurred by a Main Entity or another CE in respect of the income of a PE. The Covered Taxes are excluded from the Adjusted Covered Taxes of the CE that incurred them and are included in the Adjusted Covered Taxes of the PE. The Covered Taxes arising in the Main Entity in respect of the PE income can be computed using a three-step process:

- *The first step* is to determine the amount of the PE income that is included in the Main Entity's local taxable income. The amount of PE income included may be readily available from the Main Entity's tax return or the work papers used to prepare that return. The amount included in the Main Entity's return may be more or less than the GloBE Income allocated to the PE under Article 3.4 because it is determined under the rules for computing taxable income in the Main Entity's jurisdiction. However, the amount of PE income included in the local taxable income is the relevant figure for measuring how much local tax was paid in respect of the PE's GloBE Income.
- *The second step* is to determine the Main Entity's tax liability arising from inclusion of the PE income. If the PE income inclusion is subject to Tax separate and apart from the other income of the Main Entity, the tax rate applicable to the included income can simply be multiplied by the amount of the income inclusion. If, on the other hand, the PE income inclusion is mixed with the Main Entity's other income, the Main Entity's pre-foreign tax credit tax liability on all the income needs to be determined and allocated between the PE income inclusion and the rest of the Main Entity's taxable income. In many cases, a pro-rata allocation will be appropriate. In cases where the PE income is mixed with other income, if the Main Entity's total taxable income is less than the PE income inclusion, all of the pre-foreign tax credit liability is attributed to the inclusion. In other words, domestic losses and losses of other PEs allowed in the Main Entity's taxable income computation under a credit method are first used against domestic income and then applied to PE income inclusions.
- *The third step* is to determine the tax credit, if any, allowed in respect of Taxes paid by the PE. In many cases, the total credit allowed in respect of these income inclusions will be easily determinable from the Main Entity's tax returns. In some cases, however, the creditable Taxes of PEs may be included in a broader base of foreign income that includes other foreign income of the Main Entity. In these cases, the amount of the foreign tax credit attributable to

the PE income has to be determined based on the rules of the jurisdiction and using reasonable assumptions where necessary.

476. The amount of Covered Taxes paid on PE income inclusions is the excess of the tax liability arising from the PE income inclusions over any credit allowed for the PE's Taxes on its income, as explained through **Illustration # 49**:

Illustration of Allocation of tax to a PE under Paragraph (a) of Article 4.3.2

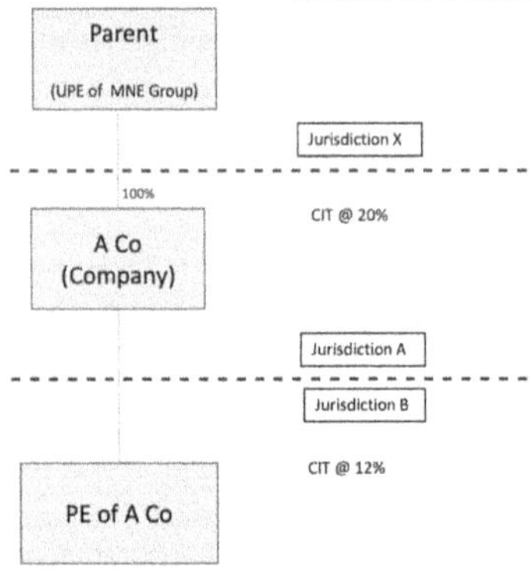

Step 1

Assumptions

- Company A incurs Tax in its residence jurisdiction on its income and the income of its PE at 20%.
- PE incurs tax at 12% in its jurisdiction. PE earns 100 of income and incurs 12 of tax in Year 1.
- Company A includes all 100 of PE income and the pre-credit tax liability in its jurisdiction is 20.
- However, a foreign tax credit is applied to reduce the tax charge on the PE income to 8.

Step 2

Application of Article 4.3.2(a)

- In this example, the 8 of tax would be excluded from Company A's Adjusted Covered Taxes and allocated to the PE because that is the actual liability with respect to the PE income.

477. *Situation when cross-crediting of Taxes is not allowed, cross-crediting of Taxes may be subject to limitations or cross-crediting may be fully allowed:* The foregoing three-step process determines the amount of Tax to exclude from the Main Entity's Covered Taxes. Once that amount is determined, however, those Taxes have to be allocated to the jurisdiction of the relevant PEs if the Main Entity was subject to tax on the income of more than one PE. Generally, this will require the MNE to determine the pre-credit tax liability for each PE income inclusion and subtract the allowed credit for foreign taxes on each inclusion from the pre-credit tax liability. The rules of the Main Entity jurisdiction, including tax credit limitations, apply in making these determinations. For example, in many cases, Tax paid by the PE will be creditable only to the extent of tax liability arising from the income inclusion of that PE. In other words, cross-crediting of Taxes is not allowed. Under those circumstances, the amount of residual Tax (i.e., Tax in excess of the allowed credit for foreign taxes) on a particular PE income inclusion is easily determined by subtracting the allowed credit from the pre-credit tax liability on the income inclusion. In other cases, the creditable Taxes may be subject to limitations or cross-crediting may be allowed. In the case of credit limitations, the MNE Group will need to determine the allowed credit for foreign taxes on each PE income inclusion based on the rules of the jurisdiction and, where necessary, make reasonable assumptions.

478. *Determining tax allocable to a PE is more complicated when cross-crediting is allowed*: Determining the amount of Tax paid on a PE income inclusion is more complicated when cross-crediting is allowed because Taxes paid by one PE are allowed to reduce the tax liability arising in respect of other PE income inclusions. Cross-crediting means that the Tax paid with respect to an income inclusion from a low-taxed PE may not equal the pre-credit tax liability on the inclusion less the tax credit allowed for Taxes paid by that PE. Where cross-crediting is allowed, the Taxes paid in respect of an inclusion should be determined by subtracting the credit allowed for Taxes paid by the particular PE and then further subtracting an appropriate amount of excess creditable Taxes paid by other PEs from the pre-credit tax liability of the PE. The appropriate amount of excess creditable taxes should be determined by allocating the total amount of excess creditable taxes among PE inclusions based on the relative residual tax liability due to each PE inclusion, taking into account only creditable taxes paid by that PE (i.e., the liability after the credit for taxes paid by the PE but before excess credits are allocated). Allocating the excess creditable taxes based on relative residual tax liability determined based solely on the PE's creditable taxes will ensure that the amount of the Main Entity's Covered Taxes allocated to PEs do not exceed the amount of Taxes actually arising on the related income inclusions. Deferred tax liabilities with respect to PE income are allocated in the same manner.

479. *Allocation of tax to a PE under Article 4.3.2(a) in case of a Flow-through Entity:* In the case of a Flow-through Entity, Article 4.3.2(a) allocates, in accordance with the allocation of GloBE Income or Loss pursuant to Article 3.5.1(a), the underlying taxes to the PE. If, for instance, the Constituent Entity-owner of a Flow-through Entity (such as a partner of Tax Transparent Entity that is a partnership which is itself also a CE) is required to pay the tax with respect to the income attributable to the PE due to the activities undertaken through a Tax Transparent Entity, that tax is allocated pursuant to Article 4.3.2 (a) from the Partner to that PE.

Allocation of tax from a Tax Transparent Entity to its Constituent Entity-owner under Paragraph (b) of Article 4.3.2

480. *Purpose of paragraph (b):* Paragraph (b) allocates taxes in connection with the income of a Tax Transparent Entity that is allocated to a Constituent Entity-owner. Generally, Tax Transparent Entities are not subject to CIT in the jurisdiction where they are created. However, some Covered Taxes could be imposed at the sub-national level or local level on Tax Transparent Entities without causing them to be considered a tax resident of that jurisdiction. In other cases, the operations carried out through the Tax Transparent Entity could give rise to source taxation that could be borne by the Tax Transparent Entity.

481. *Tax borne by a Tax Transparent Entity that is attributable to a PE is first allocated to the PE:* In most cases, where the Tax Transparent Entity is liable to Tax on net income in a jurisdiction, it will be because the activities and operations of that entity give rise to a PE in that jurisdiction (see paragraph (b) of the definition of PE in Article 10.1). In those cases, the appropriate portion of the income of the Tax Transparent Entity that is attributable to the PE is first allocated to the PE under Article 3.5.1(a), and so is the tax.

482. *Tax borne by a Tax Transparent Entity that is not attributable to a PE is allocated to Constituent Entity-owners:* Consistent with Article 3.5.1(b), Covered Taxes that are not allocated to a PE will be assigned to the Constituent Entity-owners of the Tax Transparent Entity. Typically, this will mean that Covered Taxes imposed on a Tax Transparent Entity's income (and not attributable to any PE) will be assigned to each Constituent Entity-owner in proportion to its share of the Tax Transparent Entity's income. In the case of a Reverse Hybrid Entity, the income and Taxes would remain with the entity itself, and, therefore, no allocation of Covered Taxes is needed in accordance with this paragraph.

Allocation of tax in a CFC Tax Regime under Paragraph (c) of Article 4.3.2

483. Similar to the allocation to Permanent Establishments in paragraph (a), paragraph (c) allocates taxes imposed pursuant to a CFC Tax Regime. The same general process described in paragraph (a) above for allocating Covered Taxes imposed on the Main Entity in respect of a PE can also be applied by a Constituent Entity-owner in respect of taxes arising under a CFC Tax Regime with the amount of any CFC Taxes included in the financial accounts of a direct or indirect Constituent Entity-owner on its share of the CFC's income being allocated to such CFC, subject to the limitations of Article 4.3.3.

Allocation of tax to Hybrid Entities under Paragraph (d) of Article 4.3.2

484. *Purpose of paragraph (d):* Paragraph (d) allocates Taxes of Constituent Entity-owners arising in connection with the income of Hybrid Entities. If a Constituent Entity-owner of a Hybrid Entity is located in a tax jurisdiction that imposes Tax on the owner's share of the Hybrid Entity's income under a fiscal transparency regime, the Covered Taxes included in the financial accounts of the Constituent Entity-owner should be assigned to the Hybrid Entity. The same general process described in paragraph (a) above for allocating Covered Taxes imposed on the Main Entity in respect of a PE can be used to determine the amount of taxes allocated by a Constituent Entity-owner to a Hybrid Entity; however, any taxes allocated to a Hybrid Entity by a Constituent Entity-owner in respect of Passive Income are subject to limitation under Article 4.3.3. If the Constituent Entity-owner is subject to a withholding tax or net basis taxes on distributions from the Hybrid Entity, such Taxes would also be allocated to the Hybrid Entity pursuant to paragraph (e).

Allocation of tax between CEs arising from dividends and other distributions under Paragraph (e) of Article 4.3.2

485. *Purpose of paragraph (e):* Paragraph (e) allocates taxes arising in connection with distributions between CEs. This includes withholding tax and net basis taxes incurred by direct Constituent Entity-owners on distributions by CEs in respect of their stock which are allocated to the distributing CE. Withholding taxes are imposed under the laws of the distributing CE and are collected at the source, but the income tax is the legal liability of the Constituent Entity-owner. The rule applies to Taxes with respect to any type of distribution with respect to the stock of the distributing CE. Thus, the rule also applies to Taxes in respect of a distribution that does not meet the definition of a dividend for tax purposes in the recipient jurisdiction or that would not be considered a distribution of retained earnings under the UPE's financial accounting standard.

486. *For simplicity, Taxes assigned to the jurisdiction of the immediate CE that distributed the dividend*: In many cases, the distributing CE is the CE that originally earned the income. In other cases, the distributing CE will be a direct or indirect shareholder of the CE that originally earned the income. Ideally, Covered Taxes incurred by CEs with respect to distributions should be assigned to the tax jurisdiction of the CE that originally earned the underlying income. However, tracking and tracing distributions through the ownership chain would be extremely complex and burdensome, particularly where an entity controls multiple CEs. Accordingly, paragraph (e) provides that such Taxes should be assigned to the jurisdiction of the immediate CE that distributed the dividend that triggered the tax liability.

4.4.3.3 Article 4.3.3.

487. Covered Taxes allocated to a Constituent Entity pursuant to Article 4.3.2(c) and (d) in respect of Passive Income are included in such Constituent Entity's Adjusted Covered Taxes in an amount equal to the lesser of:

(a) the Covered Taxes allocated in respect of such Passive Income; or
(b) the Top-up Tax Percentage for the Constituent Entity's jurisdiction, determined without regard to the Covered Taxes incurred with respect to such Passive Income by the Constituent Entity-owner, multiplied by the amount of the Constituent Entity's Passive Income includible under any Controlled Foreign Company Tax Regime or fiscal transparency rule.

Any Covered Taxes of the Constituent Entity-owner incurred with respect to such Passive Income that remain after the application of this article shall not be allocated under Article 4.3.2(c) or (d).

488. The term Passive Income mentioned *supra* is defined in Article 10.1 as below:

> Passive Income means income included in GloBE Income that is:
>
> (a) a dividend or dividend equivalents;
> (b) interest or interest equivalent;
> (c) rent;
> (d) royalty;
> (e) annuity; or
> (f) net gains from property of a type that produces income described in paragraphs (a) to (e),
>
> but only to the extent a Constituent Entity-owner is subject to tax on such income under a Controlled Foreign Company Tax Regime or as a result of an Ownership Interest in a Hybrid Entity.

489. *Objective of the Article*: Article 4.3.3 imposes a limitation on the 'push-down' of Taxes from a Constituent Entity-owner that are attributable to Passive Income of the subsidiary CE. This rule is designed to maintain the integrity of the jurisdictional blending rules in relation to mobile income. In the absence of Article 4.3.3, the rules in Article 4.3.2(c) and (d), which allocate Taxes paid by a Constituent Entity-owner under a CFC Tax Regime or in respect of a Hybrid Entity, would effectively blend the Taxes paid on that mobile income in the Constituent Entity-owner's high-tax jurisdiction with other income arising in the Low-Tax Jurisdiction. Without the rule of Article 4.3.3, an MNE Group could shift mobile income from high-tax jurisdictions to Low-Tax Jurisdictions to reduce overall tax liability (including Top-up Tax liability) in the MNE Group.

490. *Practical effect of the Article*: Under Article 4.3.3, the amount of Covered Taxes allocated pursuant to Articles 4.3.2(c) and (d) from a Constituent Entity-owner to a subsidiary in respect of Passive Income is limited to the lesser of the actual amount of Covered Taxes in respect of such Passive Income or the Top-up Tax Percentage that applies in the subsidiary jurisdiction, (determined without regard to the taxes to be pushed down to the subsidiary under the CFC Tax Regime or fiscal transparency rule), multiplied by the amount of the subsidiary's Passive Income that is includible under the CFC Tax Regime or fiscal transparency rule. Any remaining Covered Taxes of the subsidiary Constituent Entity-owner incurred with respect to such Passive Income after the application of this article are included in the Constituent Entity-owner's Adjusted Covered Taxes. The practical effect of this rule is therefore to cap the total Covered Taxes on such passive income (including the taxes allocated to the subsidiary under the CFC or tax transparency regime) to the minimum rate.

491. The CFC Tax push-down limitation under Article 4.3.3. on Adjusted Covered Taxes is explained through **Illustration # 50**:

Illustration of CFC Tax push-down limitation under Article 4.3.3

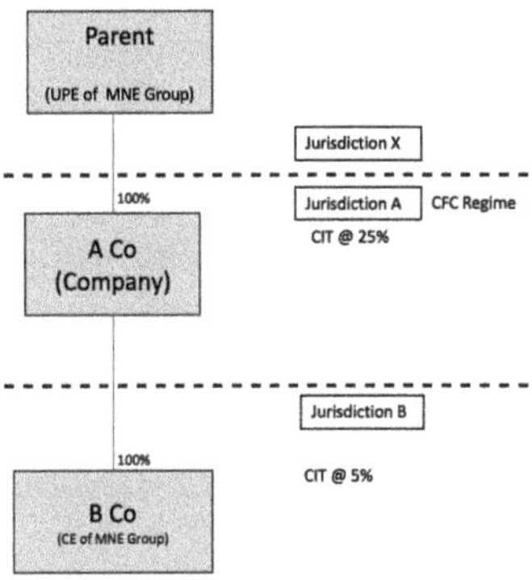

Assumptions Step 1

- A Co is a CE of a MNE Group in Country A. Country A imposes a 25% CIT rate and has a CFC Tax Regime which imposes Taxes on shareholders in respect of Passive Income derived by foreign (CFC) subsidiaries. A Co has no other operating income in Year 1.
- A Co wholly owns B Co, which is located in Country B. Country B imposes a 5% CIT rate. B Co is the only CE located in Country B.
- In Year 1, B Co has GloBE Income of EUR 100, of which EUR 50 is Passive Income that is subject to the CFC Tax Regime of Country A.
- Country A imposes its CFC charge on the EUR 50 of Passive Income earned by B Co. This CFC charge is computed by applying the Country A CIT rate of 25% to the Passive Income earned by B Co, less any applicable foreign tax credit (FTC). Accordingly, the Country A CFC charge is 10 ((25% x 50) – (5% x 50)). The tax calculation for both A Co and B Co is as below:

A Co (Country A)		B Co (Country B)	
Country A Income		Country B Income	
Operating Income	0	Operating Income	50
CFC Inclusion (B Co)	50	Passive Income	50
Total Taxable Income	50	Total Taxable Income	100
Country A Tax		Country B Tax	
Tax on Operating Income (25%)	0	Tax on Operating Income (5%)	2.5
Tax on CFC Inclusion (25%)	12.5	Tax on Passive Income (5%)	2.5
Foreign Tax Credit (CFC Inclusion)	(2.5)		
Total Country A Tax*	10	Total Country B Tax	5

* Entirely attributable to CFC inclusion since there is no other income

Application of Article 4.3.3 Step 2

- The amount of any CFC Taxes included in the financial accounts of a direct or indirect Constituent Entity-owner on its share of the CFC's income is allocated to such CFC under Article 4.3.2(c). The allocation of CFC Taxes, however, is subject to the limitations of Article 4.3.3.
- Under Article 4.3.3, the allocation of CFC Taxes is limited to the lesser of:
  (a) the actual amount of Covered Taxes in respect of such Passive Income; or
  (b) the Top-up Tax Percentage that applies in the subsidiary jurisdiction, multiplied by the amount of the subsidiary's Passive Income that is includible under the CFC Tax Regime.

  For the purposes of this formula, the Top-up Tax Percentage is determined without regard to the Covered Taxes to be allocated to the subsidiary under the CFC Tax Regime.
- The maximum amount of CFC Taxes that can be allocated from Country A to Country B (to increase its ETR) under Article 4.3.3 is therefore computed as follows:
  Step 1: the Top-up Tax Percentage for Country B is determined without regard to any Covered Taxes of the Constituent Entity-owner on such Passive Income. This amount is 10% (15% - 5%).
  Step 2: the Top-up Tax Percentage calculated under Step 1 is multiplied by the amount of the Constituent Entity's Passive Income includible under the CFC Tax Regime of Country A. This amount is EUR 5 (10% x EUR 50).
  Step 3: the lesser of the Step 2 amount or the actual CFC Taxes with respect to the Passive Income is allocated to B Co.

Solution Step 3

- In this case the Step 2 amount is 5, while the actual CFC Tax amount is 10. Therefore, Covered Tax of 5 may be allocated under Article 4.3.3 from Country A to Country B.
- Absent the limitation in Article 4.3.3, Article 4.3.2 (c) would have allocated the full CFC Tax of EUR 10 to Country B.
- Article 4.3.3 ensures that the CFC Tax allocated from Country A to Country B is sufficient to reach the Minimum Rate with respect to the income brought into charge under the CFC Tax Regime.
- The remaining Covered Tax of EUR 5 in Country A stays with A Co and is included in its Adjusted Covered Taxes for purposes of determining the ETR in Country A.
- A table illustrates the GloBE Calculations after Application of Article 4.3.3.

A Co (Country A)		B Co (Country B)	
GloBE Income	0	GloBE Income	100
Covered Taxes		Covered Taxes	
Country A Tax	10	Country B Tax	5
CFC Tax Allocated to Country B	(5)	CFC Tax Allocated from Country A	5
Total Country A Adjusted Covered Taxes	5	Total Country B Adjusted Covered Taxes	10
ETR	-	ETR	10%
Top-up Tax	-	Top-up Tax	5

4.4.3.4 Article 4.3.4.

492. Where the GloBE Income of a Permanent Establishment is treated as GloBE Income of the Main Entity pursuant to Article 3.4.5, any Covered Taxes arising in the location of the Permanent Establishment and associated with such income are treated as Covered Taxes of the Main Entity up to an amount not exceeding such income multiplied by the highest corporate tax rate on ordinary income in the jurisdiction where the Main Entity is located.

493. *Purpose of the Article*: Article 4.3.4 ensures that in cases where the GloBE Income of a PE is treated as GloBE Income of the Main Entity pursuant to Article 3.4.5, any

Adjusted Covered Taxes associated with such income are treated as Adjusted Covered Taxes of the Main Entity, in an amount not exceeding such income multiplied by the highest corporate tax rate on ordinary income in the jurisdiction. The highest corporate tax rate on ordinary income means the full marginal rate which a jurisdiction generally applies to categories of income which do not benefit from any exemption, exclusion, credit or other tax relief applicable to particular types of payments. This concept is further considered in paragraph 32 of the OECD's 2015 Final Report on Action 2: Neutralising the Effects of Hybrid Mismatch Arrangements.[98] This also does not include rates which are only applied to particular business sectors.

494. The situation to apply Article 4.3.4 arises after a loss of a PE has been treated as a loss of a Main Entity under Article 3.4.5. In most cases, there will not be Taxes in the location of the PE, either because the jurisdiction allows the PE to carry-forward its loss or, more rarely, because the PE is not subject to Tax in the jurisdiction.

495. *Deferred tax assets*: When a GloBE Loss of a PE is treated as an expense of a Main Entity under Article 3.4.5, any deferred tax asset established with respect to a tax loss of the PE jurisdiction shall not reduce the Adjusted Covered Taxes of the PE jurisdiction or the Main Entity jurisdiction. Conversely, when the deferred tax asset established by the PE reverses in the PE jurisdiction, the Adjusted Covered Taxes of the PE jurisdiction or Main Entity jurisdiction shall not be increased. Deferred tax attributes generated or used in the Main Entity jurisdiction with respect to a loss of the PE are available for use and remain subject to the other provisions of Chapter 4.

4.4.4 Article 4.4. (Mechanism to Address Temporary Differences)

496. *Objective of the Article*: Article 4.4 provides the mechanism to address temporary differences which arise when income or loss is recognised in a different year for financial accounting and tax. The principal mechanism that the GloBE Rules use to address temporary differences is set forth in Article 4.4 and builds on deferred tax accounting, with key adjustments to protect the integrity of the GloBE Rules, as explained through **Illustration # 51**:

98. Refer 'Action 2: BEPS 2015 Final Report, OECD/G20 Base Erosion and Profit Shifting Project' http://www.oecd.org/tax/beps-2015-final-reports.htm.

Illustration to address temporary differences set forth in Article 4.4

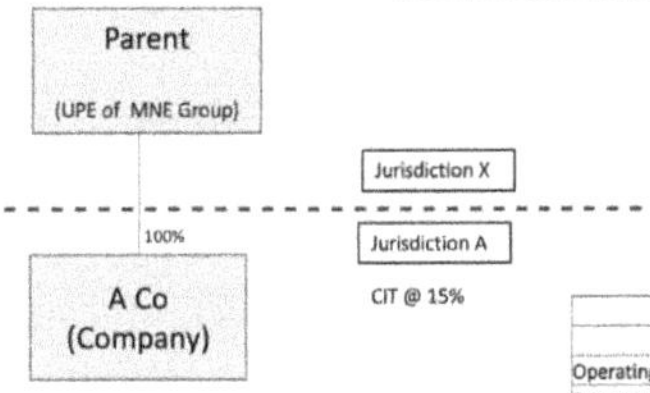

Assumptions Step 1

- Company A is located in Country A which imposes a 15% CIT.
- In the first Fiscal Year, Company A purchases Asset M for 100 that benefits from immediate expensing under the tax laws of Country Z, but that must be amortised over five years for financial accounting purposes.
- Company A earns 100 of operating income in that same Fiscal Year.
- For domestic tax purposes, Company A has no taxable income due to the immediate expensing of Asset M.
- However, for financial accounting and GloBE purposes, Company A has 80 of income (100 of operating income, less 20 of amortisation).
- Absent Article 4.4.1, Top-up Tax of 12 would be due in the first Fiscal Year, given the 80 of income with no tax paid as computed in the Table below:

Year 1			
Domestic Tax Computation		**Financial Accounting**	
Operating Income	100	Operating Income	100
Depreciation on asset costing 100 @ 100%	-100	Depreciation on asset costing 100 @ 20%	-20
Taxable Income	0	Taxable Income	80
Tax Paid	0	Top-up Tax in Year 1 as Tax paid is Nil	12

Application of Article 4.4 Step 2

- Article 4.4.1 operates to adjust for this timing difference by permitting the deferred tax assets and liabilities of Company A to be taken into account.
- The temporary difference amount is 80 (i.e., the amount of income that is GloBE Income in the current Fiscal Year and that will reverse as the asset is amortised for financial accounting purposes over the next four years).
- To prevent this timing difference from resulting in Top-up Tax, 80 of GloBE Income should be sheltered by the Article 4.4 rules.
- Accordingly, the Article 4.4.1 rules, following standard tax accounting principles, will permit a deferred tax liability to be recognised in the first Fiscal Year of 12, which provides shelter for 80 of GloBE Income at the 15% Minimum Rate, as summarised in the Table here.

Year 1	
Financial Accounting for GloBE purposes	
Operating Income	100
Depreciation on asset costing 100 @ 20%	-20
Taxable Income	80
Current Tax @15%	12
Deferred Tax Adjustment (on 80 at minimum rate of 15%)	(12)
Top-up Tax	0

497. While Article 4.4 uses existing deferred tax accounts maintained by MNE Groups to the greatest extent possible to simplify compliance, certain adjustments are required to protect the integrity of the GloBE Rules, which include:

- using the lower of the Minimum Rate or the applicable tax rate to calculate deferred tax assets and liabilities in order to prevent deferred tax amounts from sheltering unrelated GloBE Income;
- the rules require the recapture of certain amounts claimed as deferred tax liabilities that are not paid within five years;
- exceptions are provided for the most common and material book-to-tax differences when they relate to substance in a jurisdiction or are not prone to taxpayer manipulation. These amounts do not require monitoring for recapture.

498. Prominent features of Article 4.4 are provided in Box 4.20.

Box 4.20 Prominent Features of Article 4.4

- Provides the mechanism to address temporary differences, which arise when income or loss is recognised in a different year for financial accounting and tax.
- Requires certain adjustments to the existing deferred tax accounts maintained by MNE Groups to protect the integrity of the GloBE Rules.
- Article 4.4.1 provides that Total Deferred Tax Adjustment Amount adjusts the Covered Taxes of a CE to take certain deferred tax assets and liabilities into account in order to address the impact of temporary differences.
- Paragraph (a) of Article 4.4.1 prevents overstatement of the jurisdictional ETR by excluding from the Total Deferred Tax Adjustment Amount the

amount of deferred tax expense with respect to any items that are excluded from the computation of GloBE Income or Loss under Chapter 3.

- Paragraph (b) of Article 4.4.1 operates to exclude deferred tax expense that relates to 'Disallowed Accruals' and 'Unclaimed Accruals' from the Total Deferred Tax Adjustment Amount.
- Paragraph (c) of Article 4.4.1 excludes valuation adjustments or accounting recognition adjustments with respect to deferred tax assets so as to achieve alignment in recording of deferred tax assets for domestic tax loss and GloBE purposes. It follows that when a loss is not available for domestic law purposes, it cannot reverse under financial accounting rules, and therefore it will not be available for GloBE purposes to increase Adjusted Covered Taxes.
- Paragraph (d) of Article 4.4.1 excludes the amount of deferred tax expense that results from a change in the applicable domestic tax rate.
- Paragraph (e) of Article 4.4.1 excludes the deferred tax benefit with respect to the generation of tax credits as well as the deferred tax expense with respect to the use of tax credits. The generation of tax credits should not give rise to Top-up Tax under Article 4.1.5
- Paragraph (a) of Article 4.4.2 operates to take into account any 'Disallowed Accrual' or 'Unclaimed Accrual' that has been paid during the Fiscal Year, as once such Taxes are paid, it is appropriate to take them into account for GloBE purposes.
- Paragraph (b) of Article 4.4.2 permits the addition of Recaptured Deferred Tax Liabilities that have been paid during the Fiscal Year.
- Paragraph (c) of Article 4.4.2 provides for the generation of a deemed deferred tax asset when a deferred tax asset should have been generated but was not due to the recognition criteria not being met. This rule is a corollary to the rule in Article 4.4.1(c) that disregards valuation adjustments or accounting recognition adjustments.
- Article 4.4.3 provides that when a deferred tax asset has been recorded at a rate lower than the Minimum Rate, such asset may be recast at the Minimum Rate when the asset is attributable to a GloBE Loss.
- Provides that to the extent an amount is recast at the Minimum Rate under Article 4.4.3, the recast must be done in the Fiscal Year in which the loss becomes a GloBE Loss to prevent distortive outcomes.
- Article 4.4.4 provides that barring Recapture Exception Accruals, deferred tax liabilities recorded in other categories that do not reverse within the five Fiscal Years must be recaptured in the Fiscal Year in which the increase in the Recaptured Deferred Tax Liability was originally included in the Total Deferred Tax Adjustment Amount.
- Article 4.4.4 ensures that deferred tax liabilities recorded with respect to categories that do not relate to specific policy-allowed categories are actually settled within the required period of time and are, therefore, required to be monitored under the rules.

- To reduce compliance burdens, Article 4.4.5 ensures certain low-risk items referred to as Recapture Exception Accrual that are certain to reverse over time are not required to be monitored under the rules in Article 4.4.4 for recapture.
- The Disallowed Accrual rule is set forth in Articles 4.4.6 and 4.4.1(b). This rule is intended to prevent accruals of tax with respect to uncertain tax positions and distributions from a CE from being included in the Adjusted Covered Taxes amount until actually paid.
- Article 4.4.7 provides a compliance simplification option with respect to the Article 4.4.4 recapture rule. This article permits a CE to exclude from the Total Deferred Tax Adjustment Amount any deferred tax liability that is not expected to be paid within the time period set forth in Article 4.4.4. This simplification allows for the exclusion of deferred tax liabilities that are almost certain to require recapture, which reduces compliance monitoring such liabilities and recalculating Top-up Tax several years later.

4.4.4.1 Article 4.4.1.

499. The Total Deferred Tax Adjustment Amount for a Constituent Entity for the Fiscal Year is equal to the deferred tax expense accrued in its financial accounts if the applicable tax rate is below the Minimum Rate or, in any other case, such deferred tax expense recast at the Minimum Rate, with respect to Covered Taxes for the Fiscal Year subject to the adjustments set forth in Articles 4.4.2 and 4.4.3 and the following exclusions:

(a) The amount of deferred tax expense with respect to items excluded from the computation of GloBE Income or Loss under Chapter 3;
(b) The amount of deferred tax expense with respect to Disallowed Accruals and Unclaimed Accruals;
(c) The impact of a valuation adjustment or accounting recognition adjustment with respect to a deferred tax asset;
(d) The amount of deferred tax expense arising from a re-measurement with respect to a change in the applicable domestic tax rate; and
(e) The amount of deferred tax expense with respect to the generation and use of tax credits.

500. *The Article addresses impact of temporary differences:* Article 4.4.1 establishes the Total Deferred Tax Adjustment Amount for a CE, which is an amount that is added to the Adjusted Covered Taxes of a CE for a Fiscal Year under Article 4.1.1(b). The Total Deferred Tax Adjustment Amount adjusts the Covered Taxes of a CE to take certain deferred tax assets and liabilities into account in order to address the impact of temporary differences.

501. *Computation of Total Deferred Tax Adjustment Amount:* The starting point for the Total Deferred Tax Adjustment Amount is the amount of deferred tax expense accrued in the financial accounts of a CE if the applicable tax rate is below the Minimum Rate or, in any other case, such deferred tax expense recast at the Minimum Rate. Deferred tax expense for the Fiscal Year is comprised of the net movement in deferred tax assets and liabilities between the beginning and end of the Fiscal Year. When established, deferred tax assets are recorded as negative tax expense (i.e., income tax benefit), whereas deferred tax liabilities are recorded as tax expense. Note that the recast of deferred tax expense may either be performed on an item-by-item basis or in the aggregate for all items recorded at the same rate, as the result should remain unchanged. When a deferred tax asset or deferred tax liability reverses, it will reverse at the same amount and rate at which it has been recorded. A reversal of a deferred tax liability is a negative deferred tax expense, whereas the reversal of a deferred tax asset equates to a deferred tax expense. The applicable tax rate is the tax rate at which the deferred tax item is recorded. For example, if a deferred tax liability of 20 is recorded with respect to income of 100, the applicable tax rate is 20% (i.e., the tax imposed on an item of income divided by that item of income). This rate is higher than the Minimum Rate and would thus be recast at the Minimum Rate, as explained through **Illustration # 52**:

Illustration explaining that deferred tax liabilities (or assets) must be recast with reference to the Minimum Rate as per Article 4.4.1

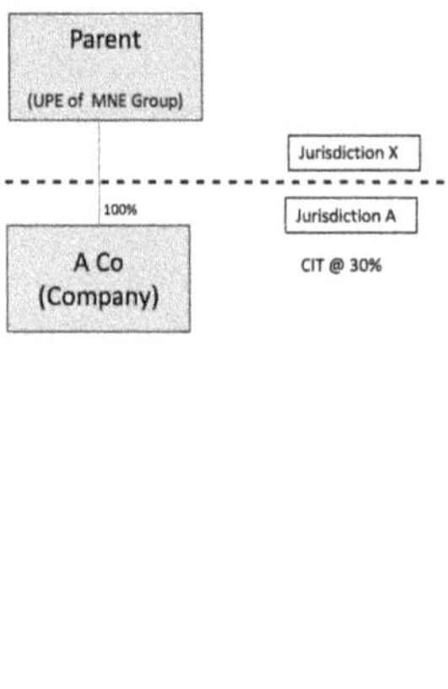

Assumptions Step 1

- Company A is located in Country A which imposes a 30% CIT.
- In the first Fiscal Year, Company A purchases Asset M for 100 that benefits from immediate expensing under the tax laws of Country Z, but that must be amortised over five years for financial accounting purposes.
- Company A earns 100 of operating income in that same Fiscal Year.
- For domestic tax purposes, Company A has no taxable income due to the immediate expensing of Asset M.
- However, for financial accounting and GloBE purposes, Company A has 80 of income (100 of operating income, less 20 of amortisation).
- Absent Article 4.4.1, Top-up Tax of 12 would be due in the first Fiscal Year, given the 80 of income with no tax paid as computed in the Table below:

Year 1				
Domestic Tax Computation			**Financial Accounting**	
Operating Income	100		Operating Income	100
Depreciation on asset costing 100 @ 100%	-100		Depreciation on asset costing 100 @ 20%	-20
Taxable Income	0		Taxable Income	80
Tax Paid	0		Top-up Tax in Year 1 as Tax paid is Nil	12

Application of Article 4.4.1 Step 2

- Article 4.4.1 operates to adjust for this timing difference by permitting the deferred tax assets and liabilities of Company A to be taken into account.
- The temporary difference amount is 80 (i.e., the amount of income that is GloBE Income in the current Fiscal Year and that will reverse as the asset is amortised for financial accounting purposes over the next four years).
- The rules in Article 4.4.1 would still recognise a deferred tax liability of 12 (i.e. 80 of additional income multiplied by the 15% Minimum Rate and not at the CIT rate of 30% imposed by the jurisdiction) in the first Fiscal Year. When such deferred tax liability reverses, the amount of the reversal will be 12.

502. To the extent deferred tax assets exceed deferred tax liabilities, deferred tax expense will be negative (i.e., an asset in lieu of a liability). This amount is typically accrued with respect to the applicable domestic tax rate (i.e., the tax rate in a jurisdiction which applies to the item of income with respect to which the deferred tax item is recorded) in a jurisdiction in order to adjust for timing differences between financial accounting recognition and domestic tax recognition. In order to use the accounts to adjust for timing differences under the GloBE Rules, the deferred tax assets and liabilities must be recast with reference to the Minimum Rate to the extent they have been recorded at a rate in excess of the Minimum Rate.

Exclusions under paragraph (a)

503. *Paragraph (a) prevents overstatement of the jurisdictional ETR:* Paragraph (a) of Article 4.4.1 excludes from the Total Deferred Tax Adjustment Amount the amount of deferred tax expense with respect to any items that are excluded from the computation of GloBE Income or Loss under Chapter 3. This paragraph operates to prevent taxes associated with items not includible in the calculation of GloBE Income or Loss from being used to increase the amount of Adjusted Covered Taxes, resulting in an overstatement of the jurisdictional ETR, as explained through **Illustration # 53**:

Illustration explaining application of Article 4.4.1(a)

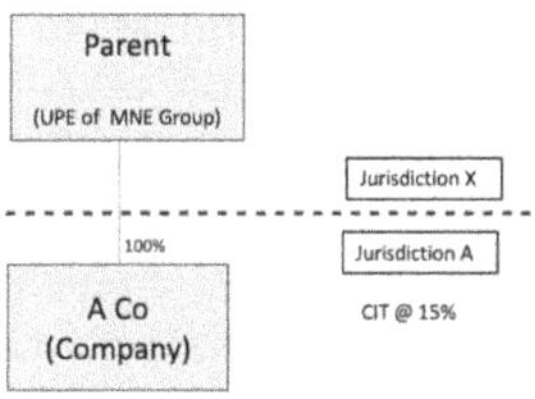

Assumptions Step 1

- Company A is located in Country A which imposes a 15% CIT and subjects to tax Excluded Equity Gains and Losses.
- In a Fiscal Year, A Co incurs a GloBE Loss of (300) and an Excluded Equity Loss of (100).
- This Excluded Equity Loss is not included in the GloBE Income or Loss for Country C, because it is an Excluded Equity Loss under Article 3.2.1(c).
- Accordingly, if there are no other differences between the GloBE base and the Country C tax base, the GloBE Loss for Country C is (300) whereas the domestic tax loss for Country C is (400).

Application of Article 4.4.1(a) Step 2

- A deferred tax asset of 60 is established for domestic tax purposes, however, for GloBE purposes only 45 may be taken into account since 15 of deferred tax asset relates to the Excluded Equity Loss of 100, as shown in Table below:

Year 1				
Domestic Tax Computation			**Deferred Tax Asset for GloBE purposes on applying Article 4.4.1 (a)**	
Operating Income	-300		Operating Income	-300
Excluded Equity Loss	-100		Excluded Equity Loss adjusted under Article 3.2.1(c)	0
Taxable Income	-400		GloBE Income	-300
Deferred Tax Asset @ 15%	(60)		Deferred Tax Asset @ 15% for GloBE purposes	(45)

Exclusions under paragraph (b)

504. *Purpose of the paragraph:* Paragraph (b) operates to exclude deferred tax expense that relates to 'Disallowed Accruals' and 'Unclaimed Accruals' from the Total Deferred Tax Adjustment Amount. These terms are further explained in the discussion on Article 4.4.6 and Article 4.4.7 *infra*. The principal reason for excluding such amounts until paid is the speculative nature as to whether such amounts will be actually paid in the case of a Disallowed Accrual or when the amounts will be paid in the case of an Unclaimed Accrual. The discussion made *supra* on Paragraph (d) of Article 4.1.3 sets out the basis for the exclusion of current tax expense that relates to uncertain tax positions.

Exclusions under paragraph (c)

505. *Purpose of the paragraph is to prevent distortions:* Paragraph (c) excludes valuation adjustments or accounting recognition adjustments with respect to deferred tax assets. When it is not probable that taxable profit will arise in the future against which all or part of a domestic tax loss can be applied, a valuation allowance or accounting recognition adjustment is generally required for financial accounting purposes. This valuation allowance or accounting recognition adjustment is applied to the extent of the loss that is not forecast to be usable. When an accounting recognition adjustment is recorded, the deferred tax asset is not recorded as a deferred tax asset in the financial statements to the extent it is not forecast to be usable in the future. When accounting rules require a valuation allowance, the deferred tax asset associated with the domestic tax loss is recorded in the financial statements as a deferred tax asset; however, an offsetting liability is recorded as a valuation allowance to the extent of the deferred tax asset that is not forecast to be usable. If financial forecasts change in a future period and it becomes probable that taxable profit will arise in the current period or a future period, the accounting recognition adjustment or valuation allowance is reversed in the period in which the forecast changes.

506. *Alignment in recording of deferred tax assets for domestic tax loss and GloBE purposes*: Because the generation of deferred tax assets reduces Adjusted Covered Taxes, it is necessary to ensure that a deferred tax asset relating to a domestic tax loss is recorded in the same year as such loss for GloBE purposes. Accordingly, the rule in paragraph (c) ensures that the deferred tax asset is recorded for GloBE purposes in the same year as the economic loss which gave rise to such asset. Because valuation allowances and accounting recognition adjustments are disregarded under the GloBE Rules, a deferred tax asset will be recorded in respect of a domestic tax loss regardless of whether there is a forecast of probable future use of such attribute. As a result, a taxpayer may have recorded a GloBE deferred tax asset in respect of a carry-forward domestic tax loss that expires. A carry-forward loss cannot be used under domestic law when it is not available to offset domestic taxable income. The financial accounting rules treat deferred tax assets arising from domestic carry-forward losses as reversed when they are used to offset domestic taxable income. Therefore, such losses will not be available for use for GloBE purposes to the extent they cannot be used under domestic law. It follows that when a loss is not available for domestic law purposes, it cannot reverse under financial accounting rules, and therefore it will not be available for GloBE purposes to increase Adjusted Covered Taxes.

507. *Example explaining application of paragraph (c):* In Year 1, a CE incurs a GloBE Loss of (100), and a deferred tax asset of (15) is generated; however, financial forecasts indicate that the tax loss will not be used in the future. Accordingly, the benefit of this tax loss is not recorded due to valuation adjustments or accounting recognition adjustments. However, this is disregarded for GloBE purposes, and the deferred tax asset is generated. In Year 2, the forecast changes and the valuation adjustment or accounting recognition adjustment is reversed. This is also disregarded for GloBE purposes. In Year 3, GloBE Income of 100 is generated, and the loss deferred tax asset is used and reversed. Absent the application of paragraph (c), in this example, the deferred tax asset would have been generated in Year 2, reducing Adjusted Covered Taxes in a year in which there is no Net GloBE Income, and Top-up Tax would have otherwise arisen under Article 4.1.5.

Exclusions under paragraph (d)

508. *Purpose of the paragraph:* Paragraph (d) excludes the amount of deferred tax expense that results from a change in the applicable domestic tax rate. This amount is excluded because amounts accrued in this respect are simply changes to amounts already accrued and should not be taken into account as additional Covered Taxes in a Fiscal Year. For example, if additional deferred tax expense comes through the financial statements because a tax rate has increased from 10% to 15%, this amount should not be added to Covered Taxes since it does not relate to GloBE Income in the current Fiscal Year. Articles 4.6.2 and 4.6.3 provide rules that govern how domestic tax rate changes are taken into account for GloBE purposes to ensure appropriate credit is given for tax paid.

Exclusions under paragraph (e)

509. *Purpose of the paragraph is to exclude tax credits to prevent distorted GloBE results:* Paragraph (e) excludes the deferred tax benefit with respect to the generation of tax credits as well as the deferred tax expense with respect to the use of tax credits. Tax credits are excluded from Article 4.4.1 Total Deferred Tax Adjustment amount because the inclusion of such amounts could lead to distortions in GloBE results.

510. *Tax credits explained*: A tax credit is an amount that taxpayers can subtract directly from taxes owed to a government. They differ from deductions, which reduce the amount of taxable income. Instead, they directly reduce the amount of tax owed. One example of a tax credit is an investment tax credit whereby the government provides the taxpayer that incurs certain qualifying expenditure with a reduction in a future tax payable that is calculated as a percentage of the expenditure incurred. A tax credit under paragraph (e) includes tax credits granted in a jurisdiction due to a tax liability imposed in another jurisdiction or imposed on profits distributed by another entity, such as foreign tax credits.

511. *Generation of tax credits should not give rise to Top-up Tax under Article 4.1.5:* Since the generation and use of tax credits are excluded from the Total Deferred Tax Adjustment Amount; hence, any movement in deferred tax expense arising from the generation and use of such tax credits is excluded from the computation of Adjusted Covered Taxes. For example, when an excess foreign tax credit carry-forward is generated, the deferred tax asset associated with such carry-forward will not reduce Adjusted Covered Taxes since it is excluded from the Total Deferred Tax Adjustment Amount under Article 4.4.1(e). Conversely, when such foreign tax credit carry-forward is used in a subsequent Fiscal Year, the use of such deferred tax asset will not result in an increase in Adjusted Covered Taxes for the same reason. This results in the same outcome as if no deferred tax asset for the carry-forward of a foreign tax credit was recorded at all. Also, since deferred tax assets arising from the generation of tax credits are excluded from the Total Deferred Tax Adjustment Amount and will not reduce Adjusted Covered Taxes, hence, the generation of tax credits should not give rise to Top-up Tax under Article 4.1.5, as explained through **Illustration # 54**:

Illustration explaining application of Article 4.4.1(e)

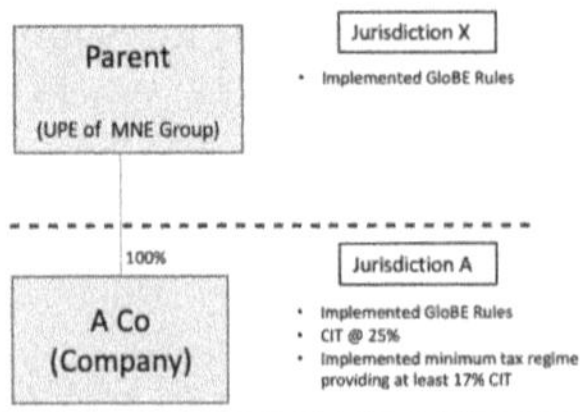

Assumptions Step 1

- A Co is a Constituent Entity of an MNE Group that is subject to the GloBE Rules. A Co is the only Constituent Entity located in Country A. The only tax imposed on A Co under Country A law is corporation tax which is imposed at the rate of 25%.
- The tax base of Country A is the same as the GloBE tax base.
- Country A has a minimum tax regime that provides at least 17% corporate income tax must be paid in a taxable year.
- In Year 1, A Co earns GloBE Income of 100 in Country A. The initial tax liability for A Co is therefore 25 but Country A provides an incentive tax credit to A Co of 15.
- Because of the Country A minimum tax regime, only 8 of the incentive tax credit may be used in Year 1 given the 17% minimum rate requirement. The remaining 7 of incentive tax credit is available for carry-forward to a future tax year.
- A Co therefore pays 17 of Country A tax in Year 1 and carries-forward an excess credit of 7.
- In Year 2, A Co earns GloBE Income of 100 and has an initial tax liability in Country A of 25. A Co applies its remaining 7 tax credit carry-forward from Year 1 and pays 18 of Country A tax in Year 2.

Application of Article 4.4.1(e) Step 2

- Because Article 4.4.1(e) excludes deferred tax expense with respect to the generation and use of tax credits, the carry-forward of 7 generated in Year 1 does not give rise to a deferred tax asset for GloBE purposes, and therefore does not reduce the Adjusted Covered Taxes for Country A in Year 1.
- Applying the same rule, the use of the credit carry-forward of 7 in Year 2 does not increase Adjusted Covered Taxes for Country A in Year 2.
- As a result, the Country A ETR is 17% in Year 1 (17/100) and 18% in Year 2 (18/100).
- Absent the rule in Article 4.4.1(e), the Country A results would have been distorted by the generation of excess tax credits in Year 1, as the credit carry-forward would give rise to a deferred tax asset that would otherwise reduce Adjusted Covered Taxes below the Minimum Rate.
- A table illustrating the numerical results of this example is given here.

Particulars	Year 1	Year 2
GloBE Income/ (Loss)	100	100
Country A Tax (25%)	(25)	(25)
Tax Credit Generated	15	0
Carry-forward Tax Credit Applied	0	7
Final Country A Tax	(17)	(18)
Country A ETR	17%	18%
Top-up Tax	0	0
Excess Tax Credit Carry-forward	7	0

4.4.4.2 *Article 4.4.2.*

512. Article 4.4.2 provides for certain adjustments to the Total Deferred Tax Adjustment Amount, which is adjusted as follows:

(a) Increased by the amount of any Disallowed Accrual or Unclaimed Accrual paid during the Fiscal Year;
(b) Increased by the amount of any Recaptured Deferred Tax Liability determined in a preceding Fiscal Year which has been paid during the Fiscal Year; and
(c) Reduced by the amount that would be a reduction to the Total Deferred Tax Adjustment Amount due to recognition of a loss deferred tax asset for a current year tax loss, where a loss deferred tax asset has not been recognised because the recognition criteria are not met.

513. *Adjustments carried out through paragraph (a):* The first adjustment in paragraph (a) operates to take into account any 'Disallowed Accrual' or 'Unclaimed Accrual' that has been paid during the Fiscal Year. As discussed in Article 4.4.1 Commentary, such amounts were not taken into account when generated due to the speculative nature of when and whether such Taxes would be paid. However, once such Taxes are paid, it is appropriate to take them into account for GloBE purposes. Although the tax paid will be included in current taxes, this may be offset by the decrease in the deferred tax liability, to the extent the deferred tax liability is included in the Total Deferred Tax Adjustment Amount and therefore in Adjusted Covered Taxes. As a result, it is necessary to include an amount in the Total Deferred Tax Adjustment Amount to ensure there is no net movement in the Total Deferred Tax Adjustment Amount in order to ensure that the tax is taken into account for GloBE purposes. Because Article 4.4.1(b) excludes the movement in deferred tax expense with respect to 'Disallowed Accruals', the decrease in deferred tax liability when a 'Disallowed Accrual' reverses should be excluded from the Total Deferred Tax Adjustment Amount. Therefore, the amount that reverses with respect to a 'Disallowed Accrual' need not be added under Article 4.4.2(a) since that amount is already accounted for in current tax expense without an offsetting deferred tax liability reversal for GloBE purposes. However, while the exclusions of deferred tax expense in Article 4.4.1 apply equally to exclude both increases and decreases in deferred tax expense, an 'Unclaimed Accrual' is defined solely by reference to an increase in a deferred tax liability, and thus any subsequent decrease will not be captured by the exclusion in Article 4.4.1(b), making the rule in Article 4.4.2(a) necessary for 'Unclaimed Accruals'.

514. *Adjustments carried out through paragraph (b):* Paragraph (b) permits the addition of Recaptured Deferred Tax Liabilities that have been paid during the Fiscal Year. As discussed in greater detail in Article 4.4.4 *infra*, certain amounts claimed as Adjusted Covered Taxes must be recaptured if not paid within the time limit set forth in Article 4.4.4. Subparagraph (b) permits taking these previously recaptured Adjusted Covered Taxes into account when such amounts are paid.

515. *Adjustments carried out through paragraph (c):* Paragraph (c) provides for the generation of a deemed deferred tax asset when a deferred tax asset should have been generated but was not due to the recognition criteria not being met. This rule is a corollary to the rule in Article 4.4.1(c) that disregards valuation adjustments or accounting recognition adjustments. However, in some cases, the deferred tax asset may not be recorded in the first place due to the criteria not being met. This paragraph provides for the generation of the deferred tax asset for GloBE purposes in the year of the loss, and the rule in Article 4.4.1(c) then subsequently disregards the generation of such deferred tax asset in subsequent years when the recognition criteria are met. This aligns the generation of the attribute with the loss to ensure that Top-up Tax is not triggered under Article 4.1.5 simply due to the fact that the recognition criteria have not been met, as illustrated through an example, providing that in Year 1, CE A generates a GloBE Loss and local tax loss of (100). No deferred tax asset (DTA) is generated for financial accounting purposes because the recognition criteria have not been met (i.e., there is no forecast of future profits). The application of this subparagraph (c) results in the generation of a DTA of 15 in Year 1 (this represents the DTA that would have otherwise been recorded at the Minimum Rate). In Year 2, CE A does not earn taxable income or GloBE Income or Loss; however, the future forecasts change, and the DTA of 15 is recorded for financial accounting purposes because the recognition criteria are met. This is disregarded under Article 4.4.1(c). In Year 3, the CE earns GloBE Income of 100 and applies its domestic tax loss carry-forward. The DTA of 15 is applied in Year 3.

4.4.4.3 Article 4.4.3.

516. A deferred tax asset that has been recorded at a rate lower than the Minimum Rate may be recast at the Minimum Rate in the Fiscal Year such deferred tax asset is recorded, if the taxpayer can demonstrate that the deferred tax asset is attributable to a GloBE Loss. The Total Deferred Tax Adjustment Amount is reduced by the amount that a deferred tax asset is increased due to being recast under this article.

517. *Purpose of the Article*: Article 4.4.3 provides that when a deferred tax asset has been recorded at a rate lower than the Minimum Rate that such asset may be recast at the Minimum Rate when the asset is attributable to a GloBE Loss. This rule preserves the basic tenet that a GloBE Loss of EUR 1 should offset a GloBE Income of EUR 1. For example, if a loss deferred tax asset was recorded at a 5% rate, a GloBE Loss of 100 would result in a deferred tax asset of 5. When 100 of income is subsequently earned, the deferred tax asset of 5 reverses and is added to Covered Taxes through the Total Deferred Tax Adjustment Amount. Absent a recast at the Minimum Rate, Top-up Tax of 10 would be due when 100 of income is subsequently earned. However, permitting a recast of the GloBE Loss at the Minimum Rate (i.e., increasing the value of the deferred tax asset recorded from 5 to 15 in respect of the GloBE Loss) prevents this outcome and provides that a loss of 100 shelters 100 of income, as depicted in the table below:

Prior to application of Article 4.4.3			
Year 1		**Year 2**	
Deferred Tax Asset for GloBE purposes		**Top-up Tax**	
Operating Income	-100	Operating Income	100
GloBE Income	-100	GloBE Income	100
Deferred Tax Asset @ 5% for GloBE purposes	(5)	Tax	15
		Deferred Tax Adjustment	(5)
		Top-up Tax	10
Post application of Article 4.4.3			
Year 1		**Year 2**	
Deferred Tax Asset for GloBE purposes		**Top-up Tax**	
Operating Income	-100	Operating Income	100
GloBE Income	-100	GloBE Income	100
Deferred Tax Asset @ 15% for GloBE purposes	(15)	Tax	15
		Deferred Tax Adjustment	(15)
		Top-up Tax	0

518. To the extent an amount is recast at the Minimum Rate under Article 4.4.3, the recast must be done in the Fiscal Year in which the loss becomes a GloBE Loss to prevent distortive outcomes. For example, recasting in a year after the GloBE Loss is incurred could result in such recast resulting in additional Top-up Tax under the operation of Article 4.1.5. To the extent a deferred tax asset is increased by operation of this rule, it follows that, like the generation of an actual deferred tax asset, that the Total Deferred Tax Adjustment Amount is decreased by the amount of incremental deferred tax asset generated.

4.4.4.4 Article 4.4.4.

519. To the extent a deferred tax liability, that is not a Recapture Exception Accrual, is taken into account under this article and such amount is not paid within the five subsequent Fiscal Years, the amount must be recaptured pursuant to this article. The Amount of the Recaptured Deferred Tax Liability determined for the current Fiscal Year shall be treated as a reduction to Covered Taxes in the fifth preceding Fiscal Year, and the ETR and Top-up Tax of such Fiscal Year shall be recalculated under the rules of Article 5.4.1. The Recaptured Deferred Tax Liability for the current Fiscal Year is the amount of the increase in a category of deferred tax liability that was included in the Total Deferred Tax Adjustment Amount in the fifth preceding Fiscal Year that has not reversed by the end of the last day of the current Fiscal Year unless such amount relates to a Recapture Exception Accrual as set forth in Article 4.4.5.

520. *Purpose of the Article*: Barring Recapture Exception Accruals, deferred tax liabilities recorded in other categories that do not reverse within the five Fiscal Years must be recaptured in the Fiscal Year in which the increase in the Recaptured Deferred Tax Liability was originally included in the Total Deferred Tax Adjustment Amount. This rule ensures that deferred tax liabilities recorded with respect to categories that do not relate to specific policy-allowed categories are actually settled within the required period of time and are, therefore, required to be monitored under the rules.

521. *Mechanics of the Article*: Each item of deferred tax expense for a CE that is not in a category that meets the Recapture Exception Accrual definition should be tested in each Fiscal Year for recapture as necessary under the mechanics of Article 4.4.4. For example, in Year 0, a Constituent Entity reports an amount as a deferred tax liability and includes that amount in Adjusted Covered Taxes. The category of income to which the deferred tax liability relates is not listed in Article 4.4.5 as a Recapture Exception Accrual. In Year 5, which is five subsequent Fiscal Years after the amount was claimed, the deferred tax liability has not reversed and is subject to recapture as a Recaptured Deferred Tax Liability. Accordingly, the Year 0 Top-up Tax calculation must be recalculated under Article 5.4, having removed such amount.

4.4.4.5 Article 4.4.5.

522. Recapture Exception Accrual means the tax expense accrued attributable to changes in associated deferred tax liabilities, in respect of:

(a) cost recovery allowances on tangible assets;
(b) the cost of a licence or similar arrangement from the government for the use of immovable property or exploitation of natural resources that entails significant investment in tangible assets;
(c) research and development expenses;
(d) decommissioning and remediation expenses;
(e) fair value accounting on unrealised net gains;

(f) foreign currency exchange net gains;
(g) insurance reserves and insurance policy deferred acquisition costs;
(h) gains from the sale of tangible property located in the same jurisdiction as the Constituent Entity that are reinvested in tangible property in the same jurisdiction; and
(i) additional amounts accrued as a result of accounting principles changes with respect to categories (a) through (h).

523. *Objective of the Article is to ease compliance burden*: The Recapture Exception Accrual rule, which provides categories of deferred tax liabilities that do not need to be monitored for recapture under Article 4.4.4, is set forth in Article 4.4.5. The list of Recapture Exception Accruals sets out the temporary differences that are both common in IF jurisdictions and that are generally material to MNE Groups. Such temporary differences are typically tied to substantive activities in a jurisdiction or are differences that are not prone to taxpayer manipulation. Accordingly, to reduce compliance burdens, these low-risk items that are certain to reverse over time are not required to be monitored under the rules in Article 4.4.4 for recapture.

524. Various categories of deferred tax liabilities under the Recapture Exception Accrual rule as listed above are discussed below:

(a) *Paragraph (a) of Article 4.4.5:* The inclusion of cost recovery allowances in paragraph (a) of Article 4.4.5 with respect to tangible assets reflects the principle that accelerated depreciation and immediate expensing regimes are common in IF jurisdictions and that such timing differences are certain to reverse over the life of an asset. Absent the rule in paragraph (a) of Article 4.4.5, the recapture mechanism in Article 4.4.4 could serve to disgorge the benefit of such regimes and result in the distortion of jurisdictional ETRs for assets that have a lifespan longer than the time period (of five Fiscal Years) set forth in Article 4.4.4. Paragraph (a) applies in the case of tangible assets that are owned or leased and *inter alia* be in the nature of Property, Plant, and Equipment or Stockpiles, natural resources, such as mineral deposits, timber, oil and gas reserves, and exploration and evaluation assets.
(b) *Paragraph (b) of Article 4.4.5*: Paragraph (b) includes the cost of a licence or similar arrangement from the government, such as a lease or concession, for the use of immovable property or the exploitation of natural resources, where this entails significant investment in tangible assets. A right to use immovable property includes licenses for the right to use radio spectrum for telecommunications services. When the right also imposes an obligation to incur significant investment in tangible assets, the cost will be within paragraph (b). Thus, where there are differences between the relevant financial accounting rules and the relevant tax accounting rules regarding the timing of recognition of the cost of the licence or similar arrangement or related costs, or the accounting rules require capitalisation of a broader range of such costs, the associated deferred tax liabilities are treated as Recapture Exception

Accruals. For example, local tax laws may require the amortisation of a radio spectrum license over a fifteen-year period, whereas, for financial accounting purposes, the useful life of such asset has been determined to be twenty years.

(c) *Paragraph (c) of Article 4.4.5*: Research and development (R&D) expenses are included in paragraph (c) of Article 4.4.5, given that tax rules in IF jurisdictions generally permit the deduction of R&D costs, whereas some of such costs may be capitalised for financial accounting purposes. Adhering to the financial accounts with respect to the capitalisation of R&D costs could lead to unintended outcomes, including increased pressure on the application of accounting standards and differences in treatment depending upon the accounting standard utilised. Accordingly, given the commonality of deductions in IF jurisdictions and the materiality of R&D expenses to MNE Groups, R&D expenses are included as a Recapture Exception Accrual.

(d) *Paragraph (d) of Article 4.4.5*: De-commissioning and remediation expenses are included in paragraph (d) of Article 4.4.5 as Recapture Exception Accruals. These costs include the costs a taxpayer will incur to decommission certain types of assets upon reaching the end of their useful life and remediating the site environment. For example, upon the end of the useful life of a nuclear power plant, the plant must be decommissioned, and environmental remediation will be required as part of the closure process. In order to reflect the economic performance of an investment accurately, accounting standards generally require the present value of anticipated decommissioning costs to be capitalised and amortised over the life of the relevant asset. Such assets may include oil rigs, a well, a mine, or a power plant. Including such costs in paragraph (d) of Article 4.4.5 avoids the unintended outcome of effectively denying a GloBE deduction for environmental and other clean-up costs.

(e) *Paragraph (e) of Article 4.4.5*: Fair value accounting on unrealised gains is included in paragraph (e) of Article 4.4.5 as a Recapture Exception Accrual. Some examples of fair value gains and losses for accounting purposes include increases in value of the investment assets of insurance companies or increases in the value of rights to timber held by a forestry company. Gains on such investments may not be brought into account for tax purposes until such amounts have been realised through a sale or other disposition of the asset. The taxation of realised gains and losses is relatively common among IF jurisdictions and can give rise to temporary differences, which can often be material to MNE Groups, both in terms of amount and length of deferral. The Recapture Exception Accrual under this paragraph (e) only applies to the extent the fair value accounting is also applied for GloBE purposes. Therefore, this paragraph would not apply to the extent the MNE Group had made an election under Article 3.2.5 in relation to such gains.

(f) *Paragraph (f) of Article 4.4.5*: Net gains of foreign currency exchange are taken into account in paragraph (f) of Article 4.4.5. Monetary items such as payables, receivables, and loans denominated in a foreign currency (i.e., different from the functional currency for financial accounting purposes of the

CE) are translated at the closing rate for accounting purposes, which is the spot exchange rate at the reporting date. These foreign exchange gains and losses are generally recognised in the financial accounting income of a CE. Domestic tax laws, however, may not recognise these unrealised foreign exchange gains and losses until a realisation event occurs, such as a repayment of a loan.

(g) *Paragraph (g) of Article 4.4.5:* Insurance reserves are provided for in paragraph (g) of Article 4.4.5 as a Recapture Exception Accrual. Insurance companies generally collect premiums, invest such premiums, and pay claims with the earnings. When a premium is collected, it is known that some portion of the premium and earnings on such premium will be needed to pay claims, generally in a subsequent period. Inclusive Framework jurisdictions generally allow a deduction with reference to the amount reserved for future claims; thus, the full premium received is not subject to CIT. The amount allowed as a tax deduction is typically determined by reference to the amount of reserve requirements set by insurance regulatory agencies, which require insurance companies to hold a certain amount of assets in high-grade, liquid investments to ensure they can pay policyholder claims. Such regulatory capital requirements typically exceed accounting reserves by a significant amount. The difference between these accounting and tax reserves creates temporary differences that may be sustained over long periods, especially in the case of life insurance. The reference to deferred acquisition costs in Article 4.4.5(g) may include the recognition of items relating to in-force contracts (for example, as part of an insurance business acquisition), where the insurer is required to recognise the difference in the fair value of the acquired insurance contracts and insurance obligations assumed on acquisition.

(h) *Paragraph (h) of Article 4.4.5:* Some IF jurisdictions permit a taxpayer to benefit from rollover or deferral relief with respect to gain on the disposition of capital assets if reinvested into a replacement asset within a prescribed time period. The gain is not recognised but is treated as a reduction to the acquisition cost of the new asset, thereby preserving the gain for future taxation. Rollover or deferral of gain treatment is equivalent to recognising the gain and then allowing an immediate expense of the same amount of the cost of the new asset. Thus, to the extent that the asset is depreciable for accounting purposes, the rollover or deferral is akin to accelerated depreciation and immediate expensing. However, in the case of land, the temporary difference will not reverse until the land is sold and the gain is not rolled over to a new investment. Such difference is material and common in IF jurisdictions, having characteristics similar to accelerated depreciation. This is because the underlying expenditure is directly connected with investment in tangible assets, and the difference will reverse over a definite period. Adherence to financial accounting treatment with respect to such property could lead to unintended outcomes, including volatility in GloBE calculations.

(i) *Paragraph (i) of Article 4.4.5:* Paragraph (i) of Article 4.4.5 provides that deferred tax expenses resulting from a change in accounting principles with respect to the categories enumerated in paragraphs (a) through (h) also benefit from the Recapture Exception Accrual rule. For example, if a change in accounting principles or policies occurs, as described in International Accounting Standards (IAS) 8, in a Fiscal Year that results in additional deferred tax expense being accrued with respect to a previously recorded cost recovery allowance on tangible property, such accrual shall benefit from the Recapture Exception Accrual rule by virtue of the application of this paragraph.

4.4.4.6 Article 4.4.6.

525. Disallowed Accrual means:

(a) any movement in deferred tax expense accrued in the financial accounts of a Constituent Entity which relates to an uncertain tax position; and
(b) any movement in deferred tax expense accrued in the financial accounts of a Constituent Entity which relates to distributions from a Constituent Entity.

526. *Purpose of Article 4.4.6 read with Article 4.4.1(b)*: The Disallowed Accrual rule is set forth in Article 4.4.6 and 4.4.1(b). This rule is intended to prevent accruals of tax with respect to uncertain tax positions and distributions from a CE from being included in the Adjusted Covered Taxes amount until actually paid.

527. *Uncertainty over tax payments:* Amounts accrued with respect to uncertain tax positions are disallowed, given the MNE Group's determination (and possibly its explicit or implicit assertion to the relevant tax authority) that the Taxes are not owed and the high uncertainty with respect to whether such amounts will be paid in a future period. Although the precise criteria may differ under Acceptable Financial Accounting Standards, uncertain tax positions generally result when a CE takes a filing position that is not more likely than not to be sustained upon examination. Financial accounting standards require that a reserve is established for such positions. If the filing position is sustained, the reserve is released. Given the nature of such accruals, these amounts may not be treated as Covered Taxes unless and until the amount is actually paid. Further, Taxes levied upon distributions, such as withholding taxes and net basis taxes on dividends received, are generally imposed when an entity makes a distribution to its shareholder(s). Given that the MNE Group generally decides the timing of such distributions between CEs, it would be inappropriate to provide a current increase to Adjusted Covered Taxes for deferred tax amounts accrued in respect of distribution taxes.

4.4.4.7 Article 4.4.7.

528. Unclaimed Accrual means any increase in a deferred tax liability recorded in the financial accounts of a Constituent Entity for a Fiscal Year that is not expected to be paid within the time period set forth in Article 4.4.4 and for which the Filing Constituent Entity makes an Annual Election not to include in Total Deferred Tax Adjustment Amount for such Fiscal Year.

529. *The Article provides a compliance simplification option*: Article 4.4.7 provides a compliance simplification option with respect to the Article 4.4.4 recapture rule. This article permits a CE to exclude from the Total Deferred Tax Adjustment Amount any deferred tax liability that is not expected to be paid within the time period set forth in Article 4.4.4. This simplification allows for the exclusion of deferred tax liabilities that are almost certain to require recapture, which reduces compliance monitoring such liabilities and recalculating Top-up Tax several years later.

530. A ready reckoner on Structure and Mechanics of Article 4.4 is provided in Figure 4.22.

Figure 4.22 A Ready Reckoner on Structure and Mechanics of Article 4.4

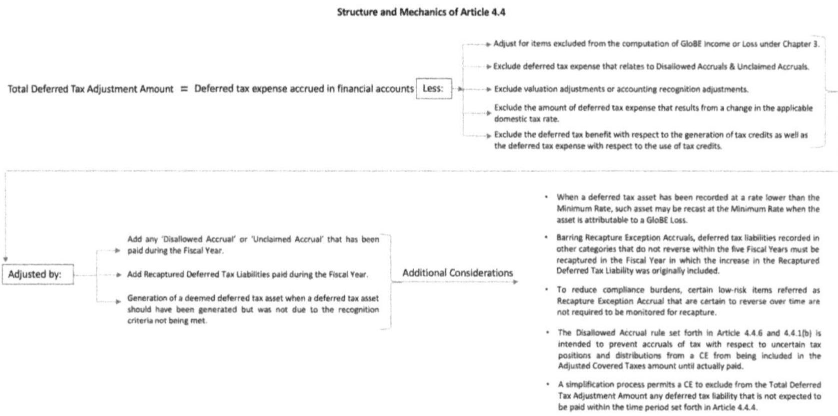

4.4.5 Article 4.5. (The GloBE Loss Election)

531. *Objective of the Article*: Article 4.5 provides an elective rule to effectively carry GloBE losses forward with a deemed deferred tax asset. When elected, Article 4.5 applies in lieu of Article 4.4 modified deferred tax accounting rules. Accordingly, Article 4.5 is generally expected to be of greatest utility as a simplification in jurisdictions that do not impose a CIT or impose one at a very low rate, given that when the election is made, Article 4.4 no longer applies, and temporary differences may result in Top-up Tax. The election may be made for any jurisdiction.

532. Prominent features of Article 4.5 are provided in Box 4.21.

Box 4.21 Prominent Features of Article 4.5

- Provides an elective rule to effectively carry GloBE losses forward with a deemed deferred tax asset. When elected, Article 4.5 applies in lieu of the Article 4.4 modified deferred tax accounting rules.
- Provides that the election may be made by the MNE Group for any jurisdiction.
- Provides that when a GloBE Loss Election is made for a jurisdiction, a GloBE Loss Deferred Tax Asset is established in each Fiscal Year in which there is a Net GloBE Loss for the jurisdiction.
- The GloBE Loss Deferred Tax Asset is equal to the Net GloBE Loss in a Fiscal Year for the jurisdiction multiplied by the Minimum Rate.
- Provides that the balance of the GloBE Loss Deferred Tax Asset is carried forward to subsequent Fiscal Years, reduced by the amount of GloBE Loss Deferred Tax Asset used in a Fiscal Year.
- Provides that the GloBE Loss Deferred Tax Asset must be used in any subsequent Fiscal Year in which there is Net GloBE Income for the jurisdiction in an amount equal to the lower of the Net GloBE Income multiplied by the Minimum Rate or the amount of available GloBE Loss Deferred Tax Asset.
- The election is useful for a jurisdiction that does not impose CIT or applies a low rate of CIT.
- Provides for an indefinite carry-forward of the GloBE Loss DTA; however, domestic law in certain circumstances may limit the practical application of the GloBE Loss DTA after a certain period of time.
- Provides that if the GloBE Loss Election is subsequently revoked, any remaining GloBE Loss Deferred Tax Asset is reduced to zero. Allowing the GloBE Loss Deferred Tax Asset to be carried forward into these subsequent Fiscal Years would potentially permit double benefit for losses and other distorted outcomes.
- Provides that the GloBE Loss Election must be filed with the first GloBE Information Return of the MNE Group that includes the jurisdiction for which the election is made, which means the GloBE Loss Election is an election that may only be made once.
- Does not allow GloBE Loss Election for a jurisdiction with an Eligible Distribution Tax System as it would result in an overstated ETR in such jurisdictions, given that distribution tax is only applicable when positive earnings are distributed.
- GloBE Loss Deferred Tax Asset is not transferred with a CE when it leaves the MNE Group.
- Provides a special rule for Flow-through Entities that are the UPE of an MNE Group where the GloBE Loss remains with the Flow-through Entity that is a UPE and can only be used to offset future GloBE Income of such UPE. Note

that other entities are not aggregated with the Flow-through Entity that is a UPE, even if a GloBE Loss Election has been made for the jurisdiction in which the UPE is located.

4.4.5.1 *Article 4.5.1.*

533. In lieu of applying the rules set forth in Article 4.4, a Filing Constituent Entity may make a GloBE Loss Election for a jurisdiction. When a GloBE Loss Election is made for a jurisdiction, a GloBE Loss Deferred Tax Asset is established in each Fiscal Year in which there is a Net GloBE Loss for the jurisdiction. The GloBE Loss Deferred Tax Asset is equal to the Net GloBE Loss in a Fiscal Year for the jurisdiction multiplied by the Minimum Rate.

534. The term Net GloBE Loss mentioned above is defined in Article 10.1 as below:

> Net GloBE Loss of a jurisdiction is the nil or negative amount, if any, computed in accordance with the following formula:

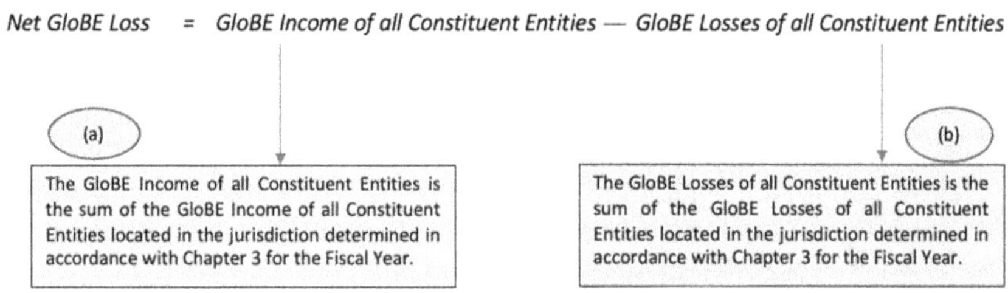

4.4.5.2 *Article 4.5.2.*

535. The balance of the GloBE Loss Deferred Tax Asset is carried forward to subsequent Fiscal Years, reduced by the amount of GloBE Loss Deferred Tax Asset used in a Fiscal Year.

4.4.5.3 *Article 4.5.3.*

536. The GloBE Loss Deferred Tax Asset must be used in any subsequent Fiscal Year in which there is Net GloBE Income for the jurisdiction in an amount equal to the lower of the Net GloBE Income multiplied by the Minimum Rate or the amount of available GloBE Loss Deferred Tax Asset.

537. *Election useful for a jurisdiction that does not impose CIT or applies a low rate of CIT:* Article 4.5.1 establishes a deemed deferred tax asset at the Minimum Rate when there is a Net GloBE Loss for a jurisdiction in a Fiscal Year. This GloBE Loss Deferred Tax Asset may be carried forward under Article 4.5.2 and used in any subsequent Fiscal

Year in which there is GloBE Income for the jurisdiction under Article 4.5.3. When a GloBE Loss Deferred Tax Asset is used in a subsequent Fiscal Year, the amount of GloBE Loss Deferred Tax Asset is added to Covered Taxes under Article 4.1.2. For example, if a CE is located in a country that does not impose a CIT, an election under Article 4.5 would provide a GloBE Loss attribute at the Minimum Rate for economic losses incurred that otherwise would not have a corresponding deferred tax asset due to the lack of a domestic CIT.

538. *Indefinite carry-forward*: While Article 4.5 provides for an indefinite carry-forward, domestic law, in certain circumstances, may limit the practical application of the GloBE Loss Deferred Tax Asset after a certain period of time. For example, a jurisdiction may prevent a taxpayer from claiming the benefit of a carry-forward loss unless they can meet certain record-keeping and evidential requirements.

4.4.5.4 Article 4.5.4.

539. If the GloBE Loss Election is subsequently revoked, any remaining GloBE Loss Deferred Tax Asset is reduced to zero, effective as of the first day of the first Fiscal Year in which the GloBE Loss Election is no longer applicable.

540. *Transition rule applicable when GloBE Loss Election is revoked*: Article 4.5.4 sets out the transition rule that is applicable if the GloBE Loss Election is subsequently revoked. This article requires that any remaining GloBE Loss Deferred Tax Asset be reduced to zero upon transition. This adjustment is required because when a jurisdiction is transitioned to the modified deferred tax accounting method set out in Article 4.4, the historical deferred tax assets and liabilities will be taken into account as if they had been calculated under Articles 4.4 and 9.1 for the prior Fiscal Years. Allowing the GloBE Loss Deferred Tax Asset to be carried forward into these subsequent Fiscal Years would potentially permit double benefit for losses and other distorted outcomes.

4.4.5.5 Article 4.5.5.

541. The GloBE Loss Election must be filed with the first GloBE Information Return of the MNE Group that includes the jurisdiction for which the election is made. A GloBE Loss Election cannot be made for a jurisdiction with an Eligible Distribution Tax System as defined in Article 7.3.

542. *Stage of GloBE Loss Election and reason for solitary election:* Article 4.5.5 provides that the GloBE Loss Election must be filed with the GloBE Information Return of the MNE Group filed for the first Fiscal Year in which the MNE Group has a CE located in the jurisdiction for which the election is made and that such election cannot be made for a jurisdiction with an Eligible Distribution Tax System as defined in Article 7.3. Because the GloBE Loss Election can only be filed with the first GloBE Information Return of the MNE Group that includes the jurisdiction for which the election is made, the GloBE Loss Election is an election that may only be made once. This rule is required to limit the applicability of Article 4.5.1 such that it not only provides a relief mechanism or simplification for jurisdictions where an MNE Group decides that an election is necessary but also does not allow for manipulation or distortions by shifting into and out of the election over time.

543. *Reason for not allowing GloBE Loss Election for a jurisdiction with an Eligible Distribution Tax System*: Permitting a deemed deferred tax asset for losses in jurisdictions with an Eligible Distribution Tax System as defined in Article 7.3 would result in an overstated ETR in such jurisdictions, given that distribution tax is only applicable when positive earnings are distributed.

544. *GloBE Loss Deferred Tax Asset is not transferred with a CE when it leaves the MNE Group*: Since the GloBE Loss Deferred Tax Asset is a jurisdictional attribute of the MNE Group, pursuant to Article 6.2.1(f), it does not transfer with a CE in the event such entity leaves the MNE Group. Accordingly, when a CE has been acquired from another MNE Group, whether such MNE Group has or has not made a GloBE Loss Election will not be relevant or taken into account for purposes of the acquiring MNE Group. Note that to the extent all CEs in a jurisdiction are transferred, the GloBE Loss Deferred Tax Asset remains with the transferor MNE Group despite the fact that it no longer has CEs in such jurisdiction. For example, MNE Group 1 has made a GloBE Loss Election with respect to Country A and then sells CE Z, which is located in Country A, to MNE Group 2. MNE Group 2 will not acquire any GloBE Loss Deferred Tax Asset with respect to the acquisition of CE Z, and the GloBE Loss Election made by MNE Group 1 has no impact on MNE Group 2. MNE Group 2 may still elect the GloBE Loss Election for Country A with its first GloBE Information Return that includes Country A if it so desires.

4.4.5.6 Article 4.5.6.

545. A Flow-through Entity that is a UPE of an MNE Group may make a GloBE Loss Election under this article. When such an election is made, the GloBE Loss Deferred Tax Asset shall be calculated in accordance with Articles 4.5.1 to 4.5.5; however, the GloBE Loss Deferred Tax Asset shall be calculated with reference to the GloBE Loss of the Flow-through Entity after reduction in accordance with Article 7.1.2.

546. *Special rule for Flow-through Entities that are the UPE of an MNE Group*: Article 4.5.6 provides a special rule for Flow-through Entities that are the UPE of an MNE Group that is made independently of an Article 4.5 election for any jurisdiction. Such entities may make a GloBE Loss Election under Article 4.5, and when the election is made, the GloBE Loss Deferred Tax Asset is calculated for the UPE in accordance with Articles 4.5.1 through 4.5.5. This special GloBE Loss Deferred Tax Asset is calculated solely with reference to the GloBE Loss of the Flow-through Entity after reduction in accordance with Article 7.1.2 to ensure losses that flow through to shareholders are not double-counted. This GloBE Loss remains with the Flow-through Entity that is a UPE and can only be used to offset future GloBE Income of such UPE. Accordingly, because other entities are not aggregated with the Flow-through Entity that is a UPE for purposes of calculating the GloBE Loss, this election is made with respect to only the

Flow-through Entity that is the UPE. Note that other entities are not aggregated with the Flow-through Entity that is a UPE, even if a GloBE Loss Election has been made for the jurisdiction in which the UPE is located.

4.4.6 Article 4.6. (Post-filing Adjustments and Tax Rate Changes)

547. *Objective of the Article*: Article 4.6 governs adjustments to amounts of Covered Taxes incurred with respect to a jurisdiction after the GloBE Information Return for the period has been filed. An MNE Group's liability for Covered Taxes may increase or decrease for various reasons, such as:

- a change in the amount of income recognised for local tax purposes due to an examination of the tax returns by the tax authority of a jurisdiction, or
- a review of the tax returns by the Entity's management or tax advisers, or
- the liability for Covered Taxes may increase or decrease due to errors, or
- a more accurate estimate of the tax liability after the GloBE Information Return has been filed.

548. *The article addresses changes in MNE Group's liability for Covered Taxes after the GloBE Information Return for the relevant year was filed:* Upward revisions would normally result in additional tax expense, and downward revisions would normally result in a refund of tax (either in cash to, or as a reduction of another tax liability of, the taxpaying entity or its shareholders) after the GloBE Information Return for the relevant year was filed. These changes to accrued tax expenses may have impacted the MNE Group's Top-up Tax liability with respect to a preceding Fiscal Year. In other words, if the final tax liability in a jurisdiction had been correctly determined when the GloBE Information Return was filed, the shareholder may have computed a different ETR and possibly paid more or less Top-up Tax and may have established a larger or smaller deferred tax liability or asset in that Fiscal Year.

549. Prominent features of Article 4.6 are provided in Box 4.22.

Box 4.22 Prominent Features of Article 4.6

- Governs adjustments to amounts of Covered Taxes incurred with respect to a jurisdiction after the GloBE Information Return for the period has been filed.
- Article 4.6.1 permits the MNE Group to:
  - treat increases to liabilities for Covered Taxes in previous Fiscal Years as current year tax increases for purposes of the GloBE Rules. This has the effect that refunds of Top-up Tax paid with respect to prior Fiscal Years will not occur under the operation of Article 4.6.1,
  - treat an immaterial decrease in Covered Taxes as a reduction to Covered Taxes in the current Fiscal Year.

- Article 4.6.1 generally requires a re-computation of the ETR and Top-up Tax for the Fiscal Year to which the tax adjustment relates in the case of a decrease in Covered Taxes. However, a taxpayer may elect to include an immaterial decrease in the current Fiscal Year.
- An immaterial decrease in Covered Taxes is an aggregate reduction that is less than EUR 1 million in the Adjusted Covered Taxes determined for the jurisdiction for a Fiscal Year.
- Provides that adjustments for material decreases must be made in respect of the relevant previous Fiscal Year to which the tax adjustment relates because the overstatement of Covered Taxes may have avoided Top-up Tax in that year, and simply reducing Covered Taxes in the current year may not effectively recapture the avoided Top-up Tax.
- Provides that a re-determination may only be carried back to the extent it does not result in a refund of Top-up Tax. To the extent a re-determination would otherwise result in a refund of Top-up Tax, such re-determination is taken into account in the re-determination year (i.e., the current Fiscal Year).
- Article 4.6.1 also applies when a domestic tax loss is carried back to a prior Fiscal Year.
- Article 4.6.2 provides that when there is a reduction to the applicable domestic tax rate to a rate below the Minimum Rate, such reduction must be taken into account under the rules of Article 4.6.1. This rule ensures that when a domestic tax rate is subsequently reduced, the deferred tax expense previously claimed as a Covered Tax is adjusted to the correct value.
- Article 4.6.3 provides the rule that is applicable when a deferred tax expense has been taken into account at a rate lower than the Minimum Rate, and the applicable tax rate is subsequently increased.
- Article 4.6.4 provides that the ETR and Top-up Tax for a jurisdiction must be recalculated in which such amount was claimed as Adjusted Covered Tax to exclude an amount of current tax expense (i.e., not deferred tax expense) that is more than EUR 1 million, and is not paid within three years of the last day of the Fiscal Year.

4.4.6.1 Article 4.6.1.

550. An adjustment to a Constituent Entity's liability for Covered Taxes for a previous Fiscal Year recorded in the financial accounts shall be treated as an adjustment to Covered Taxes in the Fiscal Year in which the adjustment is made unless the adjustment relates to a Fiscal Year in which there is a decrease in Covered Taxes for the jurisdiction. In the case of a decrease in Covered Taxes included in the Constituent Entity's Adjusted Covered Taxes for a previous Fiscal Year, the ETR and Top-up Tax for such Fiscal Year must be recalculated under Article 5.4.1. In the Article 5.4.1 recalculations, the Adjusted Covered Taxes determined for the Fiscal Year shall be reduced by the amount of the decrease in Covered Taxes and GloBE Income determined for the Fiscal Year, and any intervening Fiscal Years shall be adjusted as necessary and appropriate. A Filing Constituent Entity may make an Annual Election to treat an immaterial decrease in Covered Taxes as an adjustment to Covered Taxes in the Fiscal Year in which the adjustment is made. An immaterial decrease in Covered Taxes is an aggregate decrease of less than EUR 1 million in the Adjusted Covered Taxes determined for the jurisdiction for a Fiscal Year.

551. *Outcomes which impact the current Fiscal Year*: Article 4.6.1 permits the MNE Group to:

- treat increases to liabilities for Covered Taxes in previous Fiscal Years as current year tax increases for purposes of the GloBE Rules,
- treat an immaterial decrease in Covered Taxes as a reduction to Covered Taxes in the current Fiscal Year.

552. *Benefit of treating increases and immaterial decreases in the current Fiscal Year*: While treating post-filing adjustments to a tax liability in the current year is not as accurate as recalculating the GloBE tax liability or potential GloBE tax liability with respect to the relevant Fiscal Years; it significantly simplifies the computation of Top-up Tax under the GloBE Rules. And these adjustments generally are not the types of adjustments that avoid Top-up Tax liabilities that might have arisen in previous years. Increases to Covered Taxes are only taken into account in the current Fiscal Year. This has the effect that refunds of Top-up Tax paid with respect to prior Fiscal Years will not occur under the operation of Article 4.6.1.

553. *Outcomes when there is a decrease in Covered Taxes:* Article 4.6.1 generally requires a re-computation of the ETR and Top-up Tax for the Fiscal Year to which the tax adjustment relates in the case of a decrease in Covered Taxes. However, a taxpayer may elect to include an immaterial decrease in the current Fiscal Year. An immaterial decrease in Covered Taxes is an aggregate reduction that is less than EUR 1 million in the Adjusted Covered Taxes determined for the jurisdiction for a Fiscal Year. The immateriality of an adjustment is determined for each Fiscal Year by reference to the aggregate increase or decrease in Covered Taxes for each Fiscal Year. Adjustments for material decreases must be made in respect of the relevant previous Fiscal Year to which the tax adjustment relates because the overstatement of Covered Taxes may have avoided Top-up Tax in that year, and simply reducing Covered Taxes in the current year may not effectively recapture the avoided Top-up Tax.

554. *Interaction of Article 4.6.1 vis-à-vis Article 3.2.1(h):* Article 3.2.1(h) generally provides that a correction of an error in the computation of GloBE Income or Loss for a previous Fiscal Year is taken into account in the current year as additional income or expense. However, under Article 4.6.1, if the error affects taxable income for a jurisdiction and results in a material decrease in Covered Taxes for a previous Fiscal Year, the correction is taken into account in the relevant prior year, subject to the limitations described *supra*. These rules ensure that the GloBE Income or Loss and the

Covered Taxes associated with such amount are taken into account in the ETR and Top-up Tax computations for the same Fiscal Year to avoid a distorted result. Thus, when the correction of an error in the determination of a liability for Taxes in a particular jurisdiction results in a material decrease in the tax liability, the MNE Group must do two things to properly apply Article 3.2.1(h) and Article 4.6.1:

- First, the MNE Group must determine if the error in the tax computation was due to an error in the computation of taxable income and whether there was a corresponding error in the computation of the relevant CE's Financial Accounting Net Income or Loss. If so, both the Taxes and the GloBE Income or Loss for the prior year are re-determined.
- Second, the ETR and Top-up Tax for the prior year must be re-determined based on the re-determined Taxes and GloBE Income or Loss (if also adjusted) in order to determine if there is any Additional Top-up Tax for the jurisdiction pursuant to Article 5.4.1. If that re-determination results in Additional Top-up Tax, such tax is included in the jurisdictional Top-up Tax computation pursuant to Article 5.2 in the Fiscal Year of the re-determination; the MNE Group does not amend its GloBE Information Return or any tax returns filed in association with the GloBE Rules for the year to which the adjustment relates.

Corrections that do not arise from a material decrease in tax liability are taken into account in the computation of the ETR and Top-up Tax prospectively pursuant to Article 4.6.1 and Article 3.2.1(h). As discussed in the previous paragraphs, a re-determination may only be carried back to the extent it does not result in a refund of Top-up Tax. To the extent a re-determination would otherwise result in a refund of Top-up Tax, such re-determination is taken into account in the re-determination year (i.e., the current Fiscal Year). Note that under Article 4.6.1, a Filing Constituent Entity may make an Annual Election to treat immaterial decreases in Covered Taxes as an adjustment to Covered Taxes in the re-determination year (i.e., the Fiscal Year in which the adjustment is made).

555. *Loss carry-back under local law:* Article 4.6.1 also applies when a domestic tax loss is carried back to a prior Fiscal Year. When a tax loss is carried back, a refund of tax for a prior Fiscal Year is issued in the current Fiscal Year. This refund is a decrease to Covered Taxes for a prior Fiscal Year and therefore falls within the scope of Article 4.6.1 as an adjustment to a CE's liability for Covered Taxes for a previous Fiscal Year. The refund of Covered Taxes relating to the prior year must be matched with a corresponding adjustment to reflect a carry-back of the domestic tax loss that results in outcomes that are consistent with the treatment of carry-forward losses. IF members have agreed that, in the case of a loss carry-back under local law, the domestic tax loss shall be treated as giving rise to a deferred tax asset in the same manner in which it would have under the GloBE Rules had the loss been set up as a carry-forward. Accordingly, unless the refund is immaterial as defined in Article 4.6.1 and the Filing Constituent Entity has elected to take such amount into account in the current Fiscal Year, a deemed deferred tax asset shall be established in the year the domestic tax loss is incurred. The amount of this deferred tax asset shall be the amount that would otherwise have been recognised in the financial accounts had the deferred tax asset been eligible to be carried forward and capped at an amount equal to the domestic tax loss multiplied by the Minimum Rate. Through the operation of Article 4.4, this recognition of this deferred tax asset will reduce Adjusted Covered Taxes in the Fiscal Year in which the loss is generated. This deferred tax asset shall be treated as reversed, thereby increasing Adjusted Covered Taxes, in the Fiscal Year that the domestic tax loss has been carried back to, simultaneous with the carry-back of the refund under Article 4.6.1. To the extent the sum of the deferred tax asset reversal and the tax refund result in a net increase to Covered Taxes for the prior Fiscal Year, the net increase shall be taken into account in the current Fiscal Year under Article 4.6.1. It may be noted that to the extent a loss carry-back is taken into account, the rule set forth in Article 4.1.5 continues to apply in the current Fiscal Year. This creation and reversal of the deemed deferred tax asset is the preferred mechanism for recognising the appropriate and necessary adjustments to be made in recognition of GloBE Income or Loss, as it preserves the overall integrity of the deferred tax accounting approach. These provisions are further explained through **Illustration # 55**:

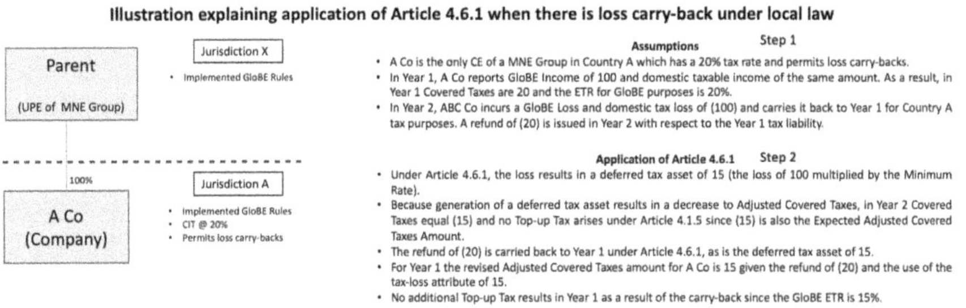

556. *The Article does not apply to an adjustment to an MNE Group's liability for Top-up Tax liability*: It should be noted that Article 4.6.1 applies when there is a change in the amount of Taxes determined for a jurisdiction. It does not apply to an adjustment to an MNE Group's liability for Top-up Tax liability as a result of the examination of a tax return that includes Top-up Tax attributable to the charging provisions in Article 2 of the GloBE Rules.

4.4.6.2 Article 4.6.2.

557. The amount of deferred tax expense resulting from a reduction to the applicable domestic tax rate shall be treated as an adjustment to a Constituent Entity's liability for Covered Taxes claimed under Article 4.1 for a previous Fiscal Year when such reduction results in the application of a rate that is less than the Minimum Rate.

558. *Objective of the Article*: Article 4.6.2 provides that when there is a reduction to the applicable domestic tax rate to a rate below the Minimum Rate, such reduction must be taken into account under the rules of Article 4.6.1. This rule ensures that when a domestic tax rate is subsequently reduced, the deferred tax expense previously claimed as a Covered Tax is adjusted to the correct value, which is the amount of such tax that will actually be paid upon reversal of the deferred tax liability. For example, in Fiscal Year 1, a Constituent Entity claims 15 of Covered Taxes resulting from a deferred tax liability on 100 of GloBE Income at 15%. In Fiscal Year 2, the jurisdiction reduces its domestic tax rate to 10%. Thus, when the deferred tax liability is ultimately paid, only 10 of tax will be paid (10% ETR). Article 4.6.1 requires (when such reduction is material) that the Fiscal Year 1 Top-up Tax must be re-computed. In this example, 5 of Top-up Tax would be due in Fiscal Year 2 owing to the re-computation.

4.4.6.3 Article 4.6.3.

559. The amount of deferred tax expense, when paid, that has resulted from an increase to the applicable domestic tax rate shall be treated as an adjustment under Article 4.6.1 to a Constituent Entity's liability for Covered Taxes claimed under Article 4.1 for a previous Fiscal Year when such amount was originally recorded at a rate less than the Minimum Rate. This adjustment is limited to an amount that is equal to an increase of deferred tax expense up to such deferred tax expense recast at the Minimum Rate.

560. *Objective of the Article*: Article 4.6.3 provides the rule that is applicable when a deferred tax expense has been taken into account at a rate lower than the Minimum Rate, and the applicable tax rate is subsequently increased. In such case, the amount of deferred tax expense that has resulted from the increase is treated as an adjustment to a Constituent Entity's liability for Covered Taxes for a previous Fiscal Year. For example, assume in Fiscal Year 1, a Constituent Entity has 100 of GloBE Income and records a deferred tax liability of 10 (10% ETR) and claims such amount as a Covered Tax. In Fiscal Year 2, the jurisdiction increases its tax rate to 15%. An additional deferred tax liability of 5 is recorded for financial accounting purposes. However, this increase of 5 is disregarded under Article 4.4.1(d) in Fiscal Year 2 and deferred until payment of the tax. In Fiscal Year 3, the tax of 15 is paid, and the full deferred tax liability reverses. The incremental 5 of deferred tax liability that reverses, which has not previously been claimed as a Covered Tax because it was disregarded, is taken into account under this article in Fiscal Year 3 upon payment and is treated as an increase to Covered Taxes through the operation of Article 4.6.1. It may be noted that had the tax rate in this example been 20%, an incremental 10 of Covered Tax would arise upon payment in Year 3, which would consist of the 5 of deferred tax liability that was previously disregarded, which is taken into account under this article, and the incremental 5 of tax liability that reflects tax in excess of the Minimum Rate, which is only taken into account when paid under Article 4.4.1.

4.4.6.4 Article 4.6.4.

561. If more than EUR 1 million of the amount accrued by a Constituent Entity as current tax expense and included in Adjusted Covered Taxes for a Fiscal Year is not paid within three years of the last day of such year, the ETR and Top-up Tax for the Fiscal Year in which the unpaid amount was claimed as a Covered Tax must be recalculated in accordance with Article 5.4.1 by excluding such unpaid amount from Adjusted Covered Taxes.

562. *Objective of the Article*: Article 4.6.4 provides that the ETR and Top-up Tax for a jurisdiction must be recalculated to exclude an amount of current tax expense (i.e., not deferred tax expense) that is more than EUR 1 million that was claimed as Adjusted Covered Tax and is not paid within three years of the last day of the Fiscal Year in which such amount was claimed as Adjusted Covered Tax. For example, in Fiscal Year 1, a CE claims 10 of current tax expense as an Adjusted Covered Tax. The CE files a local tax return reporting the 10 of tax due but does not pay such Tax by the end of Fiscal Year 4. The Fiscal Year 1 Top-up Tax must be re-computed under Article 5.4.1 without such 10 of Tax included in the calculation as a result of the non-payment of such Tax.

4.5 CHAPTER 5 OF GLOBE RULES (COMPUTATION OF ETR AND TOP-UP TAX)[99]

563. The Chapter comprises important computational rules for determining the ETR of jurisdictions in which the MNE operates and for determining the Top-up Tax for a Low-Tax Jurisdiction. The calculation of Top-up Tax for a Low-Tax Jurisdiction also includes rules for determining the amount of income that is excluded from the GloBE Rules by virtue of the Substance-based Income Exclusion. The Chapter also includes a *De Minimis* Exclusion for the CEs located in the same jurisdiction when their aggregated revenue and income do not exceed certain thresholds.

4.5.1 Article 5.1. (Determination of ETR)

564. Prominent features of Article 5.1 are provided in Box 4.23.

Box 4.23 Prominent Features of Article 5.1

- Provides that ETR computation in Article 5.1 is used to determine:
  - whether in a Fiscal Year, the MNE Group is subject to a minimum level of tax on its income arising in a particular jurisdiction, and
  - whether the jurisdiction's ETR is below the Minimum Rate (i.e., the jurisdiction is a Low-Tax Jurisdiction in respect of the MNE Group in that Fiscal Year).
- Provides that ETRs are generally computed on a jurisdictional basis.

99. Based on OECD's GloBE Model Rules, its Commentary and Illustrative Examples.

- Provides that Stateless CEs are treated as being the only CE in a jurisdiction, i.e., each Stateless CE shall be treated as a single CE located in a separate jurisdiction.
- Provides that ETR of the MNE Group for a jurisdiction with Net GloBE Income shall be calculated for each Fiscal Year.
- The ETR for a jurisdiction is equal to the sum of the Adjusted Covered Taxes of each CE located in the jurisdiction for the Fiscal Year divided by the Net GloBE Income of the jurisdiction.
- A jurisdictional blending calculation based on the aggregate income and taxes of all CEs in the same MNE Group means that when the Parent Entity applying the IIR is not the UPE, the ETR of a jurisdiction is not computed solely by reference to the CEs owned by that Parent Entity. Rather the ETR is computed by reference to all the CEs of the MNE Group 'located' in that jurisdiction.
- The approach to jurisdictional blending avoids risks that would otherwise arise to the integrity of the rules from shifting income and taxes between CEs located in the same jurisdiction and avoids potential distortions caused by particular features of the domestic tax system (such as loss-surrender and tax consolidation mechanisms). It also simplifies the mechanic for the attribution and allocation of Top-up Taxes under the IIR and UTPR.
- Provides that there are three specific exceptions to the jurisdictional ETR computation:
  - The first exception is for Investment Entities and Insurance Investment Entities.
  - The second exception applies to CEs in which the UPE holds 30% or less of the Ownership Interests but nonetheless has a Controlling Interest in the Entity, i.e., Minority-Owned Constituent Entities.
  - Finally, each Stateless Constituent Entity is treated as a single CE located in a separate jurisdiction.
- If the GloBE Losses of the CEs are equal to or exceed GloBE Income of the CEs located in that jurisdiction, there is no Net GloBE Income under Article 5.1.2, and therefore, there can be no Top-up Tax computed under Article 5.2 with respect to the jurisdiction. Consequently, the ETR for the jurisdiction need not be computed. It may, however, be noted that there may be cases in which Top-up Tax is determined under Article 4.1.5 for a jurisdiction that has a Net GloBE Loss.
- Provides that the Adjusted Covered Taxes and GloBE Income or Loss of Investment Entities and Insurance Investment Entities located in a jurisdiction are excluded from the jurisdictional ETR computation (subject to provisions of Articles 1.5.1, 1.5.2 and subject to special rules in Chapter 7).
- Provides that the rule in Article 5.1.3 is not relevant in the case of an Investment Entity or an Insurance Investment Entity that is a Tax Transparent Entity.

565. *The Article is the nucleus of GloBE Rules*: The ETR computation in Article 5.1 is the central element of the GloBE Rules. It is used to determine:

- whether in a Fiscal Year, the MNE Group is subject to a minimum level of tax on its income arising in a particular jurisdiction, and
- whether the jurisdiction's ETR is below the Minimum Rate (i.e., the jurisdiction is a Low-Tax Jurisdiction in respect of the MNE Group in that Fiscal Year).

566. *Conspicuous features associated with ETR computation*: ETRs are generally computed on a jurisdictional basis. Stateless CEs are treated as being the only CE in a jurisdiction. Certain Investment Entities and Insurance Investment Entities generally compute their ETR on a stand-alone basis under Article 7.4, but if the MNE Group has two Investment Entities in the same jurisdiction, their ETR is computed by taking into account Covered Taxes and GloBE Income or Loss of both entities. Similarly, if the MNE Group has a Minority-Owned Subgroup, a separate ETR computation is necessary for the Minority-Owned CEs located in a jurisdiction separate from the calculation made for the other CEs. Thus, in some cases, within the same jurisdiction, an MNE Group will compute:

- an ETR for a jurisdiction that is relevant for ordinary CEs located in the jurisdiction,
- another ETR that is relevant for Investment Entities or Insurance Investment Entities located in the jurisdiction, and
- another ETR that is relevant for Minority-Owned CEs of a Minority-Owned Subgroup.

The information necessary to compute the ETR of each jurisdiction will be included in the GloBE Information Return in accordance with the requirements of Article 8.1.

567. The term Insurance Investment Entity mentioned *supra* is defined in Article 10.1 as below:

> Insurance Investment Entity means an Entity that would meet the definition of an Investment Fund or a Real Estate Investment Vehicle except that it is established in relation to liabilities under an insurance or annuity contract and is wholly-owned by an Entity that is subject to regulation in its location as an insurance company.

4.5.1.1 Article 5.1.1.

568. The ETR of the MNE Group for a jurisdiction with Net GloBE Income shall be calculated for each Fiscal Year. The ETR of the MNE Group for a jurisdiction is equal to the sum of the Adjusted Covered Taxes of each Constituent Entity located in the jurisdiction divided by the Net GloBE Income of the jurisdiction for the Fiscal Year. For purposes of Chapter 5, each Stateless Constituent Entity shall be treated as a single Constituent Entity located in a separate jurisdiction.

569. *Objective of the Article*: Article 5.1.1 sets out the formula for computing the jurisdictional ETR. The ETR for a jurisdiction is equal to the sum of the Adjusted Covered Taxes of each CE located in the jurisdiction for the Fiscal Year divided by the Net GloBE Income of the jurisdiction. The result is expressed as a percentage rounded to the fourth decimal place (e.g., 14.12346% = 14.1235%) for purposes of the GloBE Rules. An ETR is not computed for a jurisdiction that has a Net GloBE Loss for the Fiscal Year. The sum of the Adjusted Covered Taxes of each CE means the sum of all of the Adjusted Covered Taxes determined under the rules of Chapter 4 for the CEs that are located in the same jurisdiction. Likewise, the Net GloBE Income or Loss of a jurisdiction is determined by aggregating all of the GloBE Income or Loss of all CEs located in the same jurisdiction. Consequently, the taxes and income attributable to Ownership Interests held by persons that are not Group Entities are taken into account in the ETR calculation.

570. *Adoption of jurisdictional blending approach*: A jurisdictional blending calculation based on the aggregate income and taxes of all CEs in the same MNE Group means that when the Parent Entity applying the IIR is not the UPE, the ETR of a jurisdiction is not computed solely by reference to the CEs owned by that Parent Entity. Rather the ETR is computed by reference to all the CEs of the MNE Group 'located' in that jurisdiction. The implication of determining the ETR based on a group-wide average ETR for the jurisdiction is that there may be cases where allocable Top-up Tax arises in respect of an Entity that would not be an LTCE if the ETR for the jurisdiction were computed on a single-entity basis or solely on the basis of taxes and income attributable to a Parent Entity's Ownership Interests in the CEs located in the jurisdiction. On the other hand, an Entity that would have been an LTCE on a stand-alone basis may not be an LTCE due to taxes paid or losses incurred by other CEs located in the jurisdiction. This approach to jurisdictional blending avoids risks that would otherwise arise to the integrity of the rules from shifting income and taxes between CEs located in the same jurisdiction and avoids potential distortions caused by particular features of the domestic tax system (such as loss-surrender and tax consolidation mechanisms). It also simplifies the mechanic for the attribution and allocation of Top-up Taxes under the IIR and UTPR.

571. *Exceptions to jurisdictional ETR computation*: There are three specific exceptions to the jurisdictional ETR computation, as mentioned below:

- The first exception is for Investment Entities and Insurance Investment Entities. Pursuant to Article 5.1.3, income and taxes of Investment Entities and Insurance Investment Entities located in a jurisdiction are excluded from the ETR computation for that jurisdiction. Special ETR computation rules are provided in Article 7.4 for such Investment Entities and Insurance Investment Entities.
- The second exception applies to CEs in which the UPE holds 30% or less of the Ownership Interests but nonetheless has a Controlling Interest in the Entity. In those cases, the rules in Article 5.6 require separate ETR computations for those CEs if they are located in a jurisdiction with ordinary CEs, and the ETR

computations for the Minority-Owned Constituent Entities make certain adjustments for income and taxes attributable to non-controlling interests.

- Finally, the last sentence of Article 5.1.1 provides a special rule under which each Stateless Constituent Entity is treated as a single CE located in a separate jurisdiction for purposes of Chapter 5. This rule adapts the general rules for computing the jurisdictional ETR to Stateless Constituent Entities. The GloBE Income or Loss and Adjusted Covered Taxes of a Stateless Constituent Entity, which go into the ETR computation, are determined in accordance with Chapters 3 and 4.

572. Location of an Entity and a Permanent Establishment is an important criterion in the determination of ETR, which is defined in Article 10.3 and is summarised in Figure 4.23.

Figure 4.23 Location of an Entity and a Permanent Establishment

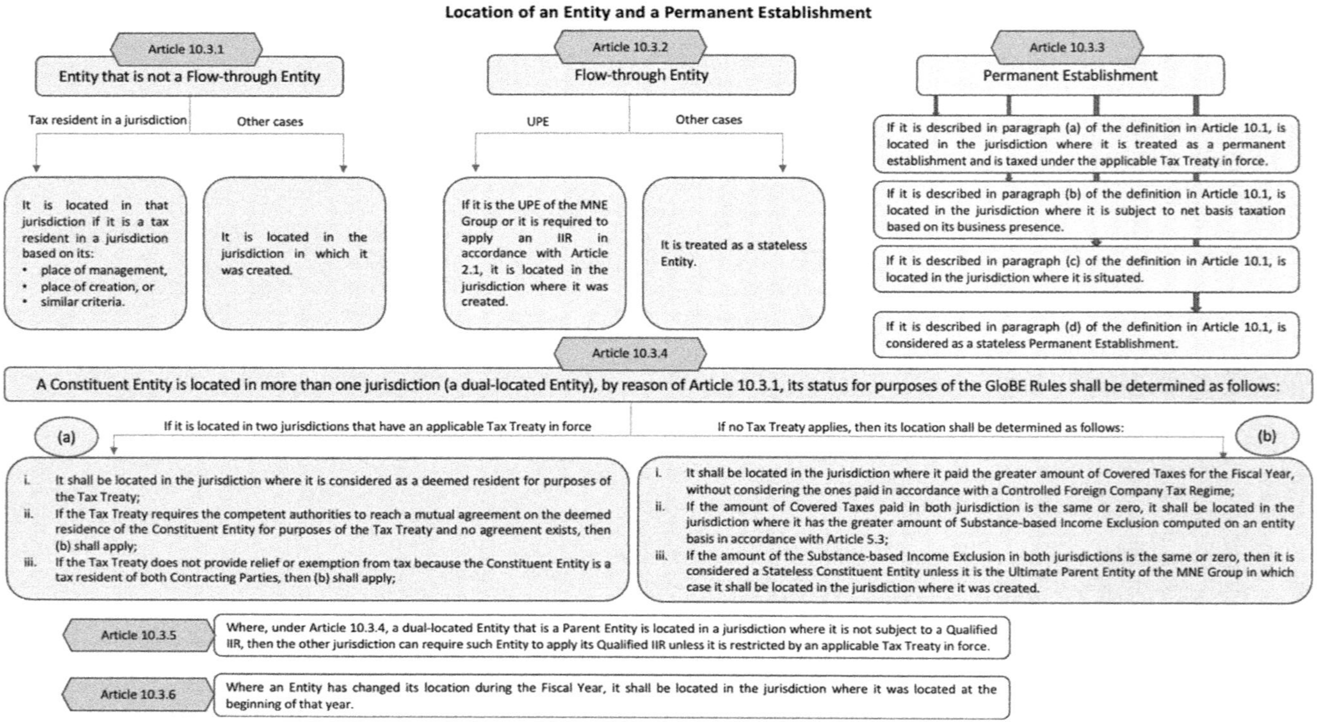

4.5.1.2 *Article 5.1.2.*

573. The Net GloBE Income of a jurisdiction for a Fiscal Year is the positive amount, if any, computed in accordance with the following formula:

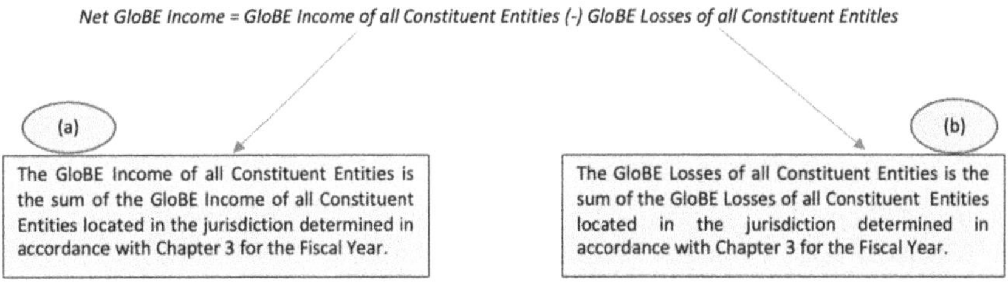

574. *Objective of the Article:* Article 5.1.2 provides the formula for computing the Net GloBE Income of a jurisdiction. The formula defines the Net GloBE Income of a jurisdiction as the positive amount, if any, obtained by subtracting GloBE Losses for the Fiscal Year of all CEs located in a jurisdiction from the GloBE Income for the Fiscal Year of all those CEs. The calculation does not include the GloBE Income or Losses of an Investment Entity, as noted in Article 5.1.3. If the GloBE Losses of the CEs are equal to or exceed the GloBE Income of the CEs located in that jurisdiction, there is no Net GloBE Income under Article 5.1.2, and therefore, there can be no Top-up Tax computed under Article 5.2 with respect to the jurisdiction. Consequently, the ETR for the jurisdiction need not be computed. It may, however, be noted that there may be cases in which Top-up Tax is determined under Article 4.1.5 for a jurisdiction that has a Net GloBE Loss.

4.5.1.3 *Article 5.1.3.*

575. Adjusted Covered Taxes and GloBE Income or Loss of Constituent Entities that are Investment Entities are excluded from the determination of the ETR in Article 5.1.1 and the determination of Net GloBE Income in Article 5.1.2.

576. *Exception provided by the Article*: Article 5.1.3 provides that the Adjusted Covered Taxes and GloBE Income or Loss of Investment Entities located in a jurisdiction are excluded from the jurisdictional ETR computation. The exception in Article 5.1.3 also extends to Insurance Investment Entities. This exclusion is necessary because an Investment Entity or an Insurance Investment Entity that is controlled by the MNE Group can be included in the GloBE Rules, but such an Investment Entity or Insurance Investment Entity would be subject to the special rules in Chapter 7 (The scope of the Excluded Entity definition in Article 1.5 applies only to an Investment Entity that is the UPE or that satisfies the requirements of Article 1.5.2). Article 5.1.3 helps to maintain the tax neutrality of controlled Investment Entities under the GloBE Rules and facilitates the application of the special rules in Chapter 7 to income earned by an MNE

Group through an Investment Entity or an Insurance Investment Entities. When necessary, the ETR of Investment Entities and Insurance Investment Entities is computed separately pursuant to Article 7.4.

577. *Situation where the Article need not apply*: The rule in Article 5.1.3 is not relevant in the case of an Investment Entity or an Insurance Investment Entity that is a Tax Transparent Entity because its income and taxes are allocated to Constituent Entity-owners, Permanent Establishments, or unrelated persons under Article 3.5.3 and Article 4.3.2.

4.5.2 Article 5.2. (Top-Up Tax)

578. Article 5.2 sets out the rules for determining the amount of Top-up Tax that is due with respect to a jurisdiction and how such Top-up Tax is allocated among the LTCEs located in that jurisdiction.

579. Prominent features of Article 5.2 are provided in Box 4.24.

Box 4.24 Prominent Features of Article 5.2

- Provides the rules for determining the amount of Top-up Tax that is due with respect to a jurisdiction and how such Top-up Tax is allocated among the LTCEs located in that jurisdiction.
- Article 5.2.1 sets out the formula for computing the Top-up Tax Percentage for each jurisdiction.
- Provides that for purposes of the GloBE Rules, a jurisdiction is considered a Low-Tax Jurisdiction in respect of the MNE Group and the CEs located in the jurisdiction are considered LTCEs when the ETR is below the Minimum Rate of 15%.
- Provides, at the same time, that if the ETR equals or exceeds the Minimum Rate, there is no Top-up Tax Percentage for the jurisdiction, and none of the CEs located in the jurisdiction will be considered LTCEs.
- Article 5.2.2 sets out the formula for determining the Excess Profit for a jurisdiction. The Excess Profit is the amount of profit, determined on a jurisdictional basis, upon which the Top-up Tax is levied.
- Article 5.2.3 provides the formula for computing the Jurisdictional Top-up Tax.
- Provides that the amount of Additional Current Top-up Tax for a jurisdiction must be computed before any reduction by a QDMTT.
- Provides that a jurisdiction is not required to adopt a QDMTT under the common approach. But if it does, the QDMTT will, in many cases, reduce the Top-up Tax to nil under Article 5.2.3.
- Provides that the amount of any excess QDMTT will not reduce the Top-up Tax under the GloBE Rules below zero or result in a refund of or credit against future Top-up Tax under the GloBE Rules.

- Article 5.2.4 allocates the Jurisdictional Top-up Tax computed for a Low-Tax Jurisdiction among the CEs in the jurisdiction.
- Provides that since the Jurisdictional Top-up Tax is computed in Article 5.2.3 by reference to the Net GloBE Income, it is allocated only to CEs that have GloBE Income for the Fiscal Year; none is allocated to CEs with GloBE Losses.
- The allocation of Top-up Tax to specific LTCEs also facilitates application of the UTPR, particularly in cases where part of an LTCE's Top-up Tax is subject to an IIR and the remainder is subject to the UTPR.
- Article 5.2.5 addresses situations where Additional Current Top-up Tax is computed for a jurisdiction under Article 5.4.1, and the jurisdiction does not have Net GloBE Income for the Fiscal Year. As a matter of convenience, Article 5.2.4 generally allocates Additional Current Top-up Tax computed under Article 5.4.1 along with Top-up Tax computed for the fiscal year among LTCEs under Article 5.2.4 based on the GloBE Income of such Entities in the fiscal years for which the recalculations under Article 5.4.1 were performed.
- It may be noted that Additional Current Top-up Tax attributable to the operation of Article 4.1.5 is not allocated pursuant to Article 5.2.5. Such Additional Current Top-up Tax is allocated separately under Article 5.4.3.

4.5.2.1 Article 5.2.1.

580. The Top-up Tax Percentage for a jurisdiction for a Fiscal Year shall be the positive percentage point difference, if any, computed in accordance with the following formula:

Top-up Tax Percentage = Minimum Rate (-) Effective Tax Rate

Where the ETR is the ETR determined in accordance with Article 5.1 for the jurisdiction for the Fiscal Year.

581. *Objective of the Article*: Article 5.2.1 sets out the formula for computing the Top-up Tax Percentage for each jurisdiction. The Top-up Tax Percentage for a jurisdiction is equal to the percentage point excess of the Minimum Rate over the ETR determined for the jurisdiction under Article 5.1 for the Fiscal Year. For this purpose, the percentage point excess of the Minimum Rate over the ETR is the positive difference, if any, between the Minimum Rate and the ETR of the jurisdiction, expressed as a percentage. For instance, assume a jurisdiction where the ETR is 7.17%, and consequently, the Top-up Tax Percentage is equal to 7.83% (= 15% - 7.17%).

582. *Situation when a jurisdiction is considered a Low-Tax Jurisdiction*: For purposes of the GloBE Rules, a jurisdiction is considered a Low-Tax Jurisdiction in respect of the MNE Group and the Constituent Entities located in the jurisdiction are considered LTCEs when the ETR is below the Minimum Rate. If the ETR equals or exceeds the

Minimum Rate, there is no Top-up Tax Percentage for the jurisdiction, and none of the Constituent Entities located in the jurisdiction will be considered LTCEs.

4.5.2.2 Article 5.2.2.

583. The Excess Profit for the jurisdiction for the Fiscal Year is the positive amount, if any, computed in accordance with the following formula:

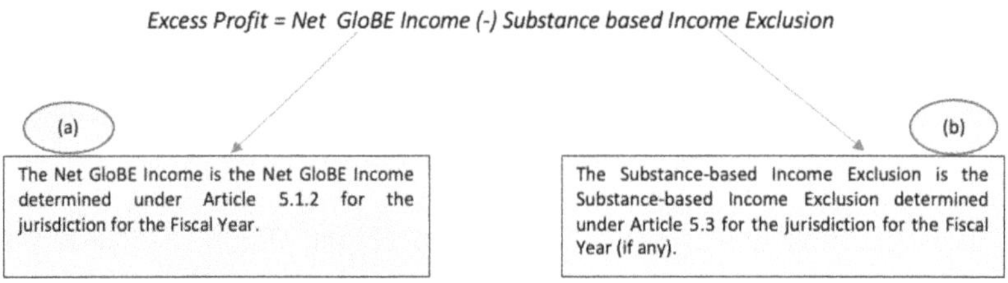

584. *Objective of the Article*: Article 5.2.2 sets out the formula for determining the Excess Profit for a jurisdiction. The Excess Profit is the amount of profit, determined on a jurisdictional basis, upon which the Top-up Tax is levied. The Excess Profit for the jurisdiction is the amount remaining after applying a Substance-based Income Exclusion (as determined under Article 5.3) for the jurisdiction. Where a taxpayer elects not to apply the Substance-based Income Exclusion, the Excess profit is equal to the Net GloBE Income for the jurisdiction. If the Substance-based Income Exclusion for the jurisdiction equals or exceeds the Net GloBE Income for the jurisdiction, there will be no Excess Profit, and thus no Top-up Tax computed for that year unless there is Additional Current Top-up Tax for that Fiscal Year. The Excess Profit formula incorporates the Substance-based Income Exclusion into the jurisdictional blending model. The Substance-based Income Exclusion for the jurisdiction is the aggregation of the exclusions computed for each CE located in the jurisdiction. The amount (of excess profit) computed for a CE is not limited by the GloBE Income of the Entity. Thus, if a CE incurs a loss or has very little profit for the Fiscal Year, its Substance-based Income Exclusion may nonetheless exclude the profit of other CEs in the jurisdiction from the reach of the Top-up Tax.

4.5.2.3 Article 5.2.3.

585. The Jurisdictional Top-up Tax for a jurisdiction for a Fiscal Year is equal to the positive amount, if any, computed in accordance with the following formula:

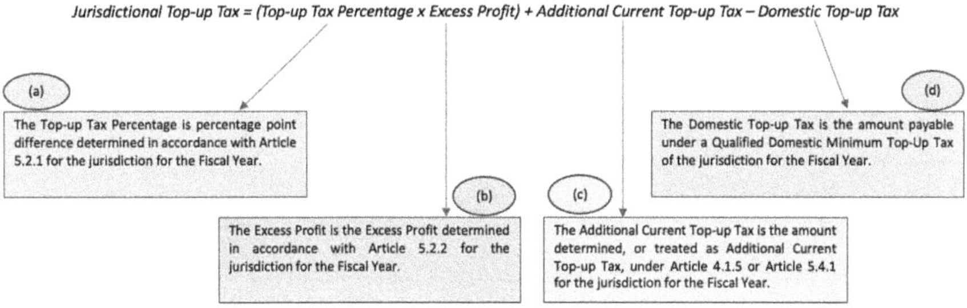

586. *Objective of the Article*: Article 5.2.3 provides the formula for computing the Jurisdictional Top-up Tax. This formula is built on the Top-up Tax Percentage computed under Article 5.2.1 and the Excess Profit computed under Article 5.2.2. The Top-up Tax Percentage is multiplied by the Excess Profit of the jurisdiction for the Fiscal Year. The product of that computation is then increased by any Additional Current Top-up Tax computed under Article 4.1.5 and Article 5.4.1 for the Fiscal Year and reduced (but not below zero) by any QDMTT in order to arrive at the Jurisdictional Top-up Tax. As provided in Article 5.4, the Additional Current Top-up Tax is an amount of Top-up Tax added to the current year that is attributable to certain recalculations of the Top-up Tax in previous years. The amount of Additional Current Top-up Tax for a jurisdiction must be computed before any reduction by a QDMTT. However, if the Top-up Tax for the jurisdiction is zero due to the application of a QDMTT, the Top-up Tax does not need to be allocated among CEs in the jurisdiction under Articles 5.2.4, 5.2.5, or 5.4.3. Any tax payable pursuant to a QDMTT is taken into account at this point in the computation so as to give full credit in the GloBE Top-up Tax computation. Thus, tax payable pursuant to a QDMTT can offset the Top-up Tax (including any Additional Current Top-up Tax calculated for the Fiscal Year) that would have been computed under Article 5.2.3 for the Fiscal Year absent the QDMTT. A jurisdiction is not required to adopt a QDMTT under the common approach. But if it does, the QDMTT will, in many cases, reduce the Top-up Tax to nil under Article 5.2.3. The amount of a QDMTT may be different from that determined under the GloBE Rules as a result of different applicable accounting standards as permitted by the definition of QDMTT in Article 10.1. This difference may result in an amount of QDMTT in excess of the amount of Top-up Tax that would otherwise be computed under Article 5.2.3. The amount of any excess, however, will not reduce the Top-up Tax under the GloBE Rules below zero or result in a refund of or credit against future Top-up Tax under the GloBE Rules.

587. The term QDMTT mentioned above is defined in Article 10.1 and explained at length in the OECD's Commentary on Article 10.1, as summarised in Figure 4.24.

Figure 4.24 Qualified Domestic Minimum Top-Up Tax

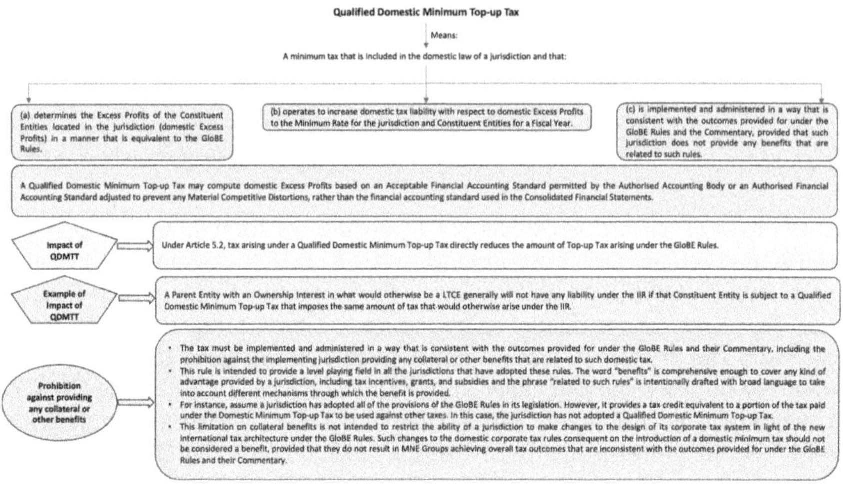

4.5.2.4 *Article 5.2.4.*

588. Except as provided in Article 5.4.3, the Top-up Tax of a Constituent Entity shall be determined for each Constituent Entity of a jurisdiction that has GloBE Income determined in accordance with Chapter 3 for the Fiscal Year included in the computation of Net GloBE Income of that jurisdiction in accordance with the following formula:

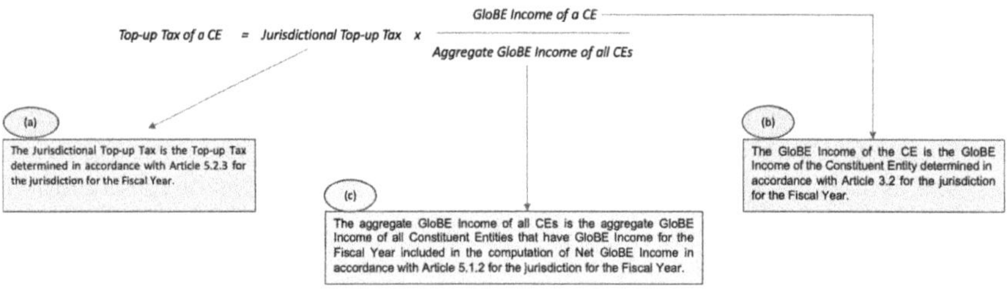

589. *Objective of the Article*: Article 5.2.4 allocates the Jurisdictional Top-up Tax computed for a Low-Tax Jurisdiction among the CEs in the jurisdiction. Because the Jurisdictional Top-up Tax is computed in Article 5.2.3 by reference to the Net GloBE Income, it is allocated only to CEs that have GloBE Income for the Fiscal Year; none is allocated to CEs with GloBE Losses. The allocation only to CEs that have GloBE Income is accomplished through an allocation key based on the ratio of each CE's GloBE Income for the Fiscal Year to the sum of the GloBE Income of all CEs located in the jurisdiction that have GloBE Income for the Fiscal Year. Although Top-up Tax is computed on a jurisdictional basis, the IIR charging provisions in Chapter 2 are based on the Parent Entity's rights to the profits of specific LTCEs. The allocation of Top-up

Tax among LTCEs under Article 5.2.4 facilitates the application of the IIR by Parent Entities other than the UPE. POPEs and some Intermediate Parent Entities do not have the same Ownership Interests in the profits of an LTCE as the UPE. If there are multiple LTCEs in the Low-Tax Jurisdiction, the Top-up Tax of each LTCE would be allocable in different proportions to Parent Entities with different Ownership Interests percentages in the various LTCEs. If, however, the UPE is applying an IIR and all of the LTCEs are wholly owned, all of the Top-up Tax computed for the jurisdiction is allocable to the UPE under Chapter 2, and therefore, as a practical matter, the UPE does not need to make the allocation among LTCEs under Article 5.2.4. The allocation of Top-up Tax to specific LTCEs also facilitates application of the UTPR, particularly in cases where part of an LTCE's Top-up Tax is subject to an IIR and the remainder is subject to the UTPR.

4.5.2.5 Article 5.2.5.

590. If the Jurisdictional Top-up Tax is attributable to a recalculation under Article 5.4.1 and the jurisdiction does not have Net GloBE Income for the current Fiscal Year, Top-up Tax shall be allocated using the formula in Article 5.2.4 based on the GloBE Income of the Constituent Entities in the Fiscal Years for which the recalculations under Article 5.4.1 were performed.

591. *Objective of the Article*: Article 5.2.5 addresses situations where Additional Current Top-up Tax is computed for a jurisdiction under Article 5.4.1, and the jurisdiction does not have Net GloBE Income for the Fiscal Year. As a matter of convenience, Article 5.2.4 generally allocates Additional Current Top-up Tax computed under Article 5.4.1 along with Top-up Tax computed for the Fiscal Year among LTCEs under Article 5.2.4 based on the GloBE Income of such Entities in the fiscal years for which the recalculations under Article 5.4.1 were performed. The charging provisions under Article 2.2 allocate Top-up Tax from LTCEs to Parent Entities based on the Parent Entity's allocable share of their GloBE Income. Where a jurisdiction lacks Net GloBE Income in the current year, it is more appropriate to allocate Additional Current Top-up Tax based on the GloBE Income of the CEs in the relevant previous years because all of the Top-up Tax was calculated by reference to the Net GloBE Income of those years. Where the UPE is subject to an IIR, the LTCEs are wholly owned, and there is no POPE in the MNE Group, allocation of Top-up Tax based on the facts of different Fiscal Years will make no difference in the end because all of the Top-up Tax of all CEs in a jurisdiction would be allocated to the UPE.

592. *Allocation of Additional Current Top-up Tax attributable to operation of Article 4.1.5:* Additional Current Top-up Tax attributable to the operation of Article 4.1.5 is not allocated pursuant to Article 5.2.5. Such Additional Current Top-up Tax is allocated separately under Article 5.4.3.

4.5.3 Article 5.3. (Substance-Based Income Exclusion)

593. Prominent features of Article 5.3 are provided in Box 4.25.

Box 4.25 Prominent Features of Article 5.3

- The policy rationale behind a formulaic, substance-based carve-out, based on payroll and tangible assets, is to exclude a fixed return for substantive activities within a jurisdiction from the application of the GloBE Rules.
- Provides that the Substance-based Income Exclusion set out in Article 5.3 only affects those MNE Groups with operations in jurisdictions that are taxed below the Minimum Rate.
- Article 5.3.1 explains the role of the Substance-based Income Exclusion in the computation of Excess Profits and Top-up Tax under Article 5.2.
- The excess of the Substance-based Income Exclusion over the Net GloBE Income of the jurisdiction for a Fiscal Year cannot be carried forward or backwards to reduce the Net GloBE Income of another Fiscal Year.
- Provides for an Election to not apply the Substance-based Income Exclusion. The Election not to apply the exclusion is provided because some MNE Groups may consider that the burden of computing the amount of the exclusion for a particular jurisdiction outweighs the potential benefits of the exclusion in that jurisdiction.
- Provides that the MNE Group is not bound to make the election for the same jurisdiction in any subsequent Fiscal Year. Thus, an MNE Group that elects not to apply the Substance-based Income Exclusion for a jurisdiction in one year may apply the exclusion in the following Fiscal Year.
- Provides that the Substance-based Income Exclusion amount for a jurisdiction is the sum of the payroll carve-out and the tangible asset carve-out for each CE, except for CEs that are Investment Entities, in that jurisdiction.
- In applying the payroll carve-out, it is necessary to identify relevant employees (Eligible Employees), the location of those employees, and the relevant payroll expenses of those Eligible Employees (Eligible Payroll Costs).
- Provides that the payroll carve-out is computed on a jurisdictional basis.
- Provides that including a broad range of tangible assets in the carve-out base recognises that all such assets are indicative of substantive activities, as it helps to level the playing field across industries that use varying types of tangible assets in their business.
- Provides that including leased tangible assets neutralises the difference between owning and leasing assets and recognises that the business decision to own or lease typically has no bearing on the intensity of substantive activities.
- The tangible asset carve-out requires that the tangible assets are located either in the same jurisdiction as the CE that owns them or, in certain

situations, in the same jurisdiction as the CE that holds the right of use of the asset.

- Provides that the computation of the carrying value of Eligible Tangible Assets for purposes of Article 5.3.4 shall be based on the average of the carrying value (net of accumulated depreciation, amortisation, or depletion and including any amount attributable to capitalisation of payroll expense) at the beginning and end of the Reporting Fiscal Year as recorded for the purposes of preparing the CFS of the UPE.
- Article 5.3.6 provides rules applicable to the computation of the amount of Eligible Payroll Costs and Eligible Tangible Assets of a PE that is a CE.
- No attribution is done to stateless PEs, i.e., no Eligible Payroll Costs and Eligible Tangible Assets are attributed to a PE described in paragraph (d) of the definition in Article 10.1.
- Article 5.3.7 explains how Eligible Payroll Costs and Eligible Tangible Assets that are included in the financial statements of a Flow-through Entity are allocated among CEs.

594. *Policy rationale*: The policy rationale behind a formulaic, substance-based carve-out, based on payroll and tangible assets, is to exclude a fixed return for substantive activities within a jurisdiction from the application of the GloBE Rules. The use of Payroll and Tangible Assets as indicators of substantive activities is justified because these factors are generally expected to be less mobile and less likely to lead to tax-induced distortions. Conceptually, excluding a fixed return from substantive activities focuses GloBE on 'excess income', such as intangible-related income, which is most susceptible to BEPS risks. The Substance-based Income Exclusion set out in Article 5.3 only affects those MNE Groups with operations in jurisdictions that are taxed below the Minimum Rate. Further, because the potential benefit is limited to a routine return and considering the computational rules of the Top-up Tax, the design avoids any tax-induced distortions of investment decisions.

4.5.3.1 Article 5.3.1.

595. The Net GloBE Income for the jurisdiction shall be reduced by the Substance-based Income Exclusion for the jurisdiction to determine the Excess Profit for purposes of computing the Top-up Tax under Article 5.2. A Filing Constituent Entity of an MNE Group may make an Annual Election not to apply the Substance-based Income Exclusion for a jurisdiction by not computing the exclusion or claiming it in the computation of Top-up Tax for the jurisdiction in the GloBE Information Return(s) filed for the Fiscal Year.

596. *Objective of the Article*: Article 5.3.1 explains the role of the Substance-based Income Exclusion in the computation of Excess Profits and Top-up Tax under Article 5.2. The exclusion is subtracted from the Net GloBE Income in the jurisdiction in order to arrive at a measure of Excess Profit. If the exclusion determined for a Fiscal Year exceeds the Net GloBE Income of the jurisdiction for that year, there will be no Excess Profit, and thus, no Top-up Tax computed for that year unless there is Additional Current Top-up Tax for that Fiscal Year. The excess of the Substance-based Income Exclusion over the Net GloBE Income of the jurisdiction for a Fiscal Year cannot be carried forward or backwards to reduce the Net GloBE Income of another Fiscal Year.

597. *Election to not apply the Substance-based Income Exclusion*: The Substance-based Income Exclusion applies by default to each jurisdiction in which the MNE Group operates. However, an MNE Group is permitted to annually elect out of the requirement to apply the exclusion on a jurisdiction-by-jurisdiction basis. The election not to apply the exclusion is provided because some MNE Groups may consider that the burden of computing the amount of the exclusion for a particular jurisdiction outweighs the potential benefits of the exclusion in that jurisdiction. The election not to apply the exclusion is made by the Filing Constituent Entity, and it is made on a jurisdiction-by-jurisdiction basis. The Filing Constituent Entity makes the election by filing a GloBE Information Return that computes Excess Profits consistent with the election, i.e., by not subtracting an exclusion amount from the Net GloBE Income of the jurisdiction. An explicit affirmative statement that the election is being made for a jurisdiction is not necessary. An election not to apply the exclusion for a Fiscal Year cannot be revoked after a GloBE Information Return for that Fiscal Year has been filed consistent with the election. However, the MNE Group is not bound to make the election for the same jurisdiction in any subsequent Fiscal Year. Thus, an MNE Group that elects not to apply the Substance-based Income Exclusion for a jurisdiction in one year may apply the exclusion in the following Fiscal Year.

4.5.3.2 Article 5.3.2.

598. The Substance-based Income Exclusion amount for a jurisdiction is the sum of the payroll carve-out and the tangible asset carve-out for each Constituent Entity, except for Constituent Entities that are Investment Entities, in that jurisdiction.

4.5.3.3 Article 5.3.3.

599. The payroll carve-out for a Constituent Entity located in a jurisdiction is equal to 5% of its Eligible Payroll Costs of Eligible Employees that perform activities for the MNE Group in such jurisdiction, except Eligible Payroll costs that are:

(a) capitalised and included in the carrying value of Eligible Tangible Assets;
(b) attributable to a Constituent Entity's International Shipping Income and Qualified Ancillary International Shipping Income under Article 3.3.5 that is excluded from the computation of GloBE Income or Loss for the Fiscal Year.

600. The term Eligible Payroll Costs mentioned above is defined in Article 10.1 as below:

> Eligible Payroll Costs means employee compensation expenditures (including salaries, wages, and other expenditures that provide a direct and separate personal benefit to the employee, such as health insurance and pension contributions), payroll and employment taxes, and employer social security contributions.

601. The term Eligible Employees mentioned above is defined in Article 10.1 as below:

> Eligible Employees means employees, including part-time employees, of a Constituent Entity that is a member of the MNE Group and independent contractors participating in the ordinary operating activities of the MNE Group under the direction and control of the MNE Group.

602. *Objective of the Article*: The payroll carve-out subtracts from the Net GloBE Income of a jurisdiction a fixed return on activities performed in that jurisdiction calculated by reference to the CE's employment costs. The payroll carve-out design recognises a CE's payroll expense as an appropriate proxy for substantive activities carried out by employees of the MNE Group in the relevant jurisdiction. In applying the payroll carve-out, it is necessary to identify relevant employees (Eligible Employees), the location of those employees, and the relevant payroll expenses of those Eligible Employees (Eligible Payroll Costs).

603. *Meaning of independent contractors:* For purposes of the payroll carve-out, independent contractors include only natural persons and may include natural persons who are employed by a staffing or employment company but whose daily activities are performed under the direction and control of the MNE Group. Independent contractors do not include employees of a corporate contractor providing goods or services to the CE.

604. *Payroll carve-out computed on a jurisdictional basis:* The payroll carve-out is computed on a jurisdictional basis and is based on the Eligible Payroll Costs of Eligible Employees that perform activities in the jurisdiction where the CE employer is located. Employees will generally perform their activity in the jurisdiction where the CE employer is located (employer's jurisdiction). However, in certain cases, the employee may also perform work for their employer outside the employer's jurisdiction.

605. *Broad approach adopted to determine Eligible Payroll Costs:* The payroll carve-out takes a broad approach to determine Eligible Payroll Costs based on a general test of whether the expenditure of the employer gives rise to a direct and separate personal benefit to the employee. Article 10.1 defines a Constituent Entity's Eligible Payroll Costs to include expenditures for salaries and wages as well as for other employee benefits or remuneration such as medical insurance, payments to a Pension Fund or other retirement benefits, bonuses and allowances payable to Eligible Employees, and stock-based compensation. Eligible Payroll Costs also include payroll taxes (or other employee expense-related taxes such as fringe benefits taxes), as well as employer social security contributions.

606. *Exclusions from Eligible Payroll Costs*: The two exclusions from Eligible Payroll Costs are as below:

- Payroll expenses capitalised into the carrying value of Eligible Tangible Assets are subject to the Tangible Assets carve-out; hence, payroll expenditures capitalised into Eligible Tangible Assets will be taken into account in the Tangible Assets carve-out. However, payroll expenditures that are capitalised to other Tangible Assets, including inventory, are included in Eligible Payroll Costs.
- The payroll carve-out computation shall not include the payroll costs attributable to a CE's International Shipping Income and Qualified Ancillary International Shipping Income under Article 3.3. Payroll costs attributable to a CE's excess income over the cap for Qualified Ancillary International Shipping Income under Article 3.3.4 are included in the payroll carve-out computation (given that such excess income would not qualify for the exclusion from the GloBE Rules, allowing the associated Substance-based Income Exclusion is warranted). The amount of payroll cost attributable to International Shipping Income and to Qualified Ancillary International Shipping Income that is excluded shall be determined under the same principles set out in Article 3.3.5. The payroll which is directly allocable to the International Shipping Income and Qualified Ancillary International Shipping that is within the cap under Article 3.3.4 shall be excluded. Payroll expenses that cannot be directly allocated shall be allocated between a CE's International Shipping Income, Qualified Ancillary International Shipping Income, and other income on a formulaic basis in proportion to its revenues from international shipping over its total revenues.

4.5.3.4 Article 5.3.4.

607. The tangible asset carve-out for a Constituent Entity located in a jurisdiction is equal to 5% of the carrying value of Eligible Tangible Assets located in such jurisdiction. Eligible Tangible Assets means:

(a) property, plant, and equipment located in that jurisdiction;
(b) natural resources located in that jurisdiction;
(c) a lessee's right-of-use of tangible assets located in that jurisdiction; and
(d) a licence or similar arrangement from the government for the use of immovable property or exploitation of natural resources that entails significant investment in tangible assets.

For this purpose, the tangible asset carve-out computation shall not include the carrying value of property (including land or buildings) that is held for sale, lease or investment. The tangible asset carve-out computation shall not include the carrying value of tangible assets used in the generation of a CE's International Shipping Income and Qualified Ancillary International Shipping Income (i.e., ships and other maritime equipment and infrastructure). The carrying value of tangible assets attributable to a CE's excess income over the cap for Qualified Ancillary International Shipping Income under Article 3.3.4 shall be included in the tangible asset carve-out computation.

608. *Objective of the Article*: The tangible asset carve-out subtracts from the Net GloBE Income of a jurisdiction a fixed return on the carrying value of Eligible Tangible Assets located in that jurisdiction. Eligible Tangible Assets include the carrying value of property, plant and equipment, natural resources, and a lessee's right-of-use assets that are located in the jurisdiction in which the CE is located. Including a broad range of tangible assets in the carve-out base recognises that all such assets are indicative of substantive activities. Moreover, it helps to level the playing field across industries that use varying types of tangible assets in their business. Including leased tangible assets neutralises the difference between owning and leasing assets and recognises that the business decision to own or lease typically has no bearing on the intensity of substantive activities.

609. *Location of tangible assets*: The tangible asset carve-out requires that the tangible assets are located in the same jurisdiction as the CE that owns them or, in the situation where the tangible asset falls into categories (c) or (d), in the same jurisdiction as the CE that holds the right-of-use of the asset. It is expected that, in most cases, the tangible asset will be located in the same jurisdiction as the CE that owns or leases the asset. However, under specific circumstances, the nature of the asset and the way it is used may be such that it is not located in any jurisdiction or is located in multiple jurisdictions (e.g., an aircraft of an international airline) at different times during the Fiscal Year.

610. *Exclusions from tangible asset carve-out computation*: The three exclusions from tangible asset carve-out computation are as below:

(1) The tangible asset carve-out computation excludes the carrying value of property (including land or buildings) held for investment, sale, or lease. While the carve-out generally seeks to recognise a broad range of tangible assets, an MNE Group should not be allowed to generate a larger carve-out by purchasing investment property in a jurisdiction. This risk is particularly relevant as it relates to buildings and land, which are commonly held as investments. To neutralise this risk, buildings and land that are held to earn rental income or for capital appreciation (or both) are excluded from the carve-out. The carve-out will still, however, take into account owner-occupied property that is directly or indirectly used in production or supply of goods and services.

(2) An MNE Group should not be allowed to generate a larger carve-out via tangible assets whose carrying cost will be recovered principally through a sale transaction instead of through continuing use in the business. Since such assets are held for sale, not use, they are a poor proxy for substantive activities. Consequently, assets held for sale are excluded from the carve-out.

In order to be considered held for sale, the asset must be available for immediate sale in its present condition, subject only to terms that are usual and customary for sales of such assets and its sale must be highly probable.

(3) The tangible asset carve-out computation shall not include the carrying value of tangible assets attributable to the generation of a CE's International Shipping Income and Qualified Ancillary International Shipping Income that is within the cap under Article 3.3.4 (i.e., ships and other maritime equipment and infrastructure). The carrying value of tangible assets used in the generation of Qualified Ancillary International Shipping Income must be excluded in proportion to the excluded income, i.e., based on the ratio of Qualified Ancillary International Shipping Income within the cap to the total Qualified Ancillary International Shipping Income.

4.5.3.5 Article 5.3.5.

611. The computation of the carrying value of Eligible Tangible Assets for purposes of Article 5.3.4 shall be based on the average of the carrying value (net of accumulated depreciation, amortisation, or depletion and including any amount attributable to capitalisation of payroll expense) at the beginning and end of the Reporting Fiscal Year as recorded for the purposes of preparing the CFS of the UPE.

612. *Objective of the Article*: Article 5.3.5 sets out the rules for determining the carrying value of Eligible Tangible Assets for purposes of the tangible asset carve-out. The article requires the MNE Group to determine the carrying value for purposes of the carve-out in conformity with the carrying value of the asset as recorded for purposes of preparing the CFS (i.e., after taking into account purchase accounting adjustments and elimination adjustments attributable to inter-company sales). The carrying value of each asset for purposes of the carve-out is the average of the beginning and end of the year carrying values. Thus, if an asset is acquired or disposed of during the Fiscal Year, its carrying value at the beginning or end of the Fiscal Year will be zero. Because the zero carrying value is included in the computation of the average, the carve-out for assets acquired or disposed of during the year will be based on half of the carrying value of asset at the end or beginning of the year. The consequence of taking into account purchase accounting adjustments in respect of Eligible Tangible Assets and ignoring inter-company sales adjustments is that the tangible asset carve-out is based on the cost of acquiring the assets from unrelated persons and reflects the MNE Group's actual investment in the relevant assets. Failure to include purchase accounting adjustments would understate the actual investment, and including inter-company sales could overstate or understate the actual investment.

4.5.3.6 *Article 5.3.6.*

613. For purposes of Articles 5.3.3 and 5.3.4, the Eligible Payroll Costs and Eligible Tangible Assets of a Constituent Entity that is a Permanent Establishment are those included in its separate financial accounts as determined by Article 3.4.1 and adjusted in accordance with Article 3.4.2, provided that the Eligible Employees and Eligible Tangible Assets are located in the jurisdiction where the Permanent Establishment is located. The Eligible Payroll Costs and Eligible Tangible Assets of a Permanent Establishment are not taken into account for the Eligible Payroll Costs and Eligible Tangible Assets of the Main Entity. The Eligible Payroll Costs and Eligible Tangible Assets of a Permanent Establishment whose income has been wholly or partly excluded in accordance with Articles 3.5.3 and 7.1.4 are excluded from the Substance-based Income Exclusion computations of the MNE Group in the same proportion.

614. *Objective of the Article*: Article 5.3.6 provides rules applicable to the computation of the amount of Eligible Payroll Costs and Eligible Tangible Assets of a PE that is a CE. This provision states that the Eligible Payroll Costs and the Eligible Tangible Assets of the PE are those included in its separate financial accounts.

615. *Mechanics of the Article*: This provision follows the same mechanics as Articles 3.4.1 and 3.4.2. The Eligible Payroll Costs and Eligible Tangible Assets are those included in the financial accounts of the PE, provided that such accounts are prepared in accordance with an Acceptable Financial Accounting Standard. If the PE does not have separate financial accounts or they are not prepared in accordance with an Acceptable Financial Accounting Standard, the amount of such Eligible Payroll Costs and Eligible Tangible Assets shall be computed as if a PE had separate financial accounts prepared in accordance with the accounting standard used in preparation of the CFS of the UPE.

616. *Tax Treaty or domestic tax law to apply*: Similar to Article 3.4.2, the Eligible Payroll Costs and Eligible Tangible Assets have to be adjusted to those that would have been attributed to a PE in accordance with the Tax Treaty or domestic tax law. In the case of PEs, as defined by paragraph (c) of the definition in Article 10.1, the Eligible Payroll Costs and Eligible Tangible Assets have to be those that would have been attributed to the PE in accordance with Article 7 of the OECD MTC and related provisions.

617. *Location of employees and assets*: A condition included in this article is that the employees and assets have to be located in the jurisdiction in which the PE is located. This condition is similar to the condition that applies to other CEs, and which is provided in Article 5.3.3 and Article 5.3.4. Where the employees and assets attributed to the PE are not located in the jurisdiction in which it is located, the costs of such employees and assets are excluded from the computation of the Substance-based Income Exclusion.

618. *No attribution to stateless PEs*: No Eligible Payroll Costs and Eligible Tangible Assets are attributed to a PE described in paragraph (d) of the definition in Article 10.1.

619. *Attribution to a PE obviates attribution to its Main Entity*: The second sentence of Article 5.3.6 states that the Eligible Payroll Costs and Eligible Tangible Assets that are attributed to a PE are not taken into account in the Eligible Payroll Costs and Eligible Tangible Assets of its Main Entity. This ensures that such costs are not taken into account twice for purposes of computing the Substance-based Income Exclusion. Furthermore, where the GloBE Income or Loss of a PE is allocated to the Main Entity in accordance with Article 3.4.5, the Eligible Payroll Costs and Eligible Tangible Assets attributed to such PE remain in the jurisdiction where it is located and therefore are not attributed to the Main Entity.

620. *Assets used to produce income if excluded from GloBE income are not taken into account*: The last sentence of Article 5.3.6 states that the Eligible Payroll Costs and Eligible Tangible Assets of a PE whose income is excluded in accordance with Articles 3.5.3 and 7.1.4 are excluded from the Substance-based Income Exclusion. If the income is partly excluded, then a reduction to the Eligible Payroll Costs and Eligible Tangible Asset has to be made in the same proportion. This ensures that the Eligible Payroll Costs and Eligible Tangible Assets that are used to produce income that is excluded from GloBE Income are not taken into account to shelter income that is included in GloBE income.

4.5.3.7 Article 5.3.7.

621. For purposes of Articles 5.3.3 and 5.3.4, Eligible Payroll Costs and Eligible Tangible Assets of a Flow-through Entity that are not allocated under Article 5.3.6 are allocated as follows:

(a) if the Financial Accounting Net Income or Loss of the Flow-through Entity has been allocated to the Constituent Entity-owner under Article 3.5.1(b), then the Entity's Eligible Payroll Costs and Eligible Tangible Assets are allocated in the same proportion to the Constituent Entity-owner provided it is located in the jurisdiction where the Eligible Employees and Eligible Tangible Assets are located;
(b) if the Flow-through Entity is the UPE, then Eligible Payroll Costs and Eligible Tangible Assets located in the jurisdiction where the UPE is located are allocated to it and reduced in proportion to the income that is excluded under Article 7.1.1; and
(c) all other Eligible Payroll Costs and Eligible Tangible Assets of the Flow-through Entity are excluded from the Substance-based Income Exclusion computations of the MNE Group.

622. *Objective of the Article*: Article 5.3.7 explains how Eligible Payroll Costs and Eligible Tangible Assets that are included in the financial statements of a Flow-through Entity are allocated properly among CEs. This provision follows the same mechanics as Article 3.5.1.

623. *Operation of the Article*: As a preliminary step, the Eligible Payroll Costs and Eligible Tangible Assets attributed to a PE in accordance with Article 5.3.6 are removed and excluded from the allocation under Article 5.3.7. This is achieved by the phrase 'not allocated under Article 5.3.6'. Article 5.3.7 then sets three different rules for different scenarios, as summarised in Figure 4.25.

Figure 4.25 Allocation of Eligible Payroll Costs and Eligible Tangible Assets of a Flow-Through Entity among CEs under Article 5.3.7

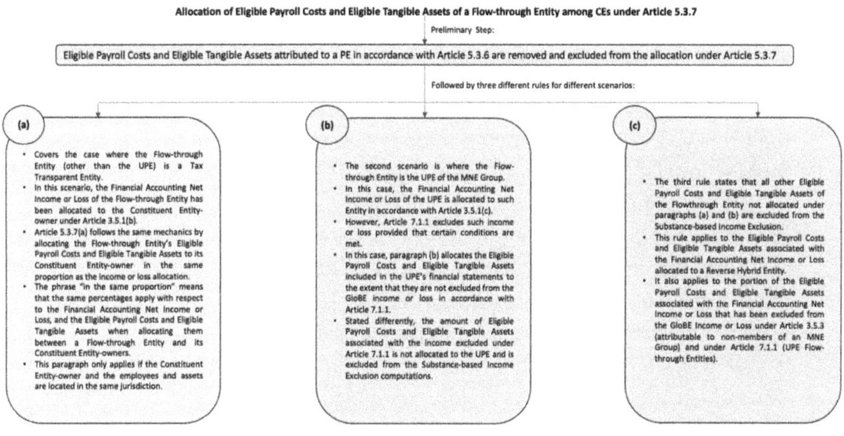

624. Illustration # 56: This example illustrates, through a flow-chart, the application of the Substance-based Income Exclusion in the situation in which a Flow-through Entity has Eligible Payroll Costs and Eligible Tangible Assets.

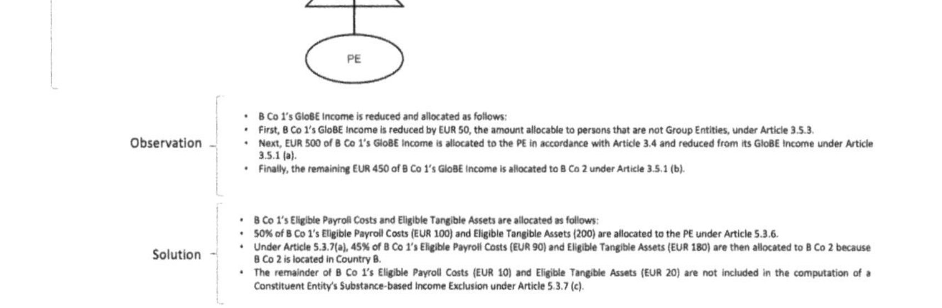

4.5.4 Article 5.4. (Additional Current Top-Up Tax)

625. Prominent features of Article 5.4 are provided in Box 4.26.

Box 4.26 Prominent Features of Article 5.4

- Certain provisions of the GloBE Rules, referred to as ETR Adjustment Articles (namely, Article 3.2.6, Article 4.4.4, Article 4.6.1, Article 4.6.4 and Article 7.3), require or permit a retroactive recalculation of the ETR and Top-up Tax for a previous Fiscal Year or Fiscal Years taking into account an adjustment to the Adjusted Covered Taxes or the Net GloBE Income (or both) for the year.
- Article 5.4.1 provides the mechanism for performing the re-calculations for the prior year and treats any additional Top-up Tax computed in respect of those prior Fiscal Years as Additional Current Top-up Tax, which is allocated to CEs in the jurisdiction under Article 5.2.
- Provides that in order to avoid the complexity and administrative burden of requiring an amended GloBE Information Return and additional separate payment of Top-up Tax, the Additional Top-Up Tax is instead charged to the Fiscal Year in which the recalculation was performed.
- Article 5.4.1 is not intended to address ordinary mistakes in the computations under the GloBE Rules or adjustments to GloBE Income arising from an examination of a CE's application of the IIR or the UTPR.
- Article 5.4.2 provides a special rule when there is additional Top-up Tax due as a result of a recalculation performed in accordance with Article 5.4.1, and there is no Net GloBE Income for the jurisdiction for the current Fiscal Year.
- Article 5.4.2 provides that the GloBE Income of the CEs in the jurisdiction shall be increased for the purposes of Article 2.2.2 in an amount equal to the additional Top-up Tax due divided by the Minimum Rate. For this purpose, any GloBE Loss determined for the Fiscal Year is disregarded.
- Article 5.4.3 sets out a special rule for allocating Top-up Taxes that arise under Article 4.1.5.
- The amount of Additional Current Top-up Tax allocated to each CE for purposes of Article 5.4.3 shall be allocated only to CEs that record an Adjusted Covered Taxes amount that is less than zero and less than the GloBE Income or Loss of such CE multiplied by the Minimum Rate.
- Article 5.4.3 requires the allocation of the Top-up Tax arising as a result of such permanent differences to the CE that generated the attribute resulting from the permanent difference.
- Provides that when Additional Current Top-up Tax arises from a re-calculation under Articles 5.4.1 to 5.4.3, Article 5.4.4 treats the CE to which the Additional Current Top-up Tax is allocated as an LTCE for purposes of Chapter 2.

- Article 5.4.4 ensures that rules of Chapter 2 apply properly to the Additional Current Top-up Tax to years in which the CE's location is not a Low-Tax Jurisdiction.

626. Certain provisions of the GloBE Rules, referred to as ETR Adjustment Articles, require or permit a retroactive recalculation of the ETR and Top-up Tax for a previous Fiscal Year or Fiscal Years, taking into account an adjustment to the Adjusted Covered Taxes or the Net GloBE Income (or both) for the year. When these provisions result in adjustments to the Adjusted Covered Taxes, the change will affect the ETR for one or more of the prior Fiscal Years. The rules for performing the necessary re-calculations for a prior year when required or permitted by an ETR Adjustment Article are set out in Articles 5.4.1 and 5.4.2. Article 5.4.3 sets out a special rule for allocating Top-up Taxes that arise under Article 4.1.5. The ETR Adjustment Articles are as below:

- Article 3.2.6: Provides an Election that permits an MNE Group to spread the effect of gains and losses from the sale of Local Tangible Assets over a period of up to five years to mitigate the effect of recognising the entire gain in a single year on the MNE Group's jurisdictional ETR computation and to match the timing of gains and losses on Local Tangible Assets.
- Article 4.4.4: Provides that barring Recapture Exception Accruals, deferred tax liabilities recorded in other categories that do not reverse within the five Fiscal Years must be recaptured in the Fiscal Year in which the increase in the Recaptured Deferred Tax Liability was originally included in the Total Deferred Tax Adjustment Amount.
- Article 4.6.1: Generally requires a re-computation of the ETR and Top-up Tax for the Fiscal Year to which the tax adjustment relates in the case of a decrease in Covered Taxes.
- Article 4.6.4: Provides that the ETR and Top-up Tax for a jurisdiction must be recalculated to exclude an amount of current tax expense (i.e., not deferred tax expense) that is more than EUR 1 million, was claimed as Adjusted Covered Tax and is not paid within three years of the last day of the Fiscal Year in which such amount was claimed as Adjusted Covered Tax.
- Article 7.3: Provides special rules in relation to certain tax regimes that subject an Entity to tax on its earnings when those earnings are distributed or deemed distributed.

4.5.4.1 Article 5.4.1.

627. If the ETR and Top-up Tax for a prior Fiscal Year is required or permitted to be recalculated pursuant to an ETR Adjustment Article,

(a) the ETR and Top-up Tax for the prior Fiscal Year shall be recalculated in accordance with the rules of Article 5.1 through Article 5.3 after taking into account the adjustments to Adjusted Covered Taxes and GloBE Income or Loss required by the relevant ETR Adjustment Article; and

(b) any amount of incremental Top-up Tax resulting from such recalculation shall be treated as Additional Current Top-up Tax under Article 5.2.3 arising in the current Fiscal Year.

628. *Objective of the Article*: If the ETR of a jurisdiction is subject to an ETR Adjustment, then Article 5.4.1 provides the mechanism for performing the recalculations for the prior year. Article 5.4.1 treats any additional Top-up Tax computed in respect of those prior Fiscal Years as Additional Current Top-up Tax, which is allocated to Constituent Entities in the jurisdiction under Article 5.2. To avoid the complexity and administrative burden of requiring an amended GloBE Information Return and additional separate payment of Top-up Tax, the Additional Top-up Tax is instead charged to the Fiscal Year in which the recalculation was performed.

629. *Applicability of the Article*: Article 5.4.1 is not intended to address ordinary mistakes in the computations under the GloBE Rules or adjustments to GloBE Income arising from an examination of a CE's application of the IIR or the UTPR. Such adjustments are not made on a prospective basis by including them in Additional Current Top-up Tax. For example, if an MNE Group erroneously excluded an item of income from the computation of its GloBE Income due to a misclassification of interest income as a dividend, it should follow the relevant administrative procedures for correcting such errors. This may entail filing an amended tax return to increase the amount of Top-up Tax payable in the jurisdiction. Similarly, if this error is discovered by the relevant tax authority on examination, the tax authority may adjust the GloBE tax liability in respect of the relevant Fiscal Year and apply its normal administrative procedures and rules, including assessment of interest or penalties, to that re-determination of tax liability. Stated differently, Article 5.4.1 applies only when there is an adjustment to a local tax item that has a follow-on effect on computations under the GloBE Rules, such as a transfer pricing adjustment that affects the income and tax liability of CEs in two or more jurisdictions.

4.5.4.2 Article 5.4.2.

630. If there is Additional Current Top-up Tax attributable to a recalculation under Article 5.4.1 and the jurisdiction does not have Net GloBE Income for the current Fiscal Year, the GloBE Income of each Constituent Entity located in the jurisdiction for purposes of Article 2.2.2 shall be equal to the result of the Top-up Tax allocated to such Entity under Articles 5.2.4 and 5.2.5 divided by the Minimum Rate.

631. *Objective of the Article*: Article 5.4.2 provides a special rule when there is additional Top-up Tax due as a result of a recalculation performed in accordance with Article 5.4.1, and there is no Net GloBE Income for the jurisdiction for the current Fiscal Year. This rule provides that the GloBE Income of the CEs in the jurisdiction shall be increased for the purposes of Article 2.2.2 in an amount equal to the additional Top-up

Tax due divided by the Minimum Rate. For this purpose, any GloBE Loss determined for the Fiscal Year is disregarded. This rule ensures that when a recalculation results in additional Top-up Tax that is payable in a Fiscal Year with no GloBE Income for a jurisdiction that there is still a mechanism in place by which the Top-up Tax that is owed can be allocated to Parent Entities that may be subject to an IIR.

4.5.4.3 Article 5.4.3.

632. If there is Additional Current Top-up Tax attributable to the operation of Article 4.1.5, the GloBE Income of each Constituent Entity located in the jurisdiction for purposes of Article 2.2.2 shall be equal to the result of the Top-up Tax allocated to such Entity under this article divided by the Minimum Rate. The amount of Additional Current Top-up Tax allocated to each Constituent Entity for purposes of this article shall be allocated only to Constituent Entities that record an Adjusted Covered Taxes amount that is less than zero and less than the GloBE Income or Loss of such Constituent Entity multiplied by the Minimum Rate. The allocation shall be made pro-rata based upon the following amount for each of those Constituent Entities:

(GloBE Income or Loss x Minimum Rate) – Adjusted Covered Taxes

633. *Objective of the Article*: Under Article 4.1.5, Top-up Tax may be due as a result of a negative Adjusted Covered Taxes Amount that represents a larger loss for the jurisdiction than the Expected Adjusted Covered Taxes Amount. Article 4.1.5 essentially requires that attributes resulting from permanent differences be paid for with additional Top-up Tax arising in the Fiscal Year in which the attribute is generated. This facilitates the continued alignment of GloBE deferred tax accounts with the accounts used for financial reporting purposes. Article 5.4.3 requires the allocation of the Top-up Tax arising as a result of such permanent differences to the CE that generated the attribute resulting from the permanent difference, as explained in **Illustration # 57**:

Illustration of Application of Article 5.4.3 read with Article 4.1.5

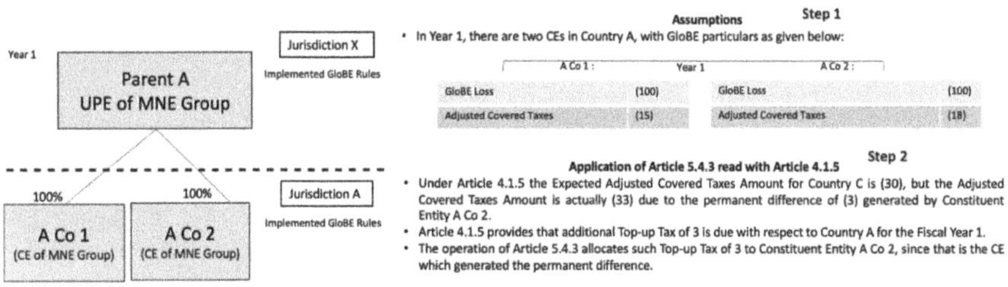

634. *GloBE Income created under Article 5.4.3*: Article 5.4.3 also creates an amount of GloBE income for each CE to which the Top-up Tax arising under Article 4.1.5 is allocated. This GloBE Income is used solely for purposes of Article 2.2 to determine a Parent Entity's Allocable Share of Top-up Tax arising under Article 4.1.5. The GloBE

Income created under Article 5.4.3 is equal to the Top-up Tax allocated to the Entity under Article 5.4.3 divided by the Minimum Rate. For this purpose, any GloBE Loss determined for the Fiscal Year is disregarded. It is possible for GloBE Income to be created for CEs in a jurisdiction for the purposes of Article 2.2.2 under both Articles 5.4.2 and 5.4.3. In this scenario, each article is applied without regard to the income created under the other article. For purposes of Article 2.2.2, the GloBE Income for any CE for which GloBE Income has been created under both articles is the sum of the income created under each article.

4.5.4.4 Article 5.4.4.

635. If a Constituent Entity is allocated Additional Current top-up Tax pursuant to this article and Article 5.2.4, such Constituent Entity shall be treated as an LTCE for the purposes of Chapter 2.

636. *Objective of the Article*: When Additional Current Top-up Tax arises from a recalculation under Articles 5.4.1 to 5.4.3, Article 5.4.4 treats the CE to which the Additional Current Top-up Tax is allocated as an LTCE for purposes of Chapter 2. Whether a jurisdiction is a Low-Tax Jurisdiction is determined annually, and the Additional Current Top-up Tax may arise in a year for which the jurisdiction is not a Low-Tax Jurisdiction. The rules of Chapter 2 apply with respect to LTCEs. Article 5.4.4 ensures that those rules apply properly to the Additional Current Top-up Tax to years in which the CE's location is not a Low-Tax Jurisdiction.

637. A ready reckoner on Structure and Mechanics of Article 5.4 is provided in Figure 4.26.

Figure 4.26 A Ready Reckoner on Structure and Mechanics of Article 5.4

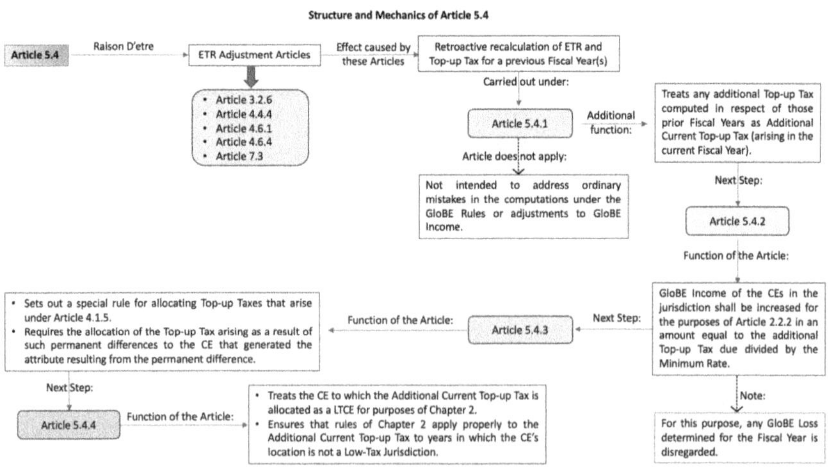

4.5.5 Article 5.5. (*De Minimis* Exclusion)

638. Prominent features of Article 5.5 are provided in Box 4.27.

Box 4.27 Prominent Features of Article 5.5

- Article 5.5 provides a jurisdictional exclusion for LTCEs of an MNE Group when both (i) the aggregated income and (ii) the revenue of those entities does not exceed agreed monetary thresholds.
- The policy intent underlying Article 5.5 is to avoid the complexities of a full ETR computation in cases where the amount of any Top-up Tax would not seem to justify the associated compliance and administrative costs.
- Article 5.5.1 provides that the Top-up Tax for the CEs located in a jurisdiction shall be deemed to be zero for a given Fiscal Year when all CEs located in the same jurisdiction meet the requirements for the *de minimis* exclusion if, for such Fiscal Year:
  - the Average GloBE Revenue of such jurisdiction is less than EUR 10 million; and
  - the Average GloBE Income or Loss of such jurisdiction is a loss or is less than EUR 1 million.
- Provides that the election is an Annual Election. This means that a jurisdiction can fall under the *de minimis* exclusion for a given Fiscal Year but not necessarily for the preceding or the following year.
- Article 5.5.1 applies at the election of the Filing Constituent Entity. As provided in Article 8.1.4 (b), the Filing Constituent Entity shall elect and provide the relevant information in its GloBE Information Return, showing that the required conditions are met to benefit from the exclusion.
- Provides that the two conditions are aggregate and cumulative. This means that the income and revenues of all CEs located in the same jurisdiction must be aggregated for the purposes of the *de minimis* exclusion, and if, for a Fiscal Year, the aggregate outcome for those CEs fail to meet one of the two conditions, the jurisdiction is not eligible for the *de minimis* exclusion for that Fiscal Year.
- Provides that the election applies notwithstanding the requirements otherwise provided in Chapter 5. This means that the election available in Article 5.5.1 does not require the MNE Group to compute the Average GloBE Revenue and Average GloBE Income or Loss of the members of a Minority-Owned Subgroup as if they were a separate MNE Group or of a Minority-Owned Constituent Entity on an entity basis. Therefore, the GloBE Revenue and the GloBE Income or Loss of those entities is taken into account for purposes of determining the Average GloBE Revenue and the Average GloBE Income or Loss of the jurisdiction where they are located.
- Article 5.5.2 provides that the values of the current Fiscal Year (whether income or loss) shall be averaged with that of the preceding two Fiscal Years

for purposes of testing whether the jurisdiction is below the threshold. Using a three-year average is intended to simplify both compliance with the rule by MNE Groups and administration of the rule by tax authorities.

- In Article 5.5.3:
  - Paragraph (a) provides that the GloBE Revenue of a jurisdiction is the sum of the revenue of all CEs located in the jurisdiction for a Fiscal Year, taking into account the adjustments calculated in accordance with Chapter 3;
  - Paragraph (b) provides that the GloBE Income or Loss of a jurisdiction is the Net GloBE Income of that jurisdiction, if any, or the Net GloBE Loss of that jurisdiction.
- Post-filing ETR Adjustments that reduce GloBE Income and/or GloBE Revenue for a previous Fiscal Year will not make a jurisdiction eligible for the *de minimis* exclusion in a previous Fiscal Year.
- Post-filing ETR Adjustments that increase the GloBE Income and/or the GloBE Revenue of the jurisdiction may result in the Average GloBE Income or the Average GloBE Revenue of the jurisdiction no longer being below the threshold for the *de minimis* exclusion for a previous Fiscal Year or Years. In such a case, Article 5.5 is no longer applicable for the relevant Fiscal Year or Years, and the Filing Constituent Entity must provide the relevant information required in the GloBE Information Return with respect to that jurisdiction for those Fiscal Years without applying Article 5.5.
- Provides that if an MNE Group acquires Entities in a merger, the GloBE Revenue and GloBE Income or Loss of those Entities determined for periods prior to the merger are not taken into account for purposes of determining the three-year averages under Article 5.5.3. Similarly, if a CE leaves the MNE Group, the GloBE Revenue and GloBE Income or Loss of that Entity determined for periods prior to the disposition of that CE are still taken into account for purposes of determining the three-year averages under Article 5.5.3.
- Provides that an election under Article 5.5 shall not apply to a CE that is a Stateless Constituent Entity or an Investment Entity, and the revenue and GloBE Income or Loss of a Stateless Constituent Entity and of an Investment Entity shall be excluded from the computations in Article 5.5.3. The election is not applicable to these CEs because their ETR is computed on an Entity basis, and they are typically not subject to tax.

639. *Policy intent*: Article 5.5 provides a jurisdictional exclusion for LTCEs of an MNE Group when both (i) the aggregated income and (ii) the revenue of those entities does not exceed agreed monetary thresholds. The policy intent underlying Article 5.5 is to avoid the complexities of a full ETR computation in cases where the amount of any Top-up Tax would not seem to justify the associated compliance and administrative costs. Article 5.5.1 sets out the effects of the exclusion as well as the required conditions to benefit from that exclusion. Articles 5.5.2 and 5.5.3 further provide the methodology for computing the relevant indicators on a jurisdictional basis.

4.5.5.1 Article 5.5.1.

640. At the election of the Filing Constituent Entity, and notwithstanding the requirements otherwise provided in Chapter 5, the Top-up Tax for the Constituent Entities located in a jurisdiction shall be deemed to be zero for a Fiscal Year if, for such Fiscal Year:

(a) the Average GloBE Revenue of such jurisdiction is less than EUR 10 million; and
(b) the Average GloBE Income or Loss of such jurisdiction is a loss or is less than EUR 1 million.

The election under this article is an Annual Election.

641. *Objective of the Article*: Article 5.5.1 provides that the Top-up Tax for the CEs located in a jurisdiction shall be deemed to be zero for a given Fiscal Year when all CEs located in the same jurisdiction meet the requirements for the *de minimis* exclusion. Article 5.5.1 further provides that this exclusion applies notwithstanding the requirements otherwise provided in Chapter 5, such as the requirement to determine the ETR of a jurisdiction and compute the Top-up Tax due if any. This means that there is no need for the MNE Group to compute the ETR of the CEs that are located in the jurisdiction that meets the *de minimis* thresholds and no need to calculate the amount of Top-up Tax that would have been due if the exclusion did not apply.

642. *Exclusion applies on an annual basis*: This means that a jurisdiction can fall under the *de minimis* exclusion for a given Fiscal Year but not necessarily for the preceding or the following year. If a CE was located in a jurisdiction to which Article 5.5.1 applied the first year when the MNE is subject to the GloBE Rules, the Transition Rules provided in Article 9.1 shall apply to such CE at the beginning of the first Fiscal Year for which Article 5.5.1 does not apply to the jurisdiction. If a CE was located in a jurisdiction to which Article 5.5.1 starts to apply one or several Fiscal Years after the MNE is subject to the GloBE Rules, the Filing Constituent Entity may nevertheless still be subject to filing obligations under the GloBE Rules during the Fiscal Year(s) where the *de minimis* exclusion applies (e.g., to ensure that an earlier deferred tax liability reversed within the required timeframe).

643. A ready reckoner on Structure and Mechanics of Article 5.5.1 is provided in Figure 4.27.

Figure 4.27 A Ready Reckoner on Structure and Mechanics of Article 5.5.1

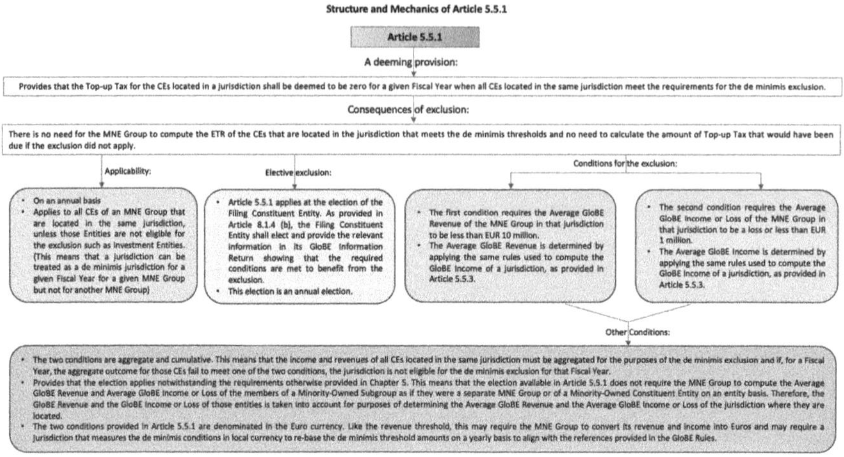

4.5.5.2 Article 5.5.2.

644. For purposes of Article 5.5.1, the Average GloBE Revenue (or GloBE Income or Loss) of a jurisdiction is the average of the GloBE Revenue (or GloBE Income or Loss) of the jurisdiction for the current and the two preceding Fiscal Years. If there were no Constituent Entities with GloBE Revenue or GloBE Losses that were located in the jurisdiction in the first or second preceding Fiscal Year, such year or years shall be excluded from the calculation of the Average GloBE Revenue and the Average GloBE Income or Loss of the relevant jurisdiction.

645. *Objective of the Article*: Article 5.5.2 provides that the GloBE Revenue and the GloBE Income or Loss of a jurisdiction shall be averaged for purposes of testing whether a jurisdiction meets the criteria for the *de minimis* exclusion. For each of those indicators, Article 5.5.2 provides that the values of the current Fiscal Year (whether income or loss) shall be averaged with that of the preceding two Fiscal Years for purposes of testing whether the jurisdiction is below the threshold. Using a three-year average is intended to simplify both compliance with the rule by MNE Groups and administration of the rule by tax authorities. At the same time, the average may result in volatile outcomes where a Fiscal Year with a significant amount of income (or loss) drops out of the three-year average.

646. *Situations leading to exclusion of some Fiscal Years*: To avoid skewing the computation of the average, the second sentence of Article 5.5.2 provides that some Fiscal Years shall be excluded from the computation of the Average GloBE Revenue and the Average GloBE Income or Loss when there are no CEs with either GloBE Revenue or GloBE Losses (in the absence of revenue) that were located in the jurisdiction for that Fiscal Year. This applies when there are no CEs located in the jurisdiction for a given Fiscal Year. It can also arise when there are only dormant CEs located in the jurisdiction. Before the GloBE Rules come into effect, there are also no CEs with GloBE Revenue or GloBE Income or Loss in any jurisdiction. This means that if, for instance, the CEs located in a given jurisdiction have an aggregate GloBE Income that equals or exceeds EUR 1 million for the first year when the GloBE Rules apply, the determination will be based solely on the revenue, income and loss of that year and the jurisdiction will not benefit from the *de minimis* exclusion for that year.

647. *Manner of computation if one Fiscal Year is shorter:* The computation of the average provided under Article 5.5.2 relies on the assumption that Fiscal Years have the same duration. If one Fiscal Year is shorter, taking into account the GloBE Revenue or the GloBE Income or Loss of that year as if it accounted for the entire year would also skew the results. In such a case, the average shall be computed by adjusting the corresponding revenue and income (or loss) calculations in proportion to the period covered by the short Fiscal Year over a calendar year in order to obtain an annual GloBE Revenue and GloBE Income or Loss for purposes of the computation, as explained in **Illustration # 58**:

Illustration of Application of Article 5.5.2 - De minimis exclusion – short Fiscal Year taken into account in the average

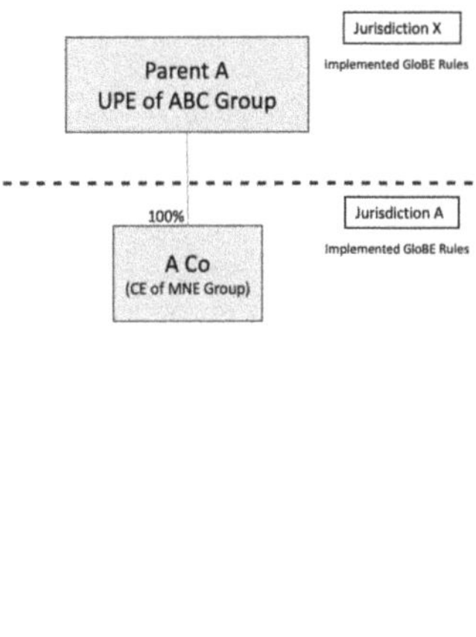

Assumptions Step 1

- Assume the ABC Group uses the calendar year as its Fiscal Year and has only one CE in Jurisdiction A, A Co.
- A Co only generates GloBE Revenue, GloBE Income, and GloBE Loss in Jurisdiction A.
- This example illustrates how the computation is performed and assesses whether the Top-up Tax for A Co may be deemed to be zero for Fiscal Year 3.
- A Co was created on 1 July in Year 1 and it's GloBE particulars are as given below:

Fiscal Year	GloBE Revenue (Euro)	GloBE Income/Loss (Euro)
Year 1	1 million	50,000
Year 2	1 million	1,00,000
Year 3	3 million	(2,00,000)

Application of Article 5.5.2 Step 2

- The computation of the average amounts under Article 5.5.2 relies on the assumption that Fiscal Years have the same duration.
- If one Fiscal Year is shorter, the average shall be computed by adjusting the corresponding GloBE Revenue and GloBE Income (or Loss) calculations in proportion to the period covered by the short Fiscal Year over a 12 month period.
- Therefore, in Year 1, as B Co's GloBE Revenue and GloBE Income were only realized over 6 months (1 July - 31 December), the GloBE Revenue and the GloBE Income of Year 1 will be multiplied by 2 (= 12/6) for the purposes of determining the average annual GloBE Revenue and GloBE Income.
- The three-year Average GloBE Revenue for this jurisdiction is as computed below:
  [(2 x 1 million) + 1 million + 3 million] / 3 = EUR 2 million
- The three-year Average GloBE Revenue or Loss for this jurisdiction is as computed below:
  [(2 x 50,000) + 100,000 + (−200,000)] / 3 = EUR 0
- The Average GloBE Revenue of Jurisdiction A is less than EUR 10 million and the Average GloBE Income or Loss of Jurisdiction A is less than EUR 1 million. As a consequence, the Top-up Tax for A Co shall be deemed to be zero for Year 3 if the Filing Constituent Entity elects for it under the GloBE Rules.

4.5.5.3 *Article 5.5.3.*

648. For purposes of Article 5.5.2:

(a) the GloBE Revenue of a jurisdiction for a Fiscal Year is the sum of the revenue of all Constituent Entities located in the jurisdiction for such Fiscal Year, taking into account the adjustments calculated in accordance with Chapter 3; and

(b) the GloBE Income or Loss of a jurisdiction for a Fiscal Year is the Net GloBE Income of that jurisdiction, if any, or the Net GloBE Loss of that jurisdiction.

649. *Objective of the Article*: In Article 5.5.3:

- Paragraph (a) provides that the GloBE Revenue of a jurisdiction is the sum of the revenue of all CEs located in the jurisdiction for a Fiscal Year, taking into account the adjustments calculated in accordance with Chapter 3;
- Paragraph (b) provides that the GloBE Income or Loss of a jurisdiction is the Net GloBE Income of that jurisdiction, if any, or the Net GloBE Loss of that jurisdiction. The Net GloBE Income of a jurisdiction is defined in Article 5.1.2 as the positive amount, if any, that is computed as the difference between the sum of the GloBE Income of all CEs and the sum of the GloBE Losses of all CEs, where both elements are determined in accordance with the rules provided in Chapter 3. If this difference is nil or negative, the outcome is a loss, and that is the Net GloBE Loss of a jurisdiction.

650. The determination of GloBE Revenue of a CE is encapsulated in Figure 4.28.

Figure 4.28 Determination of GloBE Revenue of a CE

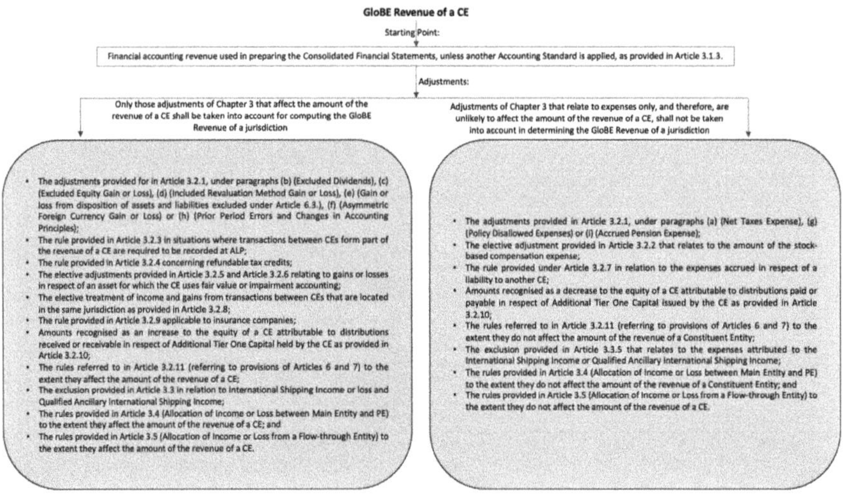

651. *Post-filing ETR Adjustments*: The GloBE Revenue and the GloBE Income or Loss of a jurisdiction are computed for each Fiscal Year to determine whether the *de minimis* exclusion applies. An ETR Adjustment Article may apply in a subsequent year such that the ETR of a jurisdiction for a previous Fiscal Year is required or permitted to be recalculated, which may also require the re-computation of the GloBE Income or Loss of that jurisdiction for that Fiscal Year or any intervening Fiscal Years. When the GloBE Income or Loss is adjusted under an ETR Adjustment Article, the GloBE Revenue shall also be adjusted as appropriate and necessary. Adjustments that reduce GloBE Income and/or GloBE Revenue for a previous Fiscal Year will not make a jurisdiction eligible for the *de minimis* exclusion in a previous Fiscal Year. However, adjustments that increase the GloBE Income and/or the GloBE Revenue of the jurisdiction may result in the Average GloBE Income or the Average GloBE Revenue of the jurisdiction no longer being below the threshold for the *de minimis* exclusion for a previous Fiscal Year or Years. In such a case, Article 5.5 is no longer applicable for the relevant Fiscal Year or Years, and the Filing Constituent Entity must provide the relevant information required in the GloBE Information Return with respect to that jurisdiction for those Fiscal Years without applying Article 5.5. For instance, in the case of a recalculation pursuant to Article 3.2.6, the GloBE Revenue for a previous Fiscal Year shall be increased by the amount of Aggregate Asset Gain set off against a Net Asset Loss for the year under paragraphs (b) or (c) and the amount allocated to the year under paragraph (d). Another example is Article 4.6.1, which addresses post-filing adjustments and provides that the ETR is re-computed for a previous Fiscal Year when post-filing adjustments result in a reduction of the ETR for that year. Those adjustments also require re-computing the GloBE Income of that Fiscal Year and the intervening Fiscal Years, as necessary and appropriate. In circumstances where the GloBE Income would need to be increased for those Fiscal Years where post-filing adjustments result in a reduction of the ETR, this may have an impact on the *de minimis* exclusion. If the adjusted GloBE Income results in the Average GloBE Income exceeding the EUR 1 million threshold provided in Article 5.5.1 for any Fiscal Year, the *de minimis* exclusion would not be applicable for those years.

652. *Changes in the Scope of the MNE Group*: Determinations of GloBE Revenue and GloBE Income or Loss of a jurisdiction under Article 5.5.3 are not adjusted to take into account periods when a CE does not belong to the MNE Group and are limited based on whether an Entity was a CE of the MNE Group in the previous Fiscal Years. Thus, if an MNE Group acquires Entities in a merger, the GloBE Revenue and GloBE Income or Loss of those Entities determined for periods prior to the merger are not taken into account for purposes of determining the three-year averages under Article 5.5.3. Similarly, if a CE leaves the MNE Group, the GloBE Revenue and GloBE Income or Loss of that Entity determined for periods prior to the disposition of that CE are still taken into account for purposes of determining the three-year averages under Article 5.5.3.

4.5.5.4 Article 5.5.4.

653. An election under Article 5.5 shall not apply to a Constituent Entity that is a Stateless Constituent Entity or an Investment Entity, and the revenue and GloBE Income or Loss of a Stateless Constituent Entity and of an Investment Entity shall be excluded from the computations in Article 5.5.3.

654. *Objective of the Article*: Article 5.5.4 provides that an election under Article 5.5 shall not apply to Stateless Constituent Entities. Equally, Article 5.5.4 further provides that an election under Article 5.5 shall not apply to a CE that is an Investment Entity. The policy intent underlying the *de minimis* exclusion is to avoid the complexities of determining the Adjusted Covered Taxes for the ETR and Top-up Tax calculations where the potential amount of Top-up Tax does not seem to justify the compliance and administrative burden. The election is not applicable to these CEs because their ETR is computed on an Entity basis, and they are typically not subject to tax. Thus, because the ETR determined for these Entities will usually be zero and the Net GloBE Income or Loss for the jurisdiction must be determined in any case to apply the exclusion, applying the exception to these Entities would not produce a significant reduction in compliance burdens, but would instead encourage MNE Groups to separate its tax-exempt income into multiple Stateless Constituent Entities and Investment Entities that qualify for the *de minimis* exclusion. Since Stateless Constituent Entities and Investment Entities are not eligible for the *de minimis* exclusion, their revenue and GloBE income are excluded from the *De Minimis* Exclusion computations in Article 5.5.3 for purposes of determining whether a jurisdiction is eligible for the *de minimis* exclusion so that such revenue or income will not cause a jurisdiction to fail the *de minimis* tests.

4.5.6 Article 5.6. (Minority-Owned Constituent Entities)

655. Prominent features of Article 5.6 are provided in Box 4.28.

Box 4.28 Prominent Features of Article 5.6

- If the income and taxes of Minority-Owned Constituent Entities were blended in the jurisdictional ETR computations, low-tax outcomes in one Entity could result in a Top-up Tax for the jurisdiction, some of which would be borne by non-Group Entity owners of a different CE. Hence, special rules are included in Article 5.6 for computing the ETR and Top-up Tax of Minority-Owned Constituent Entities.
- The special rules in Article 5.6 can also apply to PEs if the Main Entity and the PE meet the definition of a Minority-Owned Constituent Entity.
- Article 5.6.1 provides that the jurisdictional computations made with respect to members of the Minority-Owned Subgroup shall be done separately from the rest of the MNE Group. Also, clarifies that the Adjusted Covered Taxes and GloBE Income or Loss of members of a Minority-Owned Subgroup are excluded from the determination of the remainder of the MNE Group's ETR in Article 5.1.1 and Net GloBE Income in Article 5.1.2.
- Provides that an MNE Group could have two or more computations with respect to CEs located in a jurisdiction, one for members of the Minority-Owned Subgroup and the other for the rest of the MNE Group.
- Provides that operation of remaining GloBE Rules (i.e., barring jurisdictional ETR and Top-up Tax computation of members of Minority-Owned Sub-group) remain unimpacted.
- Article 5.6.2 provides that the ETR and Top-up Tax of a Minority-Owned Constituent Entity that is not a member of a Minority-Owned Subgroup are computed on an entity basis in accordance with Chapters 3 to 7 and Article 8.2. Also, clarifies that the Adjusted Covered Taxes and GloBE Income or

Loss of the Minority-Owned Constituent Entity are excluded from the determination of the remainder of the MNE Group's ETR in Article 5.1.1 and Net GloBE Income in Article 5.1.2.

- Article 5.6.2 has no effect on the eligibility of a jurisdiction for the *de minimis* exclusion provided in Article 5.5.
- Article 5.6.2 does not apply if the Minority-Owned Constituent Entity is an Investment Entity. Therefore, the special provisions applicable to Investment Entities in Articles 7.4 and 7.5 have priority and apply in these situations.

656. *Reasons for adopting special rules for computing ETR and Top-up Tax of Minority-Owned Constituent Entities*: Special rules are included in Article 5.6 for computing the ETR and Top-up Tax of Minority-Owned Constituent Entities. A Minority-Owned Constituent Entity is a CE of the MNE Group where the UPE holds directly or indirectly 30% or less of its Ownership Interests. The Entities are CEs because the UPE holds their Controlling Interests, despite the small ownership percentage. Special rules are needed for Minority–Owned Constituent Entities because a UPE may have several Minority-Owned Constituent Entities with operations in the same jurisdiction but with different groups of owners that are not Group Entities. If the income and taxes of these different CEs were blended in the jurisdictional ETR computations, low-tax outcomes in one Entity could result in a Top-up Tax for the jurisdiction, some of which would be borne by non-Group Entity owners of a different CE. While this can occur to some extent under the normal jurisdictional blending rules, the magnitude of the effect in the context of Minority-Owned Constituent Entities and the potential detrimental impact on these investment structures justifies a different rule.

657. *Special rules may apply to a PE in certain conditions*: The special rules in Article 5.6 can also apply to PEs if the Main Entity and the PE meet the definition of a Minority-Owned Constituent Entity.

4.5.6.1 Article 5.6.1.

658. The computation of the ETR and Top-up Tax for a jurisdiction in accordance with Chapters 3 to 7 and Article 8.2 with respect to members of a Minority-Owned Subgroup shall apply as if they were a separate MNE Group. The Adjusted Covered Taxes and GloBE Income or Loss of members of a Minority-Owned Subgroup are excluded from the determination of the remainder of the MNE Group's ETR in Article 5.1.1 and Net GloBE Income in Article 5.1.2.

659. The term Minority-Owned Subgroup mentioned *supra* is defined in Article 10.1 as below:

> Minority-Owned Subgroup means a Minority-Owned Parent Entity and its Minority-Owned Subsidiaries.

660. The term Minority-Owned Parent Entity mentioned *supra* is defined in Article 10.1 as below:

> Minority-Owned Parent Entity means a Minority-Owned Constituent Entity that holds, directly or indirectly, the Controlling Interests of another Minority-Owned Constituent Entity, except where the Controlling Interests of the first-mentioned Entity are held, directly or indirectly, by another Minority-Owned Constituent Entity.

661. The term Minority-Owned Subsidiary mentioned *supra* is defined in Article 10.1 as below:

> Minority-Owned Subsidiary means a Minority-Owned Constituent Entity whose Controlling Interests are held, directly or indirectly, by a Minority-Owned Parent Entity.

662. The term Controlling Interest mentioned *supra* is defined in Article 10.1 as below:

> Controlling Interest means an Ownership Interest in an entity such that the interest holder:
>
> (a) is required to consolidate the assets, liabilities, income, expenses and cash flows of the entity on a line-by-line basis in accordance with an Acceptable Financial Accounting Standard; or
> (b) would have been required to consolidate the assets, liabilities, income, expenses and cash flows of the entity on a line-by-line basis if the interest holder had prepared CFS.
>
> A Main Entity is deemed to have the Controlling Interests of its PEs.

663. The term Ownership Interest mentioned *supra* is defined in Article 10.1 as below:

> Ownership Interest means any equity interest that carries rights to the profits, capital or reserves of an Entity, including the profits, capital or reserves of a Main Entity's Permanent Establishment(s).

664. The term Constituent Entity-owner is defined in Article 10.1 as below:

> Constituent Entity-owner means a Constituent Entity that directly or indirectly owns an Ownership Interest in another Constituent Entity of the same MNE Group.

665. Not all Constituent Entities whose Controlling Interests are held by a Minority-Owned Parent Entity are considered Minority-Owned Subsidiaries and members of a Minority-Owned Subgroup. They must also meet the definition of a Minority-Owned Constituent Entity, as explained in **Illustration # 59**:

Illustration of definition of a Minority-Owned Constituent Entity in Article 10.1

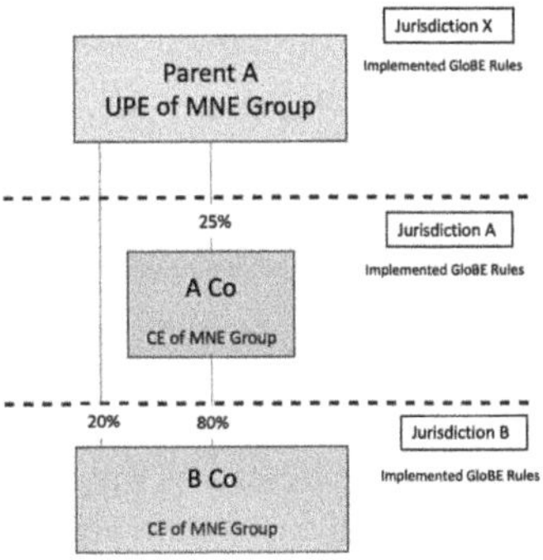

Assumptions Step 1

- Assume that UPE holds 40% of the Ownership Interests of B Co, but the Controlling Interests of B Co are held through A Co, a Constituent Entity that is the Minority-Owned Parent Entity of a Minority-Owned Subgroup

Definition of a Minority-Owned Constituent Entity in Article 10.1 Step 2

- In this case, B Co does not meet the requirements to be a Minority-Owned Constituent Entity because the UPE holds more than 30% of its Ownership Interests. The fact that its Controlling Interests are held through a Minority-Owned Parent Entity does not make it a Minority-Owned Subsidiary and member of the Minority-Owned Subgroup.

666. *Objective of the Article*: Article 5.6.1 is a special rule that only applies to Minority-owned Constituent Entities that are members of a Minority-Owned Subgroup. It states that the computation of the ETR and Top-up Tax for a jurisdiction in accordance with Chapters 3 to 7 and Article 8.2 shall apply as if they were a separate MNE Group. This means that jurisdictional computations made with respect to members of the Minority-Owned Subgroup shall be done separately from the rest of the MNE Group. The second sentence further clarifies that the Adjusted Covered Taxes and GloBE Income or Loss of members of a Minority-Owned Subgroup are excluded from the determination of the remainder of the MNE Group's ETR in Article 5.1.1 and Net GloBE Income in Article 5.1.2.

667. *MNE Group may have two or more ETR and Top-up Tax computations in a jurisdiction*: An MNE Group could have two or more computations with respect to CEs located in a jurisdiction, one for members of the Minority-Owned Subgroup and the other for the rest of the MNE Group. The result does not change regardless that a portion of the Ownership Interests is held directly by the UPE or other Parent Entities that are not part of the Minority-Owned Subgroup, as explained in **Illustration # 60**:

Illustration of Application of Article 5.6.1

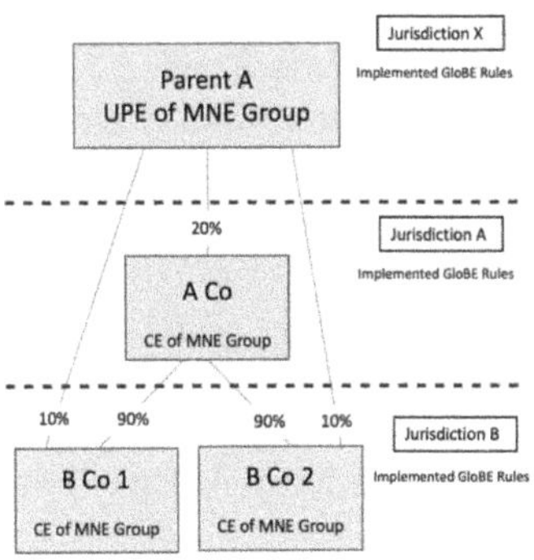

Assumptions Step 1

- The UPE holds 20% of the Ownership Interests of A Co, which owns 90% of B Co 1 and B Co 2 (located in jurisdiction B).
- The remainder 10% of the Ownership Interests of B Co 1 and B Co 2 are held directly by the UPE.
- All Entities are Constituent Entities of an MNE Group.
- A Co is a Minority-Owned Parent Entity, while B Co 1 and B Co 2 are its Minority-Owned Subsidiaries.

Application of Article 5.6.1 Step 2

- In this situation, B Co 1 and B Co 2 are Minority-Owned Constituent Entities of the MNE Group where the UPE holds directly or indirectly 30% or less of their Ownership Interests (which is 28% comprising 10% (direct) + 18% (indirect, as 90% x 20% = 18%).
- The ETR of jurisdiction B with respect to B Co 1 and B Co 2 is computed separately from the ETR computation of any other Constituent Entities of the MNE Group located in jurisdiction B.

668. *Operation of remaining GloBE Rules (i.e., barring jurisdictional ETR and Top-up Tax computation of members of Minority-Owned Subgroup) remain unimpacted:* Article 5.6.1 does not change the mechanics of the provisions of GloBE Rules other than the computation of the jurisdictional ETR and the consequential changes to the Top-up Tax computation of the members of the Minority-Owned Subgroup. For instance, if the Minority-Owned Parent Entity is a Flow-through Entity, its Financial Accounting Net Income or Loss is allocated to its Constituent Entity-owners in accordance with Article 3.5.1(b) (unless it has been allocated to a PE under Article 3.5.1(a)). Equally, Article 5.6.1 has no effect on the eligibility of a jurisdiction for the *de minimis* exclusion provided in Article 5.5. Furthermore, the charging provisions in Chapter 2 apply normally. For example, the Minority-Owned Parent Entity is not treated as the UPE of the Minority-Owned Subgroup. The UPE of the MNE Group is still required to apply the IIR with respect to the members of the Minority-Owned Subgroup. Similarly, the Minority-Owned Parent Entity and any other Parent Entity that is a POPE are still required to apply the IIR with respect to their Ownership Interests in the Minority-Owned Constituent Entities of the Minority-Owned Subgroup.

4.5.6.2 Article 5.6.2.

669. The ETR and Top-up Tax of a Minority-Owned Constituent Entity that is not a member of a Minority-Owned Subgroup are computed on an entity basis in accordance with Chapters 3 to 7 and Article 8.2. The Adjusted Covered Taxes and GloBE Income or Loss of the Minority-Owned Constituent Entity are excluded from the determination of the remainder of the MNE Group's ETR in Article 5.1.1 and Net GloBE Income in Article 5.1.2. This provision does not apply if the Minority-Owned Constituent Entity is an Investment Entity.

670. *Objective of the Article*: Article 5.6.2 is a rule that applies only to a Minority-Owned Constituent Entity that is not a member of a Minority-Owned Subgroup. This provision prevents the 70% or more of the Net Income or Loss and Adjusted Covered Taxes of the Entity, which do not effectively belong to the UPE, from being blended with the Net Income or Loss and Adjusted Covered Taxes of the other CEs of the MNE Group. However, Article 5.6.2 has no effect on the eligibility of a jurisdiction for the *de minimis* exclusion provided in Article 5.5 (*The election available in Article 5.5.1 does not require the MNE Group to compute the Average GloBE Revenue and Average GloBE Income or Loss of the members of a Minority-Owned Subgroup as if they were a separate MNE Group or of a Minority-Owned Constituent Entity on an entity basis. Therefore, the GloBE Revenue and the GloBE Income or Loss of those entities is taken into account for purposes of determining the Average GloBE Revenue and the Average GloBE Income or Loss of the jurisdiction where they are located*). The last sentence of this provision states that it does not apply if the Minority-Owned Constituent Entity is an Investment Entity. Therefore, the special provisions applicable to Investment Entities in Articles 7.4 and 7.5 have priority and apply in these situations.

4.6 CHAPTER 6 OF GLOBE RULES (CORPORATE RESTRUCTURINGS AND HOLDING STRUCTURES)[100]

671. Chapter 6 contains special rules dealing with corporate restructurings (including mergers, acquisitions, and demergers) as well as Articles that address the application of the GloBE Rules to certain holding structures such as JV investments and Multi-Parented MNE Groups.

Background: Purchase Accounting and Business Acquisitions

672. *Financial accounting of gain or loss on disposition of assets or liabilities*: Financial accounting standards used in preparing CFS do not usually provide for non-recognition of gain or loss on the disposition of assets or liabilities, either individually or as part of the disposition of an entire business. This is true regardless of whether the assets and liabilities are disposed of directly or whether the disposition is carried out through a sale of Ownership Interests in a CE. In addition, the Ownership Interests of a CE are not recognised as an asset in the CFS; instead, the assets and liabilities of the CE are consolidated with those of the MNE Group. Thus, when they are disposed of (even via a sale of the Ownership Interests), the gains and losses on the underlying assets and liabilities are generally included in the MNE Group's Financial Accounting Net Income or Loss in the CFS. Financial accounting depends on:

- whether a stand-alone business is acquired (also referred to as a business combination). Financial accounting standards generally require the acquirer to record acquired assets and liabilities at their acquisition date fair value, irrespective of the acquisition price. If the acquisition price exceeds the fair value of the acquired assets, financial accounting rules generally treat the excess as a goodwill asset. And if the acquisition price is less than the fair value of the acquired assets, financial accounting rules generally treat the shortfall as a bargain purchase and require a corresponding income inclusion. In many cases, particularly for Entity acquisitions, the fair value adjustments to the carrying value of assets and liabilities are reflected in the consolidated financial accounts rather than the separate financial accounts of the acquired CE or the CE that acquired the assets and liabilities.
- acquisition of assets or liabilities which is not considered to be a stand-alone business. The acquired assets are typically accounted for at cost (i.e., the acquisition price).

673. *For GloBE purposes, the Financial Accounting Net Income or Loss is determined using the separate entity position of the CE used in preparing the CFS:* Given the GloBE Rules primarily focus on the position of individual Entities rather than the full consolidated position of the MNE Group, it is important to distinguish between the accounting for an acquisition of a business through a share acquisition (i.e., acquiring

100. Based on OECD's GloBE Model Rules, its Commentary and Illustrative Examples.

the Ownership Interest in the Entity) and an asset acquisition (i.e., acquiring the underlying assets and liabilities of the business). From a consolidation perspective, the accounting is the same; however, the individual Entity position is often different. In a share acquisition, the individual Entity position is often unaffected as all that has changed from the Entity's perspective is the shareholder, whereas, in an asset acquisition, new assets and liabilities will be brought onto the balance sheet. As a result, the purchase accounting adjustments to fair value are usually reflected in the individual Entity position for an asset acquisition, whereas for a share acquisition, they are usually only reflected as a consolidation adjustment to get to the full consolidated position.

674. *Difference in the financial accounting and tax carrying value of assets and liabilities*: Generally, when there is a difference in the financial accounting and tax carrying value (basis or amount) of assets and liabilities, financial accounting rules require the MNE Group to establish deferred tax liabilities or deferred tax assets because the difference will manifest itself as a temporary difference in the computation of taxable and accounting income. In a business combination, financial accounting rules generally require creation of deferred tax liabilities and assets to the extent that the acquiring Entity will be subject to tax on the differences in carrying value. Unlike most deferred tax assets and liabilities, the ones created in connection with a business combination do not affect the income tax expense computation when they arise because the net effect of recognition of such deferred tax assets and liabilities is recorded in accounting goodwill and not as income tax expense. Consequently, recognition of deferred tax assets and liabilities will not give rise to Adjusted Covered Taxes for GloBE purposes at the time of the business combination. They only affect the income tax expense computation when they reverse, as explained in **Illustration # 61**:

Illustration explaining consequences of difference in the financial accounting and tax carrying value of assets and liabilities

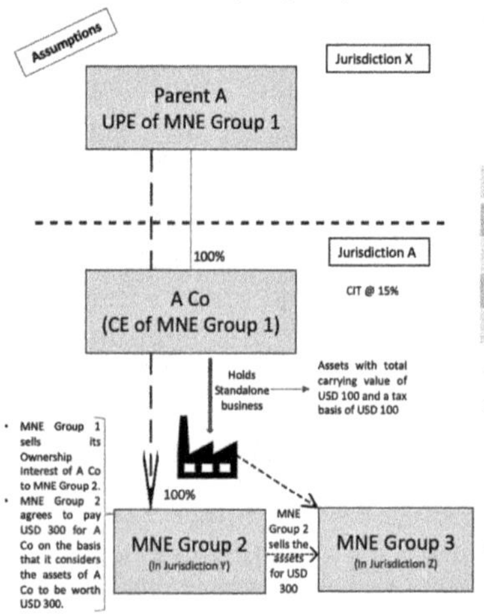

- MNE Group 1 decides to sell its Ownership Interest of A Co to MNE Group 2.
- MNE Group 2 agrees to pay USD 300 for A Co on the basis that it considers the assets of A Co to be worth USD 300.
- In this scenario, the tax basis of the underlying assets is unaffected by the acquisition. As a result, there is now a difference between the financial accounting carrying value in the consolidated financial statements (USD 300) and the tax carrying value (USD 100) of A Co's assets, and deferred tax liabilities should be recognised in relation to these temporary differences (USD 30 = (USD 300 – USD 100) * 15%)).

	Amount (USD)
Fair value of net assets acquired	300
Deferred tax liabilities recognised on acquisition (30 = (300 – 100) * 15%)	(30)
Goodwill (balancing amount to arrive at total purchase consideration of 300)	30
Total Carrying value (equal to purchase consideration)	300

- There would be no deferred tax expense arising from the recognition of the deferred tax liabilities, instead a goodwill asset is recognised.
- Thereafter, when MNE Group 2 sells the assets for USD 300, it has no financial accounting gain or loss because the carrying value of the assets is USD 300 (assuming no changes to fair value since the original acquisition). There will be a gain for tax purposes because the assets are sold for USD 300 but the tax base is USD 100, which represents the tax deduction available on sale of the assets. This gives rise to a taxable gain of USD 200 and a tax charge of USD 30 (= USD 200 * 15%), however this is offset by a reversal of the deferred tax liability of USD 30 recognised on the original acquisition. As a result the nil accounting impact from this disposal is mirrored by the nil total tax (current tax plus deferred tax) impact.
- It may be noted that the deferred tax liability of USD 30 recognised on the acquisition would only be recognised in the consolidated financial statements of MNE Group 2 and not in the individual entity position.

675. *Purchase accounting adjustments not to be taken into account*: Financial accounting adjustments to the carrying value of assets and liabilities arising in connection with purchase accounting for a business combination generally are not taken into account in the computation of GloBE Income or Loss, as discussed in Article 3.1.2. For example, purchase accounting adjustments and the corresponding deferred tax assets and liabilities are not taken into account in respect of a transaction governed by Article 6.2.1. After such transactions, the historical carrying values of the acquired assets and liabilities (i.e., the values excluding any purchase accounting adjustments made on acquisition) must be used to compute the GloBE Income or Loss, which will generally be consistent with the computation of taxable income under the local tax rules. Therefore, any deferred tax assets and liabilities associated with purchase accounting adjustments in the financial accounts must also be excluded from the computation of Adjusted Covered Taxes under Article 4.1 to prevent distortions in the ETR computations. The same is true for purchase accounting adjustments and associated deferred tax assets and liabilities in the financial accounts arising in connection with a GloBE Reorganisation that is subject to the rules of Article 6.3.2.

676. *Purchase accounting adjustments to be taken into account*: In some cases, it is appropriate to reflect purchase accounting adjustments in the GloBE income or loss. Purchase accounting adjustments arising in connection with transactions governed by Article 6.2.2, Article 6.3.1 and Article 6.3.4 should be taken into account even if those adjustments are reflected in the financial accounts at the consolidated level rather than the CE level. Purchase accounting adjustments arising in connection with transactions governed by Article 6.3.3 should be taken into account to the extent they relate to Non-Qualifying Gain or Loss. In most cases, those transactions will be fully taxable at the local level, and there may be deferred tax assets and liabilities recognised as the fair value of each of the assets and liabilities recognised in the financial accounts may not be the same as tax basis[101] of assets and liabilities recognised for tax purposes. Similarly, not all of the assets recognised for accounting purposes may be recognised for tax purposes, and the value of some accounting assets might be merged or allocated to the basis of another asset for tax purposes. In the case of tax-deductible goodwill, there may be deferred tax assets recognised at the time of initial recognition of accounting goodwill, representing fair value of accounting goodwill and future tax deductions of goodwill over a future period or upon disposal of goodwill. Future accounting amortisation and impairment on such assets recognised at acquisition date may also impact the deferred tax expense. Such deferred tax assets and liabilities that

101. A tax basis is the value of an asset that is used when determining the gain or loss when the asset is sold. Generally, it equals the asset purchase price minus any accumulated depreciation. On the other hand, carrying value is a measure of value for a company's assets. Carrying value is typically measured as the original cost of the asset, minus any depreciating factors. The depreciating factors for an asset vary based on the nature of the asset. The carrying amount is the value of an asset as treated with accounting standards. The tax base is the value of an asset as treated by tax standards. The tax base of an asset is the amount that will be deductible for tax purposes against any taxable economic benefits that will flow to an entity when it recovers the carrying amount of the asset. If those economic benefits will not be taxable, the tax base of the asset is equal to its carrying amount.

arise in connection with the transaction should be taken into account in the computation of Adjusted Covered Taxes under Article 4.1 to the extent gain or loss on those transactions is included in the computation of GloBE Income or Loss.

4.6.1 Article 6.1. (Application of Consolidated Revenue Threshold to Group Mergers and Demergers)

677. Article 6.1 explains how the consolidated revenue threshold is applied after a merger and a demerger. In the case of a merger, this article sets out special rules for measuring the consolidated revenue of the Entities or Groups involved in the merger for purposes of the four-year revenue threshold test in Article 1.1.1. In the case of a demerger, the article includes an additional rule that supplements the revenue threshold test in Article 1.1.1. The article also defines mergers and demergers for these purposes.

678. Prominent features of Article 6.1 are provided in Box 4.29.

Box 4.29 Prominent Features of Article 6.1

- Explains how the consolidated revenue threshold of EUR 750 million or more in at least two of the four Fiscal Years is applied after a merger and a demerger.
- Paragraph (a) of Article 6.1.1 provides that where two or more Groups merge to form a single Group, it is deemed that the revenue threshold is met in a given preceding year if the sum of the revenue included in each Group's CFS for that year is equal to or greater than EUR 750 million.
- This determination has to be made for each of the Fiscal Years that are tested under the consolidated revenue test in Article 1.1.
- Neither Group's pre-merger revenues are adjusted for transactions that occurred between the Groups in the preceding years, notwithstanding that the transactions between Entities will be eliminated in consolidation after the merger.
- Paragraph (b) of Article 6.1.1 applies where:
  - two single Entities that are not part of a Group are brought together to form a Group and, prior to this merger, only individual (i.e., not consolidated) financial statements were prepared by these entities, or
  - a single Entity that does not prepare CFS becomes part of a Group, or
  - as part of the same arrangement, two or more Groups merge with one Entity; one Group merges with two or more Entities; and two or more Groups merge with two or more Entities.

Paragraph (b) of Article 6.1.1 modifies the application of the consolidated revenue threshold in these cases by aggregating the combined revenue of the Entity(ies) and Group(s) of a given year for purposes of the four-year revenue test.

- The deeming rule in paragraph (b) is applied to each of the four Fiscal Years prior to the tested Fiscal Year in order to determine whether the newly formed Group falls within the scope of the GloBE Rules. This means that if the combined revenue in two out of the four Fiscal Years prior to the tested Fiscal Year equals or exceeds EUR 750 million, then the consolidated revenue threshold in Article 1.1 is met, and the MNE Group is subject to the GloBE Rules in the tested Fiscal Year. In practice, this rule is irrelevant where the acquiring MNE Group meets the revenue threshold under Article 1.1 in the Fiscal Year in which the merger takes place.
- Paragraph (c) of Article 6.1.1 deals with an MNE Group that was in the scope of the GloBE Rules but then is split into separate Groups raising the issue of how to apply the consolidated revenue threshold to these separate Groups following the demerger.
- Paragraph (c) of Article 6.1.1 is divided into two subparagraphs. Subparagraph (i) covers the first tested Fiscal Year after the demerger, while subparagraph (ii) covers the second to the fourth tested Fiscal Year after the demerger.
- The rules apply separately to each of the Groups that were formed from or remained following the demerger.
- Article 6.1.2 sets out the definition of a merger that is used in applying the rules in Article 6.1.1. The definition of 'merger' applies only for the purposes of Article 6.1.1 and is broader than the commonly understood meaning of merger.
- Article 6.1.3 defines the term 'demerger' for purposes of Article 6.1.1(c). As a general rule, the disposal of a single CE is not a demerger because, after the disposal, it would become a stand-alone Entity and not a Group. However, where the disposed of CE has a PE in another jurisdiction, then the stand-alone Entity and its PE are considered a Group in accordance with Article 1.2.3, and therefore, a new Group would exist for the purposes of Article 6.1.3.

4.6.1.1 Article 6.1.1.

679. For the purposes of Article 1.1

(a) If two or more Groups merge to form a single Group in any of the four Fiscal Years prior to the tested Fiscal Year, then the consolidated revenue threshold of the MNE Group for any Fiscal Year prior to the merger is deemed to be met for that year if the sum of the revenue included in each of their CFS for that year is equal to or greater than EUR 750 million.

(b) Where an Entity that is not a member of any Group (target) merges with an Entity or Group (acquirer) in the tested Fiscal Year and the target or acquirer does not have CFS in any of the four Fiscal Years prior to the tested Fiscal Year because it was not a member of any Group in that year, the consolidated revenue threshold of the MNE Group is deemed to be met for that year if the sum of the revenue included in each of their Financial Statements or CFS for that year is equal to or greater than EUR 750 million.

(c) Where a single MNE Group within the scope of the GloBE Rules demerges into two or more Groups (each a demerged Group), the consolidated revenue threshold is deemed to be met by a demerged Group:
   (i) with respect to the first tested Fiscal Year ending after the demerger, if the demerged Group has annual revenues of EUR 750 million or more in that year;
   (ii) with respect to the second to fourth tested Fiscal Years ending after the demerger, if the demerged Group has annual revenues of EUR 750 million or more in at least two of the Fiscal Years following the year of the demerger.

680. *Objective of the Article*: As set out in Article 1.1, the GloBE Rules apply to MNE Groups with consolidated revenue of EUR 750 million or more in at least two of the four Fiscal Years immediately preceding the tested Fiscal Year. Article 6.1 complements this four-year revenue test in three scenarios, as mentioned *supra*. These three scenarios, contained in paragraphs (a), (b) and (c) of Article 6.1.1, are encapsulated in Figures 4.29, 4.30 and 4.31, respectively, with illustrations, as below.

Figure 4.29 Provisions of Paragraph (a) of Article 6.1.1 with Illustrations

Provisions of Paragraph (a) of Article 6.1.1

For the purposes of Article 1.1:

(a)

Where two or more Groups merge to form a single Group:

- In the first scenario, the recently merged MNE Group does not have a single consolidated revenue because each of the Groups had their own separate CFS.
- Deems the revenue threshold to be met in a given preceding year if the sum of the revenue included in each Group's CFS for that year is equal to or greater than EUR 750 million.
- Neither Group's pre-merger revenues are adjusted for transactions that occurred between the Groups in the preceding years, notwithstanding that transactions between Entities will be eliminated in consolidation after the merger.
- This determination has to be made for each of the Fiscal Years that are tested under the consolidated revenue test in Article 1.1.

Illustration

Assumptions

- Assume that A Group and B Group reported separately consolidated revenue of EUR 400 million, EUR 300 million, EUR 300 million and EUR 400 million each for years 1 to 4 respectively.
- The A Group and B Group merge in year 5 into the AB MNE Group.

Amounts in EUR Million

Entity	Year 1	Year 2	Year 3	Year 4	Year 5
A Group	400	300	300	400	The A Group and B Group merge in year 5 into the AB MNE Group.
B Group	400	300	300	400	
Total	800	600	600	800	

Application of Paragraph (a) of Article 6.1.1

- Under these facts, the AB MNE Group is subject to the GloBE Rules in year 5 because in two of the four preceding Fiscal Years the sum of their consolidated revenue included in each of their CFS was EUR 750 million or more (i.e. in year 1, the combined revenue was of EUR 800 million and in year 4, the combined revenue was of EUR 800 million).

Figure 4.30 Provisions of Paragraph (b) of Article 6.1.1 with Illustrations

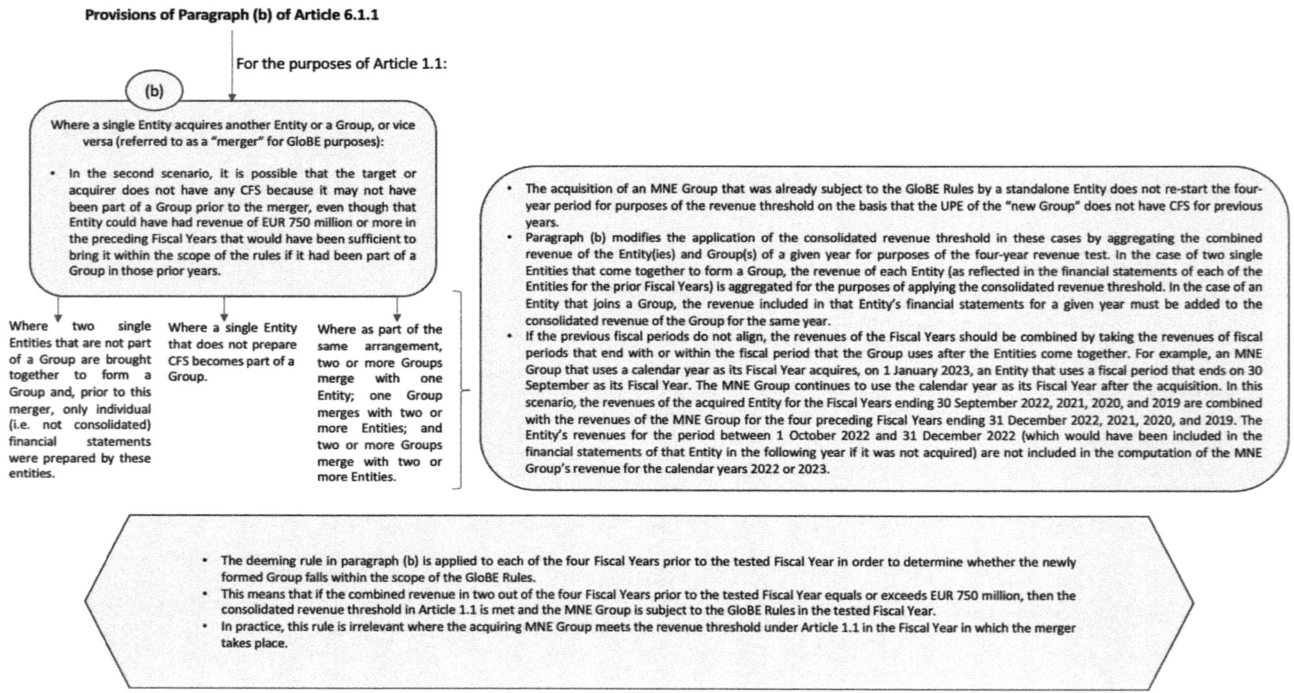

Illustration
Paragraph (b) of Article 6.1.1

Assumptions

- Assume from Fiscal Years 1 to 4, A Co and B Co (located in different jurisdictions) were single Entities and that A Co reported revenue of EUR 600 million and B Co reported revenue of EUR 400 million in each of those years.
- In Fiscal Year 5, A Co acquires B Co, creating a Group and an MNE Group which reports a consolidated revenue of EUR 1 billion in its Consolidated Financial Statements of Fiscal Year 5.

Amounts in EUR Million

Entity	Year 1	Year 2	Year 3	Year 4	Year 5
A Co	600	600	600	600	A Co acquires B Co, creating a Group and an MNE Group which reports a consolidated revenue of EUR 1 billion in its CFS of Fiscal Year 5.
B Co	400	400	400	400	
Total	1000	1000	1000	1000	

Application of Paragraph (b) of Article 6.1.1

- In this case, the recently formed AB Group is required to apply the GloBE Rules in Year 5 (i.e. the tested Fiscal Year) because their combined revenue met the EUR 750 million threshold in at least two of the prior 4 Fiscal Years.

Assumptions

- Assume A Group reported consolidated revenue of EUR 500 million in each of Fiscal Years 1 to 4.
- In Fiscal Year 5, A Group acquired an Entity B Co with reported revenue of EUR 800 million in each of Fiscal Years 1 to 4.

Amounts in EUR Million

Entity	Year 1	Year 2	Year 3	Year 4	Year 5
A Group	500	500	500	500	In Fiscal Year 5, A Group acquired an Entity B Co.
B Co	800	800	800	800	
Total	1300	1300	1300	1300	

Application of Paragraph (b) of Article 6.1.1

- In this case, the consolidated revenue threshold is met for Fiscal Year 5 (i.e. the tested Fiscal Year) because the A Group is deemed to have met the EUR 750 million consolidated revenues test by virtue of the acquired Entity's revenue of EUR 800 million in at least two of the preceding four years.

Figure 4.31 Provisions of Paragraph (c) of Article 6.1.1 with Illustrations

Provisions of Paragraph (c) of Article 6.1.1

(c) For the purposes of Article 1.1:

Where an MNE Group within the scope of the GloBE Rules demerges into two or more Groups:

- The third scenario deals with an MNE Group that was in the scope of the GloBE Rules but then is split into separate Groups raising the issue of how to apply the consolidated revenue threshold to these separate Groups following the demerger.
- This paragraph applies where the MNE Group is within the scope of the GloBE Rules in the Fiscal Year that the demerger takes place.
- Paragraph (c) applies irrespective of the form of the demerger provided that it falls within the definition of a demerger in Article 6.1.3.
- Paragraph (c) is applied separately to each of the demerged Groups.
- Paragraph (c) is a standalone revenue threshold test that applies in addition to the test in Article 1.1.1.
- The rules in paragraph (c) are intended to ensure that each Group resulting from the demerger of the in-scope MNE Group, that meet the revenue threshold in the Fiscal Year ending after the demerger, remain subject to the GloBE Rules even if the demerged Group does not meet the requirements of Article 1.1 in that year.
- Paragraph (c) is divided into two subparagraphs. Subparagraph (i) covers the first tested Fiscal Year after the demerger, while subparagraph (ii) covers from the second to the fourth tested Fiscal Years after the demerger.

Para (c) is divided into two subparas:

(i)

- Subparagraph (i) covers the first tested Fiscal Year after the demerger.
- Under subparagraph (i), the consolidated revenue threshold set out in Article 1.1 is deemed to be met by a demerged Group if the demerged Group has annual revenues of EUR 750 million or more in the first tested fiscal year after the demerger.
- This means that instead of applying a test that considers previous fiscal years, this rule is triggered for each demerged Group that has annual revenues of EUR 750 million or more in the Fiscal Year that is being tested.
- Note that this paragraph only applies to demerged Groups. The sale of a controlling interest in a single Entity will therefore not fall within the scope of paragraph (c).
- Sub-paragraph (i) applies to a Group in the Fiscal Year "ending after the demerger".
- For example, Assume Group A has a Fiscal Year that is the same as the calendar year. The UPE of Group A distributed all of the shares of subgroup B to its shareholders in 30 June of Year 1. This distribution will be considered a demerger under Article 6.1.3 and result in the creation of Group B. The Fiscal Year of Group A ends on the 31 of December of Year 1. In this case, paragraph (i) tests Group A's consolidated revenue for Year 1 because it is the first tested Fiscal Year that ends after the demerger. Paragraph (i) also tests Group B's consolidated revenue for its first tested Fiscal Year that ends after the demerger. Thus, if Group B adopts or retains the calendar year as its Fiscal Year, paragraph (i) will apply to its Fiscal Year ending 31 December of Year 1 because that is Group B's first tested year that ends after the demerger. However, because Group B's first tested Fiscal Year is composed of a period other than 12 months, then the EUR 750 million threshold has to be adjusted proportionally consistent with Article 1.1.2.

(ii)

- Subparagraph (ii) covers from the second to the fourth tested Fiscal Years after the demerger.
- Subparagraph (ii) states that the consolidated revenue threshold set out in Article 1.1 is deemed to be met by a demerged Group if it has annual revenues of EUR 750 million or more in at least two Fiscal Years following the demerger.
- As for paragraph (i), this rule also takes into account the annual revenue of the Fiscal Year that is being tested.
- For example, a demerged Group meets the test in the second Fiscal Year (i.e. the tested Fiscal Year), if it has consolidated revenues of EUR 750 million or more in Fiscal Years 1 and 2 following the demerger.

4.6.1.2 Article 6.1.2.

681. For the purposes of Article 6.1.1, a merger is any arrangement where:

(a) all or substantially all of the Group Entities of two or more separate Groups are brought under common control such that they constitute Group Entities of a combined Group; or
(b) an Entity that is not a member of any Group is brought under common control with another Entity or Group such that they constitute Group Entities of a combined Group.

682. *Objective of the Article*: Article 6.1.2 sets out the definition of merger that is used in applying the rules in Article 6.1.1. The definition of 'merger' applies only for the purposes of Article 6.1.1 and is broader than the commonly understood meaning of merger. The term applies to any merger or acquisition transaction that results in all or substantially all of the Entities of the two or more Groups being brought under common control. Article 6.1.2 is divided into two paragraphs with two different definitions. The rule in Article 6.1.1 (a) or (b) will apply if either one of the definitions in Article 6.1.2 applies. Paragraphs (a) and (b) of Article 6.1.2 are explained in Figure 4.32.

Figure 4.32 Provisions of Paragraphs (a) and (b) of Article 6.1.2

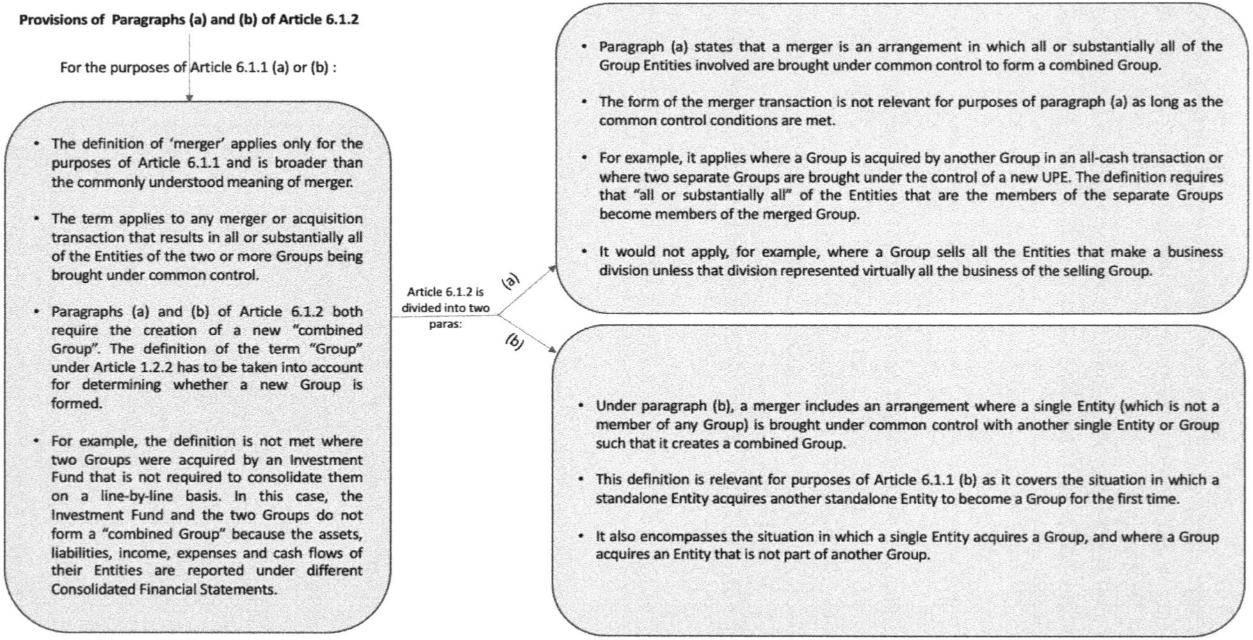

4.6.1.3 Article 6.1.3.

683. For the purposes of Article 6.1.1, a demerger is any arrangement where the Group Entities of a single Group are separated into two or more Groups that are no longer consolidated by the same UPE.

684. *Objective of the Article*: Article 6.1.3 defines the term 'demerger' for purposes of Article 6.1.1(c). After a demerger, the disposed of Group Entities are no longer consolidated on a line-by-line basis by the same UPE but continue to be consolidated on a line-by-line basis by two or more UPEs of different MNE Groups from the date of the demerger.

685. *Criteria of demerger*: The definition relies on the consolidation test, and the definition of a Group included in Articles 1.2.2 and 1.2.3. Therefore, whether a Group is separated into two or more Groups depends on whether each separated collection of Entities meets the definition of a Group and has its own CFS as defined by Article 10.1. As a general rule, the disposal of a single CE is not a demerger because, after the disposal, it would become a stand-alone Entity and not a Group. However, where the disposed of CE has a PE in another jurisdiction, then the stand-alone Entity and its PE are considered a Group in accordance with Article 1.2.3, and therefore, a new Group would exist for the purposes of Article 6.1.3. This definition does not cover the situations in which an MNE Group disposes of one or more CEs, and the acquirer is another Group. In these cases, the disposed of Entities are joining an existing Group, not creating a new one. A sale of one or more CEs to another MNE Group may, however, fall within the definition of a merger in Article 6.1.2(a) or (b) with respect to the acquiring MNE Group, where, for example, the sale of those Entities represented virtually all the business of the selling Group.

4.6.2 Article 6.2. (Constituent Entities Joining and Leaving an MNE Group)

686. Prominent features of Article 6.2 are provided in Box 4.30.

Box 4.30 Prominent Features of Article 6.2

- Provides that when an acquisition or disposition of a Controlling Interest in a CE (referred to in Article 6.2 as the target) takes place during the Fiscal Year, Article 6.2 modifies or clarifies the operation of the GloBE Rules in order to ensure the appropriate outcomes for both the buyer and seller. The rules are intended to produce a smooth separation of the target from the seller Group and a smooth integration of the target into the acquiring MNE Group.
- Article 6.2.1 includes provisions that apply in the Fiscal Year the Entity leaves or joins the Group (i.e., the acquisition year) as well as rules that

apply for the purposes of determining the ongoing tax attributes of an Entity that joins the Group in the years following the acquisition year.

- Paragraph (a) of Article 6.2.1 confirms that the target will be treated as a CE of both the acquiring and disposing of MNE Group, notwithstanding that its financial performance for the entire Fiscal Year is not consolidated on a line-by-line basis.
- Paragraph (b) of Article 6.2.1 states that in the acquisition year, the amount of Financial Accounting Net Income or Loss and the amount of Adjusted Covered Taxes taken into account for calculating a GloBE tax liability for each MNE Group shall be the amount that is taken into account in the CFS of each MNE Group.
- Paragraph (c) of Article 6.2.1 provides that an MNE Group that acquires a Controlling Interest in a CE will ignore the effect of any purchase accounting consolidation adjustments attributable to the acquisition and treat the acquired target, for GloBE purposes, as having the same carrying value in its assets that it has prior to the transfer (i.e., the historical carrying value).
  - In other words, the acquisition of a Controlling Interest in a target does not result in any change to the carrying value of the target's assets and liabilities for the purposes of determining GloBE Income or Loss.
  - Any adjustment to the carrying value of intangible assets that results from the acquisition, such as goodwill, customer lists, or workforce-in-place, are ignored in the computation of GloBE Income or Loss.
- Paragraph (d) of Article 6.2.1 states that the amount of Eligible Payroll Costs referred to in Article 5.3.3 shall be adjusted by taking into account only the costs that are reflected in the CFS prepared by the UPE of the MNE Group. Thus, each MNE Group takes into account the Eligible Payroll Costs arising during its period of ownership and for which it bears economic responsibility.
- Paragraph (e) of Article 6.2.1 provides that the amount of the Eligible Tangible Assets referred to in Article 5.3.4 shall be adjusted proportionally to correspond to the length of the period during the Fiscal Year that the target was a CE of the MNE Group. The carrying value of the Eligible Tangible Assets is determined based on the amount recorded for the purpose of preparing the CFS, including any purchase accounting consolidation adjustments attributable to the acquisition.
  - The difference in treatment between paragraphs (d) and (e) can be explained on the grounds that the tangible asset carve-out is based on the economic cost of the investment made by the MNE Group in the tangible asset located in the relevant jurisdiction, which is more accurately determined by looking to the fair value of that asset at the time of acquisition than the historical cost of that asset as recorded by the target.
- Paragraph (f) of Article 6.2.1 generally provides that deferred tax assets and liabilities of a CE that are transferred between MNE Groups are taken into account by the acquiring MNE Group in the same manner and to the same

extent as they would have been taken into account if the acquiring MNE Group had controlled the CE when they arose.
  - Article 6.2.1(f) does not apply to a GloBE Loss Deferred Tax Asset.
- Paragraph (g) of Article 6.2.1 is intended to relieve the disposing MNE Group of the need to recapture deferred tax liabilities that do not reverse (through payment or otherwise) within the five-year period required by Article 4.4.4.
  - This is achieved by treating any deferred tax liability of a CE that leaves an MNE Group as reversed when the Entity leaves the MNE Group.
  - The paragraph also starts or restarts the five-year period in Article 4.4.4 with respect to deferred tax liabilities of a CE when it joins an MNE Group. By restarting the five-year period in Article 4.4.4, paragraph (g) reduces compliance and administrative burdens that would arise if the deferred tax liabilities were subject to recapture based on their accrual dates in the disposing MNE Group.
  - Paragraph (g) does not apply to Recapture Exception Accruals described in Article 4.4.5 because they are not subject to the requirements of Article 4.4.4 before or after the acquisition date.
- Paragraph (h) of Article 6.2.1 deals with the situation in which the target is required to apply the IIR as a Parent Entity of one or both MNE Groups.
  - Paragraph (h) provides that the target shall apply the IIR separately to its Allocable Shares of the Top-up Tax of LTCEs determined for each MNE Group.
  - Thus, this rule applies where the target has an Ownership Interest in an LTCE and is a Parent Entity required to apply the IIR under the top-down approach or split-ownership rules applicable to one or both MNE Groups.
- Under Article 6.2.2, if a transfer of a Controlling Interest in a CE is treated as a transfer of assets and liabilities rather than a transfer of Ownership Interests by the jurisdiction where the target is located, then it will be treated as a transfer of assets and liabilities for GloBE purposes as well. In that case, the rules in Article 6.3 apply.
  - As a result, the gain or loss on the transfer that is treated as a sale of assets and liabilities of the target are included in the disposing MNE Group's ETR computation for the jurisdiction that imposed that treatment for local tax purposes, rather than the jurisdiction of the seller of the Ownership Interests.

687. Article 6.2 deals with cases where an Entity joins or leaves the MNE Group. In these cases, special rules are needed to apply the GloBE Rules in respect of the CE that enters or leaves an MNE Group during the Fiscal Year. The rules impact the calculations for the GloBE Income or Loss, Adjusted Covered Taxes, and Substance-based Income Exclusion and the way the IIR is applied under these circumstances.

Background of the Article

688. The GloBE Rules and Commentary are generally drafted on a steady-state basis that assume the MNE Group is comprised of the same CEs throughout the entire Fiscal Year. When an acquisition or disposition of a Controlling Interest in a CE (referred to in Article 6.2 as the target) takes place during the Fiscal Year, Article 6.2 modifies or clarifies the operation of the GloBE Rules in order to ensure the appropriate outcomes for both the buyer and seller. The rules are intended to produce a smooth separation of the target from the seller Group and a smooth integration of the target into the acquiring MNE Group. Article 6.2 also provides a special ordering rule for applying the IIR where the target is a Parent Entity that is required to apply the IIR as a member of one or both MNE Groups. Special rules are required to determine whether a target should apply the IIR for all or part of the year because the application of the IIR by the target depends on whether a Controlling Interest in the target is held by a Group Entity that is subject to a Qualified IIR. Specific ordering rules are not required for the application of the UTPR in these cases because the impact of a CE leaving or joining an MNE Group is automatically taken into account as part of the allocation methodology of the UTPR.[102]

4.6.2.1 Article 6.2.1.

689. Article 6.2.1 includes provisions that apply in the Fiscal Year the Entity leaves or joins the Group (i.e., the acquisition year) as well as rules that apply for the purposes of determining the ongoing tax attributes of an Entity that joins the Group in the years following the acquisition year. In relation to a target, it addresses the question of when the target is treated as joining or leaving a Group and apportions its income and expenses, including its Covered Taxes, between the Groups for the purposes of the GloBE Rules.

690. Except to the extent provided in Article 6.2.2, the following provisions apply where an Entity (the target) becomes or ceases to be a Constituent Entity of an MNE Group as a result of a transfer of direct or indirect Ownership Interests in such Entity during the Fiscal Year (the acquisition year):

(a) where the target joins or leaves a Group, or the target becomes the UPE of a new Group, the target will be treated as a member of the Group for the purposes of the GloBE Rules if any portion of its assets, liabilities, income, expenses or cash flows are included on a line-by-line basis in the CFS of the UPE in the acquisition year;
(b) in the acquisition year, an MNE Group shall take into account only the Financial Accounting Net Income or Loss and Adjusted Covered Taxes of the target that are taken into account in the CFS of the UPE for purposes of applying the GloBE Rules;

102. The allocation of top-up tax under the UTPR is governed by Article 2.6.

(c) in the acquisition year and each succeeding year, the target shall determine its GloBE Income or Loss and Adjusted Covered Taxes using historical carrying value of the assets and liabilities;
(d) the computation of the target's Eligible Payroll Costs under Article 5.3.3 shall take into account only those costs reflected in the CFS of the UPE;
(e) the computation of the carrying value of the target's Eligible Tangible Assets for purposes of Article 5.3.4 shall be adjusted proportionally to correspond with the length of the relevant Fiscal Year that the target was a member of the MNE Group;
(f) with the exception of the GloBE Loss Deferred Tax Asset, the deferred tax assets and deferred tax liabilities of a Constituent Entity that are transferred between MNE Groups shall be taken into account under the GloBE Rules by the acquiring MNE Group in the same manner and to the same extent as if the acquiring MNE Group controlled the Constituent Entity when such assets and liabilities arose;
(g) deferred tax liabilities of a target that have previously been included in its Total Deferred Tax Adjustment Amount shall be treated as reversed for purposes of applying Article 4.4.4 by the disposing MNE Group and treated as arising in the acquisition year for purposes of applying Article 4.4.4 by the acquiring MNE Group, except that in such cases any subsequent reduction to Covered Taxes under Article 4.4.4 shall have effect in the year in which the amount is recaptured; and
(h) if the target is a Parent Entity and it is a Group Entity of two or more MNE Groups during the acquisition year, it shall apply the provisions of the IIR separately to its Allocable Shares of the Top-up Tax of LTCE determined for each MNE Group.

691. The rules of Article 6.2.1 apply to all CEs that leave or join an MNE Group as a result of a direct or indirect disposition or acquisition of a Controlling Interest in that Entity. Accordingly, the term 'target', as used in the Commentary to this article, refers to all such Entities. The provisions of paragraphs (a) to (h) are explained in Figure 4.33

Figure 4.33 Provisions of Paragraphs (a) to (h) of Article 6.2.1

Paragraphs (a) to (h) of Article 6.2.1

Para (a)

- Paragraph (a) confirms that the target will be treated as a CE of both the acquiring and disposing MNE Group notwithstanding that its financial performance for the entire Fiscal Year is not consolidated on a line-by-line basis.
- Paragraph (a) follows the accounting treatment such that if any portion of the target's assets, liabilities, income, expenses and cash flows are included in the UPE's CFS in the acquisition year, then it will be treated as a member of the MNE Group for that year.
- In practice, if an MNE Group disposes a Controlling Interest in a CE during a Fiscal Year, it is likely that a portion of its income and expenses would be included in the CFS of the disposing MNE Group based on the period in which the CE was a member of the Group.
- Similarly, it is likely that all of the CE's assets and liabilities would be included in the CFS of the acquiring MNE Group and a portion of its income, expenses, and cash flows would be included based on the period in which the CE was a member of the Group.
- The remaining paragraphs of Article 6.2 set out specific rules designed to ensure an equitable apportioning of tax outcomes and tax attributes between the two MNE Groups.

Para (b)

- Paragraph (b) states that in the acquisition year, the amount of Financial Accounting Net Income or Loss and the amount of Adjusted Covered Taxes taken into account for calculating a GloBE tax liability for each MNE Group, shall be the amount that is taken into account in the CFS of each MNE Group.
- This approach follows the general approach adopted by the GloBE Rules of relying on the amounts reflected in the financial accounts that are used for the preparation of the CFS.

Para (c)

- Under Article 6.2.1(c), an MNE Group that acquires a Controlling Interest in a CE will ignore the effect of any purchase accounting consolidation adjustments attributable to the acquisition and treat the acquired target, for GloBE purposes, as having the same carrying value in its assets that it has prior to the transfer (i.e. the historical carrying value).
- In other words, the acquisition of a Controlling Interest in a target does not result in any change to the carrying value of the target's assets and liabilities for the purposes of determining GloBE Income or Loss.
- Moreover, any adjustment to the carrying value of intangible assets that results from the acquisition, such as goodwill, customer lists, or workforce-in-place, are ignored in the computation of GloBE Income or Loss. Denying a step-up in the target's inside basis in its assets and liabilities matches the treatment of the seller and purchaser under the GloBE Rules and ensures that gains or losses on the assets and liabilities of a CE are not permanently excluded from taxation under the GloBE Rules by virtue of a transfer of its Ownership Interests. Paragraph (c) is also expected to align outcomes under the GloBE rules with those provided under the domestic laws of most IF jurisdictions and avoid potential differences in treatment across financial accounting standards.
- This rule is consistent with the prohibition on taking into account purchase accounting adjustments in the computation of GloBE Income or Loss under Article 3.2 and applies irrespective of whether the Controlling Interest was acquired before or after the applicability date of the GloBE Rules.
- Where the financial accounting standard used by the UPE in preparing its CFS permit the UPE to "push down" adjustments to the carrying value of assets and liabilities that were attributable to a purchase of a business to the separate accounts of the acquired CE, the CE may use the carrying value reflected in its separate accounts if the acquisition occurred prior to 1 December 2021 and the MNE Group does not have sufficient records to determine its Financial Accounting Net Income or Loss with reasonable accuracy based on the unadjusted carrying values of the acquired assets and liabilities. In such cases, however, the CE must also take into account any deferred tax assets and liabilities arising in connection with the purchase in the computation of its Financial Accounting Net Income or Loss and its Adjusted Covered Taxes.

Para (d)

- The Substance-based Income Exclusion is computed for each CE under Article 5.3 by aggregating a percentage of Eligible Payroll Costs and Eligible Tangible Assets. Paragraphs (d) and (e) adjust the determination of Eligible Payroll Costs and Eligible Tangible Assets in the case of a target that is acquired or disposed part way through the Fiscal Year.
- Without such a rule, the Substance-based Income Exclusion calculated for the acquiring and disposing MNE Groups could take into account expenses and costs that were incurred prior to, or after, the target was a member of the MNE Group, possibly duplicating the effect of the expenses and costs.
- Paragraph (d) states that the amount of Eligible Payroll Costs referred in Article 5.3.3 shall be adjusted by taking into account only the costs that are reflected in the CFS prepared by the UPE of the MNE Group. Thus, each MNE Group takes into account the Eligible Payroll Costs arising during its period of ownership and that it bears economic responsibility for.

Para (e)

- Paragraph (e) provides that the amount of the Eligible Tangible Assets referred in Article 5.3.4 shall be adjusted proportionally to correspond to the length of the period during the Fiscal Year that the target was a CE of the MNE Group. The carrying value of the Eligible Tangible Assets is determined based on the amount recorded for the purpose of preparing the CFS, including any purchase accounting consolidation adjustments attributable to the acquisition.
- This means that the acquisition of a Controlling Interest in a target will result in a step-up in a target's inside basis in its assets for the purposes of the Substance-based Income Exclusion, notwithstanding that it does not produce a similar step-up for the purposes of calculating GloBE Income or Loss.
- The difference in treatment between paragraphs (d) and (e) can be explained on the grounds that the tangible asset carveout is based on the economic cost of the investment made by the MNE Group in the tangible asset located in the relevant jurisdiction which is more accurately determined by looking to the fair value of that asset at the time of acquisition than the historical cost of that asset as recorded by the target.

Para (f)

- Paragraph (f) generally provides that deferred tax assets and liabilities of a CE that are transferred between MNE Groups are taken into account by the acquiring MNE Group in the same manner and to the same extent as they would have been taken into account if the acquiring MNE Group had controlled the CE when they arose.
- Thus, if the acquiring MNE Group acquires a deferred tax liability that qualifies as a Recapture Exception Accrual, Article 4.4.4 does not apply to that deferred tax liability. On the other hand, if the deferred tax liability does not fall within the Recapture Exception Accruals, it will be subject to recapture under Article 4.4.4, after taking into account the rule in paragraph (g) related to the recapture period for acquired deferred tax liabilities. Whether a deferred tax asset or liability is transferred depends on its treatment under the applicable financial accounting standard. This accounting treatment will depend in large part on how the tax laws of the jurisdiction allocate the relevant items of deferred income and expense between the disposing and acquiring MNE Groups.
- The exception to paragraph (f) is the GloBE Loss Deferred Tax Asset. Ordinary deferred tax assets and liabilities arise with respect to specific CEs and are accounted for accordingly. They feed into the computation of the CE's Total Deferred Tax Adjustment Amount under Article 4.4.1. A GloBE Loss Deferred Tax Asset, on the other hand, arises in connection with a GloBE Loss Election under Article 4.5 with respect to a particular jurisdiction. It is an attribute that arises pursuant to an election under the GloBE Rules, but is not found in the CE's or the MNE Group's financial accounts. Because the GloBE Loss Deferred Tax Asset arises in respect of a Net GloBE Loss in a particular jurisdiction of the MNE Group that makes the election, it is considered a jurisdictional attribute of the electing MNE Group, rather than an attribute of the CEs located in the jurisdiction and cannot be transferred to another MNE Group. Accordingly, Article 6.2.1(f) does not apply to a GloBE Loss Deferred Tax Asset.

Para (g)

- Paragraph (g) is intended to relieve the disposing MNE Group of the need to recapture deferred tax liabilities that do not reverse (through payment or otherwise) within the five-year period required by Article 4.4.4.
- This is achieved by treating any deferred tax liability of a CE that leaves an MNE Group as reversed when the Entity leaves the MNE Group.
- The paragraph also starts, or re-starts the five-year period in Article 4.4.4 with respect to deferred tax liabilities of a CE when it joins an MNE Group. By re-starting the five-year period in Article 4.4.4, paragraph (g) reduces compliance and administrative burdens that would arise if the deferred tax liabilities were subject to recapture based on their accrual dates in the disposing MNE Group.
- Thus, a CE that leaves one MNE Group and joins another MNE Group will not be required to recapture any deferred tax liabilities under Article 4.4.4 when it leaves the first MNE Group and will start a new five-year period under Article 4.4.4 for all of its deferred tax liabilities when it joins the second MNE Group.
- Paragraph (g) does not apply to Recapture Exception Accruals described in Article 4.4.5 because they are not subject to the requirements of Article 4.4.4 before or after the acquisition date.
- Paragraph (g) also modifies the process for handling deferred tax liabilities that do not reverse within the five-year period after the date of acquisition. This is necessary because the normal rule under Article 4.4.4 invokes the procedures of Article 5.4.1, which requires a re-calculation of the ETR and Top-up Tax for the year in which the liability first accrued. The acquiring MNE Group did not perform an original calculation of the ETR and Top-up Tax for the relevant year based on the deferred tax liabilities of the acquired CE and thus Article 5.4.1 does not function properly in this context. Accordingly, when an acquired deferred tax liability fails to reverse before the end of the fifth Fiscal Year after the acquisition date, paragraph (g) reduces Covered Taxes in that Fiscal Year.
- To the extent Covered Taxes in a jurisdiction in that Fiscal Year are negative as a result of this reduction, Additional Current Top-up Tax may result from the application of Article 4.1.5 if the other conditions for applying Article 4.1.5 are met.

Note : Deferred tax assets and liabilities arising in connection with a business combination generally are not taken into account under the GloBE Rules because the purchase accounting adjustments to the carrying value of assets and liabilities are not taken into account in the computation of GloBE Income or Loss (subject to exceptions for Articles 6.2.2, 6.3.1, 6.3.3, and 6.3.4). Where the deferred tax assets and liabilities arising in connection with a business combination are not taken into account under the GloBE Rules, the deferred tax assets and liabilities referred to in Article 6.2.1 (f) and (g) refer to the deferred tax assets and liabilities of an acquired CE that existed before the CE joined the MNE Group, i.e., pre-acquisition deferred tax assets and liabilities.

Para (h)

- Paragraph (h) deals with the situation in which the target is required to apply the IIR as a Parent Entity of one or both MNE Groups.
- Paragraph (h) provides that the target shall apply the IIR separately to its Allocable Shares of the Top-up Tax of LTCEs determined for each MNE Group.
- Thus, this rule applies where the target has an Ownership Interest in an LTCE and is a Parent Entity required to apply the IIR under the top-down approach or split-ownership rules applicable to one or both MNE Groups.
- The determination of whether a CE in which the target has an Ownership Interest is an LTCE must be made separately with respect to both the MNE Group that the target left and the MNE Group that the target joined. Whether a CE in which the target has an Ownership Interest is an LTCE is determined based on jurisdictional blending which means that the taxes and income of other CEs owned by each MNE Group that are located in the same jurisdiction as the target will impact on the jurisdictional ETR and therefore whether the target is considered to have an Ownership Interest in an LTCE. In fact, the same CE could be an LTCE of the disposing MNE Group but not an LTCE of the acquiring MNE Group, or vice-versa. This could occur, for example, because one MNE Group has high-taxed CEs located in the same jurisdiction sheltering the low-tax outcome of the target. This outcome is consistent with the policies or principles underlying the GloBE Rules because the tax attributes of the CEs would be subject to two different computations for each of the MNE Groups involved.
- Similarly, whether the target is a Parent Entity required to apply the IIR must be determined based on the facts of each MNE Group. If the target is an Intermediate Parent Entity and the UPEs of the MNE Groups involved are located in a jurisdiction with a Qualified IIR, the target would not be required to apply the IIR under Article 2.1.3(a). However, if only one of the UPEs is located in a jurisdiction with a Qualified IIR, then the target may be required to apply the IIR with respect to the MNE Group whose UPE is not subject to the IIR. Stated differently, Article 2.1.3(a) deactivates the IIR applicable to the target in the case of the MNE Group whose UPE is subject to a Qualified IIR, but not in the case of the MNE Group whose UPE is not subject to a Qualified IIR. If both UPEs are not located in a jurisdiction with a Qualified IIR, then the target may be required to apply the IIR with respect to each MNE Group based on its Allocable Share of the Top-up Tax, if any, computed with respect to the LTCE by each MNE Group.

692. Illustration # 62: The illustration, through a flow-chart, explains the application of Article 6.2.1(e) when a CE leaves and joins an MNE Group.

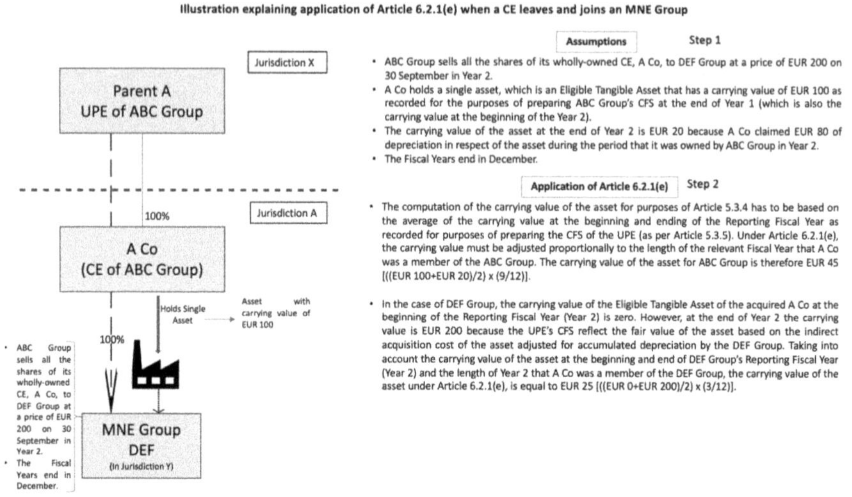

4.6.2.2 Article 6.2.2.

693. For purposes of the GloBE Rules, the acquisition or disposal of a Controlling Interest in a Constituent Entity will be treated as an acquisition or disposal of the assets and liabilities if the jurisdiction in which the target Constituent Entity is located, or in the case of a Tax Transparent Entity, the jurisdiction in which the assets are located, treats the acquisition or disposal of that Controlling Interest in the same or similar manner as an acquisition or disposition of the assets and liabilities and imposes a Covered Tax on the seller based on the difference between the tax basis and the consideration paid in exchange for the Controlling Interest or the fair value of the assets and liabilities.

694. *Objective of the Article*: Under Article 6.2.2, if a transfer of a Controlling Interest in a CE is treated as a transfer of assets and liabilities rather than a transfer of Ownership Interests by the jurisdiction where the target is located, then it will be treated as a transfer of assets and liabilities for GloBE purposes as well. In that case, the rules in Article 6.3 apply.

695. *The Article provides for an exception to Article 6.2.1*: Article 6.2.2 provides for an exception to Article 6.2.1 aimed at providing consistent treatment of an acquisition and disposition of assets and liabilities for GloBE purposes, regardless of the form in which the transaction is undertaken. When Article 6.2.2 applies to a transaction, the seller is treated as selling its Ownership Interests and the gain or loss on that sale is excluded from Article 3.2.1(c) in the jurisdiction in which it is located. At the same time, the target is treated as selling its assets and liabilities to the acquiring MNE Group in exchange for the consideration received by the seller in a transaction that is subject to Article 6.3.1. The target's gain or loss and Covered Taxes on the sale of its assets and liabilities are taken into account in computing its GloBE Income or Loss and Adjusted Covered Taxes and the disposing MNE Group's ETR for the target's jurisdiction for the Fiscal Year that includes the acquisition date. As a result of this treatment, the gain or loss on the transfer that is treated as a sale of assets and liabilities of the target are included in the disposing MNE Group's ETR computation for the jurisdiction that imposed that treatment for local tax purposes, rather than the jurisdiction of the seller of the Ownership Interests.

696. Article 6.2.2 and the two conditions for the article to apply are further explained in Figure 4.34.

Figure 4.34 Article 6.2.2 and Its Two Conditions

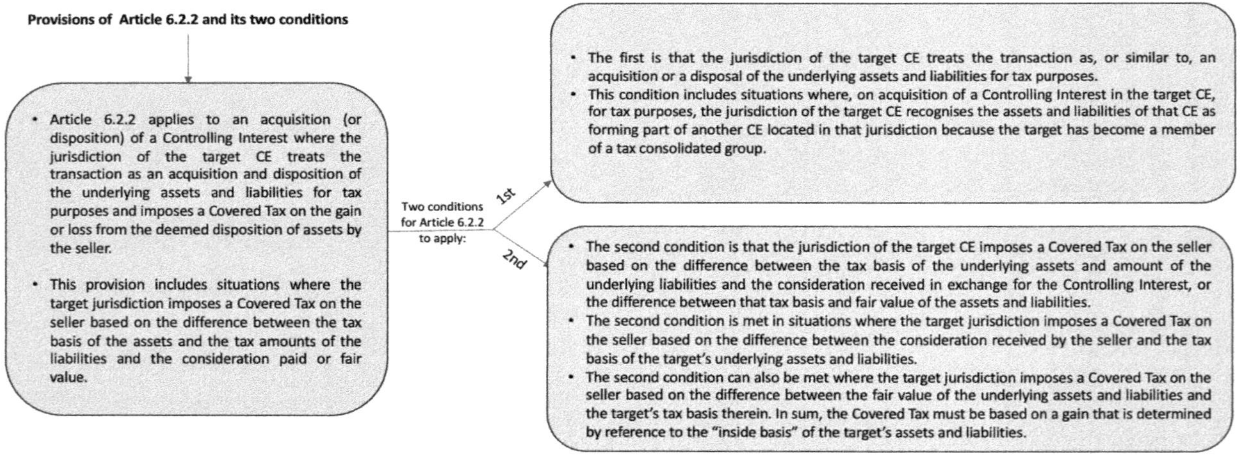

Note : A Controlling Interest is acquired when a CE that was not in control of the target acquires Ownership Interests that give it control of the target. The rule in Article 6.2.2 does not require the CE to acquire all of its Ownership Interests in the transaction in which it gains control. Thus, acquisition of an Ownership Interest, no matter how small, that combined with Ownership Interests already owned by the CE may result in the CE acquiring a Controlling Interest. Once a CE has a Controlling Interest, acquisition of additional Ownership interests in the target are not acquisitions of a Controlling Interest. However, the tax laws of the target's jurisdiction may treat a transaction as a sale of assets only when the control is acquired in a single or series of related transactions.

4.6.3 Article 6.3. (Transfer of Assets and Liabilities)

697. Prominent features of Article 6.3 are provided in Box 4.31.

Box 4.31 Prominent Features of Article 6.3

- Deals with situations in which the assets and liabilities of a CE are disposed of or acquired directly, including as part of a GloBE Reorganisation.
- Provides rules to determine whether and the extent to which gain or loss is recognised on the disposition and the carrying value to be used by the acquirer for the purposes of determining its GloBE Income or Loss in subsequent Fiscal Years.
- Article 6.3.1 relates to an acquisition or disposition of assets and liabilities that is not part of a GloBE Reorganisation.
  - For GloBE purposes, the disposing Entity must include gain or loss from the disposition of assets and liabilities in its computation of GloBE Income or Loss, and the acquiring Entity must use the adjusted carrying value as determined under the financial accounting standard used in preparing the CFS of the UPE.
  - In a transfer to which Article 6.2.2 applies, the carrying value of the acquired assets and liabilities for GloBE purposes is based on their fair value to the extent gain or loss on those assets and liabilities was included in the GloBE Income or Loss computation of the selling MNE Group.
  - Amortisation of the intangible assets or the bargain purchase gain will be included in the computation of GloBE Income or Loss only to the extent included in the acquiring Entity's Financial Accounting Net Income or Loss.
- Article 6.3.2 sets out the general treatment of an acquisition or disposition of assets and liabilities as part of a GloBE Reorganisation.
  - Article 6.3.2(a) provides that the disposing CE will not recognise the gain or loss from the transfer of the assets and liabilities for GloBE purposes.
  - Pursuant to Article 6.3.2(b), future GloBE profit or loss of the acquiring CE will be determined on the basis of the historical carrying amounts of the acquired assets and liabilities.
  - The CE must maintain accounting records to support the computation of GloBE Income or Loss by reference to the historical carrying amounts of the acquired assets and liabilities.
- Article 6.3.3 addresses instances where a GloBE Reorganisation results in recognition of Non-qualifying Gain or Loss under the laws of the disposing Entity's jurisdiction.
  - Provides that the disposing CE will include a gain or loss to the extent of the Non-Qualifying Gain or Loss. This means that the computation of

GloBE Income or Loss will include the lesser of the amount of gain or loss reflected in the financial accounts or the amount of the taxable gain or loss arising from the GloBE Reorganisation.
    - Provides that the acquiring CE will increase or decrease the carrying amounts of the acquired assets and liabilities to account for the Non-qualifying Gain or Loss. The changes in carrying value for GloBE purposes must be allocated among assets and liabilities in a manner consistent with the increases and decreases of those assets under the tax law applicable to the acquiring CE.
    - Provides that the increase or decrease in carrying value of assets and liabilities for GloBE purposes cannot exceed the Non-qualifying Gain or Loss.
- Article 6.3.4 provides an MNE Group with an election to adjust the basis of its assets and the amount of its liabilities to fair value for tax purposes in the jurisdiction in which it is located and seeks to align the outcomes under the GloBE with those that apply under local tax law.
    - When an election under Article 6.3.4 is made, the CE recognises gain or loss and adjusts the carrying value of its assets and liabilities for purposes of the GloBE Rules.
    - The election, however, does not apply to ordinary sales of assets (e.g., sales of inventory) by a CE or transfer pricing adjustments.

698. Article 6.3 deals with situations in which the assets and liabilities of a Constituent Entity are disposed of or acquired directly, including as part of a GloBE Reorganisation (where the seller is not subject to tax on the gain (or loss), in whole or part). Article 6.3 provides rules to determine whether and the extent to which gain or loss is recognised on the disposition and the carrying value to be used by the acquirer for the purposes of determining its GloBE Income or Loss in subsequent Fiscal Years.

4.6.3.1 Article 6.3.1.

699. In the case of a disposition or acquisition of assets and liabilities, a disposing Constituent Entity will include the gain or loss on disposition in the computation of its GloBE Income or Loss, and an acquiring Constituent Entity will determine its GloBE Income or Loss using the acquiring Constituent Entity's carrying value of the acquired assets and liabilities determined under the accounting standard used in preparing CFS of the UPE.

700. *Objective of the Article*: Article 6.3.1 relates to an acquisition or disposition of assets and liabilities that is not part of a GloBE Reorganisation. The article follows the accounting treatment for both the disposing Entity and the acquiring Entity. Financial accounting rules generally recognise a seller's gain or loss on the disposition of assets and liabilities and require the acquirer to use the acquisition price, which is generally the fair value of the assets, to measure the assets and liabilities upon its acquisition. As such, for GloBE purposes, the disposing Entity must include gain or loss from the disposition of assets and liabilities in its computation of GloBE Income or Loss, and the acquiring Entity must use the adjusted carrying value as determined under the financial accounting standard used in preparing the CFS of the UPE.

701. *Transfer to which Article 6.2.2 applies*: In a transfer to which Article 6.2.2 applies, the carrying value of the acquired assets and liabilities for GloBE purposes is based on their fair value to the extent gain or loss on those assets and liabilities was included in the GloBE Income or Loss computation of the selling MNE Group. The fair value must be used in the computation of the acquiring Entity's computation of GloBE Income or Loss in the acquisition year and subsequent Fiscal Years, irrespective of whether the fair value adjustments are reflected in the Entity's financial accounts or the MNE Group's consolidated financial accounts.

702. *Treatment of goodwill or other intangible assets by the acquiring Entity*: The acquiring Entity may be required under the applicable accounting standard to recognise assets and liabilities that were not recognised in the financial accounts of the disposing Entity, such as goodwill or other intangible assets. In addition, the acquiring Entity may be required to recognise bargain purchase gains under the applicable accounting standard. In such cases, amortisation of the intangible assets or the bargain purchase gain will be included in the computation of GloBE Income or Loss only to the extent included in the acquiring Entity's Financial Accounting Net Income or Loss.

4.6.3.2 Article 6.3.2.

703. If the disposition or acquisition of assets and liabilities is part of a GloBE Reorganisation, Article 6.3.1 shall not apply and:

(a) a disposing Constituent Entity will exclude any gain or loss on the disposition from the computation of its GloBE Income or Loss; and
(b) an acquiring Constituent Entity will determine its GloBE Income or Loss after the acquisition using the disposing Entity's carrying values of the acquired assets and liabilities upon disposition.

704. The term GloBE Reorganisation mentioned *supra* is defined in Article 10.1 as below:

> GloBE Reorganisation means a transformation or transfer of assets and liabilities such as in a merger, demerger, liquidation, or similar transaction where:
>
> (a) the consideration for the transfer is, in whole or in significant part, equity interests issued by the acquiring Constituent Entity or by a person connected with the acquiring Constituent Entity, or, in the case of a liquidation, equity interests of the target (or, when no consideration is provided, where the issuance of an equity interest would have no economic significance);
> (b) the disposing Constituent Entity's gain or loss on those assets is not subject to tax, in whole or in part; and

(c) the tax laws of the jurisdiction in which the acquiring Constituent Entity is located require the acquiring Constituent Entity to compute taxable income after the disposition or acquisition using the disposing Constituent Entity's tax basis in the assets, adjusted for any Non-qualifying Gain or Loss on the disposition or acquisition.

705. *Objective of the Article*: Article 6.3.2 sets out the general treatment of an acquisition or disposition of assets and liabilities as part of a GloBE Reorganisation. Article 6.3.2 aligns the GloBE Rules with the tax deferral treatment of reorganisations under domestic provisions. The requirements to qualify as a GloBE Reorganisation in paragraphs (b) and (c) of the definition relate to the tax treatment of the transformation or transaction under local tax law. These paragraphs consider the tax treatment of the transferor/disposing and transferee/acquiring entities, and both paragraphs must be met for the transaction to qualify as a GloBE Reorganisation. Consistent treatment of the transferor/disposing and transferee/acquiring entities will ordinarily occur in a purely domestic transformation or transaction and may occur in a cross-border transformation or transaction. However, consistent treatment will not always occur in a cross-border transformation or transaction. Article 6.3.2(a) provides that the disposing CE will not recognise the gain or loss from the transfer of the assets and liabilities for GloBE purposes. Pursuant to Article 6.3.2(b), future profit or loss of the acquiring CE will be determined on the basis of the historical carrying amounts of the acquired assets and liabilities. The CE must maintain accounting records to support the computation of GloBE Income or Loss by reference to the historical carrying amounts of the acquired assets and liabilities.

4.6.3.3 Article 6.3.3.

706. If a disposition or acquisition of assets and liabilities is part of a GloBE Reorganisation in which a disposing Constituent Entity recognises Non-qualifying Gain or Loss, Articles 6.3.1 and 6.3.2 shall not apply and:

(a) the disposing Constituent Entity will include gain or loss on the disposition in its GloBE Income or Loss computation to the extent of the Non-qualifying Gain or Loss; and
(b) an acquiring Constituent Entity will determine its GloBE Income or Loss after the acquisition using the disposing Entity's carrying value of the acquired assets and liabilities upon disposition adjusted consistent with local tax rules to account for the Non-qualifying Gain or Loss.

707. The term Non-qualifying Gain or Loss mentioned *supra* is defined in Article 10.1, as below:

Non-qualifying Gain or Loss means the lesser of the gain or loss of the disposing Constituent Entity arising in connection with a GloBE Reorganisation that is subject to tax in the disposing Constituent Entity's location and the financial accounting gain or loss arising in connection with the GloBE Reorganisation.

708. *Objective of the Article:* Article 6.3.3 addresses instances where a GloBE Reorganisation results in recognition of Non-qualifying Gain or Loss under the laws of the disposing Entity's jurisdiction. This may be the case under tax rules in IF jurisdictions, for example, where there is a limit to the amount of non-equity consideration that can be paid as part of the consideration for the transaction to qualify as a GloBE Reorganisation. Amounts paid over that limit may constitute taxable consideration that triggers the recognition of a gain or loss in respect of the assets transferred pursuant to the reorganisation. In the context of such GloBE Reorganisations, Article 6.3.3 provides that the disposing CE will include a gain or loss to the extent of the Non-Qualifying Gain or Loss. This means that the computation of GloBE Income or Loss will include the lesser of the amount of gain or loss reflected in the financial accounts or the amount of the taxable gain or loss arising from the GloBE Reorganisation. Further, the acquiring CE will increase or decrease the carrying amounts of the acquired assets and liabilities to account for the Non-qualifying Gain or Loss. The changes in carrying value for GloBE purposes must be allocated among assets and liabilities in a manner consistent with the increases and decreases of those assets under the tax law applicable to the acquiring CE. For example, if the CE is required by local tax rules to allocate the basis increases due to the tax gain, first to depreciable assets up to the amount of built-in gain on such assets, and then to inventory and other current assets, the CE must do the same for GloBE purposes. However, the increase or decrease in carrying value of assets and liabilities for GloBE purposes cannot exceed the Non-qualifying Gain or Loss.

4.6.3.4 *Article 6.3.4.*

709. At the election of the Filing Constituent Entity, a Constituent Entity of an MNE Group that is required or permitted to adjust the basis of its assets and the amount of its liabilities to fair value for tax purposes in the jurisdiction in which it is located, shall:

(a) Include in the computation of its GloBE Income or Loss an amount of gain or loss in respect of each of its assets and liabilities that is equal to:
  (i) the difference between the carrying value for financial accounting purposes of the asset or liability immediately before and the fair value of the asset or liability immediately after the date of the event that triggered the tax adjustment (the triggering event);
  (ii) decreased (or increased) by the Non-Qualifying Gain (or Loss), if any, arising in connection with the triggering event;

(b) use the fair value for financial accounting purposes of the asset or liability immediately after the triggering event to determine GloBE Income or Loss in Fiscal Years ending after the triggering event; and

(c) include the net total of the amounts determined in 6.3.4(a) in the Constituent Entity's GloBE Income or Loss in one of the following ways:

(i) the net total of the amounts is included in the Fiscal Year in which the triggering event occurs; or

(ii) an amount equal to the net total of the amounts divided by five is included in the Fiscal Year in which the triggering event occurs and in each of the immediate four subsequent Fiscal Years, unless the Constituent Entity leaves the MNE Group in a Fiscal Year within this period, in which case the remaining amount will be wholly included in that Fiscal Year.

710. *Objective of the Article:* A CE may be required or permitted to adjust the tax basis of its assets or the tax amount of its liabilities for a variety of reasons. Perhaps the most common circumstance is where a CE is subject to an exit tax because of a cross-border reorganisation or a change in the Entity's tax residence. In addition, a CE may be required to adjust the tax basis or amount of some or all of its assets and liabilities when it joins or leaves a tax consolidated group. In other cases, the CE (or its owners) may be permitted to make an election that adjusts the tax basis of assets and tax amount of liabilities. The adjustments required by these local tax rules are usually, but not always, based on the fair value of the asset or liability. Article 6.3.4 provides an MNE Group with an election for these situations, which seeks to align the outcomes under GloBE with those that apply under local tax law. When an election under Article 6.3.4 is made, the CE recognises gain or loss and adjusts the carrying value of its assets and liabilities for purposes of the GloBE Rules. The election, however, does not apply to ordinary sales of assets (e.g., sales of inventory) by a CE or transfer pricing adjustments. Moreover, if an election is made under this article in connection with the acquisition of a Controlling Interest in a CE that is governed by Article 6.2.1, the election does not affect the application of Article 3.2.1(c) to the seller. Paragraphs (a) to (c) of Article 6.3.4 are further explained in Figure 4.35.

Figure 4.35 Paragraphs (a) to (c) of Article 6.3.4

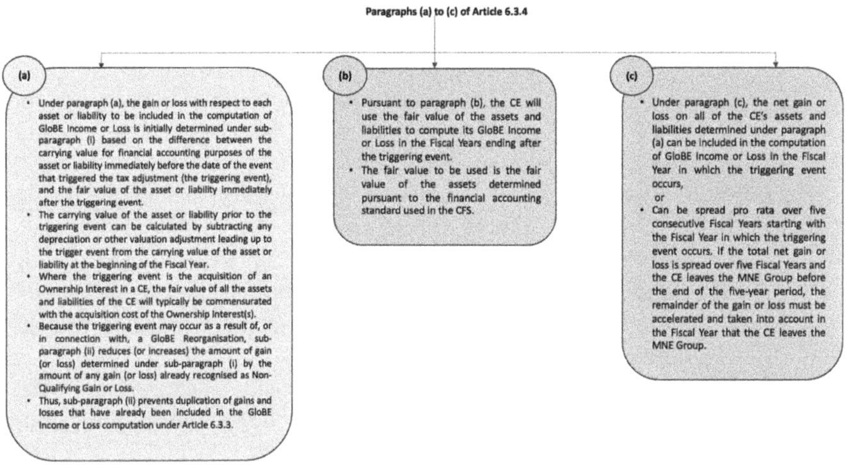

4.6.4 Article 6.4. (Joint Ventures)

711. Article 6.4 establishes special rules for JVs. These rules apply where a UPE holds, directly or indirectly, at least 50% of the Ownership Interest of a JV that is reported under the equity method in its CFS. Article 6.4 brings such JVs into scope of the GloBE Rules, along with their JV Subsidiaries.

712. Prominent features of Article 6.4 are provided in Box 4.32.

Box 4.32 Prominent Features of Article 6.4

- Article 6.4 extends the application of the GloBE Rules to Entities in which the UPE of an MNE Group owns 50% or more of the Ownership Interests (such Entities are JVs under the GloBE Rules). This ensures that all of the income of a 50/50 JV owned, directly or indirectly, by the UPE of an MNE Group will be subject to the GloBE Rules and that the rule extends to any venture in which the MNE Group holds 50% or more of the Ownership Interests (without having unilateral control).
- Article 6.4 does not, however, require the JV or its JV Subsidiaries to apply the IIR or the UTPR directly. Rather it requires the MNE Group to determine Top-up Tax in respect of a JV (or its JV Subsidiaries) located in a Low-Taxed Jurisdiction and allocates any resulting Top-up Tax to a CE within the MNE Group under the IIR or the UTPR.
- Situations when an entity is not considered a JV for GloBE purposes are as below:
  - An Entity is not a JV under the GloBE Rules, where the UPE holds less than 50% of its Ownership Interests.

  - An Entity commonly referred to as an 'associate' under accounting rules typically would not meet the GloBE definition of a JV because the UPE may not reach the 50% ownership threshold.
  - If it is an Excluded Entity or the Ownership Interests of the Entity held by the MNE Group are held directly by an Excluded Entity.
  - If it is a UPE of an MNE Group that is already within the scope of the GloBE Rules because such Group meets the consolidated revenue threshold set out in Article 1.1.
- Paragraph (a) of Article 6.4.1 provides special rules for computing the Top-up Tax of the JV and its JV Subsidiaries.
  - It states that the Top-up Tax of the JV Group shall be computed in accordance with Chapters 3 to 7 and Article 8.2 as if the members of the JV Group were CEs of a separate MNE Group and as if the JV was the UPE of that Group.
  - This means that all the provisions included in Chapters 3 to 7 and Article 8.2 of the GloBE Rules related to the computation of the Top-up Tax are applicable to the members of JV Group, including the provisions on the Substance-based Income Exclusion and Safe Harbours.
  - The Top-up Tax computation for the JV Group under Chapter 5 is made as if the JV was the UPE of a separate MNE Group.
  - The transitional rules in Articles 9.1 and 9.2 also apply with respect to JVs on the grounds that they complement the provisions in Chapters 4 and 5.
- Paragraph (b) of Article 6.4.1 regulates the application of the IIR by Parent Entities with respect to the Top-up Tax of a JV and a JV Subsidiary.
  - Paragraph (b) only applies to Parent Entities that have Ownership Interest in the JV or the JV Subsidiary.
  - It requires such Parent Entities to apply the IIR in accordance with Articles 2.1 to 2.3.
  - This means that the UPE and other Parent Entities are required to apply the IIR in accordance with the top-down approach and split-ownership rules.
  - The UPE or any other Parent Entity applying the IIR must allocate the Top-up Tax of the JV or JV Subsidiary based on its Allocable Share of the Top-up Tax.
- Paragraph (c) describes how the UTPR is applied in the context of JVs.
  - In practice, the UTPR only applies with respect to a member of a JV Group, where the UPE or other Parent Entities have not brought into charge the JV Group Top-up Tax under a Qualified IIR in accordance with paragraph (b).
  - Paragraph (c) requires the JV Group Top-up Tax to be added to the Total UTPR Top-up Tax Amount after it has been reduced by the amount that has already been brought into charge under the IIR.

- The amount is computed on the basis of the UPE's Allocable Share of the Top-up Tax of the JV or its JV Subsidiaries.

713. *Article 6.4 brings JVs into the scope of GloBE Rules*: A common business practice undertaken by MNE Groups is entering into joint ventures with third parties. Generally, for accounting purposes, a joint venture is a business enterprise that is jointly controlled by two or more persons or Entities. Because the enterprise is not controlled exclusively by one person, its accounting results are not consolidated with any of its owners on a line-by-line basis. Instead, the financial results of joint ventures are commonly reported by MNE Groups using the equity method in their CFS. Absent a special rule, this accounting treatment would exclude them from the scope of the GloBE Rules because they do not meet the definition of a CE under Article 1.3, which requires an Entity to be consolidated on a line-by-line basis. Thus, if two MNE Groups subject to the GloBE Rules, each owned 50% of the Ownership Interests of a joint venture, neither MNE Group would be subject to the GloBE Rules on its share of the JV's income in the absence of Article 6.4. Thus, Article 6.4 extends the application of the GloBE Rules to Entities in which the UPE of an MNE Group owns 50% or more of the Ownership Interests (such Entities are JVs under the GloBE Rules). This ensures that all of the income of a 50/50 JV owned, directly or indirectly, by the UPE of an MNE Group will be subject to the GloBE Rules and that the rule extends to any venture in which the MNE Group holds 50% or more of the Ownership Interests (without having unilateral control). Article 6.4 does not, however, require the JV or its JV Subsidiaries to apply the IIR or the UTPR directly. Rather it requires the MNE Group to determine Top-up Tax in respect of a JV (or its JV Subsidiaries) located in a Low-Taxed Jurisdiction and allocates any resulting Top-up Tax to a CE within the MNE Group under the IIR or the UTPR.

4.6.4.1 Article 6.4.1.

714. The GloBE Rules shall apply to a Joint Venture and its JV Subsidiaries as follows for each Fiscal Year:

(a) Chapters 3 to 7 and Article 8.2 shall apply for purposes of computing any Top-Up Tax of the Joint Venture and its JV Subsidiaries as if they were Constituent Entities of a separate MNE Group and as if the Joint Venture was the UPE of that Group;
(b) a Parent Entity that holds directly or indirectly Ownership Interests in the Joint Venture or a JV Subsidiary shall apply the IIR with respect to its Allocable Share of the Top-up Tax of a member of the JV Group in accordance with Article 2.1 to Article 2.3; and
(c) the JV Group Top-up Tax shall be reduced by each Parent Entity's Allocable Share of the Top-up Tax of each member of the JV Group that is brought into charge under a Qualified IIR under paragraph (b), and any remaining amount

shall be added to the Total UTPR Top-up Tax Amount taken into account under Article 2.5.1.

715. The term Joint Venture (JV) mentioned above is defined in Article 10.1 as below:

> Joint Venture (JV) means an Entity whose financial results are reported under the equity method in the Consolidated Financial Statements of the Ultimate Parent Entity provided that the Ultimate Parent Entity holds directly or indirectly at least 50% of its Ownership Interests. A Joint Venture does not include:
>
> (a) an Ultimate Parent Entity of an MNE Group that is subject to the GloBE Rules;
> (b) an Excluded Entity as defined by Article 1.5.1;
> (c) an Entity whose Ownership Interest held by the MNE Group are held directly through an Excluded Entity referred in Article 1.5.1 and the Entity:
>   (i) operates exclusively or almost exclusively to hold assets or invest funds for the benefit of its investors;
>   (ii) carries out activities that are ancillary to those carried out by the Excluded Entity; or
>   (iii) substantially all of its income is excluded from the computation of GloBE Income or Loss in accordance with Articles 3.2.1(b) and (c).
> (d) an Entity that is held by an MNE Group composed exclusively of Excluded Entities; or
> (e) a JV Subsidiary.

716. *Situations when an entity is not considered a JV for GloBE purposes:* Such situations arise in the circumstances mentioned below:

- An Entity is not a JV under the GloBE Rules, where the UPE holds less than 50% of its Ownership Interests despite that it could still be considered as a JV under accounting rules if it is jointly controlled by the MNE Group (definition of a JV under the GloBE Rules departs from the one commonly used in accounting rules).
- An Entity commonly referred to as an 'associate' under accounting rules (e.g., IAS 28 (IFRS Foundation, 2022)) and also reported under the equity method typically would not meet the GloBE definition of a JV because the UPE would not reach the 50% ownership threshold. In this case, the MNE Group would have significant influence over the Entity instead of joint control, which is a difference between 'associates' and JVs under accounting rules. However, such factor is not decisive in the GloBE definition of a JV.
- An Entity is not considered a JV for GloBE purposes if it is an Excluded Entity or the Ownership Interests of the Entity held by the MNE Group are held directly by an Excluded Entity.
- An Entity is excluded from the definition of a JV if it is a UPE of an MNE Group that is already within the scope of the GloBE Rules because such Group meets the consolidated revenue threshold set out in Article 1.1.

717. The term JV Group mentioned above is defined in Article 10.1 as below:

> JV Group means a Joint Venture and its JV Subsidiaries.

718. *Members of JV Group treated as CEs*: The members of a JV Group are not required to apply the charging provisions in Chapter 2. However, they are treated as if they were CEs for purposes of computing their jurisdictional ETR and Top-up Taxes.

719. The term JV Group top-up tax mentioned above is defined in Article 10.1 as below:

> JV Group Top-up Tax means the Ultimate Parent Entity's Allocable Share of the Top-up Tax of all members of the JV Group.

720. The term JV Subsidiary mentioned above is defined in Article 10.1 as below:

> JV Subsidiary means an Entity whose assets, liabilities, income, expenses and cash flows are consolidated by a Joint Venture under an Acceptable Financial Accounting Standard (or would have been required had it been required to consolidate such items in accordance with an Acceptable Financial Accounting Standard). A Permanent Establishment whose Main Entity is the Joint Venture or a JV Subsidiary shall be treated as a separate JV Subsidiary.

721. *JV or its JV Subsidiaries not to apply the IIR or UTPR*: Article 6.4.1 brings a JV and its JV Subsidiaries into scope of the GloBE Rules but only with respect to the UPE's share of the JV and its JV Subsidiaries. If the JV is an LTCE, the GloBE Rules would apply similarly to the way they apply to CEs. However, Article 6.4.1 does not require a JV or its JV Subsidiaries to apply the IIR or UTPR.

722. Paragraphs (a) to (c) of Article 6.4.1 are further explained in Figure 4.36.

Figure 4.36 Paragraphs (a) to (c) of Article 6.4.1

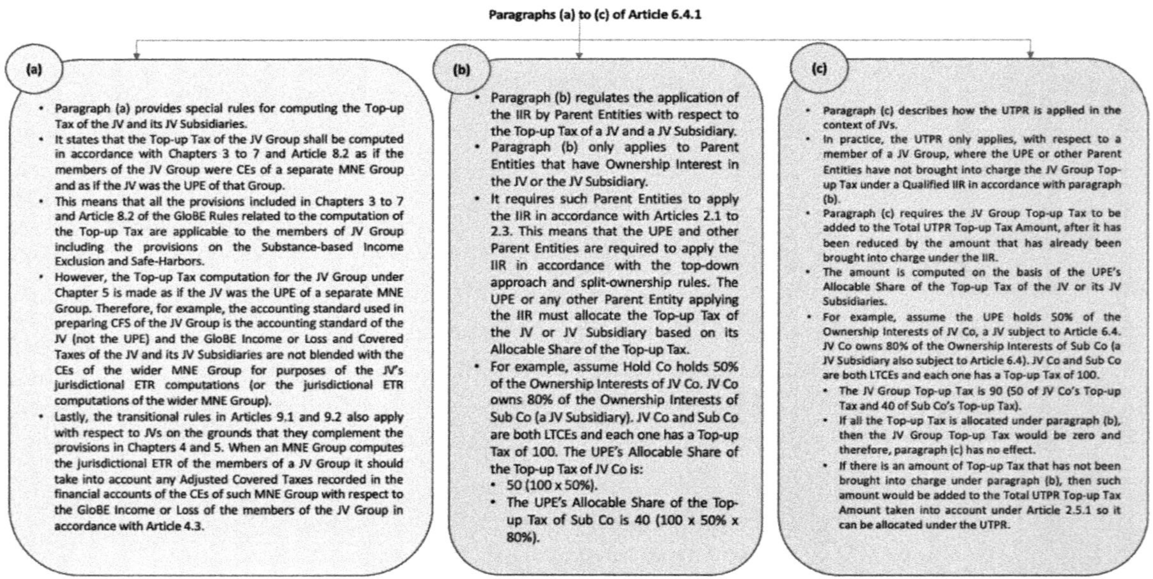

4.6.5 Article 6.5. (Multi-Parented MNE Groups)

723. Prominent features of Article 6.5 are provided in Box 4.33.

Box 4.33 Prominent Features of Article 6.5

- Provides special rules for the treatment of Multi-Parented MNE Groups under the GloBE Rules.
- Covers the situation in which two or more Groups prepare CFS in which the financial performance of these Groups is presented as a single economic unit in accordance with a Dual-listed Arrangement or a Stapled Structure.
- Ensures that the GloBE Rules apply to a Dual-listed Arrangement or a Stapled Structure in the same way they would apply to a Group with a single UPE with an appropriate allocation of Top-up Tax among the CEs of the combined MNE Group.
- Paragraph (a) of Article 6.5.1 states that the Entities and CEs of each Group are treated as if they were members of a single MNE Group for purposes of the GloBE Rules. This paragraph refers to 'Entities' and 'Constituent Entities' because it has two objectives.
  - The first objective is to determine the composition of the combined Group. Similar to Article 1.2.2, this test refers to all Entities regardless of whether they are CEs or Excluded Entities. This is important for applying the consolidated revenue threshold in Article 1.1, which takes into account the revenue of Entities that are members of the combined Group regardless of whether they are Excluded Entities.
  - The second objective is to identify the CEs of the Multi-Parented MNE Group for the purpose of applying the mechanical provisions of the GloBE Rules.
- Paragraph (b) of Article 6.5.1 states that an Entity (other than an Excluded Entity) shall be treated as a CE of the Multi-Parented MNE Group if it is consolidated on a line-by-line basis by such Group or its Controlling Interests are held by Entities of such Group.
  - The purpose of paragraph (b) is to extend the definition of CE to those Entities that would not meet the definition if each Group were tested separately but that are, nevertheless, included on a line-by-line basis in the CFS of the Multi-Parented MNE Group.
  - Furthermore, these Entities are considered as CEs if they are not consolidated on a line-by-line basis by the Multi-Parented MNE Group, but their Controlling Interest is held by Entities of the Multi-Parented MNE Group.
- Paragraph (c) of Article 6.5.1 states that the CFS of the Multi-Parented MNE Group are those referred to in the definition of Stapled Structure or Dual-listed Arrangement.

- Paragraph (d) of Article 6.5.1 clarifies that the UPEs of the Groups that comprise the Multi-Parented MNE Group are still considered the UPEs of the Multi-Parented MNE Group.
  - This clarification is important because it confirms that in these cases, there would be more than one UPE.
- Paragraph (e) of Article 6.5.1 indicates that the Parent Entities of the Multi-Parented MNE Group shall apply the IIR in accordance with Articles 2.1 to 2.3 with respect to their Allocable Shares of the Top-up Tax of the LTCE.
  - This means that under Article 2.1, each of the UPEs is required to apply the IIR under the top-down approach in the jurisdiction in which they are located.
  - This means that split-ownership rules are also applicable. However, the determination of whether an Entity is a POPE shall take into account both of the UPEs' Ownership Interests in the Entity.
- Paragraph (f) of Article 6.5.1 states that all the CEs of the Multi-Parented MNE Group are required to apply the UTPR in accordance with Articles 2.4 to 2.6.
  - It further clarifies that the UTPR shall take into account the Top-up Tax computed in respect of any LTCE that is a member of the Multi-Parented MNE Group. This means a single UTPR Top-up Tax Amount is calculated for the whole Multi-Parented MNE Group by aggregating the Top-up Tax of all the members of the Multi-Parented MNE Group, taking into account the other relevant provisions such as Article 9.3.
  - This also means that an Entity that would otherwise be a CE of only one of the Groups can be required to apply the UTPR with respect to an amount of Top-up Tax of another CE that would otherwise be a CE of another Group.
- Paragraph (g) of Article 6.5.1 clarifies that all of the UPEs are required to submit a GloBE Information Return in accordance with Article 8.1.
  - The Article contains an exception to this rule where they appoint a single Designated Filing Entity, which could be one of the UPEs or another CE of the Multi-Parented MNE Group.

724. Article 6.5 provides special rules for the treatment of Multi-Parented MNE Groups under the GloBE Rules. The article covers the situation in which two or more Groups prepare CFS in which the financial performance of these Groups is presented as a single economic unit in accordance with a Dual-listed Arrangement or a Stapled Structure. The rules in this article ensure that the GloBE Rules apply to these structures in the same way they would apply to a Group with a single UPE with an appropriate allocation of Top-up Tax among the CEs of the combined MNE Group.

4.6.5.1 Article 6.5.1.

725. The following provisions apply to Multi-Parented MNE Groups:

(a) the Entities and Constituent Entities of each Group are treated as members of a single MNE Group for purposes of the GloBE Rules (the Multi-Parented MNE Group);
(b) an Entity (other than an Excluded Entity) shall be treated as a Constituent Entity if it is consolidated on a line-by-line basis by the Multi-Parented MNE Group or its Controlling Interests are held by Entities in the Multi-Parented MNE Group;
(c) the CFS of the Multi-Parented MNE Group shall be the CFS referred to in the definition of Stapled Structure or Dual-listed arrangement (as relevant) prepared under an Acceptable Financial Accounting Standard, which is deemed to be the accounting standard of the UPE;
(d) the UPEs of the separate Groups that comprise the Multi-Parented MNE Group shall be the UPEs of the Multi-Parented MNE Group (when applying the GloBE Rules in respect of a Multi-Parented MNE Group, references to a UPE shall apply, as required, as if they were references to multiple UPEs);
(e) the Parent Entities of the Multi-Parented MNE Group (including each UPE) located in the jurisdiction that has implemented GloBE Rules shall apply the IIR in accordance with Article 2.1 to Article 2.3 with respect to their Allocable Share of the Top-up Tax of the LTCE;
(f) all of the Constituent Entities of the Multi-Parented MNE Group located in the jurisdiction that has implemented GloBE Rules shall apply the UTPR in accordance with Article 2.4 to Article 2.6, taking into account the Top-up Tax of each LTCE of the Multi-Parented MNE Group; and
(g) the UPEs are required to submit the GloBE Information Return in accordance with Article 8.1 unless they appoint a single Designated Filing Entity, and that return shall include the information concerning each of the Groups that comprise the Multi-Parented MNE Group.

726. The term Multi-Parented MNE Group mentioned above is defined in Article 10.1 as below:

> Multi-Parented MNE Group means two or more Groups where:
>
> (a) the Ultimate Parent Entities of those Groups enter into an arrangement that is a Stapled Structure or a Dual-listed Arrangement; and
> (b) at least one Entity or Permanent Establishment of the combined Group is located in a different jurisdiction with respect to the location of the other Entities of the combined Group.

727. *Reason for inclusion of the phrase 'combined Group' in the term Multi-Parented MNE Group*: The phrase 'combined Group' was included in the definition to accommodate the situation in which two domestic Groups hold Ownership Interests of an Entity located in another jurisdiction, but they only hold the Controlling Interests of the Entity when they act as a combined Group. For instance, two separate domestic Groups may each hold 50% of the Ownership Interests of an Entity located in another jurisdiction (or domestic Entity with a PE in another jurisdiction). In this case, the Entity would be treated as a JV by each Group individually. However, where the UPEs of both Groups are part of a Stapled Structure or Dual-listed Arrangement, the JV becomes a CE of the combined Group, and because that Entity is located in another jurisdiction, the combined Group becomes a Multi-Parented MNE Group.

728. The term Stapled Structure mentioned above is defined in Article 10.1 as below:

> Stapled Structure means an arrangement entered into by two or more Ultimate Parent Entities of separate Groups, under which:
>
> (a) 50% or more of the Ownership Interests in the Ultimate Parent Entities of the separate Groups are by reason of the form of ownership, restrictions on transfer, or other terms or conditions combined with each other and cannot be transferred or traded independently. If the combined Ownership Interests are listed, they are quoted at a single price; and
> (b) one of those Ultimate Parent Entities prepares Consolidated Financial Statements in which the assets, liabilities, income, expenses and cash flows of all the Entities of the Groups are presented together as those of a single economic unit and that are required by a regulatory regime to be externally audited.

729. The term Dual-listed arrangement mentioned above is defined in Article 10.1 as below:

> Dual-listed Arrangement means an arrangement entered into by two or more Ultimate Parent Entities of separate Groups, under which:
>
> (a) the Ultimate Parent Entities agree to combine their business by contract alone;
> (b) pursuant to contractual arrangements, the Ultimate Parent Entities will make distributions (with respect to dividends and in liquidation) to their shareholders based on a fixed ratio;
> (c) their activities are managed as a single economic entity under contractual arrangements while retaining their separate legal identities;
> (d) the Ownership Interests in the Ultimate Parent Entities comprising the agreement are quoted, traded or transferred independently in different capital markets; and
> (e) the Ultimate Parent Entities prepare Consolidated Financial Statements in which the assets, liabilities, income, expenses and cash flows of all the Entities of the Groups are presented together as those of a single economic unit and that are required by a regulatory regime to be externally audited.

730. The features of Stapled Structure and Dual-listed Arrangement are captured in Table 4.2.

Table 4.2 Features of Stapled Structure and Dual-Listed Arrangement

S. N.	*Feature/Characteristic*	*Stapled Structure*	*Dual-listed Arrangement*
1	Type of arrangement	50% or more of the Ownership Interests in the UPEs are 'stapled' together as if they were the Ownership Interests of a single Entity.	Two or more UPEs combine their businesses through 'contract' rather than bringing them under the ownership and control of a single entity.
2	Can the arrangement be transferred or traded independently?	No, Stapled Ownership Interests are combined together (through their form of ownership, restrictions on transfer, or other terms or conditions) in a way that they cannot be transferred or traded independently.	Yes, ownership Interests in the UPEs under a Dual-listed Arrangement are quoted, traded or transferred independently in different capital markets.
3	Mechanism of quotation on the stock exchange	Stapled Ownership Interests that are listed on a securities exchange are quoted on that exchange at a single price for the combined Ownership Interests.	Since a Dual-listed Arrangement is traded or transferred independently in different capital markets, hence, quoted prices of two or more UPEs involved in the arrangement may vary.
4	Preparation of CFS*	One of the UPEs prepares CFS in which assets, liabilities, income, expenses and cash flows of the Entities in all of the Groups are presented together as those of a single economic unit.	One of the UPEs prepares CFS in which the assets, liabilities, income, expenses and cash flows of all the Entities of the Groups are presented together as those of a single economic unit.

* Under their respective definitions, both a Stapled Structure and a Dual-listed Arrangement must prepare the CFS that are externally audited pursuant to a regulatory regime. This requirement is satisfied where a UPE prepares CFS in accordance with an Acceptable Financial Accounting Standard, where it requires that the CFS must present fairly the financial position and performance of the Entities and are audited by a professional external auditor in accordance with the auditing standards issued by the auditing standards board in the jurisdiction of the location of the UPE.

731. Article 6.5.1 is divided into several paragraphs, each of which contains a different rule that applies particularly to Multi-Parented MNE Groups, as explained in Figure 4.37.

Figure 4.37 Paragraphs (a) to (g) of Article 6.5.1

Paragraphs (a) to (g) of Article 6.5.1

Para (a)

- Paragraph (a) states that the Entities and CEs of each Group are treated as if they were members of a single MNE Group for purposes of the GloBE Rules. This paragraph refers to "Entities" and "Constituent Entities" because it has two objectives.
- The first objective is determining the composition of the combined Group. Similar to Article 1.2.2, this test refers to all Entities regardless of whether they are CEs or Excluded Entities. This is important for applying the consolidated revenue threshold in Article 1.1, which takes into account the revenue of Entities that are members of the combined Group regardless of whether they are Excluded Entities.
- The second objective is to identify the CEs of the Multi-Parented MNE Group for the purposes of applying the mechanical provisions of the GloBE Rules.
- Under this paragraph, the CEs, including PEs, of each of the Groups are treated as CEs of a single Multi-Parented MNE Group.

Para (b)

- Paragraph (b) states that an Entity (other than an Excluded Entity) shall be treated as a CE of the Multi-Parented MNE Group if it is consolidated on a line-by-line basis by such Group or its Controlling Interests are held by Entities of such Group.
- The purpose of paragraph (b) is to extend the definition of CE to those Entities that would not meet the definition if each Group were tested separately but that are, nevertheless, included on a line-by-line basis in the CFS of the Multi-Parented MNE Group.
- Furthermore, these Entities are considered as CEs if they are not consolidated on a line-by-line basis by the Multi-Parented MNE Group but their Controlling Interest are held by Entities of the Multi-Parented MNE Group.
- For example, MNE Group 1 and MNE Group 2 together constitute a Multi-Parented MNE Group. The UPEs of each MNE Group hold 50% of the Ownership Interests of an Entity. If each MNE Group were treated as a separate Group under the rules, the financial performance of the Entity would have been reported under the equity method and therefore, the Entity would have been treated as a JV. However, given that the Multi-Parented MNE Group collectively holds the Controlling Interests of the Entity it is expected that such Entity would be consolidated on a line-by-line basis and therefore, considered as a CE of the MNE Group. In the case that such Entity was not consolidated on a line-by-line basis, it will still be considered as a CE because its Controlling Interests are held by Entities of the Multi-Parented MNE Group. The same would apply, for instance, if each MNE Group held 30% of the Controlling Interests of the Entity.

Para (c)

- Paragraph (c) states that the CFS of the Multi-Parented MNE Group are those referred to in the definition of Stapled Structure or Dual-listed Arrangement.
- Accordingly, the CFS of the Multi-Parented MNE Group created under a Stapled Structure are those referred in paragraph (b) of the definition of Stapled Structure.
- Similarly, the CFS of the Multi-Parented MNE Group created under a Dual-listed Arrangement are those referred in paragraph (e) of the definition of Dual-listed Arrangement.
- These statements must meet the definition of CFS to be used for purposes of the GloBE Rules.
- The last part of paragraph (c) clarifies that whenever there is a reference to the accounting standard of the UPE, then it should be deemed to be the accounting standard that has been used by the Multi-Parented MNE Group to prepare its combined CFS.

Para (d)

- Paragraph (d) clarifies that the UPEs of the Groups that comprise the Multi-Parented MNE Group are still considered as the UPEs of the Multi-Parented MNE Group.
- This clarification is important because it confirms that in these cases there would be more than one UPE.
- The text in the parenthesis at the end of paragraph (d) further clarifies that any references to the UPE in the GloBE Rules refers to the UPEs of the Multi-Parented MNE Group.

Para (e)

- Paragraph (e) indicates that the Parent Entities of the Multi-Parented MNE Group shall apply the IIR in accordance with Articles 2.1 to 2.3 with respect to their Allocable Shares of the Top-up Tax of the LTCE. This means that under Article 2.1, each of the UPEs are required to apply the IIR under the top-down approach in the jurisdiction in which they are located. This means that split-ownership rules are also applicable. However, the determination of whether an Entity is a POPE shall take into account both of the UPEs Ownership Interests in the Entity.
- It is possible that only one of the UPEs of the Multi-Parented MNE Group is subject to a Qualified IIR. In such a case, the application of the top-down approach under Article 2.1.3 will depend on the legal holding structure of the Multi-Parented MNE Group.
- For example, if all of the Ownership Interests of an Intermediate Parent Entity, that are held by the Multi-Parented MNE Group, are held by the UPE that is subject to a Qualified IIR, then Article 2.1.3 (a) deactivates the obligation of the Intermediate Parent Entity from applying the IIR. However, if both UPEs hold Ownership Interests in the Intermediate Parent Entity, then Article 2.1.3(a) does not apply because one of its UPEs is not subject to a Qualified IIR. In this latter case, the Intermediate Parent Entity is required to apply the IIR based on its Allocable Share of the Top-up Tax of the LTCE and the UPE that is subject to a Qualified IIR would reduce its Allocable Share of the Top-up Tax of the LTCE in accordance with Article 2.3.
- The computation of each Parent Entity's Allocable Share of the Top-up Tax of LTCEs in accordance with Article 2.2 is not affected by Article 6.5. This also applies to the UPEs of the Multi-Parented MNE Group notwithstanding any arrangement that require such Entities to share the profits of their subsidiaries.

Para (f)

- Paragraph (f) states that all the CEs of the Multi-Parented MNE Group are required to apply the UTPR in accordance with Articles 2.4 to 2.6.
- It further clarifies that the UTPR shall take into account the Top-up Tax computed in respect of any LTCE that is a member of the Multi-Parented MNE Group. This means a single UTPR Top-up Tax Amount is calculated for the whole Multi-Parented MNE Group by aggregating the Top-up Tax of all the members of the Multi-Parented MNE Group, taking into account the other relevant provisions such as Article 9.3.
- This also means that an Entity that would otherwise be a CE of only one of the Groups can be required to apply the UTPR with respect to an amount of Top-up Tax of another CE that would otherwise be a CE of another Group.

Para (g)

- Paragraph (g) clarifies that all of the UPEs are required to submit a GloBE Information Return in accordance with Article 8.1. The Article contains an exception to this rule where they appoint a single Designated Filing Entity, which could be one of the UPEs or another CE of the Multi-Parented MNE Group.
- Furthermore, paragraph (g) states that the GloBE Information Return shall include the information of all Groups that are part of the Multi-Parented MNE Group. The information required under Chapter 8 should be reported as if all of the Groups were a single MNE Group.
- Paragraph (g) does not otherwise alter the rules in Article 8.1, such as the obligation of all CEs located in a jurisdiction to submit a GloBE Information Return in case it is not submitted by a Designated Local Entity, or by the UPEs or a Designated Filing Constituent Entity located in a jurisdiction with a Qualifying Competent Authority Agreement.

732. Illustration # 63: The illustration, through a flow-chart, explains that under Article 6.5.1(e), the determination of whether an Entity is a POPE shall take into account both of the UPEs' Ownership Interests in the Entity.

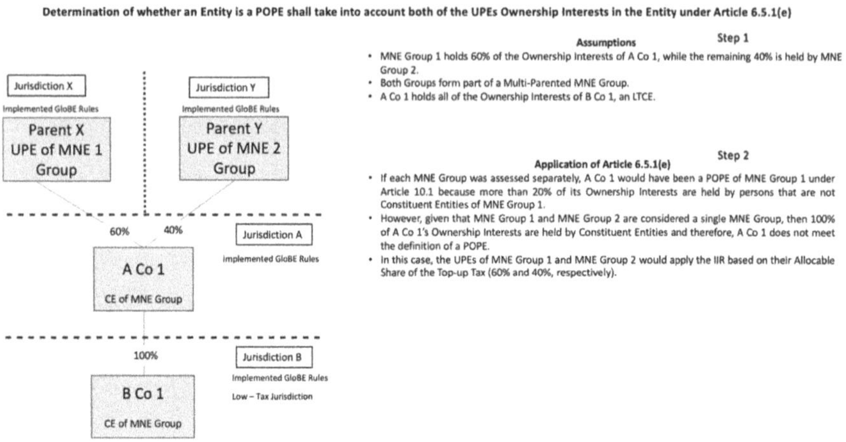

4.7 CHAPTER 7 OF GLOBE RULES (TAX NEUTRALITY AND DISTRIBUTION REGIMES)[103]

733. Chapter 7 contains special rules that are applicable to certain tax neutrality[104] and distribution tax regimes, whereby these special rules adapt the GloBE Rules to the unique features of these regimes.

4.7.1 Article 7.1. (UPE That Is a Flow-Through Entity)

734. Prominent features of Article 7.1 are provided in Box 4.34.

Box 4.34 Prominent Features of Article 7.1

- Provides reduction to the GloBE income of the UPE corresponding to the share of its income that is subject to tax at or above the minimum rate in the hands of its owners (and thereby reducing, perhaps eliminating, any exposure to Top-up Tax).
- Article 7.1.1 provides that the UPE will reduce its GloBE Income by the amount of GloBE Income attributable to each Ownership Interest that meets a criterion in paragraphs (a) to (c).

103. Based on OECD's GloBE Model Rules, its Commentary and Illustrative Examples.
104. A regime that achieves a single level of taxation on business income.

  - The remainder of the income, if any, will be included in the computation of the UPE's GloBE Income or Loss and included in the computation of the Net GloBE Income for the jurisdiction under Article 5.1.2.
  - Article 7.1.1 applies with respect to each Ownership Interest.
- Paragraph (a) of Article 7.1.1 sets out two tests that must be met with respect to each Ownership Interest for the reduction in GloBE Income for a Fiscal Year of a Flow-through Entity that is the UPE of an MNE Group:
  - A taxable period test,
  - A minimum tax test.
- Paragraph (b) of Article 7.1.1 provides a safe harbour to a Flow-through UPE with owners that are natural persons that hold small Ownership Interests in the UPE.
- Paragraph (c) of Article 7.1.1 applies to a Flow-through UPE where the holder of the Ownership Interest in the UPE is a Governmental Entity, International Organisation, a Non-profit Organisation, or a Pension Fund.
- Article 7.1.2 provides a corollary to Article 7.1.1 for losses.
  - Provides that the GloBE Losses incurred by a UPE that is a Flow-through Entity must also be reduced by the amount attributable to each Ownership Interest, except to the extent that the holders of Ownership Interests are not allowed to use the loss in computing their separate taxable income.
  - Without this rule, losses that are passed through to the holders of Ownership Interests would also be available for use in the jurisdictional ETR calculation to shield GloBE income of other CEs located in the UPE's Jurisdiction.
  - Applies with respect to each Ownership Interest, similar to Article 7.1.1.
- Article 7.1.3 requires the UPE to reduce its Covered Taxes, if any, in proportion to the income reduction under Article 7.1.1.
- Article 7.1.4 extends the treatment of Article 7.1.1 to 7.1.3 to certain PEs through which the UPE and certain other Flow-through Entities of the MNE Group conduct their business.
  - Provides that to the extent that the conditions of Article 7.1.1 are met by a holder of an Ownership Interest in the UPE with respect to the income of the PE, the PE's GloBE Income is reduced pursuant to Article 7.1.4.
  - Paragraph (a) of Article 7.1.4 covers the case where the business of the flow-through UPE is wholly or partly carried out through a PE.
  - Paragraph (b) of Article 7.1.4 allows Article 7.1.4 to also apply to PEs held by the UPE through a chain of Tax Transparent Entities.

735. The principle underlying the rules in Article 7.1 is that to the extent that the tax neutrality regime imposes tax on the UPE's owners (e.g., partners, beneficiaries or shareholders) at or above the Minimum Rate on the UPE's income contemporaneously or within a short time, the UPE's exposure to Top-up Tax will likewise be reduced. This is achieved by a reduction to the GloBE income of the UPE corresponding to the share of its income that is subject to tax at or above the minimum rate in the hands of its owners (and thereby reducing, perhaps eliminating, any exposure to Top-up Tax).

Background

736. A jurisdiction's tax system may contain rules designed to achieve a single level of taxation on business income by adopting either criterion mentioned below:

- some jurisdictions may achieve a single level of taxation on business income by adjusting the treatment of income in the hands of the owner (e.g., by exempting distributions received by shareholders),
- others may provide for a similar result by adjusting the treatment of income in the hands of the business entity (e.g., by treating certain entities or arrangements as transparent for tax purposes or permitting that entity or arrangement to deduct distributions to its investors from its taxable income).
  - These regimes are premised on the idea that the tax on the entity's income is effectively collected at the level of the owner, either by taxing that owner directly on its allocable share of the entity's income (in the case of a Tax Transparent Entity) or by taxing the owners on a Deductible Dividend paid by the entity.
  - These approaches to single-level taxation could result in unintended outcomes under the GloBE Rules when they apply to the UPE. This is because the ETR of the UPE itself will be nil (or very low), potentially resulting in a significant Top-up Tax charge even though the burden of taxation has not been avoided but rather is borne by the Entity's owners.
  - Such an outcome, mentioned *supra*, would result from an application of the relevant rules in Chapters 3 and 4. While the income allocation rules for a Tax Transparent Entity under Article 3.5.1(a) and (b) ordinarily match the income with the Covered Taxes (i.e., both in the hands of the owners or PEs), this does not work where the Tax Transparent Entity is the UPE, because its owners are not Group Entities. Accordingly, Article. 3.5.1(c) allocates the income of a Tax Transparent Entity that is the UPE to the Entity itself. Furthermore, Article 4.3, which allocates Covered Taxes paid by one CE in connection with income earned by another CE, does not apply in the case of taxes paid by persons that are not Group Entities. Allocating the taxes accrued by the owners that are outside the MNE Group would be both against the policy intention of the GloBE Rules (which is to ensure that a minimum tax is paid by MNE Groups) and administratively difficult (to obtain the necessary information from, and extract the relevant portion of taxes paid by, unrelated or uncontrolled owners of the UPE).
  - The rules in Article 7.1 resolve this issue of unintended multiple taxation for certain situations.

4.7.1.1 Article 7.1.1.

737. The GloBE Income for a Fiscal Year of a Flow-through Entity that is the UPE of an MNE Group shall be reduced by the amount of GloBE Income attributable to each Ownership Interest if:

(a) the holder of the Ownership Interest is subject to tax on such income for a taxable period that ends within twelve months of the end of the MNE Group's Fiscal Year and:
  (i) the holder of the Ownership Interest is subject to tax on the full amount of such income at a nominal rate that equals or exceeds the Minimum Rate; or
  (ii) it can be reasonably expected that the aggregate amount of Adjusted Covered Taxes of the UPE and Taxes of the holder of the Ownership Interest on such income equals or exceeds the amount that results from multiplying the full amount of such income by the Minimum Rate; or
(b) the holder is a natural person that:
  (i) is a tax resident in the UPE Jurisdiction; and
  (ii) holds Ownership Interests that, in the aggregate, are a right to 5% or less of the profits and assets of the UPE; or
(c) the holder is a Governmental Entity, an International Organisation, a Non-profit Organisation, or a Pension Fund that
  (i) is resident in the UPE Jurisdiction; and
  (ii) holds Ownership Interests that, in the aggregate, are a right to 5% or less of the profits and assets of the UPE.

738. *Objective of the Article:* The rules of Article 7.1.1 apply with respect to each Ownership Interest. The UPE will reduce its GloBE Income by the amount of GloBE Income attributable to each Ownership Interest that meets a criterion in paragraphs (a) to (c). The remainder of the income, if any, will be included in the computation of the UPE's GloBE Income or Loss and included in the computation of the Net GloBE Income for the jurisdiction under Article 5.1.2. The three situations described in paragraphs (a) to (c) are explained in Figure 4.38.

Figure 4.38 Paragraphs (a) to (c) of Article 7.1.1

Paragraph (a) of Article 7.1.1

Sets out two tests that must be met with respect to each Ownership Interest for the reduction in GloBE Income for a Fiscal Year of a Flow-through Entity that is the Ultimate Parent Entity of an MNE Group:

A taxable period test → Included at the beginning of paragraph (a)

Requirements:

- The holder is subject to current taxation on such income.
- The holder must be subject to tax on its share of the UPE's GloBE Income for a taxable period that ends within 12 months of the end of the MNE Group's Fiscal Year.
- The holder is not required to pay its tax liability within 12 months of the end of the MNE Group's Fiscal Year to meet this test. It is sufficient that the holder's share of the UPE's GloBE Income is included in its taxable income for a taxable year that ends within 12 months of the MNE Group's Fiscal Year end.
- A holder is subject to tax on its share of the UPE's GloBE Income if that income is includible in the holder's taxable income under the laws of the jurisdiction in which the holder is tax resident or includible in taxable income of a PE of the holder.

A minimum tax test → Conditions set in subparagraphs (i) or (ii) are met

Requirements:

- The conditions in subparagraphs (i) to (ii) are alternatives; thus, the conditions in only one of the subparagraphs need to be satisfied.
- Subparagraph (i) is met if the holder is subject to tax on the full amount of its share of the GloBE Income (that is, for example, without the benefit of an exemption) and subject to tax at a nominal rate that equals or exceeds the Minimum Rate (meaning no ETR calculation is required in respect of the holder).
- Temporary difference (i.e. a timing difference) between the time an item of income or expense is included in the computation of GloBE Income or Loss and the UPE's taxable income will not cause a holder to fail the requirement that it be subject to tax on the full amount of such income (as well as meeting the 12 month requirement in paragraph (a)). For example, if the UPE is allowed to use an accelerated depreciation method to compute the taxable income allocable to its holders, the difference in the timing of the income will not cause the holders to be considered subject to tax on less than the full amount of the UPE's GloBE Income. A holder is considered subject to tax on the full amount of its GloBE Income even if its taxable income includes expenses or losses related to other investments or businesses or profit-seeking activities.
- For purposes of subparagraph (i), the nominal rate is the statutory rate applicable to the holder on its share of the UPE's income. If the holder is subject to graduated rates, the nominal rate is the highest rate applicable to the holder determined as if its share of the UPE's GloBE income were its total taxable income.
- The conditions in subparagraph (i) are met with respect to holders that are not residents of the UPE Jurisdiction if the UPE Jurisdiction subjects them to tax at or above the Minimum Rate either because they are treated as having a PE in the UPE Jurisdiction or because the income is sourced in the UPE's jurisdiction and subject to a withholding or similar source-based tax. In the event that the non-resident holders are not subject to tax in the UPE's jurisdiction at a nominal rate that equals or exceeds the Minimum Rate, additional information will be required in order for the UPE to demonstrate that those holders are subject to tax on their share of the income within 12 months at a nominal rate that equals or exceeds the Minimum Rate.
- The alternative conditions under subparagraph (ii) are met if it can be reasonably expected that the aggregate amount of Covered Taxes (paid by the UPE and other Entities that are part of the Tax Transparent Structure) and taxes paid by the holder on the income attributable to the Ownership Interest equals or exceeds the amount that results from multiplying the full amount of such income by the Minimum Rate. Whether the taxes paid can be reasonably expected to equal or exceed the tax at the Minimum Rate is determined based on all the facts and circumstances. The MNE Group bears the burden of proving that the expectations are reasonable.
- Subparagraph (ii) does not require an ETR computation.
- Its conditions are met if the UPE demonstrates that it is reasonable to expect that its income will be subject to an amount of tax that equals or exceeds the tax liability on that income at the Minimum Rate.
- Subparagraph (ii) takes into account the net amount of taxes paid by the UPE and other Entities that are part of the Tax Transparent Structure and by the holder of the UPE's Ownership Interest on its share of the UPE's income. It requires that the taxes paid by the UPE and other Entities that are part of the Tax Transparent Structure are Covered Taxes and that the taxes paid by the holders are taxes on the income of the UPE. For instance, the UPE could be required to pay a local Covered Tax notwithstanding that its income is allocated to its holders under federal law. In this case, subparagraph (ii) is met if it is expected that the net amount of tax paid by the UPE itself and the holder equals or exceeds the minimum tax on that income.

Paragraph (b) of Article 7.1.1

Provides a safe harbour to a Flow-through UPE with owners that are natural persons that hold small Ownership Interests in the UPE:

- This safe harbour only applies where the two conditions in subparagraphs (i) and (ii) are met.

Tax residence test

Included in subparagraph (i)

Requirements:

- Subparagraph (i) requires the natural person to be a tax resident of the UPE Jurisdiction.
- A natural person is tax resident in a jurisdiction only if the person is subject to individual income tax in such jurisdiction. Consequently, a natural person cannot be tax resident in a jurisdiction that does not impose an individual income tax.
- Therefore, there is an expectation that the UPE's income is subject to tax in the hands of the natural person because they are both located in the same jurisdiction and therefore subject to the same tax laws regarding fiscal transparency.
- It is further reasonable to expect that the jurisdiction is subjecting natural persons to tax at a rate that equals or exceeds the Minimum Rate on their income derived from Flow-through Entities.
- Therefore, it is assumed that such persons are going to be subject to tax on the full amount of income attributable to their Ownership Interests at a rate that equals or exceeds the Minimum Rate.
- The UPE may use reasonable means of determining whether its owners are tax resident in the jurisdiction. For example, a UPE in a jurisdiction that imposes a withholding tax on the profits or distributions from the UPE with respect to foreign owners of the UPE may rely on an owner's representation as to whether it is exempt from a withholding tax or eligible for a lower withholding tax rate based on a Tax Treaty.

Ownership interest test

Included in subparagraph (ii)

Requirements:

- Subparagraph (ii) limits the safe harbour to natural persons that each hold Ownership Interests that in aggregate carry rights to 5% or less of the profits and 5% or less of the assets of the UPE.
- For example, this means that an Ownership Interest giving rights to 51% of profits would fall outside the safe harbour in 7.1.1(b), despite giving rights to less than 5% of the assets.
- The extent of each person's Ownership Interests is determined as of the end of the Fiscal Year.
- This subparagraph only applies where the Ownership Interests of the UPE are held directly by natural persons.
- Determining the tax position of minority owners may be burdensome for the UPE.
- Because natural persons are typically not eligible for preferential tax rates on income derived through a Tax Transparent Entity, it is reasonable not to require the UPE to determine the tax position of a natural person that holds Ownership Interests that in aggregate carry rights to 5% or less of the profits and assets of the UPE.
- This rule means that a UPE could be required to determine the tax position of no more than 19 natural persons, and such persons would have relatively significant stakes in the UPE.

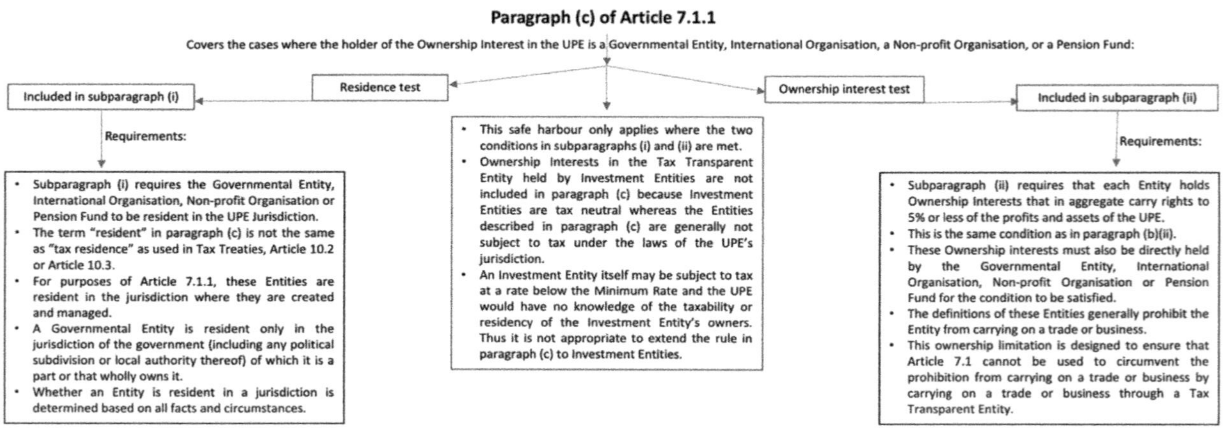
Paragraph (c) of Article 7.1.1
Covers the cases where the holder of the Ownership Interest in the UPE is a Governmental Entity, International Organisation, a Non-profit Organisation, or a Pension Fund:
Residence test
Ownership interest test
Included in subparagraph (i)
Requirements:
• Subparagraph (i) requires the Governmental Entity, International Organisation, Non-profit Organisation or Pension Fund to be resident in the UPE Jurisdiction.
• The term "resident" in paragraph (c) is not the same as "tax residence" as used in Tax Treaties, Article 10.2 or Article 10.3.
• For purposes of Article 7.1.1, these Entities are resident in the jurisdiction where they are created and managed.
• A Governmental Entity is resident only in the jurisdiction of the government (including any political subdivision or local authority thereof) of which it is a part or that wholly owns it.
• Whether an Entity is resident in a jurisdiction is determined based on all facts and circumstances.
• This safe harbour only applies where the two conditions in subparagraphs (i) and (ii) are met.
• Ownership Interests in the Tax Transparent Entity held by Investment Entities are not included in paragraph (c) because Investment Entities are tax neutral whereas the Entities described in paragraph (c) are generally not subject to tax under the laws of the UPE's jurisdiction.
• An Investment Entity itself may be subject to tax at a rate below the Minimum Rate and the UPE would have no knowledge of the taxability or residency of the Investment Entity's owners. Thus it is not appropriate to extend the rule in paragraph (c) to Investment Entities.
Included in subparagraph (ii)
Requirements:
• Subparagraph (ii) requires that each Entity holds Ownership Interests that in aggregate carry rights to 5% or less of the profits and assets of the UPE.
• This is the same condition as in paragraph (b)(ii).
• These Ownership interests must also be directly held by the Governmental Entity, International Organisation, Non-profit Organisation or Pension Fund for the condition to be satisfied.
• The definitions of these Entities generally prohibit the Entity from carrying on a trade or business.
• This ownership limitation is designed to ensure that Article 7.1 cannot be used to circumvent the prohibition from carrying on a trade or business by carrying on a trade or business through a Tax Transparent Entity.

739. Illustration # 64: The illustration, through a flow-chart, explains application of Article 7.1.1(a)(i) when UPE is a Flow-through Entity.

Illustration explaining application of Article 7.1.1(a)(i) when Ultimate Parent Entity is a Flow-through Entity

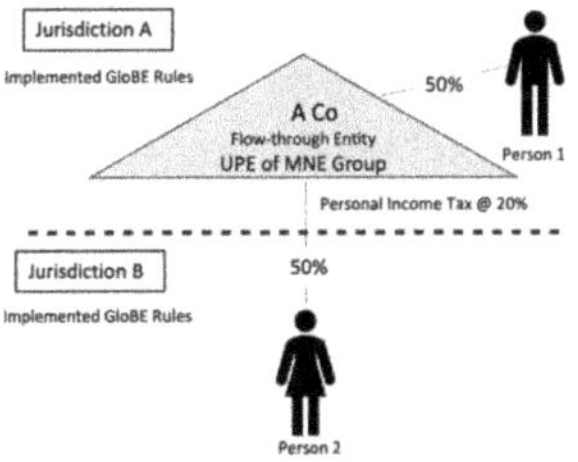

Assumptions Step 1

- A Co is a Flow-through Entity that is the UPE of an MNE Group. A Co is located in Country A and has a Fiscal Year that ends on 31 January.
- Person 1 is an individual tax resident in Country A while Person 2 is an individual tax resident in Country B. Person 1 and Person 2 each hold a 50% of the Ownership Interests in A Co.
- For the Fiscal Year ended 31 January Year 1, A Co reports EUR 140,000 of income both for domestic income tax and GloBE purposes.
- Under the tax laws of Country A, EUR 70,000 of A Co's income is included in the taxable income of Person 1 for the calendar year ended 31 December Year 1. The computation of the taxable income of Person 1 also includes a loss of EUR 50,000 from another business conducted in Country A. The taxable income of Person 1 under the tax laws of Country A is EUR 20,000 (= 70,000 – 50,000) and Person 1 is subject to tax in Country A at a rate of 20% on such taxable income.
- Under the tax laws of Country A, Person 2 is treated as having a PE in Country A and the taxable income of that PE includes EUR 70,000 of A Co's taxable income. Person 2 is subject to tax in Country A at a rate of 20% on the income of its PE for the calendar year ended 31 December Year 1.

Application of Article 7.1.1(a)(i) Step 2

- A Flow-Through Entity that is the UPE reduces its GloBE Income pursuant to Article 7.1.1(a)(i) by the amount of GloBE Income attributable to an Ownership Interest if (1) the holder is subject to tax on that income for a taxable period that ends within 12 months of the end of the MNE Group's Fiscal Year and (2) the holder of the Ownership Interest is subject to tax on the full amount of such income at a nominal rate that equals or exceeds the Minimum Rate.
- Person 1 is subject to tax on his/her share of A Co's GloBE Income for a taxable period that ends on 31 December Year 1, which is within 12 months of the end of A Co's Fiscal Year ended on 31 January Year 1, notwithstanding that payment of Person 1's tax liability is not due within 12 months of the end of A Co's Fiscal Year. Further, Person 1 is subject to tax on his/her share of A Co's GloBE income at a nominal rate that equals or exceeds the Minimum Rate.
- Person 1 is subject to tax on the full amount of such income notwithstanding that he/she was allowed to offset his/her share of A Co's GloBE Income with a loss from another business in computing his/her Country A taxable income. Accordingly, A Co reduces its GloBE Income for the Fiscal Year ended 31 January Year 1 pursuant to Article 7.1.1(a)(i) by EUR 70,000 in respect of the Ownership Interests held by Person 1. A Co will reduce its Covered Taxes proportionately under Article 7.1.3.
- Person 2 is subject to tax on his/her share of A Co's GloBE Income for a taxable period that ends within 12 months of the end of A Co's Fiscal Year. Person 2 is also subject to tax on the full amount of such income at a nominal rate that equals or exceeds the Minimum Rate. Accordingly, A Co reduces its GloBE Income for the Fiscal Year ended 31 January Year 1 pursuant to Article 7.1.1(a)(i) by EUR 70,000 in respect of the Ownership Interests held by Person 2.

740. Illustration # 65: The illustration, through a flow-chart, explains application of Article 7.1.1(a)(ii) when UPE is a Flow-through Entity.

Illustration explaining application of Article 7.1.1(a)(ii) when Ultimate Parent Entity is a Flow-through Entity

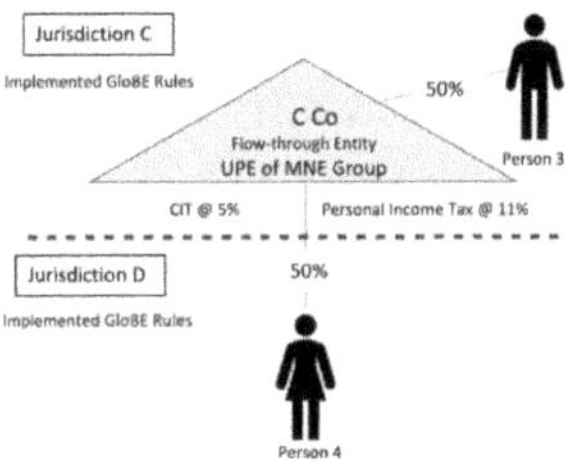

Assumptions Step 1

- C Co is a Flow-through Entity and a Tax Transparent Entity that is the UPE of an MNE Group.
- C Co is located in Country C where a 5% CIT rate applies. C Co's taxable income and GloBE Income for the Fiscal Year ended on 31 December Year 1 is EUR 200,000. The Adjusted Covered Taxes of C Co on its income are EUR 10,000 (= 5%* EUR 200,000) and such taxes meet the definition of Covered Taxes.
- Person 3 is an individual tax resident in Country C that holds a 50% Ownership Interest in C Co.
- Person 3's share of C Co's income for Year 1 is EUR 95,000 (= 50% * [EUR 200,000 – 10,000]).
- Person 3 is subject to a nominal 11% personal income tax rate on a calendar year basis.
- Person 3's share of C Co's income for the Fiscal Year ended on 31 December Year 1 is included in Person 3's Country C taxable income for the calendar year that ended 31 December Year 1.
- Person 3 is not entitled to reduce its Country C tax imposed on its share of C Co's income as a result of Country C taxes imposed on such income.
- This illustration is restricted to C Co and Person 3.

Application of Article 7.1.1(a)(ii) Step 2

- C Co cannot reduce its GloBE Income pursuant to subparagraph (i) of Article 7.1.1(a) because the personal income tax rate applicable to Person 3 is 11%, which is a nominal rate below the Minimum Rate.
- However, a Flow-Through Entity that is the UPE reduces its GloBE Income pursuant to subparagraph (ii) of Article 7.1.1(a) by the amount of GloBE Income attributable to an Ownership Interest if (1) the holder is subject to tax on that income for a taxable period that ends within 12 months of the end of the MNE Group's Fiscal Year and (2) it can reasonably be expected that the aggregate amount of Adjusted Covered Taxes of the UPE and Taxes of the holder of the Ownership Interest on such income equals or exceeds the amount that results from multiplying the full amount of such income by the Minimum Rate (as per Article 7.1.1 (a)(ii)).
- Person 3 is reasonably expected to pay EUR 10,450 of Taxes (= 11% * EUR 95,000 after-tax income of C Co) in Country C. The sum of the Taxes paid by Person 3 and C Co on the EUR 100,000 of GloBE income attributable to Person 3 is EUR 15,450 (= EUR 10,450 paid by Person 3 + EUR 5,000 paid by C Co), which exceeds the amount (EUR 15,000) that results from multiplying the full amount of such income by the Minimum Rate (EUR 100,000 * 15%). C Co will therefore reduce its EUR 200,000 GloBE Income in Year 1 by the EUR 100,000 GloBE Income attributable to Person 3's Ownership Interest. C Co will reduce its Covered Taxes proportionally under Article 7.1.3.
- C Co would not have been entitled to reduce its GloBE Income if Person 3 was granted a tax credit in Country C equal to the amount of Taxes paid by C Co. In that case, it would not be reasonable to expect the aggregate amount of Taxes (EUR 11,000) paid by Person 3 (EUR 6,000) and C Co (EUR 5,000) to equal or exceed the amount that results from multiplying the full amount of GloBE Income by the Minimum Rate (EUR 100,000 * 15% = EUR 15,000).

4.7.1.2 *Article 7.1.2.*

741. In computing its GloBE Loss for a Fiscal Year, a Flow-through Entity that is the UPE of an MNE Group shall reduce its GloBE Loss for such Fiscal Year by the amount of GloBE Loss attributable to each Ownership Interest, except to the extent that the holders of Ownership Interests are not allowed to use the loss in computing their separate taxable income.

742. *Background of the Article:* Article 7.1.2 provides a corollary to Article 7.1.1 for losses. Losses incurred by a Flow-through Entity typically flow through to the holders and are allowed as a deduction in computing the holder's taxable income or loss, and may even contribute to a loss carry-back or carry-forward that reduces the holder's share of prior or future income from the Flow-through Entity or other income. In some jurisdictions, however, losses of a Flow-through Entity are retained by the Entity and carried forward in the determination of the Entity's future taxable income.

743. *Objective of the Article:* Article 7.1.2 provides that the GloBE Losses incurred by a UPE that is a Flow-through Entity must also be reduced by the amount attributable to each Ownership Interest, except to the extent that the holders of Ownership Interests are not allowed to use the loss in computing their separate taxable income. This means that the GloBE Loss is not reduced to zero only if the loss does not flow through, in its entirety, to the holders of Ownership Interests under the tax laws applicable to the Entity and to the holders so as to allow the holders to use their share of such loss in computing their separate taxable income. To the extent that the GloBE Loss is not reduced to zero, the remaining GloBE Loss stays with the Flow-through UPE. Without this rule, losses that are passed through to the holders of Ownership Interests would also be available for use in the jurisdictional ETR calculation to shield GloBE income of other CEs located in the UPE's Jurisdiction.

744. *Filing Constituent Entity may make a GloBE Loss Election*: To the extent that a GloBE loss of a Flow-through UPE is not reduced to zero pursuant to Article 7.1.2 (and thus stays with the Flow-through UPE), a Filing Constituent Entity may make a GloBE Loss Election that is limited to the UPE under Article 4.5.6, and carry forward the balance as a GloBE Loss Deferred Tax Asset to subsequent Fiscal Years. The GloBE Loss Deferred Tax Asset is computed based on the amount of the GloBE Loss remaining after application of Article 7.1.2 and may be included in the UPE's Adjusted Covered Taxes in a subsequent year for purposes of applying Article 7.1.1(a)(ii).

745. *The Article applies with respect to each Ownership Interest*: Article 7.1.2 applies with respect to each Ownership Interest, similar to Article 7.1.1. Therefore, the MNE Group is required to demonstrate that each of its holders is not able to deduct losses attributed to their Ownership Interest in the computation of their separate taxable income in order to include their share of the loss in the GloBE Loss Deferred Tax Asset computed under Article 4.5.6.

4.7.1.3 Article 7.1.3.

746. A Flow-through Entity that reduces its GloBE Income pursuant to Article 7.1.1 shall reduce its Covered Taxes proportionally.

747. *Objective of the Article:* Article 7.1.3 requires the UPE to reduce its Covered Taxes, if any, in proportion to the income reduction under Article 7.1.1. Thus, if the UPE reduces its GloBE Income by 80% pursuant to Article 7.1.1, the UPE must also reduce its Covered Taxes by 80%. In many cases, by virtue of the tax transparency regime, the

UPE may not have any Covered Taxes. However, it is possible that Covered Taxes other than the national CIT are imposed on Flow-through Entities, such as those imposed by a local, sub-national government. Although the Covered Taxes excluded by Article 7.1.3 are not taken into account in the ETR computation for the UPE Jurisdiction, they are taken into account under Article 7.1.1(a)(ii) in determining whether the taxes on the holder's share of the UPE's GloBE Income equal or exceed the tax at the Minimum Rate on that income. Article 7.1.1 reduces the Flow-through Entity's GloBE Income by all of the GloBE Income (determined after adding back Covered Taxes) allocable to an Ownership Interest. Accordingly, no further adjustment is required to reduce the Entity's GloBE Income by the related Covered Taxes as required under Article 7.2.2.

4.7.1.4 Article 7.1.4.

748. Articles 7.1.1 through 7.1.3 shall apply to a Permanent Establishment:

(a) through which a Flow-Through Entity that is the UPE of an MNE Group wholly or partly carries out its business; or
(b) through which the business of a Tax Transparent Entity is wholly or partly carried out if the UPE's Ownership Interest in that Tax Transparent Entity is held directly or through a Tax Transparent Structure.

749. *Objective of the Article:* Article 7.1.4 extends the treatment of Article 7.1.1 to 7.1.3 to certain PEs through which the UPE and certain other Flow-through Entities of the MNE Group conduct their business. The situations described in paragraphs (a) and (b) of the article are explained in Figure 4.39.

Figure 4.39 Paragraphs (a) and (b) of Article 7.1.4

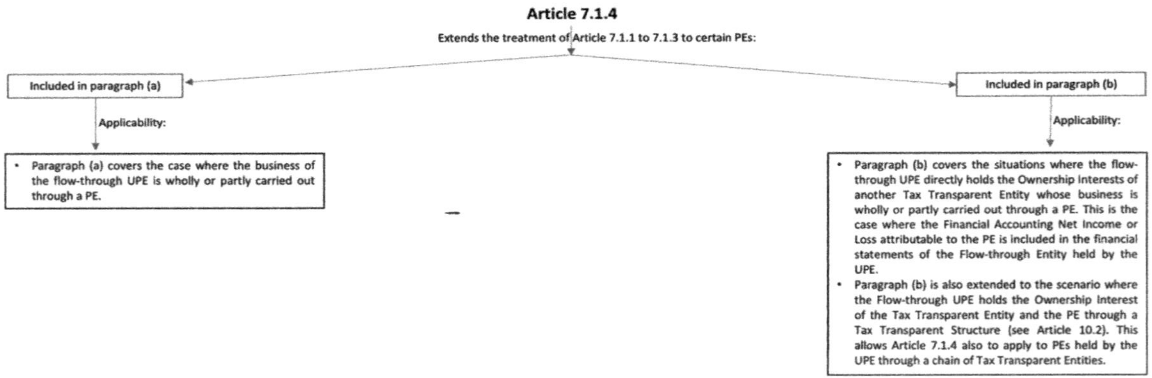

750. In the above situations, the Financial Accounting Net Income or Loss attributable to the PE is included in the financial statements of the UPE, but liability for the tax on that income may be borne by the UPE or by the holders of the UPE. Where the tax on the income of the PE is borne by the holders, the PE's GloBE Income is reduced to the extent the conditions of Article 7.1.1(a) or (b) are met. In such cases, Article 7.1.1(b) takes into account any tax paid or payable in the jurisdiction where the PE is located regardless of whether that tax is paid or payable by a CE or by the holders of the UPE.

751. *PE is treated separately from the UPE under Article 7.1.4*: The test in Article 7.1.1 applicable to the GloBE Income of the PE is separate from the test applicable to the GloBE Income that has been allocated to the UPE. This means that the GloBE Income or Loss of the PE is not included in the GloBE Income of the UPE for purposes of applying 7.1.1 to the UPE. The PE is treated separately from the UPE under Article 7.1.4 because it is a separate Constituent Entity, and its income does not flow through to the UPE under Chapter 3, as does the income of a Tax Transparent Entity. However, to the extent that the conditions of Article 7.1.1 are met by a holder of an Ownership Interest in the UPE with respect to the income of the PE, the PE's GloBE Income is reduced pursuant to Article 7.1.4.

752. Illustration # 66: The illustration, through a flow-chart, explains application of Article 7.1.4 when UPE is a Flow-through Entity which carries out business operations through a PE also.

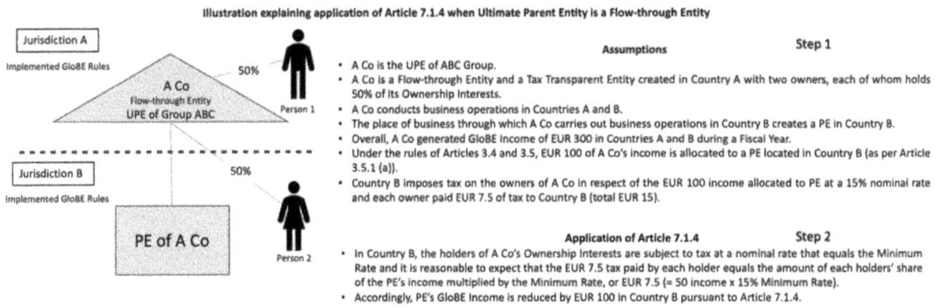

4.7.2 Article 7.2. (UPE Subject to Deductible Dividend Regime)

753. Prominent features of Article 7.2 are provided in Box 4.35.

Box 4.35 Prominent Features of Article 7.2

- Contains a set of rules for UPEs that are subject to a Deductible Dividend Regime.
  - These rules allow a deduction in the computation of the GloBE Income or Loss for Deductible Dividends.
  - Although a Deductible Dividend Regime may apply to both Entities that qualify as Investment Entities under the GloBE Rules and other similar

purpose Entities that do not meet the Investment Entity definition, the rules in Article 7.2 are needed only for those Entities that do not meet the Investment Entity definition because an Investment Entity that is the UPE is an Excluded Entity.
    - Unlike the treatment of losses incurred by a Tax Transparent Entity under local tax rules, the losses of an Entity subject to a Deductible Dividend Regime do not flow through to the owners.
- Article 7.2.1 (similar to Article 7.1.1) allows for a reduction of the UPE's GloBE Income (but not below zero) by the amount of Deductible Dividends if the UPE is subject to a Deductible Distribution Regime.
- Paragraph (a) of Article 7.2.1 requires that the Deductible Dividends are subject to tax in the hands of the recipient within twelve months of the end of the UPE's Fiscal Year.
    - Under the primary test provided under subparagraph (i) of paragraph (a) of Article 7.2.1, the UPE's GloBE Income is reduced by Deductible Dividends to recipients that are subject to a nominal tax rate that equals or exceeds the Minimum Rate.
    - The conditions under subparagraph (ii) of paragraph (a) of Article 7.2.1 are met if it can be reasonably expected that the aggregate amount of Covered Taxes (paid by the UPE) and taxes paid by the owner on the income attributable to its Ownership Interest equals or exceeds the amount that results from multiplying the full amount of such income by the Minimum Rate.
    - Subparagraph (iii) of Paragraph (a) of Article 7.2.1 contains a special rule for patronage dividends distributed to natural persons that are members of supply Cooperatives.
- Paragraph (b) of Article 7.2.1 provides a safe harbour to a Flow-through UPE where dividend recipients are natural persons that hold small Ownership Interests in the UPE.
- Paragraph (c) of Article 7.2.1 covers the cases where the dividend recipient is a Governmental Entity, International Organisation, a Non-profit Organisation, or a Pension Fund (that is not a Pension Services Entity).
- Article 7.2.2 is similar to Article 7.1.3 and generally requires a reduction of the UPE's Covered Taxes in proportion to the income distributed as a Deductible Dividend.
    - Requires a reduction of the UPE's GloBE Income by the amount of the reduction in the Covered Taxes.
- Article 7.2.3 is similar to Article 7.1.4 and extends the rules applicable to the UPE to other CEs located in the UPE Jurisdiction that are subject to the Deductible Dividend Regime and held through an ownership chain made up exclusively of such Entities.
- Article 7.2.4 provides rules to clarify the application of Article 7.2.1 with respect to certain patronage dividends distributed by supply Cooperatives.
    - The rule applies to dividend recipients other than natural persons because distributions from supply Cooperatives to natural persons are

always treated as a reduction to the UPE's GloBE Income under Article 7.2.1(a)(iii).

754. *Background:* Article 7.2 contains a set of rules for UPEs that are subject to a Deductible Dividend Regime. These rules allow a deduction in the computation of the GloBE Income or Loss for Deductible Dividends. Deductible Dividend Regimes typically apply to investment companies as well as Cooperatives. Although a Deductible Dividend Regime may apply to both Entities that qualify as Investment Entities under the GloBE Rules and other similar purpose Entities that do not meet the Investment Entity definition, the rules in Article 7.2 are needed only for those Entities that do not meet the Investment Entity definition because an Investment Entity that is the UPE is an Excluded Entity. A Deductible Dividend Regime is a tax regime designed to yield a single level of taxation on the owners of an Entity through the allowance of a deduction from the income of the Entity for distributions of profits to the owners. The owners are subject to tax on the dividends, and the Entity is subject to tax on earnings that are not distributed. Patronage dividends of a Cooperative are treated as distributions to owners under the definition of Deductible Dividend Regime in Article 10.1, and thus tax regimes intended to yield a single level of taxation for Cooperatives and their patrons will typically qualify as Deductible Dividend Regimes. Because the definition of Deductible Dividend Regime includes Cooperatives that are subject to an exemption regime, application of Article 7.2 to Cooperatives is not dependent upon the allowance of a deduction from taxable income at the Cooperative level; Article 7.2 equally applies in the case of a Cooperative that is tax exempt under the laws of the jurisdiction in which it is located.

755. *Substantive rules applicable to UPEs subject to Deductible Dividend Regimes vis-à-vis rules for UPEs that are Tax Transparent Entities:* The substantive rules applicable to UPEs that are subject to Deductible Dividend Regimes are similar to the rules for UPEs that are Tax Transparent Entities. An important difference, however, is the treatment of losses incurred by the CE. Unlike the treatment of losses incurred by a Tax Transparent Entity under local tax rules, the losses of an Entity subject to a Deductible Dividend Regime do not flow through to the owners. Accordingly, the GloBE Rules applicable to Deductible Dividend Regimes do not contain special rules for a GloBE Loss determined for a CE. Such losses are taken into account in the computation of the Net GloBE Income for the jurisdiction in which the Entity is located.

4.7.2.1 Article 7.2.1.

756. For purposes of computing its GloBE Income or Loss for a Fiscal year, a UPE that is subject to a Deductible Dividend Regime shall reduce (but not below zero) its GloBE Income for such Fiscal Year by the amount that is distributed as a Deductible Dividend within twelve months of the end of the Fiscal Year if:

(a) the dividend is subject to tax in the hands of the dividend recipient for a taxable period that ends within twelve months of the end of the MNE Group's Fiscal Year, and:
   (i) the dividend recipient is subject to tax on such dividend at a nominal rate that equals or exceeds the Minimum Rate;
   (ii) it can be reasonably expected that the aggregate amount of Adjusted Covered Taxes of the UPE and Taxes paid by the dividend recipient on the dividend income equals or exceeds the amount that results from multiplying the full amount of such income by the Minimum Rate; or
   (iii) the dividend recipient is a natural person, and the dividend is a patronage dividend from a supply Cooperative; or
(b) the dividend recipient is a natural person that:
   (i) is a tax resident in the UPE Jurisdiction; and
   (ii) holds Ownership Interests that, in the aggregate, are a right to 5% or less of the profits and assets of the UPE.
(c) the dividend recipient is resident in the UPE Jurisdiction and is:
   (i) a Governmental Entity,
   (ii) an International Organisation,
   (iii) a Non-profit Organisation or
   (iv) a Pension Fund that is not a Pension Services Entity.

757. The term Cooperative mentioned *supra* is defined in Article 10.1 as below:

> Cooperative means an Entity that collectively markets or acquires goods or services on behalf of its members and that is subject to a tax regime in the jurisdiction in which it is located that is designed to ensure tax neutrality in respect of members' property or services sold through the cooperative and property or services acquired by members through the cooperative.

758. The term Deductible Dividend mentioned *supra* is defined in Article 10.1 as below:

> Deductible Dividend means, with respect to a Constituent Entity that is subject to a Deductible Dividend Regime,
>
> (a) a distribution of profits to the holder of an Ownership Interest that is deductible from taxable income of the Constituent Entity under the laws of the jurisdiction in which it is located; or
> (b) a patronage dividend to a member of a Cooperative.

759. The term Deductible Dividend Regime mentioned *supra* is defined in Article 10.1 as below:

> Deductible Dividend Regime means a tax regime designed to yield a single level of taxation on the owners of an Entity through a deduction from the income of the Entity for distributions of profits to the owners. For this purpose, patronage dividends of a Cooperative are treated as distributions to owners. A Deductible

Dividend Regime also includes a regime applicable to Cooperatives that exempts the Cooperative from taxation.

760. *Objective of the Article:* Similar to Article 7.1.1, Article 7.2.1 allows for a reduction of the UPE's GloBE Income (but not below zero) by the amount of Deductible Dividends if the UPE is subject to a Deductible Distribution Regime. The provision applies if the Deductible Dividends are distributed within twelve months of the end of the UPE's Fiscal Year. The CE must maintain records sufficient to demonstrate the amount of GloBE Income for a Fiscal Year that was distributed within twelve months of the end of the Fiscal Year. Furthermore, it only applies in the cases described in paragraphs (a) to (c), which are explained in Figure 4.40.

Figure 4.40 Paragraphs (a) to (c) of Article 7.2.1

Paragraph (a) of Article 7.2.1

↓

Paragraph (a) requires that the Deductible Dividends are subject to tax in the hands of the recipient within 12 months of the end of the UPE's Fiscal Year.

↓

Conditions set in subparagraphs (i) to (iii) are to be met

Requirements:

- Subparagraph (i) sets out the general test for determining whether the Deductible Dividends reduce the UPE's GloBE Income for the Fiscal Year.
- Under the primary test, the UPE's GloBE Income is reduced by Deductible Dividends to recipients that are subject to a nominal tax rate that equals or exceeds the Minimum Rate.

- Subparagraph (ii) sets out an alternative, independent test.
- The conditions under subparagraph (ii) are met if it can be reasonably expected that the aggregate amount of Covered Taxes (paid by the UPE) and taxes paid by the owner on the income attributable to its Ownership Interest equals or exceeds the amount that results from multiplying the full amount of such income by the Minimum Rate.
- Subparagraph (ii) does not require an ETR computation.
- The conditions under this paragraph are met if the UPE demonstrates that it is reasonable to expect that tax paid in respect of its income will equal or exceed the tax liability on that income at the minimum rate.

- Subparagraph (iii) contains a special rule for patronage dividends distributed to natural persons that are members of supply Cooperatives.
- A supply Cooperative is a Cooperative that purchases goods or services and resells them to its members or patrons. Profits earned by the supply Cooperative are distributed to the members, typically in proportion to their purchases from the Cooperative. Most supply Cooperatives are organised for the acquisition of goods for a group of merchants. However, some supply Cooperatives are organised for the benefit of consumers that are natural persons. Unless they are engaged in business as a sole proprietor, natural persons generally are not able to deduct the cost of the goods acquired through a supply Cooperative.
- To ensure that the GloBE Rules accommodate supply Cooperatives with members that are consumers, patronage dividends paid to natural persons from a supply Cooperative are treated in the same manner as distributions that are subject to tax at or above the Minimum Rate.
- This special rule means that such dividends are treated as subject to tax when received irrespective of whether they are in fact taxable receipts of the recipient.

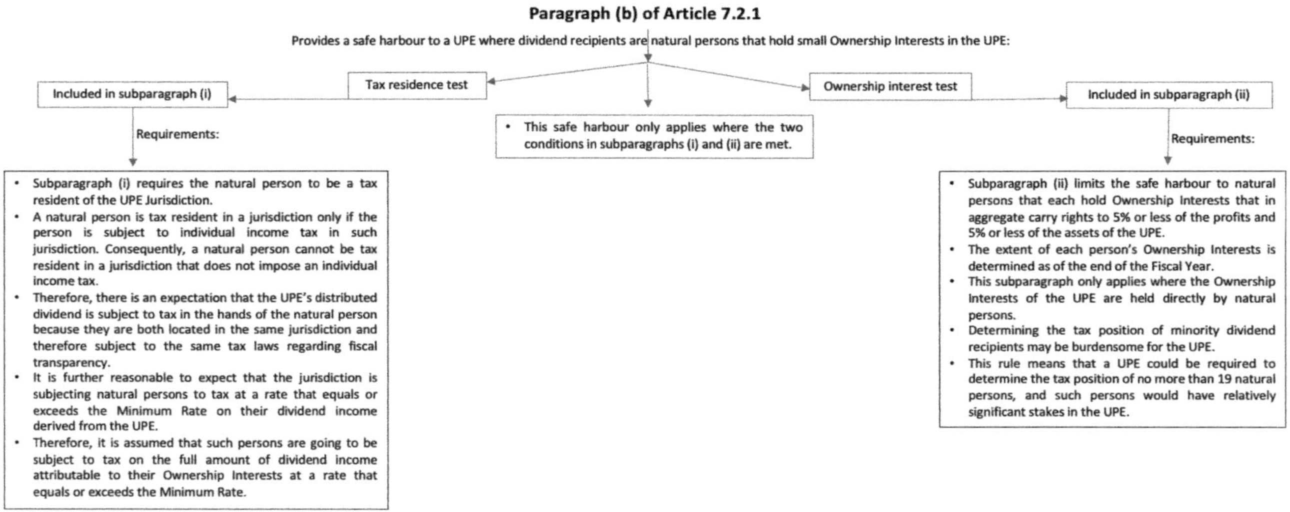
Paragraph (b) of Article 7.2.1
Provides a safe harbour to a UPE where dividend recipients are natural persons that hold small Ownership Interests in the UPE:
Tax residence test
Included in subparagraph (i)
Requirements:
• Subparagraph (i) requires the natural person to be a tax resident of the UPE Jurisdiction.
• A natural person is tax resident in a jurisdiction only if the person is subject to individual income tax in such jurisdiction. Consequently, a natural person cannot be tax resident in a jurisdiction that does not impose an individual income tax.
• Therefore, there is an expectation that the UPE's distributed dividend is subject to tax in the hands of the natural person because they are both located in the same jurisdiction and therefore subject to the same tax laws regarding fiscal transparency.
• It is further reasonable to expect that the jurisdiction is subjecting natural persons to tax at a rate that equals or exceeds the Minimum Rate on their dividend income derived from the UPE.
• Therefore, it is assumed that such persons are going to be subject to tax on the full amount of dividend income attributable to their Ownership Interests at a rate that equals or exceeds the Minimum Rate.
• This safe harbour only applies where the two conditions in subparagraphs (i) and (ii) are met.
Ownership interest test
Included in subparagraph (ii)
Requirements:
• Subparagraph (ii) limits the safe harbour to natural persons that each hold Ownership Interests that in aggregate carry rights to 5% or less of the profits and 5% or less of the assets of the UPE.
• The extent of each person's Ownership Interests is determined as of the end of the Fiscal Year.
• This subparagraph only applies where the Ownership Interests of the UPE are held directly by natural persons.
• Determining the tax position of minority dividend recipients may be burdensome for the UPE.
• This rule means that a UPE could be required to determine the tax position of no more than 19 natural persons, and such persons would have relatively significant stakes in the UPE.

Paragraph (c) of Article 7.2.1

Covers the cases where the dividend recipient is a Governmental Entity, International Organisation, a Non-profit Organisation, or a Pension Fund (that is not a Pension Services Entity):

↓

Residence test

↓ Requirements:

- Requires the Governmental Entity, International Organisation, Non-profit Organisation or Pension Fund (that is not a Pension Services Entity) to be resident in the UPE Jurisdiction.
- The term "resident" in paragraph (c) is not the same as "tax residence" as used in Tax Treaties or Article 10.2.
- For purposes of Article 7.2.1, these Entities are resident in the jurisdiction where they are created and managed.
- A Governmental Entity is resident only in the jurisdiction of the government (including any political subdivision or local authority thereof) of which it is a part or that wholly owns it.
- Whether an Entity is resident in a jurisdiction is determined based on all facts and circumstances.

Note:
Paragraph (c) of Article 7.2.1 differs from paragraph (c) of Article 7.1.1 in that:

- it only applies in the case of a Pension Fund that is not a Pension Services Entity. Thus, Article 7.2.1(c) only applies in relation to a dividend paid to the parent Pension Fund by a UPE in the Pension Fund's jurisdiction. Without this limitation, Article 7.2.1(c) could allow Pension Funds to take advantage of Deductible Dividend Regimes to earn income exempt from the GloBE Rules from UPEs located anywhere in the world by simply establishing a Pension Services Entity in the UPE's jurisdiction.
- by not imposing a limitation on the amount that can be owned by the Entities. As explained in the Commentary to Article 7.1.1(c), that limitation prevents circumvention of the rules that generally prevent these Entities from carrying on a trade or business. Deductible Dividend Regimes typically apply to Entities that engage in investment activities or to Cooperatives, and are more difficult to use, and thus less likely to be used, as a means of circumventing the prohibition on carrying on a trade or business.

4.7.2.2 Article 7.2.2.

761. A UPE that reduces its GloBE Income pursuant to Article 7.2.1 shall reduce its Covered Taxes (other than the Taxes for which the dividend deduction was allowed) proportionally and shall reduce its GloBE Income by the same amount.

762. *Objective of the Article:* Article 7.2.2 is similar to Article 7.1.3. It generally requires a reduction of the UPE's Covered Taxes in proportion to the income distributed as a Deductible Dividend. However, this reduction does not apply to any taxes paid on undistributed GloBE Income pursuant to the Deductible Dividend Regime itself (including taxes that are based on corporate equity or retained earnings). All of the tax paid under the Deductible Dividend Regime (including taxes that are based on corporate equity or retained earnings) in respect of undistributed income is included in the Entity's Covered Taxes and taken into account along with the undistributed income in determining the ETR for the jurisdiction.

763. Article 7.2.2 also requires a reduction of the UPE's GloBE Income by the amount of the reduction in the Covered Taxes. This is necessary because of two features of the GloBE Rules concerning Deductible Dividend Regimes:

- First, GloBE Income is computed under Article 3.2 by adding back Covered Taxes to the Financial Accounting Net Income or Loss.
- Second, Article 7.2.1 reduces the UPE's income by the amount of distributions, which are necessarily comprised of after-tax income.

Thus, if the UPE incurs any taxes related to distributed income, the amount of the distribution will not reduce the UPE's GloBE Income to zero; the GloBE income must also be reduced by the tax that was included in the GloBE Income under Article 3.2. Without this rule, Top-up Tax could arise even where all of the UPE's earnings were distributed as Deductible Dividends. For example, assume that a UPE has 90 of Financial Accounting Net Income, which includes 10 of accrued Covered Tax expense. The UPE distributes the 90 of income for which it receives a deduction under the applicable Deductible Dividend Regime. The UPE's GloBE Income, however, is 100 because the 10 of Covered Taxes is added back to Financial Accounting Net Income or Loss pursuant to Article 3.2.1(a). Accordingly, the 90 distribution will not reduce its 100 GloBE Income to zero. Article 7.2.2 requires a further reduction of 10 to the UPE's GloBE Income to ensure that the MNE Group is not subject to Top-up Tax in respect of the Covered Taxes added back to the determination of GloBE Income or Loss.

4.7.2.3 Article 7.2.3.

764. If the UPE holds an Ownership Interest in another Constituent Entity subject to the Deductible Dividend Regime (directly or through a chain of such Constituent Entities), Articles 7.2.1 and 7.2.2 shall apply to each other Constituent Entity in the UPE Jurisdiction that is subject to the Deductible Dividend Regime to the extent that its

GloBE Income is further distributed by the UPE to recipients that meet the requirements of Article 7.2.1.

765. *Objective of the Article:* Article 7.2.3 is similar to Article 7.1.4. It extends the rules applicable to the UPE to other CEs located in the UPE Jurisdiction that are subject to the Deductible Dividend Regime and held through an ownership chain made up exclusively of such Entities. However, the income of the CEs that are not the UPE is reduced only to the extent it is distributed to the UPE and then by the UPE to recipients that meet the requirements of Article 7.2.1. The UPE must maintain records sufficient to demonstrate that such distributions occurred within twelve months of the end of the Fiscal Year of the subsidiary Entity subject to the Deductible Dividend Regime. The UPE may use any reasonable method of determining the source of any intragroup distributions from other Entities, including determining the income of Entities that are subject to a Deductible Dividend Regime and Entities that are subject to an ordinary income tax that has not been distributed to the UPE's owners.

4.7.2.4 Article 7.2.4.

766. Patronage dividends from a supply Cooperative are subject to tax to the extent they reduce an expense or cost that is deductible in the computation of the recipient's taxable income.

767. *Objective of the Article:* Article 7.2.4 provides rules to clarify the application of Article 7.2.1 with respect to certain patronage dividends distributed by supply Cooperatives. The rule applies to dividend recipients other than natural persons because distributions from supply Cooperatives to natural persons are always treated as a reduction to the UPE's GloBE Income under Article 7.2.1(a)(iii).

768. *Supply Cooperative vis-à-vis marketing Cooperative*: Patronage dividends from a supply Cooperative may not be subject to tax in the same way that patronage dividends from a marketing cooperative are subject to tax. A marketing Cooperative is one in which members sell their products or services to the Cooperative, and the Cooperative resells those products or services to its customers. Patronage dividends received by a business from a marketing cooperative essentially represent additional sales price for the goods or services provided by the cooperative member. Patronage dividends received by a business from a supply cooperative, on the other hand, essentially represent a reduction in the cost of goods or services acquired through the cooperative. Because of the difference in the character, from an accounting and perhaps tax perspective, Article 7.2.4 treats patronage dividends from a supply Cooperative as 'subject to tax' in the hands of the recipient to the extent they reduce an expense or cost that is deductible in the computation of the dividend recipient's taxable income. Whether the dividend is then subject to tax at a rate above the Minimum Rate is determined based on the relevant rules in Article 7.2.1.

4.7.3 Article 7.3. (Eligible Distribution Tax Systems)

769. Prominent features of Article 7.3 are provided in Box 4.36.

Box 4.36 Prominent Features of Article 7.3

- Allows certain distribution tax regimes to be accommodated within the structure of the GloBE Rules, subject to certain safeguards and recapture rules.
- Mitigates the differences between the time the income accrues in the financial accounts and the time it is subject to distribution tax to the extent that distributions are made within a four-year period.
- Article 7.3.1 allows the Filing Constituent Entity to make an annual election in respect of a CE that is subject to an Eligible Distribution Tax System to add the Deemed Distribution Tax to the Adjusted Covered Taxes for the Fiscal Year.
  - An election under Article 7.3.1 is subject to the other provisions of Article 7.3.
- Article 7.3.2 determines the amount of Deemed Distribution Tax.
  - The purpose of the limitation in paragraph (b) of Article 7.3.2 is to ensure that under ordinary circumstances, the Deemed Distribution Tax does not exceed the amount of tax that could possibly arise under the relevant distribution tax system for a Fiscal Year if all earnings earned in the year were distributed.
- In order to track the extent to which Deemed Distribution Tax is paid within the four-year period, Article 7.3.3 provides that a Deemed Distribution Tax Recapture Account for each Fiscal Year in which the election was made must be maintained and be made available for examination by the tax authorities of jurisdictions imposing the GloBE Rules.
  - The Deemed Distribution Tax Recapture Accounts are maintained on a jurisdictional basis.
  - These annual accounts can be reduced in three ways in a chronological order beginning with the account established for the earliest Fiscal Year.
  - These annual accounts cannot be reduced below zero.
- Article 7.3.4 provides that when there is a Net GloBE Loss for the jurisdiction that exceeds the amount in all of the Deemed Distribution Tax Recapture Accounts, a Recapture Account Loss Carry-forward is created.
  - The said account ensures that the MNE Group is not taxed under the GloBE Rules in excess of its economic income earned through Entities subject to a Distribution Tax Regime.
  - The Recapture Account Loss Carry-forward may be carried forward indefinitely.

- Article 7.3.5 requires the MNE Group to re-calculate the ETR and the amount of Top-up Tax under Article 5.4.1 for the Election Year if the Deemed Distribution Tax Recapture Account established for the year is not reduced to zero before the end of the fourth Fiscal Year after the Fiscal Year for which it was established.
  - Mandates that an election under Article 7.3.1 applies to all CEs located in the jurisdiction.
  - The result of Article 7.3.5 should be that the Top-up Tax liability in respect of the Election Year is the same as the Top-up Tax liability that would have been determined for the year if the distribution taxes paid in the following four Fiscal Years had been paid in the Election Year.
- Article 7.3.6 ensures that payments of distribution taxes, whether as a result of actual or deemed distributions, are not counted once as a reduction to a Deemed Distribution Tax Recapture Account and a second time as Adjusted Covered Taxes.
- Article 7.3.7 provides that when a CE located in the jurisdiction leaves the MNE Group or when substantially all of the assets of a CE are transferred outside the MNE Group or outside the jurisdiction, the ETR and Top-up Tax for the jurisdiction must be re-calculated under Article 5.4.1 by reducing the Covered Taxes by the balance of the Deemed Distribution Tax Recapture Account at the end of that Fiscal Year.
  - Does not impose tax on gains attributable to a transfer of assets. Accordingly, the rule is not dependent upon whether the transaction is eligible for treatment as a GloBE Reorganisation under Article 6.3.
  - If the Departing Constituent Entity had a GloBE Loss for a Fiscal Year, the Disposition Recapture Ratio for that year will be zero, and there will be no recapture amount for that Fiscal Year.
- Article 7.3.8 provides the definition of Disposition Recapture Ratio.

770. *Background:* Article 7.3 allows certain distribution tax regimes to be accommodated within the structure of the GloBE Rules, subject to certain safeguards and recapture rules. A distribution tax regime is a tax system that:

- generally, imposes income tax on a corporation when the corporation's income is distributed or deemed to be distributed to its shareholders, rather than when it is earned;
- also imposes current tax in respect of certain non-business expenses. Current taxation based on these disallowed expenditures is equivalent to disallowing a deduction for such expenses under a more traditional income tax. Because these non-business expenditures reduce distributable earnings, they cannot be subject to tax on distribution as a practical matter.

771. *Raison d'etre of Article 7.3*: The tax rates applicable under a distribution tax regime may equal or exceed the Minimum Rate such that the income is not subject to a low rate of tax when the earnings are eventually distributed. Absent a distribution or deemed distribution, however, much of the income is not subject to tax in the year it is earned and reported in the financial accounts. Moreover, the rules in Article 4.3 generally do not permit deferred tax liabilities in respect of taxes payable upon distribution to be included in the computation of the Total Deferred Tax Adjustment Amount. This means that the CE's GloBE Income likely would be subject to tax under the GloBE Rules in those years in which there is not an actual or deemed distribution because the Adjusted Covered Taxes for the Fiscal Year will be very small or nil. Moreover, in years where distributions are made, the amount of the distributions may bear no relationship to the income arising in those years, which may result in low or even extremely high ETRs. Article 7.3 mitigates these differences between the time the income accrues in the financial accounts and the time it is subject to distribution tax to the extent that distributions are made within a four-year period.

4.7.3.1 Article 7.3.1.

772. A Filing Constituent Entity may make an annual election with respect to a Constituent Entity that is subject to an Eligible Distribution Tax System to add the amount of Deemed Distribution Tax determined under Article 7.3.2 to Adjusted Covered Taxes for the Fiscal Year. An election under this article shall apply to all Constituent Entities located in the jurisdiction.

773. The term Eligible Distribution Tax System mentioned *supra* is defined in Article 10.1, as below:

> Eligible Distribution Tax System means a corporate income tax system that
>
> (a) imposes an income tax on the corporation with the tax generally payable only when the corporation distributes profits to shareholders, is deemed to distribute profits to shareholders, or incurs certain non-business expenses;
> (b) imposes tax at a rate equal to or in excess of the Minimum Rate; and
> (c) was in force on or before 1 July 2021.

774. *Objective of the Article:* Article 7.3.1 allows the Filing Constituent Entity to make an annual election in respect of a CE that is subject to an Eligible Distribution Tax System to add the Deemed Distribution Tax (defined in Article 7.3.2 *infra*) to the Adjusted Covered Taxes for the Fiscal Year. An election under Article 7.3.1 is subject to the other provisions of Article 7.3.

4.7.3.2 Article 7.3.2.

775. The amount of Deemed Distribution Tax is the lesser of:

(a) the amount of Adjusted Covered Taxes necessary to increase the ETR computed under Article 5.2.1 for the jurisdiction for the Fiscal Year to the Minimum Rate;

or

(b) the amount of tax that would have been due if the Constituent Entities located in the jurisdiction had distributed all of their income that is subject to the Eligible Distribution Tax Regime during such year.

776. *Objective of the Article:* Article 7.3.2 determines the amount of Deemed Distribution Tax. It is lesser of (a) or (b) stated above. If the GloBE Income for the Fiscal Year were to exceed the amount of earnings that could be distributed and subject to tax upon distribution for that Fiscal Year, the Deemed Distribution Tax would be limited under paragraph (b) to the amount of tax that would arise if all taxable earnings for the Fiscal Year were distributed. The purpose of the limitation in paragraph (b) is to ensure that under ordinary circumstances, the Deemed Distribution Tax does not exceed the amount of tax that could possibly arise under the relevant distribution tax system for a Fiscal Year if all earnings earned in the year were distributed. The rule is not intended to supplant or interfere with the rules in Articles 7.3.3 and 7.3.4 for establishing and using a Recapture Account Loss Carry-forward. Thus, the computation under paragraph (b) is made without regard to any negative balance in the accumulated earnings of CEs in the jurisdiction as of the end of the preceding Fiscal Year.

4.7.3.3 Article 7.3.3.

777. An annual Deemed Distribution Tax Recapture Account is established for each Fiscal Year in which the election in Article 7.3.1 applies. A Deemed Distribution Tax Recapture Account is increased by the amount of the Deemed Distribution Tax determined under Article 7.3.2 for the jurisdiction for the Fiscal Year for which it was established. At the end of each succeeding Fiscal Year, the outstanding balances of Deemed Distribution Tax Recapture Accounts established for prior Fiscal Years are reduced in chronological order and to the extent thereof, but not below zero:

(a) first by Taxes paid by the Constituent Entities during the Fiscal Year in relation to actual or deemed distributions;
(b) then by the amount of any Net GloBE Loss of the jurisdiction multiplied by the Minimum Rate; and
(c) then by any amount of Recapture Account Loss Carry-forward applied to the current Fiscal Year pursuant to Article 7.3.4.

778. The term Deemed Distribution Tax Recapture Account mentioned *supra* is defined in Article 10.1 as below:

> Deemed Distribution Tax Recapture Account means an account maintained in accordance with Article 7.3.3.

779. *Objective of the Article:* In order to track the extent to which Deemed Distribution Tax is paid within the four-year period, a Deemed Distribution Tax Recapture Account for each Fiscal Year in which the election was made must be maintained and available for examination by the tax authorities of jurisdictions imposing the GloBE Rules. The Deemed Distribution Tax Recapture Accounts are maintained on a jurisdictional basis, as

- this facilitates jurisdictional blending of income;
- ensures that the adjustments to the recapture accounts accommodate a consolidation or group relief system in the jurisdiction and allows distributions from any CE to eliminate the account.

780. A Deemed Distribution Tax Recapture Account is established for each Fiscal Year in an amount equal to the Deemed Distribution Tax. These annual accounts can be reduced in the three ways described in Figure 4.41. The accounts are reduced in chronological order beginning with the account established for the earliest Fiscal Year, and cannot be reduced below zero.

Figure 4.41 Mechanics of Deemed Distribution Tax Recapture Account under Article 7.3.3

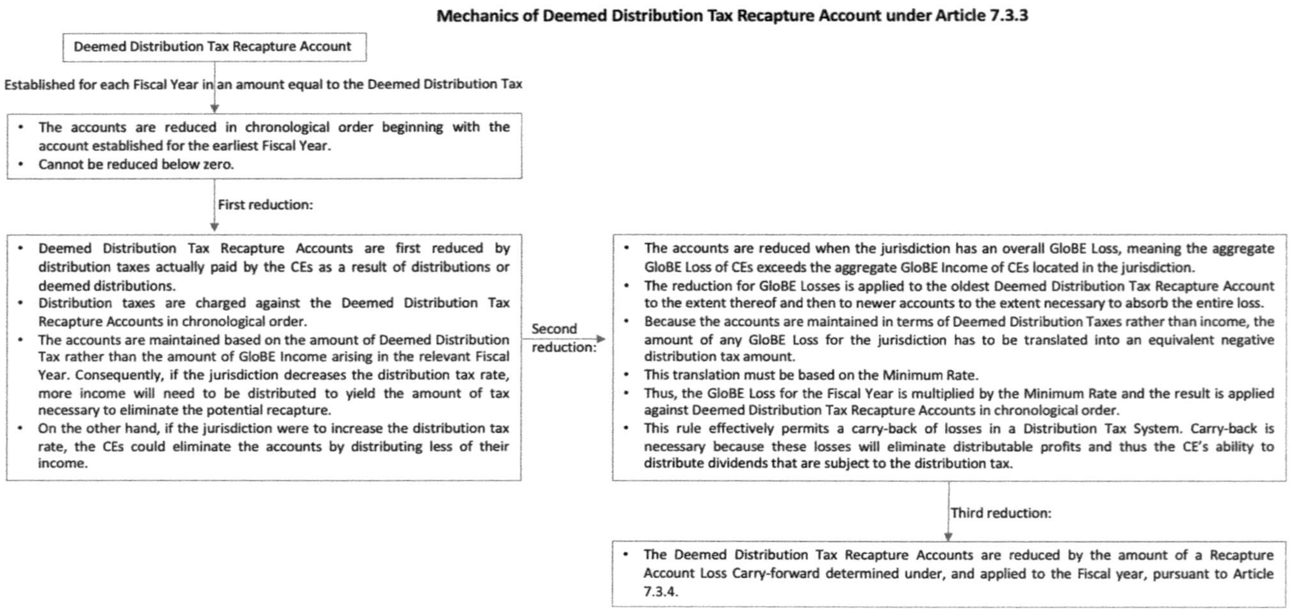

4.7.3.4 Article 7.3.4.

781. A Recapture Account Loss Carry-forward shall be established for the jurisdiction when the amount described in Article 7.3.3(b) exceeds the outstanding balance of the Deemed Distribution Tax Recapture Accounts. The Recapture Account Loss Carry-forward shall be in an amount equal to such excess and shall be taken into account in subsequent Fiscal Years as a reduction to Deemed Distribution Tax Recapture Accounts in such Fiscal Years. When such amount is taken into account in a subsequent Fiscal Year, the Recapture Account Loss Carry-forward must be reduced by that amount.

782. *Objective of the Article:* When there is a Net GloBE Loss for the jurisdiction that exceeds the amount in all of the Deemed Distribution Tax Recapture Accounts, a Recapture Account Loss Carry-forward is created. This account is reduced in subsequent years as the loss carry-forward is applied to reduce the GloBE income that would otherwise be subject to the Deemed Distribution Tax. The account ensures that the MNE Group is not taxed under the GloBE Rules in excess of its economic income earned through Entities subject to a Distribution Tax Regime.

783. *Situation when a CE leaves the MNE Group*: When a CE located in the jurisdiction leaves the MNE Group or when substantially all of the assets of a CE are transferred outside the MNE Group or outside the jurisdiction, the Recapture Account Loss Carry-forward must be reduced to the extent it is attributable to such CE. The amount attributable to a CE is determined by multiplying the Recapture Account Loss Carry-forward by the ratio of the GloBE Loss of that CE in the Fiscal Year(s) that produced a Net GloBE Loss in excess of the Deemed Distribution Tax Recapture Accounts to the total of the GloBE Losses of all CEs in the jurisdiction for that Fiscal Year(s).

784. *Indefinite carry-forward permissible*: The Recapture Account Loss Carry-forward may be carried forward indefinitely. However, the Filing Constituent Entity bears the burden of proof in respect of any Recapture Account Loss Carry-forward used in the computation of the Net GloBE Income of the jurisdiction for a Fiscal Year.

785. Illustration # 67: The illustration, through a flow-chart, explains Recapture Account Loss Carry-forward under Article 7.3.4.

Illustration explaining Recapture Account Loss Carry-forward under Article 7.3.4

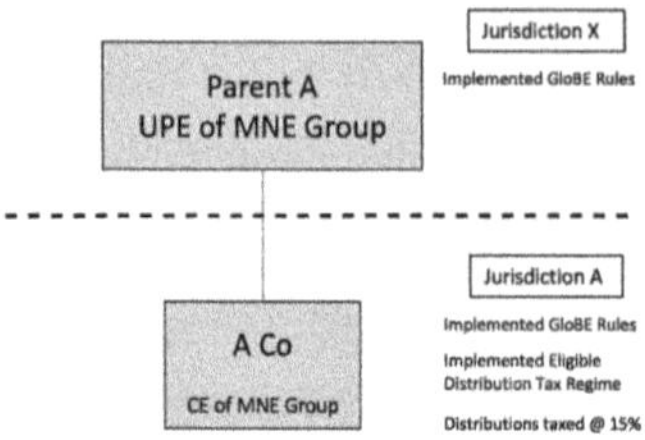

Assumptions **Step 1**

- A Co is a CE of an MNE Group and it is located in a jurisdiction with an Eligible Distribution Tax Regime.
- Distributions (and deemed distributions) are subject to tax at a 15% rate.
- An election pursuant to Article 7.3.1 is made for Year 1, Year 2, and Year 3 with respect to the jurisdiction.
- A Co makes no actual or deemed distributions in Year 1, Year 2, or Year 3.
- In Year 1, A Co earns GloBE Income of EUR 100 and records Deemed Distribution Tax of EUR 15 pursuant to Article 7.3.2(a).
- In Year 2, A Co incurs a Net GloBE Loss of EUR 120.
- In Year 3, A Co earns GloBE Income of EUR 100 and Deemed Distribution Tax of EUR 15 is recorded to achieve the Minimum Rate (as per Article 7.3.2(a)).

Application of Article 7.3.4 **Step 2**

- In Year 1, A Co has earned GloBE Income of EUR 100 and recorded Deemed Distribution Tax of EUR 15 pursuant to Article 7.3.2(a). Accordingly, the balance of the Deemed Distribution Tax Recapture Account at the end of Year 1 is EUR 15.
- In Year 2, A Co has incurred a Net GloBE Loss of EUR 120. Under Article 7.3.3, the Net GloBE Loss is multiplied by the Minimum Rate (i.e., EUR 120 x 15% = EUR 18) and EUR 15 is applied to reduce the Deemed Distribution Tax Recapture Account to EUR 0 (as per Article 7.3.3(b)).
- In Year 2, the excess over the Deemed Distribution Tax Recapture Account, EUR 3 (= EUR 18 – EUR 15), is added to a Recapture Account Loss Carry-forward under Article 7.3.4.
- In Year 3, A Co has earned GloBE Income of EUR 100 and Deemed Distribution Tax of EUR 15 is recorded to achieve the Minimum Rate (as per Article 7.3.2(a)).
- In Year 3, the Deemed Distribution Tax Recapture Account is increased by EUR 15 and then reduced by EUR 3, the balance of the Recapture Account Loss Carry-forward from Year 2, leaving a balance of EUR 12 in the Deemed Distribution Tax Recapture Account established for Year 3.
- A table illustrating the numerical results of this example is given here.

Amount in EURO

Particulars	Year 1	Year 2	Year 3
GloBE Income (or Loss)	100	(120)	100
Tax at Minimum Rate	15	(18)	15
Deemed Distribution Tax Recapture Account	15	0	12
Recapture Account Loss Carry-forward	0	3	0

4.7.3.5 Article 7.3.5.

786. If there is an outstanding balance of a Deemed Distribution Tax Recapture Account (maintained in accordance with Article 7.3.3) on the last day of the fourth Fiscal Year after the Fiscal Year for which such account was established, the Effective Tax Rate and Top-up Tax for the Fiscal Year for which the account was established must be recalculated under Article 5.4.1 by treating the balance of the Deemed Distribution Tax Recapture Account as a reduction to the Adjusted Covered Taxes previously determined for such year.

787. *Objective of the Article:* Article 7.3.5 requires the MNE Group to recalculate the ETR and the amount of Top-up Tax under Article 5.4.1 for the Election Year if the Deemed Distribution Tax Recapture Account established for the year is not reduced to zero before the end of the fourth Fiscal Year after the Fiscal Year for which it was established. The recalculations under Article 5.4.1 are done by reducing the Adjusted Covered Taxes for the Election Year by the outstanding balance (at the end of the relevant period) of the Deemed Distribution Tax Recapture Account for that year. Article 7.3.5 mandates that an election under Article 7.3.1 applies to all CEs located in the jurisdiction. The result of Article 7.3.5 should be that the Top-up Tax liability in respect of the Election Year is the same as the Top-up Tax liability that would have been determined for the year if the distribution taxes paid in the following four Fiscal Years had been paid in the Election Year.

4.7.3.6 Article 7.3.6.

788. Taxes paid during the Fiscal Year in relation to actual or deemed distributions are not included in Adjusted Covered Taxes to the extent they reduce a Deemed Distribution Tax Recapture Account under Article 7.3.3.

789. *Objective of the Article:* Article 7.3.6 ensures that payments of distribution taxes, whether as a result of actual or deemed distributions, are not counted once as a reduction to a Deemed Distribution Tax Recapture Account and a second time as Adjusted Covered Taxes. Only distribution taxes paid after all Deemed Distribution Tax Recapture Accounts have been reduced to zero are treated as Covered Taxes for the Fiscal Year. Taxes paid under an Eligible Distribution Tax Regime in respect of non-business expenses, however, are Covered Taxes and taken into account as such under the rules of Chapter 4 (refer Article 4.2.1(b)).

4.7.3.7 Article 7.3.7.

790. In the Fiscal Year that a Departing Constituent Entity leaves the MNE Group or transfers substantially all of its assets,

(a) the ETR and Top-up Tax for each preceding year for which a Deemed Distribution Tax Recapture Account is outstanding is recalculated in accordance with the principles of Article 5.4.1. by treating the balance of the Deemed Distribution Tax Recapture Account as a reduction to the Adjusted Covered Taxes previously determined for such year; and
(b) any amount of incremental Top-up Tax resulting from such recalculation shall be multiplied by the Disposition Recapture Ratio to determine the Additional Current Top-up Tax for purposes of Article 5.2.3.

791. The term Departing Constituent Entity mentioned supra is defined in Article 10.1 as below:

> Departing Constituent Entity means a Constituent Entity that is subject to an election under Article 7.3.1 and that leaves the MNE Group or transfers substantially all of its assets to a person that is not a Constituent Entity of the same MNE Group located in the same jurisdiction.

792. *Objective of the Article:* When a CE located in the jurisdiction leaves the MNE Group or when substantially all of the assets of a CE are transferred outside the MNE Group or outside the jurisdiction, the ETR and Top-up Tax for the jurisdiction must be recalculated under Article 5.4.1 by reducing the Covered Taxes by the balance of the Deemed Distribution Tax Recapture Account at the end of that Fiscal Year. If the recalculation under Article 5.4.1 results in Top-up Tax, that amount is multiplied by the Disposition Recapture Ratio (defined in Article 7.3.8 *infra*), and the result is included in the Additional Top-up Tax for the Fiscal Year. This rule recaptures the Deemed

Distribution Tax when the CE ceases to be in a position to distribute assets that would yield distribution tax to eliminate the balance in the recapture accounts. Article 7.3.7 does not impose tax on gains attributable to a transfer of assets. Accordingly, the rule is not dependent upon whether the transaction is eligible for treatment as a GloBE Reorganisation under Article 6.3.

793. *Manner of recalculations under Article 7.3.7:* Under Article 7.3.7, the MNE Group applies Article 5.4.1 to all of its Deemed Distribution Tax Recapture Accounts in the Fiscal Year that the Departing Constituent Entity leaves the MNE Group or disposes of substantially all of its assets. The recalculations under Article 7.3.7 are done in the same manner as under Article 7.3.5. The incremental Top-up Tax computed for each Deemed Distribution Tax Recapture Account is then multiplied by the Disposition Recapture Ratio determined under Article 7.3.8 to determine the amount of Additional Top-up Tax to include for the Fiscal Year under Article 5.2.3. If the Departing Constituent Entity had a GloBE Loss for a Fiscal Year, the Disposition Recapture Ratio for that year will be zero, and there will be no recapture amount for that Fiscal Year.

4.7.3.8 Article 7.3.8.

794. The Disposition Recapture Ratio is determined for each Departing Constituent Entity using the following formula:

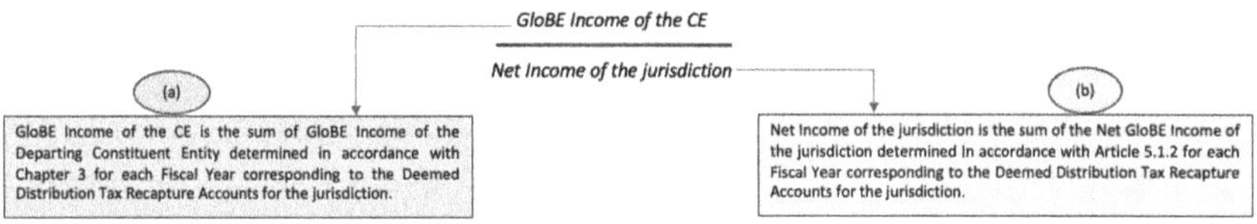

795. *Objective of the Article:* The Disposition Recapture Ratio is set out in Article 7.3.8. In conjunction with Article 7.3.7, it recaptures the outstanding balance of the Deemed Distribution Tax Recapture Accounts based on the ratio of the sum of the GloBE Income of the Departing Constituent Entity in the Fiscal Years for which a Deemed Distribution Tax Recapture Account is outstanding to the sum of the Net GloBE income of the jurisdiction for those Fiscal Years. Thus, if there are two annual recapture accounts outstanding, the Constituent Entity's GloBE Income or Loss for those two years is compared to the total Net GloBE Income for those two years, and the resulting ratio is multiplied by the incremental Top-up Tax computed for each Deemed Distribution Tax Recapture Account under Article 5.4.1 to determine the amount of Additional Top-up Tax to include for the Fiscal Year under Article 5.2.3. If the Departing Constituent Entity had a GloBE Loss in a Fiscal Year for which a Deemed Distribution Tax Recapture Account was established, that GloBE Loss and the account for that Fiscal Year are ignored in the computation of the Disposition Recapture Ratio because the account for that Fiscal Year was not attributable to GloBE income of the Departing Constituent Entity.

4.7.4 Article 7.4. (ETR Computation for Investment Entities)

796. Prominent features of Article 7.4 are provided in Box 4.37.

Box 4.37 Prominent Features of Article 7.4

- Even though Investment Entities that are the UPE are excluded from the operation of the GloBE Rules because they are not CEs of any MNE Group, the income of a controlled Investment Entity is consolidated with the MNE Group and brought within the GloBE Rules.
- Overall function of Article 7.4 is to provide special rules applicable to controlled Investment Entities and Insurance Investment Entities.
  - Provides a mechanism for calculating the ETR of a controlled Investment Entity or Insurance Investment Entity that is not subject to an election under Articles 7.5 or 7.6 (as applicable).
  - Calculates the ETR and Top-up Tax of these Entities on a stand-alone basis to prevent an MNE Group from blending low-taxed income with income of other CEs.
  - Calculates the ETR and Top-up Tax of a controlled Investment Entity only to the extent that the income is attributable to the MNE Group to ensure that minority investors are not subject to Top-up Tax on their interest in a low-taxed Investment Entity controlled by an MNE Group.
- Article 7.4.1 provides that rules of Article 7.4 apply to CEs that meet the definition of an Investment Entity.
  - Does not apply on Investment Entities and Insurance Investment Entities that are Tax Transparent Entities, as the rules contained in Article 3.5 continue to apply to the income of Investment Entities and Insurance Investment Entities that are Tax Transparent Entities.
  - Does not apply to the portion of an Investment Entity's or an Insurance Investment Entity's income that is subject to an election under Article 7.5 or Article 7.6.
- Article 7.4.2 describes the rules for computing the ETR of an Investment Entity or Insurance Investment Entity.
  - The ETR is calculated separately from any other CEs in the same jurisdiction (in other words, the GloBE Income or Loss and Covered Taxes are not blended with those of other CEs in the jurisdiction).
  - If the MNE Group owns interests in multiple Investment Entities or Insurance Investment Entities located in the same jurisdiction, a single ETR is computed for all such Entities in the jurisdiction.
  - The ETR is the Investment Entity's or Insurance Investment Entity's Adjusted Covered Taxes (defined in Article 7.4.3) divided by the MNE Group's Allocable Share of the Investment Entity's or Insurance Investment Entity's GloBE Income determined under Chapter 3.

- Article 7.4.3 provides the calculation of an Investment Entity's or Insurance Investment Entity's Adjusted Covered Taxes.
  - It is the sum of Covered Taxes accrued by the Investment Entity pursuant to Article 4.1 and the Covered Taxes accrued by its Constituent Entity-owners allocable to the Investment Entity or Insurance Investment Entity pursuant to Article 4.3.
  - The Covered Taxes paid by the Investment Entity are only those that correspond to the MNE Group's Allocable Share of the Investment Entity's GloBE Income.
  - The Covered Taxes accrued by Constituent Entity-owners taken into account under Article 7.4.3 are only those that arise with respect to their share of the Investment Entity's or Insurance Investment Entity's income.
- Article 7.4.4 defines the MNE Group's Allocable Share of the Investment Entity's or Insurance Investment Entity's GloBE Income.
  - It is calculated in the same way as would have been determined by the UPE in accordance with the rules of Article 2.2.2, taking into account only Ownership Interests in the Investment Entity or Insurance Investment Entity that are not subject to an election under Article 7.5 or Article 7.6.
  - By excluding interests subject to an election under Articles 7.5 and 7.6, the ETR computation for the Investment Entity does not double-count taxes that will be taken into account under those elections.
- Article 7.4.5 provides the rules for computing the Top-up Tax for each Investment Entity or Insurance Investment Entity.
  - These rules are designed to ensure that Top-up Tax arises only with respect to the MNE Group's interest in the Investment Entity or Insurance Investment Entity and taking into account all Covered Taxes arising in respect of that interest.
  - If there is more than one Investment Entity or Insurance Investment Entity located in the jurisdiction, their attributes determined under Articles 7.4.2 to 7.4.4 are combined to determine the Top-up Tax for all such Entities.
- Article 7.4.6 provides a special rule for computing the Substance-based Income Exclusion of Investment Entities.
  - Reduces the Substance-based Income Exclusion proportionally to correspond to the MNE Group's Allocable Share of the Investment Entity's or Insurance Investment Entity's GloBE Income or Loss.
  - If there are multiple Investment Entities located in the same jurisdiction, their Substance-based Income Exclusions are combined and offset against the Net GloBE Income of those Entities to determine their aggregate Excess Profit.
  - Article 7.4.6 applies notwithstanding the rule in Article 5.3.2, which generally excludes assets and payroll expenses of an Investment Entity or Insurance Investment Entity from the computation of the Substance-

based Income Exclusion. The rule in Article 5.3.2 is intended to prevent those assets and payroll expenses from being included in the computation of the carve-outs for both the jurisdiction and the Investment Entity or Insurance Investment Entity.

797. *Background:* Article 1.5.1(e) provides that Investment Entities that are the UPE are excluded from the operation of the GloBE Rules because they are not CEs of any MNE Group. However, the income of a controlled Investment Entity is consolidated with the MNE Group and brought within the GloBE Rules. The overall function of Article 7.4 is as below:

- provides special rules applicable to controlled Investment Entities and Insurance Investment Entities.
- provides a mechanism for calculating the ETR of a controlled Investment Entity or Insurance Investment Entity that is not subject to an election under Articles 7.5 or 7.6 (as applicable).
- The income of Investment Entities and Insurance Investment Entities is often subject to little or no tax at the entity level. Article 7.4 calculates the ETR and Top-up Tax of these Entities on a stand-alone basis to prevent an MNE Group from blending this low-taxed income with income of other CEs.
- seeks to ensure that minority investors are not subject to Top-up Tax on their interest in a low-taxed Investment Entity controlled by an MNE Group. It does so by calculating the ETR and Top-up Tax of a controlled Investment Entity only to the extent that the income is attributable to the MNE Group.

4.7.4.1 Article 7.4.1.

798. The rules of Article 7.4 apply to Constituent Entities that meet the definition of an Investment Entity, except Investment Entities that are Tax Transparent Entities or subject to an election under Article 7.5 or Article 7.6.

799. The term Investment Entity mentioned above is defined in Article 10.1 as below:

Investment Entity means:

(a) an Investment Fund or a Real Estate Investment Vehicle;
(b) an Entity that is at least 95% owned directly by an Entity described in paragraph (a) or through a chain of such Entities and that operates exclusively or almost exclusively to hold assets or invest funds for the benefit of such Investment Entities; and
(c) an Entity where at least 85% of the value of the Entity is owned by an Entity referred to in paragraph (a) provided that substantially all of the Entity's income is Excluded Dividends or Excluded Equity Gain or Loss that is excluded from the computation of GloBE Income or Loss in accordance with Articles 3.2.1 (b) or (c).

800. The term Insurance Investment Entity mentioned *supra* is defined in Article 10.1 as below:

> Insurance Investment Entity means an Entity that would meet the definition of an Investment Fund or a Real Estate Investment Vehicle except that it is established in relation to liabilities under an insurance or annuity contract and is wholly owned by an Entity that is subject to regulation in its location as an insurance company.

801. *Objective of the Article:* Applicability of Article 7.4 lies on Investment Entities and Insurance Investment Entities in accordance with the following situations:

- Investment Entities and Insurance Investment Entities that are not Tax Transparent Entities, as the rules contained in Article 3.5 continue to apply to the income of Investment Entities and Insurance Investment Entities that are Tax Transparent Entities.
- does not apply to the portion of an Investment Entity's or an Insurance Investment Entity's income that is subject to an election under Article 7.5 or Article 7.6.
- where an Investment Entity or Insurance Investment Entity is a Tax Transparent Entity in part and a Reverse Hybrid Entity in part, Article 7.4.1. applies with respect to its income, expenditure, profit or loss to the extent that it is not fiscally transparent in the jurisdiction in which the owner is located. For example, if an Investment Entity is organised as a trust and taxable on its income that is not distributed to beneficiaries, Article 7.4.1 applies to the extent the Investment Entity's or Insurance Investment Entity's income is not distributed.

4.7.4.2 Article 7.4.2.

802. The ETR for an Investment Entity that is a Constituent Entity shall be calculated separately from the Effective Tax Rate of the jurisdiction in which it is located. The Effective Tax Rate for each such Investment Entity is equal to the Investment Entity's Adjusted Covered Taxes divided by the MNE Group's Allocable Share of the Investment Entity's GloBE Income determined under Chapter 3. If there is more than one Investment Entity located in the jurisdiction, the Adjusted Covered Taxes and the MNE Group's Allocable Share of each Investment Entity's GloBE Income or Loss determined for each such Investment Entity are combined to compute the Effective Tax Rate of all such Investment Entities.

803. *Objective of the Article:* Article 7.4.2 describes the rules for computing the ETR of an Investment Entity or Insurance Investment Entity. The ETR is calculated separately from any other CEs in the same jurisdiction (in other words, the GloBE Income or Loss and Covered Taxes are not blended with those of other CEs in the jurisdiction). However, if the MNE Group owns interests in multiple Investment Entities or Insurance

Investment Entities located in the same jurisdiction, a single ETR is computed for all such Entities in the jurisdiction. The ETR is the Investment Entity's or Insurance Investment Entity's Adjusted Covered Taxes (defined in Article 7.4.3) divided by the MNE Group's Allocable Share of the Investment Entity's or Insurance Investment Entity's GloBE Income determined under Chapter 3.

4.7.4.3 Article 7.4.3.

804. An Investment Entity's Adjusted Covered Taxes is the sum of the Adjusted Covered Taxes determined for the Investment Entity under Article 4.1 attributable to the MNE Group's Allocable Share of the Investment Entity's GloBE Income and the Covered Taxes allocated to the Investment Entity under Article 4.3. The Investment Entity's Adjusted Covered Taxes does not include any Covered Taxes accrued by the Investment Entity attributable to income that is not part of the MNE Group's Allocable Share of the Investment Entity's GloBE Income.

805. *Objective of the Article:* Article 7.4.3 provides the calculation of an Investment Entity's or Insurance Investment Entity's Adjusted Covered Taxes. It is the sum of Covered Taxes accrued by the Investment Entity pursuant to Article 4.1 and the Covered Taxes accrued by its Constituent Entity-owners allocable to the Investment Entity or Insurance Investment Entity pursuant to Article 4.3. The Covered Taxes paid by the Investment Entity are only those that correspond to the MNE Group's Allocable Share of the Investment Entity's GloBE Income. The Covered Taxes accrued by Constituent Entity-owners taken into account under Article 7.4.3 are only those that arise with respect to their share of the Investment Entity's or Insurance Investment Entity's income.

4.7.4.4 Article 7.4.4.

806. The MNE Group's Allocable Share of the Investment Entity's GloBE Income is equal to the Allocable Share of the Investment Entity's GloBE Income or Loss that would be determined for the UPE in accordance with the rules of Article 2.2.2 taking into account only interests that are not subject to an election under Article 7.5 or Article 7.6.

807. *Objective of the Article:* Article 7.4.4 defines the MNE Group's Allocable Share of the Investment Entity's or Insurance Investment Entity's GloBE Income. It must be calculated in the same way as would have been determined by the UPE in accordance with the rules of Article 2.2.2, taking into account only Ownership Interests in the Investment Entity or Insurance Investment Entity that are not subject to an election under Article 7.5 or Article 7.6. By excluding interests subject to an election under Articles 7.5 and 7.6, the ETR computation for the Investment Entity does not double-count taxes that will be taken into account under those elections.

4.7.4.5 Article 7.4.5.

808. The Top-up Tax of a Constituent Entity that is an Investment Entity shall be an amount equal to the Top-up Tax Percentage for the Investment Entity multiplied by the excess of the MNE Group's Allocable Share of the Investment Entity's GloBE Income over the Substance-based Income Exclusion for the Investment Entity. The Top-up Tax Percentage for an Investment Entity shall be the percentage point excess, if any, of the Minimum Rate over the ETR of the Investment Entity. If there is more than one Investment Entity located in the jurisdiction, the MNE Group's Allocable Share of the Investment Entity's GloBE Income and the Substance-based Income Exclusion determined for each such Investment Entity are combined to compute the ETR of all such Investment Entities.

809. *Objective of the Article:* Article 7.4.5 provides the rules for computing the Top-up Tax for each Investment Entity or Insurance Investment Entity. These rules are designed to ensure that Top-up Tax arises only with respect to the MNE Group's interest in the Investment Entity or Insurance Investment Entity and taking into account all Covered Taxes arising in respect of that interest.

810. *Method of computation of Top-up Tax*: The rules of Article 7.4.5 generally follow the jurisdictional Top-up Tax computational rules in Article 5.2. First, the Top-up Tax Percentage for the Investment Entity or Insurance Investment Entity is computed by subtracting the ETR computed under Article 7.4.2 from the Minimum Rate. Then, the Investment Entity's or Insurance Investment Entity's Substance-based Income Exclusion (computed pursuant to Article 7.4.6) is deducted from the MNE Group's Allocable Share of the Investment Entity's or Insurance Investment Entity's GloBE income under Article 7.4.4. The excess of the MNE Group's Allocable Share of the Investment Entity's or Insurance Investment Entity's GloBE income over its Substance-based Income Exclusion is then multiplied by the Top-up Tax Percentage to determine the Top-up Tax. If there is more than one Investment Entity or Insurance Investment Entity located in the jurisdiction, their attributes determined under Articles 7.4.2 to 7.4.4 are combined to determine the Top-up Tax for all such Entities. In applying Article 2.2, Parent Entities must adjust the computation of their Inclusion Ratio of an Investment Entity that is an LTCE to account for the fact that the Top-up Tax computed for the Entity under Article 7.4.5 has, in effect, already been reduced by the amount that would have been attributable to other owners that are not Group Entities. For example, assume a CE owns 90% of the Ownership Interests that carry rights to 90% of the profits of an Investment Entity, and the remaining Ownership Interests are held by persons that are not Group Entities. The Investment Entity earns 100 of GloBE income for the Fiscal Year and has no Covered Taxes. Article 7.4.5 computes 13.5 of Top-up Tax based on the CE's share of the income, or 90. The Parent Entity's Inclusion Ratio is 1.0, and thus the Parent Entity is allocated all 13.5 of the Investment Entity's Top-up Tax.

4.7.4.6 Article 7.4.6.

811. The Substance-based Income Exclusion for an Investment Entity shall be determined in accordance with the principles in Article 5.3 without regard to the exception in Article 5.3.2 and by taking into account only Eligible Tangible Assets and Eligible Payroll Costs of Eligible Employees of the Investment Entities reduced in proportion to the MNE Group's Allocable Share of the Investment Entity's GloBE Income to the Investment Entity's total GloBE Income.

812. *Objective of the Article:* Generally, only Eligible Tangible Assets and Eligible Payroll Costs of Eligible Employees of the Investment Entities located in the jurisdiction are included in the calculation of the Substance-based Income Exclusion. Article 7.4.6 provides a special rule for computing the Substance-based Income Exclusion of Investment Entities. Article 7.4.6 reduces the Substance-based Income Exclusion proportionally to correspond to the MNE Group's Allocable Share of the Investment Entity's or Insurance Investment Entity's GloBE Income or Loss. If there are multiple Investment Entities located in the same jurisdiction, their Substance-based Income Exclusions are combined and offset against the Net GloBE Income of those Entities to determine their aggregate Excess Profit. Article 7.4.6 applies notwithstanding the rule in Article 5.3.2, which generally excludes assets and payroll expenses of an Investment Entity or Insurance Investment Entity from the computation of the Substance-based Income Exclusion. The rule in Article 5.3.2 is intended to prevent those assets and payroll expenses from being included in the computation of the carve-outs for both the jurisdiction and the Investment Entity or Insurance Investment Entity.

813. A ready reckoner on Structure and Mechanics of Article 7.4 is provided in Figure 4.42.

Figure 4.42 A Ready Reckoner on Structure and Mechanics of Article 7.4

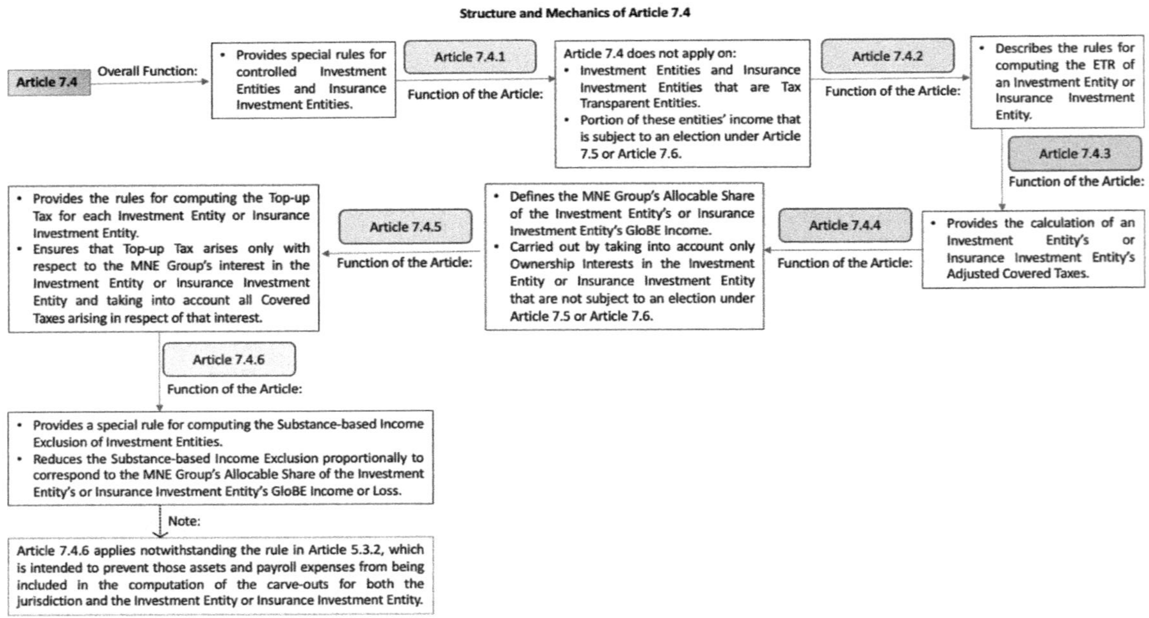

4.7.5 Article 7.5. (Investment Entity Tax Transparency Election)

814. Prominent features of Article 7.5 are provided in Box 4.38.

Box 4.38 Prominent Features of Article 7.5

- Provides an election to treat an Investment Entity or an Insurance Investment Entity as a Tax Transparent Entity.
  - Investment Entities and Insurance Investment Entities that meet the definition of a Tax Transparent Entity in Article 10.2.1 do not need to make the election.
  - Under the election, the income and Covered Taxes of the Investment Entity or Insurance Investment Entity flow through to the Constituent Entity-owner and thus, the special rules in Article 7.4 are not needed to compute the Investment Entity's ETR.
- Article 7.5.1 provides a Five-Year election to treat an Investment Entity or Insurance Investment Entity as a Tax Transparent Entity.
  - The election is available to Constituent Entity-owners of Investment Entities or Insurance Investment Entities that are subject to a mark-to-market or similar tax regime on investments in Investment Entities and Insurance Investment Entities.
  - Election under Article 7.5.1 renders Article 7.4 otiose.
  - The election allows the MNE Group to include the Constituent Entity-owner's share of the Investment Entity's results as income of the Constituent Entity-owner for GloBE purposes.
  - The election is available for both directly owned Investment Entities and Insurance Investment Entities, as well as such Entities that are indirectly owned through other Investment Entities or Insurance Investment Entities.
  - The election allows the Constituent Entity-owner to apply the Substance-based Income Exclusion with respect to its share of the income of the Investment Entity.
- Article 7.5.2 provides that the Article 7.5.1 election is a Five-Year Election.
  - Article 7.5.2 further provides transition rules for revocation of the election.
  - If the election is revoked, gains or losses from the disposition of an asset or liability held by the Investment Entity shall be determined based on the fair value of the assets or liabilities on the first day of the revocation year.

815. *Background:* The overall function of Article 7.5 is as below:

- provides special rules applicable to controlled Investment Entities and Insurance Investment Entities.

- provides an election to treat an Investment Entity or an Insurance Investment Entity as a Tax Transparent Entity (Investment Entities and Insurance Investment Entities that meet the definition of a Tax Transparent Entity in Article 10.2.1 do not need to make the election).
- under the election, the income and Covered Taxes of the Investment Entity or Insurance Investment Entity flow through to the Constituent Entity-owner and thus, the special rules in Article 7.4 are not needed to compute the Investment Entity's ETR.

4.7.5.1 Article 7.5.1.

816. A Filing Constituent Entity may elect to treat a Constituent Entity that is an Investment Entity or an Insurance Investment Entity as a Tax Transparent Entity if the Constituent Entity-owner is subject to tax in its location under a mark-to-market or similar regime based on the annual changes in the fair value of its Ownership Interest in the Entity and the tax rate applicable to the Constituent Entity-owner with respect to such income equals or exceeds the Minimum Rate. For this purpose, a Constituent Entity that indirectly owns an Ownership Interest in an Investment Entity or Insurance Investment Entity through a direct Ownership Interest in another Investment Entity or Insurance Investment Entity is considered to be subject to tax under a mark-to-market or similar regime with respect to the indirect Ownership Interest in the first-mentioned Entity if it is subject to a mark-to-market or similar regime with respect to the direct Ownership Interest in the second-mentioned Entity.

817. *Objective of the Article:* Article 7.5.1 provides a Five-Year election to treat an Investment Entity or Insurance Investment Entity as a Tax Transparent Entity. The election is available to Constituent Entity-owners of Investment Entities or Insurance Investment Entities that are subject to a mark-to-market or similar tax regime on investments in Investment Entities and Insurance Investment Entities. The treatment as a Tax Transparent Entity applies for all purposes of the GloBE Rules, including Article 3.5.

818. *Election under Article 7.5.1 renders Article 7.4 otiose:* If an election under Article 7.5.1 is made with respect to an Investment Entity or an Insurance Investment Entity, the rules in Article 7.4 do not apply.

819. *Conditions under which the election under Article 7.5.1 is available:* The election, which is made by the Filing Constituent Entity, is only available where:

- the Constituent Entity-owner is subject to tax in its location on changes in the value of its interest in the Investment Entity or Insurance Investment Entity (or its underlying investments) under a mark-to-market or similar regime at a rate that equals or exceeds the Minimum Rate.
- the election does not need to be made with respect to all Constituent Entity-owners of the Investment Entity.

- the election applies to all of a Constituent Entity-owner's interests in the Investment Entity.

820. *Consequences of treating the Investment Entity as tax transparent*: The election allows the MNE Group to include the Constituent Entity-owner's share of the Investment Entity's results as income of the Constituent Entity-owner for GloBE purposes. This election matches the timing and location of income earned through an Investment Entity under the GloBE Rules and the local tax rules where the Constituent Entity-owner is subject to a mark-to-market or similar regime.

821. *Entities eligible for Election*: The election is available for both directly owned Investment Entities and Insurance Investment Entities, as well as such Entities that are indirectly owned through other Investment Entities or Insurance Investment Entities. Thus, the tax effect of changes in value of a lower-tier Investment Entity or Insurance Investment Entity in a chain of such Entities that is reflected in the valuation of the interest in a directly held Investment Entity or Insurance Investment Entity can be matched with the GloBE Income or Loss of that Entity. The tax method and the financial accounting method of computing fair value may not be exactly the same, and thus, there may be timing differences even with the election. However, those differences will occur less frequently and in smaller amounts.

822. *Determination of share of Constituent Entity-owner*: The Constituent Entity-owner's share of the GloBE Income or Loss of the Investment Entity or the Insurance Investment Entity should not be counted twice by the Constituent Entity-owner. Only the Constituent Entity-owner's share of the GloBE Income or Loss computed for the Investment Entity or Insurance Investment Entity should be taken into account pursuant to an election under Article 7.5. The income of the Investment Entity or Insurance Investment is likely to be determined using fair value accounting in the preparation of the CFS.

823. *Financial accounting of Net Income or Loss by Constituent Entity-owner:* The Constituent Entity-owner should not account for its Ownership Interest in a CE that is an Investment Entity or an Insurance Investment Entity using a fair value accounting method, even if, on a separate entity accounting basis, the Constituent Entity-owner does not control the Investment Entity or Insurance Investment Entity. The Constituent Entity-owner's Financial Accounting Net Income or Loss should be determined pursuant to Chapter 3 using the accounting standard that was used to determine the CE's income in preparing the CFS. However, if, for some reason, the Constituent Entity-owner did account for its interest in the Investment Entity or Insurance Investment Entity using a fair value method, that income or loss should be excluded from the computation of its GloBE Income or Loss, as demonstrated in **Illustration # 68**:

Illustration of Application of Article 7.5.1

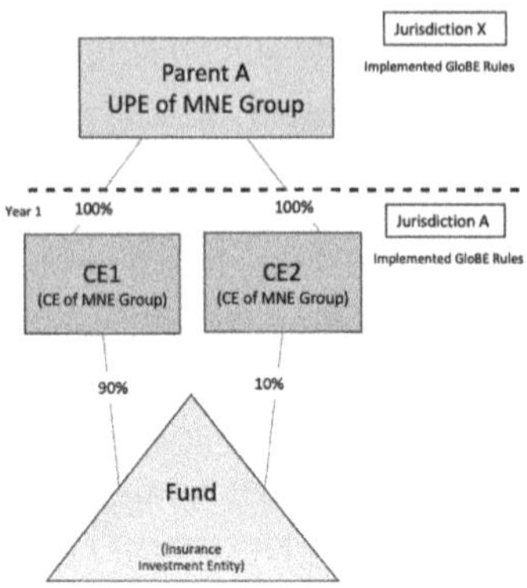

Assumptions **Step 1**

- Assume that UPE owns 100% of the Ownership Interests of CE1 and CE2.
- CE1 and CE2 own 90% and 10%, respectively, of the Ownership Interests in Fund, an Insurance Investment Entity.
- Fund earns 100 of net income in Year 1, pays no tax. and makes no distributions.
- An election under Article 7.5 is made on behalf of CE1 and CE2.
- Accordingly, CE1 and CE2 include their share of Fund's income, 90 and 10, respectively, in the computation of their GloBE Income or Loss.

Application of Article 7.5.1 **Step 2**

- On a standalone basis, CE1 controls Fund and thus would consolidate its accounts even if CE2 were an unrelated company.
- CE2, on the other hand, owns only 10% of Fund and on a standalone basis might be required to apply fair value accounting to its interest in Fund under the Acceptable Financial Accounting Standard used in the CFS.
- For purposes of the GloBE Rules, however, CE2 does not include any fair value gains or distributions from CEs. Otherwise, in this case, CE2 would recognise 10 of fair value gain in addition to the 10 of income included in its income under the Article 7.5 election.

824. *Substance-based Income Exclusion*: The election allows the Constituent Entity-owner to apply the Substance-based Income Exclusion with respect to its share of the income of the Investment Entity. In many cases, the MNE Group's Eligible Payroll Expenses and Eligible Tangible Assets related to managing the Investment Entity's or Insurance Investment Entity's activities will not arise in the Investment Entity or Insurance Investment Entity itself but instead will be those of the Constituent Entity-owners.

4.7.5.2 Article 7.5.2.

825. The election under this article is a Five-Year Election. If the election is revoked, gain or loss from the disposition of an asset or liability held by the Investment Entity shall be determined based on the fair value of the assets or liabilities on the first day of the revocation year.

826. *Objective of the Article:* Article 7.5.2 provides that the Article 7.5.1 election is a Five-Year Election. Article 7.5.2 further provides transition rules for revocation of the election. If the election is revoked, gains or losses from the disposition of an asset or liability held by the Investment Entity shall be determined based on the fair value of the assets or liabilities on the first day of the revocation year. The fair value at the beginning of the revocation year is the starting point. If the Investment Entity's income is determined using a realisation method, that value will continue to be the value of the asset for purposes of determining gains or losses under the GloBE Rules until it is disposed of. If, on the other hand, the Investment Entity's income is determined using a fair value method for the assets, then that method will revalue the assets at regular intervals and include the gains or losses in Financial Accounting Net Income or Loss. That revaluation will apply for GloBE purposes as well.

4.7.6 Article 7.6. (Taxable Distribution Method Election)

827. Prominent features of Article 7.6 are provided in Box 4.39.

Box 4.39 Prominent Features of Article 7.6

- The overall function of Article 7.6 is that it provides a special rule applicable to controlled Investment Entities.
  - Provides another alternative to the rule in Article 7.4 in the form of Taxable Distribution Method.
  - Provides that the Taxable Distribution Method reduces the exposure to Top-up Tax to the extent that the Investment Entity makes distributions of its income within a four-year period that are taxable in the hands of the recipients at or above the Minimum Rate.
- Article 7.6.1 provides for a Five-Year election to use the Taxable Distribution Method.
  - The election is made by the Filing Constituent Entity and is only available in the case of the Constituent Entity-owners that are subject to tax in their location on distributions from the Investment Entity and only if the Constituent Entity-owner can be reasonably expected to be subject to tax on such distributions at a rate that equals or exceeds the Minimum Rate.
- Article 7.6.2 sets out the operation of the Taxable Distribution Method.
  - Paragraph (a) of Article 7.6.2 requires the Constituent Entity-owner to include actual and deemed distributions in the computation of its GloBE Income in the Fiscal Year for which it is subject to tax on the distribution. The reference to deemed distribution in paragraph (a) is intended to ensure that the Taxable Distribution Method is coordinated with the tax treatment under local tax rules.
  - Paragraph (b) of Article 7.6.2 requires the Constituent Entity-owner to include the Local Creditable Tax Gross-up in its GloBE Income and Adjusted Covered Taxes.
  - Paragraph (c) of Article 7.6.2 provides that the Constituent Entity-owner's proportionate share of the Investment Entity's Undistributed Net GloBE Income is treated as GloBE Income of the Investment Entity for the Reporting Fiscal Year, and the result of multiplying the Minimum Rate by such GloBE Income is treated as Top-up Tax of a Low-Tax Constituent Entity in the Fiscal Year for purposes of Chapter 2.
  - Paragraph (d) of Article 7.6.2 provides that to achieve the intended result of attributing income (and tax consequences) of the Investment Entity to the Constituent Entity-owners rather than the Investment Entity, Article 5.1.3 requires that the Investment Entity's GloBE Income or Loss for the Fiscal Year, and any Adjusted Covered Taxes attributable to such income, are excluded from all ETR computations under

Chapter 5 and Articles 7.4.1 to 7.4.5, except to the extent the Adjusted Covered Taxes are included in the Constituent Entity-owners GloBE Income or Loss and Adjusted Covered Taxes pursuant to paragraph (b) of the Article.

- Article 7.6.3 defines the Undistributed Net GloBE Income.
  - The definition of Undistributed Net GloBE Income tests whether the GloBE Income arising in the Tested Year was distributed or offset by losses by the end of the Testing Period.
  - The Undistributed Net GloBE Income is calculated for the entire Investment Entity, but Top-up Tax is computed based on the Constituent Entity-owner's share of the Undistributed Net GloBE Income.
- Article 7.6.4 provides that distributions only reduce Undistributed Net GloBE Income of one year, i.e., they cannot be double-counted.
  - The Undistributed Net GloBE Income is further reduced by GloBE Losses, if any, arising in the Testing Period and any Investment Loss Carry-forward from a prior period.
  - There will not be any Undistributed Net GloBE Income for the first three years in which the MNE Group owns an interest in the Investment Entity.
- Article 7.6.5 defines certain terms related to the Taxable Distribution Method that are used in Article 7.6.
- Article 7.6.6 provides that the Article 7.6.1 election is a Five-Year Election to use the Taxable Distribution Method.
  - Provides rules to address consequences of revocation of election.

828. *Background:* Article 7.6 provides another alternative to the rule in Article 7.4. This alternative is the Taxable Distribution Method. This method reduces the exposure to Top-up Tax to the extent that the Investment Entity makes distributions of its income within a four-year period that are taxable in the hands of the recipients at or above the Minimum Rate. The overall function of Article 7.6 is as below:

- provides a special rule applicable to controlled Investment Entities.
- provides an election for the Constituent Entity-owner of a controlled Investment Entity.
- under the election, the Constituent Entity-owner includes distributions received from the Entity in the computation of its GloBE Income or Loss. The Constituent Entity-owner's share of the Investment Entity's income is excluded from the MNE Group's GloBE Income or Loss computations so long as it is distributed to the Constituent Entity-owner within four years.

4.7.6.1 Article 7.6.1.

829. At the election of the Filing Constituent Entity, a Constituent Entity-owner that is not an Investment Entity may apply the Taxable Distribution Method with respect to its Ownership Interest in a Constituent Entity that is an Investment Entity if the Constituent Entity-owner can be reasonably expected to be subject to tax on distributions from the Investment Entity at a tax rate that equals or exceeds the Minimum Rate.

830. *Objective of the Article:* Article 7.6.1 provides for a Five-Year election to use the Taxable Distribution Method. The election is made by the Filing Constituent Entity and is only available in the case of the Constituent Entity-owners that are subject to tax in their location on distributions from the Investment Entity and only if the Constituent Entity-owner can be reasonably expected to be subject to tax on such distributions at a rate that equals or exceeds the Minimum Rate. The election need not be made with respect to all Constituent Entity-owners of the Investment Entity. However, the election applies to all of the Constituent Entity-owner's Ownership Interests in the Investment Entity.

4.7.6.2 Article 7.6.2.

831. Under the Taxable Distribution Method:

(a) distributions and deemed distributions of the Investment Entity's GloBE Income are included in the GloBE Income of the Constituent Entity-owner (other than an Investment Entity) that received the distribution;
(b) the Local Creditable Tax Gross-up is included in the GloBE Income and Adjusted Covered Taxes of the Constituent Entity-owner (other than an Investment Entity) that received the distribution;
(c) the Constituent Entity-owner's proportionate share of the Investment Entity's Undistributed Net GloBE Income for the Tested Year is treated as GloBE Income of the Investment Entity for the Reporting Fiscal Year, and the result of multiplying the Minimum Rate by such GloBE Income is treated as Top-up Tax of a Low-Tax Constituent Entity in the Fiscal Year for purposes of Chapter 2; and
(d) the Investment Entity's GloBE Income or Loss for the Fiscal Year and any Adjusted Covered Taxes attributable to such income are excluded from all ETR computations under Chapter 5 and Articles 7.4.2 to 7.4.5, except as provided in paragraph (b).

832. *Objective of the Article:* Article 7.6.2 sets out the operation of the Taxable Distribution Method, encompassed in paragraphs (a) to (d), which are explained in Figure 4.43.

Figure 4.43 Operation of Taxable Distribution Method under Article 7.6.2

Operation of Taxable Distribution Method under Article 7.6.2

(a)

- Paragraph (a) requires the Constituent Entity-owner to include actual and deemed* distributions in the computation of its GloBE Income in the Fiscal Year for which it is subject to tax on the distribution. The reference to deemed distribution in paragraph (a) is intended to ensure that the Taxable Distribution Method is coordinated with the tax treatment under local tax rules.
- Thus, deemed distributions under the Taxable Distribution Method are generally determined by reference to the law applicable to the Constituent Entity-owner. This feature of the Taxable Distribution Method is a departure from the ordinary GloBE Rules, where distributions from CEs are excluded from GloBE Income. The Taxable Distribution Method is intended to match both the timing and location of the income earned by an MNE Group through the Investment Entity with the tax on that income in the location where the Constituent Entity-owner is subject to tax on the distributions.
- A Constituent Entity-owner that is itself an Investment Fund, i.e. an intermediate Investment Fund, does not include the distribution in its GloBE Income or Loss, to preserve the tax neutrality of Investment Entities. However, distributions to intermediate Investment Entities do not re-start the four-year clock on distributions to the Constituent Entity-owner for which the election is made.
- Distributions do not reduce the Undistributed Net GloBE Income until they reach a CE that is not an Investment Entity.

* Note : The GloBE Rules do not have an independent definition of deemed distribution, although Article 7.6.5(c) treats certain transfers of an Ownership Interest as a deemed distribution.

(b)

- Paragraph (b) requires the Constituent Entity-owner to include the Local Creditable Tax Gross-up in its GloBE Income and Adjusted Covered Taxes.
- The Local Creditable Tax Gross-up is defined in Article 7.6.5(d). It is generally the amount of Covered Taxes paid by the Investment Entity that is allowed as a credit in the computation of the Constituent Entity-owner's tax liability in respect of a distribution from the Investment Entity.
- Rather than creating a separate regime for tracking and managing Covered Taxes associated with each Constituent Entity-owner's share of the Investment Entity's GloBE Income that is subject to the Taxable Distribution Method, the GloBE Rules rely on the tax credit rules in the Constituent Entity-owner's location.
- Thus, the rule effectively provides credit for Covered Taxes paid by the Investment Entity under the GloBE Rules to the same extent a credit is allowed for local tax purposes.
- The rule also requires that the Local Creditable Tax Gross-up be treated as additional GloBE Income so that the tax credit does not have the same effect as allowing both a deduction and a credit.

(c)

- Paragraph (c) provides that the Constituent Entity-owner's proportionate share of the Investment Entity's Undistributed Net GloBE Income is treated as GloBE Income of the Investment Entity for the Reporting Fiscal Year and the result of multiplying the Minimum Rate by such GloBE Income is treated as Top-up Tax of a Low-Tax Constituent Entity in the Fiscal Year for purposes of Chapter 2.
- Liability for this Top-up Tax is determined pursuant to Chapter 2.

(d)

- To achieve the intended result of attributing income (and tax consequences) of the Investment Entity to the Constituent Entity-owners rather than the Investment Entity, Article 5.1.3 requires that the Investment Entity's GloBE Income or Loss for the Fiscal Year, and any Adjusted Covered Taxes attributable to such income, are excluded from all ETR computations under Chapter 5 and Articles 7.4.1 to 7.4.5, except to the extent the Adjusted Covered Taxes are included in the Constituent Entity-owners GloBE Income or Loss and Adjusted Covered Taxes pursuant to paragraph (b) of the Article.

4.7.6.3 Article 7.6.3.

833. The Undistributed Net GloBE Income for a Fiscal Year is the amount of the Investment Entity's GloBE Income, if any, for the Tested Year reduced (but not below zero) by:

(a) any Covered Taxes of the Investment Entity;
(b) distributions and deemed distributions to shareholders other than Constituent Entities that are Investment Entities in the Testing Period;
(c) GloBE Losses arising in the Testing Period; and
(d) Investment Loss Carry-forwards.

834. *Objective of the Article*: Article 7.6.3 defines the Undistributed Net GloBE Income. The definition of Undistributed Net GloBE Income tests whether the GloBE Income arising in the Tested Year was distributed or offset by losses by the end of the Testing Period. Thus, as a practical matter, the MNE Group must maintain an Undistributed Net GloBE Income account for each Tested Year. The Undistributed Net GloBE Income is calculated for the entire Investment Entity, but Top-up Tax is computed based on the Constituent Entity-owner's share of the Undistributed Net GloBE Income.

835. *Testing Period:* Under Article 7.6.5, the Tested Year is the third Fiscal year preceding the Reporting Fiscal Year. The Testing Period is the four-year period beginning with the Tested Year and ending with the Reporting Fiscal Year. For example, if the Investment Entity fully distributed its GloBE Income to its Constituent Entity-owners over the course of this four-year period, no Top-up Tax could be imposed under the Taxable Distribution Method. The owner could, of course, be subject to Top-up Tax in one of those years based on its own circumstances.

836. The mechanics of Undistributed Net GloBE Income under Article 7.6.3 is explained in Figure 4.44.

Figure 4.44 Mechanics of Undistributed Net GloBE Income under Article 7.6.3

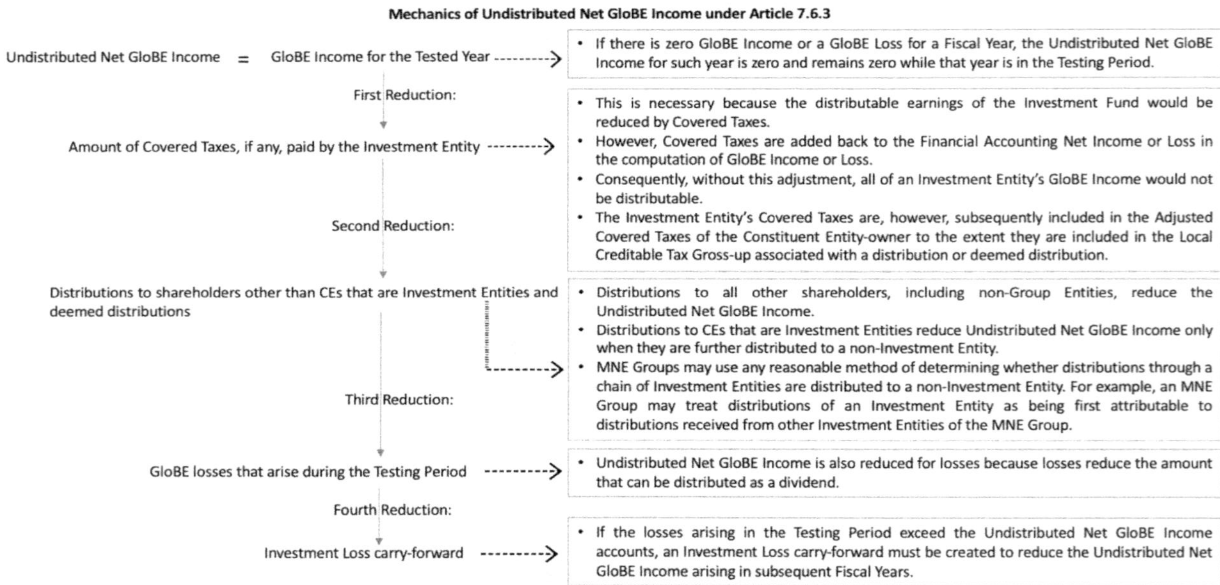

4.7.6.4 Article 7.6.4.

837. Undistributed Net GloBE Income for the Tested Year cannot be reduced by distributions or deemed distributions to the extent that such distributions were treated as a reduction to Undistributed Net GloBE Income of a previous Tested Year. For purposes of computing Undistributed Net GloBE Income, a GloBE Loss is reduced to the extent it reduced Undistributed Net GloBE Income at the end of a previous Fiscal Year. If a GloBE Loss for a Fiscal Year is not reduced to zero before the end of the last Tested Period that includes such Fiscal Year, the remainder becomes an Investment Loss Carry-forward and is reduced in the same manner as a GloBE Loss in subsequent Fiscal Years.

838. *Objective of the Article*: Article 7.6.4 provides that distributions only reduce Undistributed Net GloBE Income of one year, i.e., they cannot be double-counted. The Undistributed Net GloBE Income is further reduced by GloBE Losses, if any, arising in the Testing Period and any Investment Loss Carry-forward from a prior period. Investment Loss Carry-forwards are the amount of GloBE Losses arising before the Tested Year that were not completely absorbed, i.e., reduced to zero, before the loss year rolled out of the Testing Period. For purposes of computing Undistributed Net GloBE Income, GloBE Losses are reduced when they are used to reduce Undistributed Net GloBE income and thus cannot be used to reduce the Undistributed Net GloBE Income of another Tested Year.

839. *Consequences of MNE Group not owning an interest in the Investment Entity on Undistributed Net GloBE Income*: If the MNE Group has not owned an interest in the Investment Entity for three consecutive years, the GloBE Income for each preceding year that it did not own an interest is considered to be zero for purposes of determining the Undistributed Net GloBE Income. Accordingly, there will not be any Undistributed Net GloBE Income for the first three years in which the MNE Group owns an interest in the Investment Entity.

4.7.6.5 Article 7.6.5.

840. For purposes of Article 7.6,

(a) the Tested Year is the third year preceding the Reporting Fiscal Year;
(b) the Testing Period is the period beginning with the first day of the Tested Year and ending with the last day of the Reporting Fiscal Year that the Ownership Interest was held by a Group Entity;
(c) a deemed distribution arises when a direct or indirect Ownership Interest in the Investment Entity is transferred to a non-Group Entity and is equal to the proportionate share of the Undistributed Net GloBE Income attributable to such Ownership Interest on the date of such transfer (determined without regard to the deemed distribution); and

(d) the Local Creditable Tax Gross-up is the amount of Covered Taxes incurred by the Investment Entity that is allowed as a credit against the Constituent Entity-owner's tax liability arising in connection with a distribution from the Investment Entity.

841. The definitions of certain terms related to the Taxable Distribution Method that are mentioned in Article 7.6 are discussed in Table 4.3.

Table 4.3 Definitions of Terms under Article 7.6.5

(a)	Tested Year	- Tested Year is the third year preceding the Reporting Fiscal Year.
(b)	Testing Period	- Testing Period is the four-year period beginning with the Tested Year and ending with the Reporting Fiscal Year. - The definition is important to the determination of an Investment Entity's Undistributed Net Globe Income. - The definition, together with the other provisions of Article 7.6.3, allows distributions in the Tested Year and the three succeeding Fiscal Years to reduce the Undistributed Net GloBE Income of the Investment Entity.
(c)	Deemed distribution	- A transfer of a direct or indirect Ownership Interest in the Investment Entity to a person that is not a Group Entity is treated as a deemed distribution. - The amount of the deemed distribution is determined based on the proportional decrease in the transferring CE's Ownership Interest. - This rule applies irrespective of whether the Constituent Entity-owner that transferred its interest is subject to tax as a result of the transfer. - Without this rule, the Undistributed Net GloBE Income attributable to the disposed Investment Entity would continue to be deferred until the end of the Testing Period.
(d)	Local Creditable Tax Gross-up	- Defined as the amount of Covered Taxes incurred by the Investment Entity that is allowed as a credit against the Constituent Entity-owner's tax liability arising in connection with a distribution from the Investment Entity. - Rather than creating a separate regime for tracking and managing Covered Taxes associated with each Constituent Entity-owner's share of the Investment Entity's GloBE Income that is subject to the Taxable Distribution Method, the GloBE Rules rely on the tax credit rules in the Constituent Entity-owner's location.

		- The provision effectively provides credit for Covered Taxes paid by the Investment Entity under the GloBE Rules to the same extent a credit is allowed for local tax purposes. - The Local Creditable Tax Gross-up is treated as additional GloBE Income so that the tax credit does not have the same effect as allowing both a deduction and a credit.

4.7.6.6 Article 7.6.6.

842. The election under this article is a Five-Year Election. If the election is revoked, Constituent Entity-owner's proportionate share of the Investment Entity's Undistributed Net GloBE Income for the Tested Year at the end of the Fiscal Year preceding the revocation year is treated as GloBE Income of the Investment Entity for the revocation year, and the result of multiplying the Minimum Rate by such GloBE Income is treated as Top-up Tax of a Low-Tax Constituent Entity in the revocation year for the purposes of Chapter 2.

843. *Objective of the Article:* Article 7.6.6 provides that the Article 7.6.1 election is a Five-Year Election to use the Taxable Distribution Method. The article also provides rules to address consequences of revocation of election, whereby, when the election is revoked, Constituent Entity-owner's proportionate share of the Investment Entity's Undistributed Net GloBE Income for the Tested Year at the end of the Fiscal Year preceding the revocation year is treated as GloBE Income of the Investment Entity for the revocation year and the result of multiplying the Minimum Rate by such GloBE Income is treated as Top-up Tax of a Low-Tax Constituent Entity in the revocation year for the purposes of Chapter 2.

4.8 CHAPTER 8 OF GLOBE RULES (ADMINISTRATION)[105]

844. Providing information to tax administrations on the tax calculations made by the MNE Group under the GloBE rules is a significant part of compliance procedure. This is achieved through filing of a GloBE information Return which shall enable tax administrations to analyse the return information, assess risk areas, audit taxpayers and collect Top-up Tax that is brought into charge under the GloBE Rules in their jurisdiction. In order to limit unnecessary compliance and administrative burden for MNE Groups and tax administrations, the GloBE Implementation Framework is exploring the development of GloBE Safe Harbours. GloBE Safe Harbours would allow an MNE Group to avoid the ETR and Top-up Tax calculation in respect of its operations that are likely to be taxable at or above the Minimum Rate. They would also provide for improved tax certainty and transparency in the use of risk assessment under the GloBE

105. Based on OECD's GloBE Model Rules and its Commentary.

Rules. Also, going forward, further guidance on the interpretation or application of the GloBE Rules may be agreed upon and published by the IF.

4.8.1 Article 8.1. (Filing Obligation)

845. Prominent features of Article 8.1 are provided in Box 4.40.

Box 4.40 Prominent Features of Article 8.1

- Providing information to tax administrations on the tax calculations made by the MNE Group under the GloBE rules is achieved under Article 8.1, which sets out the requirements for the filing of a GloBE Information Return with the local tax administration.
  - The return can be filed by each CE directly with its local tax administration or through a Designated Local Entity on behalf of one or more CEs located in the same jurisdiction.
  - A Stateless Constituent Entity, such as a Flow-through Entity that is not a UPE, would not be required to file this return because it is not located in the implementing jurisdiction.
  - The Constituent Entity-owners of the Flow-through Entity would be required to submit a GloBE Information Return as would any other CE located in a jurisdiction by virtue of the first sentence of Article 8.1.1.
  - Where the Flow-through Entity is the UPE or is required to apply the IIR, it would be located in the jurisdiction where it was created in accordance with Article 10.3.2(a), and, therefore, it would be required to submit a GloBE Information Return.
  - PEs are CEs and, therefore, are required to file a GloBE Information Return in the jurisdiction where they are located.
  - An Entity treated as a JV in the CFS of an MNE Group is not required to submit a GloBE Information Return in accordance with Article 8.1.1 because it is not a CE of that MNE Group despite being treated as such solely for purposes of the computation of its Top-up Tax in accordance with Article 6.4.1 (a).
  - An Entity treated as a JV Subsidiary by an MNE Group is not required to submit a GloBE Information Return for that Group.
- Article 8.1.2 states that all CEs (including the Designated Local Entity) are discharged from the requirement to file a GloBE Information Return if the return has been filed by the UPE or by a Designated Filing Entity appointed by the MNE Group, provided that the CA of the jurisdiction in which the Filing Constituent Entity is located has a Qualifying Competent Authority Agreement with the CA of the jurisdiction where the CE is located.
- Article 8.1.3 requires a CE (either directly or through a Designated Local Entity) to notify its local tax administration of the identity and location of the

UPE or the Designated Filing Entity that will be filing the GloBE Information Return.
   - This provides the tax administration with notice that it will receive the return through information exchange channels.
- Article 8.1.4 states that the GloBE Information Return has to be filed in a standard template that is developed in accordance with the GloBE Implementation Framework and sets out the items of information that should be included in the GloBE Information Return.
   - While Article 8.1.4 relates to information in the GloBE Information Return, it is not intended to prevent a local tax administration from requesting further necessary supporting information to verify compliance with the GloBE Rules in accordance with its domestic law.
- Article 8.1.5 states that the GloBE Information Return shall apply the definitions and instructions contained in the standard template that is developed in accordance with the GloBE Implementation Framework.
- In order to allow MNE Groups time to prepare the required information, Article 8.1.6 provides them with up to fifteen months after the last day of the Reporting Fiscal Year to file the GloBE Information Return and the notifications with the relevant tax administrations.
   - There is no special provision under Article 8.1 regarding amendments to a GloBE Information Return.
- In order to provide some flexibility to jurisdictions, Article 8.1.7 provides that a tax administration may modify the information, filing and notification requirements in respect of the GloBE Information Return, where this is agreed upon as part of the GloBE Implementation Framework.
- Article 8.1.8 requires that the laws of each jurisdiction with respect to penalties, sanctions, and confidentiality of the returns (including the information in the returns) shall also apply to the GloBE Information Return.

846. *Background:* The GloBE Rules should be implemented and administered in such a way that any Top-up Tax liabilities incurred are due and paid within a reasonable period and in line with the intended outcomes under the GloBE Rules and the Commentary. Providing information to tax administrations on the tax calculations made by the MNE Group under the GloBE rules is achieved under Article 8.1, which sets out the requirements for the filing of a GloBE Information Return with the local tax administration. This return can be filed by each CE directly with its local tax administration or through a Designated Local Entity on behalf of one or more CEs located in the same jurisdiction. Article 8.1 recognises that a CE may not be in the best position to collect the information necessary to complete the GloBE Information Return, particularly if most of the information on that return concerns other members of the MNE Group. In many cases, it is expected that the UPE or a Designated Filing Entity appointed by the MNE Group would be in a better position to collect such information, much of which may already be collected in the preparation of the MNE Group's CFS. However, it may be noted that the rules set out in Article 8.1 do not seek to harmonise tax filing and payment obligations for the GloBE Rules themselves. Instead, they aim to provide core information to jurisdictions implementing the GloBE Rules information reporting requirements. The operation of tax filing and payment obligation rules, including, for example, late payment interest and time limits for auditing and correcting returns, is left to the determination of each implementing jurisdiction based on the design of that jurisdiction's existing tax filing and payment procedures.

4.8.1.1 Article 8.1.1.

847. Subject to Article 8.1.2, each Constituent Entity located in a Jurisdiction that has implemented GloBE Rules shall file a GloBE Information Return conforming to the requirements of Articles 8.1.4 to 8.1.6 with the tax administration of that Jurisdiction. The return may be filed by either the Constituent Entity itself or by a Designated Local Entity on its behalf.

848. *Objective of the Article:* Article 8.1.1 casts an obligation on either the CE or a Designated Local Entity on its behalf to file a GloBE Information Return conforming to the requirements of Articles 8.1.4 to 8.1.6 with the tax administration of the Jurisdiction that has implemented GloBE Rules. The mechanics of Article 8.1.1 are further explained in Figure 4.45.

Figure 4.45 Mechanics of Article 8.1.1

Mechanics of Article 8.1.1

Article 8.1.1 is subject to Article 8.1.2

1st sentence of Article 8.1.1

- Each CE of an MNE Group would be required to prepare a GloBE Information Return and file it with its tax administration.

Filing obligation for a Stateless CE, PE, JV and others:

- A Stateless Constituent Entity, such as a Flow-through Entity that is not a UPE, would not be required to file this return because it is not located in the implementing jurisdiction.
- For example, a partnership that is a Flow-through Entity and is not treated as tax resident in the jurisdiction where it is organized would not generally be required to submit a GloBE Information Return. In most cases this is consistent with its tax treatment in the jurisdiction where it was organized.
- However, the Constituent Entity-owners of the Flow-through Entity would be required to submit a GloBE Information Return as would any other CE located in a jurisdiction by virtue of the first sentence of Article 8.1.1.
- Where the Flow-through Entity is the UPE or is required to apply the IIR, it would be located in the jurisdiction where it was created in accordance with Article 10.3.2(a) and therefore, it would be required to submit a GloBE Information Return. In these cases, the GloBE Information Return could be filed by an authorised entity such as a trustee or manager on behalf of the Flow-through Entity.
- PEs are CEs and therefore, required to file a GloBE Information Return in the jurisdiction where they are located.
- An Entity treated as a JV in the CFS of an MNE Group is not required to submit a GloBE Information Return in accordance with Article 8.1.1, because it is not a CE of that MNE Group despite being treated as such solely for purposes of the computation of its Top-up Tax in accordance with Article 6.4.1 (a).
- For the same reasons, an Entity treated as a JV Subsidiary by an MNE Group is not required to submit a GloBE Information Return for that Group.

Note : In some cases, a Flow-through Entity may have some formal obligations under domestic tax law such as submitting information returns. In these situations, jurisdictions are free to extend the obligation in Article 8.1.1 to such Entities provided that they are created under their domestic law.

2nd sentence of Article 8.1.1

- Where there are two or more CEs located in the same jurisdiction, one of them, i.e., the Designated Local Entity, is required to file a single GloBE Information Return on behalf of the others (and itself).
- When a Designated Local Entity files a GloBE Information Return on behalf of other CEs located in the same jurisdiction, the obligation of those CEs to file their own return is discharged.
- Although Article 8.1 places the default filing obligation on each local CE, it would be acceptable for implementing jurisdictions to make a Designated Local Entity the sole CE that is legally responsible for this filing obligation, provided this approach achieves the intended purpose of ensuring an information return is filed on behalf of the MNE Group.

4.8.1.2 Article 8.1.2.

849. A Constituent Entity is not obligated to file a GloBE Information Return with the tax administration of a Jurisdiction that has implemented GloBE Rules if a GloBE Information Return conforming to the requirements of Articles 8.1.4 to 8.1.6 has been filed by either:

(a) the UPE located in a jurisdiction that has a Qualifying Competent Authority Agreement in effect with the Jurisdiction that has implemented GloBE Rules for the Reporting Fiscal Year; or
(b) the Designated Filing Entity located in a jurisdiction that has a Qualifying Competent Authority Agreement in effect with the Jurisdiction that has implemented GloBE Rules for the Reporting Fiscal Year.

850. The term Qualifying Competent Authority Agreement mentioned supra is defined in Article 10.1 as below:

> Qualifying Competent Authority Agreement means a bilateral or multilateral agreement or arrangement between Competent Authorities that provides for the automatic exchange of annual GloBE Information Returns.

851. The term Designated Filing Entity mentioned supra is defined in Article 10.1 as below:

> Designated Filing Entity means the Constituent Entity, other than the Ultimate Parent Entity, that has been appointed by the MNE Group to file the GloBE Information Return on behalf of the MNE Group.

852. *Objective of the Article:* Article 8.1.2 states that all CEs (including the Designated Local Entity) are discharged from the requirement to file a GloBE Information Return if the return has been filed by the UPE or by a Designated Filing Entity appointed by the MNE Group provided that the Competent Authority (CA) of the jurisdiction in which the Filing Constituent Entity is located has a Qualifying Competent Authority Agreement with the CA of the jurisdiction where the CE is located. Thus, by reason of the Qualifying Competent Authority Agreement, the CA of the jurisdiction where the CE is located should obtain the GloBE Information Return on an automatic basis from the CA of the jurisdiction where the UPE or Designated Filing Entity is located.

853. *Information exchange mechanism allowed under Article 8.1.2:* The information exchange mechanism allowed under Article 8.1.2 means that many, and perhaps most, tax administrations will receive the GloBE Information Return through an exchange of information mechanism and that a local filing obligation will only apply, in practice, where the return has not otherwise been filed in a jurisdiction with a Qualifying Competent Authority Agreement. The Qualifying Competent Authority Agreement mechanism allows the MNE Group to minimise compliance burdens by having the

UPE, or appoint a single Designated Filing Entity, prepare and file the GloBE Information Return centrally for distribution to tax administrations in other jurisdictions. While, in many cases, the UPE will fulfil this function of filing returns on behalf of the Group Entities, there may be reasons why another CE is better placed to do so, and, therefore, the MNE Group may appoint another CE as the Designated Filing Entity. For example, the jurisdiction where the Designated Filing Entity is located may have a wider network of international exchange agreements in effect and therefore a greater ability to reduce the local filing obligations throughout the MNE Group.

4.8.1.3 Article 8.1.3.

854. Where Article 8.1.2 applies, a Constituent Entity located in a Jurisdiction that has implemented GloBE Rules or the Designated Local Entity on its behalf shall notify the tax administration of that Jurisdiction of the identity of the Entity that is filing the GloBE Information Return and the jurisdiction in which it is located.

855. The term Designated Local Entity mentioned *supra* is defined in Article 10.1 as below:

> Designated Local Entity means the Constituent Entity of an MNE Group that is located in a jurisdiction that has implemented GloBE Rules and that has been appointed by the other Constituent Entities located in that jurisdiction of the MNE Group to file the GloBE Information Return, or to submit the notifications under Article 8.1.3.

856. *Objective of the Article:* Article 8.1.3 requires a CE (either directly or through a Designated Local Entity) to notify its local tax administration of the identity and location of the UPE or the Designated Filing Entity that will be filing the GloBE Information Return. This provides the tax administration with notice that it will receive the return through information exchange channels.

4.8.1.4 Article 8.1.4.

857. The GloBE Information Return shall be filed in a standard template that is developed in accordance with the GloBE Implementation Framework and shall include the following information concerning the MNE Group (which shall be specified, expanded or restricted in accordance with the GloBE Implementation Framework, including through the development of simplified reporting procedures):

(a) identification of the Constituent Entities, including their tax identification numbers (if they exist), the jurisdiction in which they are located and their status under the GloBE Rules,

(b) Information on the overall corporate structure of the MNE Group, including the Controlling Interests in the Constituent Entities held by other Constituent Entities;

(c) the information necessary to compute:
   (i) the ETR for each jurisdiction and the Top-up Tax of each Constituent Entity under Chapter 5;
   (ii) the Top-up Tax of a member of the JV Group under Chapter 6;
   (iii) the allocation of Top-up Tax under the IIR, and the UTPR Top-up Tax Amount to each jurisdiction, under Chapter 2;
(d) a record of the elections made in accordance with the relevant provisions of the GloBE Rules; and
(e) other information that is agreed upon as part of the GloBE Implementation Framework and is necessary to carry out the administration of the GloBE Rules.

858. *Objective of the Article:* Article 8.1.4 states that the GloBE Information Return has to be filed in a standard template that is developed in accordance with the GloBE Implementation Framework and sets out the items of information that should be included in the GloBE Information Return. While Article 8.1.4 relates to information in the GloBE Information Return, it is not intended to prevent a local tax administration from requesting further necessary supporting information to verify compliance with the GloBE Rules in accordance with its domestic law. It is anticipated that a standard template of the GloBE Information Return that is developed in accordance with the GloBE Implementation Framework will contain fields for all of the required information. The various contents and requirements of information to be disclosed in the GloBE Information Return are captured in Figure 4.46.

Figure 4.46 Contents of GloBE Information Return under Article 8.1.4

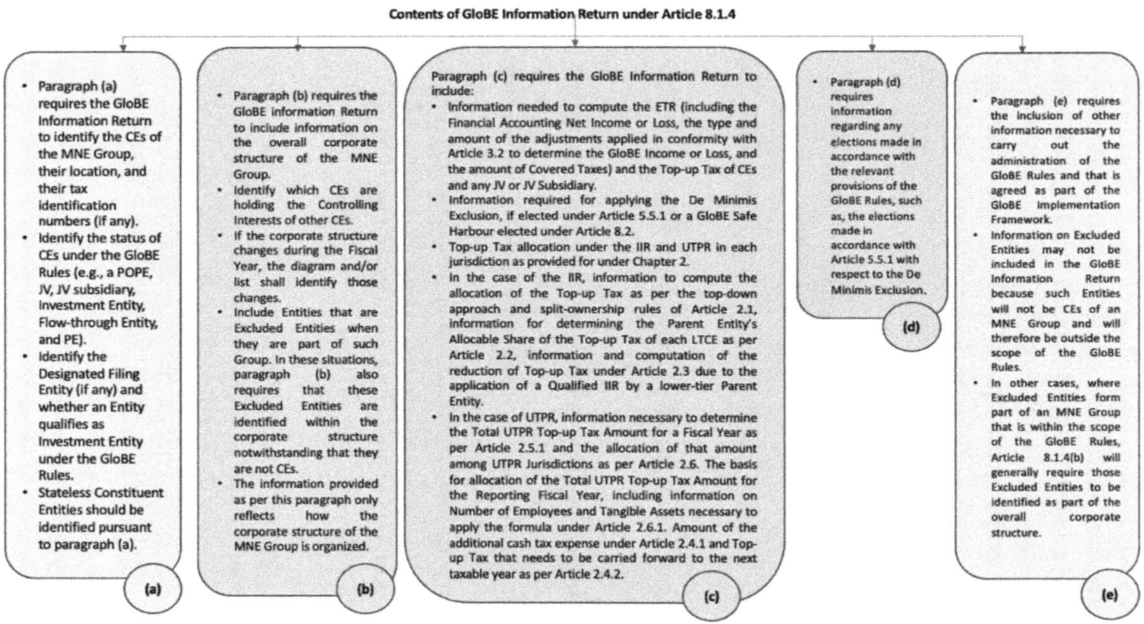

4.8.1.5 Article 8.1.5.

859. The GloBE Information Return shall apply the definitions and instructions contained in the standard template that is developed in accordance with the GloBE Implementation Framework.

860. *Objective of the Article:* Article 8.1.5 states that the GloBE Information Return shall apply the definitions and instructions contained in the standard template that is developed in accordance with the GloBE Implementation Framework. These definitions and instructions would be developed by the members of the IF on BEPS.

4.8.1.6 Article 8.1.6.

861. The GloBE Information Return and the notifications pursuant to this article shall be filed with the tax administration of the Jurisdiction that has implemented GloBE Rules no later than fifteen months after the last day of the Reporting Fiscal Year.

862. The term Reporting Fiscal Year mentioned supra is defined in Article 10.1 as below:

> Reporting Fiscal Year means the Fiscal Year that is the subject of the GloBE Information Return.

863. *Objective of the Article:* In order to allow MNE Groups time to prepare the required information, Article 8.1.6 provides MNE Groups with up to fifteen months after the last day of the Reporting Fiscal Year to file the GloBE Information Return and the notifications with the relevant tax administrations. The timing for filing notifications is aligned with the timing for filing the GloBE Information Return (i.e., within fifteen months after the last day of the Reporting Fiscal Year). This gives a CE or a Designated Local Entity ample opportunity to notify its local tax administration of the identity and location of the UPE or Designated Filing Entity that will be filing the GloBE Information Return on its behalf.

864. *Amendments to GloBE Information Return*: There is no special provision under Article 8.1 regarding amendments to a GloBE Information Return. It has been left to jurisdictions to decide whether their current domestic rules regarding amendments to tax or information returns will apply to the GloBE Information Return, or they are expected to introduce new provisions that apply only to the GloBE Information Return.

4.8.1.7 Article 8.1.7.

865. The tax administration of the Jurisdiction that has implemented GloBE Rules may modify the information, filing, and notification requirements of the GloBE Information Return to align those requirements with those provided under the GloBE Implementation Framework (including the development of simplified reporting procedures).

866. *Objective of the Article:* Article 8.1.7 provides that a tax administration may modify the information, filing and notification requirements in respect of the GloBE Information Return, where this is agreed upon as part of the GloBE Implementation Framework. This provision is intended to provide some flexibility to jurisdictions and their tax administrations in the implementation of the filing and notification requirements that are developed under the GloBE Implementation Framework (including additional, simplified or modified filing requirements) but after the enactment of the legislation, regulations, or other guidance implementing the GloBE Rules.

4.8.1.8 Article 8.1.8.

867. The laws of the Jurisdiction that has implemented GloBE Rules with respect to penalties, sanctions and the confidentiality of returns and return information shall apply to the GloBE Information Return.

868. *Objective of the Article:* Article 8.1.8 requires that the laws of each jurisdiction with respect to penalties, sanctions, and confidentiality of the returns (including the information in the returns) shall also apply to the GloBE Information Return. In the case of penalties and sanctions, this means that domestic penalties and sanctions would apply if the GloBE Information Return is not submitted on time or if there is any false or incomplete information. Jurisdictions are free to extend existing penalties or sanctions (as well as any penalty or sanction mitigation provisions) or to create new ones for the GloBE Information Return. New penalties and sanctions in respect of the GloBE Information Return should be commensurate with penalties or sanctions in respect of other information returns and other information return filing obligations in the jurisdiction.

869. *Confidentiality associated with GloBE Information Return*: In respect of confidentiality of the returns, the information gathered under the GloBE Information Return shall have at least the same level of protection as the information obtained through domestic tax or information returns. GloBE Information Returns received by a tax administration through exchange of information would further be subject to the confidentiality rules of the applicable Tax Treaty, tax information exchange agreement or other international agreement for the exchange of information.

4.8.2 Article 8.2. (Safe Harbours)

870. Prominent features of Article 8.2 are provided in Box 4.41.

Box 4.41 Prominent Features of Article 8.2

- Provides that in order to limit unnecessary compliance and administrative burden for MNE Groups and tax administrations, the GloBE Implementation Framework will seek to explore the development of GloBE Safe Harbours.

  - GloBE Safe Harbours would allow an MNE Group to avoid the ETR and Top-up Tax calculation in respect of its operations that are likely to be taxable at or above the Minimum Rate.
  - They would also provide for improved tax certainty and transparency in the use of risk assessment under the GloBE Rules.
- In anticipation of the GloBE Safe Harbours that may be developed as part of the GloBE Implementation Framework, the provisions of Article 8.2.1 would allow a Filing Constituent Entity to make an election with respect to CEs that qualify for that GloBE Safe Harbour.
  - The effect of the GloBE Safe Harbour would be to exempt the MNE Group from the need to compute the jurisdictional ETR and allow a tax administration to deem the Top-up Tax for the CEs located in the safe harbour jurisdiction to be zero for a Fiscal Year when the MNE Group can demonstrate that those CEs meet the requirements of the GloBE Safe Harbour.
  - The election for a GloBE Safe Harbour would be made on an annual basis.
- Article 8.2.2 provides for a coordinated and balanced framework under which another tax administration could challenge a taxpayer's election to apply a GloBE Safe Harbour in circumstances that may have materially affected the eligibility of the MNE Group for the relevant GloBE Safe Harbour.
  - Paragraph (a) of Article 8.2.2 provides that only a jurisdiction that could be allocated Top-up Tax under the GloBE Rules if the ETR of the safe harbour jurisdiction was below the Minimum Rate could challenge the use of a GloBE Safe Harbour with respect to the safe harbour jurisdiction.
  - Paragraph (b) of Article 8.2.2 provides that the tax administration that wishes to challenge the use of a GloBE Safe Harbour notifies the Liable Constituent Entity (or Entities) within thirty-six months after the GloBE Information Return is filed. The timeframe for clarification by the Liable Constituent Entity (or Entities) is six months.
  - Paragraph (c) of Article 8.2.2 provides that if the Liable Constituent Entity (or Entities) fails to demonstrate that the facts and circumstances identified by the tax administration did not materially affect the eligibility of the MNE for the GloBE Safe Harbour for this jurisdiction within the six-month response period, the GloBE Safe Harbour would not be applicable.

871. *Background:* MNE Groups need to collect, adjust and aggregate information on a jurisdictional basis in order to identify and allocate Top-up Tax in respect of their operations in Low-Tax Jurisdictions. At the same time, tax administrations need to analyse the return information, assess risk areas, audit taxpayers and collect Top-up Tax that is brought into charge under the GloBE Rules in their jurisdiction. It is, therefore, likely that MNE Groups and tax administrations will incur incremental compliance and administration costs in respect of the application of the GloBE Rules. In order to limit unnecessary compliance and administrative burden for MNE Groups and tax administrations, the GloBE Implementation Framework will seek to explore the development of GloBE Safe Harbours. GloBE Safe Harbours would allow an MNE Group to avoid the ETR and Top-up Tax calculation in respect of its operations that are likely to be taxable at or above the Minimum Rate. They would also provide for improved tax certainty and transparency in the use of risk assessment under the GloBE Rules.

4.8.2.1 Article 8.2.1.

872. At the election of the Filing Constituent Entity, and notwithstanding Chapter 5, the Top-up Tax for a jurisdiction (the safe harbour jurisdiction) shall be deemed to be zero for a Fiscal Year when the Constituent Entities located in this jurisdiction are eligible for a GloBE Safe Harbour, pursuant to the conditions provided under the GloBE Implementation Framework and applicable for that Fiscal Year.

873. The term GloBE Safe Harbour mentioned *supra* is defined in Article 10.1 as below:

> GloBE Safe Harbour means the exception provided in Article 8.2.1 to facilitate compliance by MNEs and administration by tax authorities. The conditions under which the Constituent Entities of an MNE Group located in a jurisdiction are eligible for the GloBE Safe Harbour will be established in accordance with a common and agreed process to be defined as part of the work undertaken by the Inclusive Framework on BEPS to develop the GloBE Implementation Framework.

874. *Objective of the Article:* In anticipation of the GloBE Safe Harbours that may be developed as part of the GloBE Implementation Framework, the provisions of Article 8.2.1 would allow a Filing Constituent Entity to make an election with respect to CEs that qualify for that GloBE Safe Harbour. The effect of the GloBE Safe Harbour would be to exempt the MNE Group from the need to compute the jurisdictional ETR and allow a tax administration to deem the Top-up Tax for the CEs located in the safe harbour jurisdiction to be zero for a Fiscal Year when the MNE Group can demonstrate that those CEs meet the requirements of the GloBE Safe Harbour. Accordingly, Article 8.2.1 allows the tax administration to treat such CEs as having zero Top-up Tax for the year. These conditions would be designed with the intent to limit compliance costs for MNE Groups as well as administrative burden for tax authorities and incorporate thresholds that ensure only those parts of the MNE Group's operations that are nearly certain to have jurisdictional ETRs above the Minimum Rate would be eligible for the GloBE Safe Harbour.

875. *Compliances expected from the MNE Group that elects to apply GloBE Safe Harbour*: If a Filing Constituent Entity elects to apply any GloBE Safe Harbour to the MNE Group's operations in a jurisdiction that would be eligible for the GloBE Safe Harbour, then the Top-up Tax for this jurisdiction would be deemed to be zero for the

Fiscal Year of the election. The election for a GloBE Safe Harbour would be made on an annual basis. An MNE Group that elects to apply the GloBE Safe Harbour in respect of its CEs in a jurisdiction (the safe harbour jurisdiction) should not be required to compute the jurisdictional ETR for those CEs under Chapters 3-5 but is required to:

- provide a record of the election to use the GloBE Safe Harbour,
- identify all the CEs in the safe harbour jurisdiction, and
- provide any other relevant information, as part of the GloBE Information Return, consistent with Article 8.1.4 (a), (d) and (e).

4.8.2.2 Article 8.2.2.

876. An election made for a jurisdiction under Article 8.2.1 shall not apply in circumstances where:

(a) A Jurisdiction that has implemented GloBE Rules could be allocated Top-up Tax under the GloBE Rules if the ETR for the safe harbour jurisdiction computed in accordance with Chapter 5 was below the Minimum Rate; and
(b) the tax administration of a Jurisdiction that has implemented GloBE Rules notifies the Liable Constituent Entity (or Entities) within thirty-six months after the filing of the GloBE Information Return of specific facts and circumstances that may have materially affected the eligibility of the Constituent Entities located in the safe harbour jurisdiction for the relevant safe harbour and invites the Liable Constituent Entity (or Entities) to clarify within six months the effect of those facts and circumstances on the eligibility of those Constituent Entities for that safe harbour; and
(c) the Liable Constituent Entity (or Entities) fail(s) to demonstrate within the response period that those facts and circumstances did not materially affect the eligibility of the Constituent Entities for the relevant safe harbour.

877. The term Liable Constituent Entity (or Entities) mentioned *supra* is defined in Article 10.1 as below:

> Liable Constituent Entity (or Entities) means one or several Constituent Entities located in a Jurisdiction that has implemented GloBE Rules that could be liable for Top-up Tax or subject to an adjustment under Chapter 2 if the GloBE Safe Harbour in Article 8.2.1 did not apply.

878. *Objective of the Article:* Where an MNE Group elects to apply a GloBE Safe Harbour, a tax administration could apply its ordinary assessment, investigation and audit processes to determine whether the GloBE Safe Harbour was applied in accordance with any criteria set out in the GloBE Implementation Framework and to assess the reasonableness of underlying data used for purposes of the GloBE Safe Harbour. As a consequence, Article 8.2.2 provides for a coordinated and balanced framework under which another tax administration could challenge a taxpayer's election to apply a GloBE Safe Harbour in circumstances that may have materially affected the eligibility of the MNE Group for the relevant GloBE Safe Harbour. Such actions by tax administrations, relevant conditions leading to such actions and necessary responses by the Liable Constituent Entity (or Entities) leading to a conclusion whether GloBE Safe Harbour is applicable or not are summarised in Figure 4.47.

Figure 4.47 Actions by Tax Administrations and Responses by the Liable Constituent Entity (or Entities) under Article 8.2.2

Actions by tax administrations and responses by the Liable Constituent Entity (or Entities) under Article 8.2.2

(a)

- Article 8.2.2(a) provides that only a jurisdiction that could be allocated Top-up Tax under the GloBE Rules if the ETR of the safe harbour jurisdiction was below the Minimum Rate could challenge the use of a GloBE Safe Harbour with respect to the safe harbour jurisdiction.
- In view of above, this paragraph ensures that the only jurisdictions that could challenge the use of a GloBE Safe Harbour are those that are affected by their use, i.e., those jurisdictions that would otherwise be allocated Top-up Tax if not for the use of a GloBE Safe Harbour.
- This paragraph would apply on an MNE Group-by-MNE Group basis and require testing whether the jurisdiction could be allocated Top-up Tax if the ETR of the safe harbour jurisdiction was below the Minimum Rate, by applying the allocation mechanics of the GloBE Rules and taking into account the MNE Group's structure.
- However, this paragraph by itself assumes that the ETR could be below the Minimum Rate and does not require the tax administration or the taxpayer to compute the ETR of the jurisdiction to test whether the ETR is below the Minimum Rate.

(b)

- Article 8.2.2(b) provides that the tax administration that wishes to challenge the use of a GloBE Safe Harbour notifies the Liable Constituent Entity (or Entities) within 36 months after the GloBE Information Return is filed.
- While the tax administration should make its best efforts to notify all Liable Constituent Entities located in the jurisdiction, there may be circumstances where it would be enough to notify substantially all Liable Constituent Entities, but not all of them, for instance because of a complex holding structure of the MNE Group in the jurisdiction.
- In addition, the tax administration may allow that only one of the Liable Constituent Entities of the MNE Group gives a response to the tax administration on behalf of the other Liable Constituent Entities, so that not all Liable Constituent Entities are required to give a response to the tax administration.
- Article 8.2.2 (b) further provides that the Liable Constituent Entity (or Entities) is invited by the tax administration to clarify the effect of those facts and circumstances on the application of the GloBE Safe Harbour.
- The timeframe for clarifying the effect of those facts and circumstances is 6 months.

(c)

- Article 8.2.2(c) provides that if the Liable Constituent Entity (or Entities) fails to demonstrate that the facts and circumstances identified by the tax administration did not affect materially the eligibility of the MNE for the GloBE Safe Harbour for this jurisdiction within the 6-month response period, the GloBE Safe Harbour would not be applicable.*
- If the Liable Constituent Entity (or Entities), instead, demonstrates that the facts and circumstances identified by the tax administration did not affect materially the eligibility of the MNE for the GloBE Safe Harbour for the CEs located in the safe harbour jurisdiction, the GloBE Safe Harbour would still be applicable and the ETR of the jurisdiction would still be treated as if it was above the Minimum Rate.

* Note : The details of the consequences where the GloBE Safe Harbour is found not applicable as a result of Article 8.2.2 shall be considered in the GloBE Implementation Framework.

4.8.3 Article 8.3. (Administrative Guidance)

879. Prominent features of Article 8.3 are provided in Box 4.42.

Box 4.42 Prominent Features of Article 8.3

- Provides that in order to address interpretational issues and also, in order to provide further clarity on GloBE Rules, the OECD shall issue Administrative Guidance, which the tax administrations of jurisdictions that have implemented GloBE Rules are required to comply with while applying the GloBE Rules, subject to any other requirements under their respective domestic law.
  - Article 8.3.1 contemplates that further guidance on the interpretation or application of the GloBE Rules may be agreed upon and published by the IF.

880. *Background:* There are a number of places in the GloBE Rules where determinations by one tax administration are likely to have corresponding consequences for the application of the GloBE Rules in other jurisdictions. In these cases, tax administrations can collaborate with each other through the IF to determine whether a coordinated solution to these questions can be agreed upon. Accordingly, to address such interpretational issues and also in order to provide further clarity on GloBE Rules, the OECD shall issue Administrative Guidance, which the tax administrations of jurisdictions that have implemented GloBE Rules are required to comply with while applying the GloBE Rules.

4.8.3.1 Article 8.3.1.

881. The tax administration of a Jurisdiction that has implemented GloBE Rules shall, subject to any requirements of domestic law, apply the GloBE Rules in accordance with any Agreed Administrative Guidance.

882. The term Agreed Administrative Guidance mentioned *supra* is defined in Article 10.1 as below:

> Agreed Administrative Guidance means guidance on the interpretation or administration of the GloBE Rules issued by the Inclusive Framework.

883. *Objective of the Article:* Article 8.3.1 contemplates that further guidance on the interpretation or application of the GloBE Rules may be agreed upon and published by the IF. This article ensures that when such guidance is issued, it is applied in a coordinated way by the tax administrations of jurisdictions that have implemented GloBE Rules. Accordingly, if the discussions at the level of the IF result in the development of Agreed Administrative Guidance, then Article 8.3.1 provides that a tax administration should interpret and apply the GloBE Rules in accordance with that Agreed Administrative Guidance, subject to any other requirements under domestic law. For example, the domestic law of some IF members would not permit them to simply refer to that Agreed Administrative Guidance to interpret and apply the GloBE Rules. Their domestic law may instead permit the tax administration to adopt that Agreed Administrative Guidance by incorporating it verbatim or in substance into its own administrative guidance. Some IF members may need parliamentary acceptance of the Agreed Administrative Guidance before it can be used to interpret or apply the GloBE Rules.

884. The Commentary released by the OECD on GloBE Rules has already identified several areas where Administrative Guidance shall be issued by the GloBE Implementation Framework, as tabulated *inter alia* in Table 4.4. Remaining areas not mentioned hereunder are separately discussed and covered *infra* under the GloBE Implementation Framework in Chapter 7.

Table 4.4 Certain Issues Where Administrative Guidance Shall Be Provided by the OECD under Article 8.3 of GloBE Rules

S. No.	*Issue Requiring Release of Administrative Guidance*	*Reference in Commentary*
1	The IF may develop further examples on the application of the GloBE Rules through Administrative Guidance.	Paragraph 3 of Introduction to the Commentary.
2	MNE Groups commonly hedge foreign currency movements in Ownership Interests in CEs. The GloBE Implementation Framework will consider providing Agreed Administrative Guidance on the extent to which such gains and losses may be treated as Excluded Equity Gains or Losses.	Paragraph 57 of Chapter 3.
3	The treatment of Pillar One taxation will be further addressed through Administrative Guidance to be developed as part of the Implementation Framework.	Paragraph 29 of Chapter 4.
4	Concerning payroll carve-out in Article 5.3.3, which is computed on a jurisdictional basis, in certain cases, the employee may perform work for their employer outside the employer's jurisdiction. Consideration will be given to the development of Agreed Administrative Guidance as part of the GloBE Implementation Framework to address those cases where the employee performs part of its activities in another jurisdiction and for those employees that perform their activity in multiple jurisdictions.	Paragraph 33 of Chapter 5.

S. No.	*Issue Requiring Release of Administrative Guidance*	*Reference in Commentary*
5	Concerning tangible asset carve-out in Article 5.3.4, under specific circumstances, the nature of the asset and the way it is used may be such that it is not located in any jurisdiction or is located in multiple jurisdictions (e.g., an aircraft of an international airline) at different times during the Fiscal Year. Consideration will be given to the development of Agreed Administrative Guidance as part of the GloBE Implementation Framework to address such cases.	Paragraph 38 of Chapter 5.
6	The special rules related to corporate restructurings in Articles 6.2 and 6.3 are intended to produce outcomes that are generally aligned with the local tax treatment of such transactions. However, the precise tax treatment of restructurings varies among IF jurisdictions, and additional guidance may be needed to address the application of the GloBE Rules in certain scenarios.	Paragraph 7 of Chapter 6.
7	For purposes of applying Article 7.1, the GloBE Implementation Framework will consider providing Agreed Administrative Guidance on the treatment of a Tax Transparent Entity that would be the UPE of the MNE Group if its Controlling Interests were not held by an Excluded Entity.	Paragraph 6 of Chapter 7.
8	The GloBE Implementation Framework will consider providing Agreed Administrative Guidance related to the measurement and treatment of items of deferred tax expense (i.e., deferred tax assets and deferred tax liabilities) in the Transition Year and subsequent years.	Paragraph 6 of Chapter 9.

4.9 CHAPTER 9 OF GLOBE RULES (TRANSITION RULES)[106]

885. *Background:* There are various stages when an MNE Group or a CE may come under the ambit of GloBE Rules:

- Where an MNE Group has revenues in excess of the revenue threshold, it will become subject to the GloBE Rules after such rules are introduced into the domestic law of a jurisdiction in which the MNE Group operates.
- Smaller MNE Groups will become subject to the GloBE Rules for the first time if they grow their revenues above the threshold, either organically or as a result of a merger or acquisition.
- A CE could also become subject to the GloBE Rules for the first time when such CE is acquired by an MNE Group that is already subject to the GloBE Rules.

106. Based on OECD's GloBE Model Rules and its Commentary.

Accordingly, at the point an MNE Group becomes subject to the GloBE Rules, it is expedient to take appropriate account of operating losses that the MNE Group has incurred in the period(s) prior to becoming subject to the GloBE Rules and also address issues arising in relation to timing differences; otherwise, taxation under the GloBE Rules may arise. These concerns and similar such concerns are addressed through Transition Rules provided in Chapter 9 of GloBE Model Rules.

4.9.1 Article 9.1. (Tax Attributes upon Transition)

886. Prominent features of Article 9.1 are provided in Box 4.43.

Box 4.43 Prominent Features of Article 9.1

- At the juncture an MNE Group becomes subject to the GloBE Rules, it is expedient to take appropriate account of operating losses that the MNE Group has incurred in the period(s) prior to becoming subject to the GloBE Rules and also address issues arising in relation to timing differences; otherwise, taxation under the GloBE Rules may arise. These concerns and similar such concerns are addressed through Transition Rules.
  - Consistent with the general mechanism to address temporary differences contained in Article 4.4, these transition rules build on deferred tax accounting concepts.
  - The transition rules allow existing deferred tax accounting attributes, including deferred tax assets resulting from prior year losses, to be used in the calculation of the ETR to prevent distortions upon entry into the GloBE regime of a CE of an MNE Group.
- Article 9.1.1 sets out the deferred tax accounting attributes of a CE that may be utilised in calculating the ETR in a jurisdiction in the Transition Year and subsequent years.
  - Article 9.1.1 provides the basis to use these attributes in determination of Covered Taxes pursuant to Article 4.4.
  - Attributes established under Article 9.1.1 are eliminated pursuant to Article 4.5.1 when a GloBE Loss Election is made under Article 4.5 because Article 4.4 does not apply when the GloBE Loss is elected under Article 4.5.
- Article 9.1.2 provides a limitation to prevent the triggering of permanent difference losses before applicability of the GloBE Rules.
  - The limitation in Article 9.1.2 applies to any deferred tax asset generated in a transaction that takes place after 30 November 2021.
  - Article 9.1.2 does not have retroactive tax implications but rather sets out rules with respect to how certain attributes are taken into account in Fiscal Years to which the GloBE Rules apply.
- Article 9.1.3 provides a limitation on intragroup asset transfers before applicability of the GloBE Rules.

- If an asset is transferred between entities of an MNE Group after 30 November 2021 and before the Transition Year, and such entities would have been CEs of that MNE Group had the GloBE Rules been in effect with respect to that MNE Group, such asset must be recorded at its historical carrying value for GloBE purposes to limit the ability to step-up the basis in such assets without including the resulting gain in the computation of GloBE Income or Loss.
- The rule in Article 9.1.3, however, does not apply to inventory because of the routine nature of intragroup inventory sales and the typically brief period that it is held before sale outside the MNE Group.
- The Article does not have retroactive tax implications.

887. *Background:* When an MNE Group comes under the ambit of GloBE Rules, the financial and accounting history of the Group may raise certain issues which, if not addressed, may result in immediate taxation under the GloBE Rules. Such issues are *inter alia* as mentioned below:

- The MNE Group will be required, under a jurisdictional blending approach, to compute the ETR on its income in each jurisdiction where it operates and compare it to the Minimum Rate. Failure to take appropriate account of operating losses that the MNE Group has incurred in the period(s) prior to becoming subject to the GloBE Rules could result in a distorted picture of the MNE Group's tax position in that jurisdiction and may subject the MNE Group to taxation in excess of its economic profit. For example, a CE may have incurred operating losses in the years prior to the MNE Group becoming subject to the GloBE Rules. Frequently, the operating losses of the CE will also be recognised for local tax purposes, and these losses may be eligible to be carried forward and be available to reduce taxable income arising in a future period in the same jurisdiction. Ignoring the effect of these prior period losses could result in an immediate GloBE tax on profits arising in subsequent periods despite the fact that the local tax jurisdiction is otherwise a high-tax jurisdiction and that the income subject to charge under the GloBE Rules represents, from the MNE Group's perspective, a recovery of prior period losses.
- A similar transition-related issue arises in relation to timing differences that straddle the applicability date of the GloBE Rules. Of particular concern are those timing differences that result in the acceleration of income for tax purposes and hence taxes paid prior to an MNE Group being subject to the GloBE Rules, which then reverse after the MNE Group is subject to the GloBE Rules (i.e., the financial accounting income is reported after the MNE Group becomes subject to the GloBE Rules). These situations may arise, for example, when local law taxes pre-payments of contractual fees upon receipt rather than over the term of the contract or prohibits deductions for estimates of future bad debts or warranty expenses (i.e., reserves for bad debts or warranty expenses). Absent a corrective rule that takes account of pre-paid taxes in respect of that

> income, the result would be a lower GloBE ETR in the year(s) of reversal and thus potential GloBE Top-up Tax in those years, despite the fact that the local tax jurisdiction is otherwise a high-tax jurisdiction. Similarly, timing differences that defer tax on financial accounting income arising before the GloBE Rules apply would, absent a special rule, reduce the GloBE tax liability on GloBE income arising within the GloBE applicability period.

888. *Need for transition rules:* In order to address the concerns stated *supra*, Article 9.1 provides for transition rules. Consistent with the general mechanism to address temporary differences contained in Article 4.4, these transition rules build on deferred tax accounting concepts. The transition rules allow existing deferred tax accounting attributes, including deferred tax assets resulting from prior year losses, to be used in the calculation of the ETR to prevent distortions upon entry into the GloBE regime of a CE of an MNE Group. At the same time, it may be noted that the transition rules differ from the general mechanisms contained in Chapter 4 in some ways.

4.9.1.1 Article 9.1.1.

889. When determining the ETR for a jurisdiction in a Transition Year and for each subsequent year, the MNE Group shall take into account all of the deferred tax assets and deferred tax liabilities reflected or disclosed in the financial accounts of all of the Constituent Entities in a jurisdiction for the Transition Year. Such deferred tax assets and liabilities must be taken into account at the lower of the Minimum Rate or the applicable domestic tax rate. A deferred tax asset that has been recorded at a rate lower than the Minimum Rate may be taken into account at the Minimum Rate if the taxpayer can demonstrate that the deferred tax asset is attributable to a GloBE Loss. For purposes of applying this article, the impact of any valuation adjustment or accounting recognition adjustment with respect to a deferred tax asset is disregarded.

890. The term Transition Year mentioned *supra* is defined in Article 10.1 as below:

> Transition Year, for a jurisdiction, means the first Fiscal Year that the MNE Group comes within the scope of the GloBE Rules in respect of that jurisdiction.

The Transition Year is determined on a jurisdictional basis. The phrase 'in respect of that jurisdiction' is used in the definition rather than 'of that jurisdiction' to make clear that the MNE Group's Transition Year for a particular jurisdiction may be initiated due to the GloBE Rules of another jurisdiction.

891. *Objective of the Article:* Article 9.1.1 sets out the deferred tax accounting attributes of a CE that may be utilised in calculating the ETR in a jurisdiction in the Transition Year and subsequent years. Rather than requiring an MNE Group to undertake complex calculations as if the CE had been subject to the GloBE Rules in prior years, it uses a simplified approach that allows the MNE Group to take into account the deferred tax accounting attributes of the MNE Group at the beginning of the Transition Year, at the lower of the Minimum Rate or the applicable domestic tax rate. The applicable domestic tax rate is the rate at which an item of deferred tax expense has been recorded in the financial accounts. However, deferred tax assets in respect of GloBE Losses that have been recorded at a rate lower than the Minimum Rate may be recast at the Minimum Rate if the taxpayer can demonstrate that the deferred tax asset is attributable to a loss that would have been a GloBE Loss had the MNE Group been subject to the GloBE Rules in the year in which the loss arose. These attributes include losses that have not been recognised due to an accounting recognition adjustment or valuation allowance.

892. *Provides the basis to use deferred tax accounting attributes*: Article 9.1.1 provides the basis to use these attributes in determination of Covered Taxes pursuant to Article 4.4. Therefore, when a pre-existing deferred tax attribute is used for financial reporting purposes in a Fiscal Year in which the GloBE Rules apply, such attribute is available for use in the application of Article 4.4, subject to the limitations of Article 9.1. For example, if a CE incurred a tax loss of (100) in a year before the GloBE applied, a deferred tax expense of (15) (i.e., deferred tax benefit) will be included in the Total Deferred Tax Adjustment Amount under Article 4.4 when the associated tax loss is used in a Fiscal Year in which the GloBE applies. It may be noted that Attributes established under Article 9.1.1 are eliminated pursuant to Article 4.5.1 when a GloBE Loss Election is made under Article 4.5 because Article 4.4 does not apply when the GloBE Loss is elected under Article 4.5.

4.9.1.2 Article 9.1.2.

893. Deferred tax assets arising from items excluded from the computation of GloBE Income or Loss under Chapter 3 must be excluded from Article 9.1.1 computation when such deferred tax assets are generated in a transaction that takes place after 30 November 2021.

894. *Objective of the Article:* Article 9.1.2 provides a limitation to prevent the triggering of permanent difference losses before applicability of the GloBE Rules. An example of this would be a CE that triggers a domestic tax loss with respect to an item that is not taken into account in the calculation of GloBE Income or Loss, such as depreciation deductions in excess of an asset's cost. Absent the Article 9.1.2 limitation, such attribute would be imported into the GloBE attributes upon becoming subject to the rules. The limitation in Article 9.1.2 applies to any deferred tax asset generated in a transaction that takes place after 30 November 2021. Article 9.1.2 does not have retroactive tax implications but rather sets out rules with respect to how certain attributes are taken into account in Fiscal Years to which the GloBE Rules apply.

895. Illustration # 69: The application of Article 9.1.2 is illustrated in the example below:

> In December, 2021, a CE purchases an asset for 100. The jurisdiction in which the CE is located imposes a 25% CIT rate and allows for immediate expensing of the asset in 2021 and an additional 300 of tax depreciation with respect to such asset as a tax incentive that will be deducted in the same Fiscal Year. After taking into

account the deductions with respect to the asset, there is a domestic tax loss of 300 for which a deferred tax asset is established. As the deferred tax asset recorded with respect to the supplemental 300 domestic tax loss reverses, it is not included in Adjusted Covered Taxes under the application of this article.

4.9.1.3 Article 9.1.3.

896. In the case of a transfer of assets between Constituent Entities after 30 November 2021 and before the commencement of a Transition Year, the basis of the acquired assets (other than inventory) shall be based upon the disposing Entity's carrying value of the transferred assets upon disposition with the deferred tax assets and liabilities brought into GloBE determined on that basis.

897. *Objective of the Article:* Article 9.1.3 provides a limitation on intragroup asset transfers before applicability of the GloBE Rules. If an asset is transferred between entities after 30 November 2021 and before the Transition Year of an MNE Group, and such entities would have been CEs of that MNE Group had the GloBE Rules been in effect with respect to that MNE Group, such asset must be recorded at its historical carrying value for GloBE purposes to limit the ability to step-up the basis in such assets without including the resulting gain in the computation of GloBE Income or Loss. It follows that when this rule applies because there is no change in asset basis, items of deferred tax expense with respect to such transaction will be recorded for GloBE purposes with respect to the historical carrying value of the assets transferred. The historical carrying value of the asset can easily be determined because the gain on the intragroup transfer and corresponding increased depreciation or amortisation must be eliminated in the CFS. The rule in Article 9.1.3, however, does not apply to inventory because of the routine nature of intragroup inventory sales and the typically brief period that it is held before sale outside the MNE Group. Like Article 9.1.2, this article does not have retroactive tax implications but rather sets out rules with respect to how certain attributes are taken into account in Fiscal Years to which the GloBE Rules apply.

4.9.2 Article 9.2. (Transitional Relief for the Substance-Based Income Exclusion)

898. Prominent features of Article 9.2 are provided in Box 4.44.

Box 4.44 Prominent Features of Article 9.2

- Provides the relevant percentages for the purpose of applying the payroll carve-out in Article 5.3.3 and tangible asset carve-out in Article 5.3.4 for Fiscal Years that begin in the transition period of ten calendar years beginning with 2023.
- Provides that in a transition period of ten years, the amount of income excluded will be:

- 10% of payroll and 8% of the carrying value of tangible assets in the year 2023,
- declining annually by 0.2 percentage points for the first five years, and
- declining annually by 0.8 percentage points for payroll and by 0.4 percentage points for tangible assets for the last five years.

- The Substance-based Income Exclusion set out in Article 5.3 and the percentages outlined for the transition period in Articles 9.2.1 and 9.2.2, respectively, affect only those MNE Groups with operations in jurisdictions that are taxed below the Minimum Rate.

899. The article provides the relevant percentages for the purpose of applying the payroll carve-out in Article 5.3.3 and tangible asset carve-out in Article 5.3.4 for Fiscal Years that begin in the transition period of ten calendar years beginning with 2023. Accordingly, in a transition period of ten years, the amount of income excluded will be:

- 10% of payroll and 8% of the carrying value of tangible assets in the year 2023,
- declining annually by 0.2 percentage points for the first five years, and
- declining annually by 0.8 percentage points for payroll and by 0.4 percentage points for tangible assets for the last five years.

4.9.2.1 Article 9.2.1.

900. For the purposes of applying Article 5.3.3, the value of 5% shall be replaced with the value set out in the table set out below for each Fiscal Year beginning in each of the following calendar years:

Fiscal Year Beginning In	Article 5.3.3 Rate (%)
2023	10
2024	9.8
2025	9.6
2026	9.4
2027	9.2
2028	9.0
2029	8.2
2030	7.4
2031	6.6
2032	5.8

901. *Objective of the Article:* The policy rationale behind a formulaic, substance-based carve-out is to exclude a fixed return for substantive activities within a jurisdiction from the application of the GloBE Rules. The Substance-based Income Exclusion set out in Article 5.3 only affects those MNE Groups with operations in jurisdictions that are taxed below the Minimum Rate. Article 9.2.1 provides the relevant percentages for the purpose of applying the payroll carve-out in Article 5.3.3 for Fiscal Years that begin in the transition period of ten calendar years beginning with 2023. For example, if an MNE Group has a Fiscal Year that commences on 1 March 2023, the applicable percentage to be applied for the Article 5.3.3 payroll carve-out in that Fiscal year is 10%. This transition period applies regardless of when an MNE Group comes within the scope of the GloBE Rules. For example, if an MNE Group first becomes subject to the GloBE Rules in the Fiscal Year that commences on 1 January 2026, the applicable percentage to be applied for Article 5.3.3 in that Fiscal Year is 9.4%.

4.9.2.2 Article 9.2.2.

902. For the purposes of applying Article 5.3.4, the value of 5% shall be replaced with the value set out in the table set out below for each Fiscal Year beginning in each of the following calendar years:

Fiscal Year Beginning In	Article 5.3.4 Rate (%)
2023	8
2024	7.8
2025	7.6
2026	7.4
2027	7.2
2028	7.0
2029	6.6
2030	6.2
2031	5.8
2032	5.4

903. *Objective of the Article:* Article 9.2.2 provides the relevant percentages for the purpose of applying the tangible asset carve-out in Article 5.3.4 for Fiscal Years that begin in the transition period of ten calendar years beginning with 2023. The principles described above for Article 9.2.1 apply *pari passu* with respect to Article 9.2.2.

4.9.3 Article 9.3. (Exclusion from the UTPR of MNE Groups in the Initial Phase of Their International Activity)

904. Prominent features of Article 9.3 are provided in Box 4.45.

Box 4.45 Prominent Features of Article 9.3

- Provides a transitional exclusion from the UTPR for MNE Groups that are in the initial phase of their international activity.
- Article 9.3.1 provides an exclusion from the UTPR for MNE Groups that meet the requirements set out in Article 9.3.2.
  - The exclusion from the UTPR is effected by reducing to zero any amount of Top-up Tax that would otherwise be taken into account for determining the UTPR Top-up Tax Amount in accordance with Article 2.5.1.
  - Provides that there is no need for the MNE Group to compute the ETR of its CEs and no need to calculate the amount of Top-up Tax that would have been due if the exclusion did not apply.
  - The exclusion provided in Article 9.3.1 applies on an annual basis.
- Article 9.3.2 provides two criteria for determining whether an MNE Group is in the initial phase of its international activity for Article 9.3.1 to apply.
  - Both of the criteria must be met for a given Fiscal Year in order for the MNE Group to qualify for the exclusion for that Fiscal Year.
  - Paragraph (a) of Article 9.3.2 provides that the exclusion in Article 9.3.1 only applies to MNE Groups that have CEs located in no more than six jurisdictions for a Fiscal Year.
  - Paragraph (a) of Article 9.3.2 provides that there is no requirement that the five other jurisdictions are the same five jurisdictions over the five-year period during which the MNE Group can benefit from the exclusion.
  - Paragraph (b) of Article 9.3.2 provides that the exclusion in Article 9.3.1 only applies to MNE Groups that have a limited amount of tangible assets (not exceeding EUR 50 million for the Fiscal Year) outside the Reference Jurisdiction.
  - Paragraph (b) of Article 9.3.2 provides that once the value of tangible assets held in jurisdictions other than the Reference Jurisdiction exceeds EUR 50 million, then the exclusion from the UTPR no longer applies.
- Article 9.3.3 provides the definition for the Reference Jurisdiction for purposes of Article 9.3.2.
  - The Reference Jurisdiction of an MNE Group is the jurisdiction where the MNE Group has the highest total value of Tangible Assets, where the total value of Tangible Assets in a jurisdiction is the sum of the Net Book Values of all Tangible Assets of all the CEs of the MNE Group that are located in that jurisdiction.
  - For purposes of Article 9.3.3, the Reference Jurisdiction is identified in respect of the first Fiscal Year for which the MNE Group originally comes within the scope of the GloBE Rules and remains unchanged

over the five-year period during which the MNE benefits from the exclusion.

- Article 9.3.4 provides that:
  - The exclusion in Article 9.3.1 only applies for a period of five years after the MNE Group has come within the scope of the GloBE Rules.
  - For MNE Groups that are in scope of the GloBE Rules when they come into effect, the period of five years will start at the time the UTPR rules come into effect.
  - The five-year period shall not be suspended by any circumstance. For instance, if the MNE Group meets the requirements provided in Article 1.1 for a Fiscal Year and its revenues decline in subsequent years such that the MNE Group is not in scope of the GloBE Rules for any subsequent year, the five-year period continues to run.
  - The first Fiscal Year for which the MNE Group is subject to the GloBE Rules is included for the purposes of counting the period of five years.
- Article 9.3.5 provides for adding an optional provision that Article 9.3.1 shall not apply where the implementing Jurisdiction is the Reference Jurisdiction of the MNE Group.
  - Prevents potential abuse of Article 9.3.1 exclusion by providing an option for the Reference Jurisdiction to apply the UTPR to MNE Groups so as to limit the risk of locally headquartered MNE Groups inverting out of the Reference Jurisdiction to escape the GloBE Rules.
  - Has the effect of preserving the ability of the Reference Jurisdiction to make an adjustment under the UTPR in respect of any amount of Top-up Tax that arises in a Low-Tax Jurisdiction.
  - Provides an additional option under paragraph (a) to jurisdictions that implement Article 9.3.5 to consider limiting the application of the UTPR under this paragraph to the Top-up Tax Amount that arises in Low-Tax Jurisdictions other than the Reference Jurisdiction. Article 9.3.5(a) achieves this by reducing the Top-up Tax Amount of an LTCE that would be taken into account under Article 2.5.1 to zero if that LTCE is located in the Reference Jurisdiction.
  - In order to allocate the full amount of Top-up Tax arising in Low-Tax Jurisdictions to the Reference Jurisdiction, Article 9.3.5(b) provides that the UTPR Percentage of the jurisdictions other than the Reference Jurisdiction is deemed to be zero.
  - The option set out in Article 9.3.5 operates as an exception from the UTPR exclusion provided under Article 9.3 and therefore is subject to the general time limit provided in Article 9.3.4.

4.9.3.1 Article 9.3.1.

905. Subject to Article 9.3.4, the Top-up Tax that would otherwise be taken into account under Article 2.5.1 shall be reduced to zero during the initial phase of an MNE Group's international activity, notwithstanding the requirements otherwise provided in Chapter 5.

906. *Objective of the Article:* Article 9.3.1 provides an exclusion from the UTPR for MNE Groups that meet the requirements set out in Article 9.3.2. More specifically, the exclusion from the UTPR is effected by reducing to zero any amount of Top-up Tax that would otherwise be taken into account for determining the UTPR Top-up Tax Amount in accordance with Article 2.5.1. Article 9.3.1 further provides that this exclusion applies notwithstanding the requirements otherwise provided in Chapter 5, such as the requirement to determine the ETR of a jurisdiction and compute the Top-up Tax due if any. This means that there is no need for the MNE Group to compute the ETR of its CEs and no need to calculate the amount of Top-up Tax that would have been due if the exclusion did not apply. The exclusion provided in Article 9.3.1 applies on an annual basis. Provided the conditions set in Article 9.3.2 are met for a Fiscal Year, the exclusion provided in Article 9.3.1 applies for that Fiscal Year.

4.9.3.2 Article 9.3.2.

907. For the purposes of Article 9.3, an MNE Group is in the initial phase of its international activity if, for a Fiscal Year:

(a) it has Constituent Entities in no more than six jurisdictions; and
(b) the sum of the Net Book Values of Tangible Assets of all Constituent Entities located in all jurisdictions other than the Reference Jurisdiction does not exceed EUR 50 million.

908. *Objective of the Article*: Article 9.3.2 provides two criteria for determining whether an MNE Group is in the initial phase of its international activity for Article 9.3.1 to apply. Both of the criteria must be met for a given Fiscal Year in order for the MNE Group to qualify for the exclusion for that Fiscal Year. The criteria provided in paragraphs (a) and (b) of Article 9.3.2 are discussed in Figure 4.48.

Figure 4.48 Paragraphs (a) and (b) of Article 9.3.2

Paragraphs (a) and (b) of Article 9.3.2

(a)

- Paragraph (a) provides that the exclusion in Article 9.3.1 only applies to MNE Groups that have CEs located in no more than six jurisdictions for a Fiscal Year.
- Thus, an MNE Group can qualify for the exclusion if it has CEs in up to five jurisdictions outside the Reference Jurisdiction.
- For this purpose, there is no requirement that the five other jurisdictions are the same five jurisdictions over the five-year period during which the MNE Group can benefit from the exclusion.
- The location* of a CE is determined by applying the rules provided in Article 10.3.
- Stateless Constituent Entities are not located in any jurisdiction, so those entities are not counted for the purposes of determining the number of jurisdictions in which the MNE Group operates under these rules.
- Location of Investment Entities that are not Excluded Entities is not taken into account for purposes of determining the number of jurisdictions in which the MNE Group has CEs under Article 9.3.2(a).
- Location of a JV and of its JV Subsidiaries is not taken into account for purposes of determining the number of jurisdictions in which the MNE Group has CEs.
- Location of Minority-Owned Constituent Entities is taken into account for purposes of determining the number of jurisdictions in which the MNE Group has CEs.

* Note : Article 10.3 has been explained in Figure 4.23 *supra* while discussing Article 5.1.1.

(b)

- Paragraph (b) provides that the exclusion in Article 9.3.1 only applies to MNE Groups that have a limited amount of tangible assets outside the Reference Jurisdiction, i.e., the jurisdiction where they conduct the majority of their substantive activities when the MNE Group originally comes within the scope of the GloBE Rules.
- More specifically, paragraph (b) provides that MNE Groups qualify for the exclusion only if the sum of the Net Book Values of Tangible Assets** of all CEs located in all jurisdictions other than the Reference Jurisdiction does not exceed EUR 50 million for the Fiscal Year.
- For purposes of Article 9.3.2(b), all Tangible Assets, as defined in Article 10.1 are taken into account, provided they are held by the CEs of the MNE Group that are located in the jurisdictions other than the Reference Jurisdiction over the relevant period.
- Provides that once the value of tangible assets held in jurisdictions other than the Reference Jurisdiction exceeds EUR 50 million, then the exclusion from the UTPR no longer applies.
- Tangible Assets of Stateless Constituent Entities are considered held by CEs located in a jurisdiction other than the Reference Jurisdiction for the purposes of assessing the EUR 50 million threshold, other than to the extent that the MNE Group demonstrates that those Tangible Assets are physically located in the Reference Jurisdiction.
- For purposes of Article 9.3.2(b), Tangible Assets of Investment Entities that are not Excluded Entities are not taken into account because those entities are excluded from the application of the UTPR.
- Tangible Assets held by a JV or its JV Subsidiaries are also not taken into account because those are not CEs for the purposes of Article 9.3 and are not required to apply the UTPR.
- The Tangible Assets held by Minority-Owned Constituent Entities are taken into account for purposes of this rule.

** Note : As provided in Article 10.1, the Net Book Value of Tangible Assets means the average of the beginning and end of year values of Tangible Assets after taking into account accumulated depreciation, depletion, and impairment, as recorded in the financial statements.

4.9.3.3 Article 9.3.3.

909. For the purposes of Article 9.3.2, the Reference Jurisdiction of an MNE Group is the jurisdiction where the MNE Group has the highest total value of Tangible Assets for the Fiscal Year in which the MNE Group originally comes within the scope of the GloBE Rules. The total value of Tangible Assets in a jurisdiction is the sum of the Net Book Values of all Tangible Assets of all the Constituent Entities of the MNE Group that are located in that jurisdiction.

910. *Objective of the Article*: Article 9.3.3 provides the definition of the Reference Jurisdiction for purposes of Article 9.3.2. The Reference Jurisdiction of an MNE Group is the jurisdiction where the MNE Group has the highest total value of Tangible Assets, where the total value of Tangible Assets in a jurisdiction is the sum of the Net Book Values of all Tangible Assets of all the CEs of the MNE Group that are located in that jurisdiction. For purposes of Article 9.3.3, all Tangible Assets, as defined in Article 10.1, are taken into account, provided they are held by the CEs of the MNE Group over the relevant period.

911. *Reference Jurisdiction remains unchanged over the five-year period*: For purposes of Article 9.3.3, the Reference Jurisdiction is identified in respect of the first Fiscal Year for which the MNE Group originally comes within the scope of the GloBE Rules and remains unchanged over the five-year period during which the MNE benefits from the exclusion.

4.9.3.4 Article 9.3.4.

912. This Article 9.3 shall not apply for any Fiscal Year that starts later than five years after the first day of the first Fiscal Year when the MNE Group originally came within the scope of the GloBE Rules. For MNE Groups that are in scope of the GloBE Rules when they come into effect, the period of five years will start at the time the UTPR rules come into effect.

913. *Objective of the Article*: Article 9.3.4 has two limbs:

- provides that the exclusion in Article 9.3.1 only applies for a period of five years after the MNE Group has come within the scope of the GloBE Rules.
- provides that for MNE Groups that are in scope of the GloBE Rules when they come into effect, the period of five years will start at the time the UTPR rules come into effect.

The five-year period provided under Article 9.3.4 shall not be suspended by any circumstance. For instance, if the MNE Group meets the requirements provided in Article 1.1 for a Fiscal Year and its revenues decline in subsequent years such that the MNE Group is not in scope of the GloBE Rules for any subsequent year, the five-year period continues to run. The provisions of Article 9.3.4 are further explained in Figure 4.49.

Figure 4.49 *Provisions of Article 9.3.4*

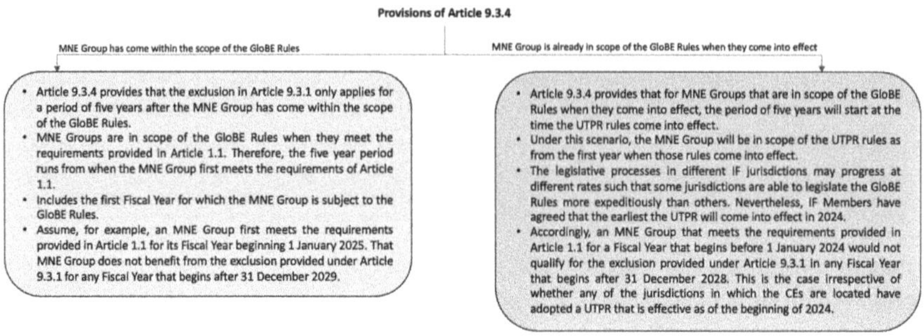

4.9.3.5 Article 9.3.5.

914. [*Optional provision*] If a jurisdiction that has implemented GloBE Rules is the Reference Jurisdiction of the MNE Group pursuant to Article 9.3.3, then Article 9.3.1 shall not apply during the initial phase of that MNE Group's international activity and, during that initial phase:

(a) [*Optional provision*] the Top-up Tax calculated for an LTCE that would be taken into account under Article 2.5.1 shall be reduced to zero if that LTCE is located in the Reference Jurisdiction, notwithstanding the requirements otherwise provided in Chapter 5; and
(b) the UTPR Percentage of jurisdictions other than the Reference Jurisdiction is deemed to be zero.

915. *Background necessitating introduction of the Article*: Article 9.3.5 contains an optional provision that allows the Reference Jurisdiction to use the UTPR to defend its tax base from a tax planning opportunity that may arise under the exclusion for MNEs in the initial phase of their international activity. Because the Article 9.3.1 exclusion treats all of the jurisdictions in which the MNE Group operates as having zero Top-up Tax, a largely domestic Group could establish a new UPE in a jurisdiction that does not have a Qualified IIR and then the Parent Entity could extract value from the domestic Group without being subject to minimum taxation under the UTPR. This gap in the coverage of the GloBE Rules could also provide a competitive advantage for UPEs located in a non-GloBE jurisdiction seeking to acquire MNE Groups. To thwart this potential abuse of the Article 9.3.1 exclusion, jurisdictions that introduce a UTPR may consider providing an optional exception to Article 9.3.1 that would exclude the operation of Article 9.3 in that jurisdiction where it is the Reference Jurisdiction in respect of an MNE Group that is in the initial phase of its international activity. The reason for including such an option in Article 9.3 for those jurisdictions that choose to implement the GloBE Rules would be to provide a level playing field between locally headquartered MNE Groups that are in the initial phase of their international activity (and would therefore be subject to the IIR in respect of their operations in Low-Tax Jurisdictions) and those MNE Groups in the initial phase of their international activity that maintain a UPE outside, but the major part of their operations within, that jurisdiction. An option for the Reference Jurisdiction to apply the UTPR to such Groups would help to limit the risk of locally headquartered MNE Groups inverting out of the Reference Jurisdiction to escape the GloBE Rules.

916. *Objective of the Article*: Jurisdictions that wish to limit the operation of Article 9.3 in the way highlighted *supra* may consider adding an optional provision (Article 9.3.5) which provides that Article 9.3.1 shall not apply where the implementing Jurisdiction is the Reference Jurisdiction of the MNE Group. This will have the effect of preserving the ability of the Reference Jurisdiction to make an adjustment under the UTPR in respect of any amount of Top-up Tax that arises in a Low-Tax Jurisdiction. In order to allocate the full amount of Top-up Tax arising in those jurisdictions to the Reference Jurisdiction, Article 9.3.5(b) provides that the UTPR Percentage of the jurisdictions other than the Reference Jurisdiction is deemed to be zero.

917. *Additional option under paragraph (a)*: Jurisdictions that implement Article 9.3.5 may also consider limiting the application of the UTPR under this paragraph to the Top-up Tax Amount that arises in Low-Tax Jurisdictions other than the Reference Jurisdiction. Article 9.3.5(a) achieves this by reducing the Top-up Tax Amount of an LTCE that would be taken into account under Article 2.5.1 to zero if that LTCE is located in the Reference Jurisdiction.

918. *Time limit for the option provided in Article 9.3.5 to operate*: The option set out in Article 9.3.5 operates as an exception from the UTPR exclusion provided under Article 9.3 and therefore is subject to the general time limit provided in Article 9.3.4.

4.9.4 Article 9.4. (Transitional Relief for Filing Obligations)

919. Prominent features of Article 9.4 are provided in Box 4.46.

Box 4.46 Prominent Features of Article 9.4

- Provides transitional relief for the filing and notification obligations pursuant to Article 8.1 with respect to the Transition Year.
- Provides that the filing and notification obligations must be fulfilled within eighteen months, rather than the normal fifteen months, after the end of the Reporting Fiscal Year, that is, the Transition Year.

4.9.4.1 Article 9.4.1.

920. Notwithstanding Article 8.1.6, the GloBE Information Return or the notifications pursuant to Article 8.1 shall be filed with the tax administration of the jurisdiction that has implemented GloBE Rules no later than eighteen months after the last day of the Reporting Fiscal Year that is the Transitional Year.

921. *Objective of the Article*: In order to provide amelioration to MNE Groups in carrying out compliance with GloBE Rules, Article 9.4.1 provides transitional relief for the filing and notification obligations pursuant to Article 8.1 with respect to the Transition Year. The filing and notification obligations must be fulfilled within eighteen months, rather than the normal fifteen months, after the end of the Reporting Fiscal Year, that is, the Transition Year.

4.10 CHAPTER 10 OF GLOBE RULES (DEFINITIONS)[107]

922. Chapter 10 of GloBE Rules is dedicated to defining various terms that are used in the GloBE Rules. It has been *inter alia* clarified in Paragraph 2 of the Commentary on Chapter 10 that when financial accounting terminology or concepts that are not defined in Article 10.1 are used in the GloBE Rules or Commentary in connection with a GloBE Rule or principle that relies on financial accounting, such terms and concepts should be interpreted consistent with the meaning given to them in financial accounting standards and guidance.

923. It may be noted that certain articles of the GloBE Rules directly define some of the terms used in the GloBE Rules, whereas the rest are defined in Chapter 10 under Articles 10.1, 10.2 and 10.3, respectively. Instead of confining all definitions of technical terms incorporated in Chapter 10 of GloBE Rules in one place, a differentiating feature of this book has been to insert the definitions depending on the relevance of the term while discussing each article of the GloBE Rules in detail or where such terms are first used in Chapter 4 of this book. At the same time, for the ease of readers, an index of definitions is provided in Table 4.5, mentioning the relevant Article(s) of GloBE Rules discussed in Chapter 4 of the book where such terms are defined.

Table 4.5 Index of Definitions

Index of Definitions Provided in Article 10.1		
S. No.	*Defined Term*	*Defined/Included in Article*
1	Acceptable Financial Accounting Standard	Included in Article 3.1.2
2	Accrued Pension Expense	Included in Article 3.2.1(i)
3	Additional Current Top-up Tax	Included in Article 4.1.5
4	Additional Tier One Capital	Included in Article 3.2.10
5	Additions to Covered Taxes	Defined in Article 4.1.2
6	Adjusted Asset Gain	Included in Article 3.2.6
7	Adjusted Covered Taxes	Defined in Article 4.1.1
8	Aggregate Asset Gain	Included in Article 3.2.6

107. Based on OECD's GloBE Model Rules and its Commentary.

Index of Definitions Provided in Article 10.1		
S. No.	*Defined Term*	*Defined/Included in Article*
9	Agreed Administrative Guidance	Included in Article 8.3.1
10	Allocable Share of the Top-up Tax	Defined in Article 2.2.1
11	Annual Election	Included in Article 3.2.6
12	Allocated Asset Gain	Included in Article 3.2.6
13	Arm's Length Principle	Included in Article 3.2.3
14	Asymmetric Foreign Currency Gains or Losses	Included in Article 3.2.1(f)
15	Authorised Accounting Body	Included in Article 3.1.2
16	Authorised Financial Accounting Standard	Included in Article 3.1.2
17	Average GloBE Income or Loss	Defined in Article 5.5.2
18	Average GloBE Revenue	Defined in Article 5.5.2
19	Commentary	Included in Article 2.1.3
20	Consolidated Financial Statements	Included in Article 1.1.1
21	Constituent Entity	Defined in Article 1.3.1
22	Constituent Entity-owner	Defined in Article 5.6.1
23	Controlled Foreign Company Tax Regime	Included in Article 4.3.2
24	Controlling Interest	Included in Articles 1.4.1 and 5.6.1
25	Cooperative	Included in Article 7.2.1
26	Covered Taxes	Defined in Article 4.2
27	Deductible Dividend	Included in Article 7.2.1
28	Deductible Dividend Regime	Included in Article 7.2.1
29	Deemed Distribution	Defined in Article 7.6.5(c)
30	Deemed Distribution Tax	Defined in Article 7.3.2
31	Deemed Distribution Tax Recapture Account	Included in Article 7.3.3
32	Departing Constituent Entity	Included in Article 7.3.7
33	Designated Filing Entity	Included in Article 8.1.2
34	Designated Local Entity	Included in Article 8.1.3
35	Disallowed Accrual	Defined in Article 4.4.6
36	Disposition Recapture Ratio	Defined in Article 7.3.8
37	Disqualified Refundable Imputation Tax	Included in Article 3.2.1(a)
38	Dual-listed Arrangement	Included in Article 6.5.1
39	Effective Tax Rate (ETR)	Defined in Article 5.1.1
40	Election Year	Included in Article 3.2.6
41	Eligible Distribution Tax System	Included in Articles 4.2.1 and 7.3.1
42	Eligible Employees	Included in Article 5.3.3
43	Eligible Payroll Costs	Included in Article 5.3.3
44	Eligible Tangible Assets	Defined in Article 5.3.4
45	Entity	Included in Article 1.1.3

Index of Definitions Provided in Article 10.1		
S. No.	*Defined Term*	*Defined/Included in Article*
46	ETR Adjustment Article	Means Article 3.2.6, 4.4.4, 4.6.1, 4.6.4, and 7.3
47	Excess Profit	Defined in Article 5.2.2
48	Excluded Dividends	Included in Article 3.2.1(b)
49	Excluded Entity	Defined in Articles 1.5.1 and 1.5.2
50	Excluded Equity Gain or Loss	Included in Article 3.2.1(c)
51	Filing Constituent Entity	Included in Article 1.5.3
52	Financial Accounting Net Income or Loss	Defined in Article 3.1.2
53	Fiscal Year	Included in Article 1.1.2
54	Five-Year Election	Included in Article 1.5.3
55	GloBE Implementation Framework	Included in Article 1.5
56	GloBE Income of all Constituent Entities	Defined in Article 5.1.2(a)
57	GloBE Income or Loss of a Constituent Entity	Defined in Article 3.1.1
58	GloBE Information Return	Included in Article 1.5
59	GloBE Loss Deferred Tax Asset	Defined in Article 4.5
60	GloBE Loss Election	Defined in Article 4.5.1
61	GloBE Losses of all Constituent Entities	Defined in Article 5.1.2(b)
62	GloBE Reorganisation	Included in Article 6.3.2
63	GloBE Revenue	Defined in Article 5.5.3(a)
64	GloBE Rules	Included in Article 1.1
65	GloBE Safe Harbour	Included in Article 8.2.1
66	Governmental Entity	Included in Article 1.5.1
67	Group	Defined in Articles 1.2.2 and 1.2.3
68	Group Entity	Included in Article 1.1.1
69	High-Tax Counterparty	Included in Article 3.2.7
70	IIR	Defined in Articles 2.1 to 2.3
71	Included Revaluation Method Gain or Loss	Included in Article 3.2.1(d)
72	Insurance Investment Entity	Included in Articles 5.1 and 7.4.1
73	Intermediate Parent Entity	Included in Article 2.1
74	International Organisation	Included in Article 1.5.1
75	International Shipping Income	Defined in Article 3.3.2
76	Intragroup Financing Arrangement	Included in Article 3.2.7
77	Investment Entity	Included in Articles 2.4.3 and 7.4.1
78	Investment Fund	Included in Article 1.5.1

Index of Definitions Provided in Article 10.1		
S. No.	*Defined Term*	*Defined/Included in Article*
79	Joint Venture	Included in Articles 2.1.1 and 6.4.1
80	JV Group	Included in Articles 2.5.1 and 6.4.1
81	JV Group Top-up Tax	Included in Articles 2.5.1 and 6.4.1
82	JV Subsidiary	Included in Article 6.4.1
83	Liable Constituent Entity (or Entities)	Included in Article 8.2.2
84	Local Creditable Tax Gross-up	Defined in Article 7.6.5(d)
85	Local Tangible Asset	Included in Article 3.2.6
86	Look-back Period	Included in Article 3.2.6
87	Loss Year	Included in Article 3.2.6
88	Low-Taxed Constituent Entity	Included in Article 1.3
89	Low-Tax Entity	Included in Article 3.2.7
90	Low-Tax Jurisdiction	Included in Article 2.1.6
91	Main Entity	Included in Article 1.4.1
92	Material Competitive Distortion	Included in Article 3.1.2
93	Minimum Rate	Means 15%
94	Minority-Owned Constituent Entity	Included in Article 2.5.1
95	Minority-Owned Parent Entity	Included in Article 5.6.1
96	Minority-Owned Subgroup	Included in Article 5.6.1
97	Minority-Owned Subsidiary	Included in Article 5.6.1
98	MNE Group	Defined in Article 1.2.1
99	MNE Group's Allocable Share of the Investment Entity's GloBE Income	Defined in Article 7.4.4
100	Multi-Parented MNE Group	Included in Article 6.5.1
101	Net Asset Gain	Included in Article 3.2.6
102	Net Asset Loss	Included in Article 3.2.6
103	Net Book Value of Tangible Assets	Included in Article 2.6.1
104	Net GloBE Income	Defined in Article 5.1.2
105	Net GloBE Loss	Included in Article 4.5.1
106	Net Taxes Expense	Included in Article 3.2.1(a)
107	Non-profit Organisation	Included in Article 1.5.1
108	Non-Qualified Refundable Tax Credit	Included in Article 3.2.4
109	Non-qualifying Gain or Loss	Included in Articles 3.2.1(e) and 6.3.3
110	Number of Employees	Included in Article 2.6.1
111	OECD Model Tax Convention	Means OECD MTC 2017
112	Other Comprehensive Income	Included in Article 3.1.2

Index of Definitions Provided in Article 10.1		
S. No.	*Defined Term*	*Defined/Included in Article*
113	Ownership Interest	Included in Articles 2.1 and 5.6.1
114	Parent Entity	Included in Article 2.1
115	Parent Entity's Inclusion Ratio	Defined in Article 2.2.2
116	Partially Owned Parent Entity	Included in Article 2.1
117	Passive Income	Included in Article 4.3.3
118	Pension Fund	Included in Article 1.5.1
119	Pension Services Entity	Included in Article 1.5.2
120	Permanent Establishment	Included in Articles 1.2.1 and 3.4
121	Policy Disallowed Expenses	Included in Article 3.2.1(g)
122	Portfolio Shareholding	Included in Article 3.2.1(b)
123	Prior Period Errors and Changes in Accounting Principles	Included in Article 3.2.1(h)
124	Qualified Ancillary International Shipping Income	Defined in Article 3.3.3
125	Qualified Domestic Minimum Top-up Tax	Included in Articles 4.2.2 and 5.2.3
126	Qualified IIR	Included in Article 2.1.3
127	Qualified Imputation Tax	Included in Article 3.2.4
128	Qualified Refundable Tax Credit	Included in Article 3.2.4
129	Qualified UTPR	Included in Article 2.4.2
130	Qualifying Competent Authority Agreement	Included in Article 8.1.2
131	Real Estate Investment Vehicle	Included in Article 1.5.1
132	Recaptured Deferred Tax Liability	Defined in Article 4.4.4
133	Recapture Exception Accrual	Defined in Article 4.4.5
134	Reductions to Covered Taxes	Defined in Article 4.1.3
135	Reference Jurisdiction	Defined in Article 9.3.3
136	Reporting Fiscal Year	Included in Article 8.1.6
137	Short-term Portfolio Shareholding	Included in Article 3.2.1(b)
138	Stapled Structure	Included in Article 6.5.1
139	Stateless Constituent Entity	Described in Articles 10.3.2(b) and 10.3.3(d)
140	Substance-based Income Exclusion	Defined in Article 5.3
141	Tangible Assets	Included in Article 2.6.1
142	Tax	Included in Article 4.2.1
143	Taxable Distribution Method	Defined in Article 7.6.2
144	Tax Treaty	Means a DTAA
145	Tested Year	Defined in Article 7.6.5(a)

Index of Definitions Provided in Article 10.1		
S. No.	*Defined Term*	*Defined/Included in Article*
146	Testing Period	Defined in Article 7.6.5(b)
147	Top-up Tax	Defined in Article 5.2
148	Top-up Tax Percentage	Defined in Article 5.2.1
149	Total Deferred Tax Adjustment Amount	Defined in Article 4.4.1
150	Total UTPR Top-up Tax Amount	Included in Article 2.5
151	Transition Year	Included in Article 9.1.1
152	Ultimate Parent Entity (UPE)	Defined in Article 1.4
153	Undistributed Net GloBE Income	Defined in Article 7.6.3
154	UPE Jurisdiction	Included in Article 2.5.2
155	UTPR	Defined in Articles 2.4 to 2.6
156	UTPR Jurisdiction	Included in Article 2.6
157	UTPR Percentage	Included in Article 2.6.1
158	UTPR Top-up Tax Amount	Included in Article 2.5.2
Index of Definitions provided in Article 10.2		
159	Flow-through Entity, Tax Transparent Entity, Reverse Hybrid Entity, and Hybrid Entity	Included in Articles 2.2.4 and 3.5
Index of Definitions provided in Article 10.3		
160	Location of an Entity and a Permanent Establishment	Included in Article 5.1.1

CHAPTER 5

Technical Discussions and Policy Considerations Concerning GloBE Rules

The GloBE Rules merit elaborate technical discussions amidst specific policy considerations, accompanied by an analysis of all the 141 IF Member Countries on certain parameters with suitable recommendations.

5.1 INTERACTION BETWEEN GLOBE RULES AND EXISTING BEPS MEASURES[108]

924. Pillar Two is designed to operate alongside a jurisdiction's existing anti-avoidance rules. This is why the GloBE Rules set out how taxes imposed under BEPS measures like CFC charges should be taken into account in the Globe ETR calculations, i.e., GloBE Rules are broadly designed to ensure taxes charged under existing anti-avoidance rules are treated as covered taxes and, where possible, then allocated to the jurisdictions in which the relevant income is recognised in the GloBE base. This ensures that the tax charged under existing BEPS measures is taken into account in the ETR calculations and therefore prevents Pillar Two from imposing additional top-up taxes on income streams that have already been subjected to tax under other BEPS measures. This aligns with the inherent objective of formulation of Pillar Two Proposals which are:

- the GloBE Rules are invoked after other anti-avoidance rules are applied;
- seek to tax any remaining low-taxed profits in the jurisdiction and, thus, address remaining BEPS issues.

108. Refer 'The HMRC's OECD Pillar 2 Consultation on implementation' https://assets.publishing.service.gov.uk/government/uploads/system/uploads/attachment_data/file/1045663/11Jan_2022_Pillar_2_Consultation_.pdf accessed on 15 May 2022.

925. The Pillar Two Proposals and existing BEPS measures can coexist on account of the following factors:

- There is not a significant overlap between Pillar Two and other BEPS measures, as the latter are designed to address specific tax planning risks. Pillar Two does not address the risks designed to shift particular streams of income out of a jurisdiction's tax base directly. While Pillar Two will reduce the incentive to shift profits to low-tax jurisdictions by reducing the tax rate arbitrage that can be achieved, it imposes a minimum tax at the jurisdictional level, hence, does not prevent the type of planning targeted by other anti-avoidance rules.
- In jurisdictions where the maximum marginal CIT is much higher than the minimum tax rate of 15% envisaged under the GloBE Rules, potential incentives and opportunities for tax planning and tax avoidance shall still exist, and they can only be addressed by other anti-avoidance rules.
- As Pillar Two only applies to MNEs with over EUR 750 million of global revenue, other BEPS measures will continue to play an important role in protecting a jurisdiction's tax base for the wider population.

926. The measures to implement minimum taxation under the GloBE Rules are unrelated to avoidance behaviour and shall continue to apply[109] in the following situations:

- even if value creation has been correctly allocated according to transfer pricing rules;
- even if CFC rules and other anti-base erosion rules preventing double non-taxation are applicable;
- even if any specific or general anti-abuse rules are applicable.

5.2 INTERACTION AND RELATION OF IIR WITH UTPR

927. The IIR works by imposing a top-up tax on a parent entity in respect of the LTCEs. The IIR applies on a top-down basis, which means that it is applied by the entity that is at, or near, the top of the ownership chain in the MNE Group, which is normally the UPE. However, in case where the UPE does not apply the IIR, one or more IPEs will have to apply the IIR to their LTCEs. The IIR is subject to a split-ownership rule for shareholdings below 80%. This means IIR will be applied by a POPE to its controlled subsidiaries of a sub-set of the MNE Group in priority to the UPE when such POPE is owned by more than 20% by shareholders outside of the MNE group. In case there are several POPEs in an MNE group, the IIR will be applied by the POPE closest in the chain

109. Refer 'Editorial titled The Pillar Two Top-Up Taxes: Interplay, Characterization, Treaties and Tax' by Ana Paula Dourado Editor-in-Chief Intertax, Volume 50, Issue 5 © 2022 Kluwer Law International BV, The Netherlands' https://kluwerlawonline.com/api/Product/CitationPDFURL?file=Journals\TAXI\TAXI2022045.pdf accessed on 22 May 2022.

of ownership to the LTCE. On the other hand, the UTPR acts as a backstop to the IIR and applies in situations where there is no qualifying IIR in the jurisdiction of the UPE or where a low level of taxation arises in the jurisdiction of the UPE. The UTPR works by allocating top-up tax to a jurisdiction to the extent the low-tax income of a CE is not subject to tax under an IIR. The UTPR allocates top-up tax to jurisdictions based on a two-factor formula, which is based on carrying value of tangible assets and number of employees in the jurisdiction.[110] Thus, by introducing an IIR in a jurisdiction, its headquartered groups will not be subject to the UTPR in respect of their foreign profits and will only be subjected to the IIR at the level of foreign intermediate parent entities in relatively limited situations where those entities are partially owned by third parties. The primacy accorded to IIR over UTPR would benefit residence States since they would receive the tax revenue that a source State did not collect as it adopted an ETR below 15% (subject to source States not adopting the QDMTT). Conceptually, the IIR will result in revenue gains, but such benefits will primarily be concentrated in developed and capital-exporting countries. However, from the perspective of residence States, it can be stated that the IIR protects the tax base of the residence country, as the source State did not tax appropriately.

928. *Factors which make UTPR a backstop rather than the primary rule*[111] – The same calculations under Chapter 5 are applied, whether the top-up tax is being charged under the IIR or the UTPR, to ensure coordinated outcomes. However, given that there will typically be subsidiaries in several different jurisdictions, the UTPR requires a higher level of administrative cooperation, which underlines the importance of the standardised information reporting requirements contained in Chapter 8. It is also one of the reasons the UTPR is a backstop rather than the primary rule.

929. *GloBE Rules provide for application of IIR as much as possible in comparison to UTPR*: In terms of allocation of top-up tax, IIR takes precedence over the UTPR. In addition, the feature of preference of IIR over UTPR embodied in GloBE Rules is also evident from an option to not elect an Entity as an Excluded Entity under Article 1.5.3. When the election is made, the GloBE Rules will apply to the Entity described in Article 1.5.2 in the same manner as they apply to any other CE of the MNE Group. For example, a Filing Constituent Entity may elect to treat an Entity as a CE rather than an Excluded Entity under Article 1.5.2 in order to apply the IIR and not the UTPR with respect to the top-up tax of the LTCE. Take, for example, an MNE Group with a UPE that is an Investment Fund which is an Excluded Entity, but which consolidates on a line-by-line basis with its subsidiaries under the Acceptable Financial Accounting Standard used to prepare its CFS. Such MNE Group may make this election so that the entity can apply the IIR to its subsidiaries instead of subjecting all of its CEs to the UTPR.

110. Refer 'European Commission's Proposal for a Council Directive on ensuring a global minimum level of taxation for multinational groups in the Union' https://eur-lex.europa.eu/legal-content/EN/TXT/?uri=CELEX%3A52021PC0823 accessed on 15 May 2022.
111. Refer 'OECD's The Pillar Two Rules in a Nutshell (Determination of the group entity liable for the top-up tax)' https://www.oecd.org/tax/beps/pillar-two-model-rules-in-a-nutshell.pdf.

930. The interaction and relation of IIR with UTPR are further explained in Figure 5.1.

Figure 5.1 Interaction and Relation of IIR with UTPR

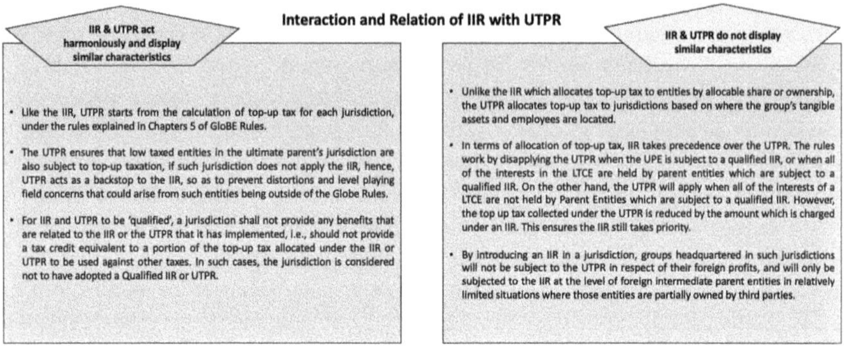

931. Some of the interactive provisions of IIR and UTPR discussed *supra* are further explained in the illustrations below:

Illustration # 70: The application of the top-down approach is illustrated through a flow-chart below:

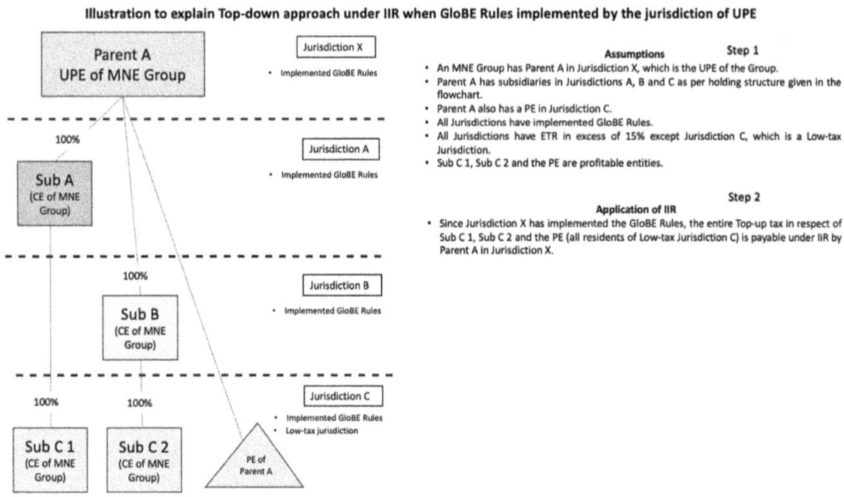

Illustration # 71: The application of top-down approach under IIR and application of UTPR when GloBE Rules are not implemented by the jurisdiction of UPE is illustrated through a flow-chart below:

Illustration to explain Top-down approach under IIR and application of UTPR when GloBE Rules not implemented by the jurisdiction of UPE

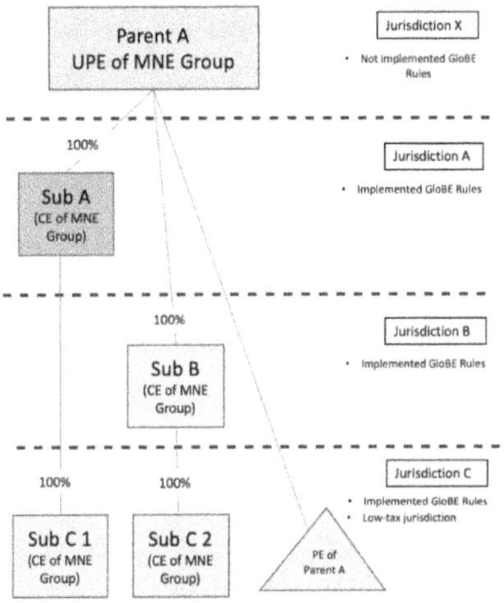

Assumptions **Step 1**

- An MNE Group has Parent A in Jurisdiction X, which is the UPE of the Group.
- Parent A has subsidiaries in Jurisdictions A, B and C as per holding structure given in the flowchart.
- Parent A also has a PE in Jurisdiction C.
- All Jurisdictions have implemented GloBE Rules, except Jurisdiction X.
- All Jurisdictions have ETR in excess of 15% except Jurisdiction C, which is a Low-tax Jurisdiction.
- Sub C 1, Sub C 2 and the PE are profitable entities.

Step 2

Application of Top-down approach under IIR and application of UTPR

- Since Jurisdiction X has not implemented the GloBE Rules, Parent A will not pay any Top-up tax in respect of Sub C 1, Sub C 2 and the PE (all residents of Low-tax Jurisdiction C) under IIR in Jurisdiction X.
- Following the Top-down approach, Intermediate Parent Entity, Sub A will pay Top-up tax in Jurisdiction A in respect of Sub C 1 (resident of Low-tax Jurisdiction C).
- Following the Top-down approach, Intermediate Parent Entity, Sub B will pay Top-up tax in Jurisdiction B in respect of Sub C 2 (resident of Low-tax Jurisdiction C).
- Top-up tax in respect of the PE in Jurisdiction C shall be recovered by applying the UTPR.

Illustration # 72: The application of UTPR is illustrated through a flow-chart below:

Illustration to explain application of UTPR

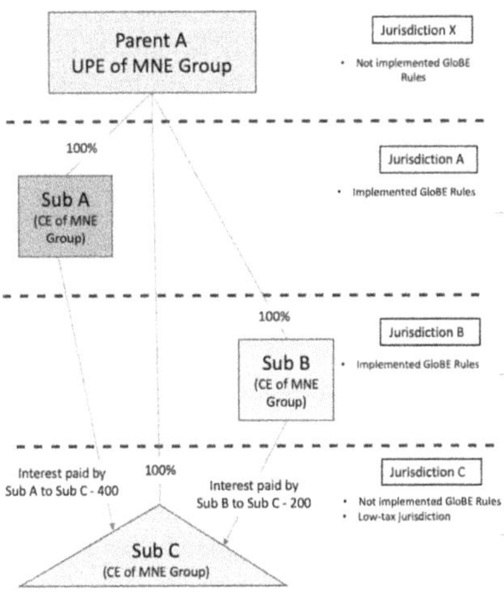

Assumptions **Step 1**

- An MNE Group has Parent A in Jurisdiction X, which is the UPE of the Group.
- Parent A has subsidiaries in Jurisdictions A, B and C as per holding structure given in the flowchart.
- Only Jurisdictions A and B have implemented GloBE Rules.
- Jurisdictions A and B have ETR in excess of 15%,i.e., 20%, whereas, Jurisdiction C is a Low-tax Jurisdiction with ETR of 10%. Relevant data of Sub A, Sub B and Sub C are as below:

Sub A		Jurisdiction A
CIT rate	A	20%
EBIT		600
Interest paid to Sub C		-400
Net Profit	B	200
CIT @ 20% [B*A]	C	40
No. of Employees	D	200
Value of Tangible Assets	E	2000

Sub B		Jurisdiction B
CIT rate	F	20%
EBIT		400
Interest paid to Sub C		-200
Net Profit	G	200
CIT @ 20% [G*F]	H	40
No. of Employees	I	400
Value of Tangible Assets	J	4000

Sub C		Jurisdiction C
CIT rate	K	10%
Interest Income from Sub A and Sub B		600
Net Profit	L	600
CIT @ 10% [L*K]	M	60
Top-up tax (%)	N	5%
UTPR Top-up tax Amount [L*N]	O	30

Illustration to explain application of UTPR

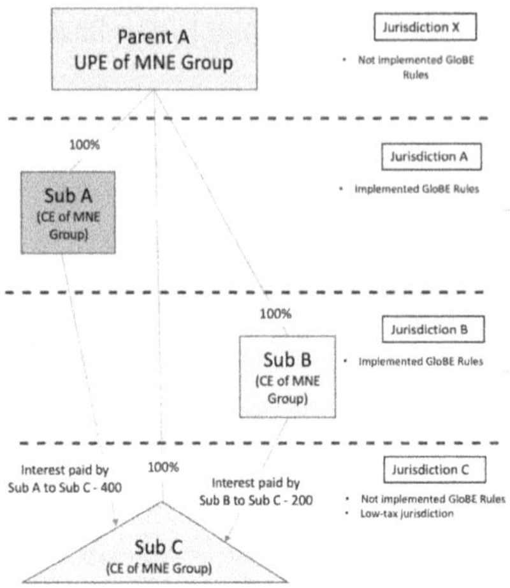

Step 2

Solution : Application of UTPR

- Since Jurisdiction X has not implemented the GloBE Rules, Parent A will not pay any Top-up tax in respect of Sub C under IIR in Jurisdiction X.
- Top-up tax in respect of Sub C in Low-tax Jurisdiction C shall be recovered through UTPR and will be allocated to Jurisdictions A and B, as per details given below:

UTPR % [50%*(D/(D+I))+50%*(E/(E+J))]	P	33.33
UTPR Top-up Tax Amount [O*P]	Q	10
Denial of deduction/equivalent adjustment [Q/A]	R	50
Revised Net Profit [B+R]	S	250
Total Tax Payable [S*A] = [C+Q]	T	50

UTPR % [50%*(I/(D+I))+50%*(J/(E+J))]	U	66.67
UTPR Top-up Tax Amount [O*U]	V	20
Denial of deduction/equivalent adjustment [V/F]	W	100
Revised Net Profit [G+W]	X	300
Total Tax Payable [X*F] = [H+V]	Y	60

5.3 INTERACTION AND RELATION OF IIR WITH CFC RULE

932. *Background of CFC rule*: CFC rules are designed to limit artificial deferral of tax by using offshore low-taxed entities. These rules aim to disincentivise businesses from moving their income to low-tax jurisdictions, as it can still be subject to domestic tax and thus protect the domestic tax base. The countries[112] which have CFC rules currently include Argentina, Australia, Austria, Belgium, Brazil, Bulgaria, Canada, Chile, China, Colombia, Croatia, Czech Republic, Denmark, Estonia, Finland, France, Germany, Greece, Hungary, Iceland, Indonesia, Ireland, Israel, Italy, Japan, Kazakhstan, Korea, Latvia, Lithuania, Luxembourg, Malta, Mauritius, Mexico, Netherlands, New Zealand, Norway, Pakistan, Peru, Poland, Portugal, Romania, Russia, Slovak Republic, Slovenia, South Africa, Spain, Sweden, Turkey, the United Kingdom and the United States.

933. *CFC and IIR similarities:*[113] The IIR rule operates similarly to a CFC rule by requiring a parent company to bring into account and tax the profits of a subsidiary that are subject to an ETR below the minimum rate. The operation of the IIR is, in some respects, based on traditional CFC rule principles and triggers an inclusion at the level of the shareholder where the income of a controlled foreign entity is taxed below the effective minimum tax rate. For the purposes of calculating the ETR under the GloBE

112. Refer 'OECD's List of countries with Controlled Foreign Company (CFC) Rules' https://qdd.oecd.org/data/CFC/.ALL accessed on 17 May 2022.
113. Refer 'South Centre's Tax Cooperation Policy Brief 22, 12 January 2022 titled Global Minimum Corporate Tax: Interaction of Income Inclusion Rule with Controlled Foreign Corporation and Tax-sparing Provisions by Kuldeep Sharma' https://www.southcentre.int/wp-content/uploads/2022/01/Tax-PB-22.pdf accessed on 17 May 2022.

rules, covered taxes *inter alia* include taxes paid in accordance with CFC rules, provided that they are imposed on the income of the CFC that is attributed to shareholders in the parent jurisdiction. Such CFC taxes are assigned, where possible, to the jurisdiction in which the underlying income arises (i.e., to the jurisdiction of the CFC) and are excluded from the ETR computation if the underlying income is excluded. In subjecting a domestic taxpayer to tax on its share of the foreign income of a controlled subsidiary, therefore, the IIR operates in a way that is closely comparable to a CFC rule.

934. *CFC and IIR dissimilarities:*[114] The CFC rule and IIR differ in various aspects, as summarised below:

- CFC rules typically do not apply to all the subsidiaries in an MNE Group, and when they do apply, they usually only capture certain types of low-tax passive income.[115] In contrast, the GloBE rules will apply to all the subsidiaries in the group and all types of income.
- Liability for the amount of top-up tax computed for a low-taxed CE is allocated to the parent entity in proportion to the parent entity's equity interest in the income of that entity. The liability for the top-up tax usually falls on the UPE of the MNE Group. However, under certain circumstances, the GloBE rules are designed so that the liability for the top-up tax shifts to one or more other CEs of the MNE Group. This coordination of IIRs among jurisdictions is part of the design of the GloBE Rules, whereas CFC rules, though they may have tax credit rules designed to avoid double taxation, typically do not have this level of coordination.
- In the case of CFC rules, the tax treatment of the income attributed to the controlling entity usually bears the same tax burden as other equivalent income and would not depend on the top-up tax, as happens with the IIR.
- In respect of countries that allow imputation tax credit,[116] income earned under the CFC rule is considered eligible, whereas IIR is not eligible for the same, as the definition of a Qualified IIR excludes an IIR where the country provides benefits relating to the IIR. The Commentary to GloBE Rules says that if a jurisdiction provides a tax credit equivalent to a portion of the tax paid under an IIR to be used against other taxes, that will not be a Qualified IIR. This is explained on the basis that the intention of the rules is to provide a level playing field among all jurisdictions to avoid inversions incentivised by differences in the implementation and application of the GloBE rules.

114. *Id.*
115. Refer 'Passive Income as defined in Article 10.1 of GloBE Model Rules', 'Action 3: BEPS 2015 Final Report (paragraph 78), OECD/G20 Base Erosion and Profit Shifting Project' http://www.oecd.org/tax/beps-2015-final-reports.htm' and 'Deloitte's Policy options for domestic implementation of a global minimum corporate tax rate' https://www.taxathand.com/article/20418/India/2021/Policy-options-for-domestic-implementation-of-a-global-minimum-corporate-tax-rate accessed on 17 May 2022.
116. Refer 'OECD Pillar Two: GloBE rules for New Zealand' https://taxpolicy.ird.govt.nz/en/publications/2022/2022-ip-oecd-pillar-two accessed on 17 May 2022.

5.3.1 IIR and CFC Rule Can Coexist in Domestic Tax Laws

935. An IIR is not included in the definition of a CFC Tax Regime. Although CFC Tax Regimes impose tax on the owners of a foreign subsidiary, they are distinguishable from an IIR in that the Top-up Tax under the IIR is initially computed on a jurisdictional basis so as to bring the tax paid on excess profits in that jurisdiction up to an agreed minimum tax rate. Those taxes are then allocated to each LTCE in proportion to that Entity's GloBE Income before being brought into charge by a Parent Entity. Given the policy and mechanical differences between the two, a jurisdiction is not required to replace an existing CFC Tax Regime by introducing an IIR and, therefore, is not prevented from employing both an IIR and a CFC Tax Regime in its domestic tax laws.[117]

936. Further, FAQs[118] issued by the OECD on GloBE Rules have clarified that despite global minimum tax rules applying on top of CFC rules, it would not lead to double taxation, as below:

> Because the GloBE Rules operate as a minimum tax, the rules are complimentary to existing corporate tax rules, such as CFC regimes. Taxes paid on income arising in a jurisdiction, including under CFC regimes, is taken into account for purposes of computing the effective tax rate in a jurisdiction. To the extent tax is paid at or above the minimum rate as a result of existing rules, including CFC rules, no additional tax is due under Pillar Two.

5.3.2 Interaction of IIR and CFC Rule with Treaty Provisions under UN and OECD MTC 2017[119]

937. *Report on Pillar Two Blueprint states IIR and CFC rule are compatible with tax treaties*: The IIR operates by requiring a parent entity, in most cases, the UPE, to bring into account as income its proportionate share of the income of each CE located in a low-tax jurisdiction in which it owns an equity interest. That income is then taxed in the parent entity's hands up to the GloBE minimum rate after crediting any covered taxes (as defined for the purposes of the GloBE) on that income. In subjecting a domestic taxpayer to tax on its share of the foreign income of a controlled subsidiary, therefore, the IIR operates in a way that is closely comparable to a CFC rule and raises the same treaty questions as raised by CFC rules. Although there are a number of differences between the IIR and the CFC rules of many jurisdictions, since CFC regimes do not conflict with treaty obligations (though some countries do not conform to this

---

117. Refer 'OECD's Commentary on GloBE Model Rules, Chapter 10 (pg. 194, paragraph 8)'.
118. Refer 'OECD's FAQs on Global Anti-Base Erosion Model Rules (Pillar Two): Sl. No. 14' https://www.oecd.org/tax/beps/pillar-two-model-GloBE-rules-faqs.pdf.
119. Refer 'South Centre's Tax Cooperation Policy Brief 22, 12 January 2022 titled Global Minimum Corporate Tax: Interaction of Income Inclusion Rule with Controlled Foreign Corporation and Tax-sparing Provisions by Kuldeep Sharma' https://www.southcentre.int/wp-content/uploads/2022/01/Tax-PB-22.pdf accessed on 17 May 2022.

view)[120] hence, for the same reasons, it can be concluded that an IIR along the lines envisaged under the GloBE is similarly compatible with the provisions of tax treaties that are generally based on the UN or OECD Model.[121]

938. *Interaction with Articles 7 and 10:* A significant number of countries have adopted CFC provisions to address issues related to the use of foreign base companies. While the design of this type of legislation varies considerably among countries, a common feature of these rules, which are now internationally recognised as a legitimate instrument to protect the domestic tax base, is that they result in a Contracting State taxing its residents on income attributable to their participation in certain foreign entities. Since such legislation results in a State taxing its own residents, paragraph 3 of Article 1 confirms that it does not conflict with tax conventions like Articles 7 and 10.[122] Though, some countries hold a viewpoint that CFC provisions are contrary to the treaty provisions.[123] The purpose of paragraph 1 of Article 7 is to limit the right of one Contracting State to tax the business profits of enterprises of the other Contracting State. As confirmed by paragraph 3 of Article 1, the paragraph does not limit the right of a Contracting State to tax its own residents under CFC provisions found in its domestic law, even though such tax imposed on these residents may be computed by reference to the part of the profits of an enterprise that is resident of the other Contracting State that is attributable to these residents' participation in that enterprise. Tax so levied by a State on its own residents does not reduce the profits of the enterprise of the other State and may not, therefore, be said to have been levied on such profits.[124] Similarly, as confirmed by paragraph 3 of Article 1, paragraph 5 of Article 10 cannot be interpreted as preventing the State of residence of a taxpayer from taxing that taxpayer, pursuant to its controlled foreign company's legislation or other rules with similar effect, on profits which have not been distributed by a foreign company. Moreover, it should be noted that the paragraph is confined to taxation at source and, thus, has no bearing on the taxation at residence under such legislation or rules.[125] Also, the UN and OECD commentaries make it clear that even if a treaty does not have a saving clause, i.e., Article 1(3), it does not mean that a State is restricted from applying its CFC rule.[126]

939. *Interaction with Article 9:* Transfer pricing rules are intended to adjust the taxable profits of associated enterprises (AEs) to eliminate distortions arising whenever the

120. Refer paragraph 110 of Commentary on Article 1 of the OECD MTC 2017. Also, refer paragraphs 27.4 to 27.7 of the Commentary on Article 1 of the OECD MTC 2014.
121. Refer 'OECD Report on Pillar Two Blueprint (paragraphs 681 to 683)' https://www.oecd.org/tax/beps/tax-challenges-arising-from-digitalisation-report-on-pillar-two-blueprint-abb4c3d1-en.htm
122. UN Model DTC 2017 (paragraph 40 of commentary on Article 1) and OECD MTC 2017 (paragraph 81 of commentary on Article 1).
123. OECD MTC 2017 (paragraph 110 of commentary on Article 1).
124. UN Model DTC 2017 (paragraph 8 of commentary on Article 7) and OECD MTC 2017 (paragraph 14 of commentary on Article 7).
125. UN Model DTC 2017 (paragraph 16 of commentary on Article 10) and OECD MTC 2017 (paragraph 37 of commentary on Article 10).
126. OECD MTC 2017 (paragraph 15 of commentary on Article 1).

prices or other conditions of transactions between those enterprises differ from what they would have been if the enterprises had been unrelated. Because CFC rules, by definition, address related parties (as the companies that are captured by such rules are controlled by another party), jurisdictions often also use these rules to combat the adjusted prices charged between related parties. In other words, CFC rules are seen as a way for a parent jurisdiction to capture income earned by a foreign subsidiary that may not have been earned had the original pricing of the income-creating asset been set correctly. CFC rules are thus often referred to as 'backstops' to transfer pricing rules. That terminology, however, is misleading in that CFC rules do not always complement transfer pricing rules. CFC rules may target the same income as transfer pricing rules in some situations, but it is unlikely that either CFC rules or transfer pricing rules, in practice, eliminate the need for the other set of rules. Instead, while CFC rules may capture some income that is not captured by transfer pricing rules (and vice versa), neither set of rules fully captures the income that the other set of rules intends to capture.[127] Transfer pricing rules, which generally rely on a facts and circumstances analysis and focus primarily on payments between related parties, do not remove the need for CFC rules. CFC rules are generally more mechanical and more targeted than transfer pricing rules, and many CFC rules automatically attribute certain categories of income that are more likely to be geographically mobile and therefore easy to shift into a low-tax foreign jurisdiction, regardless of whether the income was earned from a related party.[128] CFC rules, similar to transfer pricing regulations, could possibly lead to economic double taxation among related parties. Consequently, specific rules which trigger economic double taxation among AEs, need to be tested with Article 9. CFC rules reallocate the profits of the CFC to the shareholder. By doing so, they are taxing the taxable base, which has been allocated to another country on an arm's length basis. Thus, as they go beyond the boundaries of Article 9, they are restricted.[129] By applying the CFC rule, the State of the shareholder is unilaterally rewriting the accounts of AEs even though the transactions between such enterprises have taken place on normal open market commercial terms (on an arm's length basis).[130] Similarly, a conflict may arise if the IIR makes income/profit reallocations beyond arm's length allocations. However, given the understanding arising from the extant IIR rules, there may not be a case of double taxation as the State of the UPE taxes the low-taxed income only up to the top-up rate (and not up to the domestic tax rate, which may be higher). That being said, double taxation may arise under IIR if the ETR of a CE complies with the ALP but is less than the minimum rate set at 15%.

---

127. Refer 'BEPS Action 3 Report (paragraph 8)' https://www.oecd.org/ctp/designing-effective-controlled-foreign-company-rules-action-3-2015-final-report-9789264241152-en.htm accessed on 17 May 2022.
128. *Id.* (paragraph 9).
129. Refer 'V. Chand, A. Turina, K. Romanovska: Tax Treaty Obstacles in Implementing the Pillar Two Global Minimum Tax Rules and a Possible Solution for Eliminating the various challenges, Vol. 14 Issue: World Tax Journal, 2022 (Volume 14), No. 1 Published online: 21 February 2022' https://research.ibfd.org/#/doc?url=/collections/wtj/html/wtj_2022_01_int_1.html accessed on 17 May 2022.
130. Refer 'OECD MTC 2017 (paragraph 2 of commentary on Article 9)'.

5.4 INTERACTION AND RELATION OF GLOBE RULES WITH GILTI AND BEAT

940. *Background of GILTI:*[131] Before the 2017 TCJA, the United States generally taxed its firms and residents on their worldwide income. However, US firms could defer the tax on foreign subsidiaries' active business earnings until those earnings were repatriated to the United States as dividends. The US Congress was concerned that completely exempting US multinationals' foreign earnings might exacerbate the incentive to shift profits to low-tax jurisdictions abroad. So, Congress in the US added a new 10.5% minimum tax on GILTI to discourage such profit shifting. GILTI is intended to approximate the income from intangible assets (such as patents, trademarks, and copyrights) held abroad. The US Congress considered intangible assets highly mobile – and sought to discourage US firms from shifting these assets offshore. More specifically, a US business must include GILTI in its gross income annually. GILTI is calculated as the total active income earned by a US firm's foreign affiliates that exceeds 10% of the firm's depreciable tangible property. A corporation (but not other businesses) can generally deduct 50% of the GILTI and claim a foreign tax credit for 80% of foreign taxes paid or accrued on GILTI. Thus, if the foreign tax rate is zero, the effective US tax rate on GILTI will be 10.5% (half of the regular 21% corporate rate because of the 50% deduction). If the foreign tax rate is 13.125% or higher, there will be no US tax after the 80% credit for foreign taxes.

941. *IIR and GILTI*: In the US, the tax rate for corporations is proposed[132] to be increased from 21% to 28%. The 28% CIT rate will consequently increase the GILTI rate in tandem, and the new GILTI effective rate would be 20% (as against the current rate of 10.5-13.125%), applied on a jurisdiction-by-jurisdiction basis (rather than the current practice of application on a global basis). Since the GILTI rules are similar in their intent to the IIR rule, the US is expected to continue to apply them rather than adopting an IIR. However, if the proposed amendments in the US do not go through, GILTI may instead be treated as a kind of CFC regime.[133] Accordingly, the OECD[134] has clarified that GILTI can coexist with GloBE Rules, and changes to the GILTI rules as a result of US legislation, such as the Build Back Better Act (BBBA), will be incorporated into this process to the extent those changes are enacted, to ensure a level playing field. These conditions, therefore, remain to be settled.

131. Refer 'Tax Policy Center's Briefing Book: What is global intangible low-taxed income and how is it taxed under the TCJA?' https://www.taxpolicycenter.org/briefing-book/what-global-intangible-low-taxed-income-and-how-it-taxed-under-tcja accessed on 17 May 2022.

132. Refer 'General Explanations of the Administration's Fiscal Year 2023 Revenue Proposals, Department of the Treasury, March 2022' https://home.treasury.gov/system/files/131/General-Explanations-FY2023.pdf accessed on 17 May 2022.

133. Refer 'OECD Pillar Two: GloBE rules for New Zealand (paragraph 3.6, footnote)' https://taxpolicy.ird.govt.nz/en/publications/2022/2022-ip-oecd-pillar-two accessed on 15 May 2022.

134. Refer 'OECD's FAQs on Global Anti-Base Erosion Model Rules (Pillar Two): Sl. No. 15' https://www.oecd.org/tax/beps/pillar-two-model-GloBE-rules-faqs.pdf.

942. *Background of BEAT:*[135] Section 59A of the Internal Revenue Code of the United States imposes a Base Erosion Anti-Abuse Tax (BEAT) liability on certain corporate taxpayers, in addition to their regular tax liability. Liability for BEAT is generally limited to corporate taxpayers with substantial gross receipts that make deductible payments to foreign-related parties above a specified threshold (referred to as a 'base erosion payment'). Taxpayers potentially liable for this additional tax have three-year average gross receipts in excess of USD 500 million and a 'base erosion percentage' exceeding a specified threshold. The base erosion percentage is generally determined by dividing the taxpayer's 'base erosion tax benefits' by the amount of all deductions allowed to the taxpayer for the taxable year. Under the BBBA, the definition of base erosion payments is further expanded with respect to inventory costs to include payments to a foreign-related party for certain direct and indirect inventory costs.

943. *UTPR and BEAT:* From the US perspective, in conjunction with the GILTI regime, adopting the UTPR ensures that income earned by a multinational company, whether based in the United States or elsewhere, is subject to a minimum rate of taxation regardless of where the income is earned. Just as GILTI ensures that a minimum per-jurisdiction rate of tax is paid by US-based multinationals on income earned through CFCs, the UTPR ensures that a minimum per-jurisdiction rate of tax is paid on income earned in each jurisdiction in which foreign-based multinationals operate. This ensures that companies cannot avoid a minimum rate of taxation by, for example, relocating their headquarters to a foreign jurisdiction that has not implemented an IIR. The UTPR is designed to encourage countries to adopt the global minimum tax agreed to as part of the international negotiations by ensuring that profits in low-tax jurisdictions are taxed at the same minimum rate. In the United States, it is proposed[136] to repeal the BEAT and replace it with a UTPR that is consistent with the UTPR described in the Pillar Two Model Rules. When another jurisdiction adopts a UTPR, it is proposed[137] to also include a DMT that would protect US revenues from the imposition of UTPR by other countries.

5.5 INTERACTION OF GLOBE RULES WITH TAX-SPARING PROVISIONS[138]

944. *Background*: By 'tax-sparing' credit, it is meant that credit is granted by a country (generally a developed or capital-exporting country) in respect of tax not only actually paid but actually forgone under the incentive legislation of another country (generally

135. Refer 'General Explanations of the Administration's Fiscal Year 2023 Revenue Proposals, Department of the Treasury, March 2022' https://home.treasury.gov/system/files/131/General-Explanations-FY2023.pdf accessed on 17 May 2022.
136. *Id.*
137. *Id.*
138. Refer 'South Centre's Tax Cooperation Policy Brief 22, 12 January 2022 titled Global Minimum Corporate Tax: Interaction of Income Inclusion Rule with Controlled Foreign Corporation and Tax-sparing Provisions by Kuldeep Sharma' https://www.southcentre.int/wp-content/uploads/2022/01/Tax-PB-22.pdf accessed on 17 May 2022.

a developing or capital-importing country).[139] Factors in favour of a tax-sparing regime include that it makes it more favourable to invest abroad, catalyses transfer of capital and technology, acts as a device to aid an emerging economy and ensures the exercise of a developing country's sovereignty by allowing it to effectively deploy a specific part of its domestic tax regime. The rationale[140] for support of developed countries under their tax system to achieve the objective of introducing tax-sparing provisions by developing countries is *inter alia* explained below:

> The effectiveness of the tax incentive measures introduced by most developing countries depends on the interrelationship between the tax systems of the developing countries and those of the capital-exporting countries from which the investment originates. It is of primary importance to developing countries to ensure that the tax incentive measures shall not be made ineffective by taxation in the capital-exporting countries using the foreign tax credit system. This undesirable result is to some extent avoided in bilateral treaties through a 'tax-sparing' credit, by which a developed country grants a credit not only for the tax paid but also for the tax spared by incentive legislation in the developing country. It is also avoided by the exemption method. Developing countries consider it necessary to underline their understanding that either the exemption method or the tax-sparing clause is, for these countries, a basic and fundamental aim in the negotiation of tax treaties. On the other hand, studies have shown that tax factors may not themselves be decisive in the process of investment decisions and, therefore, tax sparing may not be an appropriate policy.

5.5.1 Viewpoint of Some Countries on Tax-Sparing

945. Industrialised countries have a fairly restrictive policy on adopting tax-sparing provisions in tax treaties. On the outer end of the scale is the United States, which has a consistent policy of not adopting tax-sparing provisions in any of its tax treaties. More recently, Norway has also taken the policy position of not adopting tax-sparing provisions in tax treaties. The United Kingdom has seemingly adopted a more balanced position and has concluded tax treaties with tax-sparing provisions as recently as 2011. Developing countries tend to be proponents of tax sparing. On the outer end of this scale is the position of Brazil, that refuses to enter into tax treaties unless the treaty includes tax sparing. China has also been a strong proponent of tax sparing.[141]

946. Factors[142] which prompt some countries to opine that tax-sparing may not be an appropriate policy *inter alia* include:

---

139. Refer 'UN Model DTC 2017 (paragraph 10 of commentary on Article 23)'.
140. *Id.*, (paragraph 4 of commentary on Article 23).
141. Refer 'The Concept of Tax Sparing: A General Analysis, and an Analysis and Assessment of the Various Features of Tax Sparing Provisions by Kristian Reinert Haugland Nilsen Master of Laws, University of Oslo' https://www.jus.uio.no/ior/english/research/projects/global-tax-tranparency/publications/the-concept-of-tax-sparing.pdf accessed on 17 May 2022.
142. Refer 'OECD's Tax Sparing – A Reconsideration' https://www.oecd-ilibrary.org/taxation/tax-sparing_9789264162433-en accessed on 17 May 2022.

- Tax sparing provisions offer ample opportunities for tax planning and tax avoidance, which undermines the tax bases of both the residence and source country.
- Investment decisions made by international investors resident in credit countries are rarely dependent upon or influenced by the existence or absence of tax sparing provisions in tax treaties.
- While negotiating tax treaties, in return for tax sparing provisions, some countries (developing) have to settle for certain concessions like lower withholding tax rates or stricter PE rules.

947. That being said, many members from both developed and developing countries are of the view that tax-sparing credits should be included in treaties between developed and developing countries where the developed country used the credit method.[143] On the other hand, the exemption method of providing relief for double taxation eliminates the undesirable effects of the residence country's taxes on the source country's tax incentive scheme.[144] The purpose of these provisions is to allow non-residents to obtain a foreign tax credit for the taxes that have been 'spared' under the incentive programme of the source State or to ensure that these taxes will be taken into account for the purposes of applying certain conditions that may be attached to exemption systems.[145]

5.5.2 Viewpoint That GloBE Rules May Force Abandonment of Tax-Sparing Provisions

948. From the African viewpoint,[146] IIR may compel countries to give up on tax incentive regimes as explained below:

> An analysis gives the average corporate tax rate for Africa as 27.46%. Tax incentives, giveaways and loopholes result in a far lower effective tax rate for African countries. For instance, with a nominal tax rate of 30%, where the actual profit of an MNE could not be established, the Nigeria tax authorities, under its laws, subject such companies to a deemed profit taxation which results in an ETR of only 6%. This means that, as far as Nigeria is concerned, the difference between the proposed global minimum effective tax rate of 15% and the 6% ETR will be taxed by the country of residence of the MNE group using the IIR. This generates a situation for developing countries in which they have to shore up their ETR by overhauling their tax incentive regimes and retooling domestic legal framework for more effective taxation of MNEs to avoid losing a significant portion of their tax right/base to a developed country.

143. Refer 'UN Model DTC 2017 (paragraph 5 of commentary on Article 23)'.
144. *Id.*, (paragraph 6 of commentary on Article 23).
145. Refer 'UN Model DTC 2017 (paragraph 73 of commentary on Article 23) and OECD MTC 2017 (paragraph 73 of commentary on Articles 23A and 23B)'.
146. Refer 'What Does the G7 Proposal on Taxation of the Digitalised Economy Mean for African countries?' https://afripoli.org/what-does-the-g7-proposal-on-taxation-of-the-digitalised-economy-mean-for-african-countries accessed on 17 May 2022.

949. Overhauling of tax incentive regimes following the introduction of IIR may have other implications as well. Interventions aimed at restructuring tax incentive regimes must cover domestic tax laws and tax-related incentives within the context of International Investment Agreements (IIAs). These Agreements are usually fraught with stabilisation clauses that guarantee a set standard of regulatory treatment to investments made pursuant to the Agreement. Some such clauses forbid the host nation from withdrawing certain incentives guaranteed under the IIA or otherwise established at the time of the investment. Though removing these kinds of tax incentives may be difficult, maintaining such boundaries may be less attractive to the MNEs if all IF members implement the IIR. This is because the MNEs will not benefit from the incentive since they would be taxed in their home jurisdiction.[147]

950. In general, tax sparing clauses oblige the State of residence to provide relief for the taxes spared by the source State. The clauses are typically found in the relief provisions similar to Article 23A or 23B of the UN and OECD MTC. The question now is whether the State of residence, when applying its CFC rule or the IIR, shall provide relief to its own resident for taxes that have been spared by the other State (in the hands of a separate taxpayer). As a start, it should be noted that the saving clause (corresponding to Article 1(3) of the UN and OECD MTC) contains an exception for Article 23. This would mean that the State enforcing the CFC rule / IIR will have to provide treaty benefits to its own residents for cases falling within the elimination of double taxation provisions. In the context of IIR, there may be a case when the UPE is taxed on the CEs income and the spared tax is not considered as covered taxes for calculating the ETR of the CE.[148]

5.5.3 OECD's Response to Allay Concerns on Potential Conflict Between GloBE Rules and Tax-Sparing Provisions

951. The OECD, in its October 2021 statement, has touched upon this issue by stating that the tax incentives provided to spur substantial economic activity will be accommodated through a carve-out. Overall, the GloBE rules will relieve pressure on developing countries to provide excessively generous tax incentives to attract foreign investment; while at the same time, there will be carve-outs for activities with real substance.[149] Thereafter, FAQs[150] issued by the OECD on GloBE Rules have further clarified, as below:

---

147. *Id.*
148. Refer 'V. Chand, A. Turina, K. Romanovska: Tax Treaty Obstacles in Implementing the Pillar Two Global Minimum Tax Rules and a Possible Solution for Eliminating the various challenges, Vol. 14 Issue: World Tax Journal, 2022 (Volume 14), No. 1 Published online: 21 February 2022' https://research.ibfd.org/#/doc?url=/collections/wtj/html/wtj_2022_01_int_1.html accessed on 17 May 2022.
149. Refer 'OECD's October 2021 Brochure – Two-Pillar Solution' https://www.oecd.org/tax/beps/brochure-two-pillar-solution-to-address-the-tax-challenges-arising-from-the-digitalisation-of-the-economy-october-2021.pdf.
150. Refer 'OECD's FAQs on Global Anti-Base Erosion Model Rules (Pillar Two): Sl. No. 7' https://www.oecd.org/tax/beps/pillar-two-model-GloBE-rules-faqs.pdf.

> A substance carve-out based on assets and payroll costs allows a jurisdiction to continue to offer tax incentives that reduce taxes on routine returns from investment in substantive activities, without triggering additional GloBE top-up tax. Given the carve-out covers investment in both tangible assets and payroll it will have broad application to a wide range of different industries.

5.5.4 OECD's Response Does Not Entirely Allay Concerns

952. Under the MLI, India has not included paragraph 3 of Article 7 while inserting Article 11 of the MLI in its tax treaties (refer India's synthesised texts[151] released), which is equivalent to Article 1(3) of the UN and OECD MTC. A probable reason for the same is that India does not subscribe to Authorised OECD Approach (AoA) advocated by the OECD since it believes that the same is more suited for countries which are net exporters of capital and technology, thereby implying that arm's length return in the source (developing) State may not be sufficient for taxation of a PE (in the market jurisdiction). A rationale for the same is that the business profits are a result of both supply as well as demand-side factors, and a FAR-based attribution ignores the contribution to business profits made by demand-side factors such as access to marketplace, etc.[152] That being the case, ascribing returns based on CFC regulations would wean taxation to the State of residence rather than to the State of source. Perhaps, that is why India has not introduced the CFC regulations as such. Also, as mentioned *supra*, some countries do not conform to the view that CFC regulations comply with Article 7(1) of the OECD MTC. That being the case, it may be an issue of conflict if IIR under Pillar Two is adopted by India or for that matter any country which does not have CFC provisions in place, though, at the same time, it cannot be said that inclusion of CFC provisions is a *sine qua non* for adopting the Pillar Two provisions. India, like many developing countries, did not have CFC rules as they would have been at odds with the tax-sparing rules. Adoption of IIR (which is an extension of CFC rules) under Pillar Two is therefore going to create conflict with the tax-sparing rules, as demonstrated by **Illustration # 73**:

> Let us assume a hypothetical situation where a Company A under an MNE Group is located in Jurisdiction A which is a low-tax jurisdiction where corporate tax rate is Nil and there is another Company B under the same MNE Group which is located in Jurisdiction B where corporate tax rate is 25%. It is further assumed that Jurisdiction B has tax sparing rules in its domestic law which allow 100% tax exemption to certain eligible corporates and for the purposes of this illustration, it is also assumed that Company B complies with all requisite conditions so as to avail the tax exemption. The amount of top-up tax under IIR in respect of the CEs in Jurisdiction A and B respectively is constructed through an illustration hereunder so as to analyse its conflict with tax-sparing rules:

151. Refer 'India's synthesized texts under the MLI' https://incometaxindia.gov.in/Pages/international-taxation/dtaa.aspx.
152. Refer 'South Centre's Comments on the OECD Secretariat Proposal for a 'Unified Approach' under Pillar One' https://www.southcentre.int/wp-content/uploads/2019/11/OECD-Tax-Pillar-One-Comments-South-Centre-Tax-Initiative-v4.pdf accessed on 17 May 2022.

CE	Globe Income	Adjusted Covered Taxes	Jurisdictional ETR	Top-up Tax Percentage	Total Carveout*	Determination of Excess Profit	Determination of amount of Top-up Tax
Company A	100	0	0	15	17	83	12.45
Company B	100	0	0	15	23	77	11.55

Calculation of Substance-based Income Exclusion					
CE	Payroll expenses	Payroll carveout (at 10%)	Carrying value of tangible assets	Tangible assets Carveout (at 8%)	Total Carveout*
Company A	50	5	150	12	17
Company B	150	15	100	8	23

The example above demonstrates that the taxes spared by Jurisdiction B are allocated to the UPE. In this illustration, the impact of Payroll and Tangible assets Carve-outs is limited to an extent, i.e., in their absence, the amount of Top-up Tax for Jurisdiction B would have been 15, whereas, with Carve-outs, it is 11.55. However, the impact of Carve-outs on lowering of amount of Top-up Tax will increase if the Payroll expenses and Carrying value of Tangible assets in Company B are substantially higher and also, let us assume that instead of 100% tax exemption, there is 50% tax exemption in Jurisdiction B, as demonstrated in the example given below:

CE	Globe Income	Adjusted Covered Taxes	Jurisdictional ETR	Top-up Tax Percentage	Total Carveout**	Determination of Excess Profit	Determination of amount of Top-up Tax
Company A	100	0	0	15	17	83	12.45
Company B	100	12.5	12.5	2.5	82	18	0.45

Calculation of Substance-based Income Exclusion					
CE	Payroll expenses	Payroll carveout (at 10%)	Carrying value of tangible assets	Tangible assets Carveout (at 8%)	Total Carveout**
Company A	50	5	150	12	17
Company B	500	50	400	32	82

It is to be noted that the higher carve-out rates (10% for Payroll Carve-out and 8% for Tangible assets Carve-out) apply in the transition period of ten years, following which, the carve-out rate will drop substantially to 5%, which implies that amount of Top-up Tax will correspondingly increase once the transition period is over. Notwithstanding the carve-out rate and the quantum of Payroll expenses and Carrying value of Tangible assets, the above illustration adequately demonstrates that taxes spared by the State of Source are getting shifted to the State of UPE under the IIR. The IIR, therefore, impinges on tax sovereignty of developing countries which have introduced tax-sparing provisions.

5.5.5 Observations

953. The importance of tax incentives for developing countries can be gauged from OECD's 'Building an investment tax incentives database'[153] findings that in 80% of countries covered, at least one tax incentive supports an area related to the Sustainable Development Goals. This is why it is difficult for most developing countries to give up on tax incentives.

954. Generally, the implementation of tax-sparing provisions in tax treaties by developing countries can be viewed as a *quid pro quo* in exchange for the lowering of withholding tax rates at source or stricter PE rules that entail adopting a tax treaty. With tax sparing benefits gone post the adoption of IIR under Pillar Two, it is unlikely that developing countries would be in a position to re-visit and re-set the already lowered withholding tax rates or re-negotiate the softening of stricter PE rules in their tax treaties.

955. Specifically, from the perspective of developing countries, the adoption of GloBE implies losing tax incentives as a tax policy instrument to attract foreign direct investment. This is why every country involved, but especially developing countries should undertake a thorough examination to determine whether such measures are convenient for their interests in the long run.[154] Also, countries may consider changing tax-based incentives to grants and other forms of subsidy to better accommodate the GloBE rules. Ongoing incentives may be grandfathered, and any potential tax ceding to another jurisdiction arising from tax sparing may be arrested/prevented through introduction of QDMTT. Future SEZ rules may be introduced in a manner which attracts MNEs that are outside the scope of Pillar Two rules.

5.6 GLOBE RULES CONTAIN MEASURES TO EASE COMPLIANCE BURDEN

956. The GloBE Rules is an innovative, elaborate but complex instrument. In order to strike a balance and ease implementation, the rules have certain in-built provisions to ameliorate compliance burden. Before such measures are discussed, let us have a cursory view of some of the complex GloBE provisions:

- Article 2.2.3, where the parent entity (other than the UPE) is required to prepare hypothetical CFS based on four assumptions.
- Paragraph (b) of Article 2.6.2 which provides that the Flow-through Entity's employees and Tangible Assets that are not allocated to PEs are allocated to any CEs that are located in the jurisdiction where the Flow-through Entity was

153. Refer 'OECD's Building an investment tax incentives database' https://www.oecd-ilibrary.org/finance-and-investment/building-an-investment-tax-incentives-database_62e075a9-en accessed on 20 May 2022.

154. Refer 'Aitor Navarro's Article titled Jurisdiction Not to Tax, Tax Sparing Clauses, and the OECD Minimum Taxation (GloBE) Proposal' https://doi.org/10.2478/ntaxj-2021-0004 accessed on 17 May 2022.

created irrespective of whether they are the Constituent Entity-owners of the Entity. This approach of allocating the employees and Tangible Assets of Flow-through Entities differs from the approach provided under Article 3.5 to allocate the Income or Loss of a Flow-Through Entity.

- The mechanism of computation of GloBE income or loss in Chapter 3 *inter alia* involves various adjustments in Article 3.2.
- It is quite tedious (to monitor) that each item of deferred tax expense for a CE that is not in a category that meets the Recapture Exception Accrual definition should be tested in each Fiscal Year for recapture as necessary under the mechanics of Article 4.4.4.
- The ETR Adjustment Articles are provided in Articles 3.2.6, 4.4.4, 4.6.1, 4.6.4, and 7.3. When these provisions result in adjustments to the Adjusted Covered Taxes, the change will affect the ETR for one or more of the prior Fiscal Years.
- The provisions of Article 6.2 involve CEs joining and leaving an MNE Group.

957. Some of the measures intended to ease compliance burden are directly linked to the complex provisions illustrated above. Such measures and other remaining provisions which have been incorporated in the GloBE Rules to ease compliance burden are *inter alia* listed below:

(a) *Option for an election under Article 3.2.8*: The MNE Group may prefer an election under Article 3.2.8 over the burden of determining arm's length prices for transactions between CEs in the same jurisdiction, particularly in cases where the CEs may not be applying an arm's length standard to same-jurisdiction (domestic) transactions in a jurisdiction that does not impose a Covered Tax.

(b) *For simplicity, taxes assigned to the jurisdiction of the immediate CE that distributed the dividend*: In many cases, the distributing CE is the CE that originally earned the income. In other cases, the distributing CE will be a direct or indirect shareholder of the CE that originally earned the income. Ideally, Covered Taxes incurred by CEs with respect to distributions should be assigned to the tax jurisdiction of the CE that originally earned the underlying income. However, tracking and tracing distributions through the ownership chain would be extremely complex and burdensome, particularly where an entity controls multiple CEs. Accordingly, paragraph (e) of Article 4.3.2 provides that such taxes should be assigned to the jurisdiction of the immediate CE that distributed the dividend that triggered the tax liability.

(c) *Provisions of Recapture Exception Accrual rule*: It provides categories of deferred tax liabilities that do not need to be monitored for recapture under Article 4.4.4, as set forth in Article 4.4.5. The list of Recapture Exception Accruals sets out the temporary differences that are both common in IF jurisdictions and that are generally material to MNE Groups. Such temporary differences are typically tied to substantive activities in a jurisdiction or are differences that are not prone to taxpayer manipulation. Accordingly, to reduce compliance burdens, these low-risk items that are certain to reverse over time are not required to be monitored under the rules in Article 4.4.4 for recapture.

(d) *Provisions of Article 4.4.7:* It provides a compliance simplification option with respect to the Article 4.4.4 recapture rule, as it permits a CE to exclude from the Total Deferred Tax Adjustment Amount any deferred tax liability that is not expected to be paid within the time period set forth in Article 4.4.4. This simplification allows for the exclusion of deferred tax liabilities that are almost certain to require recapture, which reduces compliance monitoring such liabilities and recalculating Top-up Tax several years later.

(e) *Provisions of Article 4.5*: It provides an elective rule to effectively carry GloBE losses forward with a deemed deferred tax asset. When elected, Article 4.5 applies in lieu of Article 4.4 modified deferred tax accounting rules. Accordingly, Article 4.5 is generally expected to be of greatest utility as a simplification in jurisdictions that do not impose a CIT or impose one at a very low rate, given that when the election is made, Article 4.4 no longer applies, and temporary differences may result in Top-up Tax.

(f) *Provisions of Article 4.6.1*: Article 4.6.1 permits the MNE Group to treat increases to liabilities for Covered Taxes in previous Fiscal Years as current year tax increases for purposes of the GloBE Rules. Similarly, an immaterial decrease in Covered Taxes may be treated as a reduction in Covered Taxes in the current Fiscal Year. Thus, under Article 4.6.1, while treating post-filing adjustments to a tax liability in the current year is not as accurate as recalculating the GloBE tax liability or potential GloBE tax liability with respect to the relevant Fiscal Years, it significantly simplifies the computation of Top-up Tax under the GloBE Rules.

(g) *Election to not apply the Substance-based Income Exclusion*: Article 5.3.1 provides for an election to not apply the Substance-based Income Exclusion, as some MNE Groups may consider that the burden of computing the amount of the exclusion for a particular jurisdiction outweighs the potential benefits of the exclusion in that jurisdiction. The MNE Group is not bound to make the election for the same jurisdiction in any subsequent Fiscal Year. Thus, an MNE Group that elects not to apply the Substance-based Income Exclusion for a jurisdiction in one year may apply the exclusion in the following Fiscal Year.

(h) *De Minimis Exclusion*: Chapter 5 includes a *De Minimis* Exclusion for the CEs located in the same jurisdiction when their aggregated revenue and income do not exceed certain thresholds. The policy intent underlying Article 5.5 is to avoid the complexities of a full ETR computation in cases where the amount of any Top-up Tax would not seem to justify the associated compliance and administrative costs.

(i) *Provisions of Article 5.4.1*: If the ETR of a jurisdiction is subject to an ETR Adjustment, then Article 5.4.1 provides the mechanism for performing the re-calculations for the prior year. Article 5.4.1 treats any additional Top-up Tax computed in respect of those prior Fiscal Years as Additional Current Top-up Tax, which is allocated to CEs in the jurisdiction under Article 5.2. To avoid the complexity and administrative burden of requiring an amended GloBE Information Return and additional separate payment of Top-up Tax, the Additional Top-up Tax is instead charged to the Fiscal Year in which the recalculation was performed. This way, the need to avoid compliance and administrative burdens outweighs competing considerations relating to accuracy in connection with the attribution of Top-up Tax based on changes in ownership interests of LTCEs between the prior year and the year the recalculation is undertaken.

(j) *Provisions of paragraph (g) of Article 6.2.1*: Article 6.2.1(g) starts or restarts the five-year period in Article 4.4.4 with respect to deferred tax liabilities of a CE when it joins an MNE Group. By restarting the five-year period in Article 4.4.4, paragraph (g) reduces compliance and administrative burdens that would arise if the deferred tax liabilities were subject to recapture based on their accrual dates in the disposing MNE Group.

(k) *Provisions of paragraph (b) of Article 7.1.1:* These provisions provide a safe harbour to a Flow-through UPE with owners that are natural persons holding small Ownership Interests in the Flow-through UPE.

(l) *Provisions of paragraph (b) of Article 7.2.1*: In respect of a UPE that is subject to a Deductible Dividend Regime, provisions of paragraph (b) of Article 7.2.1 provide a safe harbour to the UPE with dividend recipients that are natural persons holding small Ownership Interests in the UPE.

(m) *Adoption of Safe Harbours under Article 8.2:* In order to limit unnecessary compliance and administrative burden for MNE Groups and tax administrations, the GloBE Implementation Framework is exploring the development of GloBE Safe Harbours. GloBE Safe Harbours would allow an MNE Group to avoid the ETR and Top-up Tax calculation in respect of its operations that are likely to be taxable at or above the Minimum Rate. They would also provide for improved tax certainty and transparency in the use of risk assessment under the GloBE Rules.

(n) *Recourse to Article 8.3*: Further guidance on the interpretation or application of the GloBE Rules may be agreed upon and published by the IF for the benefit of various stakeholders.

(o) *Transition Rules provided in Chapter 9*: The transitional rules described in this chapter are *inter alia* as below:

  (a) *Allow* higher percentages to be used in calculating the substance-based income exclusion in the first ten years of the GloBE rules. The percentages start at 10% for payroll costs and 8% for tangible assets and taper down to the 5% rates over a ten-year period.

  (b) Allow for a longer filing deadline in an MNE's Transition Year. An MNE is normally required to file its GloBE return and other notifications within fifteen months after the end of its accounting period. In an MNE's Transition Year, this deadline is extended to eighteen months.

  (c) Address the treatment of losses and other timing differences. Where there are losses and other timing differences arising before a Transition Year, the MNE will generally be treated as though it were already subject to the

GloBE rules at the time the losses or timing differences arose. This is done by taking into account existing deferred tax accounting attributes (including deferred tax assets from earlier losses) in the ETR calculation described in Chapter 5. Consistent with that treatment, deferred tax assets and deferred tax liabilities are generally taken into account at the lower of 15% and the applicable domestic tax rate. However, deferred tax assets generated after 30 November 2021 from items that are excluded from the GloBE base must be disregarded for GloBE purposes. In addition, the GloBE tax basis in assets acquired in an intragroup transaction after 30 November 2021 must be based on historical carrying values and related deferred tax assets and liabilities must similarly be determined based on historical carrying values. The purpose of this is to defeat inappropriate tax planning transactions.

(d) Provide temporary relief from the application of UTPR for MNEs in the initial phase of international activity. An MNE is considered in its 'initial phase of international activity' if it has CEs in no more than six jurisdictions and has less than EUR 50 million of tangible assets (by book value) outside of the jurisdiction in which it has the most tangible assets (again, by book value). The relief applies on an annual basis. Since this rule does not apply to the IIR, this relief is only relevant for groups that are headquartered in a country that does not have an IIR, and even then, it will be somewhat undercut if the group has a lower-tier parent company in a country with an IIR. The temporary relief expires after the MNE has been in scope of the GloBE Rules for five years. This five-year period is not suspended even if the MNE's revenues decline, so it falls outside the scope of the rules during those five years, as explained in **Illustration # 74**:

Illustration demonstrating that temporary relief expires after the MNE Group has been in scope of the GloBE Rules for five years

S. No.	Fiscal Year ending 31 December	Revenue (Euro Million)
1	2030	760
2	2031	780
3	2032	600
4	2033	640
5	2034	720

- An MNE Group crosses the Euro 750 million consolidated annual revenue threshold for the first time in its fiscal year ended 31 December 2030.

- The first year in which the GloBE Rules apply to the MNE Group is 2032, as it has been provided that the GloBE Rules apply to MNEs that have consolidated annual revenues of at least Euro 750 million in at least two of the last four fiscal years.

- Assuming the MNE Group meets the other requirements for the initial phase relief from the UTPR, it will qualify for the relief in 2032 and the last year it can obtain the relief is for the year 2036.
- It does not matter that the MNE Group's annual revenues fell below the Euro 750 million threshold from 2032 to 2034.

5.7 GLOBE RULES CONTAIN ANTI-ABUSE PROVISIONS AND MEASURES

958. GloBE (an acronym for Global Anti-Base Erosion) Rules is an anti-BEPS instrument itself. The Pillar Two Proposal, which *inter alia* incorporates the GloBE Rules, is designed to operate alongside a jurisdiction's existing anti-avoidance rules. In addition, during the course of formulation of these entirely new set of rules, the IF has been cognisant of the fact that in the course of implementation, MNEs do not exploit the GloBE Rules to their advantage, following which, specific anti-abuse provisions have been incorporated at various places, as discussed below:

(a) *Provisions of Article 3.2.3*: This article requires transactions between Group Entities to be priced consistently with the ALP and recorded at the same price for GloBE purposes for all CEs that are parties to the transaction.
(b) *Provisions of Article 3.2.7*: This article prevents MNE Groups from engaging in transactions that are intended to increase the ETR in a jurisdiction that is below the Minimum Rate.
(c) *Provisions of paragraph (e) of Article 4.1.3*: Under paragraph (e), if the taxpayer has no expectation to pay the tax within the three-year timeframe, it may not be included in the computation of Adjusted Covered Taxes. Since timely payment of liability for Covered Taxes is within the control of the MNE Group, there is no mechanism to include amounts paid after expiration of the three-year period in Adjusted Covered Taxes. This also prevents an abuse whereby a CE could assert that it does not intend to pay the tax in a year where the CE is well over the Minimum Rate and then subsequently pays the tax liability in a year in which it is below the Minimum Rate, using the rule to escape what would otherwise be Top-up Tax liability. Paragraph (e) applies with respect to amounts of current tax expense; accordingly, post-filing adjustments, such as additional tax liability resulting from a subsequent audit, will not fall within the scope of this paragraph since such amounts are not included in current tax expense. It may be noted that Article 4.6 provides the rules with respect to Covered Taxes paid as a result of a post-filing adjustment. In addition, there is a special rule set forth in Article 4.1.2(c) to include amounts paid with respect to uncertain tax positions, which permits the inclusion of such amounts irrespective of the operation of paragraph (e).
(d) *Provisions of Article 4.3.3*: This article prevents potential abuse arising out of application of Article 4.3.2(c), (d). Without the rule of Article 4.3.3, an MNE Group could shift mobile income from high-tax jurisdictions to Low-Tax Jurisdictions to reduce overall tax liability (including Top-up Tax liability) in the MNE Group.
(e) *Provisions of Article 4.6.4*: If more than EUR 1 million of the amount accrued by a CE as current tax expense and included in Adjusted Covered Taxes for a Fiscal Year is not paid within three years of the last day of such year, the ETR and Top-up Tax for the Fiscal Year in which the unpaid amount was claimed as a Covered Tax must be recalculated in accordance with Article 5.4.1 by excluding such unpaid amount from Adjusted Covered Taxes.
(f) *The approach to jurisdictional blending*: Under Article 5.1.1, the jurisdictional blending approach avoids risks that would otherwise arise to the integrity of the rules from shifting income and taxes between CEs located in the same jurisdiction and avoids potential distortions caused by particular features of

the domestic tax system (such as loss-surrender and tax consolidation mechanisms).

(g) *Provisions of Article 7.1.2*: Article 7.1.2 provides that the GloBE Losses incurred by a UPE that is a Flow-through Entity must also be reduced by the amount attributable to each Ownership Interest, except to the extent that the holders of Ownership Interests are not allowed to use the loss in computing their separate taxable income. Without Article 7.1.2, losses that are passed through to the holders of Ownership Interests would also be available for use in the jurisdictional ETR calculation to shield GloBE income of other CEs located in the UPE's Jurisdiction.

(h) *Provisions of paragraph (c) of Article 7.2.1 inter alia applicable only in the case of a Pension Fund that is not a Pension Services Entity*: Provisions of paragraph (c) of Article 7.2.1 only apply in the case of a Pension Fund that is not a Pension Services Entity and to this extent, differ from the provisions of paragraph (c) of Article 7.1.1. Thus, Article 7.2.1(c) only applies in relation to a dividend paid to the parent Pension Fund by a UPE in the Pension Fund's jurisdiction. Without this limitation, Article 7.2.1(c) could allow Pension Funds to take advantage of Deductible Dividend Regimes to earn income exempt from the GloBE Rules from UPEs located anywhere in the world by simply establishing a Pension Services Entity in the UPE's jurisdiction.

(i) *Provisions of Article 9.1.3*: This article provides a limitation on intragroup asset transfers before applicability of the GloBE Rules. If an asset is transferred between entities after 30 November 2021 and before the Transition Year of an MNE Group, and such entities would have been CEs of that MNE Group had the GloBE Rules been in effect with respect to that MNE Group, such asset must be recorded at its historical carrying value for GloBE purposes to limit the ability to step-up the basis in such assets without including the resulting gain in the computation of GloBE Income or Loss. The rule in Article 9.1.3, however, does not apply to inventory because of the routine nature of intragroup inventory sales and the typically brief period that it is held before sale outside the MNE Group.

(j) *Provisions of Article 9.3.5:* Article 9.3.5 contains an optional provision that allows the Reference Jurisdiction to use the UTPR to defend its tax base from a tax planning opportunity that may arise under the exclusion for MNEs in the initial phase of their international activity. The GloBE Rules contain an optional provision in Article 9.3.5 for implementing jurisdictions that is intended to reduce the risk of locally headquartered MNEs establishing a new UPE in a jurisdiction without an IIR in order to take advantage of the initial transition phase relief. Since the temporary relief only applies to the UTPR, an MNE Group headquartered in a jurisdiction in the initial phase of its international activity with LTCEs would still be charged top-up tax in that jurisdiction under the IIR (assuming that jurisdiction was to adopt the IIR). If, however, it established a new UPE in a jurisdiction without an IIR and transferred the LTCEs to that new UPE, it might not be charged top-up tax in respect of its LTCEs at all during the five-year period it qualified for temporary relief. The optional provision under Article 9.3.5 is intended to address this risk. The optional provision under Article 9.3.5 would allow the Reference Jurisdiction to collect the full amount of top-up tax arising in a low-tax jurisdiction under the UTPR, no matter where the UPE is located, as demonstrated in **Illustration # 75**:

Illustration of Application of Optional Provision under Article 9.3.5

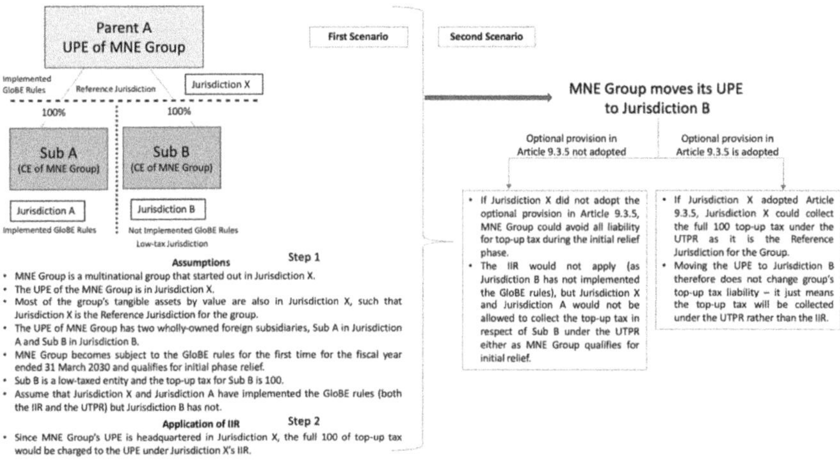

If a Jurisdiction decides to adopt the optional provision in Article 9.3.5, there is a further sub-option in Article 9.3.5(a) of the GloBE Rules for it to limit the application of the UTPR to top-up tax arising in jurisdictions other than itself. Adopting this sub-option would mean that, where a Jurisdiction is the Reference Jurisdiction for an MNE, it will be able to collect top-up tax under the UTPR in respect of the MNE's low-taxed entities located in any jurisdiction other than itself. But top-up tax in respect of any low-taxed entities in that jurisdiction will not be collected by it or any other jurisdiction. The effect of this sub-option is to preserve the tax outcomes that arise under that jurisdiction's tax law (so as to prevent over-taxation), even if those outcomes mean that its MNE's ETR is less than 15%. If this sub-option were not adopted, top-up tax arising in that jurisdiction during an MNE's initial phase would be collected by it under the UTPR, even though no other country would be allowed to collect that tax, as demonstrated in **Illustration # 76**:

Illustration of Application of Optional Provision under Article 9.3.5 and Article 9.3.5 (a)

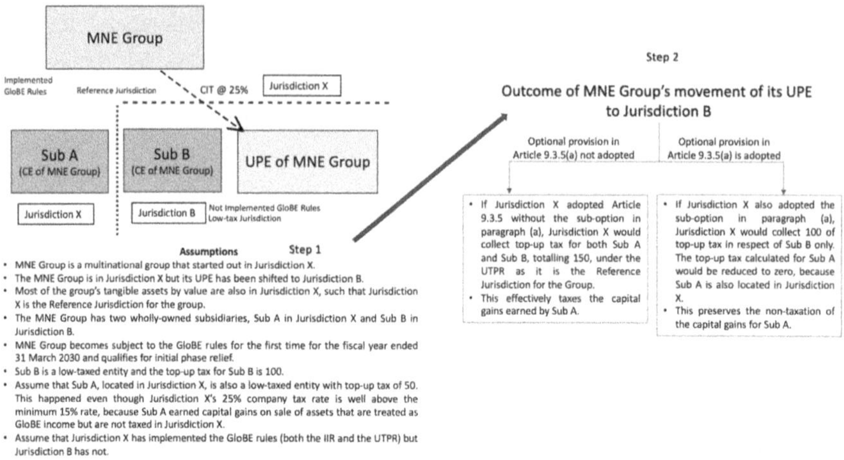

5.8 REQUIREMENT TO MAINTAIN ROBUST DOCUMENTATION

959. Although the taxpayers are required to maintain adequate and robust documentation to demonstrate that GloBE Rules have been sufficiently complied with, it has been outlined in the Commentary to GloBE Rules that there is a need for supporting documentation to facilitate adequate examination and satisfaction of tax authorities concerned, *inter alia,* in respect of the following articles of GloBE Rules:

(a) *Filing of GloBE Information Return under Article 8.1*: The GloBE Information Return is a return in a standardised template form that provides a tax administration with the information it needs to evaluate the correctness of a CE's tax liability under the GloBE Rules. Hence, all CEs of an MNE Group are expected to prepare and maintain sufficient information and documentation for filing of the GloBE Information Return, either by itself or any Designated Local Entity or facilitate its filing by the UPE or a Designated Filing Entity appointed by the MNE Group.

(b) *Maintain Transfer Pricing documentation under Article 3.2.3*: Article 3.2.3 requires transactions between Group Entities to be priced consistently with the ALP and recorded at the same price for GloBE purposes for all CEs that are parties to the transaction, and consequently, the MNE Group is expected to maintain a transfer pricing policy and connected supporting documents to justify ALP.

(c) *Requirements of Article 3.3.6 for a CE's International Shipping Income and Qualified Ancillary International Shipping Income to qualify for the exclusion from its GloBE Income or Loss*: Article 3.3.6 imposes a substance criterion in order to qualify for the exclusion. Article 3.3.6 is aimed at ensuring that the strategic or commercial management of all ships deployed in earning International Shipping Income is effectively carried on from within the jurisdiction where the CE is located. The strategic or commercial management of the ships concerned is limited to those deployed in earning International Shipping Income and must be effectively carried out in the jurisdiction where the CE is located in order to qualify for the exclusion. The carrying on strategic or commercial management from within the jurisdiction where the CE is located is effectively determined on the basis of the relevant facts and circumstances and taking into account all relevant factors depending on the item of income. Accordingly, the CE is expected to maintain sufficient details and documentation to support carrying on strategic or commercial management from within the jurisdiction.

(d) *Requirements of Article 7.2.1:* The CE must maintain records sufficient to demonstrate the amount of GloBE Income for a Fiscal Year that was distributed within twelve months of the end of the Fiscal Year.

(e) *Requirements of Article 7.2.3*: The UPE must maintain records sufficient to demonstrate that distributions occurred within twelve months of the end of the Fiscal Year of the subsidiary Entity subject to the Deductible Dividend Regime.

(f) *Requirements of Article 7.3.3*: In order to track the extent to which Deemed Distribution Tax is paid within the four-year period, a Deemed Distribution Tax Recapture Account for each Fiscal Year in which the election was made must be maintained and available for examination by the tax authorities of jurisdictions imposing the GloBE Rules.

5.9 ANALYSIS OF IF MEMBER COUNTRIES AND CONSEQUENT POLICY CONSIDERATIONS

960. To secure a minimum level of substance is the nucleus of the OECD BEPS Project, with equal importance bestowed on transparency rules so that tax administrations can apply their tax rules effectively. Prescribing a minimum tax rate of 15% is the core element of GloBE Rules which *inter alia* require intragroup transactions to be at ALP with an expectation that MNEs perform real economic activity (having substance) and pay their fair share of taxes in a transparent manner. Accordingly, an analysis of domestic law of IF member countries is required to evaluate the extent of policy and legal modifications required, especially in light of the fact that GloBE Rules are being implemented as a common approach and that these new set of rules are to be implemented through domestic law of respective countries. Therefore, first of all, it is expedient to understand the primary features[155] of domestic laws of IF[156] member countries, for which a compilation has been done in Table 5.1 to ascertain the

155. Refer 'IBFD' https://research.ibfd.org/#/search?N = 3 + 10 + 4293744764&Ne = 7487&Nu = global_rollup_key&Np = 2&Ns = sort_country_one|0||subcategory|0||sort_jurisdiction|0||sort_state_province|0 accessed on 20 May 2022.

156. Refer 'Members of the OECD/G20 Inclusive Framework on BEPS, updated: November 2021' https://www.oecd.org/tax/beps/inclusive-framework-on-beps-composition.pdf accessed on 20 May 2022.

prevalence of CIT regime, applicable CIT rate, availability of TP procedures and commitment to AEOI.[157]

Table 5.1 Analysis of IF Member Countries

S. No.	*IF Member Country*	*Applicability of CIT*	*CIT =/> 15%*	*Availability of TP provisions*	*AEOI: Status of Commitment*
1	Albania	Yes	Yes	Yes	2021
2	Andorra	Yes	No	Yes	2018
3	Angola	Yes	Yes	Yes	No commitment as yet
4	Anguilla	No	No	No	2017
5	Antigua and Barbuda	Yes	Yes	No	2018
6	Argentina	Yes	Yes	Yes	2017
7	Armenia	Yes	Yes	Yes	No commitment as yet
8	Aruba	Yes	Yes	Yes	2018
9	Australia	Yes	Yes	Yes	2018
10	Austria	Yes	Yes	Yes	2018
11	Bahamas	No	No	No	2018
12	Bahrain	No	No	No	2018
13	Barbados	Yes	No	No	2018
14	Belarus	Yes	Yes	Yes	No commitment as yet
15	Belgium	Yes	Yes	Yes	2017
16	Belize	Yes	No	No	2018
17	Benin	Yes	Yes	Yes	No commitment as yet
18	Bermuda	No	No	No	2017
19	Bosnia and Herzegovina	Yes	No	Yes	No commitment as yet
20	Botswana	Yes	Yes	Yes	No commitment as yet
21	Brazil	Yes	Yes	Yes	2018
22	British Virgin Islands	No	No	No	2017
23	Brunei Darussalam	Yes	Yes	No	2018

157. Refer 'OECD's Global Forum on Transparency and Exchange of Information for tax purposes, Automatic Exchange of Information (AEOI): Status of Commitments as of 5 January 2022' https://www.oecd.org/tax/transparency/AEOI-commitments.pdf accessed on 20 May 2022.

S. No.	*IF Member Country*	*Applicability of CIT*	*CIT =/> 15%*	*Availability of TP provisions*	*AEOI: Status of Commitment*
24	Bulgaria	Yes	No	Yes	2017
25	Burkina Faso	Yes	Yes	Yes	No commitment as yet
26	Cabo Verde	Yes	Yes	Yes	No commitment as yet
27	Cameroon	Yes	Yes	Yes	No commitment as yet
28	Canada	Yes	Yes	Yes	2018
29	Cayman Islands	No	No	No	2017
30	Chile	Yes	Yes	Yes	2018
31	China	Yes	Yes	Yes	2018
32	Colombia	Yes	Yes	Yes	2017
33	Congo	Yes	Yes	Yes	No commitment as yet
34	Cook Islands	Yes	Yes	Yes	2018
35	Costa Rica	Yes	Yes	Yes	2018
36	Côte d'Ivoire	N/A	N/A	N/A	No commitment as yet
37	Croatia	Yes	Yes	Yes	2017
38	Curaçao	Yes	Yes	Yes	2018
39	Czech Republic	Yes	Yes	Yes	2017
40	Democratic Republic of the Congo	Yes	Yes	Yes	No commitment as yet
41	Denmark	Yes	Yes	Yes	2017
42	Djibouti	Yes	Yes	Yes	No commitment as yet
43	Dominica	Yes	Yes	No	2018
44	Dominican Republic	Yes	Yes	Yes	No commitment as yet
45	Egypt	Yes	Yes	Yes	No commitment as yet
46	Estonia	Yes	Yes	Yes	2017
47	Eswatini	Yes	Yes	Yes	No commitment as yet
48	Faroe Islands	N/A	N/A	N/A	2017
49	Finland	Yes	Yes	Yes	2017
50	France	Yes	Yes	Yes	2017
51	Gabon	Yes	Yes	Yes	No commitment as yet

S. No.	IF Member Country	Applicability of CIT	CIT =/> 15%	Availability of TP provisions	AEOI: Status of Commitment
52	Georgia	Yes	Yes	Yes	2024
53	Germany	Yes	Yes	Yes	2017
54	Gibraltar	Yes	No	No	2017
55	Greece	Yes	Yes	Yes	2017
56	Greenland	Yes	Yes	Yes	2018
57	Grenada	Yes	Yes	No	2018
58	Guernsey	Yes	No	No	2017
59	Haiti	Yes[158]	Yes[159]	Yes[160]	No commitment as yet
60	Honduras	Yes	Yes	Yes	No commitment as yet
61	Hong Kong	Yes	Yes	Yes	2018
62	Hungary	Yes	No	Yes	2017
63	Iceland	Yes	Yes	Yes	2017
64	India	Yes	Yes	Yes	2017
65	Indonesia	Yes	Yes	Yes	2018
66	Ireland	Yes	No	Yes	2017
67	Isle of Man	Yes	No	No	2017
68	Israel	Yes	Yes	Yes	2018
69	Italy	Yes	Yes	Yes	2017
70	Jamaica	Yes	Yes	Yes	2022
71	Japan	Yes	Yes	Yes	2018
72	Jersey	Yes	No	No	2017
73	Jordan	Yes	Yes	Yes	2023
74	Kazakhstan	Yes	Yes	Yes	2021
75	Kenya*	Yes	Yes	Yes	2022
76	Korea	Yes	Yes	Yes	2017
77	Latvia	Yes	Yes	Yes	2017
78	Liberia	Yes	Yes	Yes	No commitment as yet
79	Liechtenstein	Yes	No	Yes	2017
80	Lithuania	Yes	Yes	Yes	2017

158. Refer 'Economy Profile of Haiti, Doing Business 2020, World Bank Group' https://www.doingbusiness.org/content/dam/doingBusiness/country/h/haiti/HTI.pdf accessed on 20 May 2022.
159. *Id.*
160. Refer 'Transfer Pricing Country Summary, Haiti, July 2018 by TPA Global' https://www.tpa-global.com/wp-content/uploads/2020/05/180712-haiti-transfer-pricing-country-summary-report-2018.pdf accessed on 20 May 2022.

S. No.	*IF Member Country*	*Applicability of CIT*	*CIT =/> 15%*	*Availability of TP provisions*	*AEOI: Status of Commitment*
81	Luxembourg	Yes	Yes	Yes	2017
82	Macau	Yes	No	No	2018
83	Malaysia	Yes	Yes	Yes	2018
84	Maldives	Yes	Yes	Yes	2022
85	Malta	Yes	Yes	No	2017
86	Mauritius	Yes	Yes	No	2018
87	Mauritania	Yes	Yes	Yes	No commitment as yet
88	Mexico	Yes	Yes	Yes	2017
89	Monaco	Yes	Yes	No	2018
90	Mongolia	Yes	Yes	Yes	No commitment as yet
91	Montenegro	Yes	Yes	Yes	2023
92	Montserrat	Yes	Yes	No	2017
93	Morocco	Yes	Yes	Yes	2022
94	Namibia	Yes	Yes	Yes	No commitment as yet
95	Netherlands	Yes	Yes	Yes	2017
96	New Zealand	Yes	Yes	Yes	2018
97	Nigeria*	Yes	Yes	Yes	2020
98	North Macedonia	Yes	No	Yes	No commitment as yet
99	Norway	Yes	Yes	Yes	2017
100	Oman	Yes	Yes	Yes	2020
101	Pakistan*	Yes	Yes	Yes	2018
102	Panama	Yes	Yes	Yes	2018
103	Papua New Guinea	Yes	Yes	Yes	No commitment as yet
104	Paraguay	Yes	No	Yes	No commitment as yet
105	Peru	Yes	Yes	Yes	2020
106	Poland	Yes	Yes	Yes	2017
107	Portugal	Yes	Yes	Yes	2017
108	Qatar	Yes	No	Yes	2018
109	Romania	Yes	Yes	Yes	2017
110	Russian Federation	Yes	Yes	Yes	2018
111	Saint Kitts and Nevis	Yes	Yes	No	2018

S. No.	*IF Member Country*	*Applicability of CIT*	*CIT =/> 15%*	*Availability of TP provisions*	*AEOI: Status of Commitment*
112	Saint Lucia	Yes	Yes	No	2018
113	Saint Vincent and the Grenadines	Yes	Yes	Yes	2018
114	Samoa	Yes	Yes	Yes	2018
115	San Marino	Yes	Yes	Yes	2017
116	Saudi Arabia	Yes	Yes	Yes	2018
117	Senegal	Yes	Yes	Yes	No commitment as yet
118	Serbia	Yes	Yes	Yes	No commitment as yet
119	Seychelles	Yes	Yes	Yes	2017
120	Sierra Leone	Yes	Yes	Yes	No commitment as yet
121	Singapore	Yes	Yes	Yes	2018
122	Slovak Republic	Yes	Yes	Yes	2017
123	Slovenia	Yes	Yes	Yes	2017
124	South Africa	Yes	Yes	Yes	2017
125	Spain	Yes	Yes	Yes	2017
126	Sri Lanka*	Yes	Yes	Yes	No commitment as yet
127	Sweden	Yes	Yes	Yes	2017
128	Switzerland	Yes	No	No	2018
129	Thailand	Yes	Yes	Yes	2023
130	Togo	Yes	Yes	Yes	No commitment as yet
131	Trinidad and Tobago	Yes	Yes	No	2018
132	Tunisia	Yes	Yes	Yes	2024
133	Turkey	Yes	Yes	Yes	2018
134	Turks and Caicos Islands	No	No	No	2017
135	Ukraine	Yes	Yes	Yes	2023
136	United Arab Emirates	No	No	No	2018
137	United Kingdom	Yes	Yes	Yes	2017
138	United States	Yes	Yes	Yes	FATCA
139	Uruguay	Yes	Yes	Yes	2018
140	Viet Nam	Yes	Yes	Yes	No commitment as yet

S. No.	*IF Member Country*	*Applicability of CIT*	*CIT =/> 15%*	*Availability of TP provisions*	*AEOI: Status of Commitment*
141	Zambia	Yes	Yes	Yes	No commitment as yet

* Kenya, Nigeria, Pakistan and Sri Lanka have not joined the Pillar Two Agreement as of now.

5.9.1 The CIT Regime and CIT Rate

961. On a perusal of Table 5.1, it is seen that some IF member countries do not have any CIT regime at present. Since these countries are part of the IF, hence, following the common approach, they are obligated to comply with the Pillar Two recommendations in light of their concurrence to these proposals. If these states do not introduce a CIT regime or do not implement GloBE Rules, the common approach embodied in these rules will ensure taxation in the home jurisdiction (state of residence) of the MNEs. Hence, to this extent, profits arising (sourced) in these jurisdictions would not get taxed in these countries if they continue to not have a CIT regime. It is also seen in Table 5.1 that some countries have corporate tax rate less than the minimum agreed rate of 15%. If the tax rate in these countries continues to be below the minimum tax rate of 15%, following the common approach, GloBE rules will ensure partial taxation in the home jurisdiction (state of residence) of the MNEs. Hence, to this extent, profits arising (sourced) in these countries would not get fully taxed there if they continue to apply ETR below 15%.

962. Accordingly, IF member countries which do not have CIT regime at present may consider introducing the same in their respective jurisdictions.

963. Even though the headline CIT rate in most IF countries are higher or equal to 15%, the ETR of MNEs in these jurisdictions may be less than 15% due to grant/availing of tax exemptions. Hence, IF countries which provide for tax exemptions may end up taxing the CEs in their respective jurisdictions to the extent of ETR that is less than 15%. The GloBE rules provide for a formulaic substance carve-out that excludes an amount of income that is 5% of the carrying value of tangible assets and payroll. In a transition period of ten years, the amount of income excluded will be 8% of the carrying value of tangible assets and 10% of payroll. It has been analysed in detail in paragraph 5.5 *supra* that despite 'Formulaic Substance Carve-Out', GloBE rules would still wean taxation to the State of residence at the expense of the State of source (which has spared taxes to attract FDI), which is apparently disadvantageous for such IF countries. Adoption of GloBE rules is, therefore, seen to be creating a conflict with the tax-sparing rules. Accordingly, such IF countries may consider a minimum ETR regime that would top up an MNE group's ETR to 15% and would apply to MNE groups operating in a particular jurisdiction with annual revenues of at least EUR 750 million in CFS of the UPE. This way, tax will not be ceded to another jurisdiction.

964. Though STTR is not part of GloBE Rules, however, since we are discussing the CIT rate in IF member countries, it would suffice to state here that the STTR under Pillar Two allows countries to levy a 'top-up' tax on certain related party payments where the recipient company in its home jurisdiction is not subject to a tax rate of at least 9% on those payments. With a statutory CIT rate of less than 9%, businesses in some IF countries may face a foreign top-up tax under the STTR. Hence, such IF countries would do well to enhance the tax rate to at least 9% in order to protect their overseas business from application of STTR.

5.9.2 Qualified Domestic Top-Up Tax

965. GloBE Model Rules released on 20 December 2021 have added a new concept of QDMTT, a concept that previously was not included in the OECD Report on Pillar Two Blueprint. Jurisdictions have been allowed under the GloBE Rules to opt into this possibility, thereby changing the ordering rule of the IIR. This allows a jurisdiction to introduce a rule which effectively duplicates the Model for top-up tax but ensures that the tax is collected by that local jurisdiction and is not ceded to another jurisdiction. Assuming low-tax jurisdictions take this path, it may reduce the complexity of the rules in many circumstances while achieving the goal of the Pillar Two project of providing a floor for tax competition.[161] In order to preserve tax sovereignty and their tax base, IF member countries may consider incorporating the QDMTT as it allows the jurisdiction in which a low-taxed entity is resident to levy the top-up tax before application of the IIR at the level of the parent company.

966. However, if an MNE records profits in a CE in a tax haven without carrying on commensurate economic activities therein, other countries might still tax those profits even if the tax haven imposes a QDMTT. Other countries' tax claims could be based on transfer pricing rules, CFC regime and other anti-avoidance doctrines. In such cases, MNEs may have an incentive to exit tax havens that adopt QDMTT.[162] Accordingly, such IF countries may adopt QDMTT depending upon the intensity of economic activities conducted by MNEs and the prevalence of support infrastructure in each country. That being said, IF countries, having well-developed financial markets, infrastructure, and trained manpower which adds a considerable amount of value to transactions undertaken for non-residents and political stability, may not witness an exodus of MNEs, as tax-saving is generally not the sole criterion prompting MNEs to shift base.

161. Refer 'KPMG's Update on Pillar 2 agreement – December 2021' https://home.kpmg/xx/en/home/insights/2021/12/inclusive-framework-beps-agreement-20-december-2021.html accessed on 20 May 2022.
162. Refer 'Noam Noked: The Case for Domestic Minimum Taxes on Multinationals' https://www.taxnotes.com/tax-notes-international/corporate-taxation/case-domestic-minimum-taxes-multinationals/2022/02/07/7d4qj?highlight=noam%20noked 20 May 2022.

5.9.3 Transfer Pricing Legislation

967. Article 3.2.3 of GloBE Rules *inter alia* provides as below:

> Any transaction between Constituent Entities located in different jurisdictions that is not recorded in the same amount in the financial accounts of both Constituent Entities or that is not consistent with the Arm's Length Principle must be adjusted so as to be in the same amount and consistent with the Arm's Length Principle. A loss from a sale or other transfer of an asset between two Constituent Entities located in the same jurisdiction that is not recorded consistent with the Arm's Length Principle shall be recomputed based on the Arm's Length Principle if that loss is included in the computation of GloBE Income or Loss.

968. The above provisions unequivocally reinforce the concept of transfer pricing. This implies that while computing GloBE income, the *inter se* transactions between CEs within or across jurisdictions are required to be aligned with the ALP. On perusal of Table 5.1, it may be seen that some IF member countries do not have TP legislation, which is a cause of concern as far as implementation of GloBE Rules is concerned. Hence, such countries would be required to incorporate TP regulations also in their domestic law and ensure that intragroup transactions are recorded at ALP.

5.9.4 Implementation of CRS for Automatic Exchange of Information

969. Under Common Reporting Standard (CRS) for Automatic Exchange of Information (AEOI), the participating jurisdictions exchange information automatically on a regular interval. Since tax and financial information is considered confidential and is protected by confidentiality provisions in most countries, the disclosure of such information to a foreign jurisdiction may be legally challenging. Also, in the absence of a legally binding agreement, there is a possibility that countries may not exchange information in a continuous and reliable manner. To address these concerns, countries enter into agreements which make it legally binding on countries and provide the legal basis for exchanging information.[163]

970. Bringing in transparency is the prime objective of all anti-BEPS measures. Implementation of CRS for AEOI is a positive demonstration by a country that it is committed to being a transparent, compliant and reputable jurisdiction. Those IF member countries who haven't committed to the CRS as of now, as evident on perusal of Table 5.1, may also consider providing their respective commitment to it at an early date in order to exhibit their willingness to be a transparent and responsible jurisdiction.

163. Refer "Financial Transparency Coalition: Automatic Exchange of Tax Information 2017" https://financialtransparency.org/wp-content/uploads/2018/05/Automatic-Exchange-of-Tax-Information.pdf accessed on 20 May 2022.

5.9.5 Domestic Legislation Required to Implement GloBE Rules

971. OECD's October statement has set out an aim for jurisdictions to legislate GloBE Rules into their respective domestic laws in 2022 so that these rules take effect from 2023. The GloBE Rules operate not by way of a multilateral instrument but by incorporation by countries in their domestic law. The procedure for legislation of GloBE Rules into domestic law may vary from country to country. The method will depend on the legal framework which governs the implementation of international rights and obligations in each jurisdiction, i.e., whether the adoption of rules automatically results in the integration of the rights and obligations set out in those rules into domestic law (a 'monist system') or whether domestic legislation is required in order to transpose the rights and obligations in such rules into domestic law (a 'dualist system'). Hence, it is recognised that legislation of some IF members would not permit them to simply refer to IF's Agreed Administrative Guidance to interpret and apply the GloBE Rules. Their domestic law may instead permit the tax administration to adopt the IF's Agreed Administrative Guidance by incorporating it verbatim or in substance into its own administrative guidance. On the other hand, some IF members may need parliamentary acceptance of the Agreed Administrative Guidance before it could be used to interpret or apply the GloBE Rules.

972. It would be pertinent to state here that Pillar Two compliances will be over and above the tax returns and filings that are already being executed by taxpayers. The GloBE has been designed as a global set of rules that will be targeted at large MNE groups and will overlay the domestic regime of a jurisdiction. Accordingly, the design of IIR and UTPR as Top-up Taxes does not restrict a jurisdiction from legislating the rules under a CIT system in its domestic law. Some of the areas where jurisdictions may have to consider introduction of legislation so as to comply with GloBE Rules (*inter alia* protecting their tax base simultaneously) are discussed *supra*. Additionally, it has been suggested in the Commentary to GloBE Rules that jurisdictions may take further necessary steps in their respective domestic law, as below:

(a) Article 2.1.6 requires the application of the IIR by the Parent Entity to LTCEs that are located outside the implementing jurisdiction. However, some IF members may wish to extend the application of the IIR domestically in order to avoid discriminating between domestic and foreign CEs that are members of the same MNE Group, as being contemplated by the European Union[164] and Jersey.[165] Such an extension of IIR to domestic LTCEs would appear logical, particularly as the UTPR would be collected by other jurisdictions anyway if

164. Refer 'European Commission's Proposal for a Council Directive on ensuring a global minimum level of taxation for multinational groups in the Union' https://eur-lex.europa.eu/legal-content/EN/TXT/?uri=CELEX%3A52021PC0823 accessed on 15 May 2022.

165. Refer 'OECD Pillars 1 & 2: Tax Policy Reflections, April 2022, Government of Jersey, paragraph 5.4.3' https://www.gov.je/SiteCollectionDocuments/Tax%20and%20your%20money/R%20OECD%20Pillars%201%20and%202%20tax%20policy%20reflections.pdf accessed on 21 May 2022.

there were insufficiently taxed profits in the local subsidiaries and branches of domestic UPEs.

(b) OECD's statement dated 8 October 2021[166] *inter alia* states that countries are free to apply the IIR to MNEs headquartered in their country even if they do not meet the threshold of EUR 750 million, an option being contemplated by the European Union.[167]

(c) Article 2.4.1 does not prescribe how the UTPR Top-up Tax Amount is allocated among the CEs that are located in the UTPR Jurisdiction. The allocation among the CEs within a UTPR Jurisdiction is to be addressed under that UTPR Jurisdiction's domestic law, which would ensure that such allocation mechanism is best coordinated with other existing domestic tax rules. The UTPR Jurisdiction may provide in its domestic law that the UTPR adjustment is imposed on only one CE or several CEs that are located in the jurisdiction. Therefore, a UTPR Jurisdiction may reallocate the UTPR Top-up Tax Amount among the CEs located in that jurisdiction, in subsequent years, in order to ensure that the UTPR Top-up Tax Amount is collected as soon as possible.

(d) There is no special provision under Article 8.1 regarding amendments to a GloBE Information Return. It is left to jurisdictions to decide whether their current domestic rules regarding amendments to tax or information returns will apply to the GloBE Information Return or to introduce new provisions that apply only to the GloBE Information Return.

(e) Article 8.1.8 requires that the laws of each jurisdiction with respect to penalties, sanctions, and confidentiality of the returns (including the information in the returns) shall also apply to the GloBE Information Return. Jurisdictions are free to extend existing penalties or sanctions or to create new ones for the GloBE Information Return.

(f) Article 8.3 provides that in order to address interpretational issues and also, in order to provide further clarity on GloBE Rules, the OECD shall issue Administrative Guidance, which the tax administrations of jurisdictions that have implemented GloBE Rules are required to comply with while applying the GloBE Rules, subject to any other requirements under their respective domestic law.

---

166. Refer 'OECD's Statement on a Two-Pillar Solution to Address the Tax Challenges Arising from the Digitalisation of the Economy – 8 October 2021' https://www.oecd.org/tax/beps/statement-on-a-two-pillar-solution-to-address-the-tax-challenges-arising-from-the-digitalisation-of-the-economy-october-2021.htm.

167. Refer 'European Commission's Proposal for a Council Directive on ensuring a global minimum level of taxation for multinational groups in the Union' https://eur-lex.europa.eu/legal-content/EN/TXT/?uri=CELEX%3A52021PC0823 accessed on 15 May 2022.

CHAPTER 6
Implementation of GloBE Rules by Jurisdictions

The GloBE implementation process of certain jurisdictions is discussed, namely, Canada, European Union, Jersey, New Zealand, Singapore, South Africa, Switzerland, United Arab Emirates, the United Kingdom and the United States of America.

973. OECD's October statement has set out an aim for jurisdictions to legislate GloBE Rules into their respective domestic laws in 2022 so that these rules take effect from 2023. It may also be noted that IF Members have agreed that the earliest the UTPR will come into effect is in 2024, as mentioned in paragraph 25 of the Commentary on Chapter 9 (Transition Rules). Accordingly, many jurisdictions have got activated to kick-start the implementation process, as discussed *infra*, which reflects the way various tax administrations have perceived GloBE Rules and their respective mechanism of implementation. Since the approach to understanding and implementation of GloBE Rules among all jurisdictions has to be common and consistent, the discussion *infra* demonstrates just that. Also, readers will get acquainted with the implementation process at a global level which, coupled with the theoretical discussion on GloBE Rules carried out in Chapter 4 of the book and Technical & Policy discussions in Chapter 5 of the book, is expected to further enhance and deepen their understanding of these rules.

6.1 IMPLEMENTATION BY CANADA[168]

974. Budget 2022 of Canada *inter alia* proposes to implement Pillar Two, along with a DMT, that would apply to Canadian entities of MNEs that are within the scope of Pillar Two. In this context, it has been stated that Pillar Two builds on the OECD/G20 BEPS project and intends to:

168. Refer 'International Tax Measures announced in Budget 2022 by Canada, Pillar Two – Global Minimum Tax' https://budget.gc.ca/2022/report-rapport/tm-mf-en.html#a4_1_2 accessed on 15 May 2022.

- reduce the incentive for MNEs to shift profits into low-tax jurisdictions.
- seeks to end the 'race to the bottom' in international corporate taxation by setting a floor on tax competition, while leaving appropriate flexibility for governments to design their income tax systems to support business investment and innovation.
- be implemented through changes to each country's domestic tax laws.

975. *Overview*: Under Pillar Two, an MNE is generally required to calculate the ETR on its profits in each jurisdiction in which it operates. If the ETR for a particular jurisdiction is below 15 %, the MNE is subject to a 'top-up tax' that brings the ETR on its profits in the jurisdiction up to the 15 % minimum rate. There is an exclusion (the Substance-based Income Exclusion) from the application of the top-up tax for an amount of income equal to a fixed percentage of the carrying value of an MNE's tangible assets and of its expenditures on labour in a jurisdiction. This is intended as a measure of the MNE's substantive economic activities in the jurisdiction.

976. *Core charging rules*: The GloBE Rules are comprised of two core charging rules for the top-up tax:

- *IIR*: The IIR is the primary rule. In general terms, if the country where the UPE of an MNE is located has implemented the IIR, it has the primary right to impose a top-up tax on the UPE with respect to income from the MNE's operations in any jurisdiction where it is taxed at an ETR below 15 %. The top-up tax brings the ETR of this low-taxed income up to 15 %. If the ultimate parent jurisdiction has not implemented the IIR, the right to impose the top-up tax under the IIR shifts to the jurisdiction of the highest-tier intermediate parent entity within the MNE's structure that has adopted the IIR.
- *UTPR*: The UTPR is a 'backstop' rule that generally applies where neither the ultimate parent jurisdiction nor any intermediate parent jurisdiction of an MNE has implemented the IIR. In that case, other jurisdictions in which the MNE operates that have implemented the UTPR would impose the top-up tax on the group entities located in their jurisdiction, with the top-up tax being allocated among those jurisdictions on a formulary basis. The UTPR provides a strong incentive for countries to adopt Pillar Two, as it ensures that MNEs whose parent entities are located in non-implementing jurisdictions are nonetheless subject to top-up tax in respect of their low-taxed income.

977. *DMT*: The GloBE Model Rules also explicitly contemplate that a jurisdiction may enact a DMT that would apply a top-up tax on low-tax income of its domestic entities. If such a tax is designed to achieve the intended outcomes under Pillar Two, it is treated as a QDMTT and is creditable dollar-for-dollar against the top-up tax liability otherwise arising under Pillar Two. In effect, this allows a jurisdiction to collect the top-up tax applicable to any low-taxed income of its domestic entities rather than allowing the top-up tax to accrue to the treasuries of other countries under the IIR or UTPR.

978. *Implementation in Canada:* Canada intends to implement GloBE Rules formulated by the OECD into its domestic law. Accordingly, as per the timeline and parameters set out in the OECD's October Statement, Budget 2022 of Canada proposes to implement Pillar Two, along with a DMT that would apply to Canadian entities of MNEs that are within the scope of Pillar Two. The government anticipates that the IIR and DMT will come into effect in 2023 as of a date to be fixed. The UTPR would come into effect no earlier than 2024. Hence, in order to allow the government to implement Pillar Two in accordance with the intended timeline, Budget 2022 has launched a public consultation on the implementation in Canada of the GloBE Model Rules and a DMT. The principal purpose of this consultation is to ensure that the draft legislation takes account of any necessary adaptations of the GloBE Model Rules to the Canadian legal and income tax context rather than to seek views on the major design aspects of the GloBE Model Rules or broader policy considerations. Accordingly, Budget 2022 has narrated (in brief) Chapters 1 to 10 of GloBE Model Rules and has invited public comments on each of the chapters as part of the consultation process.

6.2 IMPLEMENTATION BY THE EUROPEAN UNION

979. The EU members of the IF are supporting the global agreement that the European Commission's proposal is implementing. The only EU Member State that is not a member of the IF[169] and, as such, has not formally committed to the agreement is Cyprus. That being said, the Commission expects that Cyprus shall also support the Directive.[170] However, as of 31 May 2022, it has been reported that Poland[171] has raised concerns that the minimum tax could enter into force without the new rules preventing big multinationals from booking profits in the most favourable countries.

980. The Commission's proposal closely follows the OECD's Pillar Two Proposals with necessary adjustments[172] on the following lines to ensure compliance with EU law:

- The Directive adjusts the scope to also include purely domestic groups, while the scope of the OECD Pillar Two is limited to multinational (MNE) groups and a parent entity subjects only its foreign subsidiaries to the IIR. This departure from the OECD Model Rules is necessary in order to comply with the EU fundamental freedoms, specifically the freedom of establishment.

169. Refer 'Members of the OECD/G20 Inclusive Framework on BEPS – Updated: November 2021' https://www.oecd.org/tax/beps/inclusive-framework-on-beps-composition.pdf accessed on 15 May 2022.
170. Refer 'European Commission's Taxation and Customs Union – Minimum corporate taxation' https://ec.europa.eu/taxation_customs/taxation-1/minimum-corporate-taxation_en accessed on 15 May 2022.
171. Refer 'Poland blocks EU compromise on global minimum corporate tax deal' https://www.reuters.com/world/europe/poland-blocks-eu-compromise-global-minimum-corporate-tax-deal-2022-04-05/ accessed on 15 May 2022 (Poland has subsequently agreed, while Hungary has objected to implementation of a global minimum tax in the EU).
172. Refer 'European Commission's Questions and Answers on Minimum corporate taxation' https://ec.europa.eu/commission/presscorner/detail/en/qanda_21_6967 accessed on 15 May 2022.

- The OECD Model Rules allow jurisdictions the option to apply a qualifying domestic minimum tax. The Commission proposal will also allow the EU Member States to exercise the option to apply a domestic top-up tax to low-taxed domestic subsidiaries. This option will allow the top-up tax due by the subsidiaries of the multinational group to be charged locally, within the respective Member State, and not at the level of the parent entity.

981. The Directive[173] issued by the European Commission on implementation of GloBE Rules by the Member States, so as to ensure a minimum level of taxation for multinational groups in the Union, is succinctly discussed below:

(a) *IIR*: Under the rules of the Directive, the IIR applies in the following situations:
  - UPE in the EU: If the UPE is located in the EU, it will be subject to the top-up tax in respect of its LTCEs in the same and other EU Member States as well as in third-country jurisdictions.
  - IPE/POPE in the EU with UPE outside the EU: If there is no UPE in the EU, the LTCEs of the MNE group in the EU would effectively be taken into account by the third-country UPE of the Group if it applies the IIR. However, if there is at least one POPE or one IPE (if the jurisdiction where the UPE is located does not apply an IIR) in the EU, then the IPE/POPE will be subject to the top-up tax in respect of their low-taxed directly or indirectly owned constituent entities in the EU and third-country jurisdictions.
  - POPE in the EU with UPE in the EU: Although a UPE located in the EU is normally charged the top-up tax in respect of its LTCEs, there is also a possibility that the primary taxing right lies with the Member State of a POPE. In these cases, one has to follow a 'bottom-up' method in identifying the POPE that is liable to tax. One will have to start from the lowest-tier wholly owned constituent entities and move up to the first POPE, which will be liable to top-up tax under the IIR in respect of its LTCEs. The other POPEs up to the UPE will also be subject to the IIR but with a right to receive a credit for top-up tax due by another POPE lower in the chain.
  - Amount of CE's top-up tax, which a Parent Entity is entitled to collect through the IIR, is, in general, based on the proportion of the parent entity's interest in the income of the LTCE.

(b) *Domestic Top-Up Tax*: In order to preserve the sovereignty of Member States, the Directive provides that a Member State can opt to apply the top-up tax domestically to CEs located in its territory, referred to as Domestic Top-up Tax. This election allows that the top-up tax is charged and collected in a jurisdiction in which a low level of taxation occurred instead of collecting all

173. Refer 'European Commission's Proposal for a COUNCIL DIRECTIVE on ensuring a global minimum level of taxation for multinational groups in the Union' https://eur-lex.europa.eu/legal-content/EN/TXT/?uri=CELEX%3A52021PC0823 accessed on 15 May 2022.

the additional tax at the level of the UPE. When this election is exercised, the parent entity applying the IIR will be obliged to give credit for the qualified domestic top-up tax when calculating the top-up tax in respect of the relevant jurisdiction.

(c) *Undertaxed Payments Rule (UTPR):* The Directive provides that the UTPR applies in the following situations:
   - In circumstances where the UPE is located outside the EU in a jurisdiction that does not apply a qualifying IIR, all its CEs in jurisdictions with an appropriate UTPR framework will be subject to the UTPR. In this circumstance, CEs of such an MNE group that are located in a Member State will be apportioned and will have to pay, in their Member State a share of the top-up tax linked to the low-taxed subsidiaries of the MNE group.
   - The Directive provides that the UTPR will also apply to situations where the jurisdiction of the UPE operates a qualifying IIR but the UPE, together with its subsidiaries located in that same jurisdiction, are low-taxed. The top-up tax corresponding to the low-taxed UPE and its domestic subsidiaries will be charged through the UTPR to all the eligible entities across the MNE Group, including entities that are located in a Member State. This should only happen when the UPE is located outside the EU because an EU-located UPE either applies the IIR principles to itself and to its domestic subsidiaries or acknowledges that top-up was locally charged via the Domestic Top-up tax. Therefore, there should be no top-up tax allocated under the UTPR when the UPE is located in the EU.
   - In line with the OECD Model Rules, the calculation and allocation of the UTPR top-up tax in the Directive is based on two factors, i.e., number of employees and the carrying value of tangible assets.

(d) *Calculation of the Qualifying Income or Loss*: The Directive provides the following rules for the determination of qualifying income, i.e., the adjusted income that will be taken into account for computing the ETR:
   - In order to compute qualifying income, start with the financial accounting net income or loss of the CE for the fiscal year, as determined for the purpose of preparing CFS.
   - Then, adjustments are made to this income or loss as defined in Article 15 (which corresponds to Article 3.2 of OECD GloBE Rules).
   - In line with the OECD Model Rules, the Directive excludes international shipping income and partly ancillary international shipping income from the application of the GloBE Model Rules.
   - Includes rules specific to CEs that are a PE or a flow-through entity. In these cases, special rules are needed in order to avoid double-counting or no counting of the income attributable to these entities. These special rules will also limit tax avoidance opportunities.

(e) *Computation of Adjusted Covered Taxes:* The Directive provides the following rules for the determination of Adjusted Covered Taxes:

- The prime principle in allocating covered taxes is to assign them to the jurisdiction where underlying profits subject to these taxes were earned.
- To ensure this principle, the Directive also provides special rules in respect of cross-border taxes or income streams in the case of a PE, transparent entity, CFC, a hybrid entity, or taxes on dividends.

(f) *Calculation of ETR and Top-Up Tax:* The Directive provides the following rules for the calculation of the ETR of an MNE group in a jurisdiction for a fiscal year:
- The effective rate is computed by dividing the adjusted covered taxes of the group by the adjusted income earned by the group in a specific jurisdiction for the fiscal year.
- In line with the global agreement, the Directive sets the minimum ETR for the purposes of the GloBE Model Rules at 15%.
- For the purpose of calculation and allocation of the top-up tax,
  - Firstly, the top-up tax percentage is computed for a jurisdiction as a difference between the minimum ETR of 15% and the ETR of the jurisdiction.
  - This top-up tax percentage is then multiplied by the income for the GloBE purposes of that jurisdiction for the year in question.
  - The substance-based income exclusion (if any) is also deducted from this amount to arrive at the jurisdictional top-up tax.
  - In line with the GloBE Model Rules, the Directive provides for a substance-based income exclusion based on payroll costs and tangible assets.
  - The filing entity of an MNE group can elect not to apply the substance-based income exclusion for a jurisdiction.
  - Finally, the top-up tax for each CE in a jurisdiction is obtained by apportioning the jurisdictional top-up tax among CEs in that jurisdiction based on the income for the GloBE purposes of each CE in that jurisdiction.
- The Directive provides that when, as a result of an adjustment made to covered taxes or qualifying income or loss to a prior fiscal year, there is an additional top-up tax to be collected, such top-up tax should be treated as additional top-up tax for the fiscal year under review.
- In order to reduce compliance burdens in low-risk situations, an exclusion applies to minimal amounts of profit, referred to as the de minimis income exclusion. This is when profits of the MNE Group's CEs in a jurisdiction are below EUR 1 million and revenues below EUR 10 million. In such circumstances and provided that the election of the *de minimis* income exclusion is taken, the top-up tax of the CEs in this jurisdiction is deemed to be zero for GloBE purposes.

(g) *Special Rules for Mergers and Acquisitions:* The Directive provides special rules in respect of mergers, acquisitions, joint ventures, and multi-parented MNE groups as below:

- Provides for the application of a consolidated revenue threshold to group members in a merger or demerger situation.
- When a CE is acquired or sold by an MNE group within the scope of the rules, such a CE should be treated as part of both groups during the year, with certain adjustments to the values of the attributes used for the operation of the GloBE Model Rules (covered taxes, eligible payroll, eligible tangible assets, GloBE deferred tax assets).
- There are rules for the recognition of a gain or loss and carrying values in a transfer of assets and liabilities, including reorganisations.
- There is a special provision to include joint ventures, which would otherwise not be included in the definition of an MNE group for GloBE purposes.
- Finally, there is a specific rule for multi-parented MNE groups in a way that group entities are treated as part of a single MNE group.

(h) *Tax Neutrality and Distribution Regimes:* The Directive contains the following rules in respect of tax neutrality regimes and distribution tax systems:
- In order to avoid unintended outcomes, such as a disproportionate UTPR top-up tax liability in an MNE Group, the Directive provides for special rules for the computation of the income of the UPE, where such an entity is a flow-through or subject to a deductible dividend regime.
- In respect of investment entities, there are specific rules for the determination of the ETR, the top-up tax, an election to treat them as tax transparent entities, and an election to apply taxable distribution method.
- In relation to distribution tax systems, the Directive provides that, on an annual election by the filing entity with respect to CEs which are subject to an eligible distribution tax system, a deemed distribution tax is included in the calculation of the adjusted covered taxes of the relevant CEs. This involves maintaining a deemed distribution tax recapture account for each fiscal year for which the election is made. If in a four-year period, no tax is paid at the minimum rate on such deemed distribution, and the CE has not incurred an allowable loss, then the top-up tax is payable based on the outstanding balance of the recapture account for the year in question.

(i) *Administrative Provisions:* The Directive contains the following rules in respect of administrative provisions, including filing obligations:
- The Directive obliges a CE of an MNE group located in a Member State to file a top-up tax information return unless the return is filed by the MNE group in another jurisdiction with which the Member State has an exchange of information agreement.
- The required return may be filed either by the CE or by another designated local entity located in the Member State on its behalf.
- If the CE is relieved from filing the return, it must nevertheless notify its tax administration of the identity and location of the CE filing the return for the MNE group.

- The returns must be filed within fifteen months after the end of the fiscal year to which they relate.
- The Directive also lays down penalties for when an MNE group fails to comply with the obligations laid down in the Directive.

(j) *Transitional Rules:* The Directive contains transitional rules as below:
- These rules outline how to determine some aspects of the GloBE Model Rules when a group has to apply them for the first time (in order to reduce the compliance burden).
- Covers transition rules for the substance-based income exclusion.
- Provides parameters for carving domestically earned income out of the IIR and UTPR for large-scale domestic groups and MNE groups, respectively, in their initial phase of activity;
- Provides transitional relief for filing obligations and portfolio shareholdings.

(k) *Specific application of the IIR to large-scale domestic groups:* The Directive provides application of the IIR to large-scale domestic groups as below:
- Extends the application of the IIR to purely domestic groups located in a Member State if they meet the EUR 750 million threshold.
- This specific aspect of the EU rules is meant to avoid any risk of discrimination in a Member State between an entity that belongs to a group with cross-border activities and a group with purely domestic activities.
- These large-scale domestic groups will compute their ETR and, where relevant, be charged any top-up tax due under the IIR.
- In order to maintain an equal treatment with regard to MNE groups that are in the first stages of their international activities, it also grants large-scale domestic groups a five-year transitional period during which their low-taxed domestic activities will be excluded from the application of the rules.

(l) *Commencement of application of the rules*: The Directive states that the commencement of the application of the rules is set for 1 January 2023, with the exception of the UTPR, for which the application is deferred to 1 January 2024.

6.3 IMPLEMENTATION BY JERSEY[174]

982. Jersey is contemplating the implications of Pillar Two and is of the view to either implement the GloBE Rules with a 15% domestic minimum tax sitting alongside the existing corporate tax framework or, since GloBE is not a minimum standard but a

174. Refer 'OECD Pillars 1 & 2: Tax Policy Reflections, April 2022, Government of Jersey' https://www.gov.je/SiteCollectionDocuments/Tax%20and%20your%20money/R%20OECD%20Pillars%201%20and%202%20tax%20policy%20reflections.pdf accessed on 21 May 2022.

common approach, it is, therefore, not mandatory for Jersey to implement it. Accordingly, Jersey is considering three options:

- Policy Option 1: No implementation of GloBE.
- Policy Option 2: Implementation of GloBE, either IIR only, or with both IIR and UTPR.
- Policy Option 3: Introduction of a domestic minimum tax in addition to GloBE.

6.4 IMPLEMENTATION BY NEW ZEALAND[175]

983. The Inland Revenue of New Zealand has released a document that provides the basis for consultation on whether New Zealand should adopt GloBE tax rules and how it should implement those rules if it does decide to adopt them, along with an interesting statement that the Government has not decided whether to adopt either Pillar One or Pillar Two and has not ruled out adopting a digital services tax. The document goes on to state that the rules are the main component of Pillar Two of the G20/OECD Two-Pillar Solution to reform the international income tax framework in response to the challenges posed by the increasing globalisation and digitalisation of the economy. Details and concomitant discussions on GloBE Rules stated in the document are *inter alia* described below:

(a) *Purpose of the rules*: GloBE rules ensure that in-scope MNEs pay at least a 15% tax on their income in each country where that income is reported for financial reporting purposes. The rules operate not by way of a multilateral instrument but by incorporation by countries in their domestic law. They are intended to apply to every in-scope MNE in the world, no matter where it has its headquarters, operations or sales. The design of the rules means this intention can be achieved even if many or most countries do not adopt the rules. But the design does require implementation by a critical mass of countries.
(b) *Focus of the rules is on taxation of more mobile forms of income*: An important aspect of the rules is that they only apply to income in excess of the substance-based income exclusion ('excess income'). The exclusion is calculated under a formula which gives a percentage return on the value of tangible assets and payroll expense in the country. The exclusion is intended to focus the rules on the taxation of more mobile forms of income, such as interest or the return to intellectual property.
(c) *Consequences of not adopting the GloBE Rules*: The only impact for New Zealand from not adopting GloBE Rules is that it forgoes the possibility of receiving any revenue from them. Non-adoption will not increase the competitiveness or reduce the compliance costs of New Zealand-headquartered groups. Nor will it make New Zealand a more attractive destination for foreign MNE investment.

175. Refer 'OECD Pillar Two: GloBE rules for New Zealand' https://taxpolicy.ird.govt.nz/en/publications/2022/2022-ip-oecd-pillar-two accessed on 15 May 2022.

(d) *Benefits of GloBE Rules*: The Inland Revenue envisages the following benefits from GloBE Rules:
- The rules will provide a significant benefit to New Zealand even if we do not adopt them. This is the benefit of reducing the incentive for MNEs to shift profits out of New Zealand. Currently, MNEs can save as much as 28 cents in the dollar by moving income out of New Zealand into a zero-tax country (imputation reduces the incentive for New Zealand groups to shift profits out of New Zealand but has no effect on foreign groups operating in New Zealand). The GloBE Rules should reduce this tax-saving to a maximum of 13 cents in the dollar and should thus reduce the incidence of such profit shifting. This is the main benefit of GloBE Rules for New Zealand.
- The GloBE rules will reduce (though they will still not eliminate) the tax advantages enjoyed by MNEs over purely domestic New Zealand businesses.
- Adoption of the rules will ensure New Zealand, rather than other countries, collects the revenue from any undertaxed CEs of New Zealand headquartered groups.
- It will also ensure that New Zealand is seen to be playing its part in the global minimum tax project, which New Zealand can expect to benefit from significantly.
- The effect of the GloBE Rules in reducing profit shifting is clearly in New Zealand's interests, and this suggests that if New Zealand's participation is of any significance, it should do its part to support adoption of the rules by enacting them itself.

(e) *GloBE Rules apply on jurisdiction-by-jurisdiction basis:* A key aspect of the GloBE Rules is that they apply on a jurisdiction-by-jurisdiction basis. Tax paid in a country where the rate is above 15% cannot be used to credit the liability for a country where the rate is below 15%. Allocating profits appropriately between jurisdictions is consequently integral to the GloBE Rules. As with the rules allocating income between jurisdictions, the Model Rules contain similar rules allocating certain covered taxes. These generally seek to assign the tax to the jurisdiction to which the income is allocated so that all of the taxes paid on this income are taken into account.

(f) *IIR:* This rule imposes a top-up tax on the top company in an MNE (or in some cases lower-tier holding companies) so that at least 15% tax is paid on the company's share of the excess income of its directly and indirectly owned subsidiaries and branches in each country where that income is reported. The IIR is similar to a CFC rule in that it imposes tax on a company in relation to the profits of its foreign subsidiaries (and branches), though there are also important differences. The IIR works on a 'top-down' basis, by imposing top-up tax on a parent entity in an MNE. The top-up tax will usually be imposed on the MNE's UPE, if that parent is resident in a jurisdiction that has a qualified IIR. There are also ordering rules that may apply if it does not, or if the group's low-taxed entities are more than 20% owned by minority investors outside the group. Countries that wish to adopt Pillar Two are supposed to bring this rule into effect in 2023.

(g) *An UTPR*: This rule is designed as a back-up to the IIR, intended to apply to the low-tax excess income of an MNE group member in a country when that income is not subject to an IIR (because no direct or indirect group company shareholder of that group member is subject to an IIR with respect to the income). Like the IIR, this rule would impose sufficient additional tax on the group to increase the tax rate on that income to 15%, but the tax would be imposed on all group members resident in countries with a UTPR, in proportion to their substance in each country. This ensures that if a jurisdiction decides not to implement the GloBE rules, MNEs cannot avoid paying the minimum 15% tax simply by moving their headquarters to that jurisdiction. This rule is supposed to be effective in 2024 for countries that wish to adopt Pillar Two.

(h) *Mechanism for Top-up tax allocated to New Zealand under the UTPR to be brought to charge among multiple CEs:* The Model Rules do not prescribe how tax allocated to a jurisdiction by the UTPR should be brought to charge. This is left to individual jurisdictions. The outcome must be to produce an additional cash tax impost in that jurisdiction equal to the top-up tax allocated to it. The amount of this impost in a particular year is subject to the limit that it should not exceed the tax benefit of tax deductions otherwise available to constituent entities in that country in that year. While the top-up tax allocated to a jurisdiction will be charged to the MNE's CEs in that jurisdiction, an MNE may have multiple CEs, and countries are free to determine how that liability is allocated and charged between them. There are two different approaches to charging the top-up tax under the UTPR:

   (i) *Option 1: Denying a deduction*

      - The first approach, which is set out in the GloBE Rules, would be to deny an income tax deduction on otherwise deductible expenses of the MNE group. The top-up tax allocated to New Zealand would be converted to denied deductions by dividing the top-up tax allocated to New Zealand by the company tax rate. For example, a top-up tax liability of 1,000 would be converted into denial of a deduction for 3,571 (1000/28%) of otherwise deductible expenditure in the year the top-up tax relates to. This would cap the top-up tax based on the total deductions of the entity. If deductions in that year were less than 3,571, the shortfall would be carried forward and used to reduce deductions in the next year. As the top-up is allocated for the jurisdiction as a whole, there would need to be rules to specify how the MNE should apply the adjustment when there are multiple entities within New Zealand. This could be achieved by specifying that the deductions should be denied first in the CE in the group with the highest taxable income (ignoring any deduction denial) and then continue on to the CE with the next highest taxable income if that is still insufficient to collect the tax and so on, as explained in **Illustration** # 77:

Illustration of allocation of top-up tax under UTPR brought to charge among multiple CEs by denying a deduction

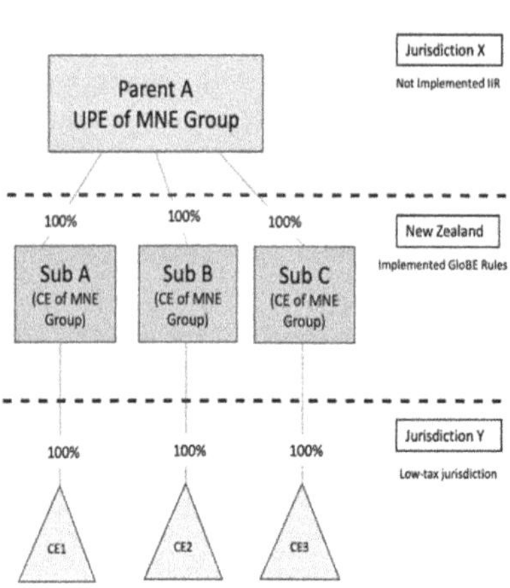

Assumptions Step 1

- An MNE has its UPE in a jurisdiction that does not have an IIR.
- For the purposes of this illustration, notwithstanding the application of IIR, assume Top-up tax of 100 has been allocated to New Zealand under the UTPR for the MNE's 2030 Fiscal Year.
- At a 28% company tax rate, the 100 of top-up tax converts to 357 of denied deductions (100 / 0.28).
- The MNE has 3 New Zealand subsidiaries. Before denying any deductions under the UTPR, the subs have the following gross income, deductions and taxable income:

Entity	Gross Income	Deductions	Taxable Income
Sub A	300	250	50
Sub B	140	100	40
Sub C	200	170	30

Step 2

Top-up tax under UTPR brought to charge among multiple CEs by denying a deduction

- If New Zealand chose to collect tax under the UTPR by denying deductions, first in the constituent entity with the highest taxable income (and so on),
  - Sub A would be denied deductions of 250,
  - Sub B would be denied deductions of 100, and
  - Sub C would be denied deductions of 7.

- There are a number of disadvantages to this approach in the New Zealand context:
  - Denying deductions to taxpayers would have flow-on effects on provisional tax liabilities of the company.
  - Denying a deduction will not result in an additional cash tax expense when the relevant New Zealand entity is in a loss position. While the additional cash tax expense may materialise at a future point if the entity becomes profitable, this may not occur for a long time. This is inconsistent with the OECD's intention that the UTPR should give rise to an additional cash tax expenses as early as possible.
  - Denying a deduction would result in a company paying more income tax, which would result in more credits to its imputation credit account. This seems particularly inappropriate in relation to tax imposed under the UTPR.
  - New Zealand allows a relatively long period for taxpayers to file tax returns compared to other jurisdictions. However, the filing dates for these income tax returns is still before the filing date for the GloBE information returns. This could result in a taxpayer having to limit deductions in an income tax return that is due for filing prior to the taxpayer calculating that denial of expenditure in their subsequent GloBE information return.

(ii) *Option 2: Separate tax liability*

- The second approach would be to treat the GloBE calculation and any resulting tax liability as a separate tax liability independent of income tax. This would apply to the UTPR as well as the IIR.

- The tax would be a joint and several liability of all New Zealand CEs.
- In relation to the UTPR, this charge would still be capped by reference to deductions in order to meet the 'equivalent adjustment' requirements in the Model Rules. But it will be capped by the total deductions claimed by all New Zealand CEs.
- This approach is seen as avoiding the disadvantages of using the income tax system to account for the UTPR as this will not impact provisional tax, and being a stand-alone tax will not have flow-on effects on other taxes. The UTPR's type of calculation and payment is better dealt with as a separate tax type.
- It will also eliminate some of the complexity of using the income tax system, such as having to identify entities with the most capacity to absorb any top-up and creating ordering rules where deductions are subject to some sort of limitation under other tax rules or where the group or a member of it has losses.

(i) *Interaction with imputation:* Generally, New Zealand income tax paid by a New Zealand company gives rise to an imputation credit, which can be passed on to the company's shareholders when the company pays a dividend (including a taxable bonus issue). This includes tax paid on income recognised under the CFC rules. However, the payment of foreign income tax does not give rise to imputation credits. Whether tax paid under the GloBE Rules should give rise to an imputation credit or not is discussed hereunder:
- *Purpose of imputation:* The broad purpose of the imputation credit regime is to ensure that income earned through a company is taxed at the shareholder's marginal rate. The exclusion of foreign income tax from the regime reflects a policy choice not to give shareholders in New Zealand companies a credit for foreign income tax paid, even though a foreign tax credit generally is available on income earned by the shareholders directly. This can be justified on the following basis:
  - The payment of foreign taxes does not benefit New Zealand, as those foreign taxes are not available for the Government to spend on services here. Accordingly, providing a deduction rather than a credit for foreign taxes maximises national welfare and encourages companies to pay taxes in New Zealand rather than offshore.
  - Foreign tax credits are also not available for New Zealand shareholders in foreign companies with respect to underlying foreign tax, that is, tax paid by the company.
  - When a foreign company earns income and pays tax in New Zealand, no foreign country gives a credit to the foreign company's shareholders for the New Zealand tax paid. There is an argument that a country should only give residents tax credits for another country's taxes if the other country reciprocates (though New Zealand gives a unilateral foreign tax credit on directly earned income).

- Tax imposed in New Zealand under the IIR is clearly New Zealand tax, which does benefit the New Zealand economy, and therefore presents a prima facie case for an imputation credit. However, there are a number of arguments against giving a credit, as discussed below:
  - First, the reason for the imposition of the IIR is that insufficient tax has been paid in a country outside New Zealand. The purpose of the GloBE rules is to correct that insufficiency. If the IIR gives rise to an imputation credit, this policy is significantly undermined. Although sufficient tax is paid at a corporate level, the entire top-up amount is available as a dollar-for-dollar tax reduction to the shareholder. This means the imposition of the IIR would be unwound on distribution.
  - Second, Pillar Two tax is conceptually different from the imposition of tax under the CFC regime. CFC regime in New Zealand generally only taxes mobile, passive income, which could as easily have been derived in New Zealand as overseas. So, the kind of income on which CFC tax is imposed does not have a sufficiently strong connection with the foreign country where it prima facie is taxable to justify exempting it from New Zealand tax. Since the income is treated effectively as income directly earned by the New Zealand shareholder, it is logical to provide an imputation credit in that case. The same analysis does not apply to IIR tax. Consistent with this line of reasoning, the GloBE Rules are explicit that if the payment of tax under New Zealand's IIR gives rise to an imputation credit, it will not be a Qualified IIR. This means that other countries' UTPRs would still apply to New Zealand headquartered MNEs (in addition to IIR). This is an unacceptable result, meaning New Zealand are effectively required by the Model Rules not to allow an imputation credit.
  - Third, allowing an imputation credit for tax paid under the UTPR seems particularly anomalous. Tax paid under the UTPR will often be paid by an MNE member other than the shareholder of the low-tax member. So, there will be no cash earnings included in the paying company's assets (either directly owned or through participation in lower-tier companies) corresponding to the tax paid.

(j) *Domestic minimum tax*: The GloBE rules contemplate that a jurisdiction may introduce a DMT, which would use the same tax base as the GloBE rules but take priority over them. For New Zealand, this tax would be closely based on the GloBE rules but would apply to undertaxed profits in New Zealand. It would mean that New Zealand would collect all of the top-up tax on such profits, rather than sharing it with other countries with Pillar Two rules. So, there would be no additional tax cost for MNEs subject to the tax, just a change in what country they pay the tax to.

A DMT could be imposed solely on New Zealand headquartered in-scope MNEs. For these MNEs, top-up tax on undertaxed New Zealand profits would ordinarily be collected under the UTPR. The UTPR allocation mechanism (based on tangible assets and the number of employees in each UTPR country) means that in many cases, much of this tax would be allocated to New Zealand, but this would depend on the level of overseas assets and employees. A DMT would avoid them having to pay any part of the Pillar Two tax on undertaxed New Zealand income in other countries under the UTPR. This would benefit New Zealand by allowing it to retain all of the tax that our MNEs would otherwise need to pay offshore under the UTPR.

A DMT could be expanded to apply also to foreign headquartered in-scope MNEs operating in New Zealand. In this case it would allow New Zealand to collect a tax equivalent to the Pillar Two tax on any low-tax New Zealand income that would otherwise arise under either another country's IIR (in most cases) or other countries' UTPRs.

6.5 IMPLEMENTATION BY SINGAPORE

984. Singapore's budget for 2022, presented on 18 February 2022,[176] is contemplating the Minimum ETR regime, with comments as below:

- Singapore is exploring a 'top-up tax' called a minimum ETR regime due to Pillar Two of BEPS 2.0.
- The minimum ETR regime would top-up an MNE group's ETR in Singapore to 15% and would apply to MNE groups in Singapore with annual revenues of at least EUR 750 million in CFS of the UPE.

985. In order to elaborate, the Budget 2022 Speech[177] has *inter alia* stated in regard to the Pillar Two Proposal as below:

- While BEPS 2.0 may have reduced the scope for tax competition, it has not reduced global competition for investments. In fact, competition is likely to intensify as governments worldwide seek to restore and rebuild their economies after the effects of the pandemic. So, there may be less tax competition, but there will be other forms of competition. We will have to take this into consideration and ensure that Singapore remains one of the best places in the world for business.
- Pillar Two introduces, among other things, a global minimum ETR of 15% for MNE groups with annual global revenues of EUR 750 million or more under its GloBE Model Rules. What this means is that if such an MNE were to have an

176. Refer 'KPMG's Singapore: Tax measures in budget 2022' https://home.kpmg/us/en/home/insights/2022/02/tnf-singapore-tax-measures-in-budget-2022.html accessed on 16 May 2022.
177. Refer 'Singapore Budget 2022 Speech' https://www.mof.gov.sg/docs/librariesprovider3/budget2022/download/pdf/fy2022_budget_statement.pdf accessed on 16 May 2022.

ETR of less than 15% in Singapore at the group level, other jurisdictions, such as its home jurisdiction, can collect the difference up to 15%.

- Singapore will adjust its tax system in response to Pillar Two GloBE Rules. Singapore is exploring a top-up tax called the Minimum Effective Tax Rate, or 'METR'. The METR will top up the MNE group's Effective Tax Rate in Singapore to 15%. IRAS will study this further and consult the industry on the design of METR.

6.6 IMPLEMENTATION BY SOUTH AFRICA[178]

986. South Africa intends to implement the Two-Pillar Solution. In this regard, in the Budget Review 2022 dated 23 February 2022 by the National Treasury, Republic of South Africa, it has been *inter alia* stated as below:

> South Africa is a member of the Steering Group of the OECD/G20 IF tasked with finding consensus-based solutions to tax challenges associated with digitalisation of the economy. In October 2021, the IF agreed on a two-pillar solution, and will work on an implementation framework to take effect by 2023. South Africa will propose legislative amendments to implement these rules once the framework has been finalised and translated into a local context.

6.7 IMPLEMENTATION BY SWITZERLAND[179]

987. In the meanwhile, Switzerland is planning to ensure a minimum taxation in accordance with Pillar Two of the OECD/G20 project by introducing a 'supplementary tax', which, in the case of large corporate groups, will bridge the gap between a lower ETR and the 15% minimum tax rate.

6.8 IMPLEMENTATION BY THE UNITED ARAB EMIRATES

988. The United Arab Emirates (UAE), a member of the IF and a leading financial hub, has concurred with the Two-Pillar Solution and is among the first countries to come up with policy formulation in its domestic law in response to the proposals.

---

178. Refer 'Budget Review 2022, National Treasury, Republic of South Africa, 23 February 2022' http://www.treasury.gov.za/documents/national%20budget/2022/review/FullBR.pdf accessed on 16 May 2022.
179. Refer 'Swiss Federal Council opens a consultation regarding the implementation of the OECD/G20 Pillar 2 model rules to ensure a minimum taxation of multinationals' http://www.internationaltaxplaza.info/homepage/news-archive/news-archive-2022/473-news-archive-march-2022/6330-swiss-federal-council-opens-a-consultation-regarding-the-implementation-of-the-oecd-g20-pillar-2-model-rules-to-ensure-a-minimum-taxation-of-multinationals.html accessed on 16 May 2022.

6.8.1 Present Tax Structure in the UAE

989. As of now, i.e., prior to adoption of GloBE Rules, the tax structure in the UAE[180] is *inter alia* as below:

- In practice, oil companies and subsidiaries of foreign banks are the only entities subject to CIT in the UAE;
- Up to AED 1,000,000, tax rate is Nil, and upwards of AED 1,000,000, it ranges between 10-55% depending upon the taxable income;
- Net operating losses incurred by the taxpayer may be carried forward indefinitely to be set off against the income of future years, although Abu Dhabi restricts the carry-forward of loss relief to one year only and allows use of this carry-forward only once every five years;
- Several emirates in the UAE have free zones where businesses are offered incentives such as exemptions from income tax and customs duties, the possibility of 100% foreign ownership, streamlined administrative procedures, etc.;
- There are currently no transfer pricing rules in the UAE. However, the UAE in 2019 introduced the CbCR obligation.

6.8.2 Corporate Tax Regime Announced by the UAE in Response to Pillar Two

990. On 26 July 2021, the Ministry of Finance issued an official statement confirming the UAE's support of the global minimum ETR as proposed under 'Pillar Two' of the OECD BEPS project.[181] In an endeavour to enhance its position as a prominent hub for investment, business and in order to meet international standards for tax transparency and harmful tax practices, UAE has proposed a headline corporate tax rate of 9% for taxable income exceeding AED 375,000 effective for financial years starting on or after 1 June 2023. A nil CIT rate for taxable income up to AED 375,000 is expected to support small- and medium-sized businesses and start-ups.

991. The prominent provisions of these regulations, as mentioned in the FAQ[182] released by the UAE Ministry of Finance, are as below:

- UAE CIT will apply to all UAE businesses and commercial activities alike, except for the extraction of natural resources, which will remain subject to Emirate-level corporate taxation;

180. Refer 'IBFD' https://research.ibfd.org/#/doc?url=/linkresolver/static/gtha_ae_s_1.&refresh=1645539407371%23gtha_ae_s_1 accessed on 17 May 2022.
181. Refer 'Press Release: The Ministry of Finance announces the introduction of a Corporate Tax in the UAE' https://www.mof.gov.ae/en/media/materials/News/Pages/31012022.aspx accessed on 17 May 2022.
182. Refer 'FAQ released by the UAE Ministry of Finance' https://www.mof.gov.ae/en/resourcesAndBudget/Pages/faq.aspx accessed on 17 May 2022.

- Dividends and capital gains earned by a UAE business from its qualifying shareholdings will be exempt from UAE CIT;
- A different tax rate (yet to be announced) for large multinationals that has consolidated global revenues in excess of EUR 750 million shall apply that meets the specific criteria set with reference to Pillar Two;
- The investment in real estate by individuals in their personal capacity will not be subject to UAE CIT, provided the individual is not required to obtain a commercial license or permit to carry out such activity in the UAE. Similarly, individuals will not be subject to UAE CIT on dividends, capital gains and other income earned from owning shares or other securities in their personal capacity. Interest and other income earned by an individual from bank deposits or saving schemes will not be subject to UAE CIT;
- Foreign entities and individuals will be subject to UAE CIT only if they conduct a trade or business in the UAE in an ongoing or regular manner. UAE CIT will generally not be levied on a foreign investor's income from dividends, capital gains, interest, royalties and other investment returns;
- Free zone businesses will be subject to UAE CIT, but the UAE CIT regime will continue to honour the CIT incentives currently being offered to free zone businesses that comply with all regulatory requirements and that do not conduct business with mainland UAE;
- Banking operations will be subject to UAE CIT;
- The UAE CIT regime will allow a business to use losses incurred (as from the UAE CIT effective date) to offset taxable income in subsequent financial periods, provided certain conditions are met. Tax losses from one group company may be used to offset taxable income of another group company, provided certain conditions are met;
- A UAE group of companies can elect to form a tax group and be treated as a single taxable person, provided certain conditions are met. A UAE tax group will only be required to file a single tax return for the entire group;
- Foreign CIT paid on UAE taxable income will be allowed as a tax credit against the UAE CIT liability;
- UAE withholding tax will not be applicable on domestic and cross-border payments of any nature under the UAE CIT regime;
- UAE businesses will need to comply with transfer pricing rules and documentation requirements set with reference to the OECD Transfer Pricing Guidelines.

6.8.3 Advantages of Introducing the New Tax Rules

992. The UAE's new corporate tax has been received in a 'positive manner' by businesses, as the new levy is going to replace most of the fees companies presently have to pay.[183] These new rules are expected to *inter alia* provide certain additional benefits as mentioned below:

- enhance UAE's position as a prominent hub for investment and business;
- meet international standards for tax transparency and harmful tax practices;
- the STTR under Pillar Two allows countries to levy a 'top-up' tax on certain related party payments where the recipient company in its home jurisdiction is not subject to a tax rate of at least 9 % on those payments. With a statutory UAE CIT rate of 9 %, UAE businesses may not face a foreign top-up tax under the STTR;
- a nil CIT rate for taxable income up to AED 375,000 is expected to support small- and medium-sized businesses and start-ups.

6.8.4 Release of Public Consultation Document on UAE Corporate Tax[184]

993. Subsequently, a Public Consultation Document was released containing information on the proposed UAE Corporate Tax regime for the purposes of obtaining input from interested parties. In addition to the information on UAE CIT regime mentioned above, the document *inter alia* contains comprehensive details, briefly mentioned below, specifically in the context of Pillar Two Proposals:

- The UAE CIT regime will have transfer pricing rules to ensure that the price of a transaction is not influenced by the relationship between the parties involved. In order to achieve this outcome, the UAE will apply the internationally recognised ALP to transactions and arrangements between related parties and with connected persons.
- The introduction of a CIT regime in the UAE will provide a basis for the UAE to execute its support of the global minimum ETR as proposed under Pillar Two and, more broadly, its commitment to enhancing tax transparency and preventing harmful tax practices.
- The UAE is working with other members of the IF to implement the Pillar Two proposals. As the work is ongoing at the IF level, further announcements on how the Pillar Two rules will be embedded into the UAE CIT regime will be made in due course.

---

183. Refer 'No UAE income tax for now, minister says in the wake of corporate tax move' https://www.arabianbusiness.com/gcc/uae/no-uae-income-tax-for-now-minister accessed on 17 May 2022.
184. Refer 'Public Consultation Document – UAE Corporate Tax' https://www.mof.gov.ae/en/resourcesAndBudget/Documents/UAE_CT-Public_Consultation_Document_English.pdf accessed on 17 May 2022.

6.9 IMPLEMENTATION BY THE UNITED KINGDOM

994. *Background*: The HMRC, the tax authority of the UK government, released the consultation[185] paper on implementation of Pillar Two in January 2022. This consultation represents the next important step in the implementation of the OECD agreed Pillar Two framework within the UK. With the policy, design framework and detailed provisions of the Pillar Two rules already having been agreed upon at international level, this consultation has specifically sought input on the UK application of the Model Rules as well as on a series of wider implementation questions.

995. *IIR*: For the benefit of various stakeholders, the HMRC has outlined the operation of UK IIR on the lines stated below:

- The rule ordering in the Model Rules means that the UK's IIR would apply at different points in the group structure depending on the particular circumstances of the group.
- The IIR will only apply to MNEs whose consolidated annual revenues are greater than EUR 750 million.
- It will apply to all such MNEs which are headquartered in the UK, with the UK IIR applied to the UPE of the group.
- The UK IIR will also apply to UK intermediate parent entities of foreign headquartered groups where those entities are more than 20% owned by minority investors or are controlled by parent entities that are not located in a jurisdiction that has introduced Pillar Two.
- The UK IIR will impose a top-up tax on the parent entities based on their interests in overseas subsidiaries and branches which are located in jurisdictions in which the MNE has an overall ETR in the jurisdiction below 15%.

996. *Top-down approach*: The GloBE Rules include a priority order which establishes the order in which the IIR is applied when the LTCE is owned by more than one parent entity. This priority order is designed to prevent the over-taxation that would result if multiple countries simultaneously sought to charge the same top-up tax. The basic structure is to follow a top-down approach. This means the UPE jurisdiction will usually have the first priority in collecting the top-up tax. Consequently, other jurisdictions cannot generally apply their IIR to other parent entities in the group when the UPE is subject to a qualified IIR. The only exception to this is when minority shareholders hold at least 20% of a parent entity, lower down the group structure. If the UPE is not subject to a qualified IIR, an intermediate parent entity will be charged the IIR. For these purposes, intermediate parent entities are entities that are controlled by the UPE and have an ownership interest in the LTCE. Where there are multiple intermediate parents that have an interest in the LTCE, in that case, in line with the top-down approach, an Intermediate Parent will not be charged the IIR if it is controlled

185. Refer 'The HMRC's OECD Pillar 2 Consultation on implementation' https://assets.publishing.service.gov.uk/government/uploads/system/uploads/attachment_data/file/1045663/11Jan_2022_Pillar_2_Consultation_.pdf accessed on 15 May 2022.

by another Intermediate Parent which is subject to a qualified IIR. However, the IIR will not be switched off when the higher Intermediate Parent does not control the lower Intermediate Parent. In this circumstance, the lower Intermediate Parent will charge its IIR, and the higher Intermediate Parent will reduce its share of the top-up tax by the tax charged by the lower intermediate parent. This maximises the amount of top-up tax collected under the IIR, which in turn reduces the residual top-up which is collected through the UTPR.

997. *UTPR*: For the benefit of various stakeholders, the HMRC has outlined the operation of UK UTPR on the lines stated below:

- The UK UTPR would only apply to groups with revenue of more than EUR 750 million.
- It would be limited to the UK entities of groups which are headquartered outside the UK.
- It would only then apply in relation to the group's overseas profits when:
  - the MNE's UPE is not subject to an IIR,
  - there are low-taxed entities within a group for which a top-up tax is due, and
  - this top-up tax has not been fully collected or charged under the IIR in other jurisdictions.
- It could also apply to the extent there are low-taxed profits in the jurisdiction in which the foreign headquartered group is parented.
- UTPR allocates the top-up tax between jurisdictions in which the group has CEs based on where the group's tangible assets and employees are located instead of by ownership.
- The top-up tax payable in the UK would be calculated by multiplying the remaining top-up due for a low-tax jurisdiction by the ratio of the MNE's tangible assets and employees in the UK over the MNE's tangible assets and employees in other jurisdictions with a UTPR.
- The top-up tax will be given effect through a denial of deduction or an equivalent adjustment.
  - The first approach (denial of deduction), which is set out in the GloBE Rules, would be to deny a Corporation Tax deduction on payments made by CEs. The top-up would be converted into payments by dividing the top-up tax allocated to the UK by the UK statutory CIT rate. This would cap the charge to the lower of the top-up tax allocated to the UK and the amount of payments made by UK CEs. As the intention would be to bring the maximum top-up into charge, the government would not restrict the type of payment which could be subject to the adjustment. This means the denial could apply to any payment made from an entity, not just in respect of related party payments to the relevant low-taxed jurisdiction. Similarly, there does not need to be any link between the type of expense which is denied and the nature of the low-taxed income. As the top-up is allocated for the jurisdiction as a whole, there would need to be rules to specify how

the MNE should apply the adjustment when there are multiple CEs in the UK. The guiding principle here would be to ensure the maximum top-up tax is collected, which could be achieved by specifying that the deduction should be made first in the most profitable company in the group and then continue onto the next company if that is still insufficient to collect the full top-up and so on.

- The second approach (equivalent adjustment) would be to introduce a new charge on a UK CE based on the top-up allocated to the UK. This charge would be capped by reference to the payments made by CEs in the UK in order to meet the 'equivalent adjustment' requirements in the GloBE Rules.
- The second approach (equivalent adjustment) is simpler to operate and may avoid some of the challenges that could arise with integrating a denial of deduction approach with the existing Corporation Tax rules on account of the following uncertainties:
  - Identifying entities with the most profit capacity to absorb the top-up tax.
  - Creating ordering rules where there are different tax rates on certain types of income, deductions are already subject to some limitation under other tax rules or where the group has losses.

998. *No application of IIR to smaller UK-headquartered groups*: While the Model rules only apply to groups that meet the revenue threshold of EUR 750 million, the IF statement does permit jurisdictions to apply the IIR to smaller groups that are headquartered in their jurisdiction. In such cases, the UPE would be charged the top-up tax in relation to any foreign LTCE. However, these profits could not be subject to a UTPR or an IIR in another jurisdiction. The HMRC does not propose to apply the IIR to smaller UK-headquartered groups owing to certain factors mentioned below:

- First, smaller UK-headquartered groups are less likely to have substantial overseas operations and are therefore less likely to pose the risks that Pillar Two is designed to protect against.
- Second, it reflects that, as these groups would also not be subject to an IIR or UTPR in another jurisdiction, introducing the IIR to these groups could damage the UK's attractiveness as a parent location for limited gains.
- Third, it reflects that smaller groups could incur substantial compliance and administrative costs complying with the Globe rules. Smaller groups may be less able to absorb these costs. They will also not have developed systems for CbCR, which underpins several areas of the Globe rules (e.g., the calculation of the substance-based carve-out).

999. *GloBE income*: The calculation of a CE's GloBE income starts from its financial accounting income. The general rule is that this income should be calculated according to the accounting standard of its UPE and therefore reflect the entries which feed into (or are derived from) its CFS. The entity's financial accounting profit is then subject to certain adjustments that are needed to reconcile the most important differences between accounting and tax definitions of profit. These adjustments are intended to bring the Globe base (denominator in the ETR calculation) more into line with a measure of taxable profit so that the ETR provides a reasonable measure of the level of taxation in that jurisdiction.

1000. *Allocating income between jurisdictions:* The GloBE Rules are designed to ensure that MNEs pay a minimum ETR of 15 % on their profits in each jurisdiction. This means high-taxed profits in one jurisdiction cannot be used to offset low-taxed profits in another jurisdiction. Allocating profits appropriately between jurisdictions is consequently integral to the GloBE Rules, which is achieved through:

- Valuing cross-border intragroup transactions in accordance with the ALP, where this is different to the transfer price used for accounting.
- Requiring financial accounting profits to be allocated between a PE and its head office entity based on the attribution of income and expenses to the PE for tax purposes.
- Transferring the Globe losses of a PE that is taxed under the credit method in the jurisdiction of its head office to the head office CE.
- Allocating the income of a tax transparent CE to its owners to the extent that the owners also treat the entity as tax transparent (i.e., tax the income) or are not members of the MNE group.

1001. *Covered taxes*: Taxes are generally limited to taxes on income. Covered Taxes will include CITs like Corporation Tax. Withholding taxes and other taxes which are imposed in lieu of a CIT also qualify. However, taxes on payroll or sales will not be counted. The amount of covered taxes is equivalent to the current tax expense recorded in the financial statements, subject to certain adjustments, for example, to exclude any tax which is paid in respect of income that has been excluded from Globe income or to add any covered taxes that have been treated as an expense in the accounts. As with the rules allocating income, the OECD Model Rules contain rules to assign certain covered taxes between jurisdictions. These generally seek to assign the tax to the jurisdiction where the income is recognised so that all of the taxes paid on this income are taken into account. Withholding taxes are generally assigned to the CEs who recognise the corresponding income in their financial accounts (i.e., the entity that suffers the burden of the tax) rather than the entity that deducts the tax on payment. There is an exception to this for withholding taxes on dividends, which also applies to net basis taxes on dividend income, which are assigned to the entity that paid the distribution. The logic behind this is that these taxes can be seen as an additional tax on the profit of the distributing entity. The timing differences[186] arising when profits are taxed in a

186. These differences typically arise from differences in when income and expenses are recognised for accounting and tax purposes.

different period to when they are recognised in GloBE income are addressed using an approach based on deferred tax accounting.[187]

1002. *ETR and top-up tax*: The ETR is calculated by dividing the aggregate tax by the aggregate profit in the jurisdiction. The GloBE Rules calculate the average ETR for the whole of a jurisdiction. This ensures that an MNE with a high ETR in a jurisdiction does not suffer a top-up tax because of isolated low-tax entities whose low level of taxation could be a function of their relationship with other jurisdictional entities. Pillar Two works by charging a top-up tax where an MNE has profits in a jurisdiction which are taxed below the minimum rate. To do this, Pillar Two needs to measure the level of taxation in each jurisdiction. This is achieved by calculating the MNE's average ETR in a jurisdiction. Where the ETR is below the minimum rate, an MNE will be charged a top-up based on the difference between this ETR and the minimum rate. The steps involved in the top-up tax calculation in the GloBE Rules are as below:

- Identify whether there is net GloBE income in the jurisdiction.
- Calculate the ETR in jurisdictions with net GloBE income to identify low-tax jurisdictions.
- Compute the top-up tax percentage.
- Calculate the substance-based carve-out.
- Deduct the substance-based carve-out from the Net Globe Income in the jurisdiction to find the Excess Profit.
- Calculate the top-up tax in the jurisdiction by multiplying the Excess Profit by the top-up tax percentage and then:
  - Adding any additional top-up tax calculated in respect of earlier years.
  - Subtracting any taxes charged under a Qualified Domestic Minimum Tax in that jurisdiction.
- Allocate the top-up tax for the jurisdiction among its CEs.

1003. *Domestic minimum tax*: The UK is exploring the idea of introducing a DMT so that, instead of allowing a foreign jurisdiction to charge top-up taxes in relation to any low-taxed profits of a group's entities in the UK, the UK would instead impose that top-up tax. The UK government visualises a couple of benefits of introducing the DMT:

- A DMT would only ensure that any additional tax on UK economic activities and profits that results from the Pillar Two minimum tax framework is to the benefit of the UK Exchequer. In other words, businesses would, in most cases, pay the same level of tax on their UK profits whether there was a DMT or not, but rather than allow another country to collect that tax, a DMT would ensure the tax is paid to the UK government.

187. Deferred tax accounting is an accounting concept which seeks to match taxes to the period when the income or expenses are recognised for accounting purposes. It does this by shifting the tax expense from the year the tax is paid (or tax deduction received) to the years in which the income or expenditure is recognised in the financial statements.

- A DMT could significantly reduce compliance burdens on UK-headquartered groups by preventing them from being subject to the UTPR in multiple countries in respect of their UK domestic operations.

The GloBE Rules reduce the amount of top-up tax that is due to be collected under the IIR or UTPR by the amount of tax charged under a Qualified Domestic Top-up Tax. This means the tax under the UK DMT would reduce any top-up taxes charged by another country under either the IIR or the UTPR. This treatment only applies to domestic minimum taxes which are qualified,[188] as these are top-up taxes which are based on the GloBE Rules and which are designed to collect the same top-up that would otherwise be collected under Pillar Two. The HMRC intends that the UK DMT is designed to closely follow the Globe Rules to ensure it is qualified.

1004. *Views solicited on consultation released by the HMRC*: The government anticipates that the parts of legislation relating to the IIR would be included in Finance Bill 2022-23 and would have effect from 1 April 2023, whereas both the UTPR and the domestic minimum tax would be introduced from 1 April 2024 at the earliest. The consultation released by the HMRC seeks views on the implementation and administration of the Pillar Two Model Rules within the UK on the lines stated below:

- Mechanism to translate Pillar Two Model Rules into UK domestic legislation;
- Administration of the Globe Rules;
- Implementation of the UTPR and introduction of a domestic minimum tax in the UK to complement Pillar Two;
- Wider reforms to existing UK BEPS measures.

6.10 IMPLEMENTATION BY THE UNITED STATES OF AMERICA[189]

1005. The revenue proposals released by the Department of the Treasury in March 2022 contain measures in response to the Pillar Two Proposals, as summarised below:

- The tax rate for corporations is proposed to be increased from 21% to 28%. The 28% CIT rate will consequently increase the GILTI rate in tandem, and the new GILTI effective rate would be 20% (as against the current rate of 10.5-13.125%), applied on a jurisdiction-by-jurisdiction basis (rather than the current practice of application on a global basis).[190]

---

188. Where a domestic minimum tax is not qualified because it is not closely based on the GloBE Rules, it would be treated as a covered tax instead and would be included in the ETR calculation for the jurisdiction. This would mean the tax on the income which is excluded from the GloBE base through the substance carve-out would be disregarded, meaning the tax rate would have to be higher to fully cover the top-up tax which would be charged under the IIR or UTPR.
189. Refer 'General Explanations of the Administration's Fiscal Year 2023 Revenue Proposals, Department of the Treasury, March 2022' https://home.treasury.gov/system/files/131/General-Explanations-FY2023.pdf accessed on 17 May 2022.
190. Since, the GILTI rules are similar in their intent to the IIR rule, the US is expected to continue to apply them rather than adopting an IIR.

- The proposal would repeal the BEAT and replace it with a UTPR that is consistent with the UTPR described in the Pillar Two Model Rules.
- When another jurisdiction adopts a UTPR, the proposal also includes a DMT that would protect US revenues from the imposition of UTPR by other countries. This top-up tax equals the excess of (a) 15% of the financial reporting group's US profit determined using the same rules as under the UTPR to determine the group's profit for a jurisdiction, over (b) all the group's income tax paid or accrued with respect to US profits (including federal and state incomes taxes, corporate alternative minimum tax, and creditable foreign income taxes incurred with respect to US profits). When another jurisdiction adopts the UTPR, the proposal would also ensure that taxpayers continue to benefit from tax credits and other tax incentives that promote US jobs and investment.
- The UTPR would primarily apply to foreign-parented multinationals operating in low-tax jurisdictions. In addition, UTPR would apply only to financial reporting groups that have global annual revenue of USD 850 million or more in at least two of the prior four years.
- The UTPR ensures that a minimum per-jurisdiction rate of tax is paid on income earned in each jurisdiction in which foreign-based multinationals operate. This ensures that companies cannot avoid a minimum rate of taxation by, for example, relocating their headquarters to a foreign jurisdiction that has not implemented an IIR. The UTPR is designed to encourage countries to adopt the global minimum tax agreed to as part of the international negotiations by ensuring that profits in low-tax jurisdictions are taxed at the same minimum rate.
- Under the UTPR, both domestic corporations that are part of a foreign-parented multinational group and domestic branches of foreign corporations would be disallowed US tax deductions in an amount determined by reference to low-taxed income of foreign entities and foreign branches that are members of the same financial reporting group. Specifically, domestic group members would be disallowed US tax deductions to the extent necessary to collect the hypothetical amount of top-up tax required for the financial reporting group to pay an Effective Tax Rate of at least 15% in each foreign jurisdiction in which the group has profits, as explained in **Illustration # 78**:

Illustration of allocation of top-up tax under UTPR in the U.S.

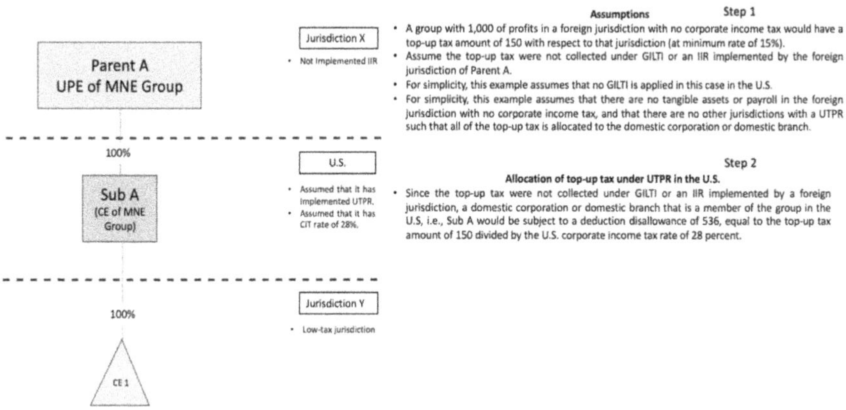

- The UTPR would not apply with respect to income subject to an IIR that is consistent with the Pillar Two Model Rules, including income that is subject to GILTI. Thus, the UTPR would generally not apply to US-parented multinationals.
- The proposal to repeal the BEAT and replace it with the UTPR would be effective for taxable years beginning after 31 December 2023.

CHAPTER 7

Conclusion

A comprehensive FAQ-cum-quick summary of the salient issues of all articles contained in Chapters 1 to 9 of GloBE Rules as a ready reckoner titled 'GloBE Rules at a Glance' has been devised, encapsulating the features, application and nuances of GloBE Rules.

1006. *Objectives of Pillar Two*: The objectives[191] of Pillar Two are being achieved through a framework of rules that require MNEs to pay a minimum of 15% of CIT on profit in each jurisdiction in which they operate. Under these rules, an adjusted accounting measure of profit will need to be calculated for a group's total operations in each jurisdiction. Where the tax paid by the group on profit in a jurisdiction (ETR) falls below the minimum tax level of 15%, the rules will then require countries to impose top-up taxes on certain entities within the group in order to bring the overall taxation of jurisdictional profit up to the minimum level of 15%. The rules include a detailed framework for determining where any required top-up tax should be imposed within the group to ensure appropriate coordination between different jurisdictions and to prevent MNEs from restructuring outside of the rules. Pillar Two also includes a treaty-based rule, the STTR, which is designed to allow jurisdictions to impose a top-up withholding tax on certain types of outbound payments that are made between related parties and are taxed at a nominal rate of less than 9%. Countries will only be required to introduce this rule in their treaties with developing IF members when requested to do so and only if they apply nominal tax rates below 9% to covered payments. This rule requires the development of a model treaty provision that is under discussion in the IF and is, therefore, outside of the scope of GloBE Rules.

1007. *Basic steps involved in calculating the ETR and top-up tax*: Under the Pillar Two framework, the basic steps involved in calculating the ETR and top-up tax payable for

191. Refer 'The HMRC's OECD Pillar 2 Consultation on implementation' https://assets.publishing.service.gov.uk/government/uploads/system/uploads/attachment_data/file/1045663/11Jan_2022_Pillar_2_Consultation_.pdf accessed on 12 April 2022.

an in-scope multinational group and then determining how that top-up will be charged are summarised[192] as under:

- Step 1: Determine the entities that a group has in a particular jurisdiction.
- Step 2: Determine the profits of those entities.
- Step 3: Determine the taxes that relate to those profits (including those which relate to timing differences).
- Step 4: Aggregate the profits and taxes found in Steps 2 and 3.
- Step 5: Calculate the group's ETR in that jurisdiction by dividing the aggregate taxes by the aggregate profits.
- Step 6: If the ETR in Step 5 is less than 15%, calculate the group's 'top-up percentage' for the jurisdiction, which is 15% less the jurisdictional ETR.
- Step 7: Calculate the jurisdictional top-up tax by taking the profit calculated in Step 2, deducting a 5% return on the tangible assets and payroll expenses in that jurisdiction, and then multiplying that amount by the 'top-up percentage' in Step 6.
- Step 8: Attribute that jurisdictional top-up tax to the group's individual entities in that jurisdiction based on their relative contribution to total profit.
- Step 9: The top-up tax attributed to an entity is first charged under the IIR, which charges this tax on the entity's parent entity.
  - The IIR is charged on a top-down basis which means the UPE will generally be charged the top-up when it is located in a jurisdiction that has introduced Pillar Two.
  - This means the IIR will only be charged at an intermediate parent level if the UPE is not subject to Pillar Two (or if the low-taxed entity is more than 20% owned by minority investors). These parents will be charged a top-up based on their ownership share in the low-taxed entity.
- Step 10: Any remaining top-up not collected under the IIR will be charged upon other group entities under the UTPR. The total amount to be collected from group entities in a jurisdiction under the UTPR will be based on the tangible assets and employees of those entities as a proportion of tangible assets and employees in all jurisdictions that have implemented the UTPR.

7.1 GLOBE RULES AT A GLANCE

1008. In line with the title of the book, for the benefit of readers, it is expedient to further summarise the salient issues of GloBE Rules as a ready reckoner for quick reference and understanding. Accordingly, a checklist titled 'GloBE Rules at a Glance' has been devised *inter alia* encapsulating the features, application and nuances of GloBE Rules in Table 7.1.

192. *Id.*

Table 7.1 GloBE Rules at a Glance

S. No.	*Query*	*Suggestive Reply*	*Basis of Reply*
Overview			
1	What is the primary purpose of the OECD/G20 project on digitalisation?	Addresses how taxing rights on income generated from cross-border activities in the digital age should be allocated among countries.	Refer BEPS Project, Public Consultation Document on 'Addressing the Tax Challenges of the Digitalisation of the Economy' https://www.oecd.org/tax/beps/public-consultation-document-addressing-the-tax-challenges-of-the-digitalisation-of-the-economy.pdf
2	What is the objective of Pillar One?	Reallocate some taxing rights over MNEs from their home countries to the markets where they have business activities and earn profits, regardless of whether firms have a physical presence there.	Refer OECD's Press Release dated 8 October 2021 titled 'International community strikes a ground-breaking tax deal for the digital age'

S. No.	*Query*	*Suggestive Reply*	*Basis of Reply*
			https://www.oecd.org/tax/international-community-strikes-a-ground-breaking-tax-deal-for-the-digital-age.htm
3	What is the objective of Pillar Two?	Introduces a global minimum corporate tax rate set at 15% and addresses remaining BEPS issues related to low-tax jurisdictions.	-do-
4	As of now, which are the IF member countries that have not agreed to the Two-Pillar Solution?	Kenya, Nigeria, Pakistan and Sri Lanka.	-do-
5	What are the components of Pillar Two Proposals?	GloBE Rules, SOR and STTR.	Refer Report on Pillar Two Blueprint.
6	What are the components of GloBE?	IIR with UTPR acting as the backdrop.	-do-
7	What is the function of IIR?	The operation of IIR is, in some respects, based on traditional CFC rule principles and triggers an inclusion at the level of the shareholder where the income of a controlled foreign entity is taxed below the effective minimum tax rate.	-do-
8	What is the function of UTPR?	It is a secondary rule and only applies where a CE is not already subject to an IIR. The UTPR is nevertheless a key part of the rule set as it serves as backstop to the IIR, ensures a level playing field and addresses inversion risks that might otherwise arise.	-do-

S. No.	*Query*	*Suggestive Reply*	*Basis of Reply*
9	What is the function of SOR?	IIR is complemented by a SOR that removes treaty obstacles from its application to certain branch structures and applies where an income tax treaty otherwise obligates a contracting state to use the exemption method.	-do-
10	What is the function of STTR?	STTR allows the source jurisdiction to impose additional taxation on certain covered payments up to the agreed minimum rate.	-do-
11	Though STTR is not part of the GloBE, despite this, how do the two interact?	Any top-up tax imposed under the STTR will be taken into account in determining the ETR for purposes of the IIR and the UTPR.	-do-
12	What is the trigger for invoking the GloBE Rules?	When an MNE's jurisdictional ETR is below the agreed minimum rate of 15%, GloBE Rules come into operation.	-do-
13	How will the GloBE Rules be implemented?	IIR and UTPR can be implemented by way of changes to domestic law of jurisdictions that implement the GloBE Rules.	-do-
14	How will the STTR and the SOR be implemented?	STTR and the SOR can only be implemented through changes to existing bilateral tax treaties, either through bilateral negotiations and amendments to individual treaties or as part of a multilateral convention.	-do-
15	What is meant by 'GloBE Rules will have the status of a common approach'?	Status of a common approach means that IF members: – are not required to adopt the GloBE rules, but if they choose to do so, they will implement and administer the rules in a way that is consistent with the outcomes provided for under Pillar Two, including in light of model rules and guidance agreed to by the IF; – accept the application of the GloBE rules applied by other IF members, including agreement as to rule order and the application of any agreed safe harbours.	Refer OECD's statement dated 1 July 2021.

S. No.	*Query*	*Suggestive Reply*	*Basis of Reply*
16	What is the Scope of GloBE Rules?	GloBE Rules apply when the consolidated revenue of the MNE Group, having foreign presence, is EUR 750 million or more. Countries are free to apply the GloBE Rules to MNEs headquartered in their country even if they do not meet the threshold of EUR 750 million.	-do-
17	What is the minimum rate for IIR and UTPR?	The minimum tax rate used for purposes of IIR and UTPR will be 15%.	Refer OECD's statement dated 8 October 2021.
18	What is the minimum rate for the STTR?	The minimum rate for the STTR will be 9%.	-do-
19	Does the system of top-up taxes, i.e., IIR and UTPR operate as a typical direct tax on income of an entity?	No, the system of top-up taxes, i.e., IIR and UTPR, applies: – to the excess profits calculated on a jurisdictional basis; – only applies to the extent those profits are subject to tax in a given year below the minimum rate of 15%; – closer in design to an international alternative minimum tax that uses standardised base and tax calculation mechanics to identify pools of low-taxed income within an MNE Group and imposes a coordinated tax charge that brings the Group's ETR on that income in each jurisdiction up to the minimum rate of 15%; – as a coordinated application of the GloBE Rules by ensuring that the aggregate amount of incremental tax payable under the rules in each jurisdiction does not cause the ETR to exceed the minimum rate.	Refer paragraph 2 of Introduction to the Commentary to GloBE Rules.
Chapter 1 of GloBE Rules			
20	What is the scope of GloBE Rules?	GloBE Rules apply to MNE Groups having foreign presence, whose annual consolidated revenues in at least two of the four preceding Fiscal Years equal or exceed EUR 750 million.	Refer paragraph 3 of Commentary on Chapter 1.

S. No.	*Query*	*Suggestive Reply*	*Basis of Reply*
21	Is consolidated revenue for the current year (i.e., the tested Fiscal Year) factored into the four-year calculation?	No, excluding the current year's results from the revenue threshold test ensures that an MNE Group knows, at the beginning of the tested Fiscal Year, whether it will be subject to the GloBE Rules in that year.	Refer paragraph 6 of Commentary on Chapter 1.
22	Are Excluded Entities subject to GloBE Rules?	No, except for purposes of calculating the revenue threshold.	Refer paragraph 16 of Commentary on Chapter 1.
23	What does 'threshold applies based on the consolidated revenue of the MNE Group' mean?	The threshold applies based on the consolidated revenue of the MNE Group, not the aggregate of the revenues of each Group Entity, i.e., revenues from transactions with other Group Entities that are eliminated in the consolidation process are excluded from the revenue threshold test.	Refer paragraph 11 of Commentary on Chapter 1.
24	What is an MNE Group?	An MNE Group means any Group that includes at least one entity or PE that is not located in the jurisdiction of the UPE. A single subsidiary or PE (even one that does not earn income) located in a jurisdiction other than the one where the UPE is located is sufficient to bring a Group within the definition of an MNE Group.	Refer Article 1.2.1 and paragraph 20 of Commentary on Chapter 1.
25	Does an entity and its foreign PE meet the definition of Group and MNE Group?	Yes.	Refer Article 1.2.1 read with Article 1.2.3.
26	Is Stateless PE excluded in determination of a Group?	Yes.	Refer paragraph 26 of Commentary on Chapter 1.
27	What is a CE?	A CE is any entity that is included in a Group and any PE of a Main Entity that is within that Group.	Refer Article 1.3.1.
28	Is a PE treated as separate from the Main Entity for the purposes of GloBE Rules?	Yes, a PE that is a CE shall be treated as separate from the Main Entity and any other PE of that Main Entity.	Refer Article 1.3.2.

S. No.	*Query*	*Suggestive Reply*	*Basis of Reply*
29	Does a CE include an entity that is an Excluded Entity?	No	Refer Article 1.3.3.
30	What are the two requirements an entity must comply with to be a UPE of the Group defined by Article 1.2.2?	The UPE is an entity that directly or indirectly owns a Controlling Interest in another entity and disqualifies an entity from being the UPE of a Group if the Controlling Interests in that entity are held by another entity.	Refer Article 1.4.1(a) and paragraphs 34, 35 of Commentary on Chapter 1.
31	Which entity is a UPE of the Group defined by Article 1.2.3?	In cases where the Group is a single entity with one or more foreign PEs, then the Main Entity is the UPE. This extended definition of UPE is necessary to ensure that a domestic entity that engages in cross-border operations through PEs is subject to the GloBE Rules.	Refer paragraph 36 of Commentary on Chapter 1.
32	What are the consequences (practical effects) for an Excluded Entity under the GloBE Rules?	– IIR and UTPR do not apply to Excluded Entities. – GloBE attributes of Excluded Entities are removed from the various computations under the GloBE Rules, except for the application of revenue threshold. – Excluded Entities do not have any administrative obligations under the GloBE Rules.	Refer paragraph 37 of Commentary on Chapter 1.
33	What is the reason for treating Investment Fund that is a UPE and Real Estate Investment Vehicle that is a UPE as Excluded Entities?	These entities are excluded from the GloBE Rules in order to protect their status as tax neutral investment vehicles. If an Investment Fund or Real Estate Investment Vehicle is not the UPE of the MNE Group, it can still be treated as a CE of the MNE Group, provided it otherwise meets the consolidation requirements of Article 1.2 and Article 1.3. However, such Investment Funds and Real Estate Investment Vehicles are considered Investment Entities and subject to special rules for calculation of ETR in Articles 7.4 through 7.6.	Refer paragraph 42 of Commentary on Chapter 1.

S. No.	*Query*	*Suggestive Reply*	*Basis of Reply*
34	What is the reason for Article 1.5.2 not to apply if the entity is held by Pension Service Entity?	Allowing a Pension Services Entity to establish a further separate controlled entity that qualified for Excluded Entity status would dilute the intended effect of the rules in Article 1.5.2, which are intended to be limited to those controlled entities that carry out functions for the Excluded Entity (such as the Governmental Entity, International or Non-profit Organisations or Pension Fund itself).	Refer paragraph 44 of Commentary on Chapter 1.
35	What is the reason for the 95% threshold in Article 1.5.2(a)?	The 95% threshold allows for situations in which there is a small minority interest holder, such as where a fund manager holds a small percentage of an Investment Fund or where domestic law requires at least two shareholders to incorporate a corporation or where an Excluded Entity invests through a partnership and is required to have another entity acting as the general partner for domestic law purposes.	Refer paragraph 47 of Commentary on Chapter 1.
36	What is the reason for keeping a lower threshold of 85% in Article 1.5.2(b)?	The ownership percentage in paragraph (b) is lower than in paragraph (a) in order to provide greater flexibility, in particular, in the context of vehicles held by Investments Funds where third parties may hold a greater stake or where the interests in the holding vehicle are issued to management or other employees of the operating company.	Refer paragraph 55 of Commentary on Chapter 1.
37	What is the reason for providing an option to an MNE Group to not elect an entity as an Excluded Entity?	To allow that entity of the MNE Group to apply the IIR to its subsidiaries instead of subjecting all of its CEs to the UTPR.	Refer paragraph 57 of Commentary on Chapter 1.

S. No.	*Query*	*Suggestive Reply*	*Basis of Reply*
Chapter 2 of GloBE Rules			
38	When does IIR apply?	IIR applies when a CE, that is, the UPE of an MNE Group, located in a jurisdiction that has implemented IIR and that owns (directly or indirectly) an Ownership Interest in an LTCE at any time during the Fiscal Year shall pay tax of an amount equal to its Allocable Share of the top-up tax of that LTCE for the Fiscal Year.	Refer Article 2.1.1.
39	What is the relevance of holding period for the purposes of applying the IIR?	The IIR applies if the UPE holds Ownership Interests of the LTCE 'at any time during the Fiscal Year'. This means that the UPE is required to apply the IIR with respect to a CE that was disposed of or acquired during the Fiscal Year. The holding period of the interests during the Fiscal Year is already reflected in the computation of the top-up tax under Chapter 5. The calculation of the top-up tax takes into account the amount of income reported in the CFS, which takes into account the holding period in which the UPE owns an LTCE for the Fiscal Year.	Refer paragraph 13 of Commentary on Chapter 2.
40	What are the rules for application of the IIR by an Intermediate Parent Entity?	An Intermediate Parent Entity of an MNE Group located in a jurisdiction that has implemented IIR and that owns (directly or indirectly) an Ownership Interest in an LTCE at any time during a Fiscal Year shall pay tax of an amount equal to its Allocable Share of the top-up tax of that LTCE for the Fiscal Year.	Refer Article 2.1.2.
41	Can PEs be treated as Parent Entities under the GloBE Rules?	In order to avoid difficult factual determinations and disputes as to whether the Ownership Interests in LTCEs are held by the PE or the Main Entity, PEs are not treated as Parent Entities under the GloBE Rules. In this context, Ownership Interests in an LTCE that are held through a PE are treated instead as held by the Main Entity.	Refer paragraph 14 of Commentary on Chapter 2.

S. No.	*Query*	*Suggestive Reply*	*Basis of Reply*
42	What is the purpose of top-down approach?	Top-down approach gives priority to applying the IIR to the Parent Entities at the top of the ownership chain. The mechanics of this provision prevents instances of double taxation that would be caused by multiple Parent Entities applying the IIR with respect to the same Ownership Interest in the LTCE.	Refer paragraph 17 of Commentary on Chapter 2.
43	Despite top-down approach, can IIR be applied by more than one Intermediate Parent Entity in the same MNE Group?	Yes, if one Intermediate Parent Entity does not have a Controlling Interest in the other Intermediate Parent Entity.	Refer paragraph 20 of Commentary on Chapter 2.
44	Shall a POPE pay its Allocable Share of top-up tax regardless of whether the UPE or an Intermediate Parent Entity is also required to apply a Qualified IIR?	Yes.	Article 2.1.4.
45	Can IIR be applied domestically and by a Parent Entity to itself?	Yes. Under this approach, a Parent Entity located in a Low-tax Jurisdiction would apply an IIR to its allocable share of top-up tax of any domestic LTCEs and also apply the IIR in respect of any top-up tax that would otherwise be allocated to the Parent Entity under Article 5.2.4. The application of a domestic IIR in this situation should be distinguished from a DMT that could be applied to all the CEs located in the same jurisdiction and regardless of whether that CE was a Parent Entity required to apply an IIR.	Refer paragraphs 24, 25 of Commentary on Chapter 2.
46	What is the essence of Inclusion Ratio?	It is the ratio of the Parent Entity's share of an LTCE's GloBE Income to its total GloBE Income for the Fiscal Year. Where a subsidiary is wholly owned, the Inclusion Ratio will always be 1, and no additional computations are required.	Refer paragraph 29 of Commentary on Chapter 2.

S. No.	*Query*	*Suggestive Reply*	*Basis of Reply*
47	What is the objective of the IIR Offset Mechanism?	IIR Offset Mechanism is intended to coordinate the application of the IIR in certain tiered or split-ownership structures to ensure that any portion of the profits of the MNE Group is subject to the IIR in only one jurisdiction (and prevent double taxation).	Refer paragraph 3c of Commentary on Chapter 2.
48	How does UTPR operate?	UTPR operates through two forms: – Denial of a deduction; or – Equivalent adjustment. The UTPR does not prescribe the mechanism by which the adjustment must be made. This is a matter of domestic law implementation that is left to the UTPR jurisdictions.	Refer paragraphs 43, 46 of Commentary on Chapter 2.
49	Does UTPR operate before or after application of domestic law?	UTPR applies after any provisions of domestic law that affect the deductibility of expenses incurred by CEs.	Refer paragraph 48 of Commentary on Chapter 2.
50	Do GloBE Rules prescribe how the UTPR top-up tax amount is allocated among the CEs that are located in the UTPR Jurisdiction?	The allocation among the CEs within a UTPR Jurisdiction should be addressed under that UTPR Jurisdiction's domestic law, which would ensure that such allocation mechanism is best coordinated with other existing domestic tax rules. The UTPR Jurisdiction may provide in its domestic law that the UTPR adjustment is imposed on only one CE or several CEs that are located in the jurisdiction.	Refer paragraph 51 of Commentary on Chapter 2.

S. No.	*Query*	*Suggestive Reply*	*Basis of Reply*
51	When can UTPR top-up tax be allocated to a partially owned CE?	Allocating top-up tax to a partially owned CE would result in the minority interest holders of such CE bearing indirectly a portion of the tax cost incurred by the application of the UTPR. A UTPR Jurisdiction may therefore provide that the top-up tax is allocated first to those CEs that are wholly owned or almost wholly owned by the MNE Group in order to minimise the extent to which those minority interest holders share the burden of top-up tax allocated from LTCEs in which they do not have an economic interest.	Refer paragraph 52 of Commentary on Chapter 2.
52	Whether the UTPR top-up tax is to be always paid by that CE that was denied a deduction (or required to make an equivalent adjustment)?	It is not required that the additional cash tax expense is to be paid by the same CEs as those that were denied a deduction (or required to make an equivalent adjustment). For instance, the UTPR jurisdiction may deny a deduction to (or impose an equivalent adjustment) on a Tax Transparent Entity, the effect of which flows through to the owners. In this case, the additional cash tax expense collected by the UTPR Jurisdiction may be levied or borne by the owners of the Tax Transparent Entity itself. As such, this additional cash tax expense may be taken into account for the purposes of assessing whether the adjustment has resulted in an additional cash tax expense that is equal to the UTPR top-up tax amount.	Refer paragraph 53 of Commentary on Chapter 2.
53	When should the adjustment arising as a result of application of UTPR top-up tax apply?	The adjustment arising as a result of application of UTPR top-up tax shall apply to the extent possible with respect to the taxable year in which the Fiscal Year ends. If this adjustment is insufficient to produce an additional cash tax expense for this taxable year equal to the UTPR top-up tax amount allocated to	Refer paragraphs 57, 60 of Commentary on Chapter 2.

S. No.	*Query*	*Suggestive Reply*	*Basis of Reply*
		the GloBE Rules implementing jurisdiction for the Fiscal Year, the difference shall be carried forward to the extent necessary to the succeeding Fiscal Years and be subject to the adjustment mentioned in Article 2.4.1 to the extent possible for each taxable year.	
54	When will a taxpayer or tax administration become aware of UTPR top-up tax amount?	It may not be possible for a taxpayer or tax administration to know the UTPR top-up tax amount that has been allocated to a jurisdiction until the GloBE Information Return is actually filed.	Refer paragraph 56 of Commentary on Chapter 2.
55	Does the carry forward mechanism of UTPR top-up tax arising as a result of incomplete adjustment in a year operate indefinitely?	Yes.	Refer paragraph 63 of Commentary on Chapter 2.
56	Is there any exception to the indefinite carry forward mechanism of UTPR top-up tax?	While Article 2.4.2 provides for an indefinite carry-forward mechanism, domestic law in certain circumstances may limit the practical application of the carry-forward after a certain period of time. For example, a jurisdiction may have a domestic statute of limitation that prevents its tax administration from applying the carry-forward mechanism to its full extent. In such a situation, the Top-up Tax Amount that has not yet been collected is not allocated to another jurisdiction.	Refer paragraph 63 of Commentary on Chapter 2.
57	Does the Carry forward mechanism operate even if the MNE Group's revenue falls below the threshold of EUR 750 million or the CE that is allocated UTPR top-up tax amount under the UTPR is not part of the MNE Group in future years?	Yes, Article 2.4.2 is not limited to the Fiscal Years in which the MNE Group is within the scope of the GloBE Rules or the Fiscal Years when the CE that is allocated UTPR top-up tax amount under the UTPR is part of the MNE Group. If the MNE Group's revenues fall below the threshold of Article 1.1, the CEs that were allocated UTPR top-up tax amounts that did not give rise to an additional cash tax expense would still be liable for the UTPR top-up tax amounts they were allocated.	Refer paragraph 64 of Commentary on Chapter 2.

S. No.	*Query*	*Suggestive Reply*	*Basis of Reply*
58	Is reallocation of UTPR top-up tax amount among CEs possible?	A UTPR Jurisdiction may reallocate the UTPR top-up tax amount among the CEs located in that jurisdiction, in subsequent years, in order to ensure that the UTPR top-up tax amount is collected as soon as possible.	Refer paragraph 65 of Commentary on Chapter 2.
59	Is a controlled Investment Entity excluded from the application of the UTPR?	Yes. This exclusion is to avoid interfering with the intended tax neutrality of these entities with respect to owners that are not Group Entities. It may be noted that Investment Entities that are the UPE of the MNE Group are Excluded Entities and are, therefore, already outside the scope of the GloBE Rules.	Refer paragraph 66 of Commentary on Chapter 2.
60	What is the benefit of single computation of the top-up tax under the IIR and the UTPR?	Common and single computation of the top-up tax under the IIR and the UTPR improves coordination between GloBE Rules in each jurisdiction and reduces implementation and compliance costs while ensuring that the rules do not result in over-taxation or taxation in excess of economic profits. In addition, relying on the same top-up tax computation under both the IIR and the UTPR aligns the expected outcomes under both rules, which allows the UTPR to operate as a meaningful backstop to the IIR. Not having a single computation of the top-up tax under both the IIR and the UTPR would either lead to less effective or harsher outcomes under the UTPR than under the IIR.	Refer paragraph 69 of Commentary on Chapter 2.
61	Does IIR take priority over the UTPR?	Yes.	Refer Article 2.5.2 and paragraph 72 of Commentary on Chapter 2.

S. No.	*Query*	*Suggestive Reply*	*Basis of Reply*
62	How is the UTPR top-up tax determined as IIR takes priority over it?	In the situation where no IIR applies at the UPE level, a lower-level Parent Entity may be required to apply the IIR as provided under Article 2.1. If the UPE's Ownership Interest in an LTCE is held indirectly through a Parent Entity that is required to apply the IIR, then no top-up tax shall be allocated under the UTPR for such LTCE. Whether or not the amount of top-up tax may be reduced to zero in accordance with this rule is determined on an entity-by-entity basis. This means that the determination is made for each LTCE.	Refer paragraph 74 of Commentary on Chapter 2.
63	The fact that the UPE is required to apply a Qualified IIR, does it mean that there is no scope for the operation of the UTPR with respect to CEs located in the UPE Jurisdiction?	No, UTPR can still be applied. Where the UPE is required to apply a Qualified IIR for the Fiscal Year, it may only be required under the laws of the UPE Jurisdiction to apply the IIR in respect of PEs and subsidiaries located in other jurisdictions. In this case, no top-up tax will be allocated under the UTPR in respect of foreign LTCEs (i.e., located outside of the UPE Jurisdiction). There could be, however, top-up tax allocable under the UTPR in respect of the domestic LTCEs (i.e., located in the UPE Jurisdiction) if the ETR of the UPE Jurisdiction is below the Minimum Rate. That top-up tax may be reduced to zero by virtue of a QDMTT payable in the UPE Jurisdiction under Article 5.2.3. In the case where the UPE is required to apply a domestic IIR with respect to domestic LTCEs, the top-up tax may also be reduced to zero under Article 2.5.2 (refer Commentary on Article 2.1.6 providing an option to jurisdictions to extend the application of the IIR domestically in order to avoid discriminating between domestic and foreign CEs that are members of the same MNE Group). If the top-up tax arising in the UPE Jurisdiction is not reduced to zero, it will be included in the UTPR top-up tax amount and allocated to each UTPR Jurisdiction in accordance with Article 2.6.	Refer paragraph 76 of Commentary on Chapter 2.

S. No.	*Query*	*Suggestive Reply*	*Basis of Reply*
64	Why 'number of employees' and 'total value of tangible assets' has been kept as the basis for determination of UTPR percentage?	The UTPR Percentage is determined on the basis of factors that reflect the relative substance of the MNE Group in each UTPR Jurisdiction. Relying on substance factors provides for a simple and transparent allocation key which facilitates the co-ordination among tax administrations. It is also expected that the jurisdictions where the MNE Group has more substance on a relative basis will be those where there is more tax capacity (such as deductible expenditure) to absorb adjustments under the UTPR.	Refer paragraph 81 of Commentary on Chapter 2.
65	What is the reason for adopting a 50% weight for the two factors, i.e., number of employees' and 'total value of tangible assets'?	This is to reflect that substance can be measured both on the basis of the Number of Employees and the Net Book Value of Tangible Assets across jurisdictions, recognising that substance may take various forms, depending on the industry and the business model of the MNE Group. Using a 50% weight for each factor avoids favouring one of the two factors over the other in the formula.	Refer paragraph 83 of Commentary on Chapter 2.
66	Can UTPR Percentage also be determined for UTPR Jurisdictions themselves that are low-tax Jurisdictions under the GloBE Rules?	The UTPR Percentage is determined for all UTPR Jurisdictions where the MNE Group is operating, even if those UTPR Jurisdictions are Low-Tax Jurisdictions under the GloBE Rules for that MNE Group. This means that: – A Low-Tax Jurisdiction that is also a UTPR Jurisdiction is allocated a portion of the UTPR Top-up Tax Amount if its UTPR Percentage is not zero (it could be zero, for instance, as a result of the provisions in Article 2.6.3). – The UPE Jurisdiction itself could be a Low-Tax Jurisdiction under the GloBE Rules and be allocated a portion of the UTPR Top-up Tax Amount that arises in respect of the CEs that are located in the UPE Jurisdiction.	Refer paragraph 86 of Commentary on Chapter 2.

S. No.	*Query*	*Suggestive Reply*	*Basis of Reply*
67	Why UTPR top-up tax amount is not allocated to any of the jurisdictions that do not have a UTPR?	The substance factors of CEs that are not located in a UTPR Jurisdiction are not taken into account for purposes of the allocation key because doing so would have the effect of allocating some of the UTPR top-up tax amount to jurisdictions without a Qualified UTPR. Allocating any of the UTPR top-up tax amount to jurisdictions that do not have a UTPR would significantly reduce the effectiveness of the rule, because the top-up tax allocated to those jurisdictions would not be collected.	Refer paragraph 87 of Commentary on Chapter 2.
68	What are the exclusions while computing a jurisdiction's UTPR percentage?	The exclusions relate to the number of employees and net book value of tangible assets held by: – an investment entity, and – a flow-through entity whose number of employees and net book value of tangible assets are not allocated either to PEs or to the CEs (if any) that are located in the jurisdiction where the Flow-through Entity was created.	Refer paragraphs 89-91 of Commentary on Chapter 2.
69	When is a UTPR Jurisdiction excluded from the allocation mechanism provided under Article 2.6.1?	A UTPR Jurisdiction shall be excluded from the allocation mechanism provided under Article 2.6.1 when the UTPR top-up tax amount allocated to that jurisdiction in a prior year has not yet resulted in an equivalent additional cash tax expense for the CEs located in that jurisdiction. Article 2.6.3 provides that, when that is the case, the UTPR percentage for the jurisdiction is zero. This mechanism ensures that no more top-up tax is allocated to such a jurisdiction until it has been able to impose	Refer paragraphs 92-94 of Commentary on Chapter 2.

S. No.	*Query*	*Suggestive Reply*	*Basis of Reply*
		the requisite amount of tax. Article 2.6.3 further provides that the Number of Employees and Tangible Assets of the CEs located in such a jurisdiction are excluded from the denominator of the formula for purposes of the allocation key. This ensures that the top-up tax that would have been allocated to the UTPR Jurisdiction with a UTPR percentage of zero is actually allocated to the other UTPR Jurisdictions. The exclusion mechanism applies on an annual basis for each Fiscal Year when the UTPR applies and is specific to a particular MNE Group. The exclusion may not apply in circumstances where the UTPR percentage for all UTPR Jurisdictions in which CEs of an MNE Group are located would be zero for a given Fiscal Year. This exception ensures that in such circumstances the UTPR top-up tax amount is still allocated to the UTPR Jurisdictions. Since it applies in situations where all UTPR Jurisdictions may have limited capacity to impose an additional top-up tax, this exception acknowledges that the UTPR top-up tax amount allocated in that year may also need to be carried forward as provided in Article 2.4.2 and be collected in a future year.	
Chapter 3 of GloBE Rules			
70	What is the starting point for computation of GloBE Income or Loss for a CE?	The starting point for computation of GloBE Income or Loss for each CE is the Financial Accounting Net Income or Loss of the CE, i.e., net income or loss for a CE, before any consolidation adjustments eliminating intragroup transactions, in preparing CFS of the UPE, which is then subjected to certain adjustments.	Refer Article 3.1.1 and Article 3.1.2.
71	What kind of adjustments are generally required in Article 3.2?	The adjustments required in Article 3.2 are generally related to permanent differences between the treatment required under financial accounting rules and local tax rules.	Refer paragraph 17 of Commentary on Chapter 3.

S. No.	*Query*	*Suggestive Reply*	*Basis of Reply*
72	What is the concomitant action of exclusion of an amount of income from the GloBE Income or Loss computation, as an outcome of Article 3.2?	To the extent an adjustment required by Article 3.2 excludes an amount of income from the GloBE Income or Loss computation, any Covered Taxes associated with that income must also be excluded from Adjusted Covered Taxes pursuant to Article 4.1.3(a).	Refer paragraph 19 of Commentary on Chapter 3.
73	What is the monetary threshold for disallowing fines/penalties and bribes/kickbacks?	There is a materiality threshold that prevents the rule from applying in the case of *de minimis* fines and the rule only applies to fines and penalties that equal or exceed EUR 50,000 (or an equivalent amount in the functional currency in which the CE's Financial Accounting Net Income or Loss was calculated). There is no such threshold for bribes and kickbacks which are always disallowed. Interest charges for late payment of tax or other liabilities to a governmental unit are not considered fines or penalties for this purpose, and do not need to be added back to Financial Accounting Net Income or Loss.	Refer paragraphs 75, 78 of Commentary on Chapter 3.
74	What is the monetary threshold for applying prior period error corrections?	The provisions requiring application of prior period error corrections do not apply to an error correction that requires a corresponding decrease in covered taxes in a previous Fiscal Year of EUR 1,000,000 or more. Such error corrections are subject to the rules of Article 4.6.1. If the adjustment is a decrease that requires re-computation of the ETR and top-up tax for a previous Fiscal Year under Article 4.6.1, an adjustment under Article 3.2.1(h) is not required because the adjustment is made in the relevant Fiscal Year pursuant to Article 4.6.1.	Refer paragraphs 79, 81 of Commentary on Chapter 3.

S. No.	*Query*	*Suggestive Reply*	*Basis of Reply*
75	What is the situation when an election is not made under Article 3.2.2?	Article 3.2.2 provides an election to substitute in the computation of GloBE Income or Loss the amount of stock-based compensation allowed as a deduction in the computation of a CE's taxable income in place of the amount expensed in its financial accounts. If the election is not made, the CE simply computes its GloBE Income or Loss taking into account the amount of stock-based compensation allowed in the computation of its Financial Accounting Net Income or Loss.	Refer paragraphs 87, 89 of Commentary on Chapter 3.
76	What is the outcome when an option expires without exercise under Article 3.2.2?	If the election is made in respect of an option that expires without exercise, the CE must treat the amount previously included as an expense in the computation of the GloBE Income or Loss pursuant to the election as additional income under the GloBE Rules. This rule prevents the CE from retaining the benefit of a deduction for an item that will never be paid.	Refer paragraph 91 of Commentary on Chapter 3.
77	How should intragroup transactions be priced for the purpose of computing GloBE income or loss?	Any transaction between CEs located in different jurisdictions that is not recorded in the same amount in the financial accounts of both CEs or that is not consistent with the ALP must be adjusted so as to be in the same amount and consistent with the ALP. A loss from a sale or other transfer of an asset between two CEs located in the same jurisdiction that is not recorded consistent with the ALP shall be re-computed based on the ALP if that loss is included in the computation of GloBE Income or Loss. This rule is intended to prevent MNE Groups from manufacturing losses in a jurisdiction through sales or other transfers between Group members at prices that are not consistent with the ALP. The rule does not apply if the loss is excluded from the CE's GloBE Income or Loss computation.	Refer paragraphs 96, 107 of Commentary on Chapter 3.

S. No.	*Query*	*Suggestive Reply*	*Basis of Reply*
78	How should transactions in the same jurisdiction between Minority-Owned CEs and other CEs, as well as, Investment Entities and other CEs be recorded?	Transactions between Minority-Owned CEs and other CEs must also be recorded in accordance with the ALP. This is necessary because Minority-Owned CEs are not included in the ETR and top-up tax computations for the jurisdiction under Articles 5.1 and 5.2, but instead compute their ETR and top-up tax separately pursuant to Article 5.6. Thus, the income and expense of the parties to the transaction will not be eliminated in the jurisdictional blending computation and failure to reflect transactions based on the ALP would distort the ETR and top-up tax calculations for the jurisdiction and the Minority-Owned CEs. Similarly, transactions between Investment Entities and other CEs located in the same jurisdiction must also be recorded in accordance with the ALP.	Refer paragraph 108 of Commentary on Chapter 3.
79	How should transactions between CEs in the same jurisdiction be recorded?	Although not explicitly stated in Article 3.2.3, transactions between CEs in the same jurisdiction must also be recorded in the same amount in both CEs. This is the expected result from applying a common accounting standard to CEs in the same jurisdiction. The principle applies, however, in all cases to prevent the exclusion of income from, or duplication of expenses in, the GloBE Income or Loss computation.	Refer paragraph 109 of Commentary on Chapter 3.
80	How are Qualified Refundable Tax Credits and Non-Qualified Refundable Tax Credits treated for the purpose of computation of GloBE Income or Loss of a CE?	Qualified Refundable Tax Credits shall be treated as income in the computation of GloBE Income or Loss of a CE, whereas, Non-Qualified Refundable Tax Credits shall not be treated as income in the computation of GloBE Income or Loss of a CE.	Refer Article 3.2.4.

S. No.	*Query*	*Suggestive Reply*	*Basis of Reply*
81	What is the objective of an election under Article 3.2.6?	Article 3.2.6 provides an election that permits an MNE Group to spread the effect of gains and losses from the sale of Local Tangible Assets over a period of up to five years to mitigate the effect of recognising the entire gain in a single year on the MNE Group's jurisdictional ETR computation and to match the timing of gains and losses on Local Tangible Assets. The policy justification for this election is that the increase in value of the asset likely accumulated over a period of years and spreading the gain over that period, up to a maximum of five years, and matching it with losses from similar property provides a better measure of whether the MNE Group has been subject to a minimum level of tax in the jurisdiction over that period. The election does not apply to sales between Group Entities because the spread period includes all years in which CEs held the property.	Refer paragraphs 119, 120 of Commentary on Chapter 3.
82	What is the purpose of provisions of Article 3.2.7 that exclude any expense attributable to an Intragroup Financing Arrangement in the course of computation of a Low-Tax Entity's GloBE Income or Loss?	This rule prevents MNE Groups from engaging in transactions that are intended to increase the ETR in a jurisdiction that is below the Minimum Rate by reducing the GloBE Income or Loss in such jurisdiction without increasing the taxable income of the counterparty to the arrangement.	Refer paragraph 127 of Commentary on Chapter 3.

S. No.	*Query*	*Suggestive Reply*	*Basis of Reply*
83	What is the purpose of an election under Article 3.2.8?	The election under Article 3.2.8 applies to transactions between CEs located in the same jurisdiction in order to prevent unintended consequences where income, expense, gains and losses from domestic intragroup transactions are treated as tax neutral intragroup transactions under local law. The MNE Group may prefer an election over the burden of determining arm's length prices for transactions between CEs in the same jurisdiction, particularly in cases where the CEs may not be applying an arm's length standard to same-jurisdiction transactions in a jurisdiction that does not impose a Covered Tax.	Refer paragraphs 133, 136 of Commentary on Chapter 3.
84	How are provisions of Article 3.2.9 and Article 4.2.2(e) inter-related?	The charge of tax (or reduction in policyholder liabilities equivalent to policyholder tax) is excluded from the computation of GloBE Income or Loss under Article 3.2.9 and any taxes arising on the policyholder returns are excluded from the definition of Covered Taxes pursuant to Article 4.2.2(e).	Refer paragraph 141 of Commentary on Chapter 3.
85	What is the objective of Article 3.2.10?	Article 3.2.10 provides that increases or decreases to the equity of a CE attributable to distributions in respect of Additional Tier One Capital shall be treated as income or expense in the computation of its GloBE Income or Loss. Equity adjustments attributable to the issuance or redemption of Additional Tier One Capital are not included in the computation of GloBE Income or Loss.	Refer paragraph 143 of Commentary on Chapter 3.
86	In what manner provisions of Article 3.2.7 interact with the provisions of Article 3.2.10?	Article 3.2.7 does not apply to deny a deduction for distributions treated as an expense pursuant to Article 3.2.10.	Refer paragraph 144 of Commentary on Chapter 3.

S. No.	*Query*	*Suggestive Reply*	*Basis of Reply*
87	What are the reasons for keeping shipping industry outside the scope of the GloBE Rules?	The international shipping industry has long been subject to industry-specific tax rules. The capital-intensive nature, the level of profitability and long economic life cycle of international shipping has led a number of jurisdictions to introduce alternative or supplementary taxation regimes for this industry. The tax regimes applicable to international shipping, such as tonnage taxes, may result in less volatile tax outcomes for shipping and provide a more stable basis for long-term investment. The widespread availability of these alternative tax regimes means that international shipping often operates outside the scope of CIT. Including international shipping within the scope of the GloBE Rules would therefore raise policy questions in light of the policy choices of these jurisdictions.	Refer paragraph 146 of Commentary on Chapter 3.
88	How are provisions of Article 3.3 and Article 4.1.3(a) inter-related?	To the extent an adjustment required by Article 3.3 excludes an amount of income from the GloBE Income or Loss computation, any Covered Taxes associated with that income must also be excluded from Adjusted Covered Taxes pursuant to Article 4.1.3(a).	Refer paragraph 148 of Commentary on Chapter 3.
89	What is the rationale for limiting the aggregated Qualified Ancillary International Shipping Income of all CEs located in a jurisdiction to not exceed 50% of those CEs' International Shipping Income?	The rationale for the limitation is that ancillary activities should only qualify for the exclusion where they are providing necessary support to the primary activity of the international shipping operation. The Qualified Ancillary Shipping Income for the jurisdiction that exceeds 50% of International Shipping Income does not qualify for the exclusion, i.e., the excess is included in the GloBE Income. The limitation applies on a jurisdictional basis.	Refer paragraphs 172, 173 of Commentary on Chapter 3.

S. No.	*Query*	*Suggestive Reply*	*Basis of Reply*
90	What is the criterion for a CE's International Shipping Income and Qualified Ancillary International Shipping Income to qualify for the exclusion from its GloBE Income or Loss?	Substance criterion is essential to qualify for exclusion, which is aimed at ensuring that the strategic or commercial management of all ships deployed in earning International Shipping Income is effectively carried on from within the jurisdiction where the CE is located. This condition is consistent with the manner in which many shipping tax regimes are designed in order to establish an economic link between the shipping company and the jurisdiction of the shipping tax regime.	Refer paragraph 180 of Commentary on Chapter 3.
91	What are the consequences for a PE that is stateless for the purposes of GloBE Rules?	A PE that is stateless for the purposes of GloBE Rules, means that the income of the PE would be subject to the GloBE Rules on a stand-alone basis without the ability to blend its income with other CEs located in that particular jurisdiction.	Refer paragraph 112 of Commentary on Chapter 10.
92	In what manner provisions of Article 3.4.4 interact with the provisions of Article 3.4.5?	The Financial Accounting Net Income or Loss of a PE is not taken into account in determining the GloBE Income or Loss of the Main Entity, except as provided in Article 3.4.5, whereby, the latter provides a rule relating to the allocation of losses of a PE. Some jurisdictions include the income or loss of a PE in the computation of the domestic taxable income of its Main Entity (e.g., jurisdictions with a worldwide tax system with a foreign tax credit system). However, GloBE Rules calculate the ETR of the Main Entity without taking into account the GloBE Income or Loss of the PE. Absent a special rule, the ETR of the Main Entity may be understated in a Fiscal Year when a PE loss is taken into account for domestic tax purposes but not for GloBE Income or Loss purposes. Under Article 3.4.5 this domestic treatment can be preserved, with the necessary corresponding adjustments.	Refer paragraphs 198, 199 of Commentary on Chapter 3.

S. No.	*Query*	*Suggestive Reply*	*Basis of Reply*
93	Why the Financial Accounting Net Income or Loss of a Flow-through Entity is reduced by the amount that is allocated to other CEs?	The Financial Accounting Net Income or Loss of a Flow-through Entity is reduced by the amount that is allocated to other CEs (Constituent Entity-owners or PEs). This is necessary to avoid double-counting under the GloBE Rules.	Refer paragraph 233 of Commentary on Chapter 3.
Chapter 4 of GloBE Rules			
94	What is the objective of making additions to covered taxes under Article 4.1.2?	The said Article requires certain additions to the Covered Taxes to be taken into account for GloBE purposes in order to ensure that all Covered Taxes are properly captured and attributed to the CE. An adjustment may be required under Article 4.1.2 because the range of items identified as income taxes in the financial statements may be narrower than the items that fall within the definition of Covered Taxes for the purposes of the GloBE Rules.	Refer paragraph 5 of Commentary on Chapter 4.
95	How are provisions of Article 4.1.3(e) supportive of application of Article 4.6.4?	Article 4.1.3(e) provides that any amount of current tax expense that is not expected to be paid within three years of the last day of the Fiscal Year shall be treated as a reduction to Covered Taxes. This rule supports the application of Article 4.6.4 which requires the recapture of material amounts previously claimed as Covered Taxes and not paid within three years of the last day of the Fiscal Year.	Refer paragraph 17 of Commentary on Chapter 4.

S. No.	*Query*	*Suggestive Reply*	*Basis of Reply*
96	What is the essence of Article 4.1.5 which provides a special rule that applies in limited circumstances when there is no Net GloBE Income in a jurisdiction for the Fiscal Year and the CE has a deferred tax asset that has arisen due to a permanent difference in the same Fiscal Year?	An Additional Current Top-up Tax charge will only arise in a Fiscal Year where the local tax loss is greater than the loss that has been recorded for GloBE purposes and the additional tax loss results from a deduction for a non-economic loss or similar permanent difference between the local tax base and GloBE Income or Loss, triggering the application of Article 4.1.5, which ensures that the permanent difference giving rise to the inflated tax loss does not result in an overstated ETR for a jurisdiction when the deferred tax attribute is later used.	Refer paragraph 21 of Commentary on Chapter 4 and Example 4.1.5 – 1.
97	What are the types of taxes that do not qualify for the definition of Covered Taxes under the GloBE Rules?	Sales Tax, VAT, Excise taxes, Digital Services Taxes, Stamp duty and ad valorem taxes, Payroll taxes (and other employment-based taxes, as well as social security contributions) and Property taxes do not qualify for the definition of Covered Taxes under the GloBE Rules.	Refer paragraph 36 of Commentary on Chapter 4.
98	Is an ordinary domestic minimum tax that is not a QDMTT considered as a Covered Tax?	An ordinary domestic minimum tax that is not a QDMTT is a Covered Tax if it otherwise meets the definition of a Covered Tax.	Refer paragraph 38 of Commentary on Chapter 4.
99	What is the overall concept of allocation of covered taxes?	Covered Taxes are generally allocated to the CE, including a stateless CE, that includes the corresponding income in the computation of its GloBE Income or Loss and then are taken into account in the ETR computation for the jurisdiction in which the entity is located. The allocation of Covered Taxes under Article 4.3.1 is not limited to the current taxes paid or accrued; it applies also to deferred taxes under Article 4.4.	Refer paragraphs 41, 42 of Commentary on Chapter 4.

S. No.	*Query*	*Suggestive Reply*	*Basis of Reply*
100	Why special allocation rules for certain cross-border taxes are provided?	Article 4.3.2 provides special allocation rules for certain cross-border taxes. These allocation rules are necessary to align the Covered Taxes with the GloBE Income to which the taxes relate, subject to certain limitations. It is intended that the GloBE Rules apply after the application of the STTR and domestic tax regimes, including regimes for the taxation of PEs or CFCs. Therefore, to preserve the intended rule order, domestic tax regimes should not provide a foreign tax credit for any tax imposed under a Qualified UTPR or IIR which is implemented in a foreign jurisdiction, otherwise the application of that domestic tax regime would create circularity issues since those Taxes have already been determined prior to applying the Qualified UTPR or IIR.	Refer paragraph 45 of Commentary on Chapter 4.
101	To which entity are Covered Taxes incurred by a Main Entity or another CE in respect of the income of a PE, allocated?	The Covered Taxes incurred by a Main Entity or another CE in respect of the income of a PE are excluded from the Adjusted Covered Taxes of the CE that incurred them and included in the Adjusted Covered Taxes of the PE.	Refer paragraph 46 of Commentary on Chapter 4.
102	How are Covered Taxes borne by a Tax Transparent Entity that are not attributable to a PE, allocated?	Covered Taxes that are not allocated to a PE will be assigned to the Constituent Entity-owners of the Tax Transparent Entity. Typically, this will mean that Covered Taxes imposed on a Tax Transparent Entity's income (and not attributable to any PE) will be assigned to each Constituent Entity-owner in proportion to its share of the Tax Transparent Entity's income. In the case of a Reverse Hybrid Entity, the income and Taxes would remain with the entity itself and therefore, no allocation of Covered Taxes is needed.	Refer paragraph 57 of Commentary on Chapter 4.

S. No.	*Query*	*Suggestive Reply*	*Basis of Reply*
103	How are Covered Taxes borne by the Constituent Entity-owners in respect of taxes arising under a CFC Tax Regime, allocated?	Similar to the allocation to PEs in paragraph (a) of Article 4.3.2, paragraph (c) of Article 4.3.2 allocates taxes imposed pursuant to a CFC Tax Regime. The same general process described in paragraph (a) of Article 4.3.2 for allocating Covered Taxes imposed on the Main Entity in respect of a PE can also be applied by a Constituent Entity-owner in respect of a taxes arising under a CFC Tax Regime with the amount of any CFC Taxes included in the financial accounts of a direct or indirect Constituent Entity-owner on its share of the CFC's income being allocated to such CFC, subject to the limitations of Article 4.3.3.	Refer paragraph 58 of Commentary on Chapter 4.
104	How are Covered Taxes borne by the Constituent Entity-owners in respect of income of Hybrid Entities, allocated?	Paragraph (d) of Article 4.3.2 allocates Taxes of Constituent Entity-owners arising in connection with the income of Hybrid Entities. If a Constituent Entity-owner of a Hybrid Entity is located in a tax jurisdiction that imposes Tax on the owner's share of the Hybrid Entity's income under a fiscal transparency regime, the Covered Taxes included in the financial accounts of the Constituent Entity-owner should be assigned to the Hybrid Entity. The same general process described in paragraph (a) of Article 4.3.2 for allocating Covered Taxes imposed on the Main Entity in respect of a PE can be used to determine the amount of taxes allocated by a Constituent Entity-owner to a Hybrid Entity, however any taxes allocated to a Hybrid Entity by a Constituent Entity-owner in respect of Passive Income are subject to limitation under Article 4.3.3.	Refer paragraph 59 of Commentary on Chapter 4.

S. No.	*Query*	*Suggestive Reply*	*Basis of Reply*
105	How does Article 4.3.3 reduce the potential abuse arising out of application of Article 4.3.2(c), (d)?	Without the rule of Article 4.3.3, an MNE Group could shift mobile income from high-tax jurisdictions to Low-Tax Jurisdictions to reduce overall tax liability (including Top-up Tax liability) in the MNE Group. The practical effect of this rule is therefore to cap the total Covered Taxes on such passive income (including the taxes allocated to the subsidiary under the CFC or tax transparency regime) to the minimum rate.	Refer paragraphs 62, 63 of Commentary on Chapter 4.
106	What is the overall function of Article 4.4?	Article 4.4 provides the mechanism to address temporary differences, which arise when income or loss is recognised in a different year for financial accounting and tax. The principal mechanism that the GloBE Rules use to address temporary differences is set forth in Article 4.4 and builds on deferred tax accounting, with key adjustments to protect the integrity of the GloBE Rules.	Refer paragraph 67 of Commentary on Chapter 4.
107	How do the provisions of Article 4.4.5 interact with Article 4.4.4?	The Recapture Exception Accrual rule, which provides categories of deferred tax liabilities that do not need to be monitored for recapture under Article 4.4.4, is set forth in Article 4.4.5. The list of Recapture Exception Accruals sets out the temporary differences that are both common in IF jurisdictions and that are generally material to MNE Groups. Such temporary differences are typically tied to substantive activities in a jurisdiction or are differences that are not prone to taxpayer manipulation. Accordingly, to reduce compliance burdens, these low-risk items that are certain to reverse over time are not required to be monitored under the rules in Article 4.4.4 for recapture.	Refer paragraph 91 of Commentary on Chapter 4.

S. No.	*Query*	*Suggestive Reply*	*Basis of Reply*
108	How do the provisions of Article 4.5 interact with Article 4.4?	Article 4.5 provides an elective rule to effectively carry GloBE losses forward with a deemed deferred tax asset. When elected, Article 4.5 applies in lieu of Article 4.4 modified deferred tax accounting rules. Accordingly, Article 4.5 is generally expected to be of greatest utility as a simplification in jurisdictions that do not impose a CIT or impose one at a very low rate, given that when the election is made, Article 4.4 no longer applies, and temporary differences may result in Top-up Tax. The election may be made for any jurisdiction.	Refer paragraph 113 of Commentary on Chapter 4.
109	What is the applicable transition rule when GloBE Loss Election is revoked?	Article 4.5.4 sets out the transition rule that is applicable if the GloBE Loss Election is subsequently revoked. This article requires that any remaining GloBE Loss Deferred Tax Asset be reduced to zero upon transition. This adjustment is required because when a jurisdiction is transitioned to the modified deferred tax accounting method set out in Article 4.4, the historical deferred tax assets and liabilities will be taken into account as if they had been calculated under Articles 4.4 and 9.1 for the prior Fiscal Years. Allowing the GloBE Loss Deferred Tax Asset to be carried forward into these subsequent Fiscal Years would potentially permit double benefit for losses and other distorted outcomes.	Refer paragraph 115 of Commentary on Chapter 4.

S. No.	*Query*	*Suggestive Reply*	*Basis of Reply*
110	What is the stage of GloBE Loss Election and the reason for solitary election?	Article 4.5.5 provides that the GloBE Loss Election must be filed with the GloBE Information Return of the MNE Group filed for the first Fiscal Year in which the MNE Group has a CE located in the jurisdiction for which the election is made and that such election cannot be made for a jurisdiction with an Eligible Distribution Tax System as defined in Article 7.3. Because the GloBE Loss Election can only be filed with the first GloBE Information Return of the MNE Group that includes the jurisdiction for which the election is made, the GloBE Loss Election is an election that may only be made once. This rule is required to limit the applicability of Article 4.5.1 such that it not only provides a relief mechanism or simplification for jurisdictions where an MNE Group decides that an election is necessary but also does not allow for manipulation or distortions by shifting into and out of the election over time.	Refer paragraph 116 of Commentary on Chapter 4.
111	Is GloBE Loss Deferred Tax Asset transferred with a CE when it leaves the MNE Group?	No, as the GloBE Loss Deferred Tax Asset is a jurisdictional attribute of the MNE Group, pursuant to Article 6.2.1(f), hence, it does not transfer with a CE in the event such entity leaves the MNE Group. Accordingly, when a CE has been acquired from another MNE Group, whether such MNE Group has or has not made a GloBE Loss Election will not be relevant or taken into account for purposes of the acquiring MNE Group.	Refer paragraph 117 of Commentary on Chapter 4.

S. No.	*Query*	*Suggestive Reply*	*Basis of Reply*
112	What is the special rule to make a GloBE Loss Election by Flow-through Entities that are the UPE of an MNE Group?	Article 4.5.6 provides a special rule for Flow-through Entities that are the UPE of an MNE Group that is made independently of an Article 4.5 election for any jurisdiction. Such entities may make a GloBE Loss Election under Article 4.5 and when the election is made, the GloBE Loss Deferred Tax Asset is calculated for the UPE in accordance with Articles 4.5.1 through 4.5.5. This GloBE Loss remains with the Flow-through Entity that is a UPE and can only be used to offset future GloBE Income of such UPE. Accordingly, because other entities are not aggregated with the Flow-through Entity that is a UPE for purposes of calculating the GloBE Loss, this election is made with respect to only the Flow-through Entity that is the UPE.	Refer paragraph 118 of Commentary on Chapter 4.
113	What is the overall function of Article 4.6?	Article 4.6 governs adjustments to amounts of Covered Taxes incurred with respect to a jurisdiction after the GloBE Information Return for the period has been filed.	Refer paragraph 119 of Commentary on Chapter 4.
114	Why are increases to Covered Taxes only taken into account in the current Fiscal Year?	Increases to Covered Taxes are only taken into account in the current Fiscal Year. This has the effect that refunds of Top-up Tax paid with respect to prior Fiscal Years will not occur under the operation of Article 4.6.1.	Refer paragraph 120 of Commentary on Chapter 4.
115	Why adjustments for material decreases in covered taxes must be made in respect of the relevant previous Fiscal Year to which the tax adjustment relates?	Adjustments for material decreases (a material decrease in Covered Taxes is an aggregate reduction that is equal to or more than EUR 1 million in the Adjusted Covered Taxes determined for the jurisdiction for a Fiscal Year) must be made in respect of the relevant previous Fiscal Year to which the tax adjustment relates because the over-statement of Covered Taxes may have avoided Top-up Tax in that year and simply reducing Covered Taxes in the current year may not effectively recapture the avoided Top-up Tax.	Refer paragraph 121 of Commentary on Chapter 4.

S. No.	*Query*	*Suggestive Reply*	*Basis of Reply*
116	How do the provisions of Article 4.6.1 interact with Article 3.2.1(h)?	Article 3.2.1(h) generally provides that a correction of an error in the computation of GloBE Income or Loss for a previous Fiscal Year is taken into account in the current year as additional income or expense. However, under Article 4.6.1, if the error affected taxable income for a jurisdiction and results in a material decrease in Covered Taxes for a previous Fiscal Year, the correction is taken into account in the relevant prior year, subject to applicable conditions, *inter alia* being that a re-determination may only be carried back to the extent it does not result in a refund of Top-up Tax. To the extent a re-determination would otherwise result in a refund of Top-up Tax, such re-determination is taken into account in the re-determination year (i.e., the current Fiscal Year).	Refer paragraphs 122, 123 of Commentary on Chapter 4.
117	How is a reduction to the applicable domestic tax rate to a rate below the Minimum Rate accounted for?	When there is a reduction to the applicable domestic tax rate to a rate below the Minimum Rate, such reduction must be taken into account under the rules of Article 4.6.1, subject to applicable conditions.	Refer paragraph 128 of Commentary on Chapter 4.
118	What is the outcome when more than EUR 1 million was claimed as Adjusted Covered Tax, and is not paid within three years of the last day of the Fiscal Year?	Article 4.6.4 provides that the ETR and Top-up Tax for a jurisdiction must be recalculated to exclude an amount of current tax expense (i.e., not deferred tax expense) that is more than EUR 1 million, was claimed as Adjusted Covered Tax, and is not paid within three years of the last day of the Fiscal Year in which such amount was claimed as Adjusted Covered Tax.	Refer paragraph 132 of Commentary on Chapter 4.
Chapter 5 of GloBE Rules			
119	What is ETR?	The ETR for a jurisdiction is equal to the sum of the Adjusted Covered Taxes of each CE located in the jurisdiction for the Fiscal Year divided by the Net GloBE Income of the jurisdiction. The result is expressed as a percentage rounded to the fourth decimal place.	Refer paragraph 3 of Commentary on Chapter 5.

S. No.	*Query*	*Suggestive Reply*	*Basis of Reply*
120	Why ETR computation in Article 5.1 is considered as the central element of the GloBE Rules?	The ETR computation in Article 5.1 is the central element of the GloBE Rules. It is used to determine: – whether in a Fiscal Year, the MNE Group is subject to a minimum level of tax on its income arising in a particular jurisdiction, and – whether the jurisdiction's ETR is below the Minimum Rate (i.e., the jurisdiction is a Low-Tax Jurisdiction in respect of the MNE Group in that Fiscal Year).	Refer paragraph 2 of Commentary on Chapter 5.
121	What are the conspicuous features associated with ETR computation?	– ETRs are generally computed on a jurisdictional basis. – Stateless CEs are treated as being the only CE in a jurisdiction. – Certain Investment Entities and Insurance Investment Entities generally compute their ETR on a stand-alone basis under Article 7.4, but if the MNE Group has two Investment Entities in the same jurisdiction, their ETR is computed by taking into account Covered Taxes and GloBE Income or Loss of both entities. – If the MNE Group has a Minority-Owned Subgroup, a separate ETR computation is necessary for the Minority-Owned CEs located in a jurisdiction separate from the calculation made for the other CEs.	Refer paragraph 2 of Commentary on Chapter 5.

S. No.	*Query*	*Suggestive Reply*	*Basis of Reply*
122	What is jurisdictional blending approach and its objective?	A jurisdictional blending calculation based on the aggregate income and taxes of all CEs in the same MNE Group means that when the Parent Entity applying the IIR is not the UPE, the ETR of a jurisdiction is not computed solely by reference to the CEs owned by that Parent Entity. Rather the ETR is computed by reference to all the CEs of the MNE Group 'located' in that jurisdiction. The implication of determining the ETR based on a group-wide average ETR for the jurisdiction is that there may be cases where allocable Top-up Tax arises in respect of an Entity that would not be an LTCE if the ETR for the jurisdiction were computed on a single-entity basis or solely on the basis of taxes and income attributable to a Parent Entity's Ownership Interests in the CEs located in the jurisdiction. On the other hand, an Entity that would have been an LTCE on a stand-alone basis may not be an LTCE due to taxes paid or losses incurred by other CEs located in the jurisdiction. This approach to jurisdictional blending avoids risks that would otherwise arise to the integrity of the rules from shifting income and taxes between CEs located in the same jurisdiction and avoids potential distortions caused by particular features of the domestic tax system (such as loss-surrender and tax consolidation mechanisms). It also simplifies the mechanic for the attribution and allocation of Top-up Taxes under the IIR and UTPR.	Refer paragraph 4 of Commentary on Chapter 5.

S. No.	*Query*	*Suggestive Reply*	*Basis of Reply*
123	What are the three specific exceptions to the jurisdictional ETR computation?	– The first exception is for Investment Entities and Insurance Investment Entities. Special ETR computation rules are provided in Article 7.4 for such Investment Entities and Insurance Investment Entities. – The second exception applies to CEs in which the UPE holds 30% or less of the Ownership Interests but nonetheless has a Controlling Interest in the Entity. – Finally, each Stateless Constituent Entity is treated as a single CE located in a separate jurisdiction for purposes of Chapter 5.	Refer paragraphs 5-8 of Commentary on Chapter 5.
124	Is there any requirement to compute ETR for a jurisdiction If the GloBE Losses of the CEs equal or exceed GloBE Income of the CEs located in that jurisdiction?	If the GloBE Losses of the CEs equal or exceed GloBE Income of the CEs located in that jurisdiction, there is no Net GloBE Income under Article 5.1.2, and therefore, there can be no Top-up Tax computed under Article 5.2 with respect to the jurisdiction. Consequently, the ETR for the jurisdiction need not be computed. It may, however, be noted that there may be cases in which Top-up Tax is determined under Article 4.1.5 for a jurisdiction that has a Net GloBE Loss.	Refer paragraph 11 of Commentary on Chapter 5.
125	What is Top-up Tax percentage for a jurisdiction?	The Top-up Tax percentage for a jurisdiction is equal to the percentage point excess of the Minimum Rate (of 15%) over the ETR determined for the jurisdiction under Article 5.1 for the Fiscal Year.	Refer paragraph 15 of Commentary on Chapter 5.

S. No.	*Query*	*Suggestive Reply*	*Basis of Reply*
126	When is a jurisdiction considered a Low-Tax Jurisdiction?	For purposes of the GloBE Rules, a jurisdiction is considered a Low-Tax Jurisdiction in respect of the MNE Group and the Constituent Entities located in the jurisdiction are considered LTCEs when the ETR is below the Minimum Rate. If the ETR equals or exceeds the Minimum Rate, there is no Top-up Tax Percentage for the jurisdiction and none of the Constituent Entities located in the jurisdiction will be considered LTCEs.	Refer paragraph 16 of Commentary on Chapter 5.
127	While computing Jurisdictional Top-up Tax, what is the *inter se* sequence of computation of Additional Current Top-up Tax and QDMTT?	The amount of Additional Current Top-up Tax for a jurisdiction must be computed before any reduction by a QDMTT.	Refer paragraph 19 of Commentary on Chapter 5.
128	What is the consequence if QDMTT is in excess of the amount of Top-up Tax that would otherwise be computed under Article 5.2.3?	The amount of a QDMTT may be different from that determined under the GloBE Rules as a result of different applicable accounting standards as permitted by the definition of QDMTT in Article 10.1. This difference may result in an amount of QDMTT in excess of the amount of Top-up Tax that would otherwise be computed under Article 5.2.3. The amount of any excess, however, will not reduce the Top-up Tax under the GloBE Rules below zero or result in a refund of, or credit against future Top-up Tax under the GloBE Rules.	Refer paragraph 20 of Commentary on Chapter 5.

S. No.	*Query*	*Suggestive Reply*	*Basis of Reply*
129	Why the Jurisdictional Top-up Tax computed for a Low-Tax Jurisdiction is allocated among the CEs in the jurisdiction?	Since the Jurisdictional Top-up Tax is computed in Article 5.2.3 by reference to the Net GloBE Income, hence, it is allocated only to CEs that have GloBE Income for the Fiscal Year; none is allocated to CEs with GloBE Losses. The allocation of Top-up Tax among LTCEs under Article 5.2.4 facilitates: – The application of the IIR by Parent Entities other than the UPE. POPEs and some Intermediate Parent Entities do not have the same Ownership Interests in the profits of an LTCE as the UPE. If there are multiple LTCEs in the Low-Tax Jurisdiction, the Top-up Tax of each LTCE would be allocable in different proportions to Parent Entities with different Ownership Interests percentages in the various LTCEs. (If, however, the UPE is applying an IIR and all of the LTCEs are wholly owned, all of the Top-up Tax computed for the jurisdiction is allocable to the UPE under Chapter 2 and therefore, as a practical matter, the UPE does not need to make the allocation among LTCEs under Article 5.2.4.) – The allocation of Top-up Tax to specific LTCEs also facilitates application of the UTPR, particularly in cases where part of an LTCE's Top-up Tax is subject to an IIR and the remainder is subject to the UTPR.	Refer paragraphs 21, 22 of Commentary on Chapter 5.

S. No.	*Query*	*Suggestive Reply*	*Basis of Reply*
130	What is the policy rationale behind a formulaic, substance-based carve-out, based on payroll and tangible assets?	The policy rationale behind a formulaic, substance-based carve-out is to exclude a fixed return for substantive activities within a jurisdiction from the application of the GloBE Rules. The use of Payroll and Tangible Assets as indicators of substantive activities is justified because these factors are generally expected to be less mobile and less likely to lead to tax-induced distortions. Conceptually, excluding a fixed return from substantive activities focuses GloBE on 'excess income', such as intangible-related income, which is most susceptible to BEPS risks. The Substance-based Income Exclusion set out in Article 5.3 only affects those MNE Groups with operations in jurisdictions that are taxed below the Minimum Rate. Further, as the potential benefit is limited to a routine return and considering the computational rules of the Top-up Tax, the design avoids any tax-induced distortions of investment decisions.	Refer paragraphs 25, 26 of Commentary on Chapter 5.
131	Can the excess of the Substance-based Income Exclusion reduce the GloBE Income of another Fiscal Year?	No, the excess of the Substance-based Income Exclusion over the Net GloBE Income of the jurisdiction for a Fiscal Year cannot be carried forward or backward to reduce the Net GloBE Income of another Fiscal Year.	Refer paragraph 27 of Commentary on Chapter 5.
132	Why an election to not apply the Substance-based Income Exclusion is provided?	The election not to apply the exclusion is provided because some MNE Groups may consider that the burden of computing the amount of the exclusion for a particular jurisdiction outweighs the potential benefits of the exclusion in that jurisdiction.	Refer paragraph 28 of Commentary on Chapter 5.

S. No.	*Query*	*Suggestive Reply*	*Basis of Reply*
133	How is the carrying value of Eligible Tangible Assets for purposes of the tangible asset carve-out computed?	The carrying value of each asset for purposes of the carve-out is the average of the beginning and end of year carrying values. Thus, if an asset is acquired or disposed during the Fiscal Year, it's carrying value at the beginning or end of the Fiscal Year will be zero. Because the zero carrying value is included in the computation of the average, the carve-out for assets acquired or disposed during the year will be based on half of the carrying value of asset at the end or beginning of the year.	Refer paragraph 49 of Commentary on Chapter 5.
134	What is the mechanism for performing recalculation of ETR for the prior year?	If the ETR of a jurisdiction is subject to an ETR Adjustment then Article 5.4.1 provides the mechanism for performing the recalculations for the prior year. Article 5.4.1 treats any additional Top-up Tax computed in respect of prior Fiscal Years as Additional Current Top-up Tax, which is allocated to CEs in the jurisdiction under Article 5.2. To avoid the complexity and administrative burden of requiring an amended GloBE Information Return and additional separate payment of Top-up Tax, the Additional Top-Up Tax is instead charged to the Fiscal Year in which the recalculation was performed.	Refer paragraph 66 of Commentary on Chapter 5.
135	In what kind of situations can recalculation of ETR under Article 5.4.1 for prior year be carried out?	Article 5.4.1 is not intended to address ordinary mistakes in the computations under the GloBE Rules or adjustments to GloBE Income arising from an examination of a CE's application of the IIR or the UTPR. It applies only when there is an adjustment to a local tax item that has a follow-on effect on computations under the GloBE Rules, such as a transfer pricing adjustment that affects the income and tax liability of CEs in two or more jurisdictions.	Refer paragraph 67 of Commentary on Chapter 5.

S. No.	*Query*	*Suggestive Reply*	*Basis of Reply*
136	What happens when a recalculation is performed in accordance with Article 5.4.1 and there is no Net GloBE Income for the jurisdiction for the current Fiscal Year?	Article 5.4.2 provides a special rule for this purpose. It provides that the GloBE Income of the CEs in the jurisdiction shall be increased for the purposes of Article 2.2.2 in an amount equal to the additional Top-up Tax due divided by the Minimum Rate. For this purpose, any GloBE Loss determined for the Fiscal Year is disregarded. This rule ensures that when a recalculation results in additional Top-up Tax that is payable in a Fiscal Year with no GloBE Income for a jurisdiction that there is still a mechanism in place by which the Top-up Tax that is owed can be allocated to Parent Entities that may be subject to an IIR.	Refer paragraph 68 of Commentary on Chapter 5.
137	Can both Articles 5.4.2 and 5.4.3 be applied simultaneously?	Yes. The GloBE Income created under Article 5.4.3 is equal to the Top-up Tax allocated to the Entity under Article 5.4.3 divided by the Minimum Rate. For this purpose, any GloBE Loss determined for the Fiscal Year is disregarded. It is possible for GloBE Income to be created for CEs in a jurisdiction for the purposes of Article 2.2.2 under both Articles 5.4.2 and 5.4.3. In this scenario, each article is applied without regard to the income created under the other article. For purposes of Article 2.2.2, the GloBE Income for any CE for which GloBE Income has been created under both articles is the sum of the income created under each article.	Refer paragraph 72 of Commentary on Chapter 5.
138	What is the policy intent underlying *De minimis* exclusion?	The policy intent underlying Article 5.5 election is to avoid the complexities of a full ETR computation in cases where the amount of any Top-up Tax would not seem to justify the associated compliance and administrative costs.	Refer paragraph 74 of Commentary on Chapter 5.

S. No.	*Query*	*Suggestive Reply*	*Basis of Reply*
139	When does *De minimis* exclusion apply?	The Top-up Tax for the CEs located in a jurisdiction shall be deemed to be zero for a Fiscal Year if, for such Fiscal Year: (a) the Average GloBE Revenue of such jurisdiction is less than EUR 10 million; and (b) the Average GloBE Income or Loss of such jurisdiction is a loss or is less than EUR 1 million. Exclusion applies on an annual basis.	Refer Article 5.5.1.
140	How are the *De minimis* thresholds computed?	Article 5.5.2 provides that the values of the current Fiscal Year (whether income or loss) shall be averaged with that of the preceding two Fiscal Years for purposes of testing whether the jurisdiction is below the threshold. Using a three-year average is intended to simplify both compliance with the rule by MNE Groups and administration of the rule by tax authorities. Those Fiscal Years shall be excluded from the computation of the Average GloBE Revenue and the Average GloBE Income or Loss when there are no CEs with either GloBE Revenue or GloBE Losses (in the absence of revenue) that were located in the jurisdiction for that Fiscal Year. This applies when there are no CEs located in the jurisdiction for a given Fiscal Year. It can also arise when there are only dormant CEs located in the jurisdiction.	Refer paragraphs 84, 85 of Commentary on Chapter 5.
141	In what manner the GloBE Income or Loss adjustment under an ETR Adjustment Article impact the *De minimis* exclusion?	When the GloBE Income or Loss is adjusted under an ETR Adjustment Article, the GloBE Revenue shall also be adjusted as appropriate and necessary. Adjustments that reduce GloBE Income and/or GloBE Revenue for a previous Fiscal Year will not make a jurisdiction eligible for the *de minimis* exclusion in	Refer paragraph 92 of Commentary on Chapter 5.

S. No.	*Query*	*Suggestive Reply*	*Basis of Reply*
		a previous Fiscal Year. However, adjustments that increase the GloBE Income and/or the GloBE Revenue of the jurisdiction may result in the Average GloBE Income or the Average GloBE Revenue of the jurisdiction no longer being below the threshold for the *de minimis* exclusion for a previous Fiscal Year or Years. In such a case, Article 5.5 is no longer applicable for the relevant Fiscal Year or Years and the Filing Constituent Entity must provide the relevant information required in the GloBE Information Return with respect to that jurisdiction for those Fiscal Years, without applying Article 5.5.	
142	How does *De minimis* exclusion apply when there are changes in the scope of the MNE Group?	If an MNE Group acquires Entities in a merger, the GloBE Revenue and GloBE Income or Loss of those Entities determined for periods prior to the merger are not taken into account for purposes of determining the three-year averages under Article 5.5.3. Similarly, if a CE leaves the MNE Group, the GloBE Revenue and GloBE Income or Loss of that Entity determined for periods prior to the disposition of that CE are still taken into account for purposes of determining the three-year averages under Article 5.5.3.	Refer paragraph 94 of Commentary on Chapter 5.
143	Is an election under Article 5.5 applicable to a CE that is a Stateless CE or an Investment Entity?	No. The election is not applicable to these CEs because their ETR is computed on an Entity basis, and they are typically not subject to tax. Since Stateless Constituent Entities and Investment Entities are not eligible for the *de minimis* exclusion, their revenue and GloBE income are excluded from the *De Minimis* Exclusion computations in Article 5.5.3 for purposes of determining whether a jurisdiction is eligible for the *de minimis* exclusion so that such revenue or income will not cause a jurisdiction to fail the *de minimis* tests.	Refer paragraphs 95, 96 of Commentary on Chapter 5.

S. No.	*Query*	*Suggestive Reply*	*Basis of Reply*
144	Why are there special rules for computing ETR and Top-up Tax of Minority-Owned Constituent Entities?	Special rules are needed for Minority–Owned Constituent Entities because a UPE may have several Minority-Owned Constituent Entities with operations in the same jurisdiction but with different groups of owners that are not Group Entities. If the income and taxes of these different CEs were blended in the jurisdictional ETR computations, low-tax outcomes in one Entity could result in a Top-up Tax for the jurisdiction, some of which would be borne by non-Group Entity owners of a different CE. While this can occur to some extent under the normal jurisdictional blending rules, the magnitude of the effect in the context of Minority-Owned Constituent Entities and the potential detrimental impact on these investment structures justifies a different rule.	Refer paragraph 97 of Commentary on Chapter 5.
145	How do provisions of Article 5.6.2 interact with Article 5.5?	Article 5.6.2 is a rule that applies only to a Minority-Owned Constituent Entity that is not a member of a Minority-Owned Subgroup. This provision prevents 70% or more of the Net Income or Loss and Adjusted Covered Taxes of the Entity, which do not effectively belong to the UPE, from being blended with the Net Income or Loss and Adjusted Covered Taxes of the other CEs of the MNE Group. However, Article 5.6.2 has no effect on the eligibility of a jurisdiction for the *de minimis* exclusion provided in Article 5.5 (The election available in Article 5.5.1 does not require the MNE Group to compute the Average GloBE Revenue and Average GloBE Income or Loss of the members of a Minority-Owned Subgroup as if they were a separate MNE Group or of a Minority-Owned Constituent Entity on an entity basis. Therefore, the GloBE Revenue and the GloBE Income or Loss of those entities is taken into account for purposes of determining the Average	Refer paragraph 106 of Commentary on Chapter 5.

S. No.	*Query*	*Suggestive Reply*	*Basis of Reply*
		GloBE Revenue and the Average GloBE Income or Loss of the jurisdiction where they are located).	
Chapter 6 of GloBE Rules			
146	When and how do GloBE Rules apply where two or more Groups merge to form a single Group?	As set out in Article 1.1, the GloBE Rules apply to MNE Groups with consolidated revenue of EUR 750 million or more in at least two of the four Fiscal Years immediately preceding the tested Fiscal Year. Neither Group's pre-merger revenues are adjusted for transactions that occurred between the Groups in the preceding years, notwithstanding that transactions between Entities will be eliminated in consolidation after the merger.	Refer paragraphs 19, 22 of Commentary on Chapter 6.
147	When and how do GloBE Rules apply where an MNE Group demerges?	GloBE Rules apply where an MNE Group (that is within the scope of GloBE Rules) demerges subject to the following conditions: – With respect to the first tested Fiscal Year after the demerger, the consolidated revenue threshold set out in Article 1.1 is deemed to be met by a demerged Group if the demerged Group has annual revenues of EUR 750 million or more in the first tested fiscal year after the demerger. This means that instead of applying a test that considers previous fiscal years, this rule is triggered for each demerged Group that has annual revenues of EUR 750 million or more in the Fiscal Year that is being tested. – With respect to second to the fourth tested Fiscal Years after the demerger, the consolidated revenue threshold set out in Article 1.1 is deemed to be met by a demerged Group if it has annual revenues of EUR 750 million or more in at least two Fiscal Years following the demerger.	Refer paragraphs 34, 36 of Commentary on Chapter 6.

S. No.	*Query*	*Suggestive Reply*	*Basis of Reply*
148	When an acquisition or disposition of a Controlling Interest in a CE takes place during the Fiscal Year, broadly, in what manner does Article 6.2 modify or clarify the operation of the GloBE Rules?	– Article 6.2 is intended to produce a smooth separation of the target from the seller Group and a smooth integration of the target into the acquiring MNE Group. – Article 6.2 provides a special ordering rule for applying the IIR where the target is a Parent Entity that is required to apply the IIR as a member of one or both MNE Groups. – Special rules are required to determine whether a target should apply the IIR for all or part of the year because the application of the IIR by the target depends on whether a Controlling Interest in the target is held by a Group Entity that is subject to a Qualified IIR. – Specific ordering rules are not required for the application of the UTPR in these cases because the impact of a CE leaving or joining an MNE Group is automatically taken into account as part of the allocation methodology of the UTPR (allocation of top-up tax under the UTPR is governed by Article 2.6).	Refer paragraphs 44, 45 of Commentary on Chapter 6.
149	What is the overall function of Article 6.3 in respect of disposal or acquisition of assets and liabilities of a CE?	Article 6.3 deals with situations in which the assets and liabilities of a Constituent Entity are disposed or acquired directly, including as part of a GloBE Reorganisation (where the seller is not subject to tax on the gain (or loss), in whole or part). Article 6.3 provides rules to determine whether and the extent to which gain or loss is recognised on the disposition and the carrying value to be used by the acquirer for the purposes of determining its GloBE Income or Loss in subsequent Fiscal Years.	Refer paragraph 4 of Commentary on Chapter 6.

S. No.	*Query*	*Suggestive Reply*	*Basis of Reply*
150	How Article 6.4 brings JVs into the scope of GloBE Rules?	Since a JV is not controlled exclusively by one person, its accounting results are not consolidated with any of its owners on a line-by-line basis. Instead, the financial results of JVs are commonly reported by MNE Groups using the equity method in their CFS. Absent a special rule, this accounting treatment would exclude them from the scope of the GloBE Rules because they do not meet the definition of a CE under Article 1.3, which requires an Entity to be consolidated on a line-by-line basis. Thus, if two MNE Groups subject to the GloBE Rules each owned 50% of the Ownership Interests of a JV, neither MNE Group would be subject to the GloBE Rules on its share of the JV's income in the absence of Article 6.4. Accordingly, Article 6.4 extends the application of the GloBE Rules to Entities in which the UPE of an MNE Group owns 50% or more of the Ownership Interests (such Entities are JVs under the GloBE Rules). This ensures that all of the income of a 50/50 JV owned, directly or indirectly, by the UPE of an MNE Group will be subject to the GloBE Rules and that the rule extends to any venture in which the MNE Group holds 50% or more of the Ownership Interests (without having unilateral control). Article 6.4 does not, however, require the JV or its JV Subsidiaries to apply the IIR or the UTPR directly. Rather it requires the MNE Group to determine Top-up Tax in respect of a JV (or its JV Subsidiaries) located in a Low-Taxed Jurisdiction and allocates any resulting Top-up Tax to a CE within the MNE Group under the IIR or the UTPR.	Refer paragraphs 83, 84 of Commentary on Chapter 6.

S. No.	*Query*	*Suggestive Reply*	*Basis of Reply*
151	What is the overall function of Article 6.5 in respect of Multi-Parented MNE Groups under the GloBE Rules?	Article 6.5 provides special rules for the treatment of Multi-Parented MNE Groups under the GloBE Rules. The article covers the situation in which two or more Groups prepare CFS in which the financial performance of these Groups is presented as a single economic unit in accordance with a Dual-listed Arrangement or a Stapled Structure. The rules in this article ensure that the GloBE Rules apply to these structures in the same way they would apply to a Group with single UPE with an appropriate allocation of Top-up Tax among the CEs of the combined MNE Group.	Refer paragraph 95 of Commentary on Chapter 6.
Chapter 7 of GloBE Rules			
152	What is the underlying principle of Article 7.1?	The principle underlying the rules in Article 7.1 is that to the extent that the tax neutrality regime imposes tax on the UPE's owners (e.g., partners, beneficiaries or shareholders) at or above the Minimum Rate on the UPE's income contemporaneously or within a short time, the UPE's exposure to Top-up Tax will likewise be reduced. This is achieved by a reduction to the GloBE income of the UPE corresponding to the share of its income that is subject to tax at or above the minimum rate in the hands of its owners (and thereby reducing, perhaps eliminating, any exposure to Top-up Tax). Likewise, GloBE Losses incurred by a UPE that is a Flow-through Entity must also be reduced by the amount attributable to each Ownership Interest, except to the extent that the holders of Ownership Interests are not allowed to use the loss in computing their separate taxable income. Without this rule, losses that are passed through to the holders of Ownership Interests would also be available for use in the jurisdictional ETR calculation to shield GloBE income of other CEs located in the UPE's Jurisdiction.	Refer paragraphs 5, 24 of Commentary on Chapter 7.

S. No.	*Query*	*Suggestive Reply*	*Basis of Reply*
153	What is the overall function of Article 7.2 in respect of UPEs that are subject to a Deductible Dividend Regime?	Article 7.2 allows a deduction in the computation of the GloBE Income or Loss for Deductible Dividends. A Deductible Dividend Regime is a tax regime designed to yield a single level of taxation on the owners of an Entity through the allowance of a deduction from the income of the Entity for distributions of profits to the owners. The owners are subject to tax on the dividends and the Entity is subject to tax on earnings that are not distributed. Deductible Dividend Regimes typically apply to investment companies as well as Cooperatives. Although a Deductible Dividend Regime may apply to both Entities that qualify as Investment Entities under the GloBE Rules and other similar purpose Entities that do not meet the Investment Entity definition, the rules in Article 7.2 are needed only for those Entities that do not meet the Investment Entity definition because an Investment Entity that is the UPE is an Excluded Entity.	Refer paragraphs 34, 35 of Commentary on Chapter 7.
154	In what manner do substantive rules applicable to UPEs subject to Deductible Dividend Regimes vary from the rules for UPEs that are Tax Transparent Entities?	The substantive rules applicable to UPEs that are subject to Deductible Dividend Regimes are similar to the rules for UPEs that are Tax Transparent Entities. An important difference, however, is the treatment of losses incurred by the CE. Unlike the treatment of losses incurred by a Tax Transparent Entity under local tax rules, the losses of an Entity subject to a Deductible Dividend Regime do not flow through to the owners. Accordingly, the GloBE Rules applicable to Deductible Dividend Regimes do not contain special rules for a GloBE Loss determined for a CE. Such losses are taken into account in the computation of the Net GloBE Income for the jurisdiction in which the Entity is located.	Refer paragraph 37 of Commentary on Chapter 7.

S. No.	*Query*	*Suggestive Reply*	*Basis of Reply*
155	What is the overall function of Article 7.3 in respect of a distribution tax regime?	The tax rates applicable under a distribution tax regime may equal or exceed the Minimum Rate such that the income is not subject to a low rate of tax when the earnings are eventually distributed. Absent a distribution or deemed distribution, however, much of the income is not subject to tax in the year it is earned and reported in the financial accounts. Moreover, the rules in Article 4.3 generally do not permit deferred tax liabilities in respect of taxes payable upon distribution to be included in the computation of the Total Deferred Tax Adjustment Amount. This means that the CE's GloBE Income likely would be subject to tax under the GloBE Rules in those years in which there is not an actual or deemed distribution because the Adjusted Covered Taxes for the Fiscal Year will be very small or nil. Moreover, in years where distributions are made, the amount of the distributions may bear no relationship to the income arising in those years, which may result in low or even extremely high ETRs. Article 7.3 mitigates these differences between the time the income accrues in the financial accounts and the time it is subject to distribution tax to the extent that distributions are made within a four-year period.	Refer paragraph 53 of Commentary on Chapter 7.
156	How application of GloBE Rules varies in respect of an Investment Entity that is the UPE and a controlled Investment Entity?	Investment Entities that are the UPE are excluded from the operation of the GloBE Rules because they are not CEs of any MNE Group (refer Article 1.5.1(e)), whereas, the income of a controlled Investment Entity is consolidated with the MNE Group and brought within the GloBE Rules.	Refer paragraph 73 of Commentary on Chapter 7.

S. No.	*Query*	*Suggestive Reply*	*Basis of Reply*
157	What is the overall function of Article 7.4 in regard to computation of ETR of controlled investment entities and Insurance Investment Entities?	The overall function of Article 7.4 is as below: – Provides special rules applicable to controlled Investment Entities and Insurance Investment Entities. – Provides a mechanism for calculating the ETR of a controlled Investment Entity or Insurance Investment Entity that is not subject to an election under Articles 7.5 or 7.6 (as applicable). – The income of Investment Entities and Insurance Investment Entities is often subject to little or no tax at the entity level. Article 7.4 calculates the ETR and Top-up Tax of these Entities on a stand-alone basis to prevent an MNE Group from blending this low-taxed income with income of other CEs. – Seeks to ensure that minority investors are not subject to Top-up Tax on their interest in a low-taxed Investment Entity controlled by an MNE Group. It does so by calculating the ETR and Top-up Tax of a controlled Investment Entity only to the extent that the income is attributable to the MNE Group.	Refer paragraph 74 of Commentary on Chapter 7.
158	How do provisions of Article 7.5 interact with provisions of Article 7.4?	The overall function of Article 7.5 is that it provides an election to treat an Investment Entity or an Insurance Investment Entity as a Tax Transparent Entity (Investment Entities and Insurance Investment Entities that meet the definition of a Tax Transparent Entity in Article 10.2.1 do not need to make the election). Under the election, the income and Covered Taxes of the Investment Entity or Insurance Investment Entity flow through to the Constituent Entity-owner and thus the special rules in Article 7.4 are not needed to compute the Investment Entity's ETR.	Refer paragraph 75 of Commentary on Chapter 7.

S. No.	*Query*	*Suggestive Reply*	*Basis of Reply*
159	How do provisions of Article 7.6 interact with provisions of Article 7.4?	Article 7.6 provides another alternative to the rule in Article 7.4. This alternative is the Taxable Distribution Method. This method reduces the exposure to Top-up Tax to the extent that the Investment Entity makes distributions of its income within a four-year period that are taxable in the hands of the recipients at or above the Minimum Rate. The overall function of Article 7.6 is that under the election, the Constituent Entity-owner includes distributions received from the Entity in the computation of its GloBE Income or Loss. The Constituent Entity-owner's share of the Investment Entity's income is excluded from the MNE Group's GloBE Income or Loss computations so long as it is distributed to the Constituent Entity-owner within four years.	Refer paragraphs 99, 76 of Commentary on Chapter 7.
Chapter 8 of GloBE Rules			
160	What are the broad obligations of various entities to file the GloBE Information Return?	– Article 8.1.1 casts an obligation on either the CE or a Designated Local Entity on its behalf to file a GloBE Information Return conforming to the requirements of Articles 8.1.4 to 8.1.6 with the tax administration of the Jurisdiction that has implemented GloBE Rules. – A Stateless Constituent Entity, such as a Flow-through Entity that is not a UPE, would not be required to file this return because it is not located in the implementing jurisdiction. – The Constituent Entity-owners of the Flow-through Entity would be required to submit a GloBE Information Return as would any other CE located in a jurisdiction by virtue of the first sentence of Article 8.1.1.	Refer paragraphs 5-9 of Commentary on Chapter 8.

S. No.	*Query*	*Suggestive Reply*	*Basis of Reply*
		– Where the Flow-through Entity is the UPE or is required to apply the IIR, it would be located in the jurisdiction where it was created in accordance with Article 10.3.2(a) and therefore, it would be required to submit a GloBE Information Return. In these cases, the GloBE Information Return could be filed by an authorised entity such as a trustee or manager on behalf of the Flow-through Entity. – PEs are CEs and, therefore, required to file a GloBE Information Return in the jurisdiction where they are located. – An Entity treated as a JV in the CFS of an MNE Group is not required to submit a GloBE Information Return in accordance with Article 8.1.1, because it is not a CE of that MNE Group despite being treated as such solely for purposes of the computation of its Top-up Tax in accordance with Article 6.4.1 (a). For the same reasons, an Entity treated as a JV Subsidiary by an MNE Group is not required to submit a GloBE Information Return for that Group. – Where there are two or more CEs located in the same jurisdiction, one of them, i.e., the Designated Local Entity, is required to file a single GloBE Information Return on behalf of the others (and itself). – When a Designated Local Entity files a GloBE Information Return on behalf of other CEs located in the same jurisdiction, the obligation of those CEs to file their own return is discharged. – Article 8.1.2 states that all CEs (including the Designated Local Entity) are discharged from the requirement to file a GloBE Information Return if the return has been filed by the UPE or by a Designated Filing Entity appointed by the MNE Group.	

S. No.	*Query*	*Suggestive Reply*	*Basis of Reply*
161	Is filing of the GloBE Information Return an end of the matter?	While Article 8.1.4 relates to information in the GloBE Information Return, it is not intended to prevent a local tax administration from requesting further necessary supporting information to verify compliance with the GloBE Rules in accordance with its domestic law.	Refer paragraph 13 of Commentary on Chapter 8.
162	How much time is allowed to the MNE Groups to file the GloBE Information Return?	In order to allow MNE Groups time to prepare the required information, Article 8.1.6 provides MNE Groups with up to fifteen months after the last day of the Reporting Fiscal Year to file the GloBE Information Return and the notifications with the relevant tax administrations. The timing for filing notifications is aligned with the timing for filing the GloBE Information Return (i.e., within fifteen months after the last day of the Reporting Fiscal Year). This gives a CE or a Designated Local Entity ample opportunity to notify its local tax administration of the identity and location of the UPE or Designated Filing Entity that will be filing the GloBE Information Return on its behalf.	Refer paragraph 25 of Commentary on Chapter 8.
163	What is the primary objective of safe harbours?	In order to limit unnecessary compliance and administrative burden for MNE Groups and tax administrations, the GloBE Implementation Framework is exploring the development of GloBE Safe Harbours. GloBE Safe Harbours would allow an MNE Group to avoid the ETR and Top-up Tax calculation in respect of its operations that are likely to be taxable at or above the Minimum Rate. They would also provide for improved tax certainty and transparency in the use of risk assessment under the GloBE Rules.	Refer paragraph 30 of Commentary on Chapter 8.

S. No.	*Query*	*Suggestive Reply*	*Basis of Reply*
164	What is the objective of issuance of Administrative Guidance by the IF?	Article 8.3.1 contemplates that further guidance on the interpretation or application of the GloBE Rules may be agreed upon and published by the IF in order to ensure that when such guidance is issued, it is applied in a coordinated way by the tax administrations of jurisdictions that have implemented GloBE Rules.	Refer paragraph 40 of Commentary on Chapter 8.
Chapter 9 of GloBE Rules			
165	What is the purpose of introducing Transition Rules in the context of tax attributes arising due to timing differences?	At the point an MNE Group becomes subject to the GloBE Rules, it is expedient to take appropriate account of operating losses that the MNE Group has incurred in the period(s) prior to becoming subject to the GloBE Rules and also, address issues arising in relation to timing differences, otherwise, taxation under the GloBE Rules may arise. Article 9.1.1 provides the basis to use deferred tax accounting attributes in determination of Covered Taxes pursuant to Article 4.4.	Refer paragraphs 2, 3, 6 of Commentary on Chapter 9.
166	What is the limitation on intragroup asset transfers before applicability of the GloBE Rules?	Article 9.1.3 provides a limitation on intragroup asset transfers before applicability of the GloBE Rules. If an asset is transferred between entities after 30 November 2021 and before the Transition Year (which means the first Fiscal Year that the MNE Group comes within the scope of the GloBE Rules in respect of that jurisdiction) of an MNE Group, and such entities would have been CEs of that MNE Group had the GloBE Rules been in effect with respect to that MNE Group, such asset must be recorded at its historical carrying value for GloBE purposes to limit the ability to step-up the basis in such assets without including the resulting gain in the computation of GloBE Income or Loss.	Refer paragraph 10 of Commentary on Chapter 9.

S. No.	*Query*	*Suggestive Reply*	*Basis of Reply*
167	What are the provisions for transitional relief for the Substance-based Income Exclusion?	Article 9.2 provides the relevant percentages for the purpose of applying the payroll carve-out in Article 5.3.3 and tangible asset carve-out in Article 5.3.4 for Fiscal Years that begin in the transition period of ten calendar years beginning with 2023. Accordingly, in a transition period of ten years, the amount of income excluded will be: – 10% of payroll and 8% of the carrying value of tangible assets in the year 2023, – declining annually by 0.2 percentage points for the first five years, and – declining annually by 0.8 percentage points for payroll and by 0.4 percentage points for tangible assets for the last five years.	Refer Article 9.2 and paragraphs 11-13 of Commentary on Chapter 9.
168	What are the requirements that must be met for an exclusion from the UTPR for MNE Groups?	When the exclusion from the UTPR applies in the initial phase of international activity, i.e., for a period of five years after the MNE Group has come within the scope of the GloBE Rules, there is no need for the MNE Group to compute the ETR of its CEs and no need to calculate the amount of Top-up Tax that would have been due if the exclusion did not apply. The exclusion applies in respect of an MNE Group on an annual basis, subject to the following conditions: – it has CEs in no more than six jurisdictions; and – the sum of the Net Book Values of Tangible Assets of all CEs located in all jurisdictions other than the Reference Jurisdiction (it is the jurisdiction where the MNE Group has the highest total value of Tangible Assets) does not exceed EUR 50 million.	Refer paragraphs 16-20 of Commentary on Chapter 9.

S. No.	*Query*	*Suggestive Reply*	*Basis of Reply*
169	What is the background of Article 9.3.5 that contains an optional provision that allows the Reference Jurisdiction to use the UTPR to defend its tax base from a tax planning opportunity that may arise under the exclusion for MNEs in the initial phase of their international activity?	Article 9.3.1 exclusion treats all jurisdictions in which the MNE Group operates as having zero Top-up Tax. A largely domestic Group could establish a new UPE in a jurisdiction that does not have a Qualified IIR, and then the Parent Entity could extract value from the domestic Group without being subject to minimum taxation under the UTPR. This gap in the coverage of the GloBE Rules could also provide a competitive advantage for UPEs located in a non-GloBE jurisdiction seeking to acquire MNE Groups. To thwart this potential abuse of the Article 9.3.1 exclusion, jurisdictions that introduce a UTPR may consider providing an optional exception to Article 9.3.1 that would exclude the operation of Article 9.3 in that jurisdiction where it is the Reference Jurisdiction in respect of an MNE Group that is in the initial phase of its international activity. The reason for including such an option in Article 9.3 for those jurisdictions that choose to implement the GloBE Rules would be to provide a level playing field between locally headquartered MNE Groups that are in the initial phase of their international activity (and would therefore be subject to the IIR in respect of their operations in Low-Tax Jurisdictions) and those MNE Groups in the initial phase of their international activity that maintain a UPE outside, but the major part of their operations within, that jurisdiction. An option for the Reference Jurisdiction to apply the UTPR to such Groups would help to limit the risk of locally headquartered MNE Groups inverting out of the Reference Jurisdiction to escape the GloBE Rules.	Refer paragraphs 27, 28 of Commentary on Chapter 9.

S. No.	*Query*	*Suggestive Reply*	*Basis of Reply*
170	What is the transitional relief for filing and notification obligations?	In order to provide amelioration to MNE Groups in carrying out compliance with GloBE Rules, Article 9.4.1 provides transitional relief for the filing and notification obligations pursuant to Article 8.1 with respect to the Transition Year. The filing and notification obligations must be fulfilled within eighteen months, rather than the normal fifteen months, after the end of the Reporting Fiscal Year, that is, the Transition Year.	Refer paragraph 32 of Commentary on Chapter 9.

7.2 GLOBE IMPLEMENTATION FRAMEWORK

1009. In accordance with the Detailed Implementation Plan accompanying OECD's October Statement, work is ongoing at the OECD to develop an Implementation Framework for public release by the end of 2022. The Implementation Framework is intended to address issues around administration of Pillar Two, including filing obligations, multilateral review processes and safe harbours that would be designed to reduce administration and compliance costs by relieving MNEs of the obligation to compute their jurisdictional ETRs in certain circumstances.

1010. As part of the GloBE Implementation Framework, the OECD is expected to undertake the following inexorable steps, *inter alia,* involving rendering Administrative Guidance (under Article 8.3), which will be released and made publicly available, to facilitate transparent, consistent, coordinated, uniform and efficacious implementation of the GloBE Rules by tax administrations and MNE Groups respectively:

- The GloBE Implementation Framework will give further consideration to the appropriate adjustments to the GloBE Income in situations where, in connection with a proceeding concerning the tax returns of two or more counterparties, the relevant tax authorities disagree as to whether or to what extent a transfer price needs to be adjusted to reflect the ALP as well as in other situations where adjustments are necessary to avoid double taxation or double non-taxation under the GloBE Rules. In addition, the GloBE Implementation framework will consider information reporting related to adjustments made by CEs pursuant to Article 3.2.3 (refer paragraph 105 of the Commentary on Chapter 3).
- In order to facilitate compliance by MNEs and administration by tax authorities, and to ensure consistent and coordinated application of Article 4.3.2 across implementing jurisdictions, the results of the further work to be carried out as part of the GloBE Implementation Framework would be released and made publicly available (refer paragraph 44 of the Commentary on Chapter 4).
- Recognising that there is significant variation in how countries impose tax on PEs (including variation in the treatment of losses and foreign tax credits), the GloBE Implementation Framework shall work on the development of a common methodology to determine the amount of Covered Taxes allocated from a CE to a PE in connection with specific country regimes (refer paragraph 54 of the Commentary on Chapter 4).
- As part of the GloBE Implementation Framework, further consideration will be given to the treatment of Insurance Investment Entities whose Constituent Entity-owners are not subject to a mark-to-market or similar tax regime on their investments in such Entities (refer paragraph 77 of the Commentary on Chapter 7).
- Bilateral and multilateral models for the Qualifying Competent Authority Agreement would be developed as part of the GloBE Implementation Framework and would be based on the Convention on Mutual Administrative

Assistance in Tax Matters, a Tax Information Exchange Agreement, a Tax Treaty with a provision equivalent to Article 26 of the OECD MTC or any other international agreement that allows automatic exchange of information (refer paragraph 11 of the Commentary on Chapter 8).

- The GloBE Information Return shall be filed in a standard template that shall be developed in accordance with the GloBE Implementation Framework (refer paragraph 13 of the Commentary on Chapter 8).
- The GloBE Information Return shall apply the definitions and instructions contained in the standard template that will be developed in accordance with the GloBE Implementation Framework (refer paragraph 24 of the Commentary on Chapter 8).
- In respect of Article 8.1.6, further guidance will be provided as part of the GloBE Implementation Framework regarding amendments to the GloBE Information Return, including the time frame and the method for the filing and exchange of information between CAs (refer paragraph 26 of the Commentary on Chapter 8).
- Pursuant to the conditions to be provided under the GloBE Implementation Framework and at the election of the Filing Constituent Entity, and notwithstanding Chapter 5, the Top-up Tax for a jurisdiction (the safe harbour jurisdiction) shall be deemed to be zero for a Fiscal Year when the CEs located in this jurisdiction are eligible for a GloBE Safe Harbour applicable for that Fiscal Year.
  - Article 8.2.1 and the definition of GloBE Safe Harbour contemplate that any GloBE Safe Harbour will be developed and released as part of the GloBE Implementation Framework. The terms of any GloBE Safe Harbour agreed under the GloBE Implementation Framework would specify the conditions that an MNE Group would need to meet in order to be able to rely on that GloBE Safe Harbour (refer paragraph 32 of the Commentary on Chapter 8).
  - The GloBE Implementation Framework could also explore whether a GloBE Safe Harbour could cover the situations where no Top-up Tax would be due, for instance, in respect of a jurisdiction where MNE Groups are subject to a QDMTT (refer paragraph 32 of the Commentary on Chapter 8).
  - The GloBE Implementation Framework shall consider the date on which the 36 month-period is considered to start in circumstances where the GloBE Information Return is received through an information exchange mechanism or by multiple domestic CEs (refer paragraph 36 of the Commentary on Chapter 8).
  - The details of the consequences where the GloBE Safe Harbour is found not applicable as a result of Article 8.2.2 shall be considered in the GloBE Implementation Framework (refer paragraph 39 of the Commentary on Chapter 8).

- Include implementing a process to assist tax administrations in determining whether a minimum tax is considered as a QDMTT (refer paragraph 118 of the Commentary on Chapter 10).
- Include implementing a process to assist tax administrations in determining whether a country has introduced a Qualified IIR (refer paragraph 127 of the Commentary on Chapter 10).
- Include guidance and processes to determine whether a set of rules is considered a Qualified UTPR (refer paragraph 143 of the Commentary on Chapter 10).

7.3 CONCLUDING REMARKS

1011. *Jurisdictions are expected to protect their turf*: It is expected that most countries which decide to implement the GloBE Rules may opt to introduce DMT in their domestic legislation. A DMT would ensure that any additional tax on local economic activities and profits that results from the Pillar Two minimum tax framework is to the benefit of the local exchequer. Also, a DMT could significantly reduce compliance burdens on local groups by preventing them from being subject to the UTPR in multiple countries in respect of their local domestic operations.

1012. *Implications of Common Approach*: Multinational groups with subsidiaries in countries that operate at a rate below the agreed minimum rate will ultimately have to face the consequences of Pillar Two. This is because the rules test the ETR per jurisdiction and apply a top-up tax to companies in the low-tax jurisdictions. As a result of either the IIR or the UTPR, a State will collect the top-up tax due at the level of the entire group if some jurisdictions where entities are based impose tax below the minimum level and do not impose any domestic top-up tax. In other words, owing to the common approach, failing to apply the Pillar Two rules will not protect jurisdictions from effectively being subject to tax, at least at the agreed minimum rate.[193]

1013. *Advantages of EUR 750 million threshold*:[194] The GloBE Rules will apply to MNEs that have consolidated revenues of EUR 750 million in at least two out of the last four years. This revenue threshold is similar to that used for CbCR purposes and shall provide concomitant synergies. The threshold is estimated to cover over 90% of the global CIT base and would keep SMEs out of the ambit of GloBE Rules.

1014. *Capacity Building*: There is a wide disparity in the existing tax administration capabilities of some developing countries that are committed to Pillar Two Solution. These capabilities will be tested further as implementation of GloBE rules may involve introduction of CIT and TP regime by certain tax administrations. Accordingly, there

193. Refer 'European Commission's Questions and Answers on Minimum corporate taxation' https://ec.europa.eu/commission/presscorner/detail/en/qanda_21_6967 accessed on 1 May 2022.
194. Refer 'OECD's FAQs on Global Anti-Base Erosion Model Rules (Pillar Two): Sl. No. 5' https://www.oecd.org/tax/beps/pillar-two-model-GloBE-rules-faqs.pdf.

will be an urgent requirement to upgrade capacity of tax officials in some countries. This can be achieved through various programmes conducted by the UN, African Tax Administration Forum, OECD and similar multilateral organisations.

1015. *OECD's Report to G7 Finance Ministers and Central Bank Governors May 2022*:[195] The implementation of the Two-Pillar Solution in developing countries will require significant tax policy and administration responses. Developing countries not yet committed to the approach will have to decide whether to implement, while those that have already decided will need to determine the legislative and regulatory reforms needed for domestic implementation, together with building administrative capacity to apply the new rules. Alongside this, the impact of Pillar Two will provide an impetus for many developing countries with significant tax incentive regimes in place to review, and potentially modify or abolish, such incentives. The design of Pillar Two with one standardised Effective Tax Rate calculation implies that the interests of countries will generally be aligned. This consistent and coordinated design means that tax administrations with less capacity may be able to rely on the filing, verification and risk assessment requirements imposed by other tax administrations with greater capacity and more experience to ensure that the right amount of tax is assessed and paid in their jurisdiction.

1016. *Expectations from the Two-Pillar Solution*: Large multinationals have the propensity to set up hundreds of offshore companies in tax havens and shift significant capital to them. In some cases, the ratio of the profits of these companies to the overall GDP of selected tax havens even exceeded 1000%.[196] Use of financial centres for moving onshore profits to low-tax regimes as well as for tax evasion and money laundering purposes needs to be highly discouraged. This is why we are now witnessing intense legislative work, both at the international and national levels, aimed at tightening tax systems in this area. The Pillar Two Proposal is one of the outcomes of these developments. The European Union lists[197] non-cooperative jurisdictions from time to time to encourage positive change in their tax legislation and practices through cooperation. It is mainly about improving the transparency of corporations' reporting of the size of their operations in different countries and eliminating the discretion of tax havens. It cannot be denied that Pillar Two would reduce the differences in Effective Tax Rate s across jurisdictions, which are one of the main drivers of profit shifting. Reducing these tax rate differentials would reduce MNEs' incentives to shift profit to low-tax jurisdictions. This would prompt MNEs to reassess their profit-shifting strategies, and it is quite likely that some MNEs would consider that the gains of certain

195. Refer 'OECD Report for the G7 Finance Ministers and Central Bank Governors May 2022, Germany' https://www.oecd.org/tax/tax-co-operation-for-the-21st-century-oecd-report-g7-may-2022-germany.pdf accessed on 31 May 2022.
196. Refer 'Małgorzata Kutera: The Role of Tax Havens in Tax Avoidance by Multinationals' https://www.researchgate.net/publication/324062993_The_Role_of_Tax_Havens_in_Tax_Avoidance_by_Multinationals/link/5c805cd592851c69505c6b8f/download accessed on 31 May 2022.
197. Refer 'Taxation: EU list of non-cooperative jurisdictions' https://www.consilium.europa.eu/en/policies/eu-list-of-non-cooperative-jurisdictions/ accessed on 31 May 2022.

profit-shifting schemes would no longer be worth the costs. Nevertheless, the reduction of profit shifting is expected to contribute significantly to the global revenue gains from Pillar Two.[198] The Two-Pillar solution is expected to have an impact on MNE investment, innovation and economic activity at global level. By raising additional tax revenues, the proposals would increase (after-tax) investment costs for the MNEs affected. This would likely have a negative effect on investment and activity, but the magnitude of this effect is estimated to be relatively small, i.e., less than 0.1 % of GDP in the medium to long term.[199]

198. Refer 'OECD's report titled Tax Challenges Arising from Digitalisation – Economic Impact Assessment' https://www.oecd-ilibrary.org/docserver/0e3cc2d4-en.pdf?expires=1645597172&id=id&accname=guest&checksum=BCDA456EF4506AF36EFDBF9351B85E5E accessed on 31 May 2022.
199. *Id.* (paragraph 30).

Bibliography

Action 1: BEPS 2015 Final Report, OECD/G20 Base Erosion and Profit Shifting Project http://www.oecd.org/tax/beps-2015-final-reports.htm

Action 2: BEPS 2015 Final Report, OECD/G20 Base Erosion and Profit Shifting Project http://www.oecd.org/tax/beps-2015-final-reports.htm

Action 3: BEPS 2015 Final Report, OECD/G20 Base Erosion and Profit Shifting Project https://www.oecd.org/ctp/designing-effective-controlled-foreign-company-rules-action-3-2015-final-report-9789264241152-en.htm accessed on 17 May 2022

Aitor Navarro's Article titled Jurisdiction Not to Tax, Tax Sparing Clauses, and the OECD Minimum Taxation (GloBE) Proposal https://doi.org/10.2478/ntaxj-2021-0004 accessed on 17 May 2022

BEPS Project Public Consultation Document on Addressing the Tax Challenges of the Digitalisation of the Economy https://www.oecd.org/tax/beps/public-consultation-document-addressing-the-tax-challenges-of-the-digitalisation-of-the-economy.pdf accessed on 7 April 2022

Budget Review 2022, National Treasury, Republic of South Africa, 23 February 2022 http://www.treasury.gov.za/documents/national%20budget/2022/review/FullBR.pdf accessed on 16 May 2022

Cover Statement by the OECD/G20 IF on BEPS on the Reports on the Blueprints of Pillar One and Pillar Two as contained on pages 10-12 of the Report on Pillar Two Blueprint

Economy Profile of Haiti, Doing Business 2020, World Bank Group https://www.doingbusiness.org/content/dam/doingBusiness/country/h/haiti/HTI.pdf accessed on 20 May 2022

Editorial titled The Pillar Two Top-Up Taxes: Interplay, Characterization, Treaties and Tax' by Ana Paula Dourado Editor-in-Chief Intertax, Volume 50, Issue 5 © 2022 Kluwer Law International BV, The Netherlands https://kluwerlawonline.com/api/Product/CitationPDFURL?file=Journals\TAXI\TAXI2022045.pdf accessed on 22 May 2022

European Commission's Proposal for a Council Directive on ensuring a global minimum level of taxation for multinational groups in the Union https://eur-lex.europa.eu/legal-content/EN/TXT/?uri=CELEX%3A52021PC0823 accessed on 15 May 2022

European Commission's Questions and Answers on Minimum corporate taxation https://ec.europa.eu/commission/presscorner/detail/en/qanda_21_6967 accessed on 1 May 2022

European Commission's Taxation and Customs Union – Minimum corporate taxation https://ec.europa.eu/taxation_customs/taxation-1/minimum-corporate-taxation_en accessed on 15 May 2022

FAQ on OECD's Model GloBE Rules dated 20 December 2021 https://www.oecd.org/tax/beps/pillar-two-model-GloBE-rules-faqs.pdf accessed on 7 April 2022

FAQ on OECD's statement dated 8 October 2021 https://www.oecd.org/tax/beps/faqs-statement-on-a-two-pillar-solution-to-address-the-tax-challenges-arising-from-the-digitalisation-of-the-economy-october-2021.pdf accessed on 5 April 2022

FAQ released by the UAE Ministry of Finance https://www.mof.gov.ae/en/resourcesAndBudget/Pages/faq.aspx accessed on 17 May 2022

Financial Transparency Coalition: Automatic Exchange of Tax Information 2017 https://financialtransparency.org/wp-content/uploads/2018/05/Automatic-Exchange-of-Tax-Information.pdf accessed on 20 May 2022

General Explanations of the Administration's Fiscal Year 2023 Revenue Proposals, Department of the Treasury, March 2022 https://home.treasury.gov/system/files/131/General-Explanations-FY2023.pdf accessed on 17 May 2022

Handbook developed by CIAT/NORAD titled Digital Economy Compliance https://www.ciat.org/Biblioteca/DocumentosTecnicos/Ingles/2021-DEC-Handbook-ing.pdf

How global corporate tax deal was struck, OECD official Grace Perez-Navarro recounts https://cfo.economictimes.indiatimes.com/news/how-global-corporate-tax-deal-was-struck-oecd-official-grace-perez-navarro-recounts/87010778 accessed on 7 April 2022

IBFD https://research.ibfd.org/#/doc?url=/linkresolver/static/gtha_ae_s_1.&refresh=1645539407371%23gtha_ae_s_1 accessed on 17 May 2022

IBFD https://research.ibfd.org/#/search?N=3+10+4293744764&Ne=7487&Nu=global_rollup_key&Np=2&Ns=sort_country_one|0||subcategory|0||sort_jurisdiction|0||sort_state_province|0 accessed on 20 May 2022

India's synthesized texts under the MLI https://incometaxindia.gov.in/Pages/international-taxation/dtaa.aspx

International Tax Measures announced in Budget 2022 by Canada, Pillar Two – Global Minimum Tax https://budget.gc.ca/2022/report-rapport/tm-mf-en.html#a4_1_2 accessed on 15 May 2022

KPMG's Singapore: Tax measures in budget 2022 https://home.kpmg/us/en/home/insights/2022/02/tnf-singapore-tax-measures-in-budget-2022.html accessed on 16 May 2022

KPMG's Update on Pillar 2 agreement – December 2021 https://home.kpmg/xx/en/home/insights/2021/12/inclusive-framework-beps-agreement-20-december-2021.html accessed on 20 May 2022

Małgorzata Kutera: The Role of Tax Havens in Tax Avoidance by Multinationals https://www.researchgate.net/publication/324062993_The_Role_of_Tax_Havens_in_Tax_Avoidance_by_Multinationals/link/5c805cd592851c69505c6b8f/download accessed on 31 May 2022

Members of the OECD/G20 Inclusive Framework on BEPS – Updated: November 2021 https://www.oecd.org/tax/beps/inclusive-framework-on-beps-composition.pdf accessed on 15 May 2022

MLI Made Easy by Kuldeep Sharma (paragraphs 9, 10), published by Wolters Kluwer https://law-store.wolterskluwer.com/s/product/mli-made-easy/01t4R00000Oibvu accessed on 8 April 2022

No UAE income tax for now, minister says in the wake of corporate tax move https://www.arabianbusiness.com/gcc/uae/no-uae-income-tax-for-now-minister accessed on 17 May 2022

Noam Noked: The Case for Domestic Minimum Taxes on Multinationals https://www.taxnotes.com/tax-notes-international/corporate-taxation/case-domestic-minimum-taxes-multinationals/2022/02/07/7d4qj?highlight=noam%20noked 20 May 2022

OECD – What is BEPS? http://www.oecd.org/tax/beps/about/ accessed on 8 April 2022

OECD Pillar Two: GloBE rules for New Zealand https://taxpolicy.ird.govt.nz/en/publications/2022/2022-ip-oecd-pillar-two accessed on 17 May 2022

OECD Pillars 1 & 2: Tax Policy Reflections, April 2022, Government of Jersey https://www.gov.je/SiteCollectionDocuments/Tax%20and%20your%20money/R%20OECD%20Pillars%201%20and%202%20tax%20policy%20reflections.pdf accessed on 21 May 2022

OECD Report for the G7 Finance Ministers and Central Bank Governors May 2022, Germany https://www.oecd.org/tax/tax-co-operation-for-the-21st-century-oecd-report-g7-may-2022-germany.pdf accessed on 31 May 2022

OECD Report on Pillar Two Blueprint https://www.oecd.org/tax/beps/tax-challenges-arising-from-digitalisation-report-on-pillar-two-blueprint-abb4c3d1-en.htm

OECD Secretary-General Tax Report to G20 Leaders in Osaka, Japan in June 2019 (pg. 9,13) https://www.oecd.org/tax/oecd-secretary-general-tax-report-g20-leaders-june-2019.pdf accessed on 8 April 2022

OECD's Building an investment tax incentives database https://www.oecd-ilibrary.org/finance-and-investment/building-an-investment-tax-incentives-database_62e075a9-en accessed on 20 May 2022

OECD's Commentary to the Global Anti-Base Erosion Model Rules (Pillar Two) https://www.oecd.org/tax/beps/tax-challenges-arising-from-the-digitalisation-of-the-economy-global-anti-base-erosion-model-rules-pillar-two-commentary.pdf

OECD's FAQs on Global Anti-Base Erosion Model Rules (Pillar Two) https://www.oecd.org/tax/beps/pillar-two-model-GloBE-rules-faqs.pdf

OECD's Global Anti-Base Erosion Model Rules (Pillar Two) Examples https://www.oecd.org/tax/beps/tax-challenges-arising-from-the-digitalisation-of-the-economy-global-anti-base-erosion-model-rules-pillar-two-examples.pdf

OECD's Global Anti-Base Erosion Model Rules (Pillar Two) https://www.oecd.org/tax/beps/tax-challenges-arising-from-the-digitalisation-of-the-economy-global-anti-base-erosion-model-rules-pillar-two.pdf

OECD's Global Forum on Transparency and Exchange of Information for tax purposes, Automatic Exchange of Information (AEOI): Status of Commitments as of 5 January 2022 https://www.oecd.org/tax/transparency/AEOI-commitments.pdf accessed on 20 May 2022

OECD's List of countries with Controlled Foreign Company (CFC) Rules https://qdd.oecd.org/data/CFC/.ALL accessed on 17 May 2022

OECD's Model Tax Convention 2017 https://www.oecd.org/ctp/treaties/model-tax-convention-on-income-and-on-capital-condensed-version-20745419.htm

OECD's October 2021 Brochure – Two-Pillar Solution https://www.oecd.org/tax/beps/brochure-two-pillar-solution-to-address-the-tax-challenges-arising-from-the-digitalisation-of-the-economy-october-2021.pdf

OECD's Pillar Two Model Rules Fact Sheets titled Overview of the Key Operating Provisions of the GloBE Rules https://www.oecd.org/tax/beps/pillar-two-GloBE-rules-fact-sheets.pdf accessed on 11 April 2022

OECD's Policy Note: Addressing the Tax Challenges of the Digitalisation of the Economy as approved by the IF on BEPS on 23 January 2019 https://www.oecd.org/tax/beps/policy-note-beps-inclusive-framework-addressing-tax-challenges-digitalisation.pdf accessed on 8 April 2022

OECD's Press Release dated 8 October 2021 titled International community strikes a ground-breaking tax deal for the digital age https://www.oecd.org/tax/international-community-strikes-a-ground-breaking-tax-deal-for-the-digital-age.htm accessed on 7 April 2022

OECD's Programme of Work to Develop a Consensus Solution to the Tax Challenges arising from the Digitalisation of the Economy https://www.oecd.org/tax/beps/programme-of-work-to-develop-a-consensus-solution-to-the-tax-challenges-arising-from-the-digitalisation-of-the-economy.pdf accessed on 8 April 2022

OECD's report titled Tax Challenges Arising from Digitalisation – Economic Impact Assessment https://www.oecd-ilibrary.org/docserver/0e3cc2d4-en.pdf?expires=1645597172&id=id&accname=guest&checksum=BCDA456EF4506AF36EFDBF9351B85E5E accessed on 31 May 2022

OECD's Statement on a Two-Pillar Solution to Address the Tax Challenges Arising From the Digitalisation of the Economy dated 1 July 2021 https://www.oecd.org/tax/beps/statement-on-a-two-pillar-solution-to-address-the-tax-challenges-arising-from-the-digitalisation-of-the-economy-july-2021.pdf accessed on 8 April 2022

OECD's Statement on a Two-Pillar Solution to Address the Tax Challenges Arising from the Digitalisation of the Economy dated 8 October 2021 https://www.oecd.org/

tax/beps/statement-on-a-two-pillar-solution-to-address-the-tax-challenges-arising-from-the-digitalisation-of-the-economy-october-2021.pdf accessed on 8 April 2022

OECD's Tax Challenges Arising from Digitalisation – Interim Report 2018 https://www.oecd.org/ctp/tax-challenges-arising-from-digitalisation-interim-report-9789264293083-en.htm accessed on 8 April 2022

OECD's Tax Sparing – A Reconsideration https://www.oecd-ilibrary.org/taxation/tax-sparing_9789264162433-en accessed on 17 May 2022

OECD's The Pillar Two Rules in a Nutshell https://www.oecd.org/tax/beps/pillar-two-model-rules-in-a-nutshell.pdf

Deloitte's Policy options for domestic implementation of a global minimum corporate tax rate https://www.taxathand.com/article/20418/India/2021/Policy-options-for-domestic-implementation-of-a-global-minimum-corporate-tax-rate accessed on 17 May 2022

Poland blocks EU compromise on global minimum corporate tax deal https://www.reuters.com/world/europe/poland-blocks-eu-compromise-global-minimum-corporate-tax-deal-2022-04-05/ accessed on 15 May 2022

Press Release: The Ministry of Finance announces the introduction of a Corporate Tax in the UAE https://www.mof.gov.ae/en/media/materials/News/Pages/31012022.aspx accessed on 17 May 2022

Public Consultation Document – UAE Corporate Tax https://www.mof.gov.ae/en/resourcesAndBudget/Documents/UAE_CT-Public_Consultation_Document_English.pdf accessed on 17 May 2022

Singapore Budget 2022 Speech https://www.mof.gov.sg/docs/librariesprovider3/budget2022/download/pdf/fy2022_budget_statement.pdf accessed on 16 May 2022

South Centre Tax Cooperation Policy Brief 14, June 2021 by Kuldeep Sharma titled The Tax Sovereignty Principle and Its Peaceful Coexistence with Article 12B of the UN Model Tax Convention https://www.southcentre.int/wp-content/uploads/2021/06/Tax-PB-14.pdf accessed on 5 April 2022

South Centre Tax Cooperation Policy Brief 22, 12 January 2022 by Kuldeep Sharma titled Global Minimum Corporate Tax: Interaction of Income Inclusion Rule with Controlled Foreign Corporation and Tax-sparing Provisions https://www.southcentre.int/tax-cooperation-policy-brief-22-12-january-2022/ accessed on 7 April 2022

South Centre's Comments on the OECD Secretariat Proposal for a 'Unified Approach' under Pillar One https://www.southcentre.int/wp-content/uploads/2019/11/OECD-Tax-Pillar-One-Comments-South-Centre-Tax-Initiative-v4.pdf accessed on 17 May 2022

Statement by the OECD/G20 IF on BEPS on the Two-Pillar Approach to Address the Tax Challenges Arising from the Digitalisation of the Economy, as approved on 29-30 January 2020 https://www.oecd.org/tax/beps/statement-by-the-oecd-g20-inclusive-framework-on-beps-january-2020.pdf accessed on 8 April 2022

Sustainable Development Goals https://www.un.org/sustainabledevelopment/sustainable-development-goals/ accessed on 5 April 2022

Swiss Federal Council opens a consultation regarding the implementation of the OECD/G20 Pillar 2 model rules to ensure a minimum taxation of multinationals http://www.internationaltaxplaza.info/homepage/news-archive/news-archive-2022/473-news-archive-march-2022/6330-swiss-federal-council-opens-a-consultation-regarding-the-implementation-of-the-oecd-g20-pillar-2-model-rules-to-ensure-a-minimum-taxation-of-multinationals.html accessed on 16 May 2022

Tax Policy Center's Briefing Book: What is global intangible low-taxed income and how is it taxed under the TCJA? https://www.taxpolicycenter.org/briefing-book/what-global-intangible-low-taxed-income-and-how-it-taxed-under-tcja accessed on 17 May 2022

Taxation: EU list of non-cooperative jurisdictions https://www.consilium.europa.eu/en/policies/eu-list-of-non-cooperative-jurisdictions/ accessed on 31 May 2022

The Concept of Tax Sparing: A General Analysis, and an Analysis and Assessment of the Various Features of Tax Sparing Provisions by Kristian Reinert Haugland Nilsen Master of Laws, University of Oslo https://www.jus.uio.no/ior/english/research/projects/global-tax-tranparency/publications/the-concept-of-tax-sparing.pdf accessed on 17 May 2022

The HMRC's OECD Pillar 2 Consultation on implementation https://assets.publishing.service.gov.uk/government/uploads/system/uploads/attachment_data/file/1045663/11Jan_2022_Pillar_2_Consultation_.pdf accessed on 12 April 2022

Transfer Pricing Country Summary, Haiti, July 2018 by TPA Global https://www.tpa-global.com/wp-content/uploads/2020/05/180712-haiti-transfer-pricing-country-summary-report-2018.pdf accessed on 20 May 2022

Transfer Pricing Developments Around the World 2020, Edited by Michael Lang, Raffaele Petruzzi, published by Wolters Kluwer, Chapter 6: Recent developments on the tax challenges arising from the digitalization of the Economy: New Profit Allocation Rules, by Giammarco Cottani, pg. 153 accessed on 31 May 2022

UN Model DTC 2017 https://www.un.org/esa/ffd/wp-content/uploads/2018/05/MDT_2017.pdf

V. Chand, A. Turina, K. Romanovska: Tax Treaty Obstacles in Implementing the Pillar Two Global Minimum Tax Rules and a Possible Solution for Eliminating the various challenges, Vol. 14 Issue: World Tax Journal, 2022 (Volume 14), No. 1 Published online: 21 February 2022 https://research.ibfd.org/#/doc?url=/collections/wtj/html/wtj_2022_01_int_1.html accessed on 17 May 2022

What Does the G7 Proposal on Taxation of the Digitalised Economy Mean for African countries? https://afripoli.org/what-does-the-g7-proposal-on-taxation-of-the-digitalised-economy-mean-for-african-countries accessed on 17 May 2022

Index

G

H

I

U

W

www.ingramcontent.com/pod-product-compliance
Ingram Content Group UK Ltd.
Pitfield, Milton Keynes, MK11 3LW, UK
UKHW020224290926
15470UKWH00001B/370

9 789403 511566